Alpheus Crosby

A Compendious Grammar of the Greek Language

Alpheus Crosby

A Compendious Grammar of the Greek Language

ISBN/EAN: 9783743393943

Manufactured in Europe, USA, Canada, Australia, Japa

Cover: Foto ©Paul-Georg Meister /pixelio.de

Manufactured and distributed by brebook publishing software (www.brebook.com)

Alpheus Crosby

A Compendious Grammar of the Greek Language

A COMPENDIOUS GRAMMAR

OF THE

GREEK LANGUAGE.

By ALPHEUS CROSBY,

PROFESSOR EMERITUS OF THE GREEK LANGUAGE AND LITERATURE IN DARTMOUTH COLLEGE.

Μηδὲν ἄγαν · πάντων μέσ' ἄριστα.
THEOGNIS.

WOOLWORTH, AINSWORTH, & COMPANY,
51, 53, & 55 JOHN STREET, NEW YORK,
111 STATE STREET, CHICAGO.
1871.

"The LANGUAGE OF THE GREEKS was truly like themselves, it was conformable to their transcendent and universal Genius. . . . . THE GREEK TONGUE, *from its propriety and universality, is made for all that is great, and all that is beautiful, in every Subject, and under every Form of writing.*" — HARRIS's *Hermes*, Bk. III., Ch. 5.

"GREEK, — the shrine of the genius of the old world; as universal as our race, as individual as ourselves; of infinite flexibility, of indefatigable strength, with the complication and the distinctness of Nature herself; to which nothing was vulgar, from which nothing was excluded; speaking to the ear like Italian, speaking to the mind like English; with words like pictures, with words like the gossamer film of the summer; at once the variety and picturesqueness of Homer, the gloom and the intensity of Æschylus; not compressed to the closest by Thucydides, not fathomed to the bottom by Plato, not sounding with all its thunders, nor lit up with all its ardors even under the Promethean touch of Demosthenes!" — COLERIDGE's *Study of the Greek Classic Poets.*

VIGNETTE: TEMPLE OF THESEUS AT ATHENS.
"Athens, the eye of Greece." — *Milton.*

Entered according to Act of Congress, in the year 1871,
BY ALPHEUS CROSBY,
in the Office of the Librarian of Congress, at Washington.

UNIVERSITY PRESS: WELCH, BIGELOW, & CO.,
CAMBRIDGE.

PREFACE.

The motto on the title-page, from old Theognis if not the older Cleobulus, indicates the principle on which this treatise has been prepared. There has been throughout an earnest effort to carry nothing to excess, neither insertion nor omission, but to write that "Middle" Grammar which, it might be hoped, the old moralist would approve, if he were at my side. The Tables, that mnemonic associations may not be disturbed, are throughout the same as in the larger grammar upon which this is based; and so little of practical precept has been omitted from the text of the latter, that many might regard this condensed edition as still large enough for the object stated in the original preface to the fuller work: "to supply what was believed to be a desideratum in the list of Greek text-books; viz., a grammar which should be portable and simple enough to be put into the hands of the beginner, and which should yet be sufficiently scientific and complete to accompany him through his whole course." Even slight variations of phraseology have been avoided, with few and unimportant exceptions; and the division here made into sections and their parts, and the references to these, apply throughout to the fuller edition; so that the two editions might even be used together in the same class without inconvenience. They are really one and the same work, *unum et idem;* except that the screw of compression, which had been before so severely applied, has here received a few more turns.

It must be confessed, however, that the arguments in favor of a short grammar have far less strength for the Greek than for the Latin. The study of the latter language is usually commenced at an earlier age, and when the learner is wholly new to philological acquisition; and it is also commenced by many who contemplate only a brief course of classical study, and who therefore find in a brief grammar, supplemented here and there by an able teacher, a supply of their wants. On the other hand, most of our students, in beginning the study of Greek, have in view a college course; and they begin it with the experience and mental strength derived from the acquisition of the Latin. They know already how to use a grammar as, what it mainly should be, a book of constant reference; and are more troubled by not finding in it what they seek, than by the presence there of much that is not immediately needed, — with which,

COMP. GR.

however, as lying before the eye, they are gaining without effort some acquaintance in anticipation of future wants. At least they will better know, — a large part of knowledge, — *where to find* what they want.

It may be added that the Greek, from the much greater fulness of its forms and variety of its constructions, cannot be as adequately treated as the Latin, except in a larger volume. Mr. MARSH, in his able Lectures on the English Language, thus distinguishes: " The grammar of the Greek language is much more flexible, more tolerant of aberration, less rigid in its requirements, than the Latin. The precision, which the regularity of Latin syntax gives to a period, the Greek more completely and clearly accomplishes by the nicety with which individual words are defined in meaning; and while the Latin trains us to be good grammarians, the Greek elevates us to the highest dignity of manhood by making us acute and powerful thinkers." The greater need of explanation which results from this fulness and freedom, calls for additional space; for, as Professor CURTIUS has well remarked, "Memory can neither accurately grasp the great variety of Greek forms nor retain them, unless it be supported by an *analyzing and combining intelligence*, which furnishes, as it were, the *hooks* and *cement* to strengthen that which has been learned, and permanently impress it upon the mind."

In respect to form, the present treatise should not be judged as an independent work, but as a condensed edition of a larger work, from the form of which it was deemed important to depart as little as possible. Thus, some references to authors, which are there fully made, are here given partially in preference to omitting them altogether. For fuller illustration and explanation on many points, will the reader pardon, once for all, a reference to the larger grammar? And will he permit the statement of principles and acknowledgments in its preface to be here understood without repetition, — the rather for a reason which will appear in the next paragraph?

The occurrence of some spaces in printing the Revised Grammar presented a temptation to adorn it with a few extracts. In the present form of printing, these spaces do not occur; and, from a reluctance to part with these gems, room has been found for them here, — where, indeed, they seem to be placed even more appropriately, as a fit introduction to the book. In their original position, they belong to sections 796, 171, 724, and 799. The last of these passages is selected the rather because its author is Professor of Modern Languages, not of Greek, and is especially eminent as a Sanskrit scholar; as that in § 800, with a quotation above, because they occur in Lectures, not on the Greek, but on the English Language, and by one who has gained such distinction, both in public life, and by his scholarship in other than classic fields. The teacher of Greek, whose judgment might be suspected of partiality, would not perhaps venture upon the strength of expression employed by the statesman-scholar.

A. C.

"THE REASONS why we spend so long a time in acquiring a mastery over the GREEK LANGUAGE are manifold. We do so partly because it is one of the most delicate and perfect instruments for the expression of thought which was ever elaborated by the mind of man, and because it is therefore admirably adapted, both by its points of resemblance to our own and other modern languages, and by its points of difference from them, to give us the IDEA, or fundamental conception, of all Grammar; i. e. of those laws which regulate the use of the forms by which we express our thoughts.

"Again, Greek is the key to one of the most astonishing and splendid regions of LITERATURE which are open for the intellect to explore, — a literature which enshrines works not only of imperishable interest, but also of imperishable importance, both directly and historically, for the development of human thought. It is the language in which the New Testament was first written; and into which the Old Testament was first translated. It was the language spoken by the greatest poets, the greatest orators, the greatest historians, the profoundest philosophers, the world has ever seen. It was the language of the most ancient, the most eloquent, and in some respects the most important of the Christian fathers. It contains the record of institutions and conceptions which lie at the base of modern civilization; and at the same time it contains the record, and presents the spectacle, of precisely those virtues in which modern civilization is most deficient.

"Nor is it an *end* only; it is also a *means*. Even for those who never succeed in reaping all the advantages which it places within their reach, it has been found to be, in various nations and ages during many hundred years, one of the very best instruments for the EXERCISE AND TRAINING OF THE MIND. It may have been studied irrationally, pedantically, and too exclusively; but though it is desirable that much should be superadded, yet with Latin it will probably ever continue to be — what the great German poet Goethe breathed a wish that it always should be — the BASIS OF ALL HIGHER CULTURE." — FARRAR's *Greek Syntax.*

INFLECTION. — "GREEK presents the MOST PERFECT SPECIMEN of an *inflectional*, or *synthetic* language. A language which gets rid of inflections as far as possible, and substitutes separate words for each part of the conception, is called an *analytic* language; and next to the Chinese, which has never attained to synthesis at all, few languages are more analytic than the English. A synthetic language will express in *one* word what requires many words for its expression in an analytic language: e. g. πεφιλήσομαι, *I shall have been loved*, Ich werde geliebt worden sein: ᾤχετο, abierat, *il s'en était allé*.

"The advantage of synthetic language lies in its compactness, precision, and beauty of form; analytic languages are clumsier, but they possibly admit of greater accuracy of expression, and are less liable to misconception. If they are inferior instruments for the imagination, they better serve the purposes of reason. Splendid efflorescence is followed by ripe fruit. The tendency of all languages, at least in historic times, is from synthesis to analysis, e. g. from case-inflections to the use of prepositions, and from tense-inflections to the use of auxiliaries. This tendency may be seen by comparing any modern language with its ancestor, e. g. Italian with Latin, Modern with Ancient Greek, Bengali with Sanskrit, Persian with Zend, German with Gothic, or English with Anglo-Saxon. "It is most important to observe that *no inflection is arbitrary*. Among all the richly multitudinous forms assumed by the Greek and Latin verbs, there is not one which does not follow some definite and ascertainable law. Parsing loses its difficulty and repulsiveness, when it is once understood that there is a definite recurrence of the same forms in the same meaning, and that the distorted shape assumed by some words is not due to arbitrary license, but to regular and well understood laws of phonetic corruption." — *Do.* (from § 7–14 of Pt. I.).

PROSODIAL DISTINCTIONS. — "Both ACCENT and QUANTITY have, and must have some play in all languages. So long as speech is dictated by thought and feeling, will men mark the more pregnant words and syllables with a superior tension of the voice. And so long as consonants remain solid, will it take a longer time to get over two of them in pronunciation than over one. In Greek, both accent and quantity were powerfully developed, so that whereas accent, the intellectual element, overbore quantity in prose, in verse on the other hand quantity, the musical element, overbore accent." — CLYDE's *Greek Syntax.*

THE GREEK PROBLEM. "What the inhabitants of the small city of Athens achieved in philosophy, in poetry, in art, in science, in politics, is known to all of us; and our admiration for them increases tenfold if, by a study of other literatures, such as the literatures of India, Persia, and China, we are enabled to compare their achievements with those of other nations of antiquity. The rudiments of almost everything, with the exception of religion, we, the people of Europe, the heirs to a fortune accumulated during twenty or thirty centuries of intellectual toil, owe to the Greeks; and, strange as it may sound, but few, I think, would gainsay it, that to the present day the achievements of these our distant ancestors and earliest masters, the songs of Homer, the dialogues of Plato, the speeches of Demosthenes, and the statues of Phidias, stand, if not unrivalled, at least unsurpassed by anything that has been achieved by their descendants and pupils.

"*How* the Greeks came to be what they were, and *how*, alone of all other nations, they opened almost every mine of thought that has since been worked by mankind; *how* they invented and perfected almost every style of poetry and prose which has since been cultivated by the greatest minds of our race; *how* they laid the lasting foundation of the principal arts and sciences, and in some of them achieved triumphs never since equalled, is a PROBLEM which neither historian nor philosopher has as yet been able to solve. Like their own goddess Athene, the people of Athens seem to spring full-armed into the arena of history; and we look in vain to Egypt, Syria, or India for more than a few of the seeds that burst into such marvellous growth on the soil of Attica." — *Lectures on the Science of Language*, by MAX MÜLLER, Professor of Modern European Languages in the University of Oxford; *Second Series.*

PREFACE TO THE TABLES.

The following tables have been prepared as part of a Greek Grammar. They are likewise published separately, for the greater convenience and economy in their use. The advantages of a tabular arrangement are too obvious to require remark; nor is it less obvious, that tables are consulted and compared with greater ease when printed together, than when scattered throughout a volume.

The principles upon which the Tables of Paradigms have been constructed are the following: —

I. *To avoid needless repetition.* There is a certain ellipsis in grammatical tables, as well as in discourse, which relieves not only the material instruments of the mind, but the mind itself, and which assists alike the understanding and the memory. When the student has learned that, in the neuter gender, the nominative, accusative, and vocative are *always* the same, why, in each neuter paradigm that he studies, must his eye and mind be taxed with the examination of nine forms instead of three? why, in his daily exercises in declension, must his tongue triple its labor, and more than triple the weariness of the teacher's ear?

II. *To represent the language according to its actual use, and not according to the theories or fancies of the Alexandrine and Byzantine grammarians.* For a single example, where not a few might be cited, the *second future active* and *middle*, which, except as a euphonic form of the first future, is purely imaginary, has been wholly rejected.

III. *To distinguish between regular and irregular usage.* What student, from the common paradigms, does not receive the impression, sometimes never corrected, that the *second perfect* and *pluperfect*, the *second aorist* and *future*, and the *third future* belong as regularly to the Greek verb, as the first tenses bearing the same name; when, in point of fact, the Attic dialect, even including poetic usage, presents only about fifty verbs which have the second perfect or pluperfect; eighty, which have the second aorist active; fifty, which have the second aorist or future passive; forty, which have the second aorist middle; and thirty which have the third future? The gleanings of all the other dialects will not double these numbers.

From the common paradigms, what student would hesitate, in writing Greek, to employ the form in -μεθον, little suspecting that it is only a variety of the first person dual, so exceedingly rare, that the learned Elmsley (perhaps too hastily) pronounced it a mere in-

vention of the Alexandrine grammarians? The teacher who meets with it in his recitation-room may almost call his class, as the crier called the Roman people upon the celebration of the secular games, "to gaze upon that which they had never seen before, and would never see again." And yet, in the single paradigm of τύπτω, as I learned it in my boyhood, this "needless *Alexandrine*,"
 "Which, like a wounded snake, drags its slow length along,"
occurs no fewer than twenty-six times, — almost nine times as often as in the whole range of the Greek classics.

To some there may appear to be an impiety in attacking the venerable shade of τύπτω, but alas! it is little more than a shade, and, with all my early and long cherished attachment to it, I am forced, after examination, to exclaim, in the language of Electra,

$$\text{Ἀντὶ φιλτάτης}$$
$$\text{Μορφῆς, σποδόν τε καὶ σκιὰν ἀνωφελῆ,}$$

and to ask why, in an age which professes such devotion to truth, a false representation of an irregular verb should be still set forth as the paradigm of regular conjugation, and made the Procrustes' bed to which all other verbs must be stretched or pruned.*

With respect to the manner in which these tables should be used, so much depends upon the age and attainments of the student, that no directions could be given which might not require to be greatly modified in particular cases. I would, however, recommend,

1. That the paradigms should not be learned *en masse*, but gradually, in connection with the study of the principles and rules of the grammar, and with other exercises.

2. That some of the paradigms should rather be used for reference, than formally committed to memory. It will be seen at once, that some of them have been inserted merely for the sake of exhibiting differences of accent, or individual peculiarities.

3. That, in learning and consulting the paradigms, the student should constantly compare them with each other, with the tables of terminations, and with the rules of the grammar.

4. That the humble volume should not be dismissed from service, till the paradigms are impressed upon the tablets of the memory as legibly as upon the printed page, — till they have become so familiar to the student, that whenever he has occasion to repeat them, "the

---

* In this edition, the example which takes the place of τύπτω is λύω, happily chosen by the sagacious Krüger as *convenient* and *economical of time* (zeitsparend), — a verb which presents, to the eye, the prefixes, stem, and affixes, with entire distinctness and regularity throughout. A method of pronunciation now becoming common in our country renders the use of βουλεύω as a verb of constant repetition less desirable than formerly, while it removes an objection to the use of λύω. This paradigm, as well as some others, has been the rather substituted as presenting a closer analogy to the Latin.

words," in the expressive language of Milton, "like so many nimble and airy servitors, shall trip about him at command, and in well-ordered files, as he would wish, fall aptly into their own places."

HANOVER, August 10, 1841.   A. C.

DURING the period that has passed since the preceding was written, such great changes have taken place in the grammars used in our schools and colleges, that some passages above seem almost to require historic notes, and the earnestness of argument in others may appear to students of the present generation like a Quixotic joust with windmills. It seems difficult to believe that it is only since that time that the use of τύπτω as a paradigm, and the tedious superfluities in -μεθον, have been dropped in our American grammars (not yet in all); and it is certainly much harder to understand, with all allowances for conservative force, why the latter are still so commonly retained in the grammars prepared for German and English students. But time and labor are accounted of less value in the Old World than in the New.

The Tables are printed, in the present edition, more compactly than they have hitherto been, and with a distinction of type to assist in the analysis of forms, which has also been made more minute. For illustration and explanation, many Latin analogies and many references to the text of the Grammar have been introduced, while other examples have been proposed for further practice. A minute Catalogue of Verbs, with many references to authors, has been brought within moderate compass, with the help of some abbreviations; while the tenses commonly cited in parsing are so distinguished by larger type, that the eye of the student will catch them at once.

It was believed that a few pages could not be better occupied than by a very brief statement of some of the chief principles, definitions, and figures of Syntax, and of a convenient System of Sentential Analysis. As these belong to General Grammar, rather than to that of any particular language, it seemed best, for economy of space and greater clearness, to present the few examples which only could find room, in our own language chiefly.

Full compensation, however, is made to the Greek in § 80, which has been condensed from Dr. Clyde's Appendix to his valuable treatise on Greek Syntax, with slight additions in brackets, and references to parallel parts of the present grammar. We are truly his debtors for presenting to us so concisely the received principles of Greek Grammar, in language such as an ancient grammarian, writing of course after the most classic period, might himself have used.

∗∗∗ The volume of Tables contains pp. 1, 2, 7-10, 13-120.

CONTENTS.

TABLES.

I. ORTHOGRAPHY AND ORTHOËPY.

1. Alphabet . . . . § 1
2. Comparison of Alphabets . . 2
3. Ligatures 3
4. Vocal Elements 4
5. Words classified according to Accent 5
6. Figures affecting Letters and Sounds 6
7. Contraction of Vowels . . 7
8. Consonant Changes . . . 8

II. ETYMOLOGY.

A. DECLENSION.

I. Cases classified 10
II. Affixes of Declension . . . 11
III. Elements of the Affixes . . 12
IV. Affixes analyzed and compared with the Latin . . 13
V. Greek and Latin Paradigms compared, λύρα, ναύτης, &c. 14
VI. Nouns of Declension I., θεά, μοῦσα, ᾠδή, μνᾶ, ταμίας, &c. 15
VII. Nouns of Declension II., χορός, νοῦς, νεώς, ᾠόν, &c. . 16
VIII. Nouns of Declension III.
  A. Mute, γύψ, θρίξ, ἐλπίς, κλείς, λέων, σῶμα, φῶς, κέρας, &c. 17
  B. Liquid, θήρ, ῥίς, ἀνήρ, &c. 18
  C. Pure, κίς, οἶς, πόλις, ἱππεύς, ἠχώ, ναῦς, γένος, ἄστυ, &c. 19
IX. Dialectic Forms of Declension 20
X. Irregular and Dialectic Declension, Ζεύς, υἱός, ὄρν, &c. 21
XI. Adjectives of Two Terminations, ἄδικος, σαφής, &c. 22
XII. Adjectives of Three Terminations, μῶρος, ἡδύς, &c. 23
XIII. Numerals, εἷς, δύο, τρεῖς, &c. 25
XIV. Active Participles, λύων, &c. 26
XV. Substantive Pronouns . . 27
XVI. Adjective Pronouns, ὁ, &c. 28

B. COMPARISON . . 29

C. CONJUGATION.

I. Distinctions classified . . . 30

II. Formation of the Tenses . . § 31
III. Analysis of the Verb . . . 32
IV. Translation of παύω . . . 34
V. Subjective Affixes analyzed and compared 35
VI. Objective Affixes analyzed and compared . . . 36
VII. General Paradigm, λύω . 37
  ἔλιπον, πέποιθα, ἐτρίβην . 38
VIII. Classes of Verbs.
  A. Mute, τρίβω, τάσσω, &c. . 39
  B. Liquid, ἀγγέλλω, φαίνω . 40
  C. Double-Consonant . . . 41
  D. Pure. i. Contract, τιμῶ, φιλῶ, δηλῶ, θηρῶ, πλέω, &c. 42
    Latin Analogies . . . 43
    ii. Barytones in -ω, θύω, &c. 44
    iii. Verbs in -μι, ἵστημι, τίθημι, δίδωμι, δείκνυμι, ἵημι, εἰμί, εἶμι, φημί, &c. 45
  E. Preteritives, οἶδα, ἧμαι, &c. 46
IX. Relation of Tenses and Stem-forms 47
X. Dialectic Forms 48
XI. Classes & Notation of Stems 49
XII. Catalogue of Verbs . . . 50

D. NUMERALS . . . 52

E. PRONOMINAL CORRELATIVES 53

F. TABLE OF DERIVATION 54

G. SIGNIFICANT ELEMENTS 55

III. SYNTAX.

A. General Principles . . . 56
B. Figures of Syntax 67
C. Forms of Analysis and Parsing 72
D. Chief Rules of Syntax . . 76

IV. PROSODY AND PRONUNCIATION.

A. Table of Feet 77
B. Metrical Description and Analysis 78
C. Methods of Pronunciation . 79

GREEK APPENDIX . . 80

CONTENTS. 11

INTRODUCTION. — DIALECTS. . . . . . §81

BOOK I. ORTHOGRAPHY AND ORTHOËPY.

CH. 1. CHARACTERS	§90	C. Apostrophe, or Elision	127
History of Orthography	97	Dialectic Variations	130
CH. 2. FIGURES	99	CH. 4. CONSONANTS	137
CH. 3. VOWELS	106	Old Semivowels	138
Syllabication	111	Euphonic Changes,	
I. Precession	113	A. In Formation of Words	147
II. Union of Syllables	117	B. In Connection of Words	161
A. Contraction	118	C. Special Rules	165
B. Crasis	124	Dialectic Variations	167

BOOK II. ETYMOLOGY.

Divisions and Definitions	172	C. Mode	269
CH. 1. PRINCIPLES OF DECLENSION	173	D. Number and Person	270
		E. History of Conjugation	271
A. Gender	174	CH. 8. PREFIXES OF CONJUGATION.	
B. Number, C. Case	178		
D. Methods and General Rules	180	I. Augment	277
E. History of Declension	186	II. Reduplication	280
CH. 2. DECLENSION OF NOUNS.		III. In Composition	282
I. First Declension	194	Dialectic Use	284
Dialectic Forms	197	CH. 9. AFFIXES OF CONJUGATION.	
II. Second Declension	199		
Dialectic Forms	201	I. Classification and Analysis	285
III. Third Declension	202	A. Tense-Signs	288
A. Mutes	203	B. Connecting Vowels	290
B. Liquids	208	C. Flexible Endings	295
C. Pures	212	II. Union with the Stem.	
Dialectic Forms	221	A. Consonant Changes	304
IV. Irregular Nouns	223	B. Vowel Changes	309
CH. 3. ADJECTIVES	229	C. -MI Form	313
CH. 4. NUMERALS	239	D. Complete Tenses	317
CH. 5. PRONOUNS.		Dialectic Forms	321
I. Substantive	243	CH. 10. STEM OF THE VERB	336
II. Adjective	249	I. Prime Stems	340
CH. 6. COMPARISON	256	II. Euphonic Stems	341
I. Of Adjectives,		III. Emphatic Stems	346
A. By -τερος, -τατος	257	IV. Adopted Stems	358
B. By -ίων, -ιστος	260	CH. 11. FORMATION OF WORDS	359
C. Irregular	262	I. Of Simple Words	362
II. Of Adverbs	263	A. Nouns	363
History of Comparison	264	B. Adjectives	373
CH. 7. PRINCIPLES OF CONJUGATION	265	C. Pronouns	377
		D. Verbs	378
A. Voice	266	E. Adverbs	380
B. Tense	267	II. Of Compound Words	383

BOOK III. SYNTAX.

General Remarks	391	I. Agreement	393
CH. 1. THE SUBSTANTIVE.		II. Use of Cases	397

CONTENTS.

A. Nominative	§ 400
B. Genitive	403
I. Of Departure	404
1. Separation	405
2. Distinction	406
II. Of Cause	410
A. 1. Origin	411
2. Material	412
3. Supply	414
4. Partitive	415
B. 1. Motive, &c.	428
2. Price, Value, &c.	431
3. Sensible and Mental Object	432
4. Time and Place	433
C. Active	434
D. Constituent	435
1. Property	440
2. Relation	441
C. Dative Objective	448
I. Of Approach	449
1. Nearness	450
2. Likeness	451
II. Of Influence	452
D. Dative Residual	465
I. Instrumental and Modal	466
II. Temporal and Local	469
E. Accusative	470
I. Of Direct Object, &c.	472
Double Accusative	480
II. Of Specification	481
III. Of Extent	482
IV. Adverbial	483
F. Vocative	484
Remarks on the Cases	485
III. Use of Numbers, Genders, and Persons	488
Rules of Agreement	492
CH. 2. ADJECTIVE AND PRONOUN.	
I. Agreement	504
II. On the Adjective	506

III. Use of Degrees	§ 510
IV. Use of the Article.	
A. Broad Use	516
B. Article Proper	520
V. On the Pronoun	535
A. Personal, &c.	536
B. Αὐτός	540
C. Demonstrative	542
D. Indefinite	548
E. Relative	549
F. Complementary and Interrogative	563
G. Ἄλλος and Ἕτερος	567
CH. 3. THE VERB.	
I. Agreement	568
II. Use of the Voices	575
A. Active	577
B. Middle	578
C. Passive	586
III. Use of the Tenses	590
A. Definite and Indefinite	591
B. Complete	599
C. Interchange	602
IV. Use of the Modes.	
A. Intellective	613
Use of ἄν	618
I. Final Clauses	624
II. Conditional	631
III. Relative & Temporal	640
IV. Complementary	643
V. Interchange	649
B. Volitive	655
C. Incorporated	657
I. Infinitive	663
II. Participle	673
III. Verbal in -τέος	682
CH. 4. THE PARTICLE	684
A. The Adverb	685
B. The Preposition	688
C. The Conjunction	700
Observations	703
CH. 5. ARRANGEMENT	718

BOOK IV. PROSODY.

CH. 1. QUANTITY AND VERSIFICATION	725
I. Natural Quantity	726
II. Local Quantity	734
III. Versification	740
A. Dactylic Verse	747
B. Anapæstic Verse	751
C. Iambic Verse	755
D. Trochaic Verse	760
E. Other Metres	764

CH. 2. ACCENT	766
I. General Laws	770
II. In Vowel Changes	772
III. In Inflection	775
IV. In Construction.	
A. Grave Accent	784
B. Anastrophe	785
C. Proclitics	786
D. Enclitics	787
V. In Formation	789

GREEK TABLES.

I. ORTHOGRAPHY AND ORTHOËPY.

1. THE ALPHABET.

(§ 90 – 92.)

Order.	Forms. Large.	Forms. Small.	Roman Letters.	Names.		Numeral Power.
I.	A	α	a	Ἄλφα	Alpha	1
II.	B	β, ϐ	b	Βῆτα	Beta	2
III.	Γ	γ, ϝ	g, n	Γάμμα	Gamma	3
IV.	Δ	δ	d	Δέλτα	Delta	4
V.	E	ε	ĕ	Ἐ ψῑλόν	Epsilon	5
VI.	Z	ζ	z	Ζῆτα	Zeta	7
VII.	H	η	ē	Ἦτα	Eta	8
VIII.	Θ	θ, ϑ	th	Θῆτα	Theta	9
IX.	I	ι	i	Ἰῶτα	Iota	10
X.	K	κ, ϰ	c	Κάππα	Kappa	20
XI.	Λ	λ	l	Λάμβδα	Lambda	30
XII.	M	μ	m	Μῦ	Mu	40
XIII.	N	ν	n	Νῦ	Nu	50
XIV.	Ξ	ξ	x	Ξῖ	Xi	60
XV.	O	ο	ŏ	Ὁ μῑκρόν	Omicron	70
XVI.	Π	π, ϖ	p	Πῖ	Pi	80
XVII.	P	ρ, ϱ	r	Ῥῶ	Rho	100
XVIII.	Σ, C	σ, ς	s	Σίγμα	Sigma	200
XIX.	T	τ, 7	t	Ταῦ	Tau	300
XX.	Υ	υ	y	Ὑ ψῑλόν	Upsilon	400
XXI.	Φ	φ	ph	Φῖ	Phi	500
XXII.	X	χ	ch	Χῖ	Chi	600
XXIII.	Ψ	ψ	ps	Ψῖ	Psi	700
XXIV.	Ω	ω	ō	Ὠ μέγα	Omega	800
EPI-SEMA.	F, ϝ, ϛ		f	Βαῦ	Vau	6
	Ϙ, ϙ		q	Κόππα	Koppa	90
	ϡ		sh	Σάν	San	900

2. Comparison of Alphabets.

(97, 98.)

Hebrew.	Greek.		Latin.		Hebrew.	Greek.		Latin.	
א Aleph	A	α Alpha	A	a	ס Samekh	Σ	σ Sigma	S	s
ב Beth	B	β Beta	B	b	ע Ayin	O	ο O micron	O	o
ג Gimel	Γ	γ Gamma	G	g	פ Pe	Π	π Pi	P	p
ד Daleth	Δ	δ Delta	D	d	צ Tsadhe	Ξ	ξ Xi	X	x
ה He	E	ε E psilon	E	e	ק Qoph	Ϙ	ϟ Koppa	Q	q
ו Vav	F	ϝ Vau	F	f	ר Resh	P	ρ Rho	R	r
ז Zayin	Z	ζ Zeta	Z	z	ש Shin	ϻ		San, Sampi	
ח Hheth	H	η Eta	H	h	ת Tav	T	τ Tau	T	t
ט Tet	Θ	θ Theta				Υ	υ U psilon	U, V, u, v, Y y	
י Yodh	I	ι Iota	I, J	i, j					
כ Kaph	K	κ Kappa	C, K	c, k		Φ	φ Phi		
ל Lamedh	Λ	λ Lambda	L	l		X	χ Chi		
מ Mem	M	μ Mu	M	m		Ψ	ψ Psi		
נ Nun	N	ν Nu	N	n		Ω	ω O mega		

3. Ligatures.

(90. 2.)

αι	αι	ὅτι	ἐπι	ϑ	σθ
ἀπο	ἀπο	ἐξ			σθαι
αυ	αυ	ευ			σσ
γὰρ	γὰρ	ην			στ
γγ	γγ	καὶ			σχ
γεν	γεν				ται
γρ	γρ	λλ			ταυ
δὲ	δὲ	μεν			τὴν
δι	δι	ος			τῆς
δια	δια	ου			το
ει	ει	περι			τοῦ
		ρα			τῶν
ἐκ	ἐκ	ρι			υν
ἐν	ἐν	ρο			ὑπο

4. Vocal Elements.

I. Vowels, Simple and Compound (106–110).

			Class I. A Sounds.	II. O Sounds.	III. E Sounds.	IV. U Sounds.	V. I Sounds.
Simple Vowels,	{	Short, 1.	ă	o	ε	ŭ	ĭ
	{	Long, 2.	ā	ω	η	ū	ī
Diphthongs in ι,	{	Proper, 3.	αι	οι	ει	υι	
	{	Improper, 4.	ᾳ	ῳ	ῃ	ῡι	
Diphthongs in υ,	{	Proper, 5.	αυ	ου	ευ		
	{	Improper, 6.	āυ	ωυ	ηυ		

II. Consonants (137, 138).

		Orders.	Class I. Labials.	Class II. Palatals.	Class III. Linguals.
MUTES.	{	1. Smooth Mutes,	π	κ	τ
		2. Middle Mutes,	β	γ	δ
		3. Rough Mutes,	φ	χ	θ
SEMI- VOWELS.	{	4. Double Consonants,	ψ	ξ	ζ
		5. Spirants,	F	I	σ
		6. Nasals,	μ	γ	ν } Liquids.
		7. Fluents,		λ ρ	

Consonants (Second Arrangement).

Mutes, { Labial, or π Mutes, π, β, φ,
Guttural, or κ Mutes, κ, γ, χ,
Dental, or τ Mutes, τ, δ, θ, } Simple Consonants.

Semivowels, { Liquids, λ, μ, ν, ρ, γ nasal,
Sibilants, { Pure, σ,
Mixed, ψ, ξ, ζ, } Double, or Compound Consonants.

III. Breathings (93).

Rough Breathing, or Aspirate (‘).
Smooth, or Soft Breathing (’).

5. Words Classified according to Accent.

Proclitic:
ὁ, οὐ, ἐν, ὡς.

Orthotone:
ὅς, ὥρα, πῦρ ·

Enclitic:
νῆσός τις.

Oxytone:
σύ, ἰδέ, ἀκοή.

Barytone:
ὕω, ἄξια, λῦε ·

Perispome:
οὖ, ὁρῶ, ἀνιῶ.

Paroxytone:
λύω, ταμίας.

Proparoxytone:
ἴδιος, ἐλύετε.

Properispome:
σῦκον, τιμᾶτε.

6. Figures affecting Letters and Sounds (99 s).

1. Adding:	2. Subtracting:	3. Transposing:	5. Uniting:
Prothesis, (*Initial*)	Aphæresis,	Metathesis.	Synæresis,
Epenthesis, (*Medial*)	Syncope,	4. Exchanging:	Contraction,
Paragoge, (*Final*)	Apocope,	Antithesis.	Crasis,
Extension.	Apostrophe.	Assimilation.	Synizesis.
6. Resolving:	7. Shortening:	8. Lengthening:	9. Attenuating:
Diæresis.	Systole.	Diastole.	Precession.

7. Contraction of Vowels (115 s).

In the columns in § 7 and 8, the *first* of the vowels or consonants affected by the change is placed at the *left*, and the *second* at the *top*, both in common type. The *result* of the change is in *full-face type*, in a line with the first and beneath the second. The parentheses enclose regular changes in the union of the stem and affixes of verbs. The labial, palatal, or lingual mute with which ν *final* combines as a, is represented by *l* or *p*. Some changes are placed below the columns, and some special cases are enclosed in brackets.

	α	αι	ᾳ	ε	ει	η	ῃ	ο	οι	ου	ω	ῳ	ι	υ(F)
α	**ᾱ** αυ ω	**αι**	**ᾳ**	(**ᾱ** η αι	**ᾳ** [Dor.	**ᾱ** η ᾱ]	**ᾳ**	**ω** εω	**ῳ** εῳ	**ω** εω	**ω**) εω	**ῳ** εῳ	**αι** ᾳ	**αυ**
ε	**η** ᾱ ει	**αι** αι ει	**ᾳ** η [Augm. ῃ]	(**ει**	**ει**	**η** [Ion. ευ	**ῃ** ευ]	**ου** ὡ	**οι** ῷ	**ου** ευ)	**ω**)	**ῳ**	**ει** ῑ	**ευ** ῡ]
η	η	**ῃ**		η	**ῃ**			ω			ω		**ῃ**	**ηυ**
ο	**ω** ᾱ ου	**αι**	(**ου** υι	**οι** ου	**ω** η	**οι** ῳ	**ου** ω	**οι**	**ου**	**ω**)	**ῳ**	**οι**	**ου**
ω	ω		**ω**										**ῳ**	**ωυ**
ι	ῑ		ῑ										ῑ	ῑ
υ	ῡ		ῡ										**υι**	ῡ

ειε & εια ει, οιε & οια οι, ονα ω & ου, υϊ ν. In Augment, ἐαυ ηὐ & αὐ, ἐευ εὐ & ηὔ, ἐο ὡ, ἐεο ἐω. In Affixes (13), αο ου & α, αε αι, οε οι & ω, οϊ ῳ.

8. Euphonic Changes of Consonants (141 s).

		σ	κ	μ	θ, σθ	τ	ντ	ν final	π, β, δ φ, ψ	π, β, γ, χ, ξ	l
π, β, φ		(ψ	φ	μμ	φθ	πτ	φατ)	la	βδ	[πφ]	[σσ, ζ]
κ, γ, χ		(ξ	χ	γμ	χθ	κτ	χατ)	pa	γδ	[κχ]	σσ, ζ
τ, δ, θ	{	(σ	κ	σμ	σθ [τθ]	στ	δατ)	la ν			σ, στ ζ, σσ
ν	{	(νε ας σσ σ	γκ κ	μμ σμ μ	νθ)			να		μπ μβ μφ μψ	ιν γγ γχ γξ

νλ λλ, νρ ῤῥ & νδρ, νθσ νσ, νζ ζ, (λσ λε, μσ με, ρσ ρε, μμμ μμ, γγμ γμ,) μλ βλ, μρ βρ, ρσ ῤῥ, σσ ττ, σδ ζ, Fρ ῥ, Fσ υσ, λl λλ.

II. ETYMOLOGY.

9. NOTES. 1. To avoid needless repetition, alike burdensome to teacher and pupil, and to accustom the student early to the application of rule, the tables of paradigms have been constructed with the following *ellipses*, which will be at once supplied from general rules:
 a. In the paradigms of DECLENSION, except the first, the *Voc. sing.* is omitted whenever it has the same form with the Nom., and the following cases are omitted throughout (see 181):
  α. The *Voc. plur.*, because it is always the same with the Nom.
  β. The *Dat. dual*, because it is always the same with the Gen.
  γ. The *Acc.* and *Voc. dual*, as always the same with the Nom.
  δ. The *Acc.* and *Voc. neut.*, in all the numbers, as always the same with the Nom.
 b. In the paradigms of ADJECTIVES, and of words similarly inflected, the *Neuter* is omitted in the *Gen.* and *Dat.* of all the numbers, and in the *Nom. dual;* because in these cases it never differs from the Masculine.
 c. In the paradigms of CONJUGATION, the 1*st Pers. dual* is omitted throughout, as having the same form with the 1st Pers. plur., and the 3*d Pers. dual* is omitted whenever it has the same form with the 2d Pers. dual, that is, in the primary tenses of the Indicative, and in the Subjunctive (299 c). For the form in -μεθον, whose empty shade has been so multiplied by grammarians, and forced to stand, for idle show, in the rank and file of numbers and persons, see 299 b.
 2. Varieties of inflection have been illustrated by some tables of still briefer form; where it seemed undesirable to cumber the page and weary the eye by the multiplication of needless details (17 s, 26, 39 s). In the shorter paradigms of verbs, the *dual* has been commonly omitted, because so little used, and so readily supplied from the general rule in 299 c.
 3. The regular formation of the tenses is exhibited in the table (31), which may be thus read: "The ——— tense is formed from the stem by affixing ———," or, "by prefixing ——— and affixing ——— (or, in the nude form, ———)." In the application of this table, the forms of the stem must be distinguished, if it has more than a single form (336).
 4. A star (*) in the tables shows that an element or form is wanting. Brackets [ ] are chiefly used to enclose what is unusual or doubtful, or may be omitted. For the common mode of representing euphonic change by the aid of parentheses, see 118 e. In this mode, *Latin Italics* have the same office as Greek full-face letters (and also, in § 42, *common Greek letters*, until a hyphen separates). For the use of the signs ¡, ‖, ⁀, see 27; of ', !, and superior figures, 36 g, 37 r; of (ν, 162 a.

A. TABLES OF DECLENSION.

10. I. CASES CLASSIFIED (397 s).

	Subjective.	Objective.	Residual.
Direct.	NOMINATIVE. Subject. *Who.*	ACCUSATIVE. Direct Object. *Whereinto.*	VOCATIVE. Compellative. *Address.*
Indirect.	GENITIVE. Origin, &c. *Whence* (from, of).	DATIVE. Indirect Object. *Whither* (to, for).	DATIVE (Ablative). Accompaniment. *Where* (at, in, with, by).

11. II. AFFIXES OF THE THREE DECLENSIONS.

	Dec. I. Masc.	Dec. I. Fem.	Dec. II. M. F.	Dec. II. Neut.	Dec. III. M. F.	Dec. III. Neut.
Sing. Nom.	ᾱς, ης	α, η	ος	ον	ς	*
Gen.	ου	ᾱς, ης	ου		ος	
Dat.	ᾳ, ῃ		ῳ		ῐ	
Acc.	αν, ην		ον		ν, ᾰ	*
Voc.	α, η		ε	ον	*	*
Plur. Nom.	αι		οι	ᾰ	ες	ᾰ
Gen.	ῶν		ων		ων	
Dat.	αις		οις		σῐ(ν	
Acc.	ᾱς		ους	ᾰ	ᾰς	ᾰ
Voc.	αι		οι	ᾰ	ες	ᾰ
Dual Nom.	ᾱ		ω		ε	
Gen.	αιν		οιν		οιν	
Dat.	αιν		οιν		οιν	
Acc.	ᾱ		ω		ε	
Voc.	ᾱ		ω		ε	

12. III. ELEMENTS OF THE AFFIXES.

In the column of Flexible Endings, the figures denote the Declensions; the small full-face letters are signs of *relation* or *case*, and the full-face capitals are signs of *number;* while those to which G. is attached also indicate *gender*. See 186–189.

	Connecting Vowels. Dec. I.	Dec. II.	Dec. III.	Flexible Endings.
Sing. Nom.	α(η)	ο	*	ς. Fem. 1, *. Neut. 2, ν G.; 3, *.
Gen.	α(η)	ο	*	(οθ) ος. 2 and Masc. 1, ο.
Dat.	α(η)	ο	*	ῐ.
Acc.	α(η)	ο	*	ν, ᾰ. Neut. 3, *.
Voc.	α(η)	ο(ε)	*	*
Plur. Nom.	α	ο	*	Eς. 1 and 2, E. Neut. ˘A G.
Gen.	α	ο	*	ωN.
Dat.	α	ο (Neut.)	*	(EΣι). 3, Σῐ. 1 and 2, ιΣ.
Acc.	α	ο	*	(νΣ) ᾰΣ. Neut. ˘A G.
Du. N. A. V.	α	ο	*	E.
G. D.	α	ο	*	ιN. 3, οιN.

§ 14. AFFIXES AND PARADIGMS COMPARED. 19

13. IV. AFFIXES ANALYZED AND COMPARED WITH THE LATIN.

The Affixes, printed in full-face type or italics, are preceded by their analyses in common type. Hyphens separate the Connecting Vowels from the Flexible Endings.

	Dec. I.		Dec. II.		Dec. III.	
	Masc. Fem.		M. F.	Neut.	M. F.	Neut.
S.N.	a-s ᾱς, ης | a-* a, η		o-s ος	o-ν ον	s	*
	a-* ᾱ		o-s ŭs	o-m ŭm	s	*
G. a-o	ου | a-os ᾱs, ης		o-o ου			os
	a-i æ [āī, ās]		o-i	ī [īŭs]		īs
D.	a-ι ᾳ, ῃ		o-ι ῳ			ī
	a-i æ		o-i	ō [ī]		ī
Ab.	a-e ā		o-e	ō		ĕ [ī]
A.	a-ν αν, ην		o-ν	ον	ν, ă	*
	a-m ăm		o-m	ŭm	ĕm [ĭm]	*
V.	a-* a, η		o-* ε	o-ν ον	*[=N.]	*
	a-* ᾱ		o-* ĕ	o-m ŭm	= N.	*
P.N.	a-ε αι		o-ε οι	*-a ă	ες	ă
	a-e æ		o-e ī	*-a ă	ēs	ă [ĭă]
G.	a-ων ῶν		o-ων ων		ων	
	a-um ārŭm [ŭm]		o-um ōrŭm[ŭm]		ŭm [ĭum]	
D.	a-ις αις		o-ις οις		σἱ(ν	
	a-is īs [ābŭs]		o-is īs [ōbŭs]		ĭbŭs[īs]	
A.	a-νs ᾱς		o-νs ους	*-a ă	νs ăs	ă
	a-ms ās		o-ms ōs	*-a ă	ems ēs [īs]	ă [ĭă]
D.N.	a-ε ā		o-ε ω		ε	
G.	a-ιν αιν		o-ιν οιν		οιν	

14. V. GREEK AND LATIN PARADIGMS COMPARED.

FIRST DECLENSION. — FEMININE.

Sing. Nom. λῠ́ρᾰ, lўra,   *a lyre* (Subject).
   Gen. λύρᾱς, { Gen. lyræ,   *of a lyre.*
                 { Abl. lyra,   *from a lyre.*
   Dat. λύρᾳ, { Dat. lyræ,   *to* or *for a lyre.*
                 { Abl. lyra,   *with* or *by a lyre.*
   Acc. λύρᾱν, lyram,   *a lyre* (Object).
   Voc. λύρᾰ, lyra,   *O lyre.*

Plur. Nom. λύραι, lyræ,   *lyres* (Subject).
   Gen. λυρῶν, { Gen. lyrārum,   *of lyres.*
                  { Abl. lyris,   *from lyres.*
   Dat. λύραις, { Dat. lyris,   *to* or *for lyres.*
                  { Abl. lyris,   *with* or *by lyres.*
   Acc. λύρᾱς, lyras,   *lyres* (Object).
   Voc. λύραι, lyræ,   *O lyres.*

Dual Nom. λύρᾱ, lyræ duæ,   *two lyres* (Subject).
   Gen. λύραιν, lyrārum duārum,   *of two lyres,* &c.

§ 14. GREEK AND LATIN DECLENSION COMPARED.

		DEC. I. MASC. *Sailor.*		DEC. II. MASC. *Wile.*		DEC. III. M. F. *Swine.*	
Sing.	Nom.	ναύτης	naut*a*	δόλος	dŏl*us*	σῦς	sūs
	Gen.	ναύτου	naut*œ*	δόλου	dol*i*	σὕός	sŭ*is*
	Dat.	ναύτῃ	naut*œ*	δόλῳ	dol*o*	σὕί	sŭ*i*
		Abl.	naut*a*		dol*o*		sŭ*e*
	Acc.	ναύτην	naut*am*	δόλον	dol*um*	σῦν	sŭ*em*
	Voc.	ναῦτἄ	naut*a*	δόλε	dol*e*	σῦ	sūs
Plur.	N. V.	ναῦται	naut*œ*	δόλοι	dol*i*	σὕες	sŭ*es*
	Gen.	ναυτῶν	naut*ārum*	δόλων	dol*ōrum*	σὕῶν	sŭ*uum*
	Dat.	ναύταις	naut*is*	δόλοις	dol*is*	σὕσί	sŭ*ibus*
	Acc.	ναύτας	naut*as*	δόλους	dol*os*	σὕας	sŭ*es*
Du.	N. A. V.	ναύτᾱ		δόλω		σὕε	
	G. D.	ναύταιν		δόλοιν		σὕοῖν	

		DEC. II. NEUT. *Gift.*			DEC. III. NEUT.		DEC. IV. N. *Knee.*	
				Fire.	*Throat.*	*Tear.*		
S.	N. A. V.	δῶρον	dōn*um*	πῦρ	guttŭr	δάκρῠ	genū
	Gen.	δώρου	don*i*	πῠρός	guttŭr*is*	δάκρῠος	gen(ŭ*is*)ūs
	Dat.	δώρῳ	don*o*	πυρί	guttur*i*	δάκρυϊ	gen(u*i*)ū
		Abl.	don*o*		gutt*ure*		gen(u*e*)ū
P.	N. A. V.	δῶρᾰ	don*a*		guttur*a*	δάκρυα	genŭ*a*
	Gen.	δώρων	don*ōrum*		guttur*um*	δακρύων	genu*um*
	Dat.	δώροις	don*is*		gutturi*bus*	δάκρυσι	genu*bus*
D.	N. A. V.	δώρω				δάκρυε	
	G. D.	δώροιν				δακρύοιν	

For σύας was also used the contract form σῦς ; for *suibus*, the syncopated *sŭbus;* and for *genubus* (genuibus), by a syncope of the *u*, *genibus*. See 225 f.

15. VI. NOUNS OF THE FIRST DECLENSION.

a. FEMININE.

		The goddess,	*fly,*	*muse,*	*table,*	*song,*	*mina.*
	Lat.	deă	musca	mūsa	mensa	ōdē	mīna
S.	N.	ἡ θεά	μυῖᾰ	μοῦσᾰ	τράπεζᾰ	ᾠδή	μνᾶ
	G.	τῆς θεᾶς	μυίᾱς	μούσης	τραπέζης	ᾠδῆς	μνᾶς
	D.	τῇ θεᾷ	μυίᾳ	μούσῃ	τραπέζῃ	ᾠδῇ	μνᾷ
	A.	τήν θεάν	μυῖᾰν	μοῦσᾰν	τράπεζᾰν	ᾠδήν	μνᾶν
P.	N.	αἱ θεαί	μυῖαι	μοῦσαι	τράπεζαι	ᾠδαί	μναῖ
	G.	τῶν θεῶν	μυιῶν	μουσῶν	τραπεζῶν	ᾠδῶν	μνῶν
	D.	ταῖς θεαῖς	μυίαις	μούσαις	τραπέζαις	ᾠδαῖς	μναῖς
	A.	τὰς θεάς	μυίᾱς	μούσᾱς	τραπέζᾱς	ᾠδάς	μνᾶς
D.	N.	τὰ θεά	μυίᾱ	μούσᾱ	τραπέζᾱ	ᾠδά	μνᾶ
	G.	ταῖν θεαῖν	μυίαιν	μούσαιν	τραπέζαιν	ᾠδαῖν	μναῖν

§ 15. c. DEC. I. 180 b, 194 s : Gender 176 ; ἡ, ὁ, 173 b ; ἄ, ᾱ, or η, in Sing., 194 s ; ποιητᾱ́ 194. 2 ; μν(αα)ᾶ, Ἑρμ(έας)ῆς, 196, 120 c ; βορρᾶ, Γωβρύου and -ᾱ, 198. 1, 93 d. Accent : θεᾶς 775 a, μυίας 771 b, μυιῶν 777 a, τραπέζης 770 a, Ἀτρεῖδαι 771 c, Ἑρμ(έας)ῆς 772. — Other Examples, σκιά *shadow*, οἰκία *house*, θύρα *door*, ὥρα hora, HOUR, μοῖρα *portion*, γλῶσσα or γλῶττα (169 a) *tongue*, δόξα *opinion*, λέαινα *lioness*, τιμή *honor*, κόρη *maiden*, σῦκ(ία)ῆ *fig-tree;* νεᾱνίας *young man*, κριτής *judge*, Πέρσης *Persian*.

§ 16. NOUNS OF THE FIRST AND SECOND DECLENSION. 21

b. MASCULINE.

	The steward,	poet,	son of Atreus,	Mercury,	north wind.	
Lat.	quæstor	poēta	Atrīdes	Hermes	boreas	
S. N.	ὁ ταμίας	ποιητής	Ἀτρείδης	Ἑρμ(έας)ῆς	βο(ρέας)ρρᾶς	
G.	τοῦ ταμίου	ποιητοῦ	Ἀτρείδου	Ἑρμ(έου)οῦ	βο(ρέου)ρρᾶ	
D.	τῷ ταμίᾳ	ποιητῇ	Ἀτρείδῃ	Ἑρμ(έᾳ)ῇ	βο(ρέᾳ)ρρᾷ	
Λ.	τὸν ταμίαν	ποιητήν	Ἀτρείδην	Ἑρμ(έαν)ῆν	βο(ρέαν)ρρᾶν	
V.	ὦ ταμία	ποιητά	Ἀτρείδη	Ἑρμ(έα)ῆ	βο(ρέα)ρρᾶ	
						Gobryas.
P. N.	οἱ ταμίαι	ποιηταί	Ἀτρεῖδαι	Ἑρμ(έαι)αῖ	N. Γωβρύας
G.	τῶν ταμιῶν	ποιητῶν	Ἀτρειδῶν	Ἑρμ(εῶν)ῶν	G. Γωβρύου,
D.	τοῖς ταμίαις	ποιηταῖς	Ἀτρείδαις	Ἑρμ(έαις)αῖς	Γωβρύᾳ
Λ.	τοὺς ταμίας	ποιητάς	Ἀτρείδας	Ἑρμ(έας)ᾶς	D. Γωβρύᾳ
D. N.	τὼ ταμία	ποιητά	Ἀτρείδα	Ἑρμ(έα)ᾶ	A. Γωβρύαν
G.	τοῖν ταμίαιν	ποιηταῖν	Ἀτρείδαιν	Ἑρμ(έαιν)αῖν	V. Γωβρύα

16. VII. NOUNS OF THE SECOND DECLENSION.

a. MASCULINE AND FEMININE.

	The choir,	island,	angel,	mind,		temple.	
Lat.	chŏrus	insŭla	angĕlus	mens		fānum	
S. N.	ὁ χορός	ἡ νῆσος	ὁ ἄγγελος	ὁ νόος,	νοῦς	ὁ νᾱός,	νεώς
G.	χοροῦ	νήσου	ἀγγέλου	νόου,	νοῦ	ναοῦ,	νεώ
D.	χορῷ	νήσῳ	ἀγγέλῳ	νόῳ,	νῷ	ναῷ,	νεῴ
Α.	χορόν	νῆσον	ἄγγελον	νόον,	νοῦν	ναόν,	νεών,
V.	χορέ	νῆσε	ἄγγελε	νόε,	νοῦ		[νεώ
P. N.	χοροί	νῆσοι	ἄγγελοι	νόοι,	νοῖ	ναοί,	νεῴ
G.	χορῶν	νήσων	ἀγγέλων	νόων,	νῶν	ναῶν,	νεών
D.	χοροῖς	νήσοις	ἀγγέλοις	νόοις	νοῖς	ναοῖς,	νεῴς
A.	χορούς	νήσους	ἀγγέλους	νόους,	νοῦς	ναούς,	νεώς
D.N.	χορώ	νήσω	ἀγγέλω	νόω,	νώ	ναώ,	νεώ
G.	χοροῖν	νήσοιν	ἀγγέλοιν	νόοιν,	νοῖν	ναοῖν,	νεῴν

b. NEUTER.

	The egg,	cave,	apple,	part,	bone.	
Lat.	ōvum	antrum	mālum	membrum	os	
S. N.	τὸ ᾠόν	ἄντρον	μῆλον	μόριον	ὀστέον,	ὀστοῦν
G.	τοῦ ᾠοῦ	ἄντρου	μήλου	μορίου	ὀστέου,	ὀστοῦ
D.	τῷ ᾠῷ	ἄντρῳ	μήλῳ	μορίῳ	ὀστέῳ,	ὀστῷ
P. N.	τὰ ᾠά	ἄντρα	μῆλα	μόρια	ὀστέα,	ὀστᾶ
G.	τῶν ᾠῶν	ἄντρων	μήλων	μορίων	ὀστέων,	ὀστῶν
D.	τοῖς ᾠοῖς	ἄντροις	μήλοις	μορίοις	ὀστέοις,	ὀστοῖς
D.N.	τὼ ᾠώ	ἄντρω	μήλω	μορίω	ὀστέω,	ὀστώ
G.	τοῖν ᾠοῖν	ἄντροιν	μήλοιν	μορίοιν	ὀστέοιν,	ὀστοῖν

§ 16. c. DEC. II. 199s: Gender 176; ν(όος)οῦς, ὀστ(έον)οῦν, 121, 120 c, 772; ν(αός)εώς 120 e, i, 772 d; A. νεώ 199. 3; ᾠόν 140. — O. E. ὁ λόγος *word*, ἡ ὁδός *way*, ὁ δῆμος *people*, ὁ ταῦρος taurus, *bull*, ὁ, ἡ ἄνθρωπος homo, *man*, ὁ θεός (182 c) deus, *god*, ὁ πλοῦς *voyage*, ὁ λεώς *people*, ὁ λαγώς *hare*, ἡ ἕως *dawn*; πτερόν *wing*, ῥόδον rosa, ROSE, σῦκον *fig*, ὄργανον *tool*.

17. v. Nouns of the Third Declension.

A. MUTE. — a. Masculine and Feminine.

	a. LABIAL.	b. PALATAL.		c. LINGUAL.	
	ὁ, vulture.	ὁ,ἡ,goat.	ἡ, hair.	ἡ, hope.	ὁ, tooth.	ἡ, key.
S. N.	γύψ	αἴξ	θρίξ	ἐλπίς	ὀδούς	κλείς clāvis
G.	γῡπός	αἰγός	τρῐχός	ἐλπίδος	ὀδόντος	κλειδός
D.	γῡπί	αἰγί	τρῐχί	ἐλπίδι	ὀδόντι	κλειδί
A.	γῦπα	αἶγα	τρίχα	ἐλπίδα	ὀδόντα	κλεῖδα, κλεῖν
P. N.	γῦπες	αἶγες	τρίχες	ἐλπίδες	ὀδόντες	κλεῖδες[κλεῖς]
G.	γῡπῶν	αἰγῶν	τρίχῶν	ἐλπίδων	ὀδόντων	κλειδῶν
D.	γῦψί	αἰξί	θριξί	ἐλπίσι	ὀδοῦσι	κλεισί
A.	γῦπας	αἶγας	τρίχας	ἐλπίδας	ὀδόντας	κλεῖδας, κλεῖς
D. N.	γῦπε	αἶγε	τρίχε	ἐλπίδε	ὀδόντε	κλεῖδε
G.	γῡποῖν	αἰγοῖν	τριχοῖν	ἐλπίδοιν	ὀδόντοιν	κλειδοῖν

	ἡ, vein.	ὁ, raven.	ὁ, lynx.	ἡ, strife.	ἡ, helmet.	ὁ, foot.
S. N.	φλέψ	κόραξ	λύγξ	ἔρις	κόρυς	πούς
G.	φλεβός	κόρακος	λυγκός	ἔριδος	κόρυθος	ποδός
D.	φλεβί	κόρακι	λυγκί	ἔριδι	κόρυθι	ποδί
A.	φλέβα	κόρακα	λύγκα	ἔριδα, ἔριν	κόρυθα, κόρυν	πόδα
P. D.	φλεψί	κόραξι	λυγξί	ἔρισι	κόρυσι	ποσί

d. LINGUAL (continued).

	ὁ,ἡ, child.	ὁ, sovereign.	ἡ, wife.	ὁ, lion.	ὁ, giant.	ἡ, Opus.
S. N.	παῖς	ἄναξ	δάμαρ	λέων	γίγας	Ὀποῦς
G.	παιδός	ἄνακτος	δάμαρτος	λέοντος	γίγαντος	Ὀποῦντος
D.	παιδί	ἄνακτι	δάμαρτι	λέοντι	γίγαντι	Ὀποῦντι
A.	παῖδα	ἄνακτα	δάμαρτα	λέοντα	γίγαντα	Ὀποῦντα
V.	παῖ	ἄνα		λέον	γίγαν	
P. D.	παισί	ἄναξι	δάμαρσι	λέουσι	γίγασι	

e. NEUTER. — LINGUAL.

	τό, body.	τό, light.	τό, liver.	τό, horn.		τό, ear.
S. N.	σῶμᾰ	φῶς	ἧπαρ	κέρᾰς	cornu	οὖς
G.	σώματος	φωτός	ἥπατος	κέρᾱτος, κέρᾱος, κέρως		ὠτός
D.	σώματι	φωτί	ἥπατι	κέρᾱτι, κέραϊ, κέρᾳ		ὠτί
P. N.	σώματα	φῶτα	ἥπατα	κέρᾱτα, κέραα, κέρᾱ		ὦτα
G.	σωμάτων	φώτων	ἡπάτων	κεράτων, κεράων, κερῶν		ὤτων
D.	σώμασι	φωσί	ἥπασι	κέρᾱσι		ὠσί
D. N.	σώματε	φῶτε	ἥπατε	κέρᾱτε, κέραε, κέρᾱ		ὦτε
G.	σωμάτοιν	φώτοιν	ἡπάτοιν	κεράτοιν, κεράοιν, κερῶν		ὤτοιν

§ 17. f. Dec. III. 202 s: Gender 177. Mutes : γύ(πs)ψ, λύγ(κs)ξ, lyn(cs)x, ἐλπί(δs)s, 151 ; γῦ(πν)πα, κλεῖ(δν)ν, 160 e, 204 a ; (θ)τριχός 159 b ; ὀδ(οντs)ούs den(ts)s, ὀδ(οντσι)οῦσι, γίγ(αντs)ᾱs gig(ants)ās, λέ(οντs)ων le(ons)o, δάμα(ρτs)ρ, 153, 156, 205 ; π(οδs)ούs pe(ds)s 214 a ; ἄν(ακτ)α, παῖ,

§ 19. LIQUIDS. PURE. 23

(a. Not syncopated.)   **18. B. LIQUID.**   (b. Syncopated.)

	ὁ, beast.	ἡ, nose.	ἡ, hand.	ὁ, man.		ὁ,ἡ,dog.	ὁ,ἡ,lamb.
S. N.	θήρ fēra	ῥίς	χείρ	ἀνήρ vir		κύων	(ἀμνός)
G.	θηρός	ῥῑνός	χειρός	ἀνέρος,	ἀνδρός	κῠνός	ἀρνός
D.	θηρί	ῥῑνί	χειρί	ἀνέρι,	ἀνδρί	κυνί	ἀρνί
A.	θῆρα	ῥῑνα	χεῖρα	ἀνέρα,	ἄνδρα	κύνα	ἄρνα
V.		ῥίν		ἄνερ		κύον	
P. N.	θῆρες	ῥῑνες	χεῖρες	ἀνέρες,	ἄνδρες	κύνες	ἄρνες
G.	θηρῶν	ῥῑνῶν	χειρῶν	ἀνέρων,	ἀνδρῶν	κυνῶν	ἀρνῶν
D.	θηρσί	ῥῑσί	χερσί	ἀνδράσι		κυσί	ἀρνάσι
A.	θῆρας	ῥῑνας	χεῖρας	ἀνέρας,	ἄνδρας	κύνας	ἄρνας
P. N.	θῆρε	ῥῑνε	χεῖρε	ἀνέρε,	ἄνδρε	κύνε	ἄρνε
G.	θηροῖν	ῥῑνοῖν	χεροῖν	ἀνέροιν,	ἀνδροῖν	κυνοῖν	ἀρνοῖν

	ὁ, orator.	ὁ, harbor.	ὁ, deity.	ὁ, pæan.	ὁ, father.
Lat.	orātor	portus	dæmon	pæān	păter
S. N.	ῥήτωρ	λιμήν	δαίμων	παιάν	πατήρ
G.	ῥήτορος	λιμένος	δαίμονος	παιᾶνος	πατέρος, πατρός
D.	ῥήτορι	λιμένι	δαίμονι	παιᾶνι	πατέρι, πατρί
A.	ῥήτορα	λιμένα	δαίμονα	παιᾶνα	πατέρα
V.	ῥῆτορ		δαῖμον		πάτερ
P. D.	ῥήτορσι	λιμέσι	δαίμοσι	παιᾶσι	πατράσι

19. C. PURE. — a. MASCULINE AND FEMININE.

	ὁ,weevil.	ὁ,ἡ,sheep.	ὁ, hero.	ὁ, ἡ, ox.	ὁ, fish.	ἡ, echo.
S. N.	κίς	οἶς ŏvis	ἥρως hērōs	βοῦς bōs	ἰχθύς	ἠχώ echo
G.	κιός	οἰός	ἥρωος	βοός bŏvis	ἰχθύος	ἠχ(όος)οῦς
D.	κῑί	οἰί	ἥρωϊ [ἥρῳ]	βοΐ bŏvi	ἰχθύϊ	ἠχ(όϊ)οῖ
A.	κίν	οἶν	ἥρωα, ἥρω	βοῦν	ἰχθύν	ἠχ(όα)ώ
V.				βοῦ	ἰχθύ	ἠχοῖ
P. N.	κίες	οἶες[οἶς]	ἥρωες	βόες	ἰχθύες [ἰχθῦς]	
G.	κιῶν	οἰῶν	ἡρώων	βοῶν boum	ἰχθύων	
D.	κῑσί	οἰσί	ἥρωσι	βουσί	ἰχθύσι	
A.	κίας	οἶας, οἶς	ἥρωας, ἥρως	βόας, βοῦς	ἰχθύας, ἰχθῦς	
D.N.	κίε	οἶε	ἥρωε	βόε	ἰχθύε [ἰχθῦ]	
G.	κῑοῖν	οἰοῖν	ἡρώοιν	βοοῖν	ἰχθύοιν	

---

204 b; σῶμ(ατ)α, φ(ωτ)ῶς, ἦπ(ατ)αρ, 160. Contraction 207: κλεῖς 122, Ὀπ(όεις)οῦς 118 d, 121 b, κέρᾳ 119, κέρα, κέρως, (οἴας) οὖς, ὠτός, 120 a, b, c. Accent: γυπός 778 a, φώτων 778 b. — O. E. ὁ γρύψ, -ῡπός, gryps, -ȳphis, GRIFFIN, Ἄραψ, -αβος, ARAB, ἡ φάλαγξ, -αγγος, phalanx, -angis, θής, θητός, hired man, ἡ λαμπάς, -άδος, torch, LAMP, ἡ χάρις, -ιτος, grace, ἡ νύξ, -κτός, nox, -ctis, NIGHT, ὁ δράκων, -οντος, draco, DRAGON, ὁ ἱμάς, -άντος, thong; τὸ ποίημα, -ατος, poēma, -atis, POEM, τὸ ἦμαρ, -ατος, day, τὸ τέρας, -ατος, prodigy, τὸ ὕδωρ, ὕδατος, water.

§ 18. c. Liquids 208 s: θή(ρς)ρ, λιμ(ενς)ήν, ῥί(νς)s, 153, 156, 208; λιμέσι, θηρσί, 154, 157; χερσί 224 f; ἄνερ 208 f; κυ[ο]νός canis, πατ[ε]ρί

THIRD DECLENSION. — PURES. § 19.

b. Masculine and Feminine (continued).

S. N.	ἡ πόλις *city*	ὁ πῆχυς *cubit*	ὁ ἱππεύς *knight*	ἡ ναῦς *ship*
G.	πόλεως	πήχεως	ἱππέως	νεώς
D.	πόλει, πόλει	πήχει, πήχει	ἱππεῖ, ἱππεῖ	νηΐ
A.	πόλιν	πῆχυν	ἱππέα	ναῦν
V.	πόλι	πῆχυ	ἱππεῦ	(γραῦ)
P. N.	πόλεες, πόλεις	πήχεες, πήχεις	ἱππέες, ἱππεῖς, -ῆς	νῆες
G.	πόλεων	πηχέων [πηχῶν]	ἱππέων	νεῶν
D.	πόλεσι	πήχεσι	ἱππεῦσι	ναυσί
A.	πόλεας, πόλεις	πήχεας, πήχεις	ἱππέας, ἱππεῖς	ναῦς
D. N.	πόλεε, πόλη	πήχεε	ἱππέε	[νῆε].
G.	πολέοιν	πηχέοιν	ἱππέοιν	νεοῖν

S. N.	Σωκράτης Socrates		Ἡρακλέης,	Ἡρακλῆς Hercules
G.	Σωκράτεος, Σωκράτους		Ἡρακλέεος,	Ἡρακλέους
D.	Σωκράτεϊ, Σωκράτει		Ἡρακλέεϊ,	Ἡρακλέει, Ἡρακλεῖ
A.	Σωκράτεα, Σωκράτη, -ην		Ἡρακλέεα,	Ἡρακλέα, Ἡρακλῆ
V.	Σώκρατες		Ἡράκλεες,	Ἡράκλεις [Ἡρακλες]

c. Neuter.

S. N.	τὸ γέρας *honor*	τὸ γένος	*race*	gĕnŭs	τὸ ἄστυ *town*
G.	γέραος, γέρως	γένεος,	γένους	generis	ἄστεος, ἄστεως
D.	γέραϊ	γέραι	γένεϊ, γένει	generi	ἄστεϊ, ἄστει
P. N.	γέραα, γέρα	γένεα	γένη	genere	ἄστεα, ἄστη
G.	γεράων, γερῶν	γενέων	γενῶν	generum	ἀστέων
D.	γέρασι	γένεσι		generibus	ἄστεσι
D. N.	γέραε, γέρα	γένεε	γένη		ἄστεε
G.	γεράοιν, γερῷν	γενέοιν, γενοῖν			ἀστέοιν

pat[e]ri, ἀρ[ε]να, 210 ; ἀνδρός 146 ; ἀρ(ενσι)νάσι 145 a. — O. E. ὁ φώρ, -ωρός, fu(rs)r, *thief*, ὁ, ἡ 'ἀήρ, -έρος, äer, AIR, ἡ μήτηρ, -τρός, mäter, -tris, MOTHER, ἡ ἀκτίς, -ῖνος, *ray*, ὁ ποιμήν, -ένος, *shepherd*, ὁ μήν, μηνός, mensis, MONTH, ὁ αἰών, -ῶνος, ævum, *age*, ὁ ἅλς, ἁλός, sa(ls)l, SALT ; τὸ νέκταρ, -apos, nectar, τὸ (FEαp) ἔαρ ἦρ vēr, *spring*.

§ 19. d. Pures 212 s : κῖς, ἰχθύς, 217 c ; κῖν 216 b, 202 a ; (ὄφις ovis) ὄϊς οἶς 21, 140 b ; [βοFs, βοFοs bovis] βοῦς, βοός, 214, 217 a, b ; ἱππ(εFs)εύς, ν(αFs)αῦς navis, πῆχυς, ἄστυ 213 a, 215 b, 216, 217 b ; πόλις 213 b, 217 g ; Σωκράτης 213 a, 217 c ; γένος 215 b, 217 d ; ἠχ(os)ώ 214 b ; V. ἠχοῖ, βοῦ, 215 c, 217 b, d ; βουσί, ναυσί, 216 d ; νηΐ 222 f ; Σωκράτην 216 c. Contraction 7, 118 s : ἤρῳ, πόλει, γέραι, 119 ; γέρα, ἄστη, γέρως, ἥρω, 120 a, b, c ; Ἡρακλέα 120 f ; νεώς 120 i, 222 f ; πόλεις, γένους, ἠχοῦς echus, οἷς, ἰχθῦ, πόλη, ἱππῆς, 121 ; A. οἷς, βοῦς, πόλεις, ναῦς, 122 ; πόλεως, ἱππέα, -ᾱς, 220 ; πηχῶν 220 f ; Ἡρακλῆς 219 c. — O. E. ὁ θώς, θωός, *jackal*, ὁ μῦς, μυός, mūs, mūris, MOUSE ; ἡ ἄρκυς, -υος, *net*, ἡ 'Ἰώ, 'Ἰοῦς, Io, Ius, ἡ τάξις, -εως, *rank*, ὁ πέλεκυς, -εως, ax, ὁ βασιλεύς *king*, ὁ Εὐμένης, -ους, ὁ Περικλ(έης)ῆς · τὸ κρέας caro, *flesh*, τὸ νέφος nūbes, *cloud*, τὸ τεῖχος *wall*.

20. IX. Dialectic Forms of Declension.

a. First Declension (197 s).

S. N. ᾱs, Ion. ης · ταμίης, βορέης.
  ης, Dor. ᾱς · ναύτᾱς, Ἀτρείδᾱς.
  Old, ᾰ · ἱππότᾰ, μητιετᾰ.
  ᾱ, Ion. η · λύρη, οἰκίη. [ση.
  ᾰ, Ion. η · Ep. ἀληθείη, κνισ-
  η, Dor. ᾱ · 'ᾱ ᾠδᾰ́, τιμᾰ́, γᾰ.
G. ου, Old, ᾱο · Ἀτρείδᾱο, Βορέᾱο.
  Ion. εω, ω · Ἀτρείδεω, Βορέω.
  Dor. ᾱ · Ἀτρείδᾱ, Ἑρμᾱ.
  ᾱς, Ion. ης · λύρης, γενεῆς.
  ης, Dor. ᾱς · τιμᾱς, μούσᾱς.
  Ep. ηθε(ν · Αἰσύμηθεν.
D. ᾳ, Ion. ῃ · ταμίῃ, λύρῃ.
  ῃ, Dor. ᾳ · ναύτᾳ, τᾳ ᾠδᾳ.
  Ep. ηφι(ν · ἦφι βίηφιν.

A. αν, { Ion. ην, εᾰ(masc.); λύρην,
       { [Ἀρισταγόρην, -εᾰ.
  ην, { Dor. ᾱν · ναύτᾱν, τιμᾱ́ν.
V. ᾱ, Ion. η · ταμίη, νεηνίη.
  ᾰ, Poet. η · Αἴητη Ap. Rh.
  η, Dor. ᾱ · Ἀτρείδᾱ, Μενάλκᾱ.
  Old, ᾰ · νύμφᾰ, Δικᾰ.
P. G. ῶν, Old, ᾱων · Ἀτρειδᾱ́ων. [ων.
  Ion. έων · Ἀτρειδέων, λυρέ-
  Dor. ᾱν · Ἀτρειδᾱν, θυρᾱν.
D. αις, Old, αισι(ν · ταῖσι θύραισιν.
  Ion. ῃσι(ν, ῃς · θεῇσι, πέτρῃς.
A. ᾱς, [Ion. εᾱς(masc.); δεσπότευς].
  Dor. ᾰς · Μοῖρᾰς, νύμφᾰς.
Æol. αις · ταῖς τιμαῖς.

b. Second Declension (201).

S. N. ος, Laconic, ορ · παλεόρ, 169 d.
G. ου, Ep. & Thes. οιο · τοῖο λόγοιο.
  Dor. ω · τῶ λόγω.
  [Ion. εω · Βάττεω, Κροίσεω.]
  Ep. οθε(ν · οὐράνοθεν.
  ω (fr. αου), Ep. ωο · Πετεῶο.
D. ῳ, Old, οι · Ἰσθμοῖ, τοῖ δάμοι.
  Ep. όφι(ν · αὐτόφι, ζυγόφιν.
  Ep. οθι · οὐρανόθι, Ἰλιόθι.

S. D. ῳ, Bœot. ῡ · αὐτῡ, τῡ δάμῡ.
P. N. οι, Bœot. ῡ · καλῡ, Ὅμηρῡ.
  [G. ων, Ion. έων · πυρέων, Σουσέων.]
D. οις, Old, οισι(ν · τοῖσι λόγοισιν.
  Bœot. ῡς · ἀλλῡς προξένῡς.
A. ους, Dor. ως, ος · τὼς λόγως, τὼς
  λύκος, παρθένος.
  Æol. οις · ἀνδρείοις πέπλοις.
Dual οιν, Ep. οιϊν · ἱπποιϊν, ὠμοιϊν.

c. Third Declension (221 s).

S. G. ατος, αος, Ion. εος · κέρεος, οὔδεος.
  εος, Ion. & Dor. ευς · θέρευς.
  έως, Ep. ῆος · βασιλῆος, ἱππῆος.
  Ion. & Dor. έος · βασιλέος.
  εως, Poet. εος, ηος · πόλεος, -ηος.
  Ion. & Dor. ιος · πόλιος.
  ιδος, Ion. & Dor. ιος · Κύπριος.
  Dor. ιτος · Θέμιτος.
  οῦς, Dor. & Æol. ῶς · ἀχῶς, αἰδῶς.
D. εῖ, Ep. ῆϊ · βασιλῆϊ, Πηλῆϊ.
  Ion. έϊ · βασιλέϊ, Πηλέϊ.
  ει, Ion. & Dor. ῑ · πόλῑ, δυνάμῑ.
  ιδι, Ion. & Dor. ῑ · Θέτῑ, ἀπόλῑ.
  υϊ, Ep. υι · νέκυι, ὀϊζυῖ.
A. ν, Poet. α · εὐρέα, ἰχθύα.
  όα, Ion. οῦν · Ἰοῦν, Λητοῦν.
  Dor. ών · Ἥρων, Λατών.
  έᾱ, Ep. ῆᾰ · βασιλῆᾰ, ἱππῆᾰ.
  Ion. & Poet. ῆ · βασιλέᾰ.
  Dor. & Poet. ῆ · βασιλῆ.
V. ες, Æol. ε · Σώκρατε.

P. N. εῖς, Old Att. ῆς · βασιλῆς.
  Ep. ῆες · βασιλῆες, ἱππῆες.
  Ion. & Dor. έες · βασιλέες.
  εις, Ion. & Dor. ιες · πόλιες.
  αα, Poet. ᾰ · γέρᾰ, κρέᾰ.
  Ion. εα · γέρεα, τέρεα.
G. ων, Ion. έων · χηνέων, ἀνδρέων.
  [Dor. ᾱν · αἰγᾱν, κυνᾱν?]
  έων, Ep. ήων · βασιλήων.
  εων, Ion. & Dor. ίων · πολίων.
D. σι(ν, Old, εσι(ν · χείρεσσι.
  Poet. εσσι(ν · ἔπεσσι.
  εσσι(ν · πόδεσσιν.
  εσι(ν, Ep. εσφι(ν · ὀχεσφιν.
  Ion. ισι(ν · πόλισι.
  εὖσι(ν, Ep. ήεσσι(ν · ἀριστήεσσι.
A. έᾱς, Ep. ῆᾰς · βασιλῆᾰς. [ᾰς.
  Ion. & Dor. έᾰς · βασιλέ-
  Comm. εῖς · βασιλεῖς.
  εις, Ion. & Dor. ιας · πόλιας.
Dual οιν, Ep. οιϊν · ποδοῖϊν.

21. x. Irregular and Dialectic Declension.

	ὁ, Jupiter.	Dor.	ὁ, Glūs.	ὁ, Œdipus.		Poet. & Ion.
S. N.	Ζεύς,	Ζάν	Γλοῦς	Οἰδίπους	[Οἰδίπος]	
G.	Διός, Ζηνός	Ζᾱνός	Γλοῦ	Οἰδίποδος, Οἰδίπου poet. Οἰδιπόδᾱο,-ᾱ,-εω
D.	Διί, Ζηνί	Ζανί	Γλοῦ	Οἰδίποδι		Οἰδιπόδᾳ, -ῃ
A.	Δία, Ζῆνα	Ζᾶνα	Γλοῦν	Οἰδίποδα, Οἰδίπουν	Οἰδιπόδᾱν,-ην
V.	Ζεῦ		Γλοῦ	Οἰδίπου		Οἰδιπόδα, -η

P. N. [Δίες, Ζῆνες]   G. Οἰδιπόδων, A. -as

	Attic. ὁ, son.	Homeric.		Doric. ἡ, ship.	Ionic.
S. N.	υἱός	υἱός		ναῦς [νᾶς]	νηῦς [νηῦς]
G.	υἱοῦ, υἱέος	υἱοῦ, υἷος, υἱέος	ναός	νηός, νεός
D.	υἱῷ, υἱεῖ	υἱῷ, υἷι, υἱέϊ, υἱεῖ	ναΐ	νηΐ
A.	υἱόν	υἱόν, υἷα, υἱέα	ναῦν [νᾶν]	νῆα, νέα [νηῦν]
V.	υἱέ	υἱέ			
P. N.	υἱοί, υἱεῖς	υἷες, υἱέες, υἱεῖς	νᾶες	νῆες, νέες
G.	υἱῶν, υἱέων υἱῶν,	υἱέων	ναῶν	νηῶν, νεῶν
D.	υἱοῖς, υἱέσι	υἱοῖσι, υἱάσι,	ναυσί,νάεσσι	νηυσί,νήεσσι,νέεσσι,
A.	υἱούς, υἱεῖς	υἷας, υἱέας	νᾶας	νῆας, νέας [ναῦφι
D. N.	υἱώ, υἱέε				
G.	υἱοῖν, υἱέοιν				

	Attic. τό, spear.	Homeric.		τό, cave.	Homeric.	ὁ, stone.
S. N.	δόρυ	Poet. δόρυ		σπέος	σπεῖος	λᾶας
G.	δόρατος,	δορός δουρός	(γούνατος)	σπείους		λᾶος
D.	δόρατι, δορί, δόρει	δουρί	δούρατι	σπῆϊ		λᾶϊ
						A. λᾶαν
P. N.	δόρατα,	δόρη δοῦρα	δούρατα	(κλέα)		
G.	δοράτων		δούρων	σπείων		λάων
D.	δόρασι		δούρεσσι, δούρασι	σπέσσι, σπήεσσι	λάεσσι
D. N.	δόρατε		δοῦρε			λᾶε
G.	δοράτοιν					

Homeric Paradigms.

	ὁ, knight.	ἡ, city.			ὁ, ἡ, sheep.
S. N.	ἱππεύς	πόλις			ὄϊς
G.	ἱππῆος (Τυδέος)	πόλιος, πτόλιος, πόλεος, πόληος	ὄϊος, οἰός
D.	ἱππῆϊ (Πηλέϊ,-εῖ)	πόλϊ, πτόλεϊ, πόλει ? πόληϊ	
A.	ἵππῆα (Τυδέα,-ῆ)	πόλιν, πτόλιν	(πόληα Hes.)	ὄϊν
V.	ἱππεῦ	(μάντι A. 106)			
P. N.	ἱππῆες, ἱππεῖς ?	πόλιες,	πόληες		ὄϊες
G.	ἱππήων	πολίων			ὄϊων, οἰῶν
D.	ἱππεῦσι (ἀριστή-	πολέεσσι (ἐπάλξεσιν)		ὀέεσσι, οἴεσι,
A.	ἱππῆας [εσσι)	πόλιας, πόλῖς or πόλεις, πόληας	ὄϊς [όεσσι

	ὁ, Ulysses.		ὁ, Patroclus.	ὁ, Mars.
S. N.	Ὀδυσσεύς,	Ὀδῠσεύς	Πάτροκλος (-ῆς Theoc.)	Ἄρης
G.	Ὀδυσσῆος,-έος,	Ὀδυσῆος, Ὀδυσεῦς	Πατρόκλου, -οιο, -ῆος	Ἄρηος, -εος
D.	(Ἀχιλλεῖ)	Ὀδυσῆϊ	Πατρόκλῳ	Ἀρηΐ,-εΐ,-ει
A.	Ὀδυσσῆα,	Ὀδυσῆα Ὀδυσῆ	Πάτροκλον, -ῆα	Ἄρηα, -ην
V.	Ὀδυσσεῦ,	Ὀδυσεῦ	Πάτροκλε, -εες or -εις	Ἄρες E. 31.

22. XI. ADJECTIVES OF TWO TERMINATIONS.

a. OF THE SECOND DECLENSION.

	ὁ, ἡ (unjust) τό		ὁ, ἡ (unfading)		τό	
S. N.	ἄδικος	ἄδικον	ἀγήραος	ἀγήρως	ἀγήραον,	ἀγήρων
G.	ἀδίκου		ἀγηράου,	ἀγήρω		
D.	ἀδίκῳ		ἀγηράῳ,	ἀγήρῳ		
A.	ἄδικον		ἀγήραον,	ἀγήρων,	ἀγήρω	
V.	ἄδικε					
P. N.	ἄδικοι	ἄδικα	ἀγήραοι,	ἀγήρῳ	ἀγήραα,	ἀγήρω
G.	ἀδίκων		ἀγηράων,	ἀγήρων		
D.	ἀδίκοις		ἀγηράοις,	ἀγήρῳς		
A.	ἀδίκους		ἀγηράους,	ἀγήρως		
D. N.	ἀδίκω		ἀγηράω,	ἀγήρω		
G.	ἀδίκοιν		ἀγηράοιν,	ἀγήρῳν		

b. OF THE THIRD DECLENSION.

	ὁ, ἡ (male) τό		ὁ, ἡ (pleasing) τό		ὁ, ἡ (two-footed) τό	
S. N.	ἄρρην	ἄρρεν	εὐχᾰρις	εὔχαρι	δίπους	δίπουν
G.	ἄρρενος		εὐχάρῐτος		δίποδος	
D.	ἄρρενι		εὐχάριτι		δίποδι	
A.	ἄρρενα		εὐχάριτα, εὔχαριν		δίποδα, δίπουν	
V.	ἄρρεν		εὔχαρι		δίπου	
P. N.	ἄρρενες	ἄρρενα	εὐχάριτες	εὐχάριτα	δίποδες	δίποδα
G.	ἀρρένων		εὐχαρίτων		διπόδων	
D.	ἄρρεσι		εὐχάρισι		δίποσι	
A.	ἄρρενας		εὐχάριτας		δίποδας	
D. N.	ἄρρενε		εὐχάριτε		δίποδε	
G.	ἀρρένοιν		εὐχαρίτοιν		διπόδοιν	

	ὁ, ἡ, (evident) τό		ὁ, ἡ (greater) τό	
S. N.	σαφής	σαφές	μείζων major	μεῖζον majus
G.	σαφέος, σαφοῦς		μείζονος majōris	
D.	σαφέϊ, σαφεῖ		μείζονι majori	
A.	σαφέα, σαφῆ		μείζονα, μείζω	
V.	σαφές		μεῖζον	
P. N.	σαφέες σαφεῖς σαφέα, σαφῆ		μείζονες, μείζους μείζονα, μείζω	
G.	σαφέων, σαφῶν		μειζόνων	
D.	σαφέσι		μείζοσι	
A.	σαφέας, σαφεῖς		μείζονας, μείζους	
D. N.	σαφέε, σαφῆ		μείζονε	
G.	σαφέοιν, σαφοῖν		μειζόνοιν	

§ 22. c. ADJ. OF TWO TERM. 231 : ἀγήρως 200, ἀγήρω 199. 3, 120 e ; ἀρρ(ενς)ην, μειζ(ονς)ων, 208 a, 157 ; εὔχαρι(τς)ς 204 ; δίπ(οδς)ους bipes, δίπουν. 214 a, 231 c, 204 a, 202 a, δίπου 215 c ; σαφής, σαφές, 213 c, 215 a, 217 d, e , σαφοῦς, σαφεῖ, 219 a, 119, 121 s ; μείζω 211. — O. E. ἥσυχος *quiet*, ἔνδοξος *glorious*, ἄν(οος)ους, -(οον)ουν, *senseless*, ἵλ(αος)εως *propitious*, εὔγεως *fertile;* εὐδαίμ(ονς)ων *fortunate*, εὐέλπι(δς)ς *hopeful*, ἀληθής, -ές, *true*, ὑγιής, -ές (120 f), *healthy*, μείων minor, *less*, πολύπους *many-footed*, polÿpus, *polyp*.

23. XII. ADJECTIVES OF THREE TERMINATIONS.

a. OF THE SECOND AND FIRST DECLENSIONS.

	ὁ (mōrus)	ἡ (foolish)	τό	M. (ἀγαθός)	F. (good)	N.
S. N.	μῶρος	μώρα	μῶρον	bŏnus	bona	bonum
G.	μώρου	μώρας		boni	bonæ	
D.	μώρῳ	μώρᾳ		bono	bonæ, Ab. -a	
A.	μῶρον	μώραν		bonum	bonam	
V.	μῶρε			bone		
P. N.	μῶροι	μῶραι	μῶρα	boni	bonæ	bona
G.	μώρων	μώρων		bonōrum	bonārum	
D.	μώροις	μώραις		bonis	bonis	
A.	μώρους	μώρας		bonos	bonas	
D. N.	μώρω	μώρα				
G.	μώροιν	μώραιν				

	ὁ (sapiens)	ἡ (wise)	τό	ὁ (simplex)	ἡ (simple)	τό
S. N.	σοφός	σοφή	σοφόν	ἁπλ(όος)οῦς	ἁπλ(όη)ῆ	ἁπλ(όον)οῦν
G.	σοφοῦ	σοφῆς		ἁπλ(όου)οῦ	ἁπλ(όης)ῆς	
D.	σοφῷ	σοφῇ		ἁπλ(όῳ)ῷ	ἁπλ(όῃ)ῇ	
A.	σοφόν	σοφήν		ἁπλ(όον)οῦν	ἁπλ(όην)ῆν	
V.	σοφέ					
P. N.	σοφοί	σοφαί	σοφά	ἁπλ(όοι)οῖ	ἁπλ(όαι)αῖ	ἁπλ(όα)ᾶ
G.	σοφῶν	σοφῶν		ἁπλ(όων)ῶν	ἁπλ(όων)ῶν	
D.	σοφοῖς	σοφαῖς		ἁπλ(όοις)οῖς	ἁπλ(όαις)αῖς	
A.	σοφούς	σοφάς		ἁπλ(όους)οῦς	ἁπλ(όας)ᾶς	
D. N.	σοφώ	σοφά		ἁπλ(όω)ώ	ἁπλ(όα)ᾶ	
G.	σοφοῖν	σοφαῖν		ἁπλ(όοιν)οῖν	ἁπλ(όαιν)αῖν	

	ὁ (aureus, golden)		ἡ		τό	
S. N.	χρύσεος,	χρῡσοῦς	χρυσέα,	χρυσῆ	χρύσεον,	χρυσοῦν
G.	χρυσέου,	χρυσοῦ	χρυσέας,	χρυσῆς		
D.	χρυσέῳ,	χρυσῷ	χρυσέᾳ,	χρυσῇ		
A.	χρύσεον,	χρυσοῦν	χρυσέαν,	χρυσῆν		
P. N.	χρύσεοι,	χρυσοῖ	χρύσεαι,	χρυσαῖ	χρύσεα,	χρυσᾶ
G.	χρυσέων,	χρυσῶν	χρυσέων,	χρυσῶν		
D.	χρυσέοις	χρυσοῖς	χρυσέαις,	χρυσαῖς		
A.	χρυσέους,	χρυσοῦς	χρυσέας,	χρυσᾶς		
D. N.	χρυσέω,	χρυσώ	χρυσέα,	χρυσᾶ		
G.	χρυσέοιν,	χρυσοῖν	χρυσέαιν,	χρυσαῖν		

§ 23. c. DEC. I. and II. 232 : μώρων 777 b ; ἁπλοῦς, χρυσοῦς, 200, 120 s, 772 c, 777 b. — O. E. φίλιος *friendly*, δίκαιος *just*, μακρός *long*, ἐχθρός *hostile*, ἀθρόος *dense*, καλός *beautiful*. μέσος medius, MIDDLE, διπλ(όος)οῦς duplex, DOUBLE, ἀργύρεος ἀργῠροῦς argenteus, *of silver*.

d. DEC. III. and I. 233 : μέλας 208 ; πᾶς, χαρίεις 205 ; ἡδύς 213 c, 217 b ; μέλαινα, ἡδεῖα, 233 a ; πᾶσα, χαρίεσσα, 233 b, 155, 156 ; μέλασι,

§ 24. OF THREE TERMINATIONS. 29

b. OF THE THIRD AND FIRST DECLENSIONS.

	ὁ (niger)	ἡ (black)	τό	ὁ (omnis)	ἡ (all)	τό
S. N.	μέλας	μέλαινα	μέλαν	πᾶς	πᾶσα	πᾶν
G.	μέλανος	μελαίνης		παντός	πάσης	
D.	μέλανι	μελαίνῃ		παντί	πάσῃ	
A.	μέλανα	μέλαιναν		πάντα	πᾶσαν	
P. N.	μέλανες	μέλαιναι	μέλανα	πάντες	πᾶσαι	πάντα
G.	μελάνων	μελαινῶν		πάντων	πασῶν	
D.	μέλασι	μελαίναις		πᾶσι	πάσαις	
A.	μέλανας	μελαίνας		πάντας	πάσας	
D. N.	μέλανε	μελαίνα		πάντε	πάσα	
G.	μελάνοιν	μελαίναιν		πάντοιν	πάσαιν	

	ὁ (gratiōsus)	ἡ (agreeable)	τό	ὁ (suāvis)	ἡ (sweet)	τό
S. N.	χαρίεις	χαρίεσσα	χαρίεν	ἡδύς	ἡδεῖα	ἡδύ
G.	χαρίεντος	χαριέσσης		ἡδέος	ἡδείας	
D.	χαρίεντι	χαριέσσῃ		ἡδέι, ἡδεῖ	ἡδείᾳ	
A.	χαρίεντα	χαρίεσσαν		ἡδύν	ἡδεῖαν	
V.	χαρίεν			ἡδύ		
P. N.	χαρίεντες	χαρίεσσαι	χαρίεντα	ἡδέες, ἡδεῖς	ἡδεῖαι	ἡδέα
G.	χαριέντων	χαριεσσῶν		ἡδέων	ἡδειῶν	
D.	χαρίεσι	χαριέσσαις		ἡδέσι	ἡδείαις	
A.	χαρίεντας	χαριέσσας		ἡδέας, ἡδεῖς	ἡδείας	
D. N.	χαρίεντε	χαριέσσα		ἡδέε	ἡδείᾱ	
G.	χαριέντοιν	χαριέσσαιν		ἡδέοιν	ἡδείαιν	

24. OF THE THREE DECLENSIONS.

	ὁ (magnus)	ἡ (great)	τό	ὁ (multus)	ἡ (much)	τό
S. N.	μέγας	μεγάλη	μέγα	πολύς	πολλή	πολύ
G.	μεγάλου	μεγάλης		πολλοῦ	πολλῆς	
D.	μεγάλῳ	μεγάλῃ		πολλῷ	πολλῇ	
A.	μέγαν	μεγάλην		πολύν	πολλήν	
V.	μεγάλε					

multi, many

P. N.	μεγάλοι	μεγάλαι	μεγάλα	πολλοί	πολλαί	πολλά
G.	μεγάλων	μεγάλων		πολλῶν	πολλῶν	
D.	μεγάλοις	μεγάλαις		πολλοῖς	πολλαῖς	
A.	μεγάλους	μεγάλας		πολλούς	πολλάς	
D. N.	μεγάλω	μεγάλα				
G.	μεγάλοιν	μεγάλαιν				

χαρίεσι, πᾶσι, 154 s; πᾶν, πάντων, πᾶσι, 729. 2, 778 b; ἡδεῖ 219. —
O. E. τάλ(ανς)ᾱς *wretched* (M. Voc. τάλᾰν), τέρ(ενς)ην *tener*, TENDER,
σύμπᾱς (σύν, πᾶς), -ᾱσα, -ᾰν, *all together*, τιμήεις *honored*, πτερόεις *winged*
(207 c), ἑκ(οντς)ών *willing*, βραχύς *brevis*, *short*, γλυκύς *dulcis*, *sweet* (168),
εὐρύς *wide*, ὀξύς *sharp*, βραδύς *tardus*, *slow*, ταχύς *swift*.

30   ADJECTIVES. — NUMERALS.   § 24.

	ὁ (mītis)	ἡ (mild)	τὸ	Γ. οἱ		αἱ	τὰ
S. N.	πρᾶος	πραεῖα	πρᾶον	πρᾶοι,	πραεῖς	πραεῖαι	πραέα
G.	πράου	πραείας			πραέων	πραειῶν	
D.	πράῳ	πραείᾳ		πράοις,	πραέσι	πραείαις	πραέσι
A.	πρᾶον	πραεῖαν		πράους,	πραεῖς	πραείας	

25. XIII. DECLENSION OF NUMERALS.

	M. (ūnus)	F. (one)	N.	M. (nullus)	F. (no one)	N.	M., none.
S. N.	εἷς	μία	ἕν	οὐδείς	οὐδεμία	οὐδέν	P. οὐδένες
G.	ἑνός	μιᾶς		οὐδενός	οὐδεμιᾶς		οὐδένων
D.	ἑνί	μιᾷ		οὐδενί	οὐδεμιᾷ		οὐδέσι
A.	ἕνα	μίαν		οὐδένα	οὐδεμίαν·		οὐδένας

	M. F. N., both.		M.F.N., two.	M.	F.	N.
D. N. A.	ἄμφω	ambo, -æ, -o	δύο, δύω	duo	duæ	duo
G. D.	ἀμφοῖν	ambōrum, &c.	δυοῖν,	late G. δυεῖν		P. late D. δυσί

	M.F.(three) N.	M. F. N.	M. F. (quatuor, four) N.
P. N.	τρεῖς τρία	tres tria	τέσσαρες, τέτταρες τέσσαρα, τέτταρα
G.	τριῶν	trium	τεσσάρων, τεττάρων
D.	τρισί	tribus	τέσσαρσι, τέτταρσι
A.	τρεῖς	tres	τέσσαρας, τέτταρας

§ 24. a. See 236 ; πολύς 213 c, 217 b ; πραεῖα 233 a, πραεῖς 121.

g. Homeric Forms of πολύς.

	ὁ	ἡ	τὸ
S. N.	πολύς, πουλύς	πολλός πολλή	πολύ, πουλύ, πολλόν
G.	πολέος		πολλῆς
D.	(πολεῖ ? Æsch.)	πολλῷ	πολλῇ
A.	πολύν, πουλύν	πολλόν	πολλήν, πουλύν
P. N.	πολέες, πολεῖς	πολλοί	πολλαί (πολέα Æsch.) πολλά
G.	πολέων	πολλῶν	πολλάων, πολλέων
D.	πολέσι, -έσσι, -έεσσι	πολλοῖσι	πολλῇσι
A.	πολέας [πολεῖς ?]	πολλούς	πολλάς

§ 25. a. NUMERALS 240 : (ἕνς) εἷς 208 d, μία 194 c, οὐδενός 973 b ; τρεῖς 218 ; τέτταρες 169 a, τέσσαρσι 157 ; (οὐδὲ εἷς) οὐδείς, μηδείς, no one, 128 a, late M. and N. (οὔτε εἷς, μήτε εἷς) οὐθείς, οὐθέν, μηθείς, μηθέν, 161 b.

b. *Dialectic Forms :* 1 : Masc. N. Ep. ἕεις 135, Hes. Th. 145, Dor. ἧς 131 d, Insc. Heracl. ; Fem. Ion. μίη, -ῆς, οὐδεμίη, 197 a, Hipp., Ep. (fr. old ἴος) ἴα, ἴης, ἰῇ, ἴαν, Δ. 437, II. 173, Λ. 174, ξ. 435 ; also Neut. ἰῷ Z. 422 ; Pl. Ion. οὐδαμοί, μηδαμοί, -αί, -ά, none, -ῶν, -οῖσι, -αῖσι, -ούς, -άς (v. l. οὐδαμέας 135 a, Hdt. 4. 114), Hdt. 1. 18, 143, &c. 2 : Ep. Du. δοιώ Γ. 236, Pl. δοιοί, -αί, -ά, -οῖσι, -οῖς, -ούς, -άς, M. 455, 464, Δ. 7, δ. 129, 526 ; Ion. Pl. δυῶν Hdt. 1. 94, δυοῖσι Ib. 32. 3 : Dor. N. A. τρῖς Insc., Poet. D. τριοῖσι Hippon. Fr. 8. 4 : Ion. τέσσερες Hdt. 2. 30, 31, Dor. τέτορες or τέττορες, Theoc. 14. 16, Tim. 96 b, Æol. and Ep. πίσυρες ε. 70 ; Poet. or late D. τέτρασι Hes. Fr. 47. 5.

26. XIV. ACTIVE PARTICIPLES.

	a. Present.			b. 2 Aorist, -μι Form.		
	ὁ (solvens)	ἡ (loosing)	τό (clearing)	ὁ (having put)	ἡ	τό
S. N.	λύων·	λύουσα	λῦον luens	θείς	θεῖσα	θέν
G.	λύοντος	λυούσης	luentis	θέντος	θείσης	
D.	λύοντι	λυούσῃ	luenti	θέντι	θείσῃ	
A.	λύοντα	λύουσαν	luentem	θέντα	θεῖσαν	
P. N.	λύοντες	λύουσαι	λύοντα luentes, -ia	θέντες	θεῖσαι	θέντα
G.	λυόντων	λυουσῶν	luentium	θέντων	θεισῶν	
D.	λύουσι	λυούσαις	luentibus	θεῖσι	θείσαις	
A.	λύοντας	λυούσᾱς	luentes	θέντας	θείσᾱς	
D. N.	λύοντε	λυούσᾱ		θέντε	θείσᾱ	
G.	λυόντοιν	λυούσαιν		θέντοιν	θείσαιν	

	c. Present Contracted.			d. Liquid Future.		
	ὁ (vīvens)	ἡ (living)	τό	ὁ (dictūrus) ἡ (about to say) τό		
S. N.	ζ(άων)ῶν	ζ(άου)ῶσα	ζ(άον)ῶν	ἐρῶν	ἐροῦσα	ἐροῦν
G.	ζ(άο)ῶντος	ζ(αού)ώσης		ἐροῦντος	ἐρούσης	
D.	ζ(άο)ῶντι	ζ(αού)ώσῃ		ἐροῦντι	ἐρούσῃ	
A.	ζ(άο)ῶντα	ζ(άου)ῶσαν		ἐροῦντα	ἐροῦσαν	
P. N.	ζ(άο)ῶντες	ζ(άου)ῶσαι	ζ(άο)ῶντα	ἐροῦντες	ἐροῦσαι	ἐροῦντα
G.	ζ(αό)ώντων	ζ(αου)ωσῶν		ἐρούντων	ἐρουσῶν	
D.	ζ(άο)ῶσι	ζ(αού)ώσαις		ἐροῦσι	ἐρούσαις	
A.	ζ(άο)ῶντας	ζ(αού)ώσᾱς		ἐροῦντας	ἐρούσᾱς	
D. N.	ζ(άο)ῶντε	ζ(αού)ώσᾱ		ἐροῦντε	ἐρούσᾱ	
G.	ζ(αό)ώντοιν	ζ(αού)ώσαιν		ἐρούντοιν	ἐρούσαιν	

	e. 1 Aorist.			f. 2 Aorist.		
	ὁ (having loosed)	ἡ	τό	ὁ (having left)	ἡ	τό
S. N.	λύσᾱς	λύσᾱσα	λῦσᾰν	λιπών	λιποῦσα	λιπόν
G.	λύσαντος	λυσάσης		λιπόντος	λιπούσης	
P. N.	λύσαντες	λύσᾱσαι	λύσαντα	λιπόντες	λιποῦσαι	λιπόντα
D.	λύσᾱσι	λυσάσαις		λιποῦσι	λιπούσαις	

	g. 2 Aorist, -μι Form.					
	ὁ (having given)	ἡ	τό	ὁ (having entered)	ἡ	τό
S. N.	δούς	δοῦσα	δόν	δύς	δῦσα	δύν
G.	δόντος	δούσης		δύντος	δύσης	
P. N.	δόντες	δοῦσαι	δόντα	δύντες	δῦσαι	δύντα
D.	δοῦσι	δούσαις		δῦσι	δύσαις	

	h. Perfect.			i. Perfect Contracted.		
	ὁ (sciens)	ἡ (knowing)	τό	ὁ (stans)	ἡ (standing)	τό
S. N.	εἰδώς	εἰδυῖα	εἰδός	ἑστώς	ἑστῶσα	ἑστώς, ἑστός
G.	εἰδότος	εἰδυίᾱς		ἑστῶτος	ἑστώσης	
P. N.	εἰδότες	εἰδυῖαι	εἰδότα	ἑστῶτες	ἑστῶσαι	ἑστῶτα
D.	εἰδόσι	εἰδυίαις		ἑστῶσι	ἑστώσαις	

§ 26. j. Participles 234. 1 : λύ(οντς)ων, λύσ(αντς)ας, θείς, δύς, 205 ; δούς 205 a ; εἰδ(οτς)ώς 214 a ; λύουσα, λύσασα, 233 b ; εἰδυῖα, ἑστῶσα, ἑστός, 233 c, a ; ζ(άων)ῶν, ζῶσα, ζῶντος, ἐστ(αώς)ώς, ἐστ(αό)ῶτος, 120 ; ἐρ(έων)ῶν, ἐρ(έου)οῦσα, ἐρ(έον)οῦν, 152, 121. — O. E. λύσων, λυθείς, λελῠκώς, 37.

27. XV. SUBSTANTIVE PRONOUNS.

The forms marked with the sign ǀ are enclitic when used without emphasis. The shorter forms, μου, μοί, μέ, are only so used. The initials affixed to dialectic forms denote, Æ. Æolic, B. Bœotic, D. Doric, E. Epic, I. Ionic, O. Old, P. Poetic. The plural *nos* and *vos* are placed beside the dual for comparison.

a. PERSONAL.

	1 Pers., *I.*		2 Pers., *thou.*		3 Pers., *of him, her, it.*	
S. Nom.	ἐγώ	ĕgo	σύ	tū	*	*
Gen.	ἐμοῦ, μοῦǀ	mei	σοῦǀ	tui	οὗǀ	sui
Dat.	ἐμοί, μοίǀ	mĭhi	σοίǀ	tĭbi	οἷǀ	sĭbi
Acc.	ἐμέ, μέǀ	mō	σέǀ	tē	ἕǀ	sĕ
P. Nom.	ἡμεῖς *we*		ὑμεῖς *you*		σφεῖς *they*	
Gen.	ἡμῶν		ὑμῶν		σφῶν	
Dat.	ἡμῖν		ὑμῖν		σφίσῐ(νǀ	
Acc.	ἡμᾶς		ὑμᾶς		σφᾶς [neut. σφέα]	
D. N. A.	νώ	nōs	σφώ	vōs	[Α. σφωέ]	
G. D.	νῷν	nostrum	σφῷν	vestrum	[σφωΐν]	

e. PERSONAL PRONOUNS: ANALYSIS, 243, 246.

	Stem. 1. 2. 3.	Conn. Vow.	Flexible Ending.	Uncontracted and Contract Forms.		
S. N.	μ- σ- ·-					
G.	μ-, ἐμ- σ- ·-	-ε-	-ο	ἐμ(έο)οῦ	σ(έο)ου	(ἕο)οῦ
D.	μ-, ἐμ- σ- ·-	-ε-	-ῐ	ἐμ(εΐ)οῖ	σ(εΐ)οῖ	(ἕϊ)οῖ
A.	μ-, ἐμ- σ- ·-	-ε-	*	ἐμέ	σέ	ἕ
P. N.	ἡμ- ὑμ- σφ-	-ε-	-ες	ἡμ(έες)εῖς	ὑμ(έες)εῖς	σφ(εες)εῖς
G.	ἡμ- ὑμ- σφ-	-ε-	-ων	ἡμ(έων)ῶν	ὑμ(έων)ῶν	σφ(έων)ῶν
D.	ἡμ- ὑμ- σφ-	-ε-(ῐ)	-ῐν, -σῐ(ν	ἡμ(εῖν)ῖν	ὑμ(εῖν)ῖν	σφίσι
A.	ἡμ- ὑμ- σφ-	-ε-	-ᾰς[n.-ᾰ]	ἡμ(έας)ᾶς	ὑμ(έας)ᾶς	σφ(έας)ᾶς[-έα]
D. N.	ν- σφ- σφ-	-ω-	-ε	ν(ὦε)ώ	σφ(ὦε)ώ	σφωέ
G.	ν- σφ- σφ-	-ω-	-ῐν	ν(ὦϊν)ῷν	σφ(ὦϊν)ῷν	σφωΐν

f. FORMS IN HOMER AND HERODOTUS.

Those following the sign ‖ are not in Herodotus, and those in brackets are not in Homer. The sign ⌢ denotes synizesis in Homer.

S. N.	ἐγώ ‖ ἐγών	σύ ‖ τύνη		
G.	ἐμέο, ἐμεῦ, μευǀ ‖ ἐμεῖο, ἐμέθεν	σέοǀ σεῦǀ ‖ σεῖο, σέθεν, τεεῖο	εὗǀ ‖ ἕοǀ εἷο, ἕθενǀ · or Ϝέοǀ Ϝεῦǀ Ϝεῖο, Ϝέθενǀ	
D.	ἐμοί, μοίǀ	σοί, τοίǀ ‖ τεΐν	οἷǀ ‖ ἑοῖ · or Ϝοῖǀ Ϝεοῖ	
A.	ἐμέ, μέǀ	σέǀ	ἕǀ μίνǀ‖ ἑέ · or Ϝέǀ Ϝεέ	
P. N.	[ἡμέες] ἡμεῖς ‖ ἄμμες	[ὑμέες] ὑμεῖς ‖ ὔμμες	[σφεῖς]	
G.	ἡμέων ‖ ἡμείων	ὑμέων ‖ ὑμείων	σφέωνǀ ‖ σφείων, σφῶν	
D.	ἡμῖν ‖ ἡμῐ͞ν, ἡμῐν, ἀμμῐ(ν	ὑμῖν ‖ ὑμῐ͞ν, ὑμμῐ(ν, ὔμμ'	σφίσῐ(νǀ σφῐ(νǀ ‖σφ'	
A.	ἡμέας, -έας ‖ ἡμᾶς,ἄμμε	ὑμέας, -έας ‖ ὔμμε	σφέαςǀ-έαςǀσφέǀ‖σφεῖας, σφᾶςǀ [n. σφέα]	
D. N.	‖νῶϊ	‖σφῶϊ, σφώ		
G.	‖νῶϊν	‖σφῶϊν		
D.	‖νῶϊν	‖σφῶϊν, σφῶν	‖σφωΐνǀ	
A.	‖νῶϊ, νώ	‖σφῶϊ, σφώ	‖σφωέǀ σφω'ǀ	

§ 27. SUBSTANTIVE. 33

b. REFLEXIVE.

1 Pers. M. (*of myself*) F.		2 Pers. M. (*of thyself*) F.		
S. G. ἐμαυτοῦ	ἐμαυτῆς	σεαυτοῦ, σαυτοῦ	σεαυτῆς, σαυτῆς	
D. ἐμαυτῷ	ἐμαυτῇ	σεαυτῷ, σαυτῷ	σεαυτῇ, σαυτῇ	
A. ἐμαυτόν	ἐμαυτήν	σεαυτόν, σαυτόν	σεαυτήν, σαυτην	
P. G. ἡμῶν αὐτῶν	ἡμῶν αὐτῶν	ὑμῶν αὐτῶν	ὑμῶν αὐτῶν	
D. ἡμῖν αὐτοῖς	ἡμῖν αὐταῖς	ὑμῖν αὐτοῖς	ὑμῖν αὐταῖς	
A. ἡμᾶς αὐτούς	ἡμᾶς αὐτάς	ὑμᾶς αὐτούς	ὑμᾶς αὐτάς	

3 Pers. M., *of himself*.		F., *of herself*.		N., *of itself*.
S. G. ἑαυτοῦ,	αὑτοῦ	ἑαυτῆς,	αὑτῆς	
D. ἑαυτῷ,	αὑτῷ	ἑαυτῇ,	αὑτῇ	
A. ἑαυτόν,	αὑτόν	ἑαυτήν,	αὑτήν	ἑαυτό, αὑτό
P. G. ἑαυτῶν,	αὑτῶν	ἑαυτῶν,	αὑτῶν	
D. ἑαυτοῖς,	αὑτοῖς	ἑαυταῖς,	αὑταῖς	
A. ἑαυτούς,	αὑτούς	ἑαυτάς,	αὑτάς	ἑαυτά, αὑτά

or P. G. σφῶν αὐτῶν, D. σφίσιν αὐτοῖς -αῖς, A. σφᾶς αὐτούς -άς

c. RECIPROCAL.

M. (*of one another*) F.	N.	M.	N.	F.
P. G. ἀλλήλων	ἀλλήλων	D. A. ἀλλήλω	ἀλλήλᾱ	
D. ἀλλήλοις	ἀλλήλαις	G. ἀλλήλοιν	ἀλλήλαιν	
A. ἀλλήλους	ἀλλήλᾱς	ἄλληλᾰ		

d. INDEFINITE.

M. F. N., *such a one*.	M.	
S. N. ὁ, ἡ, τὸ δεῖνα	P. οἱ δεῖνες	
G. τοῦ, τῆς δεῖνος	τῶν δείνων	
D. τῷ, τῇ δεῖνι	*	
A. τόν, τήν, τὸ δεῖνα	τοὺς δεῖνας	

g. ADDITIONAL FORMS.

S. N. ἰών, ἰώ B.	τῦ D., τού tū, B.	
G. ἐμέος, ἐμεῦς, ἐμοῦς, με- θέν| D.	τέο, τεῦ| τέος| τεῦς| τεοῦς, τεοῦ D.	Γέθεν| Æ., ἑοῦς D. B., ἑεῖο E.
D. ἐμίν D., ἐμύ B.	τίν D. B.	Foἷ| Æ., ἳν or ἳν D., ὗ B.
A.	τέ te, τύ| τίν D.	Fέ| Æ., νῦν| D. P.
P. N. 'ἁμές D. [Æ.	ὑμές D.	
G. 'ἁμέων, -ῶν D., ἀμμέων	ὑμμέων Æ.	
D. ἡμίν P., 'ἁμίν D., ἀμμε-	ὑμίν, ὑμῖν D. P.	φίν| ψίν| D., ἄσφι Æ.
A. 'ἁμέ D. [σι(ν Æ.	ὑμέ, ὑμμε D.	ψέ| D., ἄσφε Æ.
D. N. νῶε B.		

h. REFLEXIVE 244, 248 : New Ion. 1 Pers. ἐμεωυτοῦ, -ῆς, -ῷ, -ῇ, -όν, -ήν · 2 Pers. σεωυτοῦ, -ῆς, -ῷ, ῇ-, -όν, -ήν · 3 Pers. ἑωυτοῦ, -ῆς, -ῷ, -ῇ, -όν, -ήν, -ό, Pl. -ῶν, -έων, -οῖσι, -ῇσι, -ούς, -άς, -ά · Hdt. Dor. 3 Pers. αὑταύτου or -ω, -ᾶς, -ῳ, -ᾳ, -ον, -ᾱν, -ο, Pl. -ων, -ᾱν, -οις, -αις, -ους or -ως, -ᾱς, -ά. Æol. Γαυτῶ for αὑτοῦ, Alc. 88 [74]. See 131 e, 130 c, 197 c, 246 d.

i. RECIPROCAL 244 : Dor. ἀλλάλων 130 a, Theoc. 14. 46, ἀλλάλοισι Pind. P. 4. 397, &c. Ep. Dual ἀλλήλοιϊν 201 b, K. 65.

GR. TAB. 2* C

28. XVI. Adjective Pronouns.

I. Definite.

a. Article.   b. Relative.   c. Iterative.

	M. (the)	F.	N.	M.(qui)	F.(who)	N.	M.(ipse)	F.(very,same)	N.
S. N.	ὁ	ἡ	τό	ὅς	ἥ	ὅ	αὐτός	αὐτή	αὐτό
G.	τοῦ	τῆς		οὗ	ἧς		αὐτοῦ	αὐτῆς	
D.	τῷ	τῇ		ᾧ	ᾗ		αὐτῷ	αὐτῇ	
A.	τόν	τήν		ὅν	ἥν		αὐτόν	αὐτήν	
P. N.	οἱ	αἱ	τά·	οἵ	αἵ	ἅ	αὐτοί	αὐταί	αὐτά
G.	τῶν	τῶν		ὧν	ὧν		αὐτῶν	αὐτῶν	
D.	τοῖς	ταῖς		οἷς	αἷς		αὐτοῖς	αὐταῖς	
A.	τούς	τάς		οὕς	ἅς		αὐτούς	αὐτάς	
D. N.	τώ	τά		ὤ	ἄ		αὐτώ	αὐτά	
G.	τοῖν	ταῖν		οἷν	αἷν		αὐτοῖν	αὐταῖν	

d. Demonstrative.

	M. (this)	F.	N.	M. (hic)	F. (this)	N.
S. N.	ὅδε hic	ἥδε haec	τόδε hoc	οὗτος	αὕτη	τοῦτο
G.	τοῦδε	τῆσδε		τούτου	ταύτης	
D.	τῷδε	τῇδε		τούτῳ	ταύτῃ	
A.	τόνδε	τήνδε		τοῦτον	ταύτην	
P. N.	οἵδε hi	αἵδε hae	τάδε haec	οὗτοι	αὗται	ταῦτα
G.	τῶνδε	τῶνδε		τούτων	τούτων	
D.	τοῖσδε	ταῖσδε		τούτοις	ταύταις	
A.	τούσδε	τάσδε		τούτους	ταύτας	
D. N.	τώδε	τάδε		τούτω	ταύτα	
G.	τοῖνδε	ταῖνδε		τούτοιν	ταύταιν	

e. Possessive.

S. 1 P. ἐμός meus, my 2 P. σός tuus, thy 3 P. ὅς suus, his, her, its
P. ἡμέτερος our ὑμέτερος your σφέτερος their

---

§ 28. i. Adjective Pronouns 234. 4, 249 s. Those of Dec. 2 and 1 have in general the dialectic forms belonging to those declensions (20, 201, 197 s, 131 d) : as, Ep. τοῖο, αὐτοῖο, τοῖιν· Old τάων, αὐτάων, τοῖσι, ταῖσι, τοισίδε, αὐτοῖσι· Ion. τῇσι, τῇς, τῃσίδε, ᾖσι, αὐτῇσι· Dor. τῶ, αὐτῶ, τώς, ᾱ, ᾱ, ᾱτις, τᾱς, αὐτᾱς, τᾷδε, ταύταν, τᾱν, αὐτᾱν· Æol. τοῖς, ταῖς.

j. Article 250: ὁ, τό, 199; τώ, τοῖν, 234 e. *Dialectic Forms:* Old Nom. Pl. τοί A. 447, Hdt. 8. 68. 1, Theoc. 1. 80, Æsch. Pers. 424, ταί Γ. 5, Pind. O. 13. 25, Ar. Eq. 1329.

k. Relative 250 : ὅ 199. *D. F.:* Ep. Gen. ὅου a. 70, ἕης Π. 208, § 135.

l. Iterative 251 : αὐτό 199. So decline ἄλλος alius, *other*, and ἐκεῖνος ille, *that* (κεῖνος P. I., B. 37, Hdt. 3. 74, κῆνος Æ., Sap. 2. 1, τῆνος D., Theoc. 1. 4). *D. F.:* M. αὐτέου, -έῳ,ͣ-έων, -έοισι, -έους, F. -έη, -έης, -ίῃ, -έην, -έων, -έῃσι, -έας, New Ion.

§ 28. ADJECTIVE. 35

II. INDEFINITE.

f. Simple Indefinite.   g. Interrogative.   h. Relative Indefinite.
Lat. aliquis, ullus   quis?   quicumque, quisquis

	M.F. (any, some) N.		M.F. (who?) N.		M. (whoever)	F.	N.
S. N.	τὶς	τὶ	τίς	τί	ὅστις	ἥτις	ὅ τι
G.	τινός, τοῦ		τίνος, τοῦ		οὗτινος, ὅτου	ἧστινος	
D.	τινί, τῷ		τίνι, τῷ		ᾧτινι, ὅτῳ	ᾗτινι	
A.	τινά		τίνα		ὅντινα	ἥντινα	
P. N.	τινές	τινά,	τίνες	τίνα	οἵτινες_	αἵτινες	ἅτινα,
G.	τινῶν	[ἄττα	τίνων		ὧντινων, ὅτων	ὧντινων	[ἄττα
D.	τισί		τίσι		οἷστισι, ὅτοις	αἷστισι	
A.	τινάς		τίνας		οὕστινας	ἅστινας	
D. N.	τινέ		τίνε		ὥτινε	ἅτινε	
G.	τινοῖν		τίνοιν		οἷντινοιν	αἷντινοιν	

m. Demonstrative 252 : οὗτος, αὕτη, 252 b. Decline τοιόσδε, -άδε, -όνδε, and τοιοῦτος, -αύτη, -οῦτον or -οῦτο (199 a), talis, *such*, τοσόσδε (232 a) and τοσοῦτος tantus, *so much*, τηλικόσδε and τηλικοῦτος *so old*, τυννοῦτος tantillus, *so small*. D. F. : for τῶνδε, τοῖσδε, by a kind of double declension, Poet. τῶνδεων Alc. 127 Bk., Ep. τοῖσδεσι φ. 93, τοῖσδεσσι(ν K. 462, β. 47 ; τουτέῳ, τουτέων, 255 b ; τοῦτοι, ταῦται, 255 a.

Paragogic Declension (252 c) :

S. N.	ὁδί	ἡδί	τοδί	οὑτοσί	αὑτηΐ	τουτί
G.	τουδί	τησδί		τουτουί	ταυτησί	
D.	τῳδί	τῃδί		τουτῳί	ταυτῃΐ	
A.	τονδί	τηνδί		τουτονί	ταυτηνί	
P. N.	οἱδί	αἱδί	ταδί	οὑτοιί	αὑταιί	ταυτί
G.	τωνδί, &c.			τουτωνί, &c.		

n. Possessive 252. D. F. : 1 Pers. Pl. 'ἁμός or 'ἀμός O., Z. 414, Æsch. Ch. 428, 'ἀμέτερος D., Theoc. 2. 31, ἀμμος, ἀμμέτερος Æ., Alc. 103, 104 ; Du. νωΐτερος E., O. 39 : 2 Pers. S. τεός D. E., γ. 122, Æsch. Pr. 162 ; Pl. ὑμός O., a. 375, ὑμμος Æ. ; Du. σφωΐτερος E., A. 216 : 3 Pers. S. ὅς P. I., Γ. 333, Hdt. 1. 205, Soph. Aj. 442, ἑός E. D., a. 409, Theoc. 17. 50, Fός Æ. ; Pl. σφός O., A. 534.

o. *Indefinite* 253 s : τὶς 208 d, ὅ τι or ὅ,τι 255 c ; τοῖσι; ὅτοισι, 253.

Forms of τὶς, τίς, and ὅτις = ὅστις, in Homer and Herodotus, marked as in 27 f :

S. N.	τὶς	τὶ	τίς	τί	‖ὅτις		ὅ τι ‖ὅ ττι
G.	τέο, τεῦ		τεῦ ‖τέο		ὅτευ ‖ὅττεο, ὅττευ		
D.	τέῳ ‖τῷ		[τέῳ]		ὅτεῳ		
A.	τινά		τίνα		‖ὅτινα		
P. N.	τινές	τινά	τίνες	τίνα		‖ὅτινα	
G.	[τέων]		τέων		ὅτεων		
D.	[τέοισι]		[τέοισι]		ὀτέοισι [f. -έῃσι]		
A.	τινάς	‖ἄσσα	[τίνας]		‖ὅτινας		ἄσσα

p. For Correlative Pronouns, see 53.

29. B. ANALYSIS OF COMPARISON.

1. Old Greek and Latin Forms. 2. Common Greek Form. 3. Second Greek Form. 4. Common Latin Form. 5. Common English Form.

BASE.	CONNECTIVE.	DEGREE-SIGN. Comp.	Sup.	EXAMPLES. Comp.	Sup.
1. Root or Pos. Stem.	α (u)i		τ m		νέατος minimus
2. Pos. Stem.	ο ω αι ες ις *	τερ	τατ	μακρότερος νεώτερος φιλαίτερος ἀκρατέστερος λαλίστερος μελάντερος	μακρότατος νεώτατος φιλαίτατος ἀκρατέστατος λαλίστατος μελάντατος
3. Root.	(I)ι	₀ον	στ	ἡδίων	ἥδιστος
4. Pos. Stem.	i	or	·ssim	longior	longissimus
5. Positive.	e	r	st	longer	longest

C. TABLES OF CONJUGATION.

30. I. DISTINCTIONS CLASSIFIED (265 s).

a. VOICES.

SUBJECTIVE. *I act*		OBJECTIVE. *I am acted upon*
(Simple Performance of the act): **ACTIVE.**	*by myself* (Both Performance and Reception): **MIDDLE**, Reflexive	*by another* (Simple Reception of the act): **PASSIVE.**
Intransitive : Transitive : ἔδραμον, ἔπαυσα, cucurri, *I stopped* *I ran.* *another.*	directly : indirectly : ἐπαυσάμην, εἱλόμην, *I stopped my- I took for my- self, I ceased. self, I chose.*	ἐπαύθην, *I was stopped by another.*

b. TENSES.

	I. PRIMARY.		II. SECONDARY.
Relations.	Time. 1. Present.	2. Future.	3. Past.
1. Definite.	PRESENT. γράφω scribo, *I am writing.*	* *I shall be writing.*	IMPERFECT. ἔγραφον scribēbam, *I was writing.*
2. Indefinite.	* *I write.*	FUTURE. γράψω scribam, *I shall write.*	AORIST. ἔγραψα scripsi, *I wrote.*
3. Complete.	PERFECT. γέγραφα scripsi, *I have written.*	FUTURE PERFECT. πεπαύσομαι desiero, *I shall have ceased.*	PLUPERFECT. ἐγεγράφειν scripseram, *I had written.*

C. MODES.
I. DISTINCT.
A. INTELLECTIVE.

1. Decided, *or* Actual.	2. Undecided, *or* Contingent.	
	a. Present Contingence.	β. Past Contingence.
INDICATIVE.	SUBJUNCTIVE.	OPTATIVE.
γράφω scribo,	γράφω scribam,	γράφοιμι scriberem,
I am writing.	*I may write.*	*I might write.*

B. VOLITIVE.
IMPERATIVE.
γράφε scribe,
Write.

II. INCORPORATED.

A. Substantive.	B. Adjective.
INFINITIVE.	PARTICIPLE.
γράφειν scribere,	γράφων scribens,
To write.	*Writing.*

31. II. FORMATION OF THE TENSES.

PREFIXES.	TENSES.		AFFIXES.	
		Active.	Middle.	Passive.
	PRESENT,	ω, μι	ομαι, μαι	
Augm.	IMPERFECT,	ον, ν	όμην, μην	
	FUTURE,	σω	σομαι	θήσομαι
	2 FUTURE,			ήσομαι
Augm.	AORIST,	σα	σάμην	θην
Augm.	2 AORIST,	ον, ν	όμην, μην	ην
Redupl.	PERFECT,	κα		μαι
Redupl.	2 PERFECT,	α		
Augm. Redupl.	PLUPERFECT,	κειν		μην
Augm. Redupl.	2 PLUPERFECT,	ειν		
Redupl.	FUTURE PERFECT,	[σω]		σομαι

32. III. ANALYSIS OF THE VERB.
I. PREFIXES (277 s).

a. The AUGMENT, prefixed to *Secondary Tenses* in the *Indicative.*
b. The REDUPLICATION, prefixed to *Complete Tenses* in *all the Modes.*

II. THE STEM (344 s), including,

c. PREFORMATIVES, additions prefixed to the Root.
d. The ROOT, the primitive element of the Verb.
e. LETTERS INSERTED or CHANGED in the Root.
f. AFFORMATIVES, additions affixed to the Root.

III. AFFIXES (285 s), including,
g. TENSE-SIGNS.

σ(ε), Future and Aorist, Active and Middle; Future Perfect.
κ, Perfect and Pluperfect Active.
θε(θη), Aorist Passive.
ε(η), 2 Aorist Passive.
θης, Future Passive.
ης, 2 Future Passive.
*, Present and Imperfect; Perfect and Pluperfect Passive; 2 Perfect and Pluperfect Active.

h. CONNECTING VOWELS (290 s).

Indicative.
ο,ε,(ω,ει), Pres., Impf., Fut., Fut. Perf.
ἄ(ε), Aor. Act. and Mid.; Perf. Act.
ει(ε), Pluperfect Active.
*, Aorist, Perfect, and Pluperfect Passive; -μι Form.
ω, η(ῃ), *Subjunctive.*
Optative.
ι, General Sign; -μι Form Middle.

ιη, Aorist Passive; -μι Form Active.
οι(οιη), Pres., Fut., Perf., Fut. Perf.
αι(ειἄ, ειε), Aorist Act. and Mid.

Imperative, Infinitive, Participle.
ε(ο), Imv. ⎫ Present, Future, Future
ε(ει), Inf. ⎬ Perfect; Perfect Ac-
ο, Par.   ⎭ tive.
ἄ(ο), Aorist Active and Middle.
*, Perf. and Aor. Pass.; -μι Form.

i. FLEXIBLE ENDINGS (295 s).

A. SUBJECTIVE.

	Sing. 1	2	3	Pl. 1	2	3	Du. 2	3
	p	p	p	p n	p n	n p	p n	p n
Pri.	-μ(μἰ,*)	-s(σθἄ)	-τ(σἰ,*)	-μεν	-τε	-ντ(νσἰ,ἄσἰ)	-τον	-τον
Sec.	-μ(ν,μι,*)	-s(σθα)	-τ(*)	-μεν	-τε	-ντ(ν,εν,σἄν)	-τον	-την
Lat.	-m(*)	-s(stī)	-t	-mŭs	-tĭs	-nt(runt,re)		
		p	pm		pn npmn pm n		p n	pmn
Imv.		-θ(θἰ,s,ε,ν,*)	-τω		-τε -ντων,-τωσἄν		-τον	-των
L.		-*(to)	-to		-tĕ -nto			
	r r r r				rd			
Inf.	-ν,-ναι,-ι			Part.	-ντ-ς (τ-s)			
L.	-rĕ(se)				-nt-s -tūr-ŭs			

B. OBJECTIVE.

	Sing. 1	2	3	Pl. 1	2	3	Du. 2	3
	p v	p v	p v	p vn		np v	p v n	p v n
Pri.	-μαι	-σαι(αι)	-ται	-μεθἄ	-σθε	-νται(ἄται)	-σθον	-σθον
Sec.	-μην	-σο(ο)	-το	-μεθα	-σθε	-ντο(ατο)	-σθον	-σθην
Lat.	-(mr)r	-rĭs(re)	-tŭr	-mŭr	-mĭni	-ntŭr		
		pv	p vm	p v n		p vmn p vm n	p v n	pvmn
Imv.		-σο(ο)	-σθω	-σθε		-σθων,-σθωσἄν	-σθον	-σθων
L.		-rĕ(tor)	-tŏr	-mĭni		-ntŏr		
	v r			r v		d		d
Inf.	-σθαι			Part. -μεν-ος		Verb.-τ-ός	-τέ-ος	
L.	-rī(i, ier, rier)					-t-ŭs(sus)	-nd-ŭs	

j. Add to the list, ν PARAGOGIC in the 3d Person, after ε or simple ι (163); LETTERS INSERTED between the stem and affix (as σ, η, ε, 307, 311); and also, in compound verbs, a preceding PREPOSITION (390).

33. NOTES. a. In 32 i, the ELEMENTS of the Flexible Endings are mostly marked, according to their force, with small letters placed above: μ, σ, θ, τ, with p, as signs of *person* (246, 271 b, c, e. 2); ν, ε, α, with n, as signs of *number* (271 b, c, e); αι, ο, θ, σθ, ην, εν, with v, as signs of *voice* (271 e, 272 a, b); ω, with m, as a sign of *mode* (272 e); ν and ι, with r, as signs of *relation* (272 a, 12); τ and τέ, with d, as suffixes of *derivation* (272 b); while letters unmarked are, for the most part, simply euphonic.

b. The TRANSLATION in 34, applies, except in the Imperative, to the 1st Person singular, and must be varied for the other persons and numbers. It is read across thus: Pres. Ind. Act. *I am stopping* another, Mid. *I am stopping* my*self*, &c.; while the different forms of the Pres. and Impf. may be also rendered, *I stop, I stopped*, &c. Some words are printed in Roman letters as explanatory or, in some combinations, inadmissible.

§ 35.   SUBJECTIVE AFFIXES.   41

AND COMPARED WITH THE LATIN.

		d. AORIST ACTIVE.	e. PERF., PLUPERF. 2 PERFECT. 2 PLUPERFECT.	f. AORIST PASS., 2 AORIST PASS.
			T. C. F.	
Primary	Ind. S. 1		κʻ-α vʻ-ī	
	2		κʻ-α-ς vʻ-i-sti	
	3		κʻ-ε vʻ-i-t	
	P. 1		κʻ-ἄ-μεν vʻ-ĭ-mus	
	2		κʻ-α-τε vʻ-i-stis	
	3		(κʻ-α-ντ)κʻᾶσι vʻ-ē-	
	D. 2		κʻ-α-τον [runt	
		T. C. F.	T. C. F. [ĕra-m	T. F.
Secondary	Ind. S. 1	σ-ἄ s-ī	κʻ-ει-ν, κʻ-η vʻ-	(θʻε-μ)θʻην
	2	σ-α-ς s-i-sti	κʻ-ει-ς vʻ-era-s	θʻη-ς
	3	σ-ε s-i-t	κʻ-ει vʻ-era-t	θʻη
	P. 1	σ-ἄ-μεν s-ĭ-mus	κʻ-ει-μεν	θʻη-μεν
	2	σ-α-τε s-i-stis	κʻ-ει-τε [σαν	θʻη-τε
	3	σ-α-ν s-ē-runt	κʻ-ει-σαν, κʻ-ε-	θʻη-σαν
	D. 2	σ-α-τον	κʻ-ει-τον	θʻη-τον
	3	σ-ά-την	κʻ-εί-την	θʻή-την
				T. C. F.
Primary	Sub. S. 1	σ-ω s-ĕri-m	κʻ-ω vʻ-ĕri-m	(θʻέ-ω-μ)θʻῶ
	2	σ-ῃ-ς s-eri-s	κʻ-ῃ-ς vʻ-eri-s	(θʻέ-η-s)θʻῇς
	3	σ-ῃ s-eri-t	κʻ-ῃ vʻ-eri-t	(θʻέ-η-τ)θʻῇ
	P. 1	σ-ω-μεν	κʻ-ω-μεν	θʻῶ-μεν
	2	σ-η-τε	κʻ-η-τε	θʻῆ-τε
	3	σ-ω-σι	κʻ-ω-σι	θʻῶ-σι
	D. 2	σ-η-τον	κʻ-η-τον	θʻῆ-τον
			T. C. F.	
Secondary	Opt. S. 1	σ-αι-μι s-isse-m	κʻ-οι-μι vʻ-isse-m	(θʻε-ιη-μ)θʻείην
	2	σ-αι-ς, σ-εια-ς	κʻ-οι-ς vʻ-isse-s	(θʻε-ιη-s)θʻείης
	3	σ-αι, σ-ειε	κʻ-οι vʻ-isse-t	(θʻε-ιη-τ)θʻείη
	P. 1	σ-αι-μεν,	κʻ-οι-μεν	θʻείη-μεν, θʻεῖ-μεν
	2	σ-αι-τε	κʻ-οι-τε	θʻείη-τε, θʻεῖ-τε
	3	σ-αι-εν, σ-εια-ν	κʻ-οι-εν	θʻείη-σαν, θʻεῖ-εν
	D. 2	σ-αι-τον	κʻ-οι-τον	θʻείη-τον, θʻεῖ-τον
	3	σ-αί-την	κʻ-οί-την	θʻειή-την, θʻεί-την
				T. F.
	Imp. S. 2	(σ-α-θ)σον	κʻ-ε	(θʻε-θ)θʻητι
	3	σ-ἄ-τω	κʻ-έ-τω	θʻή-τω
	P. 2	σ-α-τε	κʻ-έ-τε	θʻη-τε
	3	σ-ά-τωσαν,	κʻ-έ-τωσαν,	θʻή-τωσαν,
		σ-ά-ντων	κʻ-ό-ντων	θʻέ-ντων
	D. 2	σ-α-τον	κʻ-ε-τον	θʻη-τον
	3	σ-ά-των	κʻ-έ-των	θʻή-των
	Infin.	σ-α-ι s-is-se	κʻ-έ-ναι vʻ-is-se	θʻῆ-ναι
	Part. N.	(σ-α-ντ-s)σᾶς	(κʻ-ο-τ-s)κʻώς	(θʻε-ντ-s)θʻείς
		(σ-α-νσ-α)σᾶσα	(κʻ-ο-νσ-α)κʻυῖα	(θʻε-νσ-α)θʻεῖσα
		(σ-α-ντ)σᾶν	(κʻ-ο-τ)κʻός	(θʻε-ντ)θʻέν
	G.	σ-α-ντ-ος	κʻ-ό-τ-ος	θʻέ-ντ-ος
		σ-άσ-ης	κʻ-υί-ᾶς	θʻείσ-ης

36. VI. OBJECTIVE AFFIXES ANALYZED

		a. NUDE.		b. EUPHONIC.	
		Pres., Perf. (2 Aor.)	Impf., Plup.	Present. (2 Aorist.)	Imperfect.
		F.		C. F.	
Ind.	S. 1	μαι		ο-μαι	ο-r
	2	σαι(αι)		(ε-αι)η, ει	ĕ-ris, -re
	3	ται		ε-ται	ĭ-tur
Primary. P.	1	μεθα		ό-μεθα	i-mur
	2	σθε		ε-σθε	i-mĭni
	3	νται		ο-νται	u-ntur
	D. 2	σθον		ε-σθον	
			F.		C. F.
Ind.	S. 1		μην		ό-μην ēba-r
	2		σο(ο)		(ε-ο)ου
	3		το		ε-το
Secondary. P.	1		μεθα		ό-μεθα
	2		σθε		ε-σθε
	3		ντο		ο-ντο
	D. 2		σθον		ε-σθον
	3		σθην		έ-σθην
Sub.	S. 1		ω-μαι	a-r	
	2		(η-αι)η	ā-ris, -re	
	3		η-ται	a-tur	
Primary. P.	1		ώ-μεθα	a-múr	
	2		η-σθε	a-mĭni	
	3		ω-νται	a-ntur	
	D. 2		η-σθον		
		C. F.		C. F.	
Opt.	S. 1	ί-μην		οί-μην	ĕre-r
	2	ι-ο		οι-ο	erĕ-ris, -re
	3	ι-το		οι-το	ere-tur
Secondary. P.	1	ί-μεθα		οί-μεθα	ere-mur
	2	ι-σθε		οι-σθε	ere-mĭni
	3	ι-ντο		οι-ντο	ere-ntur
	D. 2	ι-σθον		οι-σθον	
	3	ί-σθην		οί-σθην	
Imv.	S. 2	σο(ο)		(ε-ο)ου	ĕ-re
	3	σθω		έ-σθω	ĭ-tor
	P. 2	σθε		ε-σθε	i-mĭni
	3	σθωσαν, σθων		έ-σθωσαν, έ-σθων	u-ntor
	D. 2	σθον		ε-σθον	
	3	σθων		έ-σθων	
		F.			
Infin.		σθαι		ε-σθαι (ĕ-rī)i	
Part. N.		μεν-ος, μέν-ος		ό-μεν-ος	
		μέν-η		ο-μέν-η	
		μεν-ον, μέν-ον		ό-μεν-ον	
G.		μέν-ου		ο-μέν-ου	
		μέν-ης		ο-μέν-ης	

f. Verbals. τ-ός, -ή, -όν, t-us, -a, -um
τέ-ος, -ά, -ον nd-us, a, um

§ 36. OBJECTIVE AFFIXES. 43

AND COMPARED WITH THE LATIN.

		c. FUTURE MIDDLE, Future Perfect.	d. AORIST MIDDLE.	e. FUT. PASS., 2 Fut. Pass.
		T. C. F.		T. C. F.
Primary.	Ind. S. 1	σ-ο-μαι b-o-r		θ'ήσ-ο-μαι
	2	(σ-ε-αι)ση, σει		θ'ήσ-η, θ'ήσ-ει
	3	σ-ε-ται		θ'ήσ-ε-ται
	P. 1	σ-ό-μεθα		θ'ησ-ό-μεθα
	2	σ-ε-σθε		θ'ήσ-ε-σθε
	3	σ-ο-νται		θ'ήσ-ο-νται
	D. 2	σ-ε-σθον		θ'ήσ-ε-σθον
			T. C. F.	
Secondary.	Ind. S. 1		σ-ά-μην	
	2		(σ-α-ο)σω	
	3		σ-α-το	
	P. 1		σ-ά-μεθα	
	2		σ-α-σθε	
	3		σ-α-ντο	
	D. 2		σ-α-σθον	
	3		σ-ά-σθην	
Primary.	Sub. S. 1	σ-ω-μαι		
	2	(σ-η-αι)ση		
	3	σ-η-ται		
	P. 1	σ-ώ-μεθα		
	2	σ-η-σθε		
	3	σ-ω-νται		
	D. 2	σ-η-σθον		
Secondary.	Opt. S. 1	σ-οί-μην	σ-αί-μην	θ'ησ-οί-μην
	2	σ-οι-ο	σ-αι-ο	θ'ήσ-οι-ο
	3	σ-οι-το	σ-αι-το	θ'ήσ-οι-το
	P. 1	σ-οί-μεθα	σ-αί-μεθα	θ'ησ-οί-μεθα
	2	σ-οι-σθε	σ-αι-σθε	θ'ήσ-οι-σθε
	3	σ-οι-ντο	σ-αι-ντο	θ'ήσ-οι-ντο
	D. 2	σ-οι-σθον	σ-αι-σθον	θ'ήσ-οι-σθον
	3	σ-οί-σθην	σ-αί-σθην	θ'ησ-οί-σθην
	Imv. S. 2		(σ-α-ο)σαι	
	3		σ-ά-σθω	
	P. 2		σ-α-σθε	
	3		σ-ά-σθωσαν, σ-ά-σθων	
	D. 2		σ-α-σθον	
	3		σ-ά-σθων	
	Infin.	σ-ε-σθαι	σ-α-σθαι	θ'ήσ-ε-σθαι
	Part. N.	σ-ό-μεν-ος	σ-ά-μεν-ος	θ'ησ-ό-μεν-ος
		σ-ο-μέν-η	σ-α-μέν-η	θ'ησ-ο-μέν-η
		σ-ό-μεν-ον	σ-ά-μεν-ον	θ'ησ-ό-μεν-ον
	G.	σ-ο-μέν-ου	σ-α-μέν-ου	θ'ησ-ο-μέν-ου
		σ-ο-μέν-ης	σ-α-μέν-ης	θ'ησ-ο-μέν-ης

g. In § 35 and 36, the small initials T, C, and F denote TENSE-SIGNS, CONNECTING VOWELS, and FLEXIBLE ENDINGS; and the hyphens mark the division into these elements. The letters κ and θ of the tense-signs, as omitted in the *second tenses* (289), are separated by the mark ' from the rest of the affix; and the Latin *v* in like manner, from its frequent omission. For the arrangement in 35 a, b, e, 36 a, b, and also 37. 1, 4, 5, sec 269 c. — Classes and Elements of Affixes 32, 284 s, 303 a. 1 Sing. (μ) μ, ν, 296, (ομ, οα) ω 291 a, α 273 c, e, (κεα) κη, κεν, 291 c, (θεμ) θην 288 a, 160; 2 S. (ες) ες 275 d, 291 a, σεις 293 d, (θ) θι, σ, ς, (εθ) ε, 160 f, 297 c, (σαθ) σον 294 a, 297 c, (θεθ, θηθι) θητι 159 c, σαι, αι, (εσαι, εαι) η or ει, σο ο, (εσο, εο) ου, (σασο, σαο) σαι, σω, σαι, 297 e, f, g, 290 b; 3 S. (τ) σι, *, 298, (ετ, εε) ει 291 a; 3 Pl. (οντ, ονσι, οασι) ουσι, (καντ, κανσι, κααστ) κᾱσι, (οντ) ον, (ντ) σαν, 300 a, 156, ντων, σθων, 301; Inf. 301, (ερ) εν 294 b, 301 a; Part. 26, (κοτε) κώς 273 e.

37. VII. General Paradigm of

(Stem λυ- ; Pass. *to be loosed ;* Mid.

A. Definite Tenses.

1. Present, or Definite System : Base λῡ-

		ACTIVE.		PASSIVE AND MIDDLE.	
	a. Present. *I am loosing.* solvo		b. Imperfect. *I was loosing.* solvēbam	c. Present. *I am loosed,* &c. solvor, &c.	d. Imperfect. *I was loosed,* &c. solvēbar, &c.
Ind. S. 1	²λύω	lŭo		λύομαι	luor
2	λύεις	lui*s*		³λύῃ, ²λύει	lu*ĕris,-re*
3	²λύει	lui*t*		λύεται	lu*ĭtur*
P. 1	λύομεν	lui*mus*		λυόμεθα	lui*mur*
2	²λύετε	lui*tis*		²λύεσθε	luim*ĭni*
3	²λύουσι'	luu*nt*		λύονται	luu*ntur*
D. 2	²λύετον			²λύεσθον	
Ind. S. 1			²ἔλῡον luĕ-		ἐλῡόμην luĕ-
2			ἔλυες [*bam*		ἐλύου _ [*bar*
3			ἔλυε'		ἐλύετο
P. 1			ἐλύομεν		ἐλυόμεθα
2			ἐλύετε		ἐλύεσθε
3			²ἔλυον		ἐλύοντο
D. 2			ἐλύετον		ἐλύεσθον
3			ἐλυέτην		ἐλυέσθην
Sub. S. 1	²λύω	luam		λύωμαι	luar
2	λύῃς	luas		³λύῃ	luāris,-re
3	³λύῃ	luat		λύηται	luatur
P. 1	λύωμεν	luāmus		λυώμεθα	luamur
2	λύητε	luatis		λύησθε	luamĭni
3	λύωσι'	luant		λύωνται	luantur
D. 2	λύητον			λύησθον	
Opt. S. 1		λύοιμι	luĕrem		λυοίμην luĕrer
2		λύοις	lueres		λύοιο luerēris,-re
3		λύοι	lueret		λύοιτο lueretur
P. 1		λύοιμεν	luerēmus		λυοίμεθα lueremur
2		λύοιτε	lueretis		λύοισθε lueremĭni
3		λύοιεν	luerent		λύοιντο luerentur
D. 2		λύοιτον			λύοισθον
3		λυοίτην			λυοίσθην
Imv. S. 2	λῦε	lue		λύου	luĕre
3	λυέτω	lu*ĭ*to		λυέσθω	lu*ĭtor*
P. 2	²λύετε	lui*te*		²λύεσθε	luim*ĭni*
3	λυέτωσαν,			λυέσθωσαν,	
●	²λυόντων	luu*nto*		²λυέσθων	luu*ntor*
D. 2	²λύετον			²λύεσθον	
3	λυέτων			²λυέσθων	
Infin.		λύειν luĕre			λύεσθαι lui
Part. N.		λύων,-ουσα,-ον ǀ luens			λυόμενος, -η, -ον
G.		λύοντος,-ούσης luentis			λυομένου, -ης

(Primary / Secondary / Primary / Secondary labels in left margin)

§ 37. GENERAL PARADIGM. 45

CONJUGATION : λύω, solvo, *to loose.*
to loose for one's self, redĭmo, *to ransom.*)

B. SIMPLE INDEFINITE TENSES.

2, 3. Future and Aorist Systems : Base λῦσ-.

	ACTIVE.		MIDDLE.	
	e. FUTURE. *I shall loose.*	f. AORIST. *I loosed.*	g. FUTURE. *I shall ransom.*	h. AORIST. *I ransomed.*
	solvam	solvi	redĭmam	redēmi
Ind.	²λύσω luam		λύσομαι luar	
2	λύσεις lues		³λύσῃ,²λύσει luēris,-re	
3	²λύσει luet		λύσεται luetur	
P. 1	λύσομεν luēmus		λυσόμεθα luemur	
2	λύσετε luetis		λύσεσθε luemĭni	
3	²λύσουσι' luent		λύσονται luentur	
D. 2	λύσετον		λύσεσθον	
		I played.		
Ind.		ἔλῦσᾰ lūsī		ἐλῦσάμην
2		ἔλυσας lusisti		ἐλύσω
3		ἔλυσε' lusit		ἐλύσατο
P. 1		ἐλύσᾰμεν lusīmus		ἐλυσάμεθα
2		ἐλύσατε lusistis		ἐλύσασθε
3		ἔλυσαν lusērunt,		ἐλύσαντο
D. 2		ἐλύσατον [-re		ἐλύσασθον
3		ἐλυσάτην		ἐλυσάσθην
Sub.		²λύσω lusĕrim		λύσωμαι
2		λύσῃς luseris		³λύσῃ
3		³λύσῃ luserit		λύσηται
P. 1		λύσωμεν		λυσώμεθα
2		λύσητε		λύσησθε
3		λύσωσι'		λύσωνται
D. 2		λύσητον		λύσησθον
Opt.	λύσοιμι	λύσαιμι lusissem	λυσοίμην	λυσαίμην
2	λύσοις	λύσαις, λύσειας	λύσοιο	λύσαιο
3	λύσοι	³λύσαι, λύσειε'	λύσοιτο	λύσαιτο
P. 1	λύσοιμεν	λύσαιμεν	λυσοίμεθα	λυσαίμεθα
2	λύσοιτε	λύσαιτε	λύσοισθε	λύσαισθε
3	λύσοιεν	λύσαιεν, λύσειαν	λύσοιντο	λύσαιντο
D. 2	λύσοιτον	λύσαιτον	λύσοισθον	λύσαισθον
3	λυσοίτην	λυσαίτην	λυσοίσθην	λυσαίσθην
Imv.		²λῦσον		³λῦσαι
3		λυσάτω		λυσάσθω
P. 2		λύσατε		λύσασθε
3		λυσάτωσαν, ² λυσάντων		λυσάσθωσαν, ²λυσάσθων
D. 2		λύσατον		λύσασθον
3		λυσάτων		²λυσάσθων
Inf.	λύσειν	[²-ον! ³λῦσαι! lusisse	λύσεσθαι	λύσασθαι
Par.	λύσων,-ουσα,	λύσᾱς,-ᾱσα,-ᾰν!	λυσόμενος,-η,-ον	λυσάμενος,-η,-ον
G.	λύσοντος,-ούσης	λύσαντος, -ᾱσης	λυσομένου, -ης	λυσαμένου, -ης

C. COMPLETE TENSES.

4. Perfect System: Base λελῠκ-. **5. Perfect Passive System:**

ACTIVE.
PASSIVE AND

	i. PERFECT. *I have loosed.* solvi	j. PLUPERFECT. *I had loosed.* solvĕram	l. PERFECT. *I have been l'd, &c.* solūtus sum, &c.	m. PLUPERFECT. *I had been l'd, &c.* solūtus ĕram, &c.

Primary.

Ind. S. 1 λέλῠκᾰ *pepŭlī* — λέλῠμαι
    2 λέλυκας *pepulisti* — λέλυσαι
    3 ²λέλυκε‘ *pepulit* — λέλυται
P. 1 λελύκᾰμεν — λελύμεθα
    2 λελύκᾰτε — ²λέλυσθε
    3 λελύκᾱσι‘ — λέλυνται
D. 2 λελύκᾰτον — λέλυσθον

Secondary.

Ind. S. 1 ἐλελύκειν *pepulĕ-* ἐλελύμην
    2 ἐλελύκεις [*ram* ἐλέλυσο
    3 ἐλελύκει ἐλέλυτο
P. 1 ἐλελύκειμεν ἐλελύμεθα
    2 ἐλελύκειτε [*kesan* ἐλέλυσθε
    3 ἐλελύκεσαν, ἐλελύ- ἐλέλυντο
D. 2 ἐλελύκειτον ἐλέλυσθον
    3 ἐλελυκείτην ἐλελύσθην

Primary.

Sub. S. 1 λελύκω *pepulĕrim* λελυμένος ὦ
    2 λελύκῃς *pepuleris* λελυμένος ᾖς
    3 λελύκῃ *pepulerit* λελυμένος ᾖ
P. 1 λελύκωμεν λελυμένοι ὦμεν
    2 λελύκητε λελυμένοι ἦτε
    3 λελύκωσι‘ λελυμένοι ὦσι‘
D. 2 λελύκητον λελυμένω ἦτον

Secondary.

Opt. S. 1 λελύκοιμι *pepulissem* λελυμένος εἴην
    2 λελύκοις *pepulisses* λελυμένος εἴης
    3 λελύκοι *pepulisset* λελυμένος εἴη
P. 1 λελύκοιμεν λελυμένοι εἴημεν
    2 λελύκοιτε λελυμένοι εἴητε
    3 λελύκοιεν λελυμένοι εἴησαν
D. 2 λελύκοιτον λελυμένω εἴητον
    3 λελυκοίτην λελυμένω εἰήτην

Imv. S. 2 ²λέλυκε λέλυσο
    3 λελυκέτω λελύσθω
P. 2 λελύκετε ²λέλυσθε
    3 λελυκέτωσαν, λελύσθωσαν,
       λελυκόντων ²λελύσθων
D. 2 λελύκετον λέλυσθον
    3 λελυκέτων ²λελύσθων

Infin. λελυκέναι! *pepulisse* λελύσθαι!

Part. N. λελυκώς!-υῖα!-ός! λελυμένος!-η,-ον!
     G. λελυκότος!-υίας λελυμένου,-ης

Ind. k. *Future Perfect* λελυκὼς ἔσομαι solvĕro, *I shall have loosed.*

§ 37. COMPLETE AND COMPOUND TENSES. 47

D. Compound Indefinite Tenses.

Bases λελῠ- and λελῡσ-. 6. Compound System: Bases λῠθε- and λῠθησ-.

MIDDLE.		PASSIVE.	
n. Future Perfect. *I shall have been loosed, &c.* solūtus ĕro, redēmĕro	o. Aorist. *I was loosed.* solūtus sum	p. Future. *I shall be loosed.* solvar	
Ind. λελύσομαι		λυθήσομαι	
2 λελύσῃ, λελύσει		λυθήσῃ, λυθήσει	
3 λελύσεται		λυθήσεται	
P. 1 λελυσόμεθα		λυθησόμεθα	
2 λελύσεσθε		λυθήσεσθε	
3 λελύσονται		λυθήσονται	
D. 2 λελύσεσθον		λυθήσεσθον	
Ind.	ἐλύθην		
2	ἐλύθης		
3	ἐλύθη		
P. 1	ἐλύθημεν		
2	ἐλύθητε		
3	ἐλύθησαν		
D. 2	ἐλύθητον		
3	ἐλυθήτην		
Sub.	λυθῶ		
2	λυθῇς		
3	λυθῇ		
P. 1	λυθῶμεν		
2	²λυθῆτε		
3	λυθῶσι⁶		
D. 2	λυθῆτον		
Opt. λελυσοίμην	λυθείην	λυθησοίμην	
2 λελύσοιο	λυθείης	λυθήσοιο	
3 λελύσοιτο	λυθείη	λυθήσοιτο	
P. 1 λελυσοίμεθα	λυθείημεν, λυθεῖμεν	λυθησοίμεθα	
2 λελύσοισθε	λυθείητε, λυθεῖτε	λυθήσοισθε	
3 λελύσοιντο	λυθείησαν, λυθεῖεν	λυθήσοιντο	
D. 2 λελύσοισθον	λυθείητον, λυθεῖτον	λυθήσοισθον	
3 λελυσοίσθην	λυθειήτην, λυθείτην	λυθησοίσθην	
Imv.	λύθητι		
3	λυθήτω		
P. 2	²λύθητε		
3	λυθήτωσαν, ²λυθέντων		
D. 2	λύθητον		
3	λυθήτων		
Inf. λελύσεσθαι	λυθῆναι!	λυθήσεσθαι	
Par. λελυσόμενος,-η,-ον	λυθείς! -εῖσα! -έν!	λυθησόμενος,-η,-ον	
G. λελυσομένου,-ης	λυθέντος!.-είσης	λυθησομένου, -ης	

r. Lat. luo, *to expiate, pay;* lūdo, *play,* pello, *drive, Pf.* lūsi, pĕpŭli. The Latin above the columns is for translation; that by the side, for comparison of forms. The sign ' affixed to a form shows that it may receive *v paragogic* (163); and the sign !, that the accent is not *recessive* (769). A small figure prefixed shows the number of forms belonging to the paradigm (some of them plur. Part. forms), which are spelled in the same way. See 36 g, 38 y, 270 d.

q. *Verbals* λῠτός! solūtus, solūbĭlis, *loosed, loosable;* λῠτέος! solvendus.

38. E. Second Tenses.

	7. 2 Aorist System.		8. 2 Perfect Syst.	9. 2 Comp. Syst.
	r. 2 Aor. Act. t. 2 Aor. Middle.		u. 2 Perfect Active.	w. 2 Aorist Passive.
	I left.	*I remained.*	*I trust,* pret.	*I was worn.*
Ind.	²ἔλἴπον liqui	ἐλ".πόμην	πέποιθΰ fīdo	ἐτρἴβην trītus sum
2	ἔλιπες	ἐλίπου	πέποιθας	ἐτρίβης
3	ἔλιπε⁴	ἐλίπετο	²πέποιθε⁴	ἐτρίβη
P. 1	ἐλίπομεν	ἐλιπόμεθα	πεποίθἄμεν	ἐτρίβημεν
2	ἐλίπετε	ἐλίπεσθε	πεποίθατε	ἐτρίβητε
3	²ἔλιπον	ἐλίποντο	πεποίθἄσι⁴	ἐτρίβησαν
D. 2	ἐλίπετον	ἐλίπεσθον	πεποίθᾰτον	ἐτρίβητον
3	ἐλιπέτην	ἐλιπέσθην		ἐτριβήτην
Sub.	λίπω	λίπωμαι	πεποίθω	τριβῶ
2	λίπῃς	²λίπῃ	πεποίθῃς	τριβῇς
3	²λίπῃ	λίπηται	πεποίθῃ	τριβῇ
P. 1	λίπωμεν	λιπώμεθα	πεποίθωμεν	τριβῶμεν
2	λίπητε	λίπησθε	πεποίθητε	²τριβῆτε
3	λίπωσι⁴	λίπωνται	πεποίθωσι⁴	τριβῶσι⁴
D. 2	λίπητον	λίπησθον	πεποίθητον	τριβῆτον
Opt.	λίποιμι	λιποίμην	πεποίθοιμι, -οίην	τριβείην
2	λίποις	λίποιο	πιποίθοις, -οίης	τριβείης
3	λίποι	λίποιτο	πεποίθοι, -οίη	τριβείη
P. 1	λίποιμεν	λιποίμεθα	πεποίθοιμεν	τριβείημεν, -εῖμεν
2	λίποιτε	λίποισθε	πεποίθοιτε	τριβείητε, -εῖτε
3	λίποιεν	λίποιντο	πεποίθοιεν	τριβείησαν, -εῖεν
D. 2	λίποιτον	λίποισθον	πεποίθοιτον	τριβείητον, -εῖτον
3	λιποίτην	λιποίσθην	πεποιθοίτην	τριβειήτην, -είτην
Imv.	λίπε	λιποῦ!	²πέποιθε	τρίβηθι
3	λιπέτω	λιπέσθω	πεποιθέτω	τριβήτω
P. 2	λίπετε	λίπεσθε	πεποίθετε	²τρίβητε
3	λιπέτωσαν, ²λιπόντων	λιπέσθωσαν, ²λιπέσθων	πεποιθέτωσαν, πεποιθόντων	τριβήτωσαν, ²τριβέντων
D. 2	λίπετον	λίπεσθον	πεποίθετον	τρίβητον
3	λιπέτων	²λιπέσθων	πεποιθέτων	τριβήτων
Inf.	λιπεῖν!	λιπέσθαι!	πεποιθέναι!	τριβῆναι!
Par.	λιπών!	λιπόμενος	πεποιθώς!-υῖα!-ός!	τριβείς!-εῖσα!-εν!
	Theme λείπω (s. λιπ-, λειπ-, 347 h) linquo, *to leave*, 50 ; F. λείψω, 2 Pf. λέλοιπα, 312 b ; λιπών decl. 26 f ; accent 780 b, 781 b, 782.		v. 2 Plup. Act. ἐπεποίθειν ἐπεποίθεις ἐπεποίθει ἐπεποίθειμεν, &c.	x. 2 Fut. Pass. τριβήσομαι τριβησοίμην τριβήσεσθαι τριβησόμενος

§ 38. y. The Second Tenses, which have no place in the regular conjugation, are here supplied from the verbs λείπω, πείθω, and τρίβω (39). See 289, 303, 336 s. Pret. πέποιθα 268, 338 b, 312 b, 317 b, 318 ; πεποιθοίην 293 c.

§ 39. c. Mute Verbs 270 c : τρίβω 347 g, τάσσω 349 i, 169 a, πείθω 347 h, ὀρίζω 349 β ; τρί(β-σω)ψω, ἔτα(γ-σα)ξα, πέπει(θ-σο)σο, πεπεί(θ-σθαι)-σθαι, 151 ; ὁρι(σω, εω)ῶ, 305 a ; τέτρι(β-κα)φα, τέτα(γ-κα)χι, ὡρί(δ-κειν)-

39. VIII. CLASSES OF VERBS. A. MUTE.

	a. LABIAL: τρίβω Stem τρῑβ-, τρῐβ-; to rub.	b. PALATAL: τάσσω τἄγ-, τασσ-; arrange.	c. LINGUAL: πείθω πῐθ-, πειθ-; persuade.
Pres. A.	τρίβω tero	τάσσω, τάττω	πείθω
P. & M.	τρίβομαι	τάσσομαι, τάττομαι	πείθομαι
Impf. A.	ἔτριβον	ἔτασσον, ἔταττον	ἔπειθον
P. & M.	ἐτριβόμην	ἐτασσόμην, ἐταττόμην	ἐπειθόμην
Fut. A.	τρίψω	τάξω	πείσω
Mid.	τρίψομαι	τάξομαι	πείσομαι
1 Aor. A.	ἔτριψα	ἔταξα	ἔπεισα
Mid.	ἐτριψάμην	ἐταξάμην	ἐπεισάμην
2 Aor. A.	ἔλᾰβον took	ἤγᾰγον led	ἔπιθον poet.
Mid.	ἐλαβόμην	ἠγαγόμην	ἐπιθόμην
1 Pf. A.	τέτρῐφα trivi	τέτᾰχα	πέπεικα
1 Pl. A.	ἐτετρίφειν	ἐτετάχειν	ἐπεπείκειν
2 Pf. A.	λέλοιπα 38 r	πέφευγα fugi	πέποιθα 38
2 Pl. A.	ἐλελοίπειν	ἐπεφεύγειν	ἐπεποίθειν
Pf. P. Ind.	τέτριμμαι	τέταγμαι	πέπεισμαι
2	τέτριψαι	τέταξαι	πέπεισαι
3	τέτριπται	τέτακται	πέπεισται
p. 1	τετρίμμεθα	τετάγμεθα	πεπείσμεθα
2	τέτριφθε	τέταχθε	πέπεισθε
3	τετριμμένοι εἰσί'	τετάχαται	πεπεισμένοι εἰσί'
Imv.	τέτριψο	τέταξο	πέπεισο
3	τετρίφθω	τετάχθω	πεπείσθω
p. 2	τέτριφθε	τέταχθε	πέπεισθε
3	τετρίφθωσαν, τετρίφθων	τετάχθωσαν, τετάχθων	πεπείσθωσαν, πεπείσθων
Inf.	τετρίφθαι !	τετάχθαι !	πεπεῖσθαι !
Par.	τετριμμένος !	τεταγμένος !	πεπεισμένος !
Pl. P. Ind.	ἐτετρίμμην	ἐτετάγμην	ἐπεπείσμην
2	ἐτέτριψο	ἐτέταξο	ἐπέπεισο
3	ἐτέτριπτο	ἐτέτακτο	ἐπέπειστο
p. 1	ἐτετρίμμεθα	ἐτετάγμεθα	ἐπεπείσμεθα
2	ἐτέτριφθε	ἐτέταχθε	ἐπέπεισθε
3	τετριμμένοι ἦσαν	ἐτετάχατο	πεπεισμένοι ἦσαν
Fut. Pf.	τετρίψομαι	τετάξομαι	λελήσομαι
1 Aor. P.	ἐτρίφθην	ἐτάχθην	ἐπείσθην
1 Fut. P.	τριφθήσομαι	ταχθήσομαι	πεισθήσομαι
2 Aor. P.	ἐτρίβην oftener	ἐτάγην rare	ἐδράθην r. or 1. [slept
2 Fut. P.	τριβήσομαι	ταγήσομαι	
Verbals	τριπτός, τριπτέος	τακτός, τακτέος	πιστός, πειστέος

κειν, 149; τέτρι(β-μαι)μμαι, ἐπεπεί(θ-μην)σμην, 148; τέτρι(β-ται)πται, ἐτέτα(γ-το)κτο, πει(θ-τεος)στέος, ἐτρί(β-θην)φθην, τα(γ-θ)χθήσομαι, ὠρί(δ-θ)σθην, 147; τέτρι(β-σθε)φθε, τετά(γ-σθω)χθω, 158; τετριμμένοι (-αι, -α) ἦσαν, τεταγμένοι (-αι, -α) εἰσί or τετάχαται, 300 b, c, 158; ὤριξον, ὤρικα, 277 c, 278 a, 280 a. Tenses supplied from other Verbs: ἔλαβον 351. 2; ἤγαγον,

VERBS. — MUTE, LIQUID. § 39.

Mute Verbs.

d. LINGUAL: ὁρίζω
ὁρῖδ-, ὁριζ-; *to bound.*

Pres.	Α. ὁρίζω finio	
P. & M.	ὁρίζομαι	
Impf.	Α. ὥριζον	
P. & M.	ὡριζόμην	
1 Aor.	Α. ὥρῖσα	
Mid.	ὡρισάμην	
2 Aor.	Α. εἶδον καιω	
Mid.	εἰδόμην	
1 Pf.	Α. ὥρῖκα	
1 Pl.	Α. ὡρίκειν	
2 Pf.	Α. οἶδα 46 a	
2 Pl.	Α. ᾔδειν	
Perf.	P. ὥρισμαι	
Plup.	P. ὡρίσμην	
1 Aor.	P. ὡρίσθην	
1 Fut.	P. ὁρισθήσομαι	
2 Aor.	P.	
2 Fut.	P. [στέος	
Verbals	ὁριστός, ὁρι-	

40. B. Liquid Verbs.

a. ἀγγέλλω nuntio
ἀγγελ-, ἀγγελλ-; *to announce.*

ἀγγέλλω	
ἀγγέλλομαι	
ἤγγελλον	
ἠγγελλόμην	
ἤγγειλα	
ἠγγειλάμην	
ἤγγελον rarer	
ἠγγελόμην	
ἤγγελκα	
ἠγγέλκειν	
ὄλωλα perii	
ὀλώλειν	
ἤγγελμαι	
ἠγγέλμην	
ἠγγέλθην	
ἀγγελθήσομαι	
ἠγγέλην late	
ἀγγελήσομαι	
ἀγγελτός, ἀγγελτέος	

b. φαίνω ostendo
φᾰν-, φαιν-; *to show.*

φαίνω
φαίνομαι
ἔφαινον
ἐφαινόμην
ἔφηνα
ἐφηνάμην
ἔβᾰλον *threw*
ἐβαλόμην
πέφαγκα
ἐπεφάγκειν
πέφηνα as mid.
ἐπεφήνειν
πέφασμαι
ἐπεφάσμην
ἐφάνθην
φανθήσομαι
ἐφάνην as mid.
φανήσομαι
φαντός, φαντέος

	Fut. Act.	Fut. Mid.	Perf. Pass. & Mid.
Fut. A. ὁρίσω, ὁρῶ	ἀγγελῶ	ἀγγελοῦμαι	Ind. πέφασμαι
Opt. ὁρίσοιμι, ὁριοῖμι	Ind. φᾰνῶ	φᾰνοῦμαι	2 πέφανσαι
	2 φανεῖς	φανῇ, φανεῖ	3 πέφανται
Inf. ὁρίσειν, ὁριεῖν	3 φανεῖ	φανεῖται	P. 1 πεφάσμεθα
	P. 1 φανοῦμεν	φανούμεθα	2 πέφανθε [εἰσί
Par. ὁρίσων, ὁριῶν	2 φανεῖτε	φανεῖσθε	3 πεφασμένοι
	3 φανοῦσι‘	φανοῦνται	Imv. πέφανσο
Fut. M. ὁρίσομαι, ὁριοῦμαι	Opt. φανοῖμι,-οίην φανοίμην		3 πέφανθω
	2 φανοῖς, -οίης φανοῖο		P. 2 πέφανθε, &c.
Opt. ὁρισοίμην, ὁριοίμην	3 φανοῖ, -οίη φανοῖτο		Inf. πεφάνθαι!
	P. 1 φανοῖμεν	φανοίμεθα	Par. πεφασμένος!
Inf. ὁρίσεσθαι, ὁριεῖσθαι	2 φανοῖτε	φανοῖσθε	Plup. Pass. & Mid.
	3 φανοῖεν	φανοῖντο	ἐπεφάσμην
Par. ὁρισόμενος, ὁριούμενος	Inf. φανεῖν	φανεῖσθαι	ἐπέφανσο
	Par. φανῶν	φανούμενος	ἐπέφαντο, &c.

---

fr. ἄγω ago, *lead*, 284 e, g; πέφευγα, fr. φεύγω fugio, *flee*, 50; λελήσομαι *shall have forgotten*, fr. λανθάνω 50; ἐδράθην 342. 3, 351. 2; εἶδον 358.
— Ο. Ε. γράφω *write*, τρέπω *turn*, κόπτω *cut*, τύπτω *strike*, πλέκω *plait*, δέχομαι *receive*, πράσσω *do*, φράζω *tell*, πλάσσω *fashion*, 50; κομίζω, -ίσω, -ιῶ, κεκόμικα, -ισμαι, ἐκομίσθην, κομιστός, *bring*; σπεύδω *hasten*.

§ 40. c. LIQUID VERBS: ἀγγέλλω 349 l, φαίνω 347 h; ἀγγε(λ-σω, λέω)λῶ, φανῶ, ἔφ(αν-σα)ηνα, ἤγγειλα, 152; φαν(έω)ῶ, -(έεις)εῖς, -(έο)οῦμεν, -(έε)εῖτε, -(έου)οῦσι, -(έοι)οῖμι, -(έων)ῶν, 121, cf. φιλέω 42; φανοίην 293 b; πέφα(ν-κα)γκα 150; πέφηνα 312 a; πέφα(ν-μαι)σμαι 150 d; πέφαν-σαι

§ 42. DOUBLE-CONSONANT, PURE. 51

41. C. Double-Consonant Verbs.

a. πέμπω mitto b. σπένδω lībo c. αὔξω or αὐξάνω augeo
πεμπ-; send.   σπενδ-; pour.   αὐξ-, αὐξᾰν-; increase.

Pres. A.	πέμπω ἄρχω	σπένδω	αὔξω, αὐξάνω	
P. & M.	πέμπομαι lead	σπένδομαι	αὔξομαι, αὐξάνομαι	
Impf. A.	ἔπεμπον ἦρχον	ἔσπενδον	ηὖξον, ηὔξανον	
P. & M.	ἐπεμπόμην	ἐσπενδόμην	ηὐξόμην, ηὐξανόμην	
Fut. A.	πέμψω ἄρξω	σπείσω	αὐξήσω μελλήσω	
Mid.	πέμψομαι	σπείσομαι	αὐξήσομαι	
Aor. A.	ἔπεμψα ἦρξα	ἔσπεισα	ηὔξησα ἤψησα	
Mid.	ἐπεμψάμην	ἐσπεισάμην	ηὐξησάμην	
1 Pf. A.	πέπομφα ἦρχα	ἔσπεικα late	ηὔξηκα ἤρρηκα	
1 Pl. A.	ἐπεπόμφειν	ἐσπείκειν	ᾐξήκειν	
2 Pf. A.	λέλαμπα blaze	πέπονθα	ὄδωδα smell	
2 Pl. A.	ἐλελάμπειν	ἐπεπόνθειν	ὀδώδειν	
Perf. P.	πέπεμμαι ἦργμαι	ἔσπεισμαι	ηὔξημαι	
Plup. P.	ἐπεπέμμην	ἐσπείσμην	ᾐξήμην	
Aor. P.	ἐπέμφθην ἤρχθην	ἐσπείσθην	ηὐξήθην	
Fut. P.	πεμφθήσομαι	σπεισθήσομαι	αὐξηθήσομαι	
Verbals	πεμπτός, πεμπτέος	σπειστέος	αὐξητός, αὐξητέος	

Perfect Passive.   (d. ἐλέγχω to confute.)   Pluperfect Passive.

Ind. πέπεμμαι	ἐλήλεγμαι	ἐπεπέμμην	ἐληλέγμην
2 πέπεμψαι	ἐλήλεγξαι	ἐπέπεμψο	ἐλήλεγξο
3 πέπεμπται	ἐλήλεγκται	ἐπέπεμπτο	ἐλήλεγκτο
P. 1 πεπέμμεθα	ἐληλέγμεθα	ἐπεπέμμεθα	ἐληλέγμεθα
2 πέπεμφθε	ἐλήλεγχθε	ἐπέπεμφθε	ἐλήλεγχθε [σαν
3 πεπεμμένοι εἰσί	ἐληλεγμένοι εἰσί	πεπεμμένοι ἦσαν	ἐληλεγμένοι ἦ-

Imv. πέπεμψο   ἐλήλεγξο   Pf. P. Inf.   Pf. P. Part.
  2 πεπέμφθω   ἐληλέγχθω   πεπέμφθαι!   πεπεμμένος!
P. 3 πέπεμφθε, &c. ἐληλέγχθε, &c. ἐληλέγχθαι!   ἐληλεγμένος!

42. D. Pure Verbs. I. Contract.

1. In -άω: τιμάω honōro 2. In -έω: φιλέω ămo 3. In -όω: δηλόω declāro

S. τῑμᾰ-; to honor.   S. φῐλε-; to love.   S. δηλο-; to manifest.

---

156 b ; πέφα(ν-σθε)νθε 158 ; ὄλωλα, fr. ὄλλῡμι destroy, 351. 4, 281 c ; ἔβαλον, fr. βάλλω 50. — O. E. στέλλω send, καθαίρω purify, δέρω flay, σπείρω sow, φθείρω destroy, μιαίνω stain, τείνω stretch, κλίνω bend, κρίνω judge, πλύνω wash, τέμνω cut, βάλλω throw, μένω remain, νέμω distribute, 50.

§ 41. e. Double-Consonant Verbs : πέπομφα 312 c ; πέπε(μπμαι)μμαι, ἐλήλεγμαι, 148 a ; σπ(ενδ-σω)είσω, ἔσπ(ενδ-μ, ενσμ)εισμαι, 151, 156, 148 ; ἔσπεικα 50 ; αὐξάνω 351. 2 ; αὐξήσω 311 a ; λέλαμπα, πέπονθα, ὄδωδα, fr. λάμπω, πάσχω suffer, ὄζω, 50 ; μελλήσω, ἤψησα, ἤρρηκα, fr. μέλλω delay, ἕψω boil, ἔρρω go away, 311 a, 50. — O. E. κάμπτω bend, σφίγγω bind, τέρπω please, κλάζω clang, βόσκω feed, ἄχθομαι be vexed.

CONJUGATION. § 42.

DEFINITE

a. Present Active.

	I honor,	live,	love,	run,	manifest.
Ind.	τιμ(άω)ῶ	ζῶ	φιλ(έω)ῶ	θέω	δηλ(όω)ῶ
2	τιμ(άεις)ᾷς	ζῇς	φιλ(έεις)εῖς	θεῖς	δηλ(όεις)οῖς
3	τιμ(άει)ᾷ	ζῇ	φιλ(έει)εῖ	θεῖ	δηλ(όει)οῖ
p. 1	τιμ(άο)ῶ-μεν	ζῶμεν	φιλ(έο)οῦ-μεν	θέομεν	δηλ(όο)οῦ-μεν
2	τιμ(άε)ᾶ-τε	ζῆτε	φιλ(έε)εῖ-τε	θεῖτε	δηλ(όε)οῦ-τε
3	τιμ(άου)ῶ-σι‘	ζῶσι‘	φιλ(έου)οῦ-σι‘	θέουσι‘	δηλ(όου)οῦ-σι‘
Sub.	τιμ(άω)ῶ	ζῶ	φιλ(έω)ῶ	θέω	δηλ(όω)ῶ
2	τιμ(άῃς)ᾷς	ζῇς	φιλ(έῃς)ῇς	θέῃς	δηλ(όῃς)οῖς
3	τιμ(άῃ)ᾷ	ζῇ	φιλ(έῃ)ῇ	θέῃ	δηλ(όῃ)οῖ
p. 1	τιμ(άω)ῶ-μεν	ζῶμεν	φιλ(έω)ῶ-μεν	θέωμεν	δηλ(όω)ῶ-μεν
2	τιμ(άῃ)ᾶ-τε	ζῆτε	φιλ(έῃ)ῆ-τε	θέητε	δηλ(όῃ)ῶ-τε
3	τιμ(άω)ῶ-σι‘	ζῶσι‘	φιλ(έω)ῶ-σι‘	θέωσι‘	δηλ(όω)ῶ-σι‘
Opt.	τιμ(άοι)ῷ-μι, -ῴην		φιλ(έοι)οῖ-μι, -οίην		δηλ(όοι)οῖ-μι, -οίην
2	τιμ(άοις)ῷς, -ῴης		φιλ(έοις)οῖς, -οίης		δηλ(όοις)οῖς, -οίης
3	τιμ(άοι)ῷ, -ῴη		φιλ(έοι)οῖ, -οίη		δηλ(όοι)οῖ, -οίη
p. 1	τιμ(άοι)ῷ-μεν,-ῴημεν		φιλ(έοι)οῖ-μεν,-οίημεν		δηλ(όοι)οῖ-μεν,-οίημεν
2	τιμ(άοι)ῷ-τε, -ῴητε		φιλ(έοι)οῖ-τε, -οίητε		δηλ(όοι)οῖ-τε, -οίητε
3	τιμ(άοι)ῷ-εν		φιλ(έοι)οῖ-εν		δηλ(όοι)οῖ-εν
Imv.	τίμ(αε)ᾶ	ζῆ	φίλ(εε)ει	θεί	δήλ(οε)ου
3	τιμ(αέ)ά-τω	ζήτω	φιλ(εέ)εί-τω	θείτω	δηλ(οέ)ού-τω
p. 2	τιμ(άε)ᾶ-τε	ζῆτε,	φιλ(έε)εῖ-τε	θεῖτε,	δηλ(όε)οῦ-τε
3	τιμ(αέ)ά-τωσαν, &c.		φιλ(εέ)εί-τωσαν, &c.		δηλ(οέ)ού-τωσαν,
	τιμ(αό)ώ-ντων		φιλ(εό)ού-ντων		δηλ(αό)ού-ντων
Inf.	τιμ(άειν)ᾶν	ζῆν	φιλ(έειν)εῖν	θεῖν	δηλ(όειν)οῦν
Par.	τιμ(άων)ῶν	ζῶν	φιλ(έων)ῶν	θέων	δηλ(όων)ῶν
	τιμ(άου)ώ-σα		φιλ(έου)οῦ-σα		δηλ(όου)οῦ-σα
	τιμ(άον)ῶν		φιλ(έον)οῦν		δηλ(όον)οῦν

b. Imperfect Active.

s. 1	ἐτίμ(αον)ων	ἔζων	ἐφίλ(εον)ουν	ἔθεον	ἐδήλ(οον)ουν
2	ἐτίμ(αες)ας	ἔζης	ἐφίλ(εες)εις	ἔθεις	ἐδήλ(οες)ους
3	ἐτίμ(αε)α	ἔζη	ἐφίλ(εε)ει	ἔθει	ἐδήλ(οε)ου
p. 1	ἐτιμ(άο)ῶ-μεν	ἐζῶμεν	ἐφιλ(έο)οῦ-μεν	ἐθέομεν	ἐδηλ(όο)οῦ-μεν
2	ἐτιμ(άε)ᾶ-τε	ἐζῆτε	ἐφιλ(έε)εῖ-τε	ἐθεῖτε	ἐδηλ(όε)οῦ-τε
3	ἐτίμ(αον)ων	ἔζων	ἐφίλ(εον)ουν	ἔθεον	ἐδήλ(οον)ουν

§ 42. e. Contract Verbs 290 b, 309, 120 s, 7; τιμ(άω)ῶ, τιμ(άο)ῶμεν, τιμ(άου)ῶσι, τιμ(άοι)ῷμι, 120 c; τιμ(άεις)ᾷς, τιμ(άε)ᾶτε, τιμ(άῃς)ᾷς, τιμ(άῃ)ᾶ-τε, 120 a, 118 d; φιλ(έω)ῶσι, φιλ(έου)οῦ, φιλ(έοι)οῖο, 121 c; φιλ(έο)οῦμαι, φιλ(έει)εῖ, φιλ(έε)εῖται, 121 a, b; φιλ(έῃ)ῇ, φιλ(έῃ)ῆται, 121 d; δηλ(όων)ῶν, δηλ(όου)ούσα, δηλ(όοις)οῖς, 121 c; δηλ(όεις)οῖς, δηλ(όῃ)οῖ, 123 a; δηλ(οε)ου, ἐδήλ(οον)ουν, 121 b; δηλ(όῃ)ῶσθε, 120 d; τιμ(άειν)ᾶν, δηλ(όειν)οῦν, 309 c; τιμῴην, φιλοίης, δηλοίη (in this second form of the Opt., the parts shown above take the place of all that follows the parentheses in the first form), 293 b, c; ζ(άεις)ῇς, ζ(άῃ)ῇ, ἐζ(αε)η, 120 g; θέω, θεῖς, 309 b; τιμήσω, θη-

§ 42.   CONTRACT VERBS.   53

TENSES.
                c. PRESENT PASSIVE AND MIDDLE.

	I am honored,	*loved,*	*manifested, &c.*
Ind.	τιμ(άο)ῶ-μαι	φιλ(έο)οῦ-μαι	δηλ(όο)οῦ-μαι
2	τιμ(άῃ)ᾷ	φιλ(έῃ)ῇ, φιλ(έει)εῖ	δηλ(όῃ)οῖ
3	τιμ(άε)ᾶ-ται	φιλ(έε)εῖ-ται	δηλ(όε)οῦ-ται
P. 1	τιμ(αό)ώ-μεθα	φιλ(εό)ού-μεθα	δηλ(οό)ού-μεθα
2	τιμ(άε)ᾶ-σθε	φιλ(έε)εῖ-σθε	δηλ(όε)οῦ-σθε
3	τιμ(άο)ῶ-νται	φιλ(έο)οῦ-νται	δηλ(όο)οῦ-νται
Sub.	τιμ(άω)ῶ-μαι	φιλ(έω)ῶ-μαι	δηλ(ύω)ῶ-μαι
2	τιμ(άῃ)ᾷ	φιλ(έῃ)ῇ	δηλ(όῃ)οῖ
3	τιμ(άῃ)ᾶ-ται	φιλ(έῃ)ῆ-ται	δηλ(όῃ)ῶ-ται
P. 1	τιμ(αώ)ώ-μεθα	φιλ(εώ)ώ-μεθα	δηλ(οώ)ώ-μεθα
2	τιμ(άῃ)ᾶ-σθε	φιλ(έῃ)ῆ-σθε	δηλ(όῃ)ῶ-σθε
3	τιμ(άω)ῶ-νται	φιλ(έω)ῶ-νται	δηλ(ύω)ῶ-νται
Opt.	τιμ(αοί)ῴ-μην	φιλ(εοί)οί-μην	δηλ(οοί)οί-μην
2	τιμ(άοι)ῷ-ο	φιλ(έοι)οῖ-ο	δηλ(όοι)οῖ-ο
3	τιμ(άοι)ῷ-το	φιλ(έοι)οῖ-το	δηλ(όοι)οῖ-το
P. 1	τιμ(αοί)ώ-μεθα	φιλ(εοί)οί-μεθα	δηλ(οοί)οί-μεθα
2	τιμ(άοι)ῷ-σθε	φιλ(έοι)οῖ-σθε	δηλ(όοι)οῖ-σθε
3	τιμ(άοι)ῷ-ντο	φιλ(έοι)οῖ-ντο	δηλ(όοι)οῖ-ντο
Imv.	τιμ(άου)ῶ	φιλ(έου)οῦ	δηλ(όου)οῦ
3	τιμ(αέ)ά-σθω	φιλ(εέ)εί-σθω	δηλ(οέ)ού-σθω
P. 2	τιμ(άε)ᾶ-σθε	φιλ(έε)εῖ-σθε	δηλ(όε)οῦ-σθε
3	τιμ(αέ)ά-σθωσαν,	φιλ(εέ)εί-σθωσαν,	δηλ(οέ)ού-σθωσαν,
	τιμ(αέ)ά-σθων	φιλ(εέ)εί-σθων	δηλ(οέ)ού-σθων
Inf.	τιμ(άε)ᾶ-σθαι	φιλ(έε)εῖ-σθαι	δηλ(όε)οῦ-σθαι
Par.	τιμ(αό)ώ-μενος	φιλ(εό)ού-μενος	δηλ(οό)ού-μενος
	τιμ(αο)ω-μένη	φιλ(εο)ου-μένη	δηλ(οο)ου-μένη
	τιμ(αό)ώ-μενον	φιλ(εό)ού-μενον	δηλ(οό)ού-μενον

                d. IMPERFECT PASSIVE AND MIDDLE.

S. 1	ἐτιμ(αό)ώ-μην	ἐφιλ(εό)ού-μην	ἐδηλ(οό)ού-μην
2	ἐτιμ(άου)ῶ	ἐφιλ(έου)οῦ	ἐδηλ(όου)οῦ
3	ἐτιμ(άε)ᾶ-το	ἐφιλ(έε)εῖ-το	ἐδηλ(όε)οῦ-το
P. 1	ἐτιμ(αό)ώ-μεθα	ἐφιλ(εό)ού-μεθα	ἐδηλ(οό)ού-μεθα
2	ἐτιμ(άε)ᾶ-σθε	ἐφιλ(έε)εῖ-σθε	ἐδηλ(όε)οῦ-σθε
3	ἐτιμ(άο)ῶ-ντο	ἐφιλ(έο)οῦ-ντο	ἐδηλ(όυ)οῦ-ντο

ῥάσω, ἐφίλησα, δεδήλωκα, 310 ; ἐτέλεσα 310 c ; πλεύσω 345 ; πλευσοῦμαι 305 d ; τετέλεσμαι, ἐπλεύσθην, 307 a, b ; ἐλ(άσω)ῶ, τελ(έσω)ῶ, 305 b ; πεπράσομαι fr. (πρα-) πιπράσκω *sell*, 50 ; κεκλήσομαι fr. καλέω, -έσω, CALL, 342. 2, 50 ; δεδήσομαι fr. δέω *bind*, 319 c, 309 b ; accent 772.— O. E. νικάω *conquer*, ὀπτάω *roast*; διψάω *thirst*, πεινάω *hunger*, 120 g ; πειράω *try*, ἐάω *permit*, ἀνιάω *vex*, ἀκροάομαι *hear*, 310, 279 c ; σπάω *draw*, γελάω *laugh*, 310 c, e, 307 a ; αἰτέω *ask*, μισέω *hate*, οἰκέω *inhabit*, ἡγέομαι *lead*, μιμέομαι imitor, *imitate* ; ζέω *boil*, αἰδέομαι *respect*, 310 c, 307 a, 309 b ; πληρόω *fill*, χρυσόω *gild* ; ῥιγόω *shiver*, 324 b ; ἀρόω *plough*, 310 c, 50.

f. Indefinite and Complete Tenses.

Fut. A.	τιμήσω	φιλήσω	δηλώσω
Mid.	τιμήσομαι	φιλήσομαι	δηλώσομαι
Aor. A.	ἐτίμησα	ἐφίλησα	ἐδήλωσα
Mid.	ἐτιμησάμην	ἐφιλησάμην	ἐδηλωσάμην
Perf. A.	τετίμηκα	πεφίληκα	δεδήλωκα
Plup. A.	ἐτετιμήκειν	ἐπεφιλήκειν	ἐδεδηλώκειν
Perf. P.	τετίμημαι	πεφίλημαι	δεδήλωμαι
Plup. P.	ἐτετιμήμην	ἐπεφιλήμην	ἐδεδηλώμην
Fut. Pf.	τετιμήσομαι	πεφιλήσομαι	δεδηλώσομαι
Aor. P.	ἐτιμήθην	ἐφιλήθην	ἐδηλώθην
Fut. P.	τιμηθήσομαι	φιληθήσομαι	δηλωθήσομαι
Verbals	τιμητός, τιμητέος	φιλητός, φιλητέος	δηλωτός, δηλωτέος

g. Other Examples.

Pres. A.	θηρ(άω)ῶ *hunt*	τελ(έω)ῶ *finish*	πλέω *sail*
P. & M.	θηρ(άο)ῶ-μαι	τελ(έο)οῦ-μαι	
Impf. A.	ἐθήρ(αον)ων	ἐτέλ(εον)ουν	ἔπλεον
P. & M.	ἐθηρ(αό)ώ-μην	ἐτελ(εό)ού-μην	
Fut. A.	θηράσω	τελέσω, τελῶ	πλεύσω late
Mid.	θηράσομαι	τελέσομαι, τελοῦμαι	πλεύσομαι, πλευσοῦ-
Aor. A.	ἐθήρᾶσα	ἐτέλεσα	ἔπλευσα [μαι
Mid.	ἐθηρᾶσάμην	ἐτελεσάμην	
Perf. A.	τεθήρᾶκα	τετέλεκα	πέπλευκα
Plup. A.	ἐτεθηράκειν	ἐτετελέκειν	ἐπεπλεύκειν
Perf. P.	τεθήραμαι	τετέλεσμαι	πέπλευσμαι
Plup. P.	ἐτεθηράμην	ἐτετελέσμην	ἐπεπλεύσμην
Fut. Pf.	πεπράσομαι	κεκλήσομαι	δεδήσομαι
Aor. P.	ἐθηράθην	ἐτελέσθην	ἐπλεύσθην late
Fut. P.	θηρᾶθήσομαι	τελεσθήσομαι	πλευσθήσομαι late
Verbals	θηρᾶτός, θηρᾶτέος	τελεστός, τελεστέος	πλευστέος

Att. } ἐλ(άσω, άω)ῶ, ἐλᾷς, ἐλᾷ, ἐλῶμεν, &c.; ἐλῷμι or ἐλῴην· ἐλᾶν· ἐλῶν.
Fut. } τελ(έσω, έω)ῶ, τέλεῖς, τελεῖ, &c.; τελοῖμι or τελοίην· τελεῖν· τελῶν.

43. Analogies from Latin Contract Verbs.

1. In -(ao)o : ama-. 2. In -eo : mone-. 3. In -io : audi-.

Active Voice.

Ind. Pr.	ăm(ăo)o *love*	mŏnĕo *warn*	audĭo *hear*
2	am(ăĭs)ās	mon(cĭs)ēs	aud(ĭīs)īs
3	am(ăĭt)ăt	mon(cĭt)ĕt	aud(ĭīt)ĭt
P. 1	am(ăĭ)āmus	mon(eĭ)ēmus	aud(ĭī)īmus
2	am(ăĭ)ātis	mon(eĭ)ētis	audiī)ītis
3	am(aŭnt)ant	mon(eŭnt)ent	audiunt
Impf.	am(ae)ābam	mon(eē)ēbam	audiēbam
Sub. Pr.	am(aam)em	moneam	andiam
Impf.	am(aĕ)ārem	mon(eĕ)ērem	aud(iĕ)īrem

§ 45. BARYTONES IN -ω AND -μι. 55

Imv. s. 2	am(ă)ā	mon(ĕ)ē	aud(ĭĕ)ī
2, 3	am(ăĭ)āto	mon(ĕĭ)ēto	aud(ĭī)īto
p. 2	am(ăĭ)āte	mon(ĕĭ)ēte	aud(ĭī)īte
3	am(ăŭ)anto	mon(ĕŭ)ento	audiunto
Inf. Pr.	am(ă)āre	mon(ĕĕ)ēre	aud(ĭĕ)īre
Par. Pr.	am(aens)ans	mon(eens)ens	audiens

PASSIVE VOICE.

Ind. Pr.	ăm(ăor)or	mŏnŏor	audĭor
2	am(ăĕ)āris, -re	mon(ĕĕ)ēris -re,	aud(ĭĕ)īris, -re
3	am(ăĭ)ātur	mon(ĕĭ)ētur	aud(ĭī)ītur
p. 1	am(ăĭ)āmur	mon(ĕĭ)ēmur	aud(ĭī)īmur
2	am(ăĭ)āmini	mon(ĕĭ)ēmini	aud(ĭī)īmini
3	am(ăŭ)antur	mon(ĕŭ)entur	audiuntur
Impf.	am(ăĕ)ābar	mon(cĕ)ēbar	audiēbar
Sub. Pr.	am(aar)er	monear	audiar
Impf.	am(ăĕ)ārer	mon(ĕĕ)ērer	aud(ĭĕ)īrer
Imv. s. 2	am(ăĕ)āre	mon(ĕĕ)ēre	aud(ĭĕ)īre
2, 3	am(ăĭ)ātor	mon(ĕĭ)ētor	aud(ĭī)ītor
p. 2	am(ăĭ)āmini	mon(ĕĭ)ēmini	aud(ĭī)īmini
3	am(ăŭ)antor	mon(ĕŭ)entor	audiuntor
Inf. Pr.	am(ăĕ)āri	mon(ĕĕ)ēri	aud(ĭĕ)īri

44. PURE VERBS. II. BARYTONES IN -ω.

S. βουλευ-, *to plan*; σει-, *shake*; θῠ-, θῠ-, *sacrifice*; και-, κα-, &c., *burn*.

Pres. A.	βουλεύω	σείω	θύω (˘υ)	καίω, o. λ. κάω
P. & M.	βουλεύομαι	σείομαι	θύομαι	καίομαι
Impf. A.	ἐβούλευον	ἔσειον	ἔθυον	ἔκαιον, ἔκᾱον
P. & M.	ἐβουλευόμην	ἐσειόμην	ἐθυόμην	ἐκαιόμην
Fut. A.	βουλεύσω	σείσω	θύσω	καύσω
Mid.	βουλεύσομαι	σείσομαι	θύσομαι	καύσομαι
Aor. A.	ἐβούλευσα	ἔσεισα	ἔθῡσα	ἔκαυσα, p. ἔκεα
Mid.	ἐβουλευσάμην	ἐσεισάμην	ἐθυσάμην	ἐκαυσάμην
Perf. A.	βεβούλευκα	σέσεικα	τέθῠκα	κέκαυκα
Plup. A.	ἐβεβουλεύκειν	ἐσεσείκειν	ἐτεθύκειν	ἐκεκαύκειν
Perf. P.	βεβούλευμαι	σέσεισμαι	τέθῠμαι	κέκαυμαι
Plup. P.	ἐβεβουλεύμην	ἐσεσείσμην	ἐτεθύμην	ἐκεκαύμην
Aor. P.	ἐβουλεύθην	ἐσείσθην	ἐτύθην	ἐκαύθην, ἐκάην
Fut. P.	βουλευθήσομαι	σεισθήσομαι	τυθήσομαι	καυθήσομαι
Verbals	βουλευτός, -τέος	σειστός, -τέος	θῠτέος	καυτός or -στός

45. PURE VERBS. III. VERBS IN -μι.

1. ἵστημι (s. στᾰ-, ἱστᾰ-) *stătuo, to set up*, STATION (Pf. and 2 Aor., *to* STAND); 2. τίθημι (θε-, τῐθε-) pōno, *to put, place*; 3. δίδωμι (δο-, διδο-) do, *to give*; 4. δείκνῡμι (δεικ-, δεικνῠ-) indĭco *to point out, show*.

---

§ 44. a. BARYTONE VERBS 309 a : βεβούλευμαι, σέσεισμαι, 307 b, d ; θύσω, τέθῠκα 310 d ; ἐτύθην 159 d ; καίω (s. καϝ-, καυ-, κᾰ-, κε-, κᾰ-, και-) 345, 341, 347 g, h. — O. E. παιδεύω *educate*; πιστεύω *trust*; τίω poet.,

PURE VERBS. § 45.

a. Present Active.

DEFINITE

Ind.	ἵστημι	τίθημι	δίδωμι	δείκνῡμι, -ύω
2	ἵστης	τίθης	δίδως	δείκνῡς
3	ἵστησι'	τίθησι'	δίδωσι'	δείκνῡσι'
P. 1	ἵστᾰμεν	τίθεμεν	δίδομεν	δείκνῠμεν
2	ἵστατε	τίθετε	δίδοτε	δείκνυτε
3	ἱστᾶσι',	τιθέᾱσι',	διδόᾱσι',	δεικνύᾱσι',
		τιθεῖσι'	διδοῦσι'	δεικνῦσι'
Sub.	ἱστῶ	τιθῶ	διδῶ	δεικνύω
2	ἱστῇς	τιθῇς	διδῷς	δεικνύῃς
3	ἱστῇ	τιθῇ	διδῷ	δεικνύῃ
P. 1	ἱστῶμεν	τιθῶμεν	διδῶμεν	δεικνύωμεν
2	ἱστῆτε	τιθῆτε	διδῶτε	δεικνύητε
3	ἱστῶσι'	τιθῶσι'	διδῶσι'	δεικνύωσι'
Opt.	ἱσταίην	τιθείην	διδοίην [διδῴην]	δεικνύοιμι
2	ἱσταίης	τιθείης	διδοίης	δεικνύοις
3	ἱσταίη	τιθείη	διδοίη	δεικνύοι
P. 1	ἱσταίημεν,-αῖμεν	τιθείημεν,-εῖμεν	διδοίημεν,-οῖμεν	δεικνύοιμεν
2	ἱσταίητε,-αῖτε	τιθείητε,-εῖτε	διδοίητε,-οῖτε	δεικνύοιτε
3	ἱσταίησαν,-αῖεν	τιθείησαν,-εῖεν	διδοίησαν,-οῖεν	δεικνύοιεν
Imv.	ἵστη	τίθει	δίδου	δείκνῡ, -υε
3	ἱστάτω	τιθέτω	διδότω	δεικνύτω
P. 2	ἵστατε	τίθετε	δίδοτε	δείκνυτε
3	ἱστάτωσαν,	τιθέτωσαν,	διδότωσαν,	δεικνύτωσαν,
	ἱστάντων	τιθέντων	διδόντων	δεικνύντων
Inf.	ἱστάναι!	τιθέναι!	διδόναι!	δεικνύναι!
Par.	ἱστάς!	τιθείς!	διδούς!	δεικνύς!-ύων
	ἱστᾶσα!	τιθεῖσα!	διδοῦσα!	δεικνῦσα!
	ἱστάν!	τιθέν!	διδόν!	δεικνύν!

b. Imperfect Active.

Ind.	ἵστην	ἐτίθην, ἐτίθουν	ἐδίδων, ἐδίδουν	ἐδείκνῡν, ἐδείκνυον
2	ἵστης	ἐτίθης, ἐτίθεις	ἐδίδως, ἐδίδους	ἐδείκνῡς, ἐδείκνυες
3	ἵστη	ἐτίθη, ἐτίθει	ἐδίδω, ἐδίδου	ἐδείκνῡ, ἐδείκνυε'
P. 1	ἱστάμεν	ἐτίθεμεν	ἐδίδομεν	ἐδείκνῠμεν
2	ἵστατε	ἐτίθετε	ἐδίδοτε	ἐδείκνυτε
3	ἵστασαν	ἐτίθεσαν	ἐδίδοσαν	ἐδείκνυσαν, -υον

---

honor; κελεύω *command,* παίω *strike,* 307 b; κλείω *shut,* κολούω *maim,* 307 e, 50; δακρύω *weep,* κωλύω (ῡ) *hinder;* κλαίω *weep,* 50.

§ 45. c. VERBS IN -μι 313 s: Stems, δο- διδο-, θε- τιθε-, 357. 1, στα- ἱστα- 357. 3, δεικ- δεικνυ- 351. 3; stem-mark lengthened 314. Affixes 35 a, 36 a, g, 32 i, 295 s; (ἱστα-μ) ἵστημι, ἵστην, 296; (ἱστα-τ) ἵστησι, ἵστη, 298; ἱστ(α-ντ, ανσι, ααι)ᾶσι, τιθέασι 300 a, 156; δείκνυμι or δεικνύω 315 a; ἱστ(ά-ω)ῶ, ἱστ(ά-ῃ)ῇς, βῇς, διδ(ό-ῃ)ῷ, δῷ, γνῷ, τιθ(έ-ω)ῶμαι, 316 a; ἱσταίην, δεικνύοιμι, 293, διδῴην, δῴην, 316 b, ἱσταῖμεν, θεῖμεν, 293 a; ἱστ(α-ε)η, τιθ(ε-ε)ει, θές, δός, στῆθι, δῦθι, 297 c; ἱστάναι, δῦναι, 301; ἱστ(α-ντ-s)άς, βάς, τιθ(ε-ντ-s)είς, γνούς, 156, 26, ἱστᾶσα, διδοῦσα, 233 b; ἐδίδουν, ἐτίθεις,

§ 45. VERBS IN -MI. 57

TENSES.

c. PRESENT PASSIVE AND MIDDLE.

Ind.	ἵστᾰμαι	τίθεμαι	δίδομαι	δείκνῠμαι
2	ἵστᾰσαι	τίθεσαι, τίθῃ	δίδοσαι	δείκνυσαι
3	ἵσταται	τίθεται	δίδοται	δείκνυται
P. 1	ἱστάμεθα	τιθέμεθα	διδόμεθα	δεικνύμεθα
2	ἵστασθε	τίθεσθε	δίδοσθε	δείκνυσθε
3	ἵστανται	τίθενται	δίδονται	δείκνυνται
Sub.	ἱστῶμαι	τιθῶμαι	διδῶμαι	δεικνύωμαι
2	ἱστῇ	τιθῇ	διδῷ	δεικνύῃ
3	ἱστῆται	τιθῆται	διδῶται	δεικνύηται
P. 1	ἱστώμεθα	τιθώμεθα	διδώμεθα	δεικνυώμεθα
2	ἱστῆσθε	τιθῆσθε	διδῶσθε	δεικνύησθε
3	ἱστῶνται	τιθῶνται	διδῶνται	δεικνύωνται
Opt.	ἱσταίμην	τιθείμην, τιθοίμην	διδοίμην	δεικνυοίμην
2	ἱσταῖο	τιθεῖο, τιθοῖο	διδοῖο	δεικνύοιο
3	ἱσταῖτο	τιθεῖτο, τιθοῖτο	διδοῖτο	δεικνύοιτο
P. 1	ἱσταίμεθα	τιθείμεθα, τιθοίμεθα	διδοίμεθα	δεικνυοίμεθα
2	ἱσταῖσθε	τιθεῖσθε, τιθοῖσθε	διδοῖσθε	δεικνύοισθε
3	ἱσταῖντο	τιθεῖντο, τιθοῖντο	διδοῖντο	δεικνύοιντο
Imv.	ἵστᾰσο, ἵστω	τίθεσο, τίθου	δίδοσο, δίδου	δείκνῠσο
3	ἱστάσθω	τιθέσθω	διδόσθω	δεικνύσθω
P. 2	ἵστασθε	τίθεσθε	δίδοσθε	δείκνυσθε
3	ἱστάσθωσαν, ἱστάσθων	τιθέσθωσαν, τιθέσθων	διδόσθωσαν, διδόσθων	δεικνύσθωσαν, δεικνύσθων
Inf.	ἵστασθαι	τίθεσθαι	δίδοσθαι	δείκνυσθαι
Par.	ἱστάμενος	τιθέμενος	διδόμενος	δεικνύμενος
	ἱσταμένη	τιθεμένη	διδομένη	δεικνυμένη
	ἱστάμενον	τιθέμενον	διδόμενον	δεικνύμενον

d. IMPERFECT PASSIVE AND MIDDLE.

Ind.	ἱστᾰ́μην	ἐτιθέμην	ἐδιδόμην	ἐδεικνῠ́μην
2	ἵστασο, ἵστω	ἐτίθεσο, ἐτίθου	ἐδίδοσο, ἐδίδου	ἐδείκνυσο
3	ἵστατο	ἐτίθετο	ἐδίδοτο	ἐδείκνυτο
P. 1	ἱστάμεθα	ἐτιθέμεθα	ἐδιδόμεθα	ἐδεικνύμεθα
2	ἵστασθε	ἐτίθεσθε	ἐδίδοσθε	ἐδείκνυσθε
3	ἵσταντο	ἐτίθεντο	ἐδίδοντο	ἐδείκνυντο

315 b; ἵστασαν 300; τίθεσαι τίθῃ (late, Pall. Ep. 79), ἵστασο ἵστω, ἐθ(εσο)ου, δ(οσο)οῦ, 297 e, h; τιθοίμην, θοίμην, 315 c; accent 772 g, h, 780 a, 781, 782 b.— O. E. πίμπλημι pleo, *fill*, πίμπρημι *burn*, ὀνίνημι *benefit*, κίχρημι *lend*; ἄγαμαι *admire*, δύναμαι *be able*, κρέμαμαι *hang*, μάρναμαι poet., *fight*; δίζημαι Ep. & Ion., *seek*: ὄνομαι Ep., *blame*; ἄγνυμι *break*, ζεύγνυμι *jungo, join*, ζώννυμι *gird*, ὀλλύμι *destroy*, ὄμνυμι *swear*, πήγνυμι *fasten*. See 50.

2 Aor. (see also above) 313 b, 314 c, d: ἔβην, ἔσβην, ἔγνων, (forms partially given in 45 h), ἔδυν, ἔδραν, 2 A. of βαίνω *go*, σβέννυμι *quench*, γιγνώσκω *gnosco*, KNOW, δύνω *enter, sink*, διδράσκω *run*, 50; ἐπριάμην (s. πρια-) as 2 A. of ὠνέομαι *buy*, 50; στᾶ 297 d; στάντων, γνόντων, 314 c; ἔθηκα,

GR. TAB. 3*

58 PURE VERBS. § 45.

INDEFINITE AND

f. Fut. A.	στήσω	θήσω	δώσω	δείξω
Mid.	στήσομαι	θήσομαι	δώσομαι	δείξομαι
1 Aor. A.	ἔστησα	ἔθηκα 306 b	ἔδωκα	ἔδειξα
Mid.	ἐστησάμην	ἐθηκάμην Ep.		ἐδειξάμην
Perf. A.	ἕ*στηκα 46	τέθεικα 310 b	δέδωκα	δέδειχα
Plup. A.	ἑστήκειν, εἱστήκειν	ἐτεθείκειν	ἐδεδώκειν	ἐδεδείχειν
F. Pf. A.	ἑστήξω 319 b			

h. SECOND AORIST

Ind. ἔστην	ἔβην	(ἔθηκα	ἔσβην	(ἔδωκα	ἔγνων	ἔδυν sank.
2 ἔστης	ἔβης	ἔθηκας	ἔσβης	ἔδωκας	ἔγνως	ἔδυς
3 ἔστη	ἔβη	ἔθηκε')	ἔσβη	ἔδωκε')	ἔγνω	ἔδυ
P. 1 ἔστημεν		ἔθεμεν		ἔδομεν		ἔδυμεν
2 ἔστητε		ἔθετε		ἔδοτε		ἔδυτε
3 ἔστησαν		ἔθεσαν		ἔδοσαν		ἔδυσαν
Sub. στῶ	βῶ	θῶ		δῶ	γνῶ	δύω
2 στῇς	βῇς	θῇς		δῷς	γνῷς	δύῃς
3 στῇ	βῇ	θῇ		δῷ	γνῷ	δύῃ
P. 1 στῶμεν	βῶμεν	θῶμεν		δῶμεν	γνῶμεν	δύωμεν
2 στῆτε	βῆτε	θῆτε		δῶτε	γνῶτε	δύητε
3 στῶσι'	βῶσι'	θῶσι'		δῶσι'	γνῶσι'	δύωσι'
Opt. σταίην	βαίην	θείην		δοίην [δῴην]		δύην Ep.
2 σταίης	βαίης	θείης		δοίης		δύης
3 σταίη	βαίη	θείη		δοίη		δύη
P. 1 σταίημεν, σταῖμεν		θείημεν, θεῖμεν		δοίημεν, δοῖμεν		δύημεν, δῦμεν
2 σταίητε, σταῖτε,		θείητε, θεῖτε		δοίητε, δοῖτε		δύητε, δῦτε
3 σταίησαν, σταῖεν		θείησαν, θεῖεν		δοίησαν, δοῖεν		δύησαν, δῦεν
Imv. στῆθι [στᾶ]		θές		δός	γνῶθι	δῦθι
3 στήτω		θέτω		δότω	γνώτω	δύτω
P. 2 στῆτε		θέτε		δότε	γνῶτε	δῦτε
3 στήτωσαν,		θέτωσαν,		δότωσαν,		δύτωσαν,
στάντων		θέντων		δόντων		δύντων
Inf. στῆναι	βῆναι	θεῖναι σβῆναι		δοῦναι γνῶναι		δῦναι
Par. στάς	βάς	θείς σβείς		δούς γνούς		δύς

ἔθεμεν, θεῖναι, ἔδωκα, ἔδομεν, δοῦναι, 306 b, c, 314 d ; δύην 316 c ; δρ(άης)ᾳς 120 h ; πρίωμαι, πρίαιο, 783 b. — O. E. ἔτλην, ἔφθην, ἔπτην, ἐπτάμην, ἔσκλην, ἑάλων or ἥλων, ἔβιων, 2 A. of τλα- endure, φθάνω anticipate, πέτομαι fly, σκέλλω dry, ἁλίσκομαι be taken, βιόω vivo, live, 50.

§ 45. j. SELECT HOMERIC FORMS OF ἵστημι, τίθημι, ἵημι, δίδωμι, &c.
ACTIVE. Pres. Ind. s. 2 leis E. 880, διδοῖς (ἵης, δίδως, Bek.), 335 a, τίθησθα, διδοῖσθα (δίδωσθα Bek.), 297 b ; 3 τιθεῖ, ἱεῖ B. 752, διδοῖ, 335 a ; P. 3 θέουσι (θέωσι Bek.) 335 a ; Sub. s. 3 ἵησι N. 234, § 328 b ; Imv. ἵστα 335 a, δίδωθι 335 d ; Inf. ἱέμεν Δ. 351, ἱέμεναι N. 114, τιθήμεναι, διδοῦναι, 333 c, 335 d : Impf. s. 1 ἵειν (ἵην Bek.) ι. 88, § 315 b ; 3 ἵστασκε τ. 574, § 332 g, τίθει (τίθη Bek.) A. 441, § 284 a, 315 b ; P. 3 τίθεν a. 112, ἵεν M. 33 (v. 1. ξύν-ιον A. 273), ἔδιδον, 330 b : Fut. Ind. s. 3 ἀν-έσει σ. 265, § 310 d ;
P. 1 διδώσομεν (s. διδο-) ν. 358 ; Inf. ἠσέμεν Υ. 361, ἠσέμεναι π. 377, θησέμεναι M. 35, δωσέμεναι δ. 7, § 233 d, διδώσειν ω. 314 : 1 Aor. στήσα δ. 582,

§ 45. VERBS IN -MI. 59

COMPLETE TENSES.

g. Perf. P. ἕστᾰμαι 310 d   τέθειμαι   δέδομαι   δέδειγμαι
Plup. P. ἑστάμην   ἐτεθείμην   ἐδεδόμην   ἐδεδείγμην
F. Pf. P. ἑστήξομαι 319 b   δεδείξομαι l.
Aor. P. ἑστᾰ́θην   ἐτέθην 159 d   ἐδόθην   ἐδείχθην
Fut. P. σταθήσομαι τεθήσομαι   δοθήσομαι δειχθήσομαι
Verbals στατός, στατέος   θετός, θετέος   δοτός, δοτέος   δεικτύς, δεικτέος

ACTIVE.   i. SECOND AORIST MIDDLE.

Ind.	ἔδρᾱν ran	ἐπριάμην bought	ἐθέμην	ἐδόμην
2	ἔδρας	ἐπρίω	ἔθου	ἔδου
3	ἔδρα	ἐπρίατο	ἔθετο	ἔδοτο
P. 1	ἔδρᾱμεν	ἐπριάμεθα	ἐθέμεθα	ἐδόμεθα
2	ἔδρατε	ἐπρίασθε	ἔθεσθε	ἔδοσθε
3	ἔδρασαν	ἐπρίαντο	ἔθεντο	ἔδοντο
Sub.	δρῶ	πρίωμαι	θῶμαι	δῶμαι
2	δρᾷς	πρίῃ	θῇ	δῷ
3	δρᾷ	πρίηται	θῆται	δῶται
P. 1	δρῶμεν	πριώμεθα	θώμεθα	δώμεθα
2	δρᾶτε	πρίησθε	θῆσθε	δῶσθε
3	δρῶσι	πρίωνται	θῶνται	δῶνται
Opt.	δραίην	πριαίμην	θείμην, θοίμην	δοίμην
2	δραίης	πρίαιο	θεῖο, θοῖο,	δοῖο
3	δραίη	πρίαιτο	θεῖτο &c.	δοῖτο
P. 1	δραίημεν, δραῖμεν	πριαίμεθα	θείμεθα	δοίμεθα
2	δραίητε, δραῖτε	πρίαισθε	θεῖσθε	δοῖσθε
3	δραίησαν, δραῖεν	πρίαιντο	θεῖντο	δοῖντο
Imv.	δρᾶθι	πρίασο, πρίω	θοῦ	δοῦ
3	δράτω	πριάσθω	θέσθω	δόσθω
P. 2	δρᾶτε	πρίασθε	θέσθε	δόσθε
3	δράτωσαν, δράντων	πριάσθωσαν, πριάσθων	θέσθωσαν, θέσθων	δόσθωσαν, δύσθων
Inf.	δρᾶναι	πρίασθαι	θέσθαι	δόσθαι
Par.	δράς	πριάμενος	θέμενος	δόμενος

δῶκα δ. 649, § 284 a, ἧκα P. 708, § 135 : Perf. Ind. p. 2 ἕστητε 335 d ; Inf. ἑστάμεν φ. 261, ἑστάμεναι N. 56, § 333 c ; Part. ἑσταότος T. 79, ἑστεῶτα N. 261, § 325 d : 2 Aor. Ind. s. 1 στῆν Λ. 744, § 284 a, δύσκον, 3 στάσκεν, 332 g ; P. 3 ἔσταν, στάν I. 193, ἔφυν, 330 b, ἔστᾰσαν M. 56, § 335 d, θέσαν B. 599, ἔσαν δ. 681, δόσαν A. 162, § 284 a, Sub. (322 a, c, 323 c, 324 c, 328 b) s. 1 βείω, θείω, εἵω A. 567, γνώω· 2 στήῃς, θείῃς or θήῃς, γνώῃς Ψ. 487 ; 3 στήῃ, βήῃ, βέῃ II. 94, 852, θείῃ or θήῃ, ἔῃ II. 590, εἴῃ or ἤῃ ε. 471, ἦσιν O. 359, δώῃ, δῷσι, δώῃσιν· I'. 1 στέωμεν, στείομεν, θ.ὦμεν, θείομεν, δώωμεν· 3 στήωσι or στείωσι, δώωσιν· D. 3 στήετον ; Inf. στήμεναι K. 55, θέμεν, θέμεναι, ἔμεν Δ. 94, δόμεν, δόμεναι, γνώμεναι, 333 c. MIDDLE. Pres. Imv. ἵστασο, ἵσταο Bek., K. 291, § 297 e ; Part. τιθήμενον 335 d : Impf. p. 3 τίθεντο H. 475 : Fut. s. 2 θήσεαι δ. 163, § 323 c : 1 Aor. s. 3 θήκατο K. 31, § 306 b : 2 Aor. Ind. s. 3 θέτο Γ. 310, ἕτο δ. 76, § 284 a ; D. 3 θέσθην χ. 141 ; Sub. s. 1 θείομαι 323 c ; 2 θῆαι (v. l. θείης) T. 403 ; Imv. θέο κ. 333, θεῦ 323 c.

Verbs in -mi (continued).

ACTIVE VOICE.

	k. ἵημι mitto S. ἑ-, ἱε-; to send. Present.	2 Aorist.	l. εἰμί sum S. ἐσ-, ἐ-; to be. Present.		m. εἶμι eo, ire S. ἴ-; to go. Present.	
Ind.	ἵημι	(ἧκα)	εἰμί |	sum	εἶμι	eo
2	ἵης	ἧκας	[εἶς |] εἶ	es	[εἶς] εἶ	is
3	ἵησι'	ἧκε')	ἐστί |'	est	εἶσι'	it
P. 1	ἵεμεν	εἷμεν	ἐσμέν |	sumus	ἴμεν	imus
2	ἵετε	εἷτε	ἐστέ |	estis	ἴτε	itis
3	ἱᾶσι', ἱεῖσι'	εἷσαν (ἧκαν)	εἰσί |'	sunt	ἴᾱσι'	eunt
D. 2	ἵετον	εἷτον, 3 εἵτην	ἐστόν |		ἴτον	
Sub.	ἱῶ	ὦ	ὦ	sim	ἴω	eam
2	ἱῇς	ᾖς	ᾖς	sis	ἴῃς	eas
3	ἱῇ	ᾖ	ᾖ	sit	ἴῃ	eat
P. 1	ἱῶμεν	ὦμεν	ὦμεν	simus	ἴωμεν	eamus
2	ἱῆτε	ἦτε	ἦτε	sitis	ἴητε	eatis
3	ἱῶσι'	ὦσι'	ὦσι'	sint	ἴωσι'	eant
D. 2	ἱῆτον	ἦτον	ἦτον		ἴητον	
Opt.	ἱείην [ἵοιμι]	εἵην	εἴην	essem	ἴοιμι, ἰοίην	
2	ἱείης	εἵης	εἴης	esses	ἴοις	ires
3	ἱείη	εἵη	εἴη	esset	ἴοι	iret
P. 1	ἱείημεν, ἱεῖμεν	εἵημην, εἷμεν	εἴημεν, εἶμεν		ἴοιμεν	
2	ἱείητε, ἱεῖτε	εἵητε, εἷτε	εἴητε, εἶτε		ἴοιτε	
3	ἱείησαν, ἱεῖεν	εἵησαν, εἷεν	εἴησαν, εἶεν		ἴοιεν	
D. 2	ἱείητον, ἱεῖτον	εἵητον, εἷτον	εἴητον, εἶτον		ἴοιτον	
3	ἱειήτην, ἱείτην	εἱήτην, εἵτην	εἰήτην, εἵτην		ἰοίτην	
Imv.	ἵει	ἕς	ἴσθι	es	ἴθι [εἶ?]	i
3	ἱέτω	ἕτω	ἔστω [ἤτω]	esto	ἴτω	ito
P. 2	ἵετε	ἕτε	ἔστε	este	ἴτε	ite
3	ἱέτωσαν, ἱέντων	ἕτωσαν, ἕντων	ἔστωσαν, ἔστων, τ. ὄντων	sunto	ἴτωσαν, ἰόντων, ἴτων	eunto
D. 2	ἵετον	ἕτον	ἔστον		ἴτον	
3	ἱέτων	ἕτων	ἔστων		ἴτων	
Inf.	ἱέναι!	εἷναι	εἶναι	esse	ἰέναι!	ire
Par.	ἱείς	εἵς	ὤν	[ens]	ἰών!	iens
	ἱεῖσα! ἱέν!	εἷσα, ἕν	οὖσα, ὄν		ἰοῦσα! ἰόν!	

	Imperfect.		Imperfect.		Imperfect.	
Ind.	ἵην,[ἵουν]ἵειν	Fut. ἥσω, ἥσοιμι,	S. 1	ἦν, ἦ, ἤμην	ᾔειν, ᾖα	ibam
2	ἵης, ἵεις	ἥσειν, ἥσων	2	[ἦς] ἦσθα	ᾔεις, ᾔεισθα	
3	ἵη, ἵει		3	ἦν erat	ᾔει'	
P. 1	ἵεμεν	1 Aor. ἧκα (Ind.	P. 1	ἦμεν	ᾔειμεν, ᾖμεν	
2	ἵετε	only) 306	2	ἦτε, ἦστε	ᾔειτε, ᾖτε	
3	ἵεσαν	Perf. εἷκα, εἱκέναι,	3	ἦσαν erant	ᾔεσαν, ᾖσαν	
D. 2	ἵετον	εἰκώς 310 b	D. 2	ᾖτον, ᾖστον	ᾔειτον, ᾖτον	
3	ἱέτην	Plup. εἵκειν	3	ᾔτην, ᾔστην	ᾐείτην, ᾖτην	

§ 45.   ʿΙΗΜΙ, ΕΙΜΙ, ΕΙΜΙ, ΚΕΙΜΑΙ.   61

PASSIVE AND MIDDLE VOICES.

n. Of ἵημι.   o. Of εἰμί, to be.   q. κεῖμαι, to lie.

	Present.	2 Aorist.	Future.	Present.
Ind.	ἵεμαι	εἵμην	ἔσομαι	κεῖμαι
2	ἵεσαι	εἷσο	ἔσῃ, ἔσει	κεῖσαι
3	ἵεται	εἷτο	[ἔσεται] ἔσται	κεῖται
P. 1	ἱέμεθα	εἵμεθα	ἐσόμεθα	κείμεθα
2	ἵεσθε	εἷσθε	ἔσεσθε	κεῖσθε
3	ἵενται	εἷντο	ἔσονται	κεῖνται
Sub.	ἱῶμαι	ὦμαι		κέωμαι
2	ἱῇ	ᾖ		κέῃ
3	ἱῆται	ἧται		κέηται
P. 1	ἱώμεθα	ὤμεθα		κεώμεθα
2	ἱῆσθε	ἧσθε		κέησθε
2	ἱῶνται	ὧνται		κέωνται
Opt.	ἱείμην, ἱοίμην	εἵμην, οἵμην	ἐσοίμην	κεοίμην
2	ἱεῖο, ἱοῖο,	εἷο, οἷο	ἔσοιο	κέοιο
3	ἱεῖτο &c.	εἷτο, οἷτο	ἔσοιτο	κέοιτο
P. 1	ἱείμεθα	εἵμεθα, οἵμεθα	ἐσοίμεθα	κεοίμεθα
2	ἱεῖσθε	εἷσθε, οἷσθε	ἔσοισθε	κέοισθε
3	ἱεῖντο	εἷντο, οἷντο	ἔσοιντο	κέοιντο
Imv.	ἵεσο, ἵου	οὗ		κεῖσο
3	ἱέσθω	ἔσθω		κείσθω
P. 2	ἵεσθε	ἔσθε		κεῖσθε
3	ἱέσθωσαν, ἱέσθων	ἔσθωσαν, ἔσθων		κείσθωσαν, κείσθων
Inf.	ἵεσθαι	ἔσθαι	ἔσεσθαι	κεῖσθαι
Par.	ἱέμενος	ἔμενος	ἐσόμενος	κείμενος

	Imperfect.			Imperfect.
Ind.	ἱέμην	Fut. M. ἥσομαι	p. To εἶμι *to go*, some as-	ἐκείμην
2	ἵεσο, ἵου	1 A. M. ἡκάμην	sign a Middle, ἵεμαι *to*	ἔκεισο
3	ἵετο	Perf. εἷμαι	*hasten*, Imperf. ἱέμην.	ἔκειτο
P. 1	ἱέμεθα	Plup. εἵμην	Others write these tenses	ἐκείμεθα
2	ἵεσθε	Aor. P. εἵθην	with a rough breathing,	ἔκεισθε
3	ἵεντο	Fut. P. ἑθήσομαι	ἵεμαι, ἱέμην, and refer	ἔκειντο
D. 2	ἵεσθον	Verb- ἑτός	them to ἵημι *to send*.	Future.
3	ἱέσθην	als ἑτέος		κείσομαι

---

§ 45. r. Stems ἑ- ἱε- 357. 3, ἐσ- ἑ- 345, ι-, φα-, 314 a, κεε-, contr. κει-, 342. 1: ἵημι, cf. τίθημι· (ἱεασι) ἱεῖσι, Att. ἱᾶσι, 122, 120 f; ἵοιμι 315 c; ἱειν 315 b; A. εἷμεν, εἵμην, εἵθην, 279 c; εἰμί, εἶμι, 50; ἐστί 298 a; ἰοίην 293 c; ἴθι, εἰ, 297 d, ἰόντων 313 c, ἔστων, ἴτων, 300 e; ἦσθα, ᾔεισθα, 297 b; ἦν, ᾔει‘, 163 b; (ᾔει)ᾖμεν 118 d, 121 d; ἔσεται Ep., A. 211, ἔσται nude (the only Att. form) 303 a; dialectic forms 50; φημί, cf. ἵστημι· ἡμί, φῄς, 50; φαθί, ἐφησθα, 297 b, d; (κέεμαι) κεῖμαι, cf. τίθεμαι· κέωμαι, κεοίμην, 315 c, 772 g. Hdt. has the uncontracted κέεται, ἐκέετο, κέεσθαι, &c.

t. Forms marked with the sign ¦ may be enclitic.

PURE VERBS. — -MI FORM. § 45.

VERBS IN -μι: u. φημί fāri, *to say* (s. φᾰ-).

	Pres. Ind.	Subj.	Opt.	Imv.	Inf.	Impf.
S. 1	φημί | ἠμί	φῶ	φαίην		φάναι	ἔφην, ἦν
2	φῄς, φής	φῇς	φαίης	φάθί | or φάθι		ἔφης, ἔφησθα
3	φησί |'	φῇ	φαίη,	φάτω	Part.	ἔφη, ἦ
P. 1	φᾰμέν |	φῶμεν	&c.		r. in Att.	ἔφᾰμεν
2	φατέ |	φῆτε		φάτε	φάς	ἔφατε
3	φᾱσί |'	φῶσι'		φάτωσαν, φάντων		ἔφασαν

Fut. φήσω, Aor. ἔφησα. MID. and PASS., little used in Att.: Pres. Inf. φάσθαι, Pt. φάμενος· Impf. ἐφάμην· Perf. Imv. πεφάσθω· Aor. P. ἐφάθην· Verb. φᾰτός, φατέος. — See 45 r, t, 50.

46. E. PRETERITIVES.

a. οἶδα novi, *I know* (s. 'ἰδ-, εἰδ-, εἰδε-).

	2 Perf. Ind.	Subj.	Opt.	Imv.		2 Plup.
S. 1	οἶδα	εἰδῶ	εἰδείην			ᾔδειν, ᾔδη
2	οἶδας, οἶσθα	εἰδῇς	εἰδείης	ἴσθι		ᾔδεις, ᾔδης, ᾔδεισθα, ᾔδησθα
3	οἶδε'	εἰδῇ	εἰδείη,	ἴστω		ᾔδει', ᾔδη
P. 1	οἴδᾰμεν, ἴσμεν	εἰδῶμεν	&c.			ᾔδειμεν, ᾖσμεν
2	οἴδατε, ἴστε	εἰδῆτε		ἴστε		ᾔδειτε, ᾖστε
3	οἴδᾱσι', ἴσᾱσι'	εἰδῶσι'		ἴστωσαν		ᾔδεσαν, ᾖσαν

Inf. εἰδέναι \| Part. εἰδώς \| Fut. εἴσομαι· less Att. Fut. εἰδήσω and Aor. εἴδησα· Verb. ἰστέος. — See ὁράω 50.

b. δέδοικα or δέδια timeo, *I am afraid* (s. δῐ-, δει-).

	2 Perf. Ind.	Subj.	Opt.	Imv.	Inf.	2 Plup.
S. 1	δέδῐα	δεδίω	δεδιείην		δεδιέναι |	ἐδεδίειν
2	δέδιας	δεδίῃς	δεδιείης	δέδιθι	Part.	ἐδεδίεις
3	δέδιε'	δεδίῃ,	δεδιείη,	δεδίτω	δεδιώς |	ἐδεδίει
P. 1	δέδιμεν	&c.	&c.			ἐδέδιμεν
2	δέδιτε			δέδιτε		ἐδέδιτε
3	δεδίᾱσι'			δεδίτωσαν		ἐδέδισαν

1 Perf. δέδοικα, 1 Plup. ἐδεδοίκειν, Fut. δείσομαι Ep. chiefly, δείσω late, Aor. ἔδεισα. — See δείδω 50.

---

§ 46. c. PRETERITIVES 268, 317 s: οἶδα, δέδοικα, ἕστηκα, 320 b; (οἰδ-σθα nude, 151) οἶσθα, ᾔδεισθα, 297 b; (ἴδμεν Θ. 32, § 148) ἴσμεν, (ᾔδ-μεν) ᾖσμεν, δέδιμεν, ἔσταμεν, 320 a; δεδίασι 156 a; εἰδῶ, ἑστώ, εἰδείην (so δεδιείην)? as fr. base δεδιε-, Pl. Phædr. 351 a), ἑσταίην, (ἰδ-θι) ἴσθι, ἑστάναι, 320 c; ἑστώς 320 d; ᾔδειν, ᾔδη, 278 d, 291 c; ἑστήκειν 280 a, Att. also εἱστήκειν 279 c; ἦμαι κάθημαι (κατά, ἧμαι) 280 a, 161 b (having forms from both ἑ- and ἕδ-, or see 307 c); cf. Lat. sĕde-o, and see 141; (ἡδ-ται) ἧσται, ἧστο, 147; καθῶμαι, καθοίμην, 317 c; ἥμενος 780 c; ἐκάθησο, καθῆσο, 282 b, 783 a, 771 c. — O. F. τέθνηκα *am dead*, β' βηκα *stand*, μέμονα *am eager*, ἄνωγα *command*, 320 e, f.

§ 47.   PRETERITIVES. FORMS OF THE STEM.   63

c. ἧμαι and κάθημαι sedeo, *I sit* (s. ἑ-, ἑδ-).

PERFECT MIDDLE.

	Indicative.	Subj.	Opt.		Imperative.
S. 1	ἧμαι	κάθημαι	καθῶμαι	καθοίμην		
2	ἧσαι	κάθησαι	καθῇ	καθοῖο	ἧσο	κάθησο
3	ἧσται	κάθηται	καθῆται	καθοῖτο	ἧσθω	καθήσθω,
P. 1	ἥμεθα	καθήμεθα	καθώμεθα	καθοίμεθα		&c.
2	ἧσθε	κάθησθε	καθῆσθε	καθοῖσθε	ἧσθε	
3	ἧνται	κάθηνται	καθῶνται	καθοῖντο	ἧσθωσαν, ἧσθων	

Infin. ἧσθαι καθῆσθαι   Part. ἥμενος καθήμενος

PLUPERFECT MIDDLE.

S. 1	ἥμην	ἐκαθήμην, καθήμην	P. 1	ἥμεθα	ἐκαθήμεθα, καθήμεθα
2	ἧσο	ἐκάθησο, καθῆσο	2	ἧσθε	ἐκάθησθε, καθῆσθε
3	ἧστο	ἐκάθητο, καθῆστο,	3	ἧντο	ἐκάθηντο, καθῆντο
		καθῆτο			

Fut. Pf. καθήσομαι late. — See ἵζω 50.

d. ἕστηκα sto, *I stand* (45 f).

FIRST AND SECOND PERFECT.

	Indicative.		Subjunctive.	Opt.	Imv.	Infin.
S. 1	ἕστηκα	*	ἑστήκω ἑστῶ	ἑσταίην		ἑστηκέναι! l.
2	ἕστηκας	*	ἑστήκῃς *	ἑσταίης	ἕστᾰθι	ἑστάναι!
3	ἕστηκε‘,	*	ἑστήκῃ, *	ἑσταίη,	ἑστάτω	Part.
P. 1	&c.	ἕστᾰμεν	&c. ἑστῶμεν	&c.		ἑστηκώς!
2		ἕστατε	*		ἕστατε·	ἑστώς! 26 i
3		ἑστᾶσι‘	ἑστῶσι‘		ἑστάτωσαν, ἑστάντων

1 PLUPERFECT.			2 PLUPERFECT.	
S. 1	ἑστήκειν, εἱστήκειν	P. ἑστήκειμεν	S. *	P. ἕστᾰμεν
2	ἑστήκεις, εἱστήκεις	ἑστήκειτε	*	ἕστατε
3	ἑστήκει, εἱστήκει	ἑστήκεσαν, &c.	*	ἕστασαν

47. IX. RELATION OF THE TENSES AND FORMS OF THE STEM.

1. DOMAIN OF THE OLD STEM :	λᾰθ-	ζῠγ-	δᾰκ-
Second Aorist System :	ἔλᾰθον		ἔδᾰκον
Second Compound System :		ἐζύγην	ἐδάκην
2. DOMAIN OF THE MIDDLE STEM :	ληθ-	ζευγ-	δηκ-
Perfect Passive System :	λέλησμαι	ἔζευγμαι	δέδηγμαι
First Compound System :	ἐλήσθην	ἐζεύχθην	ἐδήχθην
Second Perfect System :	λέληθα		
First Perfect System :		ἔζευχα	δέδηχα
First Aorist System :	ἔλησα	ἔζευξα	ἔδηξα
Future System :	λήσω	ζεύξω	δήξομαι
3. DOMAIN OF THE NEW STEM : -	λανθᾰν-	ζευγνῠ-	δακν-
Present System :	λανθάνω	ζεύγνῡμι	δάκνω

48. x. Dialectic Forms. a. General Table (321 s).

Subjective.

Singular.

1 *Ind. Pr.* ω, Old μ· ὁρημι, φίλημι, κάλημι.
   ἑων, ῶ, Ion. ἑω · ὁρέω, φοιτέω, χρέω.
       Ep. ὁω, ὁω · ὁρόω, μενοινόω.
   ἑω, ῶ, Ep. εἰω · νεικείω, πνείω, τελείω.
Fut. ω, Dor. ῶ · ἑσῶ, οἰσῶ, πεμψῶ.
   σω, Dor. ξῶ · δικαξῶ, κομιξῶ.
   ῶ, Ion. ἑω · ἀγγελέω, φανέω, ἐρέω.
Impf. v, Iter. σκον · ἔχεσκον, φέρεσκον.
Aor. σα, Dor. ξα · ἐκόμιξα, ἐφθαξα. [σκον.
   αον, ων, Ion. εον, Dor. ευν & Dor. ευν · ἠγά-
   Iter. σασκον · στρέψασκον, ὤσα-
Plup. εν, Ion. εα · ᾔδεα, ἐτεθήπεα.
Sub. ω, Ep. ωμι · ἐθέλωμι, ἴδωμι, ἴκωμι.
       Old Att. η · ᾔδη, ἐπεπόνθη.
   ῶ, Ion. ἑω · λυθέω, φανέω, θέω.
       Ep. ἑίω, ἑω, &c. ; θείω, γνώω.

2 s, Old σθα · εἴπησθα, βάλοισθα, ἔχεισθα.
   ας, Dor. ες · ἀμέλγες, λέγες, συρίσδες.
   ἑας, ᾷς, Dor. ῇς · ὁρῇς, ἐρῇς, τολμῇς, λῇς.
   ἑης, ᾷς · ὁρᾷς, ἀντιᾷς, ἑάρς.

3 σι, Dor. τι · τίθητι, δίδωτι, φατί.
Sub. ῃ, Ep. ῃσι · ἄγῃσι, παύσῃσι, θέῃσι.

Plural.

1 μεν, Dor. μες · εὕρομες, δεδόλκαμες, ἥμες.
Sub. ωμεν, Ep. ομεν · ἀγείρομεν, ἴομεν.
2 *Sub.* ῆτε, Ep. ετε · εἴδετε, νεμεσήσετε.

---

3 νσι, Dor. ντι · φαντί, ἔχοντι, μένοντι.
   ουσι, Æol. οισι · κρύπτοισι, οἰκήσοισι.
   ἀουσι, ῶσι, Ep. ἑωσι, ῶωσι · βοόωσι, δρώ-
   Dor. ἁντι · πευθάντι, νικᾶντι. [ωσι.
   ἑουσι, οῦσι, Ion. εῦσι · ποιεῦσι, ἀμυνεῦσι.
   Dor. εὗντι · φιλεῦντι, μενεῦντι.
   ᾶσι, Ion. ἑᾶσι · ἱστέᾶσι, ἑστέᾶσι.
   ᾶσι, Æol. αισι · φαῖσι, κεκρίκαισιν.
   ᾶσι, Alex. ὦ · ἔγνωκαν, εἴρηκαν, ἔοργαν.
   σαν, Old ν · ἔσταν, ἴεν· ἔγνον, ἤγερθεν.
   αν, Alex. σαν · εἴποσαν, ὀλέσαυσαν.
Inf. ναι, Æol. ν · μεθύσθην, τάφην, ἀπλην.
       Dor. & Ep. μεν · κραθῆμεν, φάμεν·
       Ep. & Æol. μεναι · μιχθήμεναι, θέ-
   εν, Dor. εν · βόσκεν, γαρύεν.   [μεναι.
   Dor. & Æol. ην · εὑρῆν, ῥιγῶν, φέρην.
   Poet. ἔμεν, ἔμεναι · ἀξέμεν, ἀξέμε-
   εἷν, Ion. ἑέν · ἰδέειν, ταθέειν.   [ναι.
   ἑαν, ᾶν, Ep. ἑαν · ὁρᾶν, ἀντιᾶν.
   Dor. ἡν · ὁρῆν, στύη.   [μεναι.
   ἑεν, ἔεν, Ep. ἤμεναι, τευνήμεναι, καλή-
   δεν, Dor. εν · ὕπνῶν, ῥιγῶν.   [θνῄσκειν.
   ἕναι, Dor. & Æol. εν, ην · δεδύκειν, τε-
   Pt.   ων, Ion. ἑων · ἀγγελέων, φανέων, ἐρέων·
   ἑων, ὦν, Ep. ὁων, ὁων · ὁρόων, μαιμώων·
   ᾶς, ὦσα, Æol. αις, αισα · ῥίψαις, γελαισα.
   ουσα, Æol. οισα, Lac. ενα · ἔχοισα, λιπῶσα.
   ἁουσα, ὦσα, Ep. ὁωσα, ὁωσα, ὁωσα
   δρόωσα, ἠβώωσα, ναιετάωσα. [τος.
   G. ἑντος, Ep. ὦτος · βεβαῶτος, κεκμηώ-

Objective.

Singular.

1 ἑομαι, οῦμαι, Ion. & Dor. εῦμαι · φοβεῦμαι.
   σομαι, Dor. σοῦμαι, σεῦμαι · ἐξοῦμαι.
   οῦμαι, Ion. ἑομαι · φανέομαι, ὀλέομαι.
   μην, Dor. μᾶν · δυναμᾶν, ἱκόμαν, γενοίμαν.
       Iter. σκόμην · τελεσκόμην, μνασασκό-
2 ῃ, Ion. εαι, *Subj.* ηαι · λύεαι, πίθηαι. [μην.
   Hel. εσαι · πίεσαι, φάγεσαι, καυχᾶσαι.
   ου, Ion. εο · ἐγένεο, ἔπλεο, φράξεο.
   Ion. & Dor. ευ · ἔπλευ, φράξευ.
   Ep. εο · ἔρεο, στεῖο.
   ω, Ion. αο · ἐγράψαο, ἐδείξαο, ἐπίστάο.
   Dor. ᾶ · ἐγράψά, ἐπάξά, ἦρά.
   σαι, στο, Ep. α, ο · μέμνηαι, βεβλήηαι, ἔσσυα.
   ἕαι, ἕεο, Ion. εαι, εο · μυθέαι, φοβέαι, φοβέο.
   ηαι, 3 ηται, Ep. εαι, εται · μίσγεαι, φθίεται.

Plural.

1 μεθα, Poet. μεσθα · ἀγώμεσθα, ἐσόμεσθα.
3 νται, ντο, Ion. αται, ατο · κέαται, ἔατο.
   ανται, αντο, Ion. ἕαται, ἕατο · δυνέαται.
   αντο, Ion. ἑατο · ἐβουλέατο, ἱκέατο. [ωνται.
   ἑονται, οῦνται, Ep. ώονται, ῴονται · ἀιτιό-
   ἕοντο, ῶντο, Ep. ὁωντο, ῴοντο · ἐμνώοντο.
   Du. 3 σθην, Dor. σθαν · κτησάσθαν, ἱκέσθαν.
   Inf. ἕεσθαι, ᾶσθαι, Ion. ἕεσθαι · χρέεσθαι.
       Ep. ἁασθαι · ὁράασθαι.
       Dor. ἦσθαι · πειρῆσθαι.
   εῖσθαι, Ion. ἑεσθαι · φανέεσθαι, ὀλέεσθαι.

§ 47. DIALECTIC FORMS. 65

b. Referred to λύω as a Model.

ACTIVE.
Pres. Ind.
S. 2 λύες, λύης D. 326 a
λύεισθα O. 297 b
3 λύησι ? E. 328 b
λύη D. 130 c
P. 1 λύομες D. 328 a
3 λύοντι D. 328 a
λύοισι Æ. 328 c
Pres. Sub.
S. 1 λύωμι E. 328 b
2 λύησθα E. 297 b
3 λύησι E., -τι D. 328 b
P. 1 λύομεν E. 326 d
λύωμες D. 328 a
2 λύετε E. 326 d
3 λύωντι D. 328 a
Pres. Opt.
S. 2 λύοισθα E. 297 b
P. 3 λύοισαν AL. 330 a
Pres. Inf.
λῦέν, λύην D. 326 a
λυέμεν E. D. 333 d
λυέμεναι E. 333 d
Pres. Part.
F. λύοισα Æ. 131 d
λύωα LAC. 334
Imperfect.
S. 1 λῦον O. 284 a
λύεσκον IT. 332
P. 3 ἐλύοσαν AL. 330 a
D. 2 ἐλυέτην A. 299 d
3 [ἐ]λύετον E. 299 d
ἐλυέτᾱν D. 328 a
Fut. Ind.
λυσῶ,-εῖς,-εῖ,&c. D.325 b
1 Aor. Ind.
S. 1 λῦσα O. 284 a
λύσασκον IT. 332

[ἐ]λῦσον E. 327 a
1 Aor. Part.
λύσαις,-αισα Æ. 131 d
Perf. Ind.
S. 1 λελύκω,-ης D. 326 b
P. 3 λελύκαντι D. 328 a
λελύκᾱσι P. 328 c
λέλυκαν AL. 330 a
Perf. Inf.
λελύκειν, -ην D. Æ. 326 b
Perf. Part.
λελύκων D. Æ. 326 b
Plup. Ind.
S. 1 λελύκεα I.,-η O.291 c
ἐλέλυκον E. 326 b
2 λελύκεας I., -ης O.
291 c   [163 b
3 λελύκεε(ν I., -ει(ν P.
2 Aor. Ind.
(λέλιπον, -ες, -ε E. 284 e
P. 3 ἔλιπαν AL. 327 b
2 Aor. Inf.
λιπέειν I. 323 d
λιπῆν D. 326 a)

PASSIVE AND MIDDLE.
Pres. Ind.
S. 2 λύεαι I. 323 a
λύεσαι HEL. 331 c
P. 1 λυόμεσθα P. 299 a
Pres. Sub.
S. 2 λύηαι I. 331 a
λύεαι E. 326 d
3 λύεται E. 326 d
P. 1 λυόμεσθα E. 299 a
Pres. Opt.
P. 3 λυοίατο I. 329 a
Pres. Imv.
S. 2 λύεο I., λύευ I.D. 323

Imperfect.
S. 1 λυόμην O. 284 a
ἐλυόμᾱν D. 328 a
λυεσκόμην IT. 332
2 [ἐ]λύεο I.,-ευ I.D.323
D. 3 [ἐ]λύεσθον E. 299 d
ἐλυέσθᾱν D. 328 a
Fut. M. Ind.
λυσεῦμαι,-ῆ,&c., D. 325 b
S. 2 λύσεαι I. 323 a
Aor. M. Ind.
S. 1 λυσάμην O. 284 a
ἐλυσάμᾱν D. 328 a
λυσασκόμην IT. 332
2 [ἐ]λύσαο I. 322 b
ἐλύσᾱ D. 322 e
Aor. M. Opt.
P. 3 λυσαίατο I. 329 a
Perf. Ind.
S. 2 λέλυαι E. 331 b
P. 3 λελύαται I. 329 a
Perf. Opt.
P. 3 λελῦντο E. 317 c
Pluperfect.
P. 3 [ἐ]λελύατο I. 329 a
Aor. P. Ind.
P. 3 ἔλυθεν P. 330 b
Aor. P. Sub.
S. 1 λυθέω I., -είω E.
323 a, c   [323 c
2 λυθείης or -ήης E.
3 λυθείη or -ήη E.323 c
P. 1 λυθέωμεν I. 323 a
2 λυθείετε E. 323 c
3 λυθέωσι I. 323 a
Aor. P. Inf.
λύθην I., -ήμεν D. 333 b
λυθήμεναι E. 333 b
2 Aor. M.
[ἐ]λύμην, -σο E. 313 b
</p>

c. Various Forms of Contract Verbs (321 s).

Uncontracted.	Contracted.	Variously Protracted.
ὁράω, ὁρέω I.	ὁρῶ	ὁρόω, μενοινώω, Pt. ὁρόων A. 350
ὁράει, ὁράῃ	ὁρᾷ	ὁρᾴᾳ, μενοινᾴᾳ, Inf. ἀντιᾶαν N. 215
ὁράοιμι	ὁρῷμι	ὁρόῳμι, ἠβώοιμι, Mid. 2 αἰτιόφῳ v. 135
ὁράουσα	ὁρῶσα	ὁρόωσα, ναιετάωσα, μαιμώωσα O. 542
ὁράοντες,-έοντες I.	ὁρῶντες	ὁρόωντες, ὁρέωντες I., ἠβώοντες κ. 6
ὁρδεσθαι	ὁρᾶσθαι	ὁρᾶσθαι σ. 4, μνᾶσθαι a. 39
νεικέω	νεικῶ	νεικείω, Inf. πλείειν o. 34, Pt. νεικείων σ. 9
νεικέῃ	νεικῇ	νεικείῃ ρ. 189, νεικείῃσι A. 579, θείῃ Z. 507
ἱδρόοντα	ἱδροῦντα	ἱδρώοντα, ὑπνώοντας, Fem. ἱδρώουσα
ἀρόουσι	ἀροῦσι	ἀρόωσι, Opt. δηϊόωεν, Mid. δηϊόωντο

49. XI. CLASSES AND NOTATION OF STEMS.

I. PRIME STEMS (a; 340).

Roots, (a^1) giving rise, and (a^2) not giving rise to Modified Stems. | Derived Stems, (a^3) giving rise, and (a^4) not giving rise to Mod. St.

II. MODIFIED STEMS. 1. EUPHONIC (341 s).

b. By Precession: b^1. Of ă to ε.
$\quad\quad\quad\quad\quad\quad$ b^2. Of ε or ο to ι.
$\quad\quad\quad\quad\quad\quad$ b^3. Of ā to ω, &c.
c^1. By Contraction.
c^2. By Syncope in the Theme.
c^3. " " in the 2 Aorist.
c^4. " " in Other Tenses.
c^5. By Metathesis in the Theme.
c^6. " " in the 2 Aorist.

c^7. By Metathesis in Other Tenses.
c^8. By Antithesis.
d^1. To avoid Double Aspiration.
d^2. From Use of both Sm. & R. Forms.
e^1. By dropping a Consonant.
e^2. By adding a Consonant.
f^1 By dropping the Digamma.
f^2. By changing the Digamma.
f^3. By changing or dropping σ.

II. MODIFIED STEMS. 2. EMPHATIC (346 s).

A. BY LENGTHENING A SHORT VOWEL.
g. To the cognate Long Vowel.
h. To a Diphthong.

B. BY ADDING SYLLABLES OR LETTERS.
I. BY ANNEXING OR INSERTING CONSONANTS.

i, j, l. The Conson. I; uniting with,
$\quad$ i^1. A Palatal Mute $\Big\}$ to form σσ,
$\quad$ i^2. A Lingual Mute $\Big\}$ or ττ.
$\quad$ i^3. A Labial Mute
$\quad$ j^1. A Lingual Mute $\Big\}$
$\quad$ j^2. A Palatal Mute $\Big\}$ to form ζ.
$\quad$ j^3. A Double Palatal $\Big\}$
$\quad$ j^4. A Labial Mute
$\quad$ l. λ to form λλ.
z. ζ : z^1. Alone.
$\quad$ z^2. With a Vowel.
k. σκ : k^1. Alone.
$\quad$ k^2. With a Vowel.
$\quad$ k^3. With preceding Consonant dropped.
$\quad$ k^4. With Transposition.
$\quad$ k^5. With the κ dropped.
$\quad$ k^6. With preceding Vowel lengthened.
$\quad$ k^7. With Precess. of a Vowel.
n. ν : n^1. ν annexed.

n^2. With preceding V. lengthened.
n^3. ν inserted.
n^4. ἄν annexed.
n^5. With ῠ inserted.
n^6. With ᾰν lengthened.
n^7. νυ annexed.
n^8. Becoming ννυ after a short V.
n^9. A Lingual or Liquid dropped.
n^{10}. νε annexed.
t. τ : t^1. Alone.
$\quad$ t^2. With a Vowel.
q. θ : q^1. Alone.
$\quad$ q^2. With a Vowel.
$\quad$ q^3. With preceding Vowel lengthened.
o. Other Consonants : o^1. Alone.
$\quad$ o^2. With a Vowel.

II. BY ANNEXING VOWELS.

u. By annexing α.
$\quad$ u^2. With change of an ε to ω.
v. By annexing ε.
$\quad$ v^2. With change of an ε to ο.
w. By annexing other Vowels.

III. BY PREFIXING SYLLABLES OR LETTERS.

p. Various Preformatives.
r. Reduplication : r^1. Proper.
$\quad\quad\quad\quad\quad\quad\quad\quad$ r^2. Attic.
$\quad\quad\quad\quad\quad\quad\quad\quad$ r^3. Improper.

IV. ADOPTED STEMS (x; 358).

§ 50. ALPHABETIC LIST. 67

§ 50. XII. Catalogue of Verbs.

Notes. a. The following Catalogue contains the principal Irregular Verbs, and some verbs which are not usually so termed; while many cognates are added (338 d). Whatever is enclosed in brackets will be understood to be dialectic; and to occur in the Epic (commonly in Homer), unless specially ascribed to another dialect or another author. The dialects are commonly denoted by initials, as in § 27; and the sign + marks the rare occurrence of a word beyond the range noted (85 c, d). Some of the less familiar forms are referred to passages where they occur.

b. The regular tense-systems in use, represented by their leading forms, are arranged in the same order as in § 37; while the Future and Perfect usually cited in parsing are printed in full-face type, and the second tenses are introduced by name. The abbreviations chiefly used in naming the tenses are "pr., ipf., f., ao. (1 a., 2 a.), pf., plp., and 3 f." The voices and modes are denoted by italics: as, *A., a., M., m., P., p.; ind., sub., opt., imv., inf., pt.* The persons and numbers are marked thus: 1 s., 1 p., 1 d., 2 s., &c. The abbreviation m. (*M.*), p. (*P.*), ao., or f., annexed to a form, shows that the corresponding *middle, passive, aorist,* or *future* is also formed after the same analogy; and the voices belonging to the aorist system are then indicated, if they are not the same with those of the future system.

c. Stems are marked by hyphens affixed; and the small letters placed immediately after these, or after the themes, denote varieties of stems according to the notation in § 49 and 340 - 358. A small ^c prefixed to a word marks it as having been found only in composition: as, ^cἥνεκα, found in ἐπ-ἤνεκα. The abbreviations l., r., po., cp., ct., and *v. l.*, stand for *late, rare, poetic, compounded, contracted,* and *various reading.* Less important forms or marks are sometimes omitted. See § 51.

A.

[ἀᾰ- *hurt, mislead;* m. 3 s. ἆται T. 91; ao. ἄασα, ct. ἆσα, m.; ἀάσθην. Aug. *ᾱ*- 279 f.]

[ἀβροτάξομεν, see ἁμαρτάνω.]

ἀγάλλω (l, ἀγαλ-) *adorn, M. glory;* ἀγαλῶ, ἤγηλα· ἠγάλθην l.

ἄγαμαι *admire;* [ἀγάσομαι, δ.181,] ao.; usu., us *mid.,* ἠγάσθην, f. l. Cog. ἀγάζω po., [ἀγάομαι, ἀγαίομαι,] *admire, envy, &c.*

ἀγγέλλω (l, ἀγγελ-), *announce;* see 40.

ἀγείρω (h, ἀγερ-) *collect;* [ἀγεροῦμαι Or. Sib.,] ἤγειρα [m., 2 a. ἀγερόμην, *pt.* sync. ἀγρόμενος]; ἀγήγερκα l., -μαι l. [plp. 3 p. ἀγηγέρατο Δ. 211, ἠγέρθην, A. 57. Cog. ἀγέρομαι, ἠγερέθομαι, *v. l.* ἠγερέομαι.]

ἄγνῡμι (n⁷, Fαγ-, ἀγ- f) *break,* usu. cp. w. κατά· ^cἄξω, ἔαξα 279 b [ἦξα, Ψ. 392]; 2 pf. ^cἔᾱγα [ἔηγα I.] *am broken,* ^cἔαγμαι l., 2 a. ἐάγην [Ep. ἄ, or ᾱ?]. It has some forms as if from ἐαγ-:

ao. *pt.* ^cἐάξας Lys. 100.5, f. ^cἐάξει Mat. 12.20. [Ao. *opt.* (κατFαξαις, καFFαξαις, 136, 142) κανάξαις Hes. Op. 664.]

ἄγω *ago, lead, bring;* ἄξω, m. (sometimes as *pass.*), ἦξα r., 2 a. ἤγαγον m. 284 g; ἦχα, later ἀγήοχα 312 d, ἦγμαι, ἤχθην f. Cog. ἠγέομαι, [ἀγῑνέω.]

[ἄδε- *be sated;* see ἄω.]

ᾄδω *sing;* ᾄσομαι, -σω r., ᾖσα· ᾖσμαι, ᾖσθην: ct. fr. po. & I. ἀείδω, ἀείσω m., ἤεισα.

ἀείρω & ἀερτάζω *raise;* see αἴρω.

ἀέξω *increase;* see αὔξω.

[ἄημι & ἄω (ἀ-, ἀε- v) *breathe, blow,* P. ἄημαι (314 b; and η in some other forms for the regular ε); ao. ἄεσα, ct. ἆσα, *breathed in sleep, slept.* Cog. ἀίω, ἀϊσθω.]

αἰδέομαι v, po. αἴδομαι, *respect;* αἰδέσομαι ao.; ᾔδεσμαι, ᾐδέσθην f. [Pr. *imv.* αἰδεῖο 323 e.]

αἰνέω *praise,* usu. cp. w. ἐπί, &c.; αἰνέσω ^cm [-ήσω], ao.; ^cἤνεκα, ^cἤνημαι 310 d, ἠνέθην ^cf. [Cog. αἴνημι, αἰνίζω, -ομαι.]

68 αἴνυμαι TABLES. ἀμπνυ- § 50.

[αἴνυμαι take, see αἴρω.]
αἱρέω take, M. choose; αἱρήσω m., ao. a. l., m. r.; ᾕρηκα, -μαι [ᾁραίρηκα, -μαι, I.], 3 f. ᾑρήσομαι r., ᾑρέθην f. 310 d.: (Faλ- x, ἁλ- f, ἑλ- b, ἁλο- w, ἁλισκ- k[7]) 2 a. εἷλον m. 279 c, e, late f. & ao. ἑλῶ m., εἷλα m.: as pass., ἁλίσκομαι be taken, captured; ἁλώσομαι, 2 a. ἑάλων & ἥλων ('ἁλῶ, -οίην, -ῶναι, -ούς); ἑάλωκα & ἥλωκα.
αἴρω (h, ἀερ-, sync. ἀρ-) raise, M. win; 'ἀρῶ m., ἦρα m. (ᾄρω, ᾁραιμι, ᾆρον, &c.), 2 a. ἠρόμην ('ἀρωμαι, &c.) po.; ἦρκα, -μαι, -θην f. Po. & I. ἀείρω m. [ἀέρρω Æ. 171 a]; 'ἀρῶ (ct. fr. ἀερῶ) m., ἤειρα m.; ᾔερμαι [plp. ἀωρτο 312 d], ἠέρθην. Cog. -ἄρνυμαι, [αἴνυμαι n[b], ἠερέθομαι, ἀερτάζω.]
αἰσθάνομαι (n[4], αἰσθ-), αἴσθομαι r., perceive; αἰσθήσομαι 311 a, 2 a. ᾐσθόμην· ᾔσθημαι, ᾐσθήθην & -άνθην f. l.
[αἴσθω & αἴω breathe; see ἄημι.]
ἀΐσσω i[1], ᾄσσω c[1], rush, po. +, M.; ἀΐξω, ᾄξω, ao. a. [m. r.; ἤϊχθην.]
ἀΐω audio, hear, po. or l.; ipf. ἄϊον 279 f, ἤϊον l., [ἐπ-ήϊσα I.]
[ἀκ- or ἀχ- acuo, sharpen, pf. pt. ἀκαχμένος sharpened, 148 b, Ξ. 12.]
[ἀκαχίζω (z, ἀχ-, ἀκαχ- r[2]) afflict, M. sorrow; ἀκαχήσω 311 c, ao. r., usu. 2 a. ἤκαχον m. 284 f.; ἀκάχημαι pret. (3 p. ἀκηχέδαται, plp. ἀκαχήατο or -εἰατο M. 179, § 329 a, pt. ἀκαχήμενος Ω. 550, or ἀκηχέμενος, E. 364). Cog. ἄχομαι, ἄχνυμαι, be grieved; Pt. ἀχέων, ἀχεύων, sorrowing.]
ἀκούω (h, ἀκο-) hear; ἀκούσομαι, -σω l., ἤκουσα· ἄκουκα D.,] 2 pf. ἀκήκοα, 2 plp. ἠκηκόειν 281 d, ἤκουσμαι l., -σθην f. Cog. ἀκροάομαι, [ἀκουάζω.]
[ἀλάλκω ward off; see ἀλέξω.]
ἀλάομαι wander, po. + [ἀλόω 322 c]; [[c]ἀλήσομαι or -ησάμην, Hes. Sc. 409]; ἀλάλημαι + pret. 284 a,] ἠλήθην. Po. cog. ἀλητεύω, ἀλαίνω, [ἠλαίνω, ἠλάσκω, ἠλασκάζω.]
ἀλδαίνω (n[6], ἀλδ-) alo, nourish, po.; l. ἤλδηνα or -ησα, [2 a. ἤλδανον. Cog. ἀλδήσκω alesco, grow.]
ἀλείφω (h, ἀλιφ-) anoint, M.; ἀλείψω m., ao.; [c]ἀλήλιφα or -ειφα, ἀλήλιμμαι or -ειμμαι Th. 4. 68, ἠλείφθην f., 2 a. ἠλίφην r.
ἀλέξω r. (k[5], ἀλεκ-, ἀλκ-c[5]), & ἀλέκω l, ward off, M. defend one's self, requite;

[ἀλεξήσω, [c]ἀλέξω r.,] m., ao., [2 a. ἄλαλκον 284 c,] 2 a. inf. ἀλκαθεῖν po. r. 353 a. [Cog. l. ἀλάλκω, -κήσω.]
ἀλεύω (f[2], ἀλεF-, ἀλε- f[1]) avert, po. [M. ἀλεύομαι & ἀλέομαι shun]; ἀλεύσω, ao. a., m. r. [ἠλεύαμην & -εάμην 306 a]. Pr. imv. ἄλευ, by apocope for ἄλευε, Æsch. Pr. 568 v. l. Po. cog. ἀλύσκω (k[8], ἀλυκ-), f. ἀλύξω m., ao.; ἀλυσκάζω, [ἀλυσκάνω, ἀλεείνω.]
ἀλέω grind; ἀλ(έσω)ῶ r. 305 b, ἤλεσα· ἀλήλεκα po. r., -εσμαι or -εμαι, ἠλέσθην l. Cog. ἀλήθω r., [ἀλητρεύω.]
[ἄλθομαι become healed, E. & I.; [c]ἀλθήσομαι, ao. l.; [c]ἠλθέσθην. Cog. ἀλθαίνω & -ίσκω or -ήσκω, cure; f. ἀλθήσω l.]
ἀλίνδω roll; see κυλίνδω.
ἁλίσκομαι be captured; see αἱρέω.
[ἀλιταίνω & -τραίνω (n[6], o, ἀλιτ-) sin, E. +, M.; ἀλίτησα r., 2 a. ἤλιτον m.; pf. pt. ἀλιτήμενος guilty.]
ἀλλάσσω or -ττω (i[1], ἀλλαγ-) change, M. barter; ἀλλάξω m., ao.; [c]ἤλλαχα, -αγμαι, -άχθην [c]f., usu. in Att. prose 2 a. ἠλλάγην f.
ἅλλομαι (l, ἁλ-) salio 141, leap; ἁλοῦμαι, ἡλάμην, comm. (exc. in Ind.) 2 a. ἡλόμην [2 s. ἅλσο, 3 s. ἅλτο, pt. ἅλμενος, 326 c, 167 c].
ἀλύσκω,-κάζω, & -κάνω, see ἀλεύω.
ἀλύω (ŭ) be excited, po. +. [Cog. ἀλύσσω, f. -ξω, ἀλυσθαίνω, ἀλυκτέω (ἀλαλύκτημαι pret., 284 a), ἀλυκτάζω, Hdt. 9. 70.]
ἀλφάνω (n[4], ἀλφ-) find, po.; [2 a. ἤλφον, opt. 3 p. ἀλφοιν for -οιεν, 135, v. 383 v. l.]
ἁμαρτάνω (n[4], ἁμαρτ-) err, miss; ἁμαρτήσομαι, -σω l. +, ao. a. l. +, 2 a. ἥμαρτον· ἡμάρτηκα, -μαι, -θην [2 a. (ἀμροτ- c[6], b[3], 167 c, ἄμβροτ- or ἄβροτ- 146 b) ἤμβροτον. Cog. 1 a. sub. 1 p. ἀβροτάξομεν 326 d, K. 65.]
ἀμβλίσκω k[7] & [c]ἀμβλόω cause miscarriage; ἀμβλώσω l., ao., 2 a. [c]ἤμβλων l.; [c]ἤμβλωκα, [c]-μαι, -θην.
[ἀμέρδω & ἀμείρω (o, h, ἀμερ-), deprive; ἀμέρσω, ao. a. +, m. l.; ἠμέρθην +.]
ἀμπλακίσκω (k[2], ἀμπλακ-), miss, err, po.; 2 a. ἤμπλακον, pt. ἀπλακών 171, Eur. Alc. 241; ἠμπλάκημαι 311, Æsch. Sup. 916.
[ἀμπνυ- take breath; see πνέω.]

§ 50.   ἀμύνω   VERBS.   βαίνω   69

ἀμύνω *avert, defend* (cf. munio), *M. repel, requite;* ἀμῠνῶ m., ἠμῦνα m., 2 a. ἠμύναθον 353 a.
ἀμφιγνοέω *doubt;* see γιγνώσκω.
ἀμφισβητέω *dispute;* see βαίνω.
ἀναίνομαι (h, ἀναν-) *refuse;* ao. ἠνηνάμην.
ἀν-ᾰλίσκω & ἀν-ᾱλόω (ἀλο-, k[7]) *expend;* ἀνᾱλώσω, m. 1., ἀνήλωσα; ἀνήλωκα, -μαι, -θην f. In the aug., a is often retained, esp. in the older Att.: ἀνάλωσα, ἀνάλωκα, Th. 7. 83, 2. 64; & in comp. w. κατά, the aug. is rarely on the prep. ἀνά: κατηνάλωσα, Isoc. 201 b. See 279 f, 282 b. For the simple verb, see ἁλέω.
ἀνδάνω (n[4], Γαδ-, ἀδ- f) *please,* po. & I.; ipf. ἥνδανον, ἐάνδανον, & ἑήνδανον, 279 b, e; ἁδήσω, 2 a. ἕαδον Hdt. 1. 151, εὕαδον 142, π. 28; ἅδηκα r., 2 p. ἔαδα E. Cog. ἥδω q. v.
[ἀνεθ- *grow*, akin to ἀνθέω · 2 pf. ᶜἤνοθα 312 b : ἀν-ήνοθεν *rises*, ρ. 270; ἐπ-εν-ήνοθε *grows upon*, β. 219.]
ἀνοίγω & -οίγνυμι *open;* see οἴγω.
ἀνύω & also Att. ἀνύτω t (acc. to some, Att. ἀ-), *accomplish*, M.; ἀνύσω m., ao.; ἤνυκα, -σμαι, -σθην f. [Nude pr. ἀνύται l.; ipf. ἤνυτο e. 243, "ἄνυμες & "ἄνυτο Theoc.] Cog. ἄνω m., po.
ἀνώγω *command*, po. & I.; ἀνώξω, ao.; 2 pf. ἄνωγα pret. & unaugm. [nude 1 p. ἀνώγμεν 320, Hom. Ap. 528], imv. ἄνωγε & ἀνωχθι 320 f. [Cog. ἀνωγέω H. 394 v. l.] See 326 c.
ἀπαυράω, ἀπούρας, see ἐπαυρέω.
[ἀπαφίσκω (k[2], ἀπαφ-) *deceive;* ἀπαφήσω 311, ao. r., 2 a. ἤπαφον +, m. See ἅπτω.]
ἀπεχθάνομαι & ἀπέχθομαι, *be hated;* see ἔχθω.
ἅπτω (t, ἀφ-, 147) *fasten, kindle*, M. *touch;* ἅψω m., ao.; ἧμμαι, ἥφθην, ᶜf. l. [ἅμμαι & ἅφθην, Hdt. 1. 86, 19, ἑάφθην 279 b, N. 543. Cog. ἀφάω or ἀφάω & ἀφάσσω, *handle*, I. +, m.; f. ᶜἀφήσω, ao. ἤφησα & ἤφασα: ἀπαφίσκω q. v.]
ἀράομαι *pray, curse;* ἀράσομαι ao.; ᶜἤρᾱμαι, ᶜ-θην 1. [Pr. *inf. a.* ἀρήμεναι 333 e, χ. 322. Cog.? *pf. pt.* ἀρημένος *oppressed*, Σ. 435.]
[ἀραρίσκω (k[2] r[2], ἀρ-) *fit;* ἦρσα m., 2 a. ἤραρον + m. 284 e (nude pt. as adj. ἄρμενος);] 2 pf. ἄρᾱρᾱ

[ἄρηρα] pret. intrans. po. +, [ἀρήρεμαι, ἤρθην.] Cog. ἁρμόζω q. v., ἀρτύω & ἀρτύνω [ἀρτέομαι I.] *prepare*, and ἀρέσκω (k, ἀρε-) *please*, M.; ἀρέσω m., ao.; ἀρήρεκα l., ἠρέσθην.
ἀριστάω *dine*, with regular forms, has in comedy 2 pf. nude 1 p. ἠρίστᾰμεν Ar. Fr. 528, *inf.* ἠριστάναι, § 320; and in imitation, δειπνέω *sup*, has δεδείπναμεν, δεδειπνάναι 1b. 243.
ἁρμόζω & Att. ἁρμόττω (j[1], i[2], ἁρμοδ-) *adjust*, M.; ἁρμόσω, m. l., ao.; ἥρμοκα, -σμαι, -σθην f. See ἀραρίσκω.
ἄρνυμαι *win;* see αἴρω.
ἀρόω aro, *plough;* ἀρόσω, ao.; [ἀρήρομαι E. I.,] ἠρώθην : [ἀρόωσιν 324 c, ἀρόμμεναι 333 c[r].]
ἁρπάζω j[12] *seize;* ἁρπάσω and oftener ἁρπάσομαι [ἁρπάξω], ao.; ἥρπακα, -σμαι (-γμαι l.), -σθην f. [-χθην, Hdt. 2. 90 +], 2 a. ἡρπάγην f. l. [Nude 2 a. *pt. m.* (ἀρπα-) ἀρπάμενος l.]
ἀρύω, -ύνω, -έομαι, see ἀραρίσκω.
ἀρύω & ἀρύτω t, *draw water*, M.; ἀρύσομαι l., ἤρυσα m.; ἠρύθην or -ύσθην 307 e. — ἄρχω *lead*, see 41.
ἄσσω *rush;* see ἀΐσσω.
αὔξω [ἀέξω E. I. +] & αὐξάνω (n[4], ἀΓεξ-, αὐξ-, δεξ-, f[12]) augeo, *increase;* see 41. F.αὐξανῶ in Lxx. Cog. αὐξέω l.
αὔω *shout*, po.; ἀὔσω (ῦ), ἤϋσα.
ἀφάω & ἀφάσσω *handle;* see ἅπτω.
ἀχέων, ἀχεύων, ἄχνυμαι & ἄχομαι *be grieved;* see ἀκαχίζω.
ἄχθομαι *be vexed;* ἀχθέσομαι 311 d; ἤχθημαι l., ἠχθέσθην f.
[ἄω *satiate;* "ἄσω m., ἆσα m.; pr. *inf.* "ἄμεναι 333 e[r]. Cog. *sub.* 1 p. ἑώμεν T. 402, ao. *opt.* 3 s. ᾽ἀδήσειεν a. 134, *pf. pt.* ᾽ἀδηκότες K. 399, as fr. ἑά- & ἀδέ- *become sated;* ἀσάομαι *be nauseated*, I. D. +.] — See ἄημι.

B.

βαίνω (n[6], βα-) vado, *go;* βήσομαι po. exc. in comp., [ἐβησάμην, usu. -σόμην 327 a,] 2 a. ἔβην 45 h, e, 322 c (imv. βῆθι, ᶜβᾶ, 297 c, d); βέβηκα (2 pf. *ind.* 3 p. βεβάᾱσι B. 134, ct. βεβᾶσι Eur. Tro. 835, § 156, *sub.* ἐμβεβῶσι Pl. Phaedr. 252 e, *inf.* βεβάναι Eur. Heracl. 610, *pt.* βεβαώς, Hes. Sc. 307, ct. βεβώς, Pl. Tim. 63 c, 2 plp. 3 p. βέβασαν P. 286, § 320 e), ᵒβέβα-

βαίνω TABLES. γηράω § 50.

μαι or -ασμαι r., ⁰ἐβάθην r., ᶜ-άσθην or -άνθην l. As trans., cause to go, f.
ᶜβήσω, ao. ἔβησα. Cog. ⁰βάω r., βάσκω po., [βιβάω, βίβημι, βιβάσθω,] βιβάζω make go 305 b. Cp. ἀμφισ-βητέω dispute; f. -ήσω m., ao. ἠμφισβήτησα & ἠμφεσβήτησα ; -ητήθην (so ipf. -ήτουν, 282 b).
βάλλω (l, βαλ-, βλα- c⁶⁷) throw, M.; βαλῶ m. (βαλλήσω 311 a, Ar. Vesp. 222), [ᶜβλήσομαι, T. 335,] 2 a. ἔβαλον m. [ἔβλην, m. ἐβλήμην, opt. 2 s. βλῆο or βλεῖο b¹, N. 288]; βέβληκα, -μαι [βεβόλημαι 114 a, 311, I. 9], 3 f. βεβλήσομαι, ἐβλήθην f.
βάπτω (t, βαφ-) dip, M.; βάψω m., ao.; βέβαμμαι, ἐβάφθην, usu. 2 a. ἐβάφην, f. l.
βαστάζω carry, po. or l.; βαστάσω, &c., later, βαστάξω, &c., 349 a.
[βεβρώθοις (eat), see βιβρώσκω.]
[βέομαι, βείομαι, live; see βιόω.]
βιβάζω, [βιβάω, -ημι, -άσθω,] see βαίνω.
βιβρώσκω (r¹ k⁶, βρο-, cf. voro) eat, mostly dial. or l.; βρώσομαι l., ᶜἔβρωσα l., [2 a. ἔβρων 313 b]; βέβρωκα (pt. βεβρώς 320 d, Soph. Ant. 1022), βέβρωμαι, [3 f. -σομαι,] ἐβρώθην, f. l. Cog. βρώθω l., [2 pf. opt. βεβρώθοις Δ. 35, or pr. fr. βεβρώθ-.]
βιόω live, M.; & βιώσκομαι k⁶ revive, usu. cp. w. ἀνά · βιώσομαι, -σω l., ao., oftener 2 ao. ἐβίων 313 b (opt. βιῴην 316 b) ; βεβίωκα, -μαι, -θην f. l. [Cog. βέομαι (βείομαι 134 a) or βίομαι, also as fut. 305 f, O. 194, X. 431, Hom. Ap. 528.] See ζάω.
βλάπτω (t, βλαβ-) hurt; βλάψω m., ao. a., m. l.; βέβλαφα, -αμμαι, 3 f. -άψομαι, ἐβλάφθην, & 2 a. ἐβλάβην f. [Cog. βλάβω r., T. 82.]
βλαστάνω & r. βλαστέω (n⁴, v, βλαστ-) sprout, bud; βλαστήσω, ao., comm. 2 a. ἔβλαστον; βεβλάστηκα & ἐβλάστηκα 280 c.
βλίττω (i², βλιτ- for μελιτ- 146 b) take honey from the hive; ἔβλισα.
βλώσκω (k⁶, 146 b, μολ-) go, po.; μολοῦμαι, 2 a. ἔμολον +; μέμβλωκα.
βοάω boo, shout, M.; βοήσομαι, -σω l., ao. a., m. l.; βεβόηκα l., -μαι l., ἐβοήθην l.: [E. & I. ᶜβώσομαι, ἔβωσα m., βέβωμαι, ἐβώσθην, 131 f.]
βόσκω feed, M. (cf. pasco, vescor);

βοσκήσω 311 a, m. l., ao. l.; ἐβοσκήθην, f. l.
βούλομαι [βόλομαι] volo, WILL, wish (2 s. βούλει 297 f); βουλήσομαι; βεβούλημαι, ἐβουλήθην & ἠβουλήθην 279 a, f. l.: [2 pf. προ-βέβουλα prefer, A. 113.] Cog. βουλεύω plan, 44.
[βραχ- resound; 2 a. ἔβραχε 337 a, E. 863.]
βρέχω (b, βραχ-) wet; βρέξω l., ao.; βέβρεγμαι, ἐβρέχθην, less Att. ἐβράχην, f. l.
[βροχ-swallow; ἔβροξα; ᶜβέβροχα, ᶜἐβρόχθην l., ᶜἐβρόχην.]
βρῡχάομαι (u, βρυχ-) roar, 355 u; ᶜβρυχήσομαι very l., ao.; 2 pf. βέβρῡχα pret., ἐβρυχήθην.
βῠνέω n¹⁰, r. βύω, stop up, M.; ᶜβύσω, ao. a., m. l.; βέβυσμαι, ᶜἐβύσθην. Cog. βύνω & βύζω r.

Γ.

γαμέω (v, γαμ-) marry (of the man), M. marry (of the woman); γαμῶ m. 152, l. γαμήσω m., ἔγημα m., later ἐγάμησα · γεγάμηκα, -μαι, ἐγαμήθην f. l.: [f. m. γαμέσσεται will provide a wife, I. 394 v. l.]
γάνυμαι, l. γάννυμαι, rejoice; [γανύσσομαι 171, Ξ. 504; γεγάνῡμαι Anact. 35.] Cog. γανόω brighten, [γανάω shine.]
γέγονα, γεγάᾱτε, γεγάκειν, γείνομαι, γεννάω, see γίγνομαι.
γεγωνέω [-ώνω] & γεγωνίσκω (v, k², γεγων- r) shout; γεγωνήσω ao.; γέγωνα pret. (sub. γεγώνω, imv. γέγωνε 318).
γελάω laugh; γελάσομαι, -σω l., ao. a.; ᶜγεγέλασμαι l., ἐγελάσθην, f.l. [Cog. γελοιάω.]
[γεν-=(&, according to some, Æol. for) ἐλ- (see αἱρέω), in 2 a. m. 3 s. γέντο took, Σ. 476. See also γίγνομαι.]
γεύω cause to taste, M. gusto, taste; γεύσω m., ao.; γέγευμαι, ἐγεύσθην 307 e. [Nude pr. 1 p. γεύμεθα Theoc. 14. 51.]
[γηθέω (v, γήθω m. l.) gaudeo, rejoice+; γηθήσω, ao.;] γέγηθα pret.
γηράω & oftener γηράσκω k¹, grow old, M.; γηράσω & -άσομαι, ao. a., 2 a. ἐγήρᾱν po. or l., 313 b (inf. γη-

§ 50. γηράω VERBS. δέω 71

ρᾶναι or -άναι Æsch. Ch. 908); γεγήρᾱκα, ^cἐγηράθην l.
γίγνομαι (r¹ c², γα-, γεν- n¹ b¹), or I. & later γίνομαι, *become;* γενήσομαι, 2 a. ἐγενόμην [nude 3 s. ἔγεντο 326 c, γέντο Hes. Th. 199]; 2 pf. γέγονα [γεγάᾱτε, for γέγατε, 320, 134 s, Hom. Batr. 143, γεγάᾱσι Δ. 41, plp. 3 d. ἐκ-γεγάτην κ. 138, *inf.* γεγάμεν 333 c, E. 248, *pt.* γεγαώς, I. 456], *pt.* po. γεγώς 320 d, Soph. Aj. 472, γεγένημαι, ἐγενήθην I. D. or l., f. r. [Pf. *inf.* γεγάκειν D. 326 b.] Cog. [^cγεγάομαι 326 c, γείνομαι X. 477 v.l.,] ao. ἐγεινάμην *begat,* po. +; γεννάω *beget.* Cf. gigno, gnascor.
γιγνώσκω (k⁶ r, γνο-), or I. & later γινώσκω, gnosco, KNOW, ^cM. I.; γνώσομαι, ao. m. l. [ἀν-έγνωσα *persuaded,* Hdt.], 2 a. ἔγνων, 45 h, e (m. opt. 3 s. συγ-γνοῖτο Æsch. Sup. 216); ἔγνωκα, -σμαι, -σθην f. Cog. γνωρίζω, -ίσω, -ιῶ, ἐγνώρικα, *make known;* ἀμφιγνοέω, -ήσω, *doubt,* aug. ἠμφιγ- & ἠμφεγ- 282 b.
γλύφω sculpo, *carve;* γλύψω l., ao. a., m. l.; γέγλυμμαι & ἔγλυμμαι 280 c, ἐγλύφθην l. & r., 2 a. ἐγλύφην l. Cf. glubo. Cog. γλάφω.
γοάω (u, γο-) *bewail,* M., po. + (in Att. only pr. & ipf. m., & pr. p.); γοήσομαι, -σω l., ao. l., 2 a. ἔγοον Z. 500 ; ἐγοήθην l.
γράφω scribo, GRAVE, *write,* M.; γράψω m., ao.; γέγραφα (γεγράφηκα l. + ?), γέγραμμαι (ἔγραμμαι l., 280 c), 3 f. γεγράψομαι, ^cἐγράφθην l., 2 a. ἐγράφην f.

Δ.

δα-, *teach, learn;* see διδάσκω.
δαίνῡμι (n⁹, δαιτ-) *feast, entertain,* po. +, M. [*opt.* δαινῦτο, -ύατο, 316 c]; δαίσω, m. l., ao.; ἐδαίσθην.
δαίομαι (h, δα-) divido, *divide,* ch. po. (pr. & f.), P.; δάσομαι ao.; δέδασμαι, Α. 125 [δέδαιμαι, a. 23], ἐδάσθην l. Cog. δατέομαι po. I. [ao. *inf.* δατέασθαι 306, Hes. Op. 765], δαινύμι q. v., δαίζω, -ίξω, *rend,* po.
δαίω (h, δαϝ-, δα-) *kindle,* po. +, M.; [2 a. ἐδάομην, T. 316 ; 2 pf. δέδηα *blaze,* pret., T. 18,] δέδαυμαι, Sim. Am. 30.

δάκνω (n¹, δακ-, δηκ- g) *bite,* 47 ; δήξομαι, -ξω l., ao. r., 2 a. ἔδακον ; δέδηχα l., δέδηγμαι, ἐδήχθην f., 2 a. ἐδάκην l. Cog. δακνάζω po.
δαμάζω (z, δαμ-) domo, *tame, subdue,* po. +, M.; δαμάσω [m., δαμῶ 305 b, A. 61], ao.; δεδάμακα l., -σμαι l. [δέδμημαι c⁷, Ε. 878, 3 f. δεδμήσομαι, Hom. Ap. 543,] ἐδαμάσθην θ. 231, Mem. 4.1.3, ἐδμήθην po., Δ. 99, oftener 2 a. ἐδάμην po., Τ. 94. Po. cog. δαμάω l., δαμαλίζω, δαμνάω, δάμνημι (M. δάμναμαι).
^cδαρθάνω (n⁴, δαρθ-) *sleep,* usu. cp. w. κατά · 2 a. ^cἐδαρθον, po. ἔδραθον c⁶, T. 143 ; ^cδεδάρθηκα 311, 2 a. ^cἐδάρθην, ^cἐδράθην r. or l.
δατέομαι *divide,* po.; see δαίομαι.
[δέατο *appeared;* see δοα-.]
[δείδω + & δίω (δι-, δειδ- o h) *fear,* δίομαι + *frighten;* δείσομαι, + ?, -σω l.,] ἔδεισα · pret. δέδοικα & 2 pf. δέδια 46 b [δείδοικα, δείδια, 134 a, δεδοίκω D., 326 b]. Cog. δειμαίνω *fear,* δεδίσσομαι [δειδίσσομαι], r. δεδίσκομαι, *frighten,* δίημι *chase* (M. δίεμαι) po., & διώκω q. v.
δείκνῡμι & δεικνύω (n⁷, δεικ-) indico, *extend the hand* to point out, *show* [M. *greet* with extended hand]; δείξω, &c., 45 [in Hdt., fr. δεκ-, ^cδέξω, ἔδεξα m., ^cδέδεγμαι, ^cἐδέχθην · Ep. δείδεγμαι 134 a, pret., η. 72]. Cog. δέχομαι q. v., δεξιόομαι *greet,* [δεδίσκομαι & δειδίσκομαι *greet,* δεικανάω *show.*]
δειπνέω sup ; see ἀριστάω.
[δέμω *build,* Hom.Merc.87 ;] ἔδειμα m.; [δέδμημαι c⁷.] Cog. δομέω l.
δέρκομαι b¹ *see,* po. or l.; δέρξομαι l., ao. l., 2 a. ἔδρακον c⁶, m. r.; δέδορκα pret., ἐδέρχθην [2 a. ἐδράκην Pind. N. 7. 4].
δέρω (b¹, δαρ-), less Att. δείρω or δαίρω h, *flay,* ^cM. r.; δερῶ, ἔδειρα · δέδαρμαι, ἐδάρθην r., 2 a. ἐδάρην, f. l.
δεύομαι *want;* see δέω.
δέχομαι *receive;* δέξομαι ao.; δέδεγμαι, 3 f. δεδέξομαι, ἐδέχθην, f. l. [Pr. 3 p. δέχαται for δέχ[ο]νται 158, M. 147, 2 a. ἐδέγμην, 326 c. Cog. δέχνυμαι, δέκομαι 167, Hdt. 9. 91 ;] see δείκνῡμι.
δέω, *bind,* M., 309 b; δήσω m., ao.; δέδεκα (r. -ηκα 310 d), δέδεμαι,

3 f. δεδήσομαι 319 c, Cyr. 4. 3. 18, έδέθην f. Cog. r. δίδημι r¹, v. 8. 24.
δέω (f¹, δεF-) need, want, M. need, beg; δεήσω m. 311 c, ao. a. [3 s. έδησεν Σ. 100]; δεδέηκα, -μαι, έδεήθην, f. l. [Ep. δεύομαι f², -ήσομαι, έδεύησα, ι. 540.] Impers. δεῖ there is need, δέῃ, ct. δῇ 309 b, δέοι, δεῖν, δέον · δεήσει, έδέησε.
δηλόω, -ώσω, &c., manifest; see 42.
δήω shall find; see διδάσκω.
διαιτάω regulate, M.; διαιτήσω, διῄτησα & έδιῄτησα, δεδιῄτηκα, &c., 282 c.
διᾱκονέω minister; -ήσω, έδιᾱκόνησα, δεδιᾱκόνηκα (less Att. διηκόνησα, δεδιηκόνηκα, &c., 282 c.
διδάσκω (k², δα-, διδαχ- r¹o) doceo, teach, M.; διδάξω m., no. [έδιδάσκησα 311, Hom. Cer. 144]; δεδίδαχα, -γμαι, έδιδάχθην, f. l. [Fr. δα- disco, learn, teach, δαήσομαι 311, 2 a. έδαον & δέδαον 284 e; δεδάηκα, θ. 134, 2 pf. δέδαα, ρ. 519, δεδάημαι Hom. Merc. 483, 2 a. έδάην +. Cog. δεδάομαι 326 c, π. 316; δήω as fut., shall find, N. 260.]
δίδημι bind; see δέω bind.
ᶜδιδράσκω (r¹ k, δρα-) run; ᶜδράσομαι, ao. a. l., 2 a. ᶜέδρᾱν 45 h; ᶜδέδρᾱκα. Cog. δραπετεύω, δρασκάζω · έδραμον, see τρέχω. See δράω.
δίδωμι (r¹, δο-) do, give, δώσω, δέδωκα, &c.; see 45.
[δίζημαι seek, E. & I., 314 b; διζήσομαι ao. Cog. δίζω M., po.]
δίημι chase, M. flee, po.; see δείδω.
διοικέω manage, -ήσω, διῴκηκα, -μαι & r. δεδιῴκημαι, 282 b.
διψάω thirst, -ήσω, &c. (διψ(δει)ῇ 120 g).
δίω fear, flee; see δείδω.
διώκω pursue, M.; διώξω and oftener διώξομαι, ao. a., 2 a. έδιώκαθον 353 a; δεδίωχα, -γμαι l., έδιώχθην, f. l. See δείδω.
[δοα-, δεα- 114 b, appear; ipf. nude δέατο ζ. 242; ao. m. δοάσσατο Ξ. 23, sub. δοάσσεται 326 d, Ψ. 339. Cog. δοιάζω or δοάζω, doubt, imagine, Ap. Rh.]
δοκέω (v, δοκ-) seem, think; δόξω ao.; δέδοχα l., -γμαι, έδόχθην l.: ch. po. δοκήσω ao., δεδόκηκα, -μαι, έδοκήθην · [pf. m. pt. δεδοκημένος pret., fixed in thought, intent, watching, O. 730.]

Cog. [δοκεύω watch,] δοκιμάζω examine.
δουπέω (e¹, γδουπε-v) sound heavily, ch. po.; δουπήσω, ao. [έγδούπησα, Λ. 45], 2 a. ᶜέδουπον l.; 2 pf. δέδουπα, έδουπήθην l.
δράσσομαι i¹, grasp, seize, A. l.; δράξομαι l., ao.; δέδραγμαι (δέδαρξαι c⁷, Eur. Tro. 745 v. l.).
δράω do; δράσω ao.; δέδρᾱκα, -αμαι, r. -ασμαι 307 e, έδράσθην. Cog. [δραίνω,] άπο-διδράσκω make off, run away.
δρέπω (b¹, δραπ-), po. l. δρέπτω t, pluck, M.; δρέψομαι po., ao. a. m., [2 a. έδραπον Pind. P. 4. 231.]
δύναμαι be able (2 s. δύνᾳ 297 h); δυνήσομαι [ao. +]; δεδύνημαι, έδυνήθην, iii. 1. 35, f. l., ήδυνήθην 279 a, Cyr. 3. 1. 30, less Att. έδυνάσθην, vii. 6. 20.
δύω [ῠ Hom.] cause to enter, enter (cf. in-duo), δυνω n¹, & less Att. δύομαι, enter (the causative sense belongs to the fut. & l ao. act., but not to the 2 ao., & very rarely to the pf. act., v. 8. 23); δύσω, δύσομαι, ao., [έδυσόμην 327 a,] 2 a. έδῡν 45 h; δέδῡκα, ᶜδέδῠμαι 310 d, ᶜέδῠθην f., [2 a. r. έδύην Hipp. Cog. δύπτω, dive.]

E.

έα- become sated, έῶμεν; see άω.
έάω permit; έάσω m., είᾱσα 279 c; είᾱκα, -μαι, -θην.
έγγυάω pledge, M.; έγγυήσω, ήγγύησα or ένεγύησα · ήγγύηκα or έγγεγύηκα, &c.; 282 c.
έγείρω (h, έγερ-) rouse, raise, M. rise; έγερῶ, m. l., ήγειρα, m. l., 2 a. ήγρόμην c⁸; έγήγερκα l., 2 pf. pret. έγρήρορα, am awake, 281 d [έγρήγορθε 320 f; in imitation, ind. 3 p. έγρηγόρθᾱσι K. 419, inf. m. έγρήγορθαι for έγηγέρθαι, K. 67], έγήγερμαι, ήγέρθην, f. l. Cog. έγρω po., έγρηγορέω & γρηγορέω l., [έγρηγοράω, έγρήσσω.]
έγκωμιάζω praise; -άσω m., ένεκωμίασα, έγκεκωμίακα, 282 c.
έδω eat; see έσθίω.
έζομαι seat one's self, sit; see ίζω.
έθέλω p & θέλω, wish; -ήσω 311 b, ηθέλησα & έθέλησα · ηθέληκα & l. τεθέληκα. Θέλω is rare & doubtful

§ 50.   ἐθέλω   VERBS.   εἰμί & εἶμι   73

in Hom., Hes., & Pind.; & is in general less common than ἐθέλω, exc. in dramatic dialogue.

ἐθίζω (z², Feθ-, ἐθ-) *accustom*, M.; ἐθίσω, -ῶ 305 a, εἴθισα 279 c; εἴθικα, -σμαι, -σθην, f. l. Intrans. 2 pf. pret. εἴωθα [ἔωθα E. I.] 312 d, *am wont*, [pr. pt. ἔθων I. 540.]

εἴδομαι *seem*, εἶδον *saw*; see ὁράω.

εἰκάζω (z², Fικ-, Feικ- h, εἰκ-) *liken*; εἰκάσω, ᶜm., εἴκασα & ἤκασα 278 d; εἴκακα l., -σμαι & ἤκασμαι, -θην f. Intrans., 2 pf. pret. ἔοικα 312 b, sometimes εἶκα or ἦκα [οἶκα I.], *seem* (nude 1 p. po. ἔοιγμεν 148, Soph. Aj. 1239, [3 d. εἴκτον δ. 27, plp. εἴκτην A. 104,] irreg. 3 p. εἴξᾶσι po. +, Ar. Av. 96, see ἴσᾶσι under ὁράω), plp. ἐῴκειν 279 d, f. r. εἴξω Ar. Nub. 1001, ipf. εἶκε Σ. 520? [Cog. ἴσκω, ἔισκω q. v.]

εἴκω (Feικ-) *yield*; εἴξω [ᵒm.], ao., 2 a. εἶκαθον 353 a.

[εἰλ-· (h, Faλ-, ἀλ-, ἐλ- b¹) *volvo, roll up, press together*, P. εἴλομαι, E. 203; εἶλσα 152 d, Λ. 413; ἔελμαι Ω. 662, 2 a. ἐάλην, N. 408.] Cog. εἴλλω or εἴλλω, ἴλλω, εἰλέω or εἰλέω [ἐολέω, Pind. P. 4. 414], -ήσω, εἰλύω po. +, -ύσω [ao. p. ἐλύσθην, Ψ. 393; deriv. εἰλῦφάω, εἰλυφάζω], ἐλίσσω [εἰλίσσω po. & I. +], -ίξω (εἴλιξα 279 c), [ἐλελίξω, -ίξω, A. 530.] — εἴβω 344.

εἶλον *took*; see αἱρέω.

εἰμί (ἐσ-) *be*, & εἶμι (l-, Lat. i-re) *go*. The Pres. of εἶμι has comm. in the ind. (in Att. prose regularly), & sometimes in the other modes, the sense of the Fut.: εἶμι, [I am going] *I shall go*. For the common forms of these verbs, see 45 l, m, o, r. Their chief dialectic forms appear below, those preceded by † belonging to εἶμι *go*, and the others to εἰμί *be*:

a. DIALECTIC FORMS OF εἰμί *to be*, AND εἶμι *to go*.

Pres. Ind.	3 ἔωσι E. I.	†ἴεμεν D., ἴναι P.	P.1 ἤμες D.
S. 1 ἔμμι Æ.	ἔωντι D.	Pres. Part.	†ἤομεν E.
2 εἶς E.I., ἐσσί P.	Pres. Opt.	ἐών, ἐοῦσα, ἐόν, G.	2 ἔατε I. [σαν I.
†εἶς, εἶσθα E.	S. 2 εἴησθα P., ἔοις	ἐόντος E. I.	3 ἔσαν P. I., ἔασσαν P.
3 ἐντί D.	3 ἔοι E. I. [E.	εὖσα, ἐᾶσα, G. εὖντος, ἔντος D.	ἔσκον It.
P.1 εἰμέν E. I.	†ἰείη, εἴη? E.	ἔοισα Æ.	εἴατο? E.
εἰμές D., ἐμέν P.	Pres. Imv.		†ἤϊσαν E. I.
3 ἔᾱσι E., ἐντί, ἐ-	S. 2 ἔσο, ἔσσο P.	Imperfect.	†ἴσαν, ἤϊον E.
†ἴσι P. [οντι D.	P.3 ἐόντω D.	S. 1 ἔα E. I., ἦα E.	D.3 †ἴτην E.
Pres. Sub.	Pres. Inf.	ἔον, ἔην? E.	Fut. Ind.
S. 1 ἔω E. I., εἴω E.	ἔμεν, ἔμεναι E.	ἔσκον It. [E.	ἔσσομαι P.
†εἴω P.	ἔμμεν E. D.	†ἤϊα E. I., ἤϊον	ἐσοῦμαι D.
2 †ἴησθα E.	ἔμμεναι F. Æ.	2 ἦς late, ἔας I.	ἐσσοῦμαι D. E.
3 ᾖσι, ἔῃσι, ἔῃ E.	ἤμεν, εἶμεν D.	ἤησθα E., ἔης P.	†εἴσομαι E.
†ἴῃσι E.	εἴμεναι D.?	3 ἤεν, ἔην, ἤην E.	
P.1 ὦμες D.	†ἴμεν, ἴμεναι E.	ἦς D., ἔσκε It.	Aor. Ind.
†ἴομεν E.	†ἴμμεναι E.	†ἤϊε I.	†εἰσάμην E.
†ἴωμες D.	†ἰέμεναι E.	†ἤε, ἴε, εἴε? E.	†ἐεισάμην E.

b. The comparison of a few cognate tongues will show more clearly that the root of εἰμί *to be*, was ἐσ-, and will also illustrate the forms of inflection. The Latin is placed first, as showing least change in the flexible endings (271 d ʳ). The harsh forms *esm, esmus*, and *esnt* became, by transposition and change of vowel (cf. 116), *sum, sumus, sunt*. In the Greek, the elements are first given (32 i), and then the results. For the relation of the Sanskrit *as-* to the *es-* of the other languages, see 114 a. In the plural, the *a* is dropped or transposed. See 271 d. In the Slavic, the *j* is to be pronounced as *y*. The Lithuanian, which shows the root entire throughout, is placed last, as a language which yet lives to link the present to the remote past.

74   εἰμί   TABLES.   εἶμι   § 50.

	Latin	Gothic.		Greek.	Sanskrit.	Old Slavic	Lithuan.
S. 1	sum	im	ἐσ-μ	εἰμί, Æ.ἔμμι	asmi	jesmi	esmi
2	es	is	ἐσ-ς	εἶς, P.ἐσσί	asi	jesi	esi
3	est	ist	ἐσ-τ	ἐστί	asti	jesti	esti
P. 1	sumus		ἐσ-μεν	ἐσμέν, D.εἰμές	smas	jesmu	esme
2	estis		ἐσ-(τσ)τε	ἐστέ	stha	jeste	este
3	sunt	sind	ἐσ-ντ	εἰσί, D.ἐντί	santi	sunti	esti

c. In εἰμί *to be*, the σ of the root was retained in some forms (before τ, θ, and μ; ἐ becoming ἰ by precession in ἴσθι, 114 d). (d) It was dropped before σ of the Fut. (ἔσομαι, cf. Lat. *ero*, 139), and between two vowels, which were then contracted: Pr. 3 p. (ἐσᾶσι) ἔᾶσι E., εἰσί, *sub.* (ἔσω) ἔω F. I., ὦ, *opt.* (ἐσίην, cf. L. *sim*) εἴην · Ipf. 1 s. (augmented ἦον, ἦσα, cf. 273ʳ c, e, and L. *cram*, 139) ἦα E., ἦ (Old Att., Ar. Av. 1363), 3 s. (ἦστ, ἦσε, 273ʳ c, e) ἦεν E. 163 b, ἦν. (e) It was also dropped before ντ, ἐ commonly passing into the kindred ὁ (cf. 114 b, c): Pr. 3 p. ἐντί D., *pt.* (ἐντ- L. *ent-*, *ὀντ-*) ὤν, ἔντος D., *inv.* 3 p. (ἐντων) ὄντων. (f) It was contracted, as ε (142), with ἰ or ἠ preceding: Pr. *ind.* (ἐσμι) εἰμί, (ἐσς) εἶς F. I., or (both sigmas apparently taken up) εἶ, (ἐσμέν) εἰμέν E. I., *inf.* (ἔσναι) εἶναι (in Lat. the *r* was assimilated, (es-re) *esse*), *imv.* (ἔστω, ἔετω, cf. 121 e) ἤτω l.; Ipf. 1 s. (ἦσον) ἦν, 2 s. (ἦσς) ἦς l., pl. ἦμεν, ἦτε (oftener than ἦστε, while in the dual ἦστον and ἦστην prevail), ἦσαν. See 139 s.

The DIALECTIC or LESS ATTIC FORMS of εἰμί *to be*, are (g) *forms uncontracted* or *like* those of *verbs in* -ω (315): ἔᾶσιν B. 125, ἔοντι Archim., ἔω ι. 18, ἔωσι Hdt. 2. 39, ἔοις I. 284, ἐν-έοι Hdt. 7. 6, ἔων B. 27, ζουσα Γ. 159, ἔοισα Pind. P. 4. 471, εὖσα, εὖντα, Theoc. 2. 3, 76, (ἐνσα, 156) ἐᾶσα Tim. Loc. 96 a, ἦα β. 313, ἦεν M. 9; (h) variously *protracted*: ἐσσί (in imitation of the other persons) A. 176, μετ-είω Ψ. 47, ἔησι 328 b, B. 366, εἴη-σθα 297 b, Theog. 715, ἔης 135, ἐησθα X. 435, ἔην M. 10, ἤην Λ. 808, ἔσκον 332, H. 153, ἔσκε Hdt. 1. 196, ἔσσομαι 171, Δ. 267 (ἔσεται 45 r, A. 211), ἐσοῦμαι 305 d, Th. 5. 77 ; (i) *shortened* or *unaugmented*: ἐμέν r., Call. Fr. 294, ἔα 329 d, ἴον Λ. 762, ἐσαν Α. 267; (j) *middle forms*: ἔσο or ἔσσο A. 302, Sap. 1. 28, ἤμην r. or l., Cyr. 6. 1. 9 v. l. (ἤμεθα Mat. 23. 30), εἴατο 329 a, v. 106 v. l.; (k) *infinitives* (333): ἔμεν Δ. 299, ἔμμεναι Sap. 2. 2, ἤμεν or εἴμεν (v. l. ἤμες or εἴμες ?) Th. 5. 77, Theoc. 14. 6, εἰμεναι or ἤμεναι Ar. Ach. 775 ?; (l) *various forms*: ἔμμι 171 a, Sap. 2. 15, εἶς (or εἶς Bek.) Π. 515, Hdt. 7. 9, εἰμέν E. 873, εἰμές, ὤμες, ἤμες, 328 a, Theoc. 15. 73, 9, 14. 29, 3 s. ἐντί 169 c, Theoc. 1. 17, 3 p. ἐντί 328 a, Th. 5. 77, ἐόντω 328 dʳ, 2 s. ἦς l., 297 b, 3 s. (ἦστ) ἦς Theoc. 2. 90, ἔσεται 45 r.

m. In εἶμι *to go*, the root ʼἰ-, in the sing. of the Pres. and commonly in the Impf. throughout, was lengthened to εἰ- (314), which augmented became ἠ- (278 d): εἶμι, εἶς, εἶσι · (ἤν, cf. 273ʳ c, e) ἤα (common in the Old and Mid. Att., Pl. Apol. 22 a, and followed in the Ep. by ἤε M. 371), ἤμεν, ἤτε, ἤσαν. The Impf., having thus a form resembling that of the old Plup. (291 c), fell into the analogy of this tense in its subsequent development, and has been often so named: ἤειν, ἤεις, &c. The shorter forms of the plur. and dual were, however, more common, except perhaps ἤσαν, which some deny to the Att., while others regard it as the true Att. form.

The DIALECTIC FORMS of εἶμι *to go*, are (n) *regular nude forms*: εἶς Hes. Op. 206 (Att. εἶ, as if in imitation of εἰμί *to be*; εἶσθα 297, K. 450), (ἴᾶσι, 156) ἴσι Theog. 716 (v. l. εἶσι), ἐξ-ἴναι Ath. 580 c, ἴσαν Γ. 8, ἴτην Α. 347 : (o) *forms with* ἦ *resolved*: (ἤα) ἤια Hdt. 1. 42, ἤιε A. 47, ἤισαν Hdt. 1. 43, ἤιον 315, ψ. 370 ; (p) *with* ʼἰ *lengthened to* εἰ, as in the Pr. *ind.*: εἴω Sophr. 2 [23], κατ-είεν ? Hes. Sc. 254, εἴσομαι Ξ. 8, εἴσατο Δ. 138, ἐείσατο O. 415 ; (q) *as from* ἰε-: ἴείη T. 209, and also ἴεμαι, ἰέμην, 45 p, if they

§ 50. εἰμί VERBS. ἕπω 75

should be thus written ; (r) *infinitives* (333): ἴμεν A. 170, ἴμμεναι Τ. 365, ἐσ-ιέμεναι χ. 480 ; (t) *various forms:* ἴησθα 297 b, K. 67, ἴησι, ἴωμες 328 b, a, ἴομεν 326 d, ἴεν, ᾔομεν, 315, B. 872, λ. 22.

εἶπον *said*, 2 aor.; see φημί.
εἴργω (h, Fεργ-, ἐργ-) *shut out;* εἴρξω m., εἶρξα ; 2 a. po. εἰργαθον m. 353 a ; εἴργμαι, -χθην : [E. I. ἔργω & ἐργνῡμι n⁷ ; ἔρξομαι, ἔρξα, 2 a. ἐργαθον m.; ἔργμαι (ἔρχαται, -το, 329 a, κ. 283, P. 354) : also ἐέργω, &c., B. 617.] Cog. Lat. arceo, urgeo ; and
εἴργω & εἴργνῡμι (h, n⁷, Fεργ-, ἐργ-) *shut in ;* εἴρξω, εἶρξα ; εἴργμαι, -χθην : ch. Ion., ᶜἔργω, ᶜἔρξω, ἔρξα, ἔρχθην. The single verb Fέργω (or ἐFέργω p) in Hom., seems to have become εἴργω & εἴργω in the Att., with a distinction of sense, which, however, was not always observed.
[εἴρομαι, εἰρωτάω, *ask;* see ἐρωτάω.]
[εἰρύω *draw;* see ἐρύω.]
[εἴρω, εἰρέω, *say;* see φημί.]
εἴρω (f³ h, σερ-) sero, *join, knit* [ipf. or ao. ἤειρε K. 499]; ᶜεἴρα [ᶜἔρσα 152 d, Hipp.]; ᶜεἴρκα, -μαι [E. ἔερμαι, σ. 296, ι. ᶜἔρμαι ?]
εἶσα *set, placed*, 1 a.; see ἵζω.
[εἴσκω & ἴσκω (k⁵, see εἰκάζω) *liken;* pret. ἤϊγμαι+, ᶜEur. Alc. 1063.]
εἴωθα *am wont*, pret.; see ἐθίζω.
ἐκκλησιάζω *hold an assembly*, -άσω, &c.; aug. ἠκκλ-, ἐξεκλ-, &c., 282 c.
ἐλαύνω (n², ἐλα-) & r. ἐλάω *drive*, M.; ἐλάσω, [ἐλάω 305 b, ἐλόω 322 c] ἐλῶ, ἐλάσομαι l., ἤλασα m.; ἐλήλακα, -μαι, -σμαι l., [plp. 3 p. ἐληλάδατο or -έδατο 329 a, η. 86,] ἠλάθην, -σθην ᶜf. l. [Cog. ἐλαστρέω E. I. +.]
[ἔλδομαι (Fελδ-) & ἐέλδομαι, *desire*.]
ἐλέγχω *examine, confute;* ἐλέγξω ao.; ἐλήλεγμαι 41, ᶜἤλεγμαι r., ἠλέγχθην f.
ἕλκω & l. ἑλκύω (w, Fελκ-, cf. vellico) *pull, draw*, M.; ἕλξω, less Att. ἑλκύσω, m. l., εἵλκυσα m., εἷλξα m. l.; εἵλκυκα, -σμαι, -σθην f., εἱλχθην f. l. [Cog. ἑλκέω, -ήσω · ἑλκυστάζω.]
ἑλληνίζω *speak Greek*, -ίσω, &c.; ἑλληνίσθην or ἡλληνίσθην 279 f.
ἐλπίζω (z², Fελπ-) *hope*, M.; ἐλπ(ίσω)ιῶ l., ἤλπισα · ἤλπικα l., -σμαι l., -σθην : [ἔλπω *give hope*, M. & 2 pf. pret. ἔολπα ε. 379, *hope*, 2 plp. ἐώλπειν 279 d, φ. 96.]
ἐλυθ- *come;* see ἔρχομαι.

ἐμέω *vomo*, VOMIT ; ἐμ(έσω)ῶ m., ἤμεσα [ἤμησα ?] ; ἐμήμεκα, -σμαι l., ἐμέθην f. l.
ἐμπολάω *traffic;* -ήσω, &c.; aug. ἠμπ- or ἐνεπ-, 282 c.
ἐναίρω (h, ἐναρ-) *kill*, po., M.; [ἔνηρα l., m. E. 59,] 2 a. ἤναρον, Eur. And. 1182. Cog.,
ἐναρίζω *kill, despoil*, po., 349 a ; [ἐναρίξω, m. l.,] ἠνάριξα, m. l., [-ισα, Anac. 100]; ᶜἠνάρισμαι, ᶜ-σθην.
ἐνέπω & ἐννέπω, & l. ἐνίσπω (ἐνεπ-, ἐνιπ- b², ἐνισπ- o), *tell, speak* (cf. inquam), po., a. 1 ; [ἐνίψω & ἐνισπήσω 311, ε. 98, ἔνιψα l.,] 2 a. ἔνισπον [mv. ἐνίσπες v, 313 b, γ. 101.] Cog. [ἐνίπτω+, & ἐνίσσω i³, *chide*, 2 a. ἐνένιπον, ἠνίπαπον, 284 e ;] εἶπον, see φημί.
[ᶜἐν-ήνοθα *grow* or *lie on ;* see ἀνεθ-.]
ᶜἕννῡμι (n⁷, Fε-, ἑ-), vestio, *clothe*, [M.; f. ἕσω (ἕσσω 171, π. 79) ᶜm., ao. (ἕσσα δ. 253, ἑέσσατο K. 23) ; pf. εἷμαι+τ. 72, & ἕσμαι, ω. 250 :] comm.
ἀμφι-έννῡμι M. ; ἀμφιέσω ε. 167, Att. ᶜἀμφιῶ 305 b, Ar. Eq. 891, ἀμφιέσομαι Cyr. 4. 3. 20, ἠμφίεσα m. 282 b, Cyr. 1. 3. 17 ; ἠμφίεσμαι, -σθην l. Cog. [ᶜεἵνῡμι E. I.;] l. ἀμφιάζω, -άσω · ἐσθεῖν pf. ἤσθημαι.
ἐνοχλέω *annoy*, -ήσω, &c.; aug. ἠνωχ-, v. l. ἠνοχ- or ἐνωχ-, 282 b.
[ἐολέω *press, trouble ;* see εἰλ-.]
ἑορτάζω *keep a feast*, -άσω, &c.; aug. ἑωρ- 279 d : [ὀρτάζω ι.]
ἐπ-αν-ορθόω *set upright*, -ώσω, &c.; aug. ἐπηνωρ- 282 b.
[ἐπ-αυρέω r. & ἐπ-αυρίσκω r. (v, k², αὐρ-) *enjoy*, M.; ἐπαυρήσομαι Z. 353, ἐπηυράμην l. +, oftener 2 a. ἐπηῦρον, p. 81,] ἐπηυρόμην Eur. Hel. 469. Cog. ἀπαυράω *take away*, po., ao. ἀπηυράμην ? [pt. ἀπούρας 114, A. 356, ἀπουράμενος, Hes. Sc. 173, f. ἀπουρήσουσιν X. 489 v. l.]
ἐπι-μέλομαι & ἐπι-μελέομαι *care for ;* see μέλω.
ἐπ-ίσταμαι *understand;* see ἵστημι.
ἕπω (f³, σεπ-, σπ- c³) *be after* or *busy with* (act. scarce used exc. in comp.), M. ἕπομαι sequor, *follow ;* ipf. εἱπόν m. 279 c ; ᶜἕψω, ἕψομαι, ao. m. ?, 2 a. ᶜἵσπον (σπω, σποιμι, &c.),

ἑσπόμην (σπῶμαι, &c.) & (by redupl. & change of initial σ, σεσπ- ἐσπ-, 284e, 345) ch. po. ἐσπόμην (ἐσπωμαι, &c.), [imv. σπεῖο 323 c; ao. p. περι-έφθην, Hdt. 6. 15.] Cog. r. or l. ἕσπω m.
ἐράω love, desire, M. po. ἐράσμαι & oftener ἔραμαι; |ἠρασάμην;] ἤρασμαι, l., -σθην f. Po. cog. ἐρασσεύω, Æsch. Pr. 893, |ἐρατίζω, Λ. 551.]
ἐργάζομαι work; ἐργάσομαι, εἰργασάμην 279 c; εἴργασμαι, -σθην f. See ἔρδω.
ἔργω, -γνῦμι, ἔργω, see εἴργω, εἴργω.
ἔρδω & ἔρδω (f, Ϝεργ- & Ϝερδ-, cf. 168, ἐργ-) WORK, do, po. & l. (ἔρδω Hdt.), M.; ἔρξω, ἔρξα [ἔρξα?]; [2 pf. ἔοργα 312 b, plp. ἐώργειν 279 d, δ. 693, εὔργεα 284 b, 291 c, Hdt. 1. 127.] Cog. ἐργάζομαι, ῥέζω, q. v.
ἐρείδω prop, ch. po., M.; ἐρείσω l., ᶜm., ao.; ᶜἤρεικα & l. ᶜἐρήρεικα, ἐρήρεισμαι & ἤρεισμαι [3 p. ἐρηρέδαται, -ατο, 329 a, 3 f. ἐρερείσομαι? Hipp.,] ἠρείσθην.
ἐρείκω (h, ἐρικ-) rend, break, ᶜM.; ἤρειξα, m. l., 2 a. ἤρικον po.; ἐρήριγμαι, ἠρείχθην l. Cog. ῥήγνῦμι q. v., [ἐρέχθω, ε. 83.]
ἐρείπω (h, ἐριπ-) throw down, r. in Att. prose; ἐρείψω, ao. a. ᶜm., 2 a. ἤριπον fell, Ε. 47, m. l.; [2 pf. ᶜἐρήριπα have fallen, Ξ. 55,] ἐρήριμμαι & l. ἤρειμμαι, ἠρείφθην, [2 a. ἠρίπην Pind. O. 2. 76.] Cog. ῥίπτω throw.
ἐρέσσω i², row, po. or l.; [ao. ἤρεσα.]
ἐρεύθω & ἐρυθαίνω (h, nᵇ, ἐρυθ-, cf. rubeo & Germ. röthen) make red, REDDEN, po. or l., M.; [ἐρεύσω? Σ. 329 v. l., ao. lb., ἐρύθηρα l., ao. p. opt. ᶜἐρευθείην, Hipp. Cog. ἐρυθαίνω, ἐρυθριάω, -άσω.
ἐρίζω (j, ἐριδ-) rixor, contend, [M. +]; ἐρίσω l., ao. a. m.; ἤρικα l., [ἐρήρισμαι. Cog. ἐριδαίνω, ao. ἐρίδηνα l., ἐριδήσασθαι or ἐριζήσασθαι Ψ. 792; ἐριδμαίνω.]
ἕρπω (f³, σερπ-) serpo, creep, po. or l.; ἕρψω, εἴρψα l. 279 c. Cog. ἐρπύζω po. +, ᶜ-ύσω, εἴρπυσα.
ἔρρω go away, cf. erro, ruo; ἐρρήσω 311, ao.; ᶜἤρρηκα. [Cog.? ao. ἀπό-ερσα swept away, Z. 348.]
ἐρυγγάνω (nᵇ, ἐρυγ-) ructo, erūgo, belch, ERUCT, [M. & ἐρεύγομαι I. & E. +; ἐρεύξομαι I.,] ao. l., 2 a. ἤρυγον.

ἐρύκω hold back, ch. po. & I., [M.; ἐρύξω,] ao., [2 a. ἠρύκακον 284 e. Cog. ἐρυκάνω & ἐρυκανάω, a. 199, κ. 429.]
ἐρύω & εἰρύω (Ϝερυ-) draw, E. & I., M. draw to one's self, protect; ἐρύσω l. (ἐρύω 305 f, X. 67) & ᶜεἰρύσω l., m., εἴρυσα m. +; εἰρῦμαι & -νσμαι, -ύσθην; see 279 c. [Nude pr. & ipf. forms (326 c): act. inf. εἰρύμεναι 333 c, Hes. Op. 816; mid. ἔρυται Ap. Rh. 2. 1208, εἰρύαται Α. 239, ἔρυσο, -ῦτο, -υντο, Χ. 507, εἴρυτο, -υντο, Π. 542, ἔρυσθαι ε. 484, εἰρυσθαι ψ. 82; pass. ἔρῦτο Hes. Th. 301. Some regard these mid. & pass. forms as pret. pf. & plf.] See ῥύομαι.
ἔρχομαι (ἐρχ-, ἐλυθ- x, ἐλευθ- h) go, come; ipf. ἠρχόμην scarcely in Att., exc. in comp.; ἐλεύσομαι scarcely in Att. prose, 2 a. ἦλθον cᴮ (po. ἤλυθον), [D. ἤνθον 168. 3, Theoc. 16. 9, Lac. ἦλσον 169 d, Ar. Lys. 105; for ἤλυθα, sync. ἦλθα, see 327 b]; 2 pf. ἐλήλυθα [εἰλήλουθα 134 a, nude 1 p. εἰλήλουθμεν 326 c, γ. 81.] For the pr. exc. in the ind., the ipf., & the fut., the Att. comm. used other verbs, esp. εἶμι.
ἐρωτάω (o², ἐρ-) inquire, ask; ἐρωτήσω & ἐρήσομαι 311, ἠρώτησα, 2 a. m. ἠρόμην [imv. ἔρειο 323 c, Λ. 611]; ἠρώτηκα, -μαι, -θην. [Ερ. & I. εἰρομαι Λ. 553 (also 2 s. ἔρεαι Hes. Cert.), -ήσομαι · εἰρωτάω & -έω 322 a, Hdt. 4. 145; ἐρέω, Η. 128; ἐρεείνω +, Ζ. 145.]
ἐσθίω, & po. + ἔσθω & ἔδω, Ω. 415, Eur. Cyc. 245 (ἐδ-, ἐσθ- q¹ 147, ἐσθιw, φαγ- x) edo, EAT; f. ἔδομαι (l. φάγομαι, ἐδοῦμαι? 305 a), 2 ao. ἔφαγον; ἐδήδοκα 312 d, iv. 8. 20, [2 pf. ἔδηδα, P. 542, ἐδήδομαι, χ. 56,] ᶜἐδήδεσμαι, ἠδέσθην. [Nude pr. inf. ἔδμεναι 326 c, 333 c, Ν. 36.]
ἐστιάω feast, entertain, M.; ἐστιάσω m., εἰστίασα 279 c, m. l.; εἰστίακα, -μαι, -θην, f. l.: [ἱστιάω Ι.]
εὕδω, comm. καθ-εύδω, sleep; ipf. ηὗδον, εὖδον, ἐκάθευδον, 278 d, 282 b; εὑδήσω 311, ᶜao.; ᶜεὔδηκα l.
εὐεργετέω benefit, -ήσω, &c.; aug. εὐερ- & εὐηρ- 283. 2.
εὑρίσκω (k², εὑρ-) find, M.; εὑρήσω m. 311 b, ao. a. l., 2 a. εὗρον or ηὗρον m. 278 d (εὑράμην 327 b); εὕρηκα, -ημαι, -έθην f. 310 d.

§ 50.   ἔχθω   VERBS.   θνήσκω   77

ἔχθω, ἐχθαίρω, & ἐχθραίνω (ο, n⁶, ἐχθ-), hate, ch. po.; ao. ἤχθηρα, m. l., ἤχθρηνα l. M. or P. ἔχθομαι & ἐχθαίρομαι be hateful or hated, f. ἐχθαροῦμαι, pf. l. ἤχθημαι· comm. ἀπεχθάνομαι n⁴; -εχθήσομαι 311, 2 a. -ηχθόμην; -ήχθημαι.

ἔχω & ἴσχω (σεχ-, ἐχ- f³, ἐχ- d, σχ- c³, σχε- c⁶, ἰσχ- r³ d) have, hold (have belonging rather to ἔχω, ἕξω, and hold to ἰσχω, σχήσω), M.; ipf. εἶχον & ἴσχον 278 s; ἕξω m. & σχήσω m., [ἔσχησα r.,] 2 a. ἔσχον m. (σχῶ, σχοίην & ᶜσχοῖμι 293 c, σχές like θές 314 d, ᶜσχε r., σχεῖν, σχών, m. σχώμαι, &c.), po. ἔσχεθον, Æsch. Pr. 16 [ᶜm. Theoc.], ἔσχηκα [pt.συν-οχωκώς, Β. 218, as for -οχωχως 312d, cf. 281c, 159], ἔσχημαι [plf. 3 p. ἐπ-ώχατο 312 d, 329 a], ἐσχέθην l. or l., f. l. Cp. ἀμπ-έχω or ἀμπ-ίσχω 159 d (ipf. m. ἠμπειχόμην 282 b, Pl. Phædo 87 b); ἀν-έχω (2 a. m. ἀνεσχόμην, oftener ἠνεσχόμην 282 b, po. ἠνσχόμην 136, Ω. 518). Cog. ᶜἰσχνέομαι n¹⁰ or ᶜἰσχέομαι v (see ὑπισχνέομαι), [ἰσχάνω, ἰσχανάω, P. 747, 572;] ὀχέω bear.

ἕψω, less Att. ἑψέω, boil, cook; ἑψήσω m. 311, ao.; ἥψηκα? l., -μαι, -θην, f. l.

Ζ.

ζάω, live, see 42 a, (nude ipf. ἔζην r. Dem. 702. 2, later imv. ζῆθι po.); ζήσω m., ao. a.; ἔζηκα. The Att. preferred ζάω in the pr. & ipf., but elsewhere βιόω q. v. Cog. po. or l., ζώω, Soph. El. 157, or r. ζόω.

ζεύγνυμι (n⁷, ζυγ-, ζευγ- h, cf. jugum, jung-o) join, YOKE, M.; ζεύξω m., ao.; ᶜἔζευχα l., -γμαι, -χθην, f. l., 2 a. ἐζύγην; 47. Cog. ζυγόω, ζυγέω.

ζώννυμι (n⁸, ζο-) gird, M.; ζώσω m. l., ao.; ἔζωκα l., -σμαι, -σθην 307 d.

Η.

ἥδω (f g, ϝαδ-) please, M. delight in; ἥσω l., ao. a. [m. ι. 353]; ἥσθην f. Cog. ἀνδάνω q. v.; old pt. as adj. (ϝαδμενος 148) ἄσμενος pleased, glad; ἡδύνω sweeten, ἥδῦνα, ἥδυσμαι 304 b, -ύνθην, l. -ύσθην.

[ἡλαίνω, ἡλάσκω, see ἀλάομαι.]
ἧμαι sit, pret.;. see ἵζω & 46 c.

ἡμί I say, ἦν I said; see φημί & 45 u. [ἡμύω bow, sink; ἡμύσω, ao. +; pf. 3 s. ὑπ-εμνήμῡκε 281 d, X. 491.]

Θ.

θάλλω (l, θαλ-) bloom, flourish; θαλλήσω l. 311, 1 a. ᶜἔθηλα l., 2 a. ἔθαλον r. or l.; 2 pf. pret. τέθηλα [pt. τεθαλυῖα 325 e. Cog. θαλέω, θαλέθω, θηλέω, τηλεθάω.]

θάπτω (t, θαφ-) bury; θάψω ao.; τέθαμμαι, 3 f. τεθάψομαι, [ἐθάφθην l.;] 2 a. ἐτάφην f. d¹. Cf. τέθηπα.

θαυμάζω wonder, M. pr. l.; θαυμάσομαι, less Att. -σω, ao. a., m. l.; τεθαύμακα, -σμαι, ἐθαυμάσθην f.: [l. θωυμάζω or θωμάζω, 131 e. Cog. θαυμαίνω.]

[θε- pray for; ao. m. 3 p. θέσσαντο Pind. N. 5. 18, pt. θεσσάμενος Hes.]

θείνω (h, θεν-) fendo, strike, smite, po.; θενῶ, [ἔθεινα, Φ. 491,] 2 a. ἔθενον.
θέλω, wish, will; see ἐθέλω.
θέρω warm, ch. po., A. r. & l., M. θέρομαι· [θέρσομαι 152 d, τ. 507; 2 a. p. ἐθέρην, ρ. 23.] Cog. [θέρμω,] θερμαίνω.

θέω (f¹², θεϝ-) run, see 42 a; θεύσομαι, -σω l. & r.; ao. & pf. supplied by τρέχω, &c:

θηράω hunt, -άσω, &c., see 42 g; oftener in Att. prose, θηρεύω, -εύσω, &c.

θιγγάνω (n⁵, θιγ-) tango, τοuch (in Att. prose r. & only 2 a., but rather ἅπτομαι); θίξομαι or -ξω, 2 a. ἔθιγον, m. l.; 3 f. τεθίξομαι?, ἐθίχθην l.

θλίβω g, press; θλίψω [m. ρ. 221], ao. a.; τέθλιφα l., -ιμμαι, ἐθλίφθην, later 2 a. ἐθλίβην, f. l.: [φλίβω l. D. 168. 2.]

θνήσκω (k⁶, θαν-, θνα- c⁵⁷) die (comm. cp. w. ἀπό in prose, exc. in the complete tenses, which are rarely cp.); θανοῦμαι (κατ-θανοῦμαι po.136 d, Eur. Med. 1386), 2 a. ἔθανον; τέθνηκα (2 pf. pl. & du. τέθναμεν, -ατε, -ᾶσι, -ατον, iv.2.17, 1.19, X.52, opt. τεθναίην Σ. 98, imv. τέθναθι X. 365, inf. τεθνάναι Th. 8. 92, po. τεθν(α-ε)ᾶναι? Æsch. Ag. 539, pt. τεθνᾱώς, Pind. N. 10. 139, ct. τεθνεώς 120 i & later τεθνώς, -ῶσα, -ώς & -ός 233 a, τ. 331, vii. 4. 19, Hdt. 1. 112, [τεθνηώς or -ειώς 325 d, P. 161,] plp. 3 p. ἐτέθνασαν Hel. 6.

4. 16), 3 f. τεθνήξω & -ομαι 319 b. See κτείνω. Cog. θανατόω put to death, θανατάω desire death, 378 d.
θοινάω feast, po., M.; -άσομαι & -ήσομαι, &c., 310 a.
θερεῖν, θόρνυμαι, leap; see θρώσκω.
θράσσω disturb: see ταράσσω.
θραύω break; θραύσω ao.; τέθραυσμαι (τεθραυμαι?), ἐθραύσθην, f. l.
θρύπτω (t, θρυφ-) crush, M. put on airs; θρύψω l., m., ᶜao. a.; τέθρυμμαι, ἐθρύφθην, f. l., [2 a. ᶜ ἐτρύφην d¹, Γ. 363.] Cog. τρυφάω.˙
θρώσκω (k⁴⁶, θορ-) leap, ch. po:; ᶜθοροῦμαι, 2 a. ἔθορον. Cog. θόρνυμαι.
[θύω rush, rage; ᶜθύσω ?l., ἔθυσα l. Cog. θύνω, θινέω, θυίω.]
θύω (ῠ) sacrifice, M.; θύσω m., ao.; τέθῠκα, -ῠμαι, ἐτύθην, f. l., 159; 44.

I.

ἰάλλω (l, ἰαλ-) send, po. (or ἰάλλω d²); ᶜἰαλῶ, [ᶜἴηλα.] Cog. ἄλλομαιq. v.
[ἰάχω shout, +; pf. ᶜἴαχα pret. B. 316.] Po. cog. ἰαχέω, ἰακχέω.
ἰδεῖν, ἰδέσθαι, see, 2 a.; see ὁράω.
ἱδρόω sudo, sweat (for ct. & prolonged forms, see 324);˛ ἱδρώσω ao.; ἵδρωκα l., -μαι l. Cog., ἰδίω, Ar. Pax 85, [l. .ι. ἰδρώω.]
ἱδρύω (ῠ E.) seat, set up, M.; ἱδρύσω m., ao.; ἵδρῠκα, -ῠμαι, -όθην & -ύνθην n¹, Γ. 78, f. l. Cog. ἵζω q. v.
ἵεμαι or ἴεμαι hasten; see 45 p.
ἵζω (j, σεδ-, ἐδ-f³, ἰδ-b², cf. sedeo, sīdo) SEAT, SET, SIT, ch. po. or dial., M. ἵζομαι & ἔζομαι sit; ᶜἰζήσω l., ao. l., 311 a; f. m. ἔσομαι 151 (ἐφ-ἐσσεσθαι I. 455, εἴσομαι l.), ao. εἷσα m. 279 c, B. 549, Eur. Iph. T. 946 [pt. ᶜεἵσας, -άμενος, Hdt. 3. 126, 1. 66]; ἵζηκα l., ἧμαι c¹, pret., see 46 c (2 s. κάθ-ῃ Acts 23. 3, cf. 331 b), ᾗσθην? In Att. prose, comm. καθίζω, M. -ίζομαι & -έζομαι; καθίσω, -ιῶ 305 a, ii. 1. 4, m. l., f. m. καθιζήσομαι & καθεδοῦμαι 305 a [καθεδήσομαι l.), ao. ἐκάθισα & καθῖσα 282 b, m., ἐκαθίζησα l., [καθεῖσα m. +;] κεκάθικα l., κάθῐμαι 46 c (comic or l. imv. κάθου Ja. 2. 3), 3 f. καθήσομαι, ἐκαθέσθην l., f. ? Cog. ἰζάνω, ἱδρύω q. v.
ἵημι (ἐ-, ἱε- r⁸) send (ch. in comp. & many forms only so found), M.

hasten, desire; pr. a. ind. 2 s. ἀφ-εῖς Rev. 2. 20, 3 p. συν-ιοῦσι Mat. 13. 13, pt. συν-ιῶν Rom. 3. 11, [imv. ξύν-ιε, inf. συν-ιεῖν, Theog. 1240, 565 ;] ipf. 1 s. ᶜἵειν or ᶜἵην 315 b, 3 s. ἠφ-ιε 282 b, Mk. 1. 34, 3 p. ἀφ-ίεσαν iv. 5. 30, ἠφίεσαν Hcl. 4. 6. 11 ; ἥσω ᶜm., ἧκα ᶜm. 306, 2 a. ᶜεἷμεν ᶜm., Λ. 642, Hier. 7. 11 ; ᶜεἷκα, ii. 3. 13, ᶜεἷμαι, Th. 1. 6 [ind. 3 p. l. ἀφ-έωνται D.? Lk. 5. 23, ἀν-έωνται or -έονται Hdt. 2. 165 v. l., pt. με-μετ-ιμένος 282 b, 167 a, Hdt. 6. 1], ᶜεἵθην, Eur. Ph. 1376, ᶜf. Ven. 7. 11. See also 45 k, n, r, j, 315. Some forms are made as from shorter themes, ἵω, ἔω.
ἱκνέομαι (n¹⁰, ἱκ-), po. ἵκάνω n⁸, [m., & ἵκω,] come, in prose usu. ἀφ-ικνέομαι · ἵξομαι [ἰξῶ D., Ar. Ach. 742], ao. a. l. [ἷξον 327 a], 2 a. m. ἱκόμην; ἷγμαι. Cog. ἥκω 114 d, ἱκετεύω supplicate.˙
ἱλάσκομαι (k, ἵλα-) propitiate [E. ἱλάομαι & ἵλαμαι]; ἱλάσομαι ao.; ἱλάσθην, f. l. Cog. ἱλέομαι po., ἱλεύομαι, [& as fr. ἵλημι be propitious, pr. imv. ἴλαθι 297 d, ἴληθι 335 dʳ, pret. sub. & opt. ἱλήκω, ἱλήκοιμι, φ. 365.]
ἵλλω roll, [ἐπ-ιλλίζω,] see εἰλ-. [ἱμάσσω i², lash; ao. ἵμασα, ε. 380.]
ἱπποτροφέω keep horses; -ήσω ao.;
ἱπποτρόφηκα or -τετρόφηκα 283 a.
ἵπταμαι fly; see πέτομαι.
[ἵσᾱμι know, D.; see ὁράω.
ἵστημι (r⁸, στα-, cf. Lat. sta-re) statuo, set up, STATION, M. sto, STAND; στήσω m., ao., 2 a. ἔστην; ἕστηκα (l. pf. trans. ἔστᾰκα & 1 ao. ἔστᾰσα; so some explain ἐστᾱσαν M. 56), [2 pf. l. ἑστέατε -ᾱσι 335 c, pt. ἑστεώς 120 i, Hdt. 2. 38,] ᶜἕσταμαι r., &c. See 45, 46. Cp. ἐπ-ίσταμαι understand (2 s. ἐπίστᾱ 297 h, I. ἐπίστεαι 322 a, Hdt. 7. 135) ; ἐπι-στήσομαι ; ἠπιστήθην 282 b. Cog. ἱστάνω, l. στήκω & ἐστήκω, Rom. 14. 4, [στεῦμαι 326 e.]
ἴσχω, ἰσχνέομαι, hold; see ἔχω.

K.

καθαίρω (h, καθαρ-) purify, M.; καθαρῶ m., ἐκάθηρα m., v. 7. 35, & ἐκάθᾱρα, Œc. 18. 8, 152 c; κεκάθαρκα l., -μαι, ἐκαθάρθην, f. l., 2 a. l. ἐκαθάρην ?

§ 50.   καθέζομαι   VERBS.   κλίνω   79

καθέζομαι, κάθημαι, καθίζω, see ἵζω.
καθ-εύδω *sleep;* see εὕδω & 282 b.
καίνυμαι (n⁹, καδ-, καιδ- h) *excel,*
po.; κέκασμαι, Eur. El. 616 [*pt.* κε-
καδμένος D., 148 b, Pind. O. 1. 42.]
καίνω (h, καν-) *kill,* in prose usu.
cp. w. κατά, i. 6. 2; κανῶ, 2 a. ἔκα-
νον; 2 pf. r. κέκονα or κέκανα, 114.
Cog. κτείνω.
καίω (h, καϝ-, καυ- f², κα- f¹, κε- b)
burn, also Att. κάω g, 44, 309 b [κήω
H. 408 r. *l.*], *M.*; καύσω, *m.* r., ἔκαυσα
[ᶜ*m.* Hdt. 8. 19, ἔκηα *m.* or ἔκεια A.
40, φ. 176,] *pl.* po. κέας, Æsch. Ag.
849; ᶜκέκαυκα, -μαι, ἐκαύθην f. [2 a.
ἐκάην E. I. +, μ. 13, f. 1.]
καλέω calo, CALL, *M.*; καλέσω *m.*,
[καλέω, Γ. 383] Att. usu. καλῶ *m.*,
305 b, ἐκάλεσα *m.*; κέκληκα cᶜ, -μαι
(*opt.* 317 c), 3 f. κεκλήσομαι, ἐκλήθην f.
Cog. κικλήσκω po., [κάλημι Æ. 335 b,
προ-καλίζομαι σ. 20;] κλητεύω *sum-
mon;* κλέω, κλῄζω, *celebrate.*
καλινδέω *roll;* see κυλίνδω.
κάμνω (n, καμ-) *labor;* καμοῦμαι,
2 a. ἔκαμον [*m.*]; κέκμηκα c⁷, 308
[*pt.* κεκμηώς 325 d, Th. 3. 59 ?].
κάμπτω (t, καμπ-) *bend, M.*; κάμψω
ao.; κέκαμμαι 148 a, 41, ἐκάμφθην, f. 1.
Cog. γνάμπτω po.
κάω *burn,* not ct.; see καίω.
κεδάννῡμι, κεδάω; see σκεδάννῡμι.
κεῖμαι (c¹, κεε-; but accented without
regard to the contraction, & deemed
by some a pret.) *lie* (cf. quie-sco), see
45 q, r [2 s. κατά-κειαι 297 h, Hom.
Merc. 254, 3 s. κέσκετο 332 d, 3 p.
κέαται, -το 329 a, κέονται (as fr. κε-,
315) X. 510; *sub.* 3 s. ct. κῆται or
(κέεται 326 d) κεῖται Ω. 554; old pr. as
fut. κέω, η. 342, κείω τ. 340, § 305 f].
κείρω (h, καρ-, κερ- b) *shear, M.*;
κερῶ *m.*, ἔκειρα *m.* [ἔκερσα *m.* 152 d,
N. 546]; ᶜκέκαρκα l., -μαι, [1 a. *pt.*
κερθείς, Pind. P. 4. 146,] 2 a. ἐκάρην
I. or l.
κεκαδήσω, κεκαδών, see χάζω.
κεκαδήσομαι, see κήδω *vex.*
κέλομαι *command,* po. +, ch. E.;
κελήσομαι ao. 311 b, 2 a. κεκλόμην or
ἐκεκλόμην 284 e. Cog. [κέκλομαι l.,]
κελεύω, -εύσω, 307 b.
κεντέω (ν, κεντ-) *prick;* κεντήσω
ao. [*inf.* κένσαι 156 b, Ψ. 337]; &c.
κεράννῡμι (n⁸, κερα-) *mix;* κεράσω

l., *m.* l., ao., [ἔκρησα E. I., η. 164];
κεκέρακα l., κέκρᾱμαι c⁴ & l. κεκέρα-
σμαι, ἐκράθην f., Th. 6. 5, & ἐκεράσθην,
v. 4. 29: [κεράω E. +, κέραιε 322 c,]
ρο., I., or l. κιρνέω & κίρνημι n³, b.
κερδαίνω (n⁶, κερδ-) *gain;* κερδα-
νῶ, ἐκέρδᾱνα 152 c, [I. or l. κερδήσω
m., ao. *a.*, 311;] κεκέρδηκα (l. -ακα
or -αγκα), -ημαι l., ἐκερδάνθην l.
κεύθω (h, κυθ-) *hide,* po.; κεύσω
[ᶜao., 2 a. ἔκυθον γ. 16, § 284 e;]
2 pf. pret. κέκευθα, [κέκευθμαι r. Cog.
κευθάνω, Γ. 453.]
[κήδω (g, καδ-) *vex;* κηδήσω ᶜao.
311 c; 2 pf. pret. κέκηδα *sorrow.*]
M. κήδομαι *sorrow, care;* ἐκηδεσάμην
r., Æsch. Th. 138; [3 f. κεκαδήσομαι,
θ. 353. Cp. ἀ-κηδέω + *neglect,* -ήσω l.,
ἀκήδεσα, Ξ. 427.]
κίδνημι *spread;* see σκεδάννῡμι.
κῑνέω, -ήσω, &c., *move; M.* [& κί-
νυμαι, Δ. 281.] Cog. κίω *go,* po., [*pt.*
κιών· 2 a. μετ-ελιᾱθον 353 a, Σ. 581.]
[κιχάνω *m.*,] Att. κιγχάνω, v. l. κιχάνω (n⁶, nᵇ, κιχ-) *find,* po.; κιχή-
σομαι, [-σω l., ao. *a.* l., *m.*,] 2 a. ἔκιχον. [Cog. κίχημι (κιχε- v; not in
pr. *ind.*), *m. pl.* κιχήμενος 314 b.].
κίχρημι *lend;* see χράω.
κλάζω (j³, κλαγ-, κλαγγ- n⁸) *clan-
go, scream,* CLANG, ch. po.; κλάγξω
ao., 2 a. ἔκλαγον; 2 pf. pret. κέκλαγγα, Ven. 3. 9 [κέκληγα, B. 222, *pt.*
κεκλήγοντες 326 b, ξ. 30, but -ῶτες
Bek.], 3 f. κεκλάγξομαι 319 b. Po. cog.
κλαγγάνω +, κλαγγαίνω, κλαγγέω.
κλαίω (h, κλαϝ-, κλαυ- f², κλα- f¹)
weep, also Att. κλάω g, 309 b, *M.*;
κλαύσομαι, -σω l. (-οῦμαι 305 d, Ar.
Pax 1081), also Att. κλαιήσω or κλᾱ-
ήσω 311 c, ἔκλαυσα *m.* [2 a.? ἔκλᾶον,
Theoc. 14. 32]; κέκλαυμαι (-σμαι l.),
3 f. κεκλαύσομαι, ἐκλαύσθην f. l.
κλάω *break, M.*; κλάσω l., ᶜ*m.* l.,
ao. *a., m.* l., [nude 2 a. *pt.* ἀπο-κλάς
Anac. 17]; κέκλασμαι, ἐκλάσθην ᶜf.
κλείω claudo, *shut;* κλείσω, ao. *a.*
ᶜ*m.*; κέκλεικα, -μαι & -σμαι 307 c;
3 f. κεκλείσομαι, ἐκλείσθην f.: [I. κληΐω,
ἐκλήϊσα, &c.;] older Att. κλῄω, -ήσω.
κλέπτω (t, κλαπ-, κλεπ- b) clepo,
steal, ᶜ*M.* l., κλέψω *m.*, ao. *a.*; κέκλοφα 312 c, κέκλεμμαι, ἐκλέφθην,
comm. 2 a. ἐκλάπην.
κλίνω (g, κλῐν-) clino, *bend,* INCLINE,

M.; κλῑνῶ ^c*m.*, ἔκλῑα *m.*; κέκλῐκα l., -μαι, 304a, ἐκλίθην f. [ἐκλίνθην+], 2 a. ^cἐκλίνην ^cf.

κλύω *hear*, po.; ipf. ἔκλυον also as ao.; unde 2 a. *imv.* κλῦθι A. 37 [κέκλῦθι 284 e, K. 284, *m. pl.* κλύμενος in-clĭtus; κέκλυκα Epich.]

κνάω *scrape, M.*, see 120g; κνήσω, &c. (ἐκνήσθην 307 d). Cog. κναίω, κνίζω, κνήθω l., κνόω po.

κολούω *maim;* κολούσω l., ao.; κεκόλουμαι or -σμαι l., ἐκολούθην or -σθην, f. l., 307 e.

κομίζω (j¹, κομιδ-) *bring;* see 39 e.

κόπτω (t, κοπ-) *cut, M. bewail;* κόψω, f. l., ao.; ^cκέκοφα [2 pf. *pl.* κεκοπώς N. 60], κέκομμαι, 3 f. ^cκεκόψομαι, i. 5. 16, 2 a. ἐκόπην f.

κορέννῡμι (n⁸, κορε-) *satiate*, ch. po., *M.*; [κορέσω Hdt. 1. 212, *m.* l., κορέω, 305 b, 323 c, N. 831,] ἐκόρεσα [*m.*; 2 pf. *pl.* intrans. κεκορηώς 325 d, σ. 372,] κεκόρεσμαι [-ημαι Ε. 1.], 3 f. κεκορήσομαι l., ἐκορέσθην, f. l.: κορέω & κορέσκω r. l.

κορύσσω (i², κορυθ-) *arm*, po., *M.*; [ao. *pl.* κορυσσάμενος Τ. 397; κεκορυθμένος 148 b, P. 3 +.]

[**κοτέω** + *be angry, M.*; κοτέσσομαι? a. 101, ao. a. *m.*; 2 pf. *pl.* κεκοτηώς 325 d, Φ. 456.] Cog. κοταίνω po., Æsch. Th. 485.

κράζω (j², κραγ-) *cry out*, pr. r.; κράξω l., *m.* l., ao. a. 1., 2 a. ^cἔκραγον v. 1. 14; 2 pf. pret. κέκρᾱγα vii. 8. 15 (*imv.* κέκραχθι 320 f), 3 f. κεκράξομαι 319 b. Cog. κεκράγω l. 326 c, κλάζω q. v., κρώζω CROAK, κλώζω.

κραίνω (h, κραν-) *fulfil*, po. & I. [κραιαίνω 135]; κρανῶ *m.*, ἔκρᾱνα, *m.* l., [ἔκρηνα, ἐκρήηνα, 130 a, 135;] pf. p. 3 s. κέκρανται Eur. Hipp. 1255 (or 3 p. for -ανται?), ἐκράνθην f.

κρεμάννῡμι (n⁸, κρεμα-) & l. κρεμάω *suspend, hang;* κρεμάσω, Att. κρεμῶ [κρεμόω 322 c], ἐκρέμασα *m.*; κεκρέμασμαι l., ἐκρεμάσθην. Cog. κρέμαμαι, -ήσομαι, iv. 1. 2; κρήμνημι po. or l.

κρίζω (j², κριγ- or κρικ-) CREAK, po.; ἔκρῐξα l., [2 a. 3 s. κρῐκε or κρίγε Π. 470;] 2 pf. *pl.* κεκρῑγότες Ar. Av. 1521.

κρίνω (g, κρῐν-) *judge, M.*; κρῐνῶ *m.*, ἔκρῑνα *m.*; κέκρῐκα, -μαι, ἐκρίθην f. [ἐκρίνθην], 304a. Cp. ἀπο-κρίνομαι

answer, -κρῐνοῦμαι, -κέκρῐμαι, ao. dπ-εκρῑνάμην & later -εκρίθην.

κρούω *beat, M.*; κροῠσω *m.*, ao. *m.*; κέκρουκα, ^c-μαι & ^c-σμαι, ἐκρούσθην, 307 e. [Cog. κροαίνω *stamp*, Z. 507.]

κρύπτω (t, κρυβ- & κρυφ-) *conceal, hide, M.*; [iter. κρύπτασκον 332 e;] κρύψω *m.*, ao., 2 a. ^cἔκρυβον *m.* l.; κέκρυφα, -μμαι,[3f.κεκρύψομαι Hipp.] ἐκρύφθην, f. l., later 2 a. ἐκρύφην r. or ἐκρύβην f.: l. ^cκρύβω & κρύφω.

κτάομαι *acquire;* κτήσομαι ao.; κέκτημαι & less Att. ἔκτημαι 280 b, *have acquired*, pret. *possess* (κεκτῶμαι, -ήμην or -ῴμην, 317 c), 3 f. κεκτήσομαι (r. ἐκτ-), ἐκτήθην as *pass.*, f. l.

κτείνω (h, κτα-, κτᾰν- n, κτεν- b) *kill* (usu. cp. with ἀπό, or κατά po.); κτενῶ [κτανέω *m.*, Σ. 309], ἔκτεινα, 2 a. po.+ ἔκτανον, po. ἔκτᾰν *m.* 314 d; 2 pf. ^cἔκτονα, later 1 pf. ^cἔκτανκα, ^cἔκτακα, & ^cἐκτόνηκα, pf. *p. inf.* ^cἐκτάνθαι Polyb. 7. 7, [ἐκτάθην] ἐκτάνθην l. Cog. κτίννῡμι b, vi. 3. 5, or κτείνῡμι n⁹; καίνω q. v. As the *pass.* of κτείνω, the Att. comm. used θνήσκω.

κτίζω (z, κτι-) *build;* κτίσω, ao. a., *m.* po. r., [2 a. *pl.* ἐϋ-κτῐμενος, B. 501;] κέκτικα or ἔκτικι l. 280 c, ἔκτισμαι, -σθην, f. l.

κτυπέω v, *sound, crash*, ch. po., *M.*; ἐκτύπησα, [2 a. ἔκτυπον +, Θ. 75.]

κυλίνδω o¹, κυλινδέω v, & r. *or* l. κυλίω, *roll, M.*; κυλινδήσω l., ^cκυλίσομαι l., ἐκύλισα, ^c*m.* l.; κεκύλισμαι, ἐκυλίσθην f., ἐκυλινδήθην l. Cog. καλινδέω *m.*; ἁλίνδω or -έω, *m.* l., ^cἥλῐσα, ^cἥλικα.

κυνέω (n¹⁰, κυ-) *kiss*, po. +; κύσω l., ao., (κυνήσομαι r., ao. a. l.) Cp. προσ-κυνέω *worship*, -ήσω, &c. Cog. κυέω (-ήσω), κύω (ἔκῡσα), κυΐσκω, *conceive*.

κύρω *m.* & κῠρέω (g, v, κῠρ-) *meet, chance*, po., I., *or* l.; κύρσω ao. 152d, & κυρήσω ao.; κεκύρηκα, -μαι.

Λ.

λαγχάνω (n⁵, λαχ-, ληχ- g, λεγχn⁸ b) *obtain by lot;* λήξομαι [λάξομαι, Hdt. 7. 144], 2 a. ἔλαχον [redupl. & causative, 284 e]; εἴληχα 281, λέλογχα po., I., *or* l. [λελόγχᾱσι 328 c*, 134 a], εἴληγμαι, ἐλήχθην.

§ 50. λαμβάνω VERBS. μάομαι 81

λαμβάνω (n⁵, λαβ-, ληβ- g) *take*, *M. lay hold of;* λήψομαι, -ψω l., 2 a. ἔλαβον m. [redupl. 284 e]; εἴληφα 281, εἴλημμαι & po. λέλημμαι, 3 f. ᶜλελήψομαι l., ἐλήφθην f. (ᶜεἰλήφθην 281 b): [Ion. f. λάμψομαι n⁸, ao.ᵒa. m. r., λελάβηκα v, ᶜλέλαμμαι, ἐλάμφθην, Hdt. 9. 108, 51, 119, 4. 79: Hellen. λήμψομαι, ᶜἐλήμφθην, Acts 1. 8, 2.] Po. & I. cog. λάζυμαι & λάζομαι.

λάμπω *shine*, *M.*; λάμψω [ᵒm. I.], ao. a.; 2 pf. pret. λέλαμπα, ᶜἐλάμφθην l., ᵒf. l. [Cog. λαμπετάω.]

λανθάνω & ch. po. λήθω (n⁵, g, λαθ-) lateo, *lie hid, escape notice; M. forget,* in prose usu. cp. w. ἐπί· λήσω m., ao. a. po. +, m. l., 2 a. ἔλαθον m. [redupl. 284 e]; 2 pf. λέληθα, λέλησμαι [-ασμαι, E. 834], 3 f. λελήσομαι, Eur. Alc. 198, [ἐλήσθην ᶜf. l. +. Cog. ἐκ-ληθάνω *cause to forget*, η. 221.]

λάσκω (k³, λάκ-, cf. loquor) *sound, utter,* po. +; λακήσομαι, ao. a., 2 a. ἔλακον m. [redupl. 284 e]; 2 pf. pret. λέλᾱκα 312 a [-ηκα, pt. λελᾱκυῖα 325 e]. Po. cog. λακάζω Æsch., [ληκέω.]

[λάω, a Dor. pres. = ἐθέλω *wish;* ind. ct. λῶ, λῇς, λῇ, λῶμες, λῆτε, λῶντι, &c., 131 c, 328 a, Ar. Lys., &c. Cog. λιλαίομαι r¹ h, *desire eagerly;* pret. λελίημαι, M. 106.]

λέγω lego, Germ. legen, LAY, *gather,* (Att. only in comp., esp. w. σύν,) *M.*; λέξω m., ao., [nude 2 a. ἐλέγμην 326 e, ι. 335, imv. λέξο & λέξεο 327 a, I. 617, *inf.* ᵒλέχθαι, pt. ᵒλέγμενος;] ᶜεἴλοχα (ᵒ-εχα l.) 281, 312 c, Dem. 522. 12, ᵒλέλεγμαι, more Att. ᶜεἴλεγμαι, Th. 2. 10, ἐλέχθην, ᵒf. l., usu. in Att. 2 ao. ᶜἐλέγην ᵒf. Some have inferred a second stem, λεχ-, fr. the noun λέχος, *bed.*

λέγω *say, tell* (the same in origin with the preceding, & borrowing, ch. l., some of its special forms), *M.*; λέξω m., ao. a. ᵒm.; λέλεχα l. (classic εἴρηκα, see φημί), λέλεγμαι, 3 f. λελέξομαι, ἐλέχθην f. Cog. λογίζομαι *reckon.*

λείβω libo, *pour,* po. εἴβω e¹, Π. 11, *M.*; ἔλειψα m.

λείπω (h, λιπ-) linquo, LEAVE, r. λιμπάνω n⁵, *M.* remain [ipf. ἔλειπτο 326 e, Ap. Rh. 1. 45]; λείψω m., ao. l., 2 a. ἔλιπον m., 38; 2 pf. λέλοιπα, λέλειμμαι, 3 f. λελείψομαι, ἐλείφθην f., 2 a. ἐλίπην l., +?

λείχω lingo, Germ. lecken, LICK, not in Att. prose; λείξω l., ao.; [2 pf. pt. λελείχμώς o¹, Hes. Th. 826], ᶜἐλείχθην l. Cog. λιχμάω, λιχμάζω. λέπω (b, λαπ-) *peel,* ch. po., *M.*; ᵒλέψω ao.; [ᵒλέλεμμαι Epich. 109,] ᶜἐλάπην, f. l.

λεύσσω LOOK, po.; λεύσω ao. l. λήθω, ληθάνω, see λανθάνω.

ληΐζομαι *plunder, A. r.*; [ληΐσσομαι] ao.; λελήϊσμαι, [ἐληΐσθην.] In Att., some would contract the ηϊ into ῃ throughout. Cog. λῃστεύω.

λιγγ-; ao. λίγξε *twanged* (both onomatopes), 337 a, Δ. 125.

[λιλαίομαι, λελίημαι; see λάω.] λιμπάνω *leave*, Th. 8. 17; see λείπω. λίσσομαι i², r. λίτομαι, *pray,* po. +; [ἐλισάμην, λ. 35, 2 a. ἐλιτόμην, Il. 47.]

λόω & λούω (f¹², λοF-) lavo, *wash,* esp. the body, *M. bathe* (the ct. forms from λόω, as ἔλου, λοῦμαι, λοῦται, &c., are the more common; pr. *a. r.*); [λούσω] m., ao. *a. m.*; λέλουμαι, ἐλούθην, -σθην l.: [E. λοέω v, -έσω l., *m.*, ao., ζ. 221, 227; r. λουέω.]

λύω [usu. ῠ Hom.] *loose,* sec 37, 48 b; [iter. (ἀνα-λ) ἀλλύεσκεν 332 c, 136; 2 a. *m.* ἐλύμην 313 b, Φ. 80, 114; pf. opt. λελῦντο or -ῦτο σ. 238, § 317 c.]

M.

μαίνω (h, μαν-) *madden,* oftener μαίνομαι *be mad, rave;* [μανοῦμαι r., Hdt. 1. 109,] ἔμηνα [m. +]; μεμάνηκα l., -μαι l., 2 pf. pret. μέμηνα *am mad,* 2 a. ἐμάνην, f. l. Cog.,

μαίομαι *seek,* po. +; see μάομαι.

μανθάνω (n⁵, μαθ-) *learn:* μαθήσομαι [μαθεῦμαι D. 305 a], 2 a. ἔμαθον; μεμάθηκα, -μαι l.

μάομαι & μαίομαι h, *desire eagerly, feel after,* po. +; [μάσομαι ᵒao., λ. 591]; 2 pf. pret. μέμονα n b, *am eager,* Æsch. Th. 686, [pl. μέμαμεν, -ατε, -άασι, H. 260, imv. μεμάτω Δ. 304, pt. μεμάως Δ. 40, plp. 3 p. μέμασαν B. 863, § 320 c, 325 d. The Dor. has forms as fr. μω-, ch. nude or ct., as 3 s. μῶται, imv. μῶσο or μώεο (Mem. 2. 1. 20), inf. μῶσθαι

GR. TAB. 4* F

82 μάομαι TABLES. νάσσω § 50.

(Pl. Crat. 406 a).] Cog. μαιμάω po., μνάομαι woo, μαίνομαι rage, &c.
μάρναμαι fight, po.; sub. &c. μάρνωμαι, -αίμην (v. l. -οίμεθα 315c^r), -αο Ο. 475, -ασθαι, -άμενος; ipf. έμαρνάμην, Η. 300, Eur. Ph. 1142.
μάρπτω (t, μαρπ-) seize, po.; μάρψω ao., Ar. Eq. 197, [2 a. έμαρπον or έμαπον c¹ (redupl. 284c); μέμαρπα.]
μάσσω (i¹, μαγ-) knead, M.; μάξω ^c m., ao.; μέμαχα, -γμαι, έμάχθην po., 2 a. ^c έμάγην.
μάχομαι fight [μαχέομαι, Α. 272, pt. -ειόμενος or -εούμενος 134 a, ρ. 471, λ. 403]; μαχέσομαι ao., [-έομαι, Β. 366] Att. μαχοΰμαι, Ε. & l. μαχήσομαι ao.; μεμάχημαι (-εσμαι?), έμαχέσθην f. l.; 311 d. Cf. di-mico.
μέδω & -έω protect, rule, po. +; M. μέδομαι care for, devise; [μεδήσομαι 311, I. 650.] Cog. μήδομαι q. v. Cf. moderor, medeor, meditor.
μεθύσκω (k¹, μεθυ-) intoxicate, 379 b, M.; μεθύσω 1., ao.; μεμέθυσμαι l., έμεθύσθην, f. l.: μεθύω intrans., be intoxicated.
μειδιάω (μειδα-, μειδια-) smile; έμειδίασα [έμείδησα O. 47].
[μείρομαι (h, μαρ-, μερ- b) obtain, I. 616; 2 pf. έμμορα 284 d, l. έμμορον as 2 a. 326 b,] είμαρμαι 281 (as if for σε-σμαρ-μαι, έεμαρμαι 141, 142), Pl., [l. μεμόρηκα, -μαι & μέμορμαι.]
μέλλω be about to, intend, delay; μελλήσω 311, m. l., έμέλλησα & ήμέλλησα 279 a.
μέλω concern (often impers.), M. (in prose ch. cp. w. έπί or μετά) care for, concern; μελήσω [m. A. 523] ao. a.; [2 pf. μέμηλα ch. pret., B. 25,] μεμέληκα, -μαι [3 s. sync. μέμβλεται, -το, 146 b, 311 d, T. 343, Φ. 516], έμελήθην ^c f. Cp. έπιμέλομαι & -μελέομαι v, care for, -μελήσομαι, ao. l., -μεμέλημαι, έπεμελήθην f. Der. μελετάω study, practice.
μέμονα am eager; see μάομαι.
μένω maneo, reMAIN, wait; μενώ, έμεινα· μεμένηκα 311 b (2 pf. μέμονα? Eur. Iph. Α. 1495). Po. cog. μίμνω r¹ c², Æsch. Ag. 74, [μιμνάζω.]
μήδομαι devise, po., Φ. 413; μήσομαι, ao. έμησ-. Æsch. Pr. 477; see μέδω.
μηκάομαι? (g u, μακ-) bleat; [2 a. pt. μακών σ. 98; 2 pf. pret. pt. μεμη-

κώς, μεμακυΐα 325 e, 2 plp. έμέμηκον 326 b.] Like onomatopes, μυκάομαι, βληχάομαι, βρυχάομαι.
μιαίνω (h, μιαν-) stain, ^c M.; μιανώ, έμίανα & less Att. -ηνα 152c; μεμίαγκα l., -ασμαι & l. -αμμαι 304 b, έμιάνθην f. [3 p. μιάνθην 330 b, 134, Δ. 146.]
μίγνυμι (n⁷, μιγ-) & μίσγω 350, misceo, Germ. mischen, MIX, M.; μίξω [m.,] ao. a., m. l., [nude 2 a. έμίγμην 326 c;] μέμιχα l., -γμαι, 3 f. μεμίξομαι, έμίχθην f., 2 a. έμίγην f. 274 b^r. [Cog. μιγάζομαι, θ. 271.]
μιμνήσκω (r¹ k⁶, μνα-) remind (cf. moneo), M. re-miniscor, re-MEMBER, MENTION; μνήσω m., ao. a., m. po. +; μέμνημαι memini, remember, pret. 268 [2 s. μέμνηαι, -νῃ, 331 b], sub. &c. μεμνώμαι, -ήμην or -ῴμην, -ησο [μέμνεο 140, 134, Hdt. 5. 105]; &c., 317 s, 3 f. μεμνήσομαι, έμνήσθην f. 307 c. The old M. μνάομαι [remember, heed, pay attention to, ipf. 3 p. έμνώοντο 322 c, pt. μνωόμενος, δ. 106, & by like protraction imv. μνώεο Ap. R. 1. 896] passed into the sense of solicit, court, woo (in Att., cp. w. πρό, vii. 3. 18); έμνησάμην. Cog. [μνήσκω remind;] μνηστεύω woo; μνημονεύω remember, -σω, έμνημόνευκα 280.
μίσγω misceo, mix; see μίγνυμι.
μνάομαι, μνημονεύω, see μιμνήσκω.
μολοΰμαι, 1. pr. μολέω go; see βλώσκω.
μύζω, -έω, l. ^c -άω, suck; έμύζησα.
μυθέω, -ήσω, &c., say, po. +; [μυθεΐαι, μυθέαι, 323 c.]
μυκάομαι (g u, μυκ-) mugio, low, bellow, A. 1.; μυκήσομαι ao., [2 a. έμυκον, E. 749; 2 pf. pret. μέμυκα +, Σ. 580.] See μηκάομαι, & pf. of μύω shut eyes or lips; μύσω 1., ao.; μέμυκα, 310 d. Late καμμύω for κατα-μύω 136, Mat. 13. 15.

N.

ναίω (h, νᾰ-) dwell, settle, po.; [νάσσομαι, ao. a.] m.; νένασμαι l., ένάσθην. Der. ναιετάω po. [ναιετάωσα or -άουσα 322 c].
νάσσω i, stuff, pr. l.; [έναξα, φ. 122;] νέναομαι, Ar.,'νέναγμαι l. +.

§ 50. νεικέω VERBS. ὁμόργνῡμι 83

[νεικέω, -είω 323 c, chide; νεικέσω, ao. Γ. 59.]
νέμω distribute, pasture, M. possess, feed; νεμῶ m. (1. νεμήσω m., ao., 311 b), ἔνειμα m.; ᵒνενέμηκα, -μαι, vii. 3. 21, ἐνεμήθην (-έθην v. l.), f. l. Cog. νωμάω u², νομεύω, [νεμέθω.]
νέομαι [ct. νεῦμαι Σ. 136] go, come (also as fut. 305 f), po. +, Cyr. 4. 1. 11. Po. cog. νίσσομαι, f. νίσομαι ao.
ᵒνεφέω v, nubilo, gather clouds (cp. w. συν); ᵒνεφήσω l.; ᵒνένοφα Ar.
νέω (f, νεF-) no, nato, swim, 309 b; νευσοῦμαι or νεύσομαι 305 d, iv. 3. 12, ᵒἔνευσα; ᵒνένευκα Pl. Rep. 441 c. Cog. νήχω ch. po.
ᵒνέω Hdt., heap up; νήσω Suid., ἔνησα, m. l.; νένημαι, v. 4. 27, & -σμαι Ar. Nub. 1203, ἐνήθην & -σθην l., 307 e. [Cog. νηέω, ᵒνηνέω.]
[νέω, Hes. Op. 775] & νήθω q³, neo, spin; νήσω, ἔνησα [m. η. 198]; νένησμαι l., ἐνήθην. Cog. νάω?
νίζω (j⁴, νιφ- or νιβ-), & ch. l. νίπτω t, wash hands or feet, M.; νίψω m., ao.; νένιμμαι, [ᵒἐνίφθην Hipp.,] 2 f. νιφήσομαι l. Lxx. Cog.? νίφω, -ψω, &c., ningo, snow (cf. nix, nivis).
νοέω, -ήσω, &c., think; [1. ω for οη 131 f.]

Ξ.

ξέω scrape; [ἔξεσα Ε. 81;] ἔξεσμαι, -σθην l. Cog. ξαίνω, ξύω· ξυρέω shave.
ξηραίνω dry; -ανῶ m., ao. a. 152 c [ἀγ-ξηράνῃ for ἀνα-ξηράνῃ, 136, Φ. 347]; ἐξήρασμαι &c. 304 b, -άνθην, f. l.

Ο.

ὀδάξω (k⁵, δακ-, ὀδακ- p, cf. δάκνω), -έω, -άω l., feel a bite, bite, M.; [ὀδαξήσομαι 311, Hipp.], ὠδαξάμην l.; ὤδαγμαι.
ὁδοιπορέω travel, ὁδοποιέω make a road; -ήσω, &c.; ὡδοιπόρηκα & ὁδοιπεπόρηκα· ὡδοπεποίηκα, -μαι & ὡδοποίημαι· 283 a.
[ὀδύ- be angry, cf. odi; ὠδῡσάμην +, a. 62; ὀδώδυσμαι pret., ε. 423.]
ὀδύρομαι p, & trag. δύρομαι lament; ὀδύρουμαι, ὠδῡράμην; ὠδύρθην l.
ὄζω (j¹, ὀδ-) odoro, oleo, emit ODOR; ὀζήσω [-έσω Hipp.] ao., 311; 2 pf. ὄδωδα: [ὄσδω D. Æ., 170 a, Theoc.]

οἴγω & οἴγνῡμι n⁷, open, very r. in prose exc. in comp., ch. with ἀνά & διά· οἴξω, ᾦξα [ᾤϊξα 132, a. 436]; ᾤχθην. Cp. ἀν-οίγω & ἀν-οίγνυμι, M. l.; ἀνοίξω, ἀνέῳξα, Th. 2. 2, & r. ἤνοιξα [ἀνῴξα po.], 279 b, 282 b, m. r. l.; ἀνέῳχα, 2 pf. ἀνέῳγα ch. l., ἀνέῳγμαι, Th. 2. 4, ἤνοιγμαι l. [ἀνῴγμαι po.|, 3 f. ἀνεῴξομαι Hel. 5. 1. 14, ἀνεῴχθην (sub. ἀνοίχθω, &c.), ἠνοίχθην f. l., 2 a. ἠνοίγην f. l., Even a triple augment occurs late: ἠνέῳξα, ἠνεῴχθην, Lxx.
οἶδα knoio, εἴσομαι· see 46 & ὁράω.
οἰδ-έω, -άνω, l. -άω & -αίνω, swell, M. r.; οἰδήσω Hipp., ao.; ᾤδηκα.
οἰκτείρω h, pity; οἰκτερῶ, ᾤκτειρα· late οἰκτείρησω Rom. 9. 15, ao. a. p.
οἰνοχοέω, -ήσω, pour wine; 279 b.
οἴομαι opinor, think (nude 1 s. οἶμαι, ipf. ᾤμην, 313 c; 2 s. οἴει 297 f); οἰήσομαι 311 c, ao. l.; ᾠήθην, f. l.: [ὀΐομαι 132, Ε. 644, ὠϊσάμην (ὀΐσ- in Hom., a. 323), ὠΐσθην. A. (pr. 1 s. only) οἴω, E. usu: ὀΐω A. 59, Lac. οἰῶ Ar. Lys. 81; in ὀί- or ὠί-, usu. ῑ.]
οἰστράω goad, -ήσω; aug. 278 d.
οἴχομαι go, be gone; οἰχήσομαι 311; οἴχωκα or ᾤχωκα 312 d, Soph. Aj. 896, ᾤχηκα E. ? & l., οἴχημαι or ᾤχημαι.

ὀκέλλω (p, κελ-) run ashore, vii. 5. 12; κέλσω ao. po. 152 d, ὤκειλα.
ὀλισθάνω, r. or l. -αίνω (n⁴, n⁶, ὀλισθ-), slip, slide; ὀλισθήσω l., ao. ch. l., 2 ao. ὤλισθον, Soph. El. 746; ὠλίσθηκα Hipp. & l.
ὄλλῡμι (ὀλ- 351. 4) perdo, destroy, lose, (po. or l. exc. in comp., ch. with ἀπό,) M. perish; ὀλέσω 311 d, [1. ὀλέω m.] Att. ὀλῶ m., ὤλεσα, m. l., 2 a. m. ὠλόμην [pt. οὐλόμενος + 134 n, A. 2]; ᵒὀλώλεκα, perdidi, 2 pf. pret. ὄλωλα perii, am undone, ὀλώλεσμαι l., ὠλέσθην, f. l. [Cog. ὀλέκω m. +, A. 10, ὀλέω, T. 135 v. l.]
ὁμαρτέω accompany, meet, po. +; [ipf. du. ὁμαρτήτην 323 f.;] ὁμαρτήσω ao., v. 87, [2 a. ὅμαρτον l.]
ὄμνῡμι (n⁷, ὀμ-, ὀμο- w) swear,ᶜM.; ὀμοῦμαι 152 (l. ὀμόσω m.), ὤμοσα ᶜm.; ὀμώμοκα, -μαι & -σμαι 307 e (ᾠμωσμαι l.), ὠμόθην & -σθην f.: [Lac. f. ὀμιώμεθα, 323 fᵛ.]
ὁμόργνῡμι (u⁷, ὀμοργ-) wipe, po. +,

84 ὀμόργνυμι TABLES. παίζω §50.

M.; ὀμόρξω ᶜm., ao. ᶜa. m., θ. 88, Pl. Gorg. 525 a; ᶜὠμόρχθην.
ὀνίνημι (ὀνα- 357. 2) *benefit, M.*; ὀνήσω m., ao. a., m. l., 2 a. *inf.* ὀνῆναι?, m. ὠνήμην 314 b & -άμην, opt. ὀναίμην, [*imv.* ὄνησο τ. 68], *inf.* δνασθαι [-ησθαι I., pl. -ήμενος β. 33 ;] ὤνημαι l., -θην.
[ὄνομαι (ὀνο-) *scorn*, E. & I.; pr. & ipf. nude, cf. δίδομαι 45 ; ὀνόσομαι ao.; ᶜὠνόσθην. Fr. ὀν-, pr. οὔνεσθε (134 a) Ω. 241, & 1 a. ὤνατο P. 25, if these forms are genuine.]
ὀπυίω or ὀπύω *marry*; ὀπύσω ὄπυσμαι: according to some, -υι- before a vowel, -ῡ- before a consonant.
ὁράω (ὁρα-) see, *M.*, ipf. ἐώρ(αον)ων 279 b, [ὁρέω I., -όω E., ipf. ὤρεον or ὤρων I., 48 c, 322 ;] ἑώρακα & esp. in comedy ἑόρακα, -μαι (later than ὤμμαι, Isoc. Antid.), ἑωράθην f. l.: (fr. ὀπ- x) f. ὄψομαι (2 s. ὄψει 297 f), ao. r.; 2 pf. ὄπωπα po. & I. +, ὦμμαι, Æsch. Pr. 998, ὤφθην f.: (fr. FIΔ- x, cf. video) 2 a. εἶδον, m. ch. po. or I., 279 c, *sub.* ἴδω, ἴδωμαι, &c. (*imv.* ἴδε, ἰδοῦ, or as exclam. ἰδέ, ἰδού); 2 pf. οἶδα (I have seen, hence) *I know* (46, 320, & below) ; *Mid.* (ch. po.) εἴδομαι h, *seem, resemble*, 1 a. εἰσάμην, Υ. 81. [Cog. ὄρημι Æ. 335 b ; m. 2 s. ὄρηαι 314 b, ξ. 343 : ὄσσομαι i³, υ. 81.]
In the pret. οἶδα, the stem has four forms: (1) ἰδ-; ἴσμεν [ἴδ-μεν 148 b, A. 124], ἴσθι, ἴστω [Β. ἴττω Ar. Ach. 911], &c., 320 a [also to shorten other forms, as below, 134] ; (2) εἰδ- h ; [*sub.* εἴδομεν, εἴδετε, 326 d,] εἰδέναι [ἴδ-μεν, ἴδμεναι, 333 c], εἰδώς [ἰδυῖα, A. 608], ᾔδειν [w. double aug. 2 s. ᾔδεις X. 280, 3 s. ᾔδη ι. 206, or -δει, or I.-δε ?, 3 p. ᾔδειεν or ᾔδειν 330 b, also (ἰδ-σαν) ἴσαν ν. 170], f. εἴσομαι: (3) οἰδ- 312 b ; οἶδα, οἶδας or οἶσθα (οἶδας very r. in Att., Eur. Alc. 780 ; the comic poets sometimes blend the two forms into οἶσθας, also Eur. Ion 999 ?): (4) εἰδε- ν ; (εἰδέ-ω) εἰδῶ [ἰδέω Ξ. 235], εἰδείην, 320 c ; f. εἰδήσω, A. 546, Isoc. 11 d [ἰδησῶ Theoc. 3. 37], ao. I. or l. In the *ind.* plur., the shorter forms were more comm. in the pf., & the longer in the plp. (also l. ᾔδεισαν Mk. 14. 40). The defects of οἶδα are ch. supplied

by γιγνώσκω. [Cog. ἴσᾱμι D. (perhaps suggested by 3 p. ἴσᾶσι) Pind. P. 4. 441, ἴσᾶς, ἴσᾶτι 328 a, Theoc. 15. 146, &c.] With the *ind.* of οἶδα, cf. the corresponding Sanskrit 1 s. vĕd-a, 2 vĕttha, 3 vĕda ; 1 p. vid-ma, 2 vida, 3 vidus.
ὀρέγω [r. ὀρέγνῡμι n⁷, X. 37] *stretch out*, REACH (cf. rego, *Germ.* recken, reichen), *M. reach for, desire*, (A. ch. po. or l.;) ὀρέξω m., ao.; [ὤρεγμαι Hipp., ὀρώρεγμαι, II. 834,] ὠρέχθην as mid. See 430 b. Cog. ὀριγνάομαι, ὀρεχθέω po.
ὁρίζω j¹ [οὑρίζω l.] *bound ;* see 39.
ὄρνῡμι (n⁷, ὀρ-) *rouse*, po., *M. arise ;* ὄρσω ao. 152 d, [f. m. ὀροῦμαι, 2 ao. ὤρορον 284 e,] 2 ao. m. ὠρόμην (ὦρτο, *imv.* ὄρσο, -εο, -ευ, *inf.* ὄρθαι, &c. 326 e, 327); 2 pf. ὄρωρα as mid., N. 78, 2 plp. ὠρώρειν 281 d, Æsch. Ag. 653 : [fr. ὀρε- v, ipf. ὀρέοντο B, 398, pf. ὀρώρεμαι, *sub.* ὀρώρηται N. 271.] Cog., ch. po., ὅρω, ὀρίνω, ὀροθύνω, ὀρούω · Lat. orior.
ὀρύσσω (i¹, ὀρυχ- or ὀρυγ- d²) *dig ;* ὀρύξω, ao. a., m. I. or l., 2 a. ὤρυγον r.; ᶜὀρώρυχα (l. ὤρυχα,) -γμαι, (plf. ὀρωρ- or ὠρωρ- 281 d,) ὠρύχθην ᶜf., 2 a. l. ὠρύχην or -γην, r.
ὀσφραίνομαι & l. ὀσφράομαι (n⁶, u, ὀσφρ-) *perceive by smell*, A. l.; ὀσφρήσομαι, ao. l., 2 a. ὠσφρόμην [ὄσφραντο? 327 b, Hdt.]; ὠσφράνθην.
[οὐτάω *wound*, + ; οὐτήσω l., ao., 2 a. οὐτάν m. 314 d, Δ. 525, λ. 40 ; οὐτήθην, Θ. 537.] Cog. οὐτάζω po.
ὀφείλω (h, ὀφελ-) *owe, ought*, [ὀφέλλω Æ. E. 171 a, θ. 462 ;] ὀφειλήσω ao. 311 b, 2 a. ὤφελον (po. & I. ἔφελον 284 b, c) expressing wish, (I ought) *O that*, utinam, (l. as a particle, Gal. 5. 12 ;) ὠφείληκα, -θην. Cog. [ὀφέλλω+ *increase*, ao. opt. 3 s. ὀφέλλειε 171 a, 325 cʳ, II. 651,] &
ὀφλισκάνω (k² n⁴, ὀφλ-) *owe, incur ;* ὀφλήσω 311, ao. r., 2 a. ὤφλον, v. 8. 1 ; ὤφληκα, -μαι : l. pr. ἔφλω.

Π.

παίζω (j, παιδ-, παιγ-, 349 a) *sport ;* παιξοῦμαι 305 d, Symp. 9. 2 (l. -ξομαι & -ξω), ἔπαισα (-ξα l.) ; πέπαικα (-χα l.), -σμαι (-γμαι l.), -χθην l.

§ 50.   παίω   VERBS.   πίμπλημι   85

παίω *strike, M.*; παίσω & po. παιήσω 311, έπαισα *m.*; πέπαικα & 1. πεπαίηκα, ᶜπέπαισμαι 1., έπαίσθην. See τύπτω.

παλιλλογέω *repeat;* [plp. έπαλιλλόγητο 284 b, Hdt. 1. 118.]

πάλλω (1, παλ-) *shake*, ch. po., *M.*; έπηλα [*m.* 1., 2 a. 3 s. nude πάλτο 326 e, Ο. 645, *pt.* άμ-πεπαλών 284e;] πέπαλμαι, 2 a. ᶜέπάλην 1.

πά- *acquire;* πάσομαι ao. po.; πέπαμαι pret. *possess,* iii. 3. 18, 3 f. πεπάσομαι r. Cf. potior.

παρανομέω *transgress;* -ήσω, παρενόμησα 282 c, & παρηνόμησα 279 a (as if cp. of παρά & άνομέω); παρανενόμηκα (l. παρηνόμηκα), -μαι, &c.

παροινέω *act the drunkard;* έπαρώνησα 282 c; πεπαρώνηκα, -μαι 1., &c.

πάσσω i², *sprinkle;* πάσω, ᵒao. a., *m.* 1.; πέπασμαι 1., έπάσθην, ᶜf. 1.

πάσχω (k³ 350, παθ-, πενθ- n³ b) *patior, suffer;* πείσομαι 156, (ao. *pt.* po. πήσας ?,) 2 a. έπαθον ; 2 pf. πέπονθα, Th. 6. 11, [πέποσχα D.; 2 p. πέποσθε 320 f, Ψ. 53, *pt.* πεπαθυίῃ ρ. 555, § 325 e.]

[πατέομαι (v, πατ-) *eat, taste,* Hdt. 2. 37;] πάσομαι po. r., ao. po., i., *or* 1., γ. 9, Soph. Ant. 202; [plp. πεπάσμην Ω. 642]. Cf. pascor.

παύω *stop, repress, M. cease,* PAUSE, 34; παύσω *m.,* ao.; πέπαυκα, -μαι, 3 f. πεπαύσομαι Soph. Ant. 91, έπαύθην (-σθην 1. or v. *l.*), f. r., 2 a. 1. έπάην ᶜf., Rev. 14. 13.

πείθω (h, πιθ-) *persuade, M. believe, obey,* 38, 39; πείσω *m.,* ao. *a., m.* 1., [πεπιθήσω 284 f., 311, & as mid. πιθήσω, φ. 369, ao. + Δ. 398,] 2 a. έπιθον *m.* po. [πέπιθον *m.* 284 f, Ψ. 40]; πέπεικα, 2 pf. pret. πέποιθα *trust,* 38. 8, Th. 2. 42, nude *imv.* r. πέπεισθι 320, Aesch. Eum. 599, [2 plp. 1 p. έπεπίθμεν B. 341,] πέπεισμαι, έπείσθην f. Cog. πιστεύω; Lat. fido.

πεινάω *hunger,* πειν(άει)ῇ 120 g; -ήσω (1. -άσω) ao.; πεπείνηκα.

πείρω (h, παρ-, περ- b) *pierce,* po., i., *or* 1.; περώ ?, έπειρα, Α. 465; πέπαρμαι, 2 a. ᶜέπάρην, Hdt. 4. 94.

πεκτέω (t², πεκ-) pecto, *comb, shear,* po., [πέκω h, σ. 316; πεξώ D. 325 b, έπεξα 1., *m.*;] έπέχθην, Ar. Nub. 1356.

πελάζω (z, πελα-), & po. πελάθω,

πελάθω q, & (πλεάθ- c⁵¹) πλάθω, *bring or come near, M.* po.; πελάσω, πελώ 305 b, έπέλασα iv. 2. 3, [2 a. *m.* έπλήμην 314 b, Θ. 63;] πέπλημαι po., po. έπελάσθην & έπλάθην. Cog. πλησιάζω, [πιλνάω n³ b, πίλναμαι, Τ. 94.]

πέλω *be,* po. +, *M.*; [ipf. 3 s. έπλε c⁴, Μ. 11, *m.* 2 s. έπλεο, -ευ, 3 s. έπλετο, Χ. 281, 116, *pt.* πλόμενος.]

πέμπω *send,* 41; *Μ.* cp. in classic prose, i. 1. 2; πέμψω, πέπομφα, &c.

πεπαρεΐν, πέπρωται; see πορίζω.

πέρδομαι (b, παρδ-) pedo, *Λ.* r.; ᶜπαρδήσομαι 311, 2 a. ᶜέπαρδον; πέπορδα; Αr.

πέρθω (b, παρθ-) *destroy, ravage,* po. +, [nude pr. *inf. p.* (περθ-σθαι, περ-σθαι, 151, 158) πέρθαι II. 708;] πέρσω *m.,* ao. *a.,* [2 a. έπραθον ᶜ*m.* c⁶, ι. 40.] Usu. πορθέω v², -ήσω.

πέρνημι *sell,* po.; see πιπράσκω.

πέσσω (i³, πεπ-), & later πέπτω t, *coquo, cook, digest, M.*; πέψω, ao. *a., m. ?*; πέπεμμαι, έπέφθην f.

πετάννυμι (n⁸, πετα-) pando, *spread, expand,* (in Att. ch. cp., esp. w. άνά·) πετάω, ᶜπετώ 305 b, έπέτασα, *m.* 1.; ᶜπεπέτακα 1., -σμαι, usu. πέπταμαι c⁴, Ar. Nub. 343, έπετάσθην. Cog. [πίτνημι n³ b, λ. 392, πίτνω,] 1. ᶜπετάω.

πέτομαι (i. 5. 3) & po. *or* 1. πέταμαι u, & ίπταμαι r³ c², *fly;* πετήσομαι 311, usu. πτήσομαι c⁴, 2 a. *a.* έπτην po. or l., *m.* έπτόμην & έπτάμην· έπετάσθην l. Po. cog. ποτάομαι, Ar. Av. 251 [nude 2 s. πότῃ Sap. 20, *pt.* ποτήμενος, Theoc. 29. 30, § 335 b], ποτήσομαι ?, πεπότημαι, λ. 222, έποτήθην· [πωτάομαι, πετάομαι ?]

πεύθομαι *inquire;* see πυνθάνομαι.

πήγνυμι (n⁷, παγ-, πηγ- g) pango, *fasten, fix, M.* (opt. πήγνῦτο 316 c); πήξω *m.,* ao., [2 a. *m.* 3 s. κατ-έπηκτο 326 e, Α. 378;] ᶜπέπηχα l., 2 pf. πέπηγα pret. *am fixed,* Γ. 135, -γμαι l., έπήχθην, usu. 2 a. έπάγην f.: l. πήσσω.

πίμπλημι (πλα-, πι-μ-πλα r¹ e²) pleo, *fill,* (esp. cp. w. έν,) *M.*; πλήσω, ᶜ*m.* l., ao., 2 a. po. έπλήμην 314 b (opt. ᶜπλήμην Ar. Ach. 236, *imv.* ᶜπλήσο, &c.); ᶜπέπληκα Pl. Apol. 23 e, -σμαι or -μαι 307 e, 3 f. πεπλήσομαι l., έπλήσθην f. In the compounds of πίμπλημι & πίμπρημι, the

πίμπλημι   TABLES.   πρίασθαι   § 50.

μ is usu. omitted after -μπ-: ἐμπίπλημι, imv. ἐμπίπλη Ar. Av. 1310 [ἐμπίπληθι 335 d ʳ, Φ. 311, pt. ἐμπιπλείς Hipp. as fr. πλε-]; so πιπλάς 171, Æsch. Ch. 360; but ipf. ἐνεπίμπλην. Cog. [πίμπλέω I. 322 a, πιμπλάνομαι, I. 679,] πληρόω · πλήθω be full (2 pf. πέπληθα, Theoc. 22. 38), whence πληθύω & πληθύνω.

πίμπρημι (rˡ e, πρα-, see πίμπλημι) burn, esp. cp. w. ἐν; πρήσω ᶜm., ao. a., ᶜm. l., [ἔπρεσε 134, 130 b, Hes. Th. 856;] ᶜπέπρηκα, -μαι & -σμαι 307 e, [3 f. ᶜπεπρήσομαι, Hdt. 6. 9,] ἐπρήσθην, f. l. Cog. ᶜπίμπρω ἰ, [ᶜπρήθω, I. 589.]

πινύσκω, πέπνῦμαι, see πνέω.

πίνω (n², πο-, πῖ- b²) pōto, bibo, drink; πίομαι (usu. ῑ; Hellen. πίεσαι 331), later πιοῦμαι, 305 f, a, 2 a. ἔπιον (imv. πίε & po. πῖθι Ar. Vesp. 1489, [r. inf. πιέναι Hipp.,] 313 cʳ); πέπωκα, πέπομαι 310 d, ἐπόθην ᶜf. Causal, ποτίζω &

πιπίσκω rˡ kˡ, give to drink, po. or ι.; πίσω, [ao. a. Hipp., m. l.; ἐπίσθην l.]

πιπράσκω l. (rˡ k, περα-, πρα- c²), & πέρνημι hˢ po., sell; [περάσω, -άω 321 s, Φ. 454, ao.;] πέπρᾱκα, -μαι [πεπερημένος Φ. 58], 3 f. πεπράσομαι, vii. 1. 36, ἐπράθην, f. l.: in Att., ch. supplied in pres. by πωλέω, & in fut. & aor. by ἀποδώσομαι & ἀπεδόμην.

πίπτω (rˡ c², πετ-, softened πεσ-, cf. 143 b, πτε- c⁷) fall; πεσοῦμαι 305 d [l. -ομαι], 2 a. ἔπεσον [ἔπετον D. 169 b, ἔπεσα m. l., Rev. 1. 17; πέπτωκα 312 c, πέπτηκα l., 2 pf. pt. po. [πεπτεώς or -ηώς 325 d] πεπτώς 320 d, Soph. Aj. 828. Po. cog. πίτνω or -έω Eur. Sup. 285.

πλάζω (jˢ, πλαγγ-) cause to wander, po. or l. +, M. πλάζομαι wander; πλάγξομαι, ἔπλαγξα, m. l.; ἐπλάγχθην, a. 2. Usu. πλανάω.

πλάσσω shape, M.; ᶜπλάσω, m. l., ao. ii. 6. 26; πέπλακα l., -σμαι, ἐπλάσθην, Pl. Rep. 377 b, ᶜf. l.

πλέκω (bˡ, πλακ-) plecto, plico, PLAIT, twine, M. po. or l.; πλέξω m. l., ao.; [ᶜπέπλοχα or ᶜ-εχα 312 c, Hipp.] πέπλεγμαι, ἐπλέχθην f., 2 a. ἐπλάκην (v. l. -έκην), f. l.

πλέω (fˡ, πλεϜ-, πλευ- f²) sail,

42 g, 309 b; πλεύσομαι & πλευσοῦμαι 305 d, v. 7. 8, 1. 10, -σω l., ἔπλευσα; πέπλευκα, -σμαι, -σθην, f. l.: [I. & po. πλώω, πλώσομαι, πέπλωκα, &c., 114, Hdt. 8. 10, 5; 2 a. ἔπλων 313 b, ᶜγ. 15, pt. ἐπι-πλώς Z. 291.] Der. πλωΐζω, Th. 1. 13, πλοΐζομαι l.

πλήσσω (iˡ, πλᾱγ-, πληγ- g) strike (pr. ch. cp. w. ἐκ or ἐπί), M.; πλήξω, m. l., ao., [2 a. πέπληγον m., ἐπέπληγον, 284 e]; 2 pf. πέπληγα, vi. 1. 5, -γμαι, 3 f. πεπλήξομαι, Ar. Eq. 272, ἐπλήχθην r., 2 a. ἐπλήγην (ἐξεπλάγην, κατ-επλάγην) f. Cog. ἐκπλήγνυμαι, Th. 4. 125. See τύπτω.

πλύνω (g, πλῠν-) wash clothes (cf. λούω, νίζω); πλῠνῶ m., ἔπλῡνα m.; πέπλῠμαι, ἐπλύθην (l. -ύνθην) f., 304 a.

πνέω (fˡ, πνεϜ-, πνευ- f², πνῠ-, 142ʳ) breathe, blow, 309 b; πνεύσομαι & πνευσοῦμαι 305 d, Ar. Ran. 1221, -σω l.,- ἔπνευσα, ᶜπέπνευκα, -σμαι or -μαι l. [πέπνῦμαι pret. am wise, Ω. 377, imv. πέπνῡο 331 b, Theog. 29, &c.], ᶜἐπνεύσθην l., ᶜf. l. Cp. ἀνα-πνέω recover breath [2 a. 3 s. ἄμ-πνυεν, 136, Q. Sm. 9. 470, imv. ἄμ-πνυε X. 222, nude 2 a. m. ἄμ-πνῡτο 314 b, ω. 349; 1 a. p. ἀμπνύνθην nˡ, E. 697]. Cog. ποιπνύω puff, 379 cʳ]; πινύσκω or πινύσσω rˡ cˡ, make wise, ch. E., Æsch.; [1 a. or ipf. 3 s. ἐπίνυσσεν Ξ. 249;] ἐπινύσθην l.

πνίγω (g, πνῑγ-) choke, v. 7. 25, esp. cp. w. ἀπό · ᶜπνίξω m., ao. a.; πέπνιγμαι, Ar. Vesp. 511, 3 f. ᶜπεπνίξομαι l., ἐπνίχθην l., 2 a. ἐπνίγην f.

ποθέω desidero, desire, miss, M. r.; ποθήσω m., ἐπόθησα & -εσα 310 d; πεπόθηκα l., -μαι l., ἐποθήθην l.

ποινάομαι punish; -άσομαι 310 a.

πονέω, -ήσω (-έσω l. +), labor.

πορίζω (z², πορ-) supply, M.; πορίσω, -ιῶ, m., ἐπόρισα m., 2 a. po. ἔπορον [πεπορεῖν, v. l. πεπαρεῖν, 284 c, Pind. P. 2. 105;] πεπόρικα, -σμαι (3 s. πέπρωται it is fated, Σ. 329, pt. πεπρωμένος, Mem. 2. 1. 33), ἐπορίσθην f. Cog. πορσύνω.

πορπάω fasten; cj. w. ᾱ or η, 310.

πράσσω (iˡ, πραγ-) do [l. πρήσσω], M. exact; πράξω m., ao., πέπρᾱχα, 2 pf. πέπρᾱγα have fared, -γμαι, 3 f. πεπράξομαι, Ar. Av. 847, ἐπράχθην f.

πρίασθαι buy; see 45 i & ὠνέομαι.

§ 50.   προφητεύω   VERBS.   σκεδάννῡμι   87

προφητεύω, -εύσω, prophesy; aug. ἐπροφ- or προεφ-, 282 c, N. T., Lxx.
πτάρνυμαι (n⁷, πταρ-) sneeze, iii. 2. 9, A. 1.; ἔπτᾱρα, usu. 2 a. ἔπτᾰρον, ρ. 541, [m. Hipp.]; ἐπτάρην.
πτήσσω (i¹, πτα-, πτακ- ο, πτηκ-g) cower, crouch; πτήξω l., ao., 2 a. ᶜἔπτακον, Æsch. Eum. 252 [3 d. καταπτήτην 314 c, Θ. 136]; ἔπτηχα, -ηκα l., [2 pf. pt. πεπτηώς 325 d, Ξ. 354, cf. πίπτω.] Cog. πτώσσω, Δ. 371, [πτωσκάζω, Δ. 372.]
πτίσσω i², pinso, pound; ἔπτισα, Hdt. 2. 92; ἔπτισμαι, -σθην l.
πτύρομαι fear, l. +; 2 a. ἐπτύρην.
πτύσσω (i¹, πτυχ- or πτυγ- d²) fold, M.; ᶜπτύξω ᶜm., ao.; ἐπτυγμαι, Hier. 2. 4, (or πέπτ- 280 c,) ᶜἐπτύχθην, [2 a. ᶜἐπτύγην Hipp.]
πτύω (ῠ) spuo, spit; πτύσω m., ao. a., Soph. Ant. 653; ἔπτυκα l., -σθην, f. l., [2 a. ἐπτύην Hipp.]
πυνθάνομαι (n⁵, πυθ-, πευθ- h), po. πεύθομαι, inquire, hear; πεύσομαι (r. -οῦμαι 305 d), 2 a. ἐπυθόμην [πεπυθ- 284 e, Z. 50]; πέπυσμαι.

P, § 146, 93 d.

ῥαίνω (h, ῥαν-, ῥαδ-) sprinkle, po. & l. +; ῥανῶ, ἔρρᾱνα [inv. ῥάσσατε v. 150], ᶜm. l.; ᶜἔρραγκα Lxx., -ασμαι [3 p. ἐρράδαται, -το, 329 a], -άνθην.
ῥάπτω (t, ῥαφ-) stitch; ᶜῥάψω, ἔρραψα m.; ἔρραμμαι, Dem. 1268. 2, 2 a. ἐρράφην, Eur. Bac. 243, ᶜf. l.
ῥέζω (j², ῥεγ- cᵇ, see ἔρδω) do, po. +; ῥέξω, ἔρρεξα Pl. Leg. 642 c, po. ἔρεξα 171, Eur. And. 838; [ἐρρέχθην, I. 250.]
ῥέω (f¹, ῥεϝ-, ῥευ- f², ῥυ- 142ʳ, cf. Lat. ruo) flow; ῥεύσομαι, -σω l., ἔρρευσα, but more Att. ῥυήσομαι, ἐρρύην (2 f. & a. p., or 2 f. m. & nude 2 a. a.); ἐρρύηκα 311 c, Isoc. 159 d.
ῥήγνῡμι (n⁷, ϝραγ-, ῥαγ- 141, ῥηγ-g) BREAK, M.; ῥήξω [m.], ἔρρηξα m.; ᶜἔρρηχα l., 2 pf. ἔρρωγα am broken, 312 c, ἔρρηγμαι r., -χθην r., 2 a. ἐρράγην f.: po. & l. ῥήσσω beat. Cog. ῥάσσω & ἀράσσω, -ξω, smite; frango.
ῥῑγέω v, shudder, po. +; ῥῑγήσω ao.; 2 pf. pret. ἔρρῑγα P. 175. Cog. ῥῑγόω, -ώσω, shiver (inf. ῥῑγῶν or ῥῑγοῦν 324 b); φρίσσω q. v.; frigeo.

ῥίπτω & ῥιπτέω (t¹², ῥιφ-) throw; [iter. ῥίπτασκον 332 e.;] ῥίψω ao., [2 a. ἔρρῑφον l.;] ἔρρῑφα, -ιμμαι [inf. ῥερίφθαι 159 eʳ], 3 f. ἐρρίψομαι l., -ίφθην ᶜf., 2 a. -ίφην, f. l. Cog. ῥιπτάζω 379 b, ἐρείπω q. v.
ῥύομαι (ch. ῡ) = ἐρύομαι draw to one's self, protect (also in Att., yet r. in prose); ῥῡσομαι, Th. 5. 63, ao.; ἐρρύσθην l. Nude ipf. 3 s. ἐρρῦτο Soph. O. T. 1352, [3 p. ῥύατο 329 a, Σ. 515, pr. inf. ῥῦσθαι O. 141; iter. 2 s. ῥύσκευ 332, 323 c, Ω. 730.]
ῥώννῡμι (nᵇ, ῥο-) strengthen; ᶜῥώσω l., ao.; ἔρρωμαι (inv. ἔρρωσο farewell, Cyr. 4. 5. 33), ἐρρώσθην, Th. 4. 72, f. l.

Σ.

σαίρω (h, σαρ-) sweep; ἔσηρα, Soph. Ant. 409; 2 pf. pret. σέσηρα grin, Ar. Pax 620. Cog. σαρόω l.
σαλπίζω (j³, σαλπιγγ-) sound a trumpet; ἐσάλπιγξα 571 b; late σαλπίσω (-ιῶ), 1 Cor. 15, 52, ao., ᶜσεσάλπισμαι & ᶜ-ιγμαι, 349 a.
[σαόω & σόω, save; see σώζω.
σάσσω i, pack; [ᶜσάσω ao. Hipp.,] ἔσαξα 349 a, Œc. 19. 11; σέσαγμαι, Ib., ἐσάχθην l.
σάω & σήθω sift, ι. & l.; ἔσησα, &c.
σβέννῡμι (nᵇ, σβε-) quench, M. be quenched, go out; σβέσω, ao. a. m., f. m. ᶜσβήσομαι 310 d, (as mid., 2 a. ἔσβην 45 h, 313 dʳ, I. 471, & pf. ᶜἔσβηκα), ἔσβεσμαι, -σθην, f. l.
σείω, -σω, σέσεικα, &c., shake, 44.
σεύομαι & σόομαι, Ar. Vesp. 458, (σεϝ-, σευ- f², σῠ- 142ʳ, σε- f¹, σο- 114,) rush, hasten, po. (3 s. σεῦται 326 e); 2 a. m. ἐσύμην 313 b; ἐσύθην +. [A. σεύω l., drive, urge; 1 ao. ἔσσευα m. 306 a, 171 (l. ᶜ-ευσα); pret. ἔσσυμαι 284 d, 2 a. 3 s. ἀπ-εσσούᾶ? Hel. 1. 1. 23, Lac. for ἀπεσύη.]
σήπω (g, σαπ-) rot, trans.; σήψω ᶜao.; 2 pf. intrans. σέσηπα, B. 135, ᶜiv. 5. 12, -μμαι, ἐσήφθην l., 2 a. ἐσάπην, Hdt. 3. 66, f. l.
σίνομαι harm; iii. 4. 16; [σινήσομαι 311, Hipp., ἐσινάμην, Id.]
σκάπτω (t, σκαφ-) dig; σκάψω ao.; ᶜἔσκαφα, Isoc. 298 a, -μμαι, -φθην l., 2 a. ἐσκάφην, ᶜf. l.
σκεδάννῡμι (nᵇ, σκεδα-) scatter (as

sub., διασκεδάννῦσι, -νται, 316 c); σκεδάσω, -ῶ, 305 b, ἐσκέδασα [c]*m*.; ἐσκέδασμαι, -σθην, f. l. Cog., ch. po. or l., σκίδνημι n[3] b, [κεδάννῦμι e[1], κίδνημι +, σκεδάω, κεδάω, κεδαίομαι.]
- σκέλλω (b[1] l, σκαλ-) *dry, parch*, ch. po. *or* l., *M*. *become dry*; σκελῶ l. [ἔσκηλα Ψ. 191]; as *mid.*, 2 ao. [c]ἔσκλην c[6] (r. Ar. Vesp. 160) & pf. ἔσκληκα, (so f. *m*. σκλήσομαι l.)
σκέπτομαι t, specio, *view*; σκέψομαι ao.; ἔσκεμμαι, 3 f. ἐσκέψομαι, Pl. Rep. 392 c, ἐσκέφθην r., *2 a. [c]ἐσκέπην, [c]f. l. In Att., the pr. & ipf. were usu. supplied by σκοπέω v[2], of which the other tenses were later. Cog. σκοπεύω, [σκοπιάζω.]
σμάω *smear*, 120 g : ἔσμησα *m*.
σμύχω (cf. *smoke*) *burn*, po. or l.; [c]ἔσμυξα, Ι. 653 ; [c]ἔσμιγμαι, [c]-χθην, Theoc. 8. 90, 2 a. [c]ἐσμύγην d[2].
σόομαι *hasten*, po.; see σεύομαι.
σπάω *draw*, -σω, ἔσπακα, &c., 307.
σπείρω (b[1] h, σπαρ-) spargo, *scatter, sow*; σπερῶ, ἔσπειρα [*m*. l.]; ἔσπαρκα l., -ρμαι, Ages. 1. 30, -ρθην?, 2 a. ἐσπάρην, Th. 2. 27, f. l.
σπένδω *pour a libation*, *M*. *make a treaty*; σπείσω *m*. 156, ao. ν. 55 ; [c]ἔσπεικα l., (ἐσπενδ-μαι, ἐσπενσμαι 148, 156) ἔσπεισμαι, Th. 4. 16, -σθην l.
σπεύδω & σπουδάζω, *hasten*, 114 b.
στάζω (j[2], σταγ-) *drop*; στάξω l., ao.; [[c]ἔσταγμαι, β. 271,] [c]-χθην, 2 a. [c]ἐστάγην l.
στείβω or στίβω *tread*; στείψω l., [c]ao., Soph.; ἐστίβημαι 311, Id.Aj. 874.
στείχω h (or στίχω) *walk*, po. or ι.; [[c]ἔστειξα, δ. 277, 2 a. ἔστιχον Π. 258. Cog. στιχάομαι, B. 92, *A*. l.]
στέλλω (b[1] l, σταλ-) *fit out, send*, *M*.; στελῶ, *m*. l., ἔστειλα *m*.; ἔσταλκα, -λμαι, iii. 2. 7, -λθην r., 2 a. ἐστάλην [c]f.
στέργω *love*; στέρξω, *m*. l., ao. *a*.; [2 pf. ἔστοργα, Hdt. 7. 104, ἔστεργμαι Emped.,] ἐστέρχθην l.
στερέω & στερίσκω (v, k[2], στερ-) *deprive*; στερήσω *m*., ἐστέρησα [-εσα ν. 262]; ἐστέρηκα, -μαι, -θην f., 2 a. po. ἐστέρην f., Eur. Alc. 200, 622. Also στέρῶ ?, στέρομαι *be deprived of, want*, (f. στερῶ, στεροῦμαι, unless these are always ct. pr.)
[στεῦμαι *stand to*, 326 e; see ἵστημι]
στόρνῦμι (n[7], στορ-, στορε- v)

sterno, STREW, ch. po., I., *or* l., *M*. (also l. στορέννῦμαι); στορέσω, Att. [c]στορῶ, ἐστόρεσα *m*., ξ. 50 ; ἐστόρεσμαι l., -σθην. Also στρώννῦμι (στροc[5]); στρώσω, *m*. l., ([c]στρωννύσω r. Luc.,) ἔστρωσα, *m*. l.; ἔστρωκα l., -μαι, Th. 2. 34, [c]-θην l., f. l.
στρέφω (b[1], στραφ-) *twist,turn,M*.; στρέψω *m*., ao.; [c]ἔστροφα l., ἔστραμμαι, iv. 7. 15, ἐστρέφθην r. in Att., E. 40, [-άφθην D. I.,] 2 a. ἐστράφην f., iii. 5. 1. Cog. στρωφάω & στροφέω ch. po., 355 a ; στρεβλόω, τρέπω.
στυγέω (v, στυγ-) *hate*, po., I., *or* l.; στυγήσομαι *will be hateful*, Soph. O. T. 672 ; ἐστύγησα, Eur. Tro. 705, [ἔστυξα, λ. 502, 2 a. ἔστυγον κ. 113;] ἐστύγηκα, -μαι l., -θην, Eur. Alc. 465.
συρίζω & συρίττω [-ισδω D. 170a] *pipe, whistle*, cf. susurro ; συρίξω *m*. l., ao. *a*., & συρίσω (-ιῶ) ao. l., 349 a.
σύρω q, *drag*, *M*.; σὔρῶ l., ἔσυρα, [c]Aesch. Pr. 1065, *m*. l.; [c]σέσυρκα l., [c]-ρμαι l., 2 a. ἐσὔρην, [c]f. l.
σφάζω & σφάττω (349 i, j, σφαγ-) *slay*; σφάξω, ao. *a*., [c]*m*. r. i. 8. 29 ; ἔσφαγμαι, λ. 45, -χθην r. Hdt. 5. 5, 2 a. ἐσφάγην f., Eur. Ph. 933: l. plp. ἐσφάκειν Dio C. See φα-.
σφάλλω (l, σφαλ·) fallo, *trip, deceive*; σφαλῶ *m*., ἔσφηλα, 2 a. ἔσφαλον *m*. l. or ?; ἔσφαλκα l., -λμαι, -λθην l. r., 2 a. ἐσφάλην f., Th. 6. 80.
σώζω (z, σαο-, σω- c[1]) *save*, *M*.; σώσω *m*., ao.; σέσωκα, Isoc. 410 c, -μαι, oftener -σμαι, ἐσώθην f. [Ep. σαόω, -όσω, A. 83, &c.; pr. *imv*. 2 s. & ipf. 3 s. (σάοε, ct. σάον, σῶ, 322 c) σάω ν. 230, Π. 363, *sub*. 2 s. (σαῆς, σαοῖς, σῴς, 322 c) σώς, 3 s. σόῳ, I. 681, 424 (v. l. σόῃς, σόῃ, as fr. σόω); ct. σώω ι. 430.]

T.

[τα-, ταγ- o, TAKE, *seize*, cf. tango; τείνω: imv. 2 s. (ταε, cf. 120 g) τῇ Ξ. 219+, 2 p. τῆτε Sophr. 100 ; 2 a. pt. τεταγών 284 e, A. 591.]
ταράσσω (i[1], ταραχ-) *disturb*; ταράξω *m*., ao. *a*.; τετάραχα l. [pret. intrans. τέτρηχα c[7] (-τραα-, ct. -τρη-), Η. 346], τετάραγμαι, ἐταράχθην f.: θράσσω c[7] [1] (τραα, θρᾶ, 159 h'), ἔθραξα, Aesch. Pr. 628, Pl. Parm. 130 d, -χθην.

§ 50.   τάσσω   VERBS.   τρέπω   89

τάσσω, -ξω, τέταχα, Œc. 4. 5, &c., arrange, 39; τετάχαται, ἐτετάχατο, τετάξομαι, Th. 3. 13, 5. 6, 71, °ταγήσομαι r. l.
τέθηπα (d¹, θαφ-, 312a) be amazed, 2 pf. pret., po., I., or l., ζ. 168; 2 a. ἔταφον d¹, π. 12. Cf. θάπτω.
τείνω (h, τα-, τεν- b¹ n) tendo, stretch, M.; τενῶ °m., ἔτεινα m.; τέτακα 304 a, -μαι, λ. 19, ἐτάθην f. [Cog. τανύω +, -ύσω, &c., nude pr. 3 s. τάνυται, P. 390, 393; τιταίνω, B. 390, ao. pt. τιτήνας. See τα-.]
τελέω, -έσω, -ῶ, τετέλεκα, Pl. Apol. 20 a, &c.; finish, 42 g. Cog. τελεόω, τελειόω, τελευτάω, & probably
τέλλω (b¹ l, ταλ-) perform, raise, (po., exc. in comp., ch. w. ἀνά, ἐν, or ἐπί,) M.; °τελῶ °m. l., ἔτειλα °m.; °τέταλκα l.; °τέταλμαι, Cyr. 5. 5. 3: po. τελέθω arise, be, Eur. And. 783.
τέμνω (n, ταμ-, τεμ- b) cut, [τάμνω E. I. D., Hdt. 2. 65,] M.; τεμῶ °m., 2 a. ἔταμον m., Γ. 94, more Att. ἔτεμον m., Th. 6. 7; τέτμηκα 308, -μαι, 3 f. τετμήσομαι, ἐτμήθην f. [Cog. τμήγω, -ξω, ao. a., m. l., 2 a. διέτμαγον η. 276; 2 a. p. ἐτμάγην II. 374, -ήγην l. Heyne & Bekker read τέμει, as pr., N. 707.]
τέρπω (b, ταρπ-) please, satisfy, M.; τέρψω, m. po., ao. a. [m. r., 2 a. m. ἐταρπόμην, τεταρπόμην 284 e, T. 19;] ἐτέρφθην, Mem. 2. 1. 24, f. l., [ἐτάρφθην ζ. 99, 2 a. ἐτάρπην, δ. 47, sub. 1 p. τραπείομεν c⁶, 323 c, 326 d, Γ. 441.]
[τερσαίνω (n⁶, τερ-, τερσ- o) torreo, dry (pr. l.), M. & τέρσομαι η. 124; τέρσω l. 152 d, ao. a. m. l., ἐτέρσηνα II. 529; 2 a. p. ἐτέρσην ζ. 98.]
[τέτμον & ἔτετμον, 2 a. as fr. τεμfind, 284 e, a. 218, Hes. Th. 610.]
°τετραίνω (r¹ n², τρα-), l. τιτράω & °τίτρημι, terebro, bore: τρήσω l., ao. a., °m. l., [°τετρανέω Hdt. 3. 12, ἐτέτρηνα, ε. 247,] °m. Ar. Th. 18, ἐτέτρηνα l., 152 c; τέτρημαι, ἐτρήθην & -άνθην l.: τιτραίνω & τετρήνω l. or ?. Cog. τορέω, τιτρώσκω, q. v.
τεύχω (h, τυχ-, τυκ- d²) prepare, make, po. +, M.; τεύξω m., ao., [2 a. τέτυκον m. 284 e; τέτευχα, as p. μ. 423, -γμαι +, β. 63, 3 f. τετεύξομαι, M. 345, ἐτεύχθην I. +,] τέτυγμαι, Ξ.

9, Eur. El. 457, ἐτύχθην. Cog. τιτύσκω r¹ k³ po., τυγχάνω, τίκτω · [pf. inf. τετευχῆσθαι to be armed, χ. 104.]
τήκω (g, τακ-) melt, THAW; τήξω [m. Hipp.], ἔτηξα [m. l.]; 2 pf. intrans. τέτηκα, iv. 5. 15; τετήγμαι l., ἐτήχθην r., 2 a. ἐτάκην, f. l. [τι- grieve; 2 pf. pt. τετιηὼς 325 d, I. 13, pf. p. 2 d. τετίησθον, pt. τετιημένος, Θ. 447, 437.]
τίθημι (r¹, θε-), put, θήσω, τέθεικα, Mem. 4. 4. 19, &c., 45: late τιθέω, τιθήσομαι, ἐτίθησα. For the pass. (not found in Hom.), κεῖμαι is often used.
τίκτω (b² t, τεκ-) beget, bring forth, pr. m. po.; τέξομαι (po. τέξω, ao. r.; for τεκεῖσθαι see 305 a], 2 a. ἔτεκον, m. po. Δ. 59; τέτοκα Ven. 5. 13, τέτεγμαι (or -ογμαι?) l., ἐτέχθην, f. l.
τιμάω, -ήσω, &c., honor, 42: τετιμήσομαι Lys. 189. 11; for f. p., usu. τιμήσομαι. Cog. τίω, τίνω, τιμωρέω.
τίνω (ī E.; n¹, τι-) pay, expiate, M., ch. po. or I., take payment, punish; τίσω m., ao.; τέτικα, °-σμαι, °ἐτίσθην: also M. τίνυμαι (less correctly τίννυμαι) po., or l., T. 260, (A. l.) Po. τίω (ĭ) pay honor to, m.r.; [τίσω, ao. +; pt. τετῑμένος v. 28.]
τιτρώσκω (r¹ k⁶, τρο-) wound [r. τρώω, φ. 293]; τρώσω [m.], ao. a.; τέτρωκα l., -μαι, ii. 5. 33, 3 f. τετρώσομαι l., ἐτρώθην f. Cog. τορέω.
τλάω (c⁶, ταλ-, ταλα- u, cf. Lat. tul-i) endure, dare, ch. po., pr. very l.; τλήσομαι (l. τλήσω & ταλάσω), ἔτλησα l. [ἐτάλασσα, P. 166, m. l.], 2 a. ἔτλην 313 b, Δ. 94, Cyr. 3. 1. 2; τέτληκα Ar. Pl. 280 [2 pf. 1 p. τέτλαμεν, opt. &c. τετλαίην, τέτλαθι, τετλάναι, τετληὼς, 2 plp. 1 p. ἐτέτλαμεν, 320 e, 325 d, v. 311, 18, 23, I. 373.] Cog. τολμάω, [ὀτλέω or -εύω l.]
[τμήγω, -ξω, cut, po.; see τέμνω.]
[°τορέω (v, τορ-) pierce, pr. r., Hom. Merc. 283; °τορήσω r., ao., 2 a. ἔτορον, Λ. 236; τετόρημαι l.;] redupl. f. τετορήσω 284 g. Cog. τορεύω, τιτρώσκω, τετραίνω.
τρέπω (b¹, τραπ-) turn [I. τράπω], M.; τρέψω m., ao., 2 a. [ἔτραπον, E. 187] m.; τέτροφα, Ar. Nub. 858, later τέτραφα Dinarch. (cf. τρέφω), τέτραμμαι, 3 f. °τετράψομαι, ἐτρέφθην [I. ἐτράφθην], 2 a. ἐτράπην usu. as

m., f. 1. Τρέπω has the six aorists, as, less surely or less simply, ἀγγέλλω & πλήσσω. Po. cog. τρωπάω, τροπέω, 355 a, τραπέω.

τρέφω (d¹, θραφ-, θρεφ- b) nourish [D. τράφω], M.; (τρέφουν 296 b;) θρέψω m., ao., [2 a. ἔτραφον usu. intrans. γ. 28 ;] τέτροφα ψ. 237, 1. τέτραφα Polyb. (cf. τρέπω), τέθραμμαι (τεθράφθαι Pl. Gorg. 525 a, v. l. τετρ-), ἐθρέφθην Eur. Hec. 351, oftener 2 a. ἐτράφην, f. 1.

τρέχω (d¹, θρεχ-, δραμ- x) run; δραμοῦμαι (r. δραμῶ & θρέξω, comic ᶜθρέξομαι Ar.), ἔθρεξα po. r., 2 a. ἔδραμον; ᶜδεδράμηκα 311, 2 pf. po. ᶜδέδρομα, ε. 412, ᶜδεδράμημαι. Cog. τροχάζω, vii. 3. 46, [τρωχάω, δρομάω.]

τρέω fear, flee; ἔτρεσα, i. 9. 6. Cog. terreo; τρέμω [τρομέω v² +] tremo, TREMBLE.

τρίβω g, rub, τρίψω, ᶜτέτρῑφα Ar. Lys. 952, τέτριμμαι [3 p. τετρίφαται 300c, Hdt. 2. 93], &c., 38, 39. Cog. τείρω tero; τρύω, τρύχω · tribulo.

τρίζω (j², τριγ-) twitter, gibber, po., i., or l., ω. 5; ἔτριξα l.; 2 pf. pret. τέτρῑγα, B. 314. An onomatope, like τρύζω murmur.

τρώγω (bˢ h, τραγ-) gnaw, eat raw food; τρώξομαι, Symp. 4. 8, [ᶜἔτρωξα,] 2 a. ἔτραγον · ᶜτέτρωγμαι.

τυγχάνω (n⁵, τυχ-, τευχ- h) happen, hit; τεύξομαι, ao. 1. r., [ἐτύχησα 311, Δ. 106,] 2 a. ἔτυχον; τετύχηκα, κ. 88, Th. 1. 32, later τετεύχα, ᶜτέτευγμαι l., ᶜἐτεύχθην l. Cog. τεύχω q. v.; [D. 1 a. ἔτοσσα, Pind.]

τύπτω (t, τυπ-) strike, M. plangor, mourn; τυπτήσω 311, Ar. Pl. 21, m. r., [τύψω l.,] ἔτυψα, N. 529, m., later ἐτύπτησα Aristl., 2 a. ἔτυπον r. Eur. Ion 767 [redupl. 284 e]; τετύπτηκα l., τέτυμμαι, N. 782, Hdt. 3. 64, τετύπτημαι l., ἐτυπτήθην & ἐτύφθην l., 2 a. ἐτύπην po. or l., Ω. 421, f.? Of the verbs signifying to strike, the Att. use of τύπτω is especially in the pres. system; of πατάσσω, in the aor. act.; & of πλήσσω, in the perf. pass. & compound systems; while παίω has a freer range of the tenses: Πατάξαι ἢ πληγῆναι, to strike or be struck, Aristl. Rh. 1. 15. Τύπτει.., καί .. πατάξας Lys. 136. 22.

τύφω (d¹g, θῡφ-) fumigate, smoke; τέθῡφα r., τέθυμμαι, 2 a. ᶜἐτύφην ᵒf.

Υ.

[ὑλάω ululo, HOWL, bark, π. 9:] ὑλάσκω po., ὑλάσσω l., ὑλακτέω, υ. 13, Ven. 3. 5, [ὑλακάω & ὑλακτιάω l.]

ὑπ-ισχνέομαι, undertake, promise, A. r. l.; ὑπο-σχήσομαι, 2 a. ὑπεσχόμην; ὑπ-έσχημαι, ὑπ-εσχέθην r.: po. or l. ὑπίσχομαι. See ἔχω.

"ὕω rain, 571 d, e; "ὕσω [m. as p. Hdt. 2. 14], ὕσα; ᶜὕσμαι 307d, Ven. 9. 5, ὕσθην, Hdt. 3. 10.

Φ.

[φα-, φεν- b¹ n, kill, +; ἔφασα l., 2 a. ἔπεφνον c³, 284 e; πέφαμαι, E. 531, -σμαι l., 3 f. πεφήσομαι, O. 140: l. πέφνω, whence some accent 2 a. pt. as pres., πέφνων.] Cog. σφάζω.

φάγομαι, ἔφαγον, see ἐσθίω eat.

φαίνω h, φανῶ, πέφαγκα ᶜDinarch., &c., show, shine, M. appear, 40; as v. l. 2 a. ἔφανον m.!; 2 a. p. iter. φάνεσκε 332 g. Po. cog. [φαείνω, γ. 2,] f. (φαενω) φᾰνῶ! Ar. Eq. 300; [φάω, pf. p. πέφαται?, 3 f. πεφήσεται P. 155, cf. φα-;] φαέθω, Soph. El. 824; πιφαύσκω, λ. 442, Æsch. Ag. 23. Cog. φημί say, Sans. bhami 271 dʳ.

φείδομαι (h, φιδ-) spare; φείσομαι ao., [πεφιδήσομαι,2a.πεφιδόμην,284f; πεφίδημαι l., 311,] πέφεισμαι l.

φέρβω feed, nourish, M. po.+, Pl. Criti. 115a; [2 plp. ἐπεφόρβει Hom. Merc. 105.] Cog. ?,

φέρω fero, BEAR, bring, M., [imv. 2 p. φέρτε 326 e:] fr. οι- x, f. οἴσω m., ao. a. r., m.?, [inf. ἀνα-οῖσαι, ct. ἀνῶσαι Hdt. 1. 157, imv. οἶσε 327 a;] f. p. οἰσθήσομαι: fr. ἐνεκ- x, ἐνεγκ- n³, 1 a. ἤνεγκα m., 306 a, 2 a. ἤνεγκον (preferred in inf. & pt.; but scarcely used in ind. exc. 1 s. po., or in imv. exc. 2 s., where 1 a. is r.: Ἐγὼ ἤνεγκόν. Ἤνεγκας σύ; Ar. Th. 742), m. not in ind. & r. Soph. O. C. 470; pf. ἐνήνοχα 281 c, 312 c, Isoc. 128 d, ἐνήνεγμαι, ἠνέχθην f., iv. 7. 12: [fr. ἐνεικ-, E. & I. 1 a. ἤνεικα m., 2 a. ἤνεικον r. φ. 178; ᵒἐνήνειγμαι, Hdt. 8. 37, ᵒἠνείχθην.] Cog. φορέω v²,

§ 50.   φέρω   VERBS.   φρύγω   91

-ήσω (l. -έσω), &c. [pr. *inf.* φορῆναι 335 b, φορήμεναι 333 e, O. 310] ; φρέω (po. 2 a. *imv.* φρές) ; [ᶜἐνείκομαι.]

φεύγω (h, φυγ-) fugio, *flee*; **φεύξομαι** & -οῦμαι 305 d, -ξω l., ao. l., [l. f. φυγοῦμαι 305 a], 2 κ. ἔφυγον ; 2 pf. πέφευγα,-α. 12, [pt. πεφυγμένος a. 18,] ἐφεύχθην l. Cog. φυγγάνω Æsch. Pr. 513 ; [as fr. φυζάω, 2 pf. *pt.* πεφυζότες Φ. 6, πεφυζηώς l., 1 a. p. φυζηθείς l.]

φημί (φα-), 45 u, 271 ʳ s, & **φάσκω**, fā-ri, (a) *say, affirm* (this stronger sense belonging esp. to φάσκω, & the fut., aor., & *mid.* fr. φα-) ; ipf. ἔφασκον & (usu. as aor.) ἔφην / M. pr. [2 p. φάσθε κ. 562, *imv.* φάο π. 168, φάσθω v. 100, *inf.* φάσθαι +, Æsch. Per. 700,] *pt.* φάμενος, Hel. 1. 6. 3, ipf. ἐφάμην ch. po. or l., A. 43 ; **φήσω** (opt. l. r.), ἔφησα (*imv.* wanting); pf. *p.* [3 s. πέφαται Ap. Rh. 2. 500,] *imv.* 3 s. πεφάσθω Pl. Tim. 72 e, ᶜἐφάθην Aristl. Int. 9. 9 : (b) fr. (Fεπ- x, cf. Lat. verbum) ἐρ- f, ῥε- cᵇ (pr. *a.* (1 s. only) εἴρω h, v. 7, *m.* l., ipf. *m.* ι. 542 ;] f. ἐρῶ, ᶜ*m.* l.; εἴρηκα 281, -μαι, 3 f. εἰρήσομαι Th. 6. 34, ἐρρήθην, -έθην r., [ɪ. εἰρέθην,] *sub.* ῥηθῶ, &c., Hdt. 3. 9, f. ῥηθήσομαι : (c) fr. (Fεπ-, Fειπ-h) εἰπ-) l a. εἶπα 306 a (*ind.* 2 s., & *imv.* exc. 2 s., esp. used opt., *inf.*, & *pt.* r. in Att.), ᶜ*m.* ɪ. or l., oftener (exc. as above) 2 a. εἶπον (εἴπω, -οιμι, -έ, -εῖν, -ών), ᶜ*m.*? l., [w. syllabic aug., ἔFειπον, ἔειπον K. 445, ἔειπα Pind. N. 9. 78.] (d) Cog. φατίζω & φημίζω ch. po. ; φαίνω *show*, q. v.; (εἰρέω, Hes. Th. 38 ;] ἐρωτάω *ask*, q. v.; [ἔπω l. r.; ἐσπ- o, in pr. or 2 a. *imv.* 2 p. ἔσπετε B. 484, pr. *m.* ἔσπομαι l.;] ἐνέπω q. v.

e. The forms with φ omitted (45 u), ἠμί [3 s. ἦσι Sap. 48], ἦν, ἦ, are used for greater vivacity or the metre. Some refer them to a distinct root, akin to the Lat. *aio*. The subject follows, if expressed : ἦν δ' ἐγώ, *quoth I*, Ar. Eq. 634 ; ἦ δ' ὅς § 518 f ; ἦ, *he spake*, A. 219 ; παῖ, ἠμί, παῖ, παῖ, *boy! I say, boy! boy!* Ar. Nub. 1145. (f) The pr. 2 s. is usu. written φής, as if ct. fr. φαείς, 120 g, [φ^σθα 297 b, ξ. 149 ; 3 s. φή fr. φαεί or φησί, 103 c, Anac. 41 ; D. φατί, 3 p. φαντί, 328.]

(g) **Φάσκω** is most used in the *pt.*, to supply the place of φάς (45 n). Hom. has only the ipf., Ν. 100. The pr. *ind.* is esp. rare. (h) The familiar forms from ἐρ- & εἰπ- have associate forms, not only as above, but also in λέγω, ἀγορεύω (ch. in comp.), &c.

φθάνω (ᾱ ᴇ.; n¹, φθα-) *anticipate*, M. l.; φθάσω, Cyr. 5. 4. 38, oftener φθήσομαι 310 d, Th. 8. 12, ἔφθασα, Th. 1. 33, 2 a. ἔφθην 313 b, λ. 58, Th. 4. 4, [*m. pt.* φθάμενος E. 119 ;] ἔφθακα, ἐφθάσθην l.

φθείρω (h, φθαρ-, φθερ- b) *corrupt*, *destroy*, esp. cp. w. διά, M. ; **φθερῶ** *m.*, ἔφθειρα, [f. ᶜφθέρσω, N. 625, ao. l., 152 d, ᶜφθαρέομαι ɪ. ;] **ἔφθαρκα**, ᵒEur. Med. 226, 2 pf. ἔφθορα ᶜIb. 349, ἔφθαρμαι, 2 a. ἐφθάρην f. Cog.,

φθίνω n¹ [ῐ ᴇ., & r. φθίω, β. 368], *decay, consume* (usu. intrans. exc. in fut. & ao.), ch. po., M.; φθίσω [ῐ ᴇ. m.,] ao. *a.* [m. l., 2 a. ᶜἐφθίσω? q¹, ε. 110 v. l.,] 2 a. *m.* ἐφθίμην 313 b, Eur. Alc. 414, *sub.* &c. [φθίωμαι, ᶜφθίμην 316 e, 3 s. φθίσθω, φθίσθαι,] φθίμενος· ἔφθῐκα l., -μαι, v. 340, -θην. Cog. φθινύθω po., φθινέω l., φθέω ?

φιλέω (v, φίλ-), -ήσω, πεφίληκα, &c., *love*, 42 : [φίλημι 335 b, φιλεῖσθα 297 b, φιλήμεναι 333 c, X. 265 ; 1 a. *m.* ἐφῑλάμην 152, E. 61.]

φλαδ-, 2 a. ἔφλαδον *burst*, Æsch.

φλέγω flagro, *burn*; **φλέξω**, ᶜ*m.* l., ao. *a.* Æsch. Pr. 582 ; πέφλεγμαι l., ἐφλέχθην, 2 a. ᶜἐφλέγην ᶜf. l. Der. φλεγέθω po., P. 738, φλογίζω.

φοβέω v², -ήσω, πεφόβηκα, &c., *terrify*, M. [& ἐφέβομαι E. 532] *fear*.

φράζω (j¹, φραδ-) *tell*, M.; **φράσω** [m.], ao., [2 a. πέφραδον, ἐπέφραδον, 284 e ;] πέφρακα Isoc. 101 a, -σμαι [ᶜπεφραδμένος 148 b, Hes. Op. 653], ἐφράσθην. [Cog. r. φραδάζω, Pind.]

φράσσω & r. **φράγνυμι** (i, n⁷, φραγ-] *fence*, M. φράγνυμαι ; *m.* ᶜφράξομαι l., ἔφραξα *m.*; 2 pf. ᶜπέφραγα (or -κα) l., -γμαι, Th. 1. 82, ἐφράχθην, ᶜf. l., 2 a. ἐφράγην l., f. l.: sometimes written φαρ for φρα, 145.

φρίσσω (i, φρικ-) *shudder*; **φρίξω** l., ao. *a.*, *m.* l.; 2 pf. pret. πέφρῑκα, Λ. 383, [pt. πεφρίκοντας 326 b.] Cog. (Fριγ-, 139, 141) ῥιγέω q. v.

φρύγω g, frīgo, *roast*; [**φρύξω**] ao. ;

φρύγω TABLES. χράω § 50.

πέφρυγμαι, Th. 6. 22, ἐφρύχθην l., ἐφρύγην I. or l. : l. φρύσσω. Cog. φώγνυμι n[7], l. [φώγω D., φώξω I.; ἔφωξα & -ωσα Hipp.;] &c.

φυλάσσω (ἰ, φυλακ-), -ξω, [c]πεφύλαχα, &c., *guard*, *M. beware;* [pr. a. imv. 2 p. προ-φύλαχθε 326 e;] 2 pf. πεφύλακα l. Lxx.

φύρω g, *mix, knead*, *M.*; ἔφυρα l. [ἔφυρσα 152 d, σ. 21, m. l.]; πέφυρμαι, [3 f. πεφύρσομαι 319,] ἐφύρθην, Æsch. Ag. 732, 2 a. ἐφύρην [c]f. l. Cog. φῡράω, -άσω · [φοςθνω & -ύσσω.]

φύω (ῠ) *produce*, *M. grow /* φύσω m., ao. a., 2 ao. ἔφῡν (φύω, φύην 316 c, φῦναι, φύς, cf. ἔδῡν 45 h) *was born or made, became*, hence *am;* πέφυκα pret., *am* (by nature), Th. 4. 61, [ἐπέφυκον 326 b, 2 pf. 3 p. πεφύᾱσι Δ. 484, sub. [c]πεφύω, pt. πεφυώς, e. 477,] [c]ἐφύθην l. r., 2 a. ἐφύην, f. l. Cog. φυτεύω, -εύσω, & φῑτύω, -ύσω, *plant;* Lat. fui.

φώγνυμι [-γω, -ξω,] : see φρύγω.

X.

[c]χάζω (j[1], χαδ-, καδ- d[2]) *drive back, M.* ch. E., *cedo, retreat* (so *A*. iv. 1. 16); [κεκαδήσω 284 f, χάσομαι, [c]ἔχασα, Pind. N. 10. 129, m. +, Δ. 535, 2 a. κέκαδον, m. Δ. 497.]

χαίνω *gape*, l. Anth.; see χάσκω.

χαίρω (h, χαρ-) *rejoice, M.*; χαιρήσω 311 b, Ar. Pl. 64, ao. l., χαροῦμαι l. Lxx., [κεχαρήσω, -σομαι, 284 f, 1 a. ἐχηράμην, Ξ. 270, 2 a. ἐχαρόμην l., κεχαρόμην 284 e, Α. 256;] κεχάρηκα, Hdt. 3. 42, [pt. κεχαρηώς 325d, H. 312,] κεχάρημαι & κέχαρμαι po., Eur. Iph. A. 200, El. 1077, ἐχάρην, f. l. Cog. χαρίζομαι *gratify*.

[χανδάνω (n[5], χαδ-, χανδ- n[8], χενδ- b) *contain*, +; (χενδ-σομαι 156) χείσομαι, σ. 17, 2 a. ἔχαδον, Δ. 24 ; 2 pf. pret. κέχανδα, δ. 96.] Cog.?,

χάσκω (k[8], χαν-), l. χαίνω h, *hisco, gape;* [c]χανοῦμαι [χήσομαι ?], 2 a. ἔχανον, Δ. 182 ; 2 pf. pret. κέχηνα Ar. Av. 264. Der. χασκάζω 379 b.

χέζω (j, χεδ-) *caco, comic* +; χεσοῦμαι 305 d, [c]χέσομαι r., ἔχεσα m., 2 a. ἔχεσον r. 327 a ; 2 pf. [c]κέχοδα, κέχεσμαι ; Ar.

χέω (f[1], χ̓εϝ-, χευ- f[2], χῠ- 142[r])

pour, ch. cp. w. ἐκ, ἐν, σύν, &c., *M.*, 309 b ; f. [c]χέω or χεῶ 305 f, b, m., [χεύω β. 222,] 1 a. ἔχεα m. 306,[ἔχευα m., H. 86, 63, 2 a. m. ἐχύμην 313 b, Δ. 526 ;] [c]κέχυκα l., -μαι, ἐχύθην f. (l. -έθην f.) : also χύω l. (χύσω, &c.), χύνω l., Acts 9. 22, χεύω (pr.) po., ch. l., (ἔχευσα). Cog. χόω q. v.

χλιδάω u, *luxuriate*, po. or l. ; 2 pf. [c]κέχλιδα. [Cog. κέχλάδα pret., Pind.]

χολόω, -ώσω, &c., *anger;* *M.* χολόομαι [χώομαι c[21], Τ. 29, χώσομαι, ao. A. 64] *be angry*; pret. κεχόλωμαι, a. 69, 3 f. κεχολώσομαι Ψ. 543.

χόω & later χώννυμι n[8], *heap up;* χώσω, ao. a. [m. l.] ; [c]κέχωκα, Dem. 1279. 20, -σμαι, ἐχώσθην f. ; Cyr. 7. 3. 11, 16, 17. Cog. χέω q. v.

[χραισμέω v, *avert, help*, pr. l. r. ; χραισμήσω, Τ. 296, ao. Σ. 62, 2 a. ἔχραισμον, Ξ. 66; not in Od.] Cog.,

χράω (χρήσω, &c., 310 a, 307 e ; χράεις χρῃς 120 g, I. or l. χρᾷς Hdt. 4. 155, &c.) *to supply need*,—

a.) The need of another, by *lending;* *M.*, one's own need, by *borrowing:* κίχρημι r[1], m. κίχράμαι · [χρήσω, Hdt. 3. 58,] ao. a. m. ; κέχρηκα l., [c]-μαι, Dem. 817. 2 : l. κιχράω.

b.) The need of one who consults an oracle, by *answering;* *M.* one's own need, by *consulting an oracle:* χράω, m. χρόσομαι · χρήσω m., ao. a. ; κέχρηκα l., -σμαι or -μαι, Hdt. 7. 141, ἐχρήσθην. Po. cog. χρήζω, Eur.

c.) One's own need, by *using* what is required : *M.* χράομαι · χρήσομαι ao. ; κέχρημαι, Hdt. 1. 42, ἐχρήσθην.

d. Impers. χρή (for χράει or nude χρῆσι, cf. φημί f), it supplies need, i. e. *it is useful* or *necessary, it must* or *ought to be;* sub. χρῇ, opt. (χρεβ[1]) χρείη Æsch. Pr. 213, inf. χρῆναι nude, & po. χρῆν Eur. Hec. 260, pt. neut. & indecl. (χράον, ct. 120 i) χρεών Th. 6. 18 ; ipf. 3 s. ἐχρῆν 163 b, oftener χρῆν 284 c ; χρήσει Hdt. 7. 8.

(e) Cp. ἀπό-χρη [l. ἀποχρᾷ Hdt. 9. 79], it fully supplies need, *it suffices* or *contents;* inf. ἀπο-χρῆν Dem. 52. 13, ipf. ἀπ-έχρη ; ἀπο-χρήσει, ἀπ-έχρησε. [So l. ἀπ-εχρέετο, κατα-χρᾷ, -χρήσει, ἐκ-χρήσει, Hdt. 8. 14, 1. 164, 3. 137.] (f) These or corresponding forms are also used personally : [Meg.

§ 51. χράω VERBS. ὠνέομαι 93

χρῆσθα *you must*, 297 b ;] ἀπό-χρη, -χρήσουσι, Ar. Av. 1603, Pl. 484, [ἐξ-έχρησε Hdt. 8. 70 ;] ἀπο-χράομαι *content one's self*, Hdt. 1. 37.

g. Forms fr. χράω sometimes agree in sense w. its cog. χρῄζω [E. I. χρητίζω, -ίσω, 132, p. 121, I. χρητίσκομαι, Hdt. 3. 117] *need, wish*, 414 c : as, χρῇ Soph. Ant. 887 ; po. pret. κέχρημαι *ne'd, wish*, Eur. Iph. A. 382, a. 13, 3 f. κεχρήσομαι, Theoc. 16. 73.

χρίω *anoint*, M.; χρίσω m., ao.; κέχρικα l. Lxx., -ισμαι or -ιμαι 307 e, Cyr. 7. 5. 22, ἐχρίσθην, f. l. Cog., χρώζω & l. χρώννῡμι (z, n⁸, χρο-) *touch, color;* ἔχρωσα l.; ᶜκέχρωκα l, κέχρωσμαι, Eur. Med. 497, ἐχρώσθην, f. l. Cog. χροΐζω po., χρωτίζω, χραίνω · (χραϜ-) χράω or χραύω *graze*.

[χώομαι, *be angry;* see χολόομαι.]

Ψ.

ψάω, ᶜψήσω, &c., *rub*, 120 g. Cog. ψήχω *rub*, ψαύω *touch*, ψάλλω *twitch*, ψηλαφάω *feel after*.

ψύχω *breathe, cool;* ψύξω ao.; πέψυχα l. 280 c, ἔψυγμαι, -χθην f., Ven. 5. 3, 2 a. ἐψύχην or -γην d², Ar. Nub. 151, f. l. Mat. 24. 12.

Ω.

ὠδίνω g, *be in travail*, Λ. 269 ; late ὠδίνω ao., & ὠδινήσω 311, Lxx., ao. a. m. p.

ὠθέω (v, ὠθ-) *push, M.;* ipf. ἐώθεον m. 279 b (ὤθ- E., I., l., & r. in Att.); ὤσω ᶜm., & po. ὠθήσω, m. l., ἔωσα m. [ὦσα m. E. I., E. 19], ὤθησα ᶜm. l.; ᶜἔωκα l., -σμαι, Cyr. 7. 1. 36, -σθην f., (I. or l. ὦσμαι, ὤσθην.) Der. ὠστίζομαι *justle*, Ar. Ach. 42.

ὠνέομαι, v. 3. 7, *buy* (pr. r. as pass. Pl. Phædo 69 b) ; ipf. ἐωνεόμην 279 b (ὠν- I., l., & r. in Att.); ὠνήσομαι vii. 2. 38, ἐωνησάμην or ὠνησάμην ch. l.; ἐώνημαι as *mid. & pass.*, Lys. 108. 26, 211. 1, -θην as *pass.*: 2 a. fr. πριαx, ἐπριάμην 45 i, a. 430 ; 2 s. ἐπρίω, πρίασο, πρίω, Ar. Vesp. 1440, Ach. 870, 34. Cog. πιπράσκω *sell*.

51. REMARKS. a. In using the preceding List, it is important to observe carefully the punctuation, as showing with what words the abbreviations, references, and various marks are connected; and also to distinguish the small Roman *letters of abbreviation* (marked by periods, as f., l., r., for *future, late, rare*), from mere *letters of reference* (not so marked, though periods may follow them for punctuation). If the latter immediately follow figures, they refer (except s) to parts of sections or pages ; but otherwise, to the notation of stems in § 49, 340 s. The articles on εἰμί, φημί, and χράω, have also division-letters. (b) If the abbreviation l., r., E., I., or po. follows ao., f., or m., its force extends back to the preceding word, unless arrested by [, (, or a comma.

c. Thus, in the paragraphs on στέλλω and σφάλλω, l first denotes the union of consonant I with λ in the stem, to form λλ ; while the following l. marks the form there noted, as *late*. Ἔσφαλον preceding is likewise so marked, as no comma intervenes, but not στελῶ · while ἐστάλθην is marked as *rare*, and ἐσφάλθην as both *late* and *rare*. In the article on χέω, f¹ denotes the dropping of F in the stem ; and f after 305, a part of the section so numbered ; while f. following is an abbreviation for *future*, showing that the Aor. ἐχύθην and the late ἐχέθην · have corresponding futures, χυθήσομαι and χεθήσομαι. It is also shown, that the Fut. χέω has only been found in composition ; and that the Fut. χεύω is dialectic, occurring in Homer. The sign + shows that χανδάνω, though also enclosed in brackets, is not wholly excluded from the Attic (Ar. Ran. 260). The references to authors have been usually, but not exclusively, attached to the less familiar forms. Before a reference, ᶜ marks the word as *there* compound, though sometimes simple. See Notes on page 67.

52. D. TABLE OF NUMERALS.

I. Adjectives.

	1. Cardinal.	2. Ordinal.
Interrog.	πόσοι; quot? *how many?*	πόστος; quotus? *which in order?* or, *one of how many?*
Indefinite	ποσοί, aliquot, *some.*	
Rel. Ind.	ὁπόσοι, quotquot.	ὁπόστος, quotuscumque, *whichsoever in order.*
Relative	ὅσοι, quot, *as many.*	
Diminut.	ὀλίγοι, pauci, *few.*	ὀλιγοστός, *one of few.*
Augment.	πολλοί, multi, *many.*	πολλοστός, *one of many,* or, *one following many.*
Demonst.	τόσοι, tot, *so many.*	

		Cardinal	Ordinal
1	α΄	εἷς, μία, ἕν, unus, *one.*	πρῶτος, -η, -ον, primus, *first..*
2	β΄	δύο, δύω, duo, *two.*	δεύτερος, -ᾱ, -ον, secundus, *second.*
3	γ΄	τρεῖς, τρία, tres, *three.*	τρίτος, -η, -ον, tertius, *third.*
4	δ΄	τέσσαρες, -α, quatuor, *four.*	τέταρτος, quartus, *fourth.*
5	ε΄	πέντε, quinque, *five.*	πέμπτος, quintus, *fifth.*
6	ς΄	ἕξ, sex, *six.*	ἕκτος, sextus, *sixth.*
7	ζ΄	ἑπτά, septem, *seven.*	ἕβδομος, septimus, *seventh.*
8	η΄	ὀκτώ, octo, *eight.*	ὄγδοος, octāvus, *eighth.*
9	θ΄	ἐννέα, novem, nine.	ἔνατος, nonus, *ninth.*
10	ι΄	δέκα, decem, *ten.*	δέκατος, decimus, *tenth.*
11	ια΄	ἕνδεκα, undecim, *eleven.*	ἑνδέκατος, undecimus, *eleventh.*
12	ιβ΄	δώδεκα, duodecim, *twelve.*	δωδέκατος, duodecimus, *twelfth.*
13	ιγ΄	τρισκαίδεκα, δεκατρεῖς, tredecim, *thirteen.* [decim.	τρισκαιδέκατος, tertius decimus, *thirteenth.*
14	ιδ΄	τεσσαρεσκαίδεκα, quatuor-	τεσσαρακαιδέκατος, quartus decimus.
15	ιε΄	πεντεκαίδεκα, quindecim.	πεντεκαιδέκατος, quintus decimus.
16	ις΄	ἑκκαίδεκα, sexdecim.	ἑκκαιδέκατος, sextus decimus.
17	ιζ΄	ἑπτακαίδεκα, septendecim.	ἑπτακαιδέκατος, septimus decimus.
18	ιη΄	ὀκτωκαίδεκα, duodeviginti.	ὀκτωκαιδέκατος, duodevicesimus.
19	ιθ΄	ἐννεακαίδεκα, undeviginti.	ἐννεακαιδέκατος, undevicesimus.
20	κ΄	εἴκοσι(ν, viginti, *twenty.*	εἰκοστός, vicesimus, *twentieth.*
21	κα΄	εἷς καὶ εἴκοσι, εἴκοσιν εἷς, viginti unus, *twenty-one.*	εἰκοστὸς πρῶτος, unus et vicesimus, *twenty-first.*
30	λ΄	τριάκοντα, triginta, *thirty.*	τριᾱκοστός, tricesimus, *thirtieth.*
40	μ΄	τεσσαράκοντα, quadraginta.	τεσσαρᾱκοστός, quadragesimus.
50	ν΄	πεντήκοντα, quinquaginta.	πεντηκοστός, quinquagesimus.
60	ξ΄	ἑξήκοντα, sexaginta, *sixty.*	ἑξηκοστός, sexagesimus, *sixtieth.*
70	ο΄	ἑβδομήκοντα, septuaginta.	ἑβδομηκοστός, septuagesimus.
80	π΄	ὀγδοήκοντα, octoginta.	ὀγδοηκοστός, octogesimus.
90	ϟ΄	ἐνενήκοντα, nonaginta.	ἐνενηκοστός, nonagesimus.
100	ρ΄	ἑκατόν, centum, *a hundred.*	ἑκατοστός, centesimus, *hundredth.*
200	σ΄	διᾱκόσιοι, -αι, -α, ducenti.	διᾱκοσιοστός, ducentesimus.
300	τ΄	τριᾱκόσιοι, trecenti.	τριᾱκοσιοστός, trecentesimus.
400	υ΄	τετρᾰκόσιοι, quadringenti.	τετρᾰκοσιοστός, quadringentesimus.
500	φ΄	πεντᾰκόσιοι, quingenti.	πεντᾰκοσιοστός, quingentesimus.

§ 52   NUMERALS.   95

600 χ´ ἑξακόσιοι, sexcenti. ἑξακοσιοστός, sexcentesimus.
700 ψ´ ἑπτακόσιοι, septingenti. ἑπτακοσιοστός, septingentesimus.
800 ω´ ὀκτακόσιοι, octingenti. ὀκτακοσιοστός, octingentesimus.
900 ϡ´ ἐνακόσιοι, nongenti. ἐνακοσιοστός, nongentesimus.
1,000 ‚α χίλιοι, -αι, -α, mille. χιλιοστός, millesimus, *thousandth.*
2,000 ‚β δισχίλιοι, duo millia. δισχιλιοστός, bis millesimus.
10,000 ‚ι μύριοι, -αι, -α, decem millia, *ten thousand.* μυριοστός, decies millesimus, *ten-thousandth.*
20,000 ‚κ δισμύριοι, viginti millia. δισμυριοστός, vicies millesimus.
100,000 ‚ρ δεκακισμύριοι, centum millia, 100 *thousand.* δεκακισμυριοστός, centies millesimus, *hundred-thousandth.*

3. Temporal.

Inter. ποσταῖος; *on what day?*

1. (αὐθήμερος, *on the same day.*)
2. δευτεραῖος, *on the second day.*
3. τριταῖος, *on the third day.*
4. τεταρταῖος, *on the fourth day.*
5. πεμπταῖος, *on the fifth day.*
6. ἑκταῖος, *on the sixth day.*
7. ἑβδομαῖος, *on the seventh day.*
8. ὀγδοαῖος, *on the eighth day.*

4. Multiple.

Augm. πολλαπλοῦς, multiplex.

ἁπλ(όος)οῦς, simplex, *simple, single.*
διπλοῦς, duplex, *double.*
τριπλοῦς, triplex, *triple.*
τετραπλοῦς, quadruplex, *quadruple.*
πενταπλοῦς, quincuplex, *quintuple.*
ἑξαπλοῦς, sextuple.
ἑπταπλοῦς, septemplex, *septuple.*
ὀκταπλοῦς, octuple.

5. Proportional.

Inter. ποσαπλάσιος; *how many fold?*
Dim.
            [fold.
Augm. πολλαπλάσιος, *many*

1. (ἴσος, æquus, *equal.*)
2. διπλάσιος, diplus, *twof.*
3. τριπλάσιος, triplus.
4. τετραπλάσιος, quadruplus, *fourfold.*
5. πενταπλάσιος, *fivefold.*
6. ἑξαπλάσιος, *sixfold.*
7. ἑπταπλάσιος, septuplus.
8. ὀκταπλάσιος, octuplus.
9. ἐννεαπλάσιος, *ninefold.*
10. δεκαπλάσιος, *tenfold.*
20. εἰκοσαπλάσιος.
100. ἑκατονταπλάσιος.
1,000. χιλιοπλάσιος.
10,000. μυριοπλάσιος, 10,000-*fold.*

II. Adverbs.

ποσάκις; quoties? *how many times?*
ὀλιγάκις, paucies, *few times.*
πολλάκις, *many times.*

ἅπαξ, semel, *once.*
δίς, bis, *twice.*
τρίς, ter, *thrice.*
τετράκις, quater, *four times.*
πεντάκις, quinquies.
ἑξάκις, sexies.
ἑπτάκις, septies.
ὀκτάκις, octies.
ἐνάκις, novies.
δεκάκις, decies.
εἰκοσάκις, vicies.
ἑκατοντάκις, centies.
χιλιάκις, millies.
μυριάκις, decies millies.

III. Substantives.

ποσότης, quantitas, *quantity, number.*
ὀλιγότης, paucitas, *fewness.*
πολλότης, multitūdo.

ἑνάς, μονάς, *monad.*
δυάς, *duad.*
τριάς, *triad.*
τετράς, τετρακτύς, *quaternion.*
πεμπάς, πεντάς.
ἑξάς, *hexade.*
ἑπτάς, ἑβδομάς.
ὀκτάς, ὀγδοάς.
ἐννεάς, *ennead.*
δεκάς, *decade.*
εἰκάς, *score.*
ἑκατοντάς, *century.*
χιλιάς, *chiliad.*
μυριάς, *myriad.*

53. E. PRONOMINAL

Obsolete Primitives are printed in capitals. Poetic, Late, and Dialectic Forms are not marked.
Latin equivalents occupy the

		ORDERS,	I. Interrogative.	II. Indefinite.	III, IV. Ob(Sub)jective. Negative.	V. Definite. Relative.	VI. Indefinite.
A. ADJECTIVES OF	**1. Distinction.**	Positive,	τίs; ΠΟΣ; quis?	τίs, ΠΟΣ 'ΑΜΟΣ aliquis	οὐ(μή)τις οὐ(μη)δαμός οὐ(μη)δείς	ὅs qui ὅσπερ ὅστε	ὅστις 'ΟΙΙΟΣ quicumque
		Comparative,	πότερος; uter?	πότερος • uter	οὐ(μη)δέτερος οὐ(μη)δοπότερος		ὁπότερος
		Superlative,	πόστος;		[neuter		ὁπόστος
	2. Property.	Quantity,	πόσος; quantus?	ποσός aliquantus		ὅσος quantus	ὁπόσος quantus
		Quality,	ποῖος; qualis?	ποιός qualis	οὑτιδανός οὐ(μη)δαμινός	οἷος qualis	ὁποῖος qualis
		Age, Size,	πηλίκος;	πηλίκος		ἡλίκος	ὁπηλίκος
		Country,	ποδαπός;				ὁποδαπός
		Day,	ποσταῖος;				ὁποσταῖος
B. ADVERBS OF	**1. Place.**	Whence,	πόθεν; unde?	ποθέν ἀμόθεν alicunde	μήποθεν οὐ(μη)δαμόθεν οὐ(μη)δετέρωθεν	ὅθεν ἔνθεν unde	ὁπόθεν undecum- . [que ὁποτέρωθεν
		Where,	ποῦ; πόθι; ubi? ποτέρωθι;	πού ἀμοῦ ποθί alicubi uspiam	οὐ(μή)που οὐ(μη)δαμοῦ οὔποθι nusquam οὐ(μη)δαμόθι οὐδετέρωθι	οὗ, ἔνθα ὁσαχοῦ ὅθι, ἵνα ubi	ὅπου ὁπόθι ubiubi ὁποτέρωθι
		Whither,	ποῖ; πόσε; quo? ποτέρωσε;	ποί ἀμοῖ aliquo	οὐ(μη)δαμοῖ οὐ(μη)δαμόσε οὐ(μη)δετέρωσε	οἷ quo	ὅποι ὁπόσε quoquo ὁποτέρωσε
	2. Way, or Place where,		πῇ; qua? ποίᾳ; ποσαχῇ;	πή ἀμῇ aliqua	οὔπη οὐδέπη οὐ(μη)δαμῇ	ᾗ, ᾗχι qua ὁσαχῇ	ὅπη quaqua ὁποσαχῇ
	3. Manner, &c.,		πῶs; quomodo? ποίως; ποτέρως; ποσαχῶς; πῶ;	πώς ἀμῶς ποσῶς πώ	οὐ(μή)πως οὐ(μη)δαμῶς οὐ(μη)δετέρως οὐ(μή)πω οὐ(μη)δέπω	ὡs ut quomodo οἵως qualiter ὁσαχῶς	ὅπως utcumque ὁποίως ὁποτέρως
	4. Time.	General,	πότε; quando?	ποτέ aliquan- [do	οὐ(μή)ποτε οὐ(μη)δέποτε [nunquam οὐ(μη)κέτι	ὅτε quum ἡνίκα ἧμος, ἐπεί ἕως, ὄφρα	ὁπότε quandōque ὁπηνίκα ὁπῆμος
		Specific,	πηνίκα;				
		Various,	πῆμος; quando?				
	5. Number,		ποσάκις; quoties?		οὐδενάκις	ὁσάκις quoties	ὁποσάκις quotiesque

DERIVATIVE NOUNS. ποσότης quantitas, ποιότης qualitas, πηλικότης, ἑτερότης, ταυτότης, ὁμοιότης, ἰσότης, οὐδένεια, ἴσωσις, ἀλλοίωσις, ὁμοίωμα, &c.

CORRELATIVES.

Of the Negative Forms, the Objective begin with οὐ-, and the Subjective with μη-. space after or below some words.

Definite or Demonstrative.			Universal.		XII.
VII. Simple.	VIII. Emphatic.	IX. Deictic.	X. Distributive.	XI. Collective.	Of Identity, Diversity, &c.
ὁ, ΤΟΣ	οὗτος hic	ὅδε hic		πᾶς omnis	ὁμός, αὐτός
ἐκεῖνος	οὑτοσί	ὁδί		ἀμφω	ἄλλος
ille	hicce	hicce		ambo	alius
ἕτερος			ἑκάτερος	ἀμφότερος	
alter			alteruter	uterque	
			ἕκαστος		αὐτότατος
τόσος tan-	τοσοῦτος	τοσόσδε			
τυννός [tus	τυννοῦτος	τοσοσδί			
τοῖος talis	τοιοῦτος	τοιόσδε		παντοῖος	ὅμοιος
ἐκεῖνινος	τοιουτοσί	τοιοσδί		omnigenus	ἀλλοῖος
τηλίκος	τηλικοῦτος	τηλικόσδε			ὁμῆλιξ
				παντοδαπός	ἀλλοδαπός
					αὐθήμερος
τόθεν inde	τουτόθεν		ἑκάστοθεν	πάντοθεν	ὁμόθεν
ἔνθεν hinc	ἐντεῦθεν	ἐνθένδε	ἑκασταχόθεν	πανταχόθεν	αὐτόθεν
ἐκεῖθεν	hinc	hinc	ἑκάτερθεν	undique	ἄλλοθεν
ἑτέρωθεν	inde	inde	ἑκατέρωθεν	ἀμφοτέρωθεν	ἀλλαχόθεν
ἔνθα hic	ἐνταῦθα	ἐνθάδε	[utrimque	πανταχοῦ	ὁμοῦ, αὐτοῦ
ἐκεῖ illic	hic	hic	ἑκασταχοῦ	ubīque	ἀλλαχοῦ
τόθι ibi	ibi	ibi	ἑκάστοθι	πάντοθι	αὐτόθι
ἐκεῖθι	ἐνταυθί	ὧδε	ἑκασταχόθι	πανταχόθι	ἄλλοθι
ἑτέρωθι		hic	ἑκατέρωθι	ἀμφοτέρωθι	ἀλλαχόθι
ἐνθάδε eo	ἐνταυθοῖ		ἑκασταχοῖ	πανταχοῖ	ὁμόσε
ἐκεῖσε	huc		quocumque	πάντοσε	αὐτόσε
illuc	eo		ἑκασταχόσε	πανταχόσε	ἄλλοσε
ἑτέρωσε			ἑκατέρωσε	ἀμφοτέρωσε	ἀλλαχόσε
τῇ ea	ταύτῃ	τῇδε		πάντῃ	ὁμῇ
ἐκείνῃ	hac	hac		ubīque	ἄλλῃ
illac	.		ἑκασταχῇ	πανταχῇ	ἀλλαχῇ
τώς, ὡς ita	οὕτως	ὧδε sic		πάντως	ὁμῶς
ἐκείνως	οὑτωσί	ὡδί		omnīno	αὔτως
τοίως	sic	τοιῶσδε		παντοίως	ὁμοίως
ἑτέρως	ita	taliter	ἑκατέρως	ἀμφοτέρως	ὡσαύτως
secus				παντάχῶς	ἄλλως
τῷ, τόσως	tot modis			πάνυ	ἀλλοίως
τότε tum			ἑκάστοτε	πάντοτε,	ἄλλοτε
tunc			semper	διαπαντός	alias
τηνίκα	τηνικαῦτα	τηνικάδε		[semper	αὐτίκα
τῆμος, νῦν	τημοῦτος	τημόσδε			statim
τέως, τόφρα					αὖ, αὖθις
τοσάκις	τοσαυτάκις toties		ἑκαστάκις		ἰσάκις
toties	τουτάκις		ἑκατεράκις	ἀμφοτεράκις	

DERIVATIVE VERBS. ὁμοιόω assimulo, ἰσόω æquo, ἀλλοιόω, τοσόω, ποιόω, ἑτεροιόω, οὐδενίζω, ἀμφοτερίζω, ἰσάζω, ὁμοιάζω, ἑκατερέω, ἀλλάσσω, &c.

54. F. TABLE OF DERIVATION.

A. Nouns (363 s).

I. From Verbs: denoting
1. The *Action*, in -σις, -σία, -τις, -η, -ά, -ος (G. -ου), -τος, -τη, -τύς, -μός, -μη, -ος (G. -εος).
2. The *Effect* or *Object*, in -μα, -ον.
3. The *Doer*, in -της, -τήρ, -τωρ, (F. -τρια, -τειρα, -τρίς, -τις,) -εύς, -ός, -μων.
4. The *Place*, *Instrument*, &c., in -τήριον, -τρον, -τρᾶ.

II. From Adjectives: expressing the *Abstract*, in -ία (-ειά, -οιά), -της (G. -τητος), -σύνη, -ος (G. -εος), -άς (G. -άδος).

III. From Other Nouns:
1. *Patrials*, in -της (-ίτης, -ήτης, -άτης, -ιάτης, -ιώτης · F. -τις), -εύς (F. -ίς).
2. *Patronymics*, in -ίδης, -άδης, -ιάδης (F. -ίς, -άς, -ιάς), -ίων, (F.-ιώνη, -ίνη) : — -ιδοῦς (F. -ιδῆ).
3. *Female Appellatives*, in -ις, -αινα, -ειά, -σσα (-ττα), -ά, -η.
4. *Diminutives*, in -ιον (-ίδιον, -άριον, -ύλλιον, -ύδριον, -ύφιον, &c.), -ίσκος (F. -ίσκη), -ίς, -ιδεύς, -ίχνη, -άκνη, -αλος, -ελος, -ιλος, -υλλίς, -ύλος, &c.
5. *Augmentatives*, in -ων, -ωνίᾶ, -αξ.
6. *Place*, *Instrument*, &c., in -αιον, -ειον, 375 ᵉ N.

B. Adjectives (373 s).

I. From Verbs: in -ικός, -τήριος, -μων, *active*; -τός, -τέος, -νός, *passive*; -ιμος, implying *fitness*; -ρός, -άς, -ός.

II. From Nouns: in -ιος (-αιος, -ειος, -οιος, -ῳος, -υιος), *pertaining to*; -ικός, -κός, -ακός, -αϊκός, *relating to*; -εος, -ινος, -εν, *material*; -ινός, *time* or *prevalence*; -ινος, -ηνός, -ᾱνός. *patrial*; -ρός, -φρός, -ηρός, -αλέος, -ηλός, -ωλός, -εις, -ώδης, *fulness* or *quality*.

III. From Adjectives and Adverbs:
1. As from Nouns.
2. Strengthened Forms: Comparative, Superlative.

C. Pronouns (53, 244 s, 377).

D. Verbs (378 s).

I. From Nouns and Adjectives; in -έω, -εύω, -άω, *to be* or *do*; -όω, -αίνω, -ύνω, *to make*; -ίζω, -άζω, *imitative*, *active*, &c.; -ιάω, -άω, *desiderative*; -ω with penult strengthened, *active*, &c.

II. From Other Verbs: in -σείω, *desiderative*; -ζω, -σκω, -λλω, *frequentative*, *intensive*, *inceptive*, *causative*, *diminutive*, &c.; reduplicated.

E. Adverbs (380 s).

I. Oblique Cases of Nouns and Adjectives:
1. *Accusatives*: of Nouns; Neut. Sing. and Plur. of Adjectives (esp. Comparatives and Superlatives).
2. *Genitives*, in -θεν, *place whence*; -ου, *place where*; -ης, &c.
3. *Datives*, in -οι, -οθι, -ησι, -ᾶσι, *place where*; -ῃ (-η), -ᾳ (-α), -αι, -ι, *way*, *manner*, *place where*, *time when*; &c.

II. Derivatives signifying,
1. *Manner*, in -ως, -ηδόν, -δόν, -δην, -άδην, -δα, -δις, -ί (ΐ), -εί, -ξ.
2. *Time when*, in -τε, -ίκα.
3. *Place whither*, in -σε, -δις.
4. *Number*, in -άκις.

III. Prepositional Forms and Phrases:
1. Prepositions with their Cases.
2. Prepositions without Cases.
3. Derivatives from Prepositions, in -ω, -θεν, -ωθεν, -τος, -δον, &c.

55. G. SIGNIFICANT ELEMENTS OF LANGUAGE.

NOTE. The term "things" is here used in its large sense, as including every object of sense, discourse, or thought; whether persons, material things, or mere abstractions. The term "actions" is used for both *actions* and *states*.

Grand Divisions.	The Signs of	Classes.	Orders.	Subdivisions.
A. Essential Elements.	Things,	I. SUBSTANTIVES,	Nouns, { Proper. / Common,	{ Appellative. / Collective. / Substantial. / Abstract. }
			Substantive Pronouns,	{ Personal, / Reflexive, / Connective, &c. }
			Infinitives (Gerunds, Supines).	
	Actions,	II. VERBS,	Transitive, Intransitive,	{ Finite Verbs. / Infinitives. / Participles. }
B. Descriptive Elements.	Properties of Things,	III. ADJECTIVES,	Articles,	{ Definite. / Indefinite. }
			Numerals,	{ Cardinal. / Ordinal. / Multiple, &c. }
			Adjective Pronouns,	{ Possessive. / Demonstrative. / Connective. / Interrogative. / Indefinite. / Distributive. / Negative, &c. }
			Participles.	
			Adjectives,	{ Of Quality. / Of Circumstance. }
	Properties of Actions or of other Properties,	IV. ADVERBS,	Of Manner, Of Place, Of Time, Of Degree, Of Number, &c.	{ Demonstrative. / Connective. / Interrogative. / Indefinite. / Negative. / Emphatic, &c. }
C. Connective Elements.	Relations of Things,	V. PREPOSITIONS,	Of Place, Time, Action, Cause, &c.	
	Relations of Sentences,	VI. CONJUNCTIONS,	Coördinate,	{ Copulative. / Adversative. / Alternative. }
			Subordinate,	{ Complementary. / Conditional. / Concessive. / Causal. / Final, &c. }
D. Instinctive Elements.	Emotions,	VII. INTERJECTIONS,	Of Pleasure, Pain, Address, &c.	

Without its ESSENTIAL ELEMENTS, language could have no existence as rational discourse; without its DESCRIPTIVE ELEMENTS, it would be vague and meagre; without its CONNECTIVE ELEMENTS, it would be disjointed; and without its INSTINCTIVE ELEMENTS, it would want sensibility and passion.

III. SYNTAX.

A. GENERAL PRINCIPLES.

56. *A thought expressed in words* forms a SENTENCE (sententia, *thought*). SYNTAX is the doctrine of sentences, as ETYMOLOGY, of words, ORTHOËPY, of vocal sounds, and ORTHOGRAPHY, of written characters.

a. To *analyze a sentence* is to divide it into its parts, observing their offices and relations. These parts, in Syntax, are of three kinds: *included sentences*, commonly called *clauses; phrases*, expressive combinations of words, yet not sentences; and *single words*, or those which in Etymology are so regarded: 'He came *when it was time*'; 'He came *in good time*'; 'He came *seasonably*.'

1. SENTENTIAL ANALYSIS.

57. 1. Every complete sentence has two *chief* or *primary elements*, the SUBJECT and PREDICATE; and may have a third, the COMPELLATIVE.

a. The subject and compellative are those substantives in the sentence which denote most directly the *persons* or *things spoken of* (subject) or *addressed* (compellative): '*Brethren, virtue* ennobles.'

b. The term *substantives* is here employed, as commonly in Syntax, to include not only nouns, substantive pronouns, and infinitives (55), but whatever is used *substantively;* as, an *adjective* or *adverb* denoting some person or thing, a *phrase* or *clause* forming an object of thought or remark, or any word spoken of *as a word:* '*Now*'s the day'; '*Above twenty* came'; '*Go* is a verb.' See 68 a, 70 a, 491.

c. The predicate is always a *verb;* and, of more than one, that which is most closely related to the subject in the expression of the thought.

(d) As the essence of a sentence is *predication*, the predicate is often taken as a representative of the sentence. Thus a word which connects or modifies a sentence, is familiarly spoken of as connecting or modifying the *verb* of the sentence: '*But perhaps* he will go.'

2. Sentences have also various *minor elements:*

e.) *Exponents*, words which mark the offices or relations of sentences or their parts: 'He said *that* he went *to* Paris *and* Rome.' See 65 s.

f.) Elements that are *grammatically independent;* as, a participial phrase absolute, interjections, &c.: '*This said*, he fell, *alas!*'

g.) *Subordinate elements*, or *modifiers*, which are joined with other elements to *modify* or *limit* them, i. e. to affect in various ways their force or application: '*Dear* brethren, *true* virtue *always* ennobles.'

h. A word which is modified by another, is termed its *principal;* and this distinction of *principals* and *modifiers* applies not only to single words, but also to phrases and sentences.

58. MODIFIERS are of three kinds: (1) WORDS OF PROPERTY, i. e. *Adjectives* and *Adverbs* (55), including all words so considered; (2) MODIFYING SUBSTANTIVES, including *Appositives* and *Adjuncts;* and (3) DEPENDENT SENTENCES.

a. MODIFYING SUBSTANTIVES. When, with *one* name of a person or thing, *another* is connected for the sake of explanation, specification, description, or emphasis, the latter is said to be *in apposition* with the former, and is termed an APPOSITIVE: 'Paul the *apostle*.' All other modifying substantives are termed ADJUNCTS: 'Saul of *Tarsus*.'

b. When two names for the same person or thing are connected as above, that should be regarded as the appositive which is added for the sake of modifying the other, whatever may be its position: 'George the *King*,' or '*King* George.' It is not, however, always easy to determine this; and two or more names are often so joined that they may be regarded as forming *one complex noun:* '*Charles James Fox*.'

c. An ADJUNCT, in respect to *form*, is either *prepositional* or *nude;* that is, it is either joined to its principal by a preposition, which serves as an *exponent* of its relation; or it is joined *immediately*, without a preposition. — In the first case, it is also termed *exponential;* and in the second, *immediate*. In the sentence, 'Give me the book,' the adjuncts *me* and *book* are both nude, or immediate; while in 'Give the book to me,' the adjunct *me* (or, prefixing the exponent, *to me*) is prepositional.

d. As to its use, an adjunct is regarded either as *completing* the idea of its principal, or as denoting some *circumstance* respecting it; and is hence distinguished as *complementary* or *circumstantial* (more briefly, as a *complement* or a *circumstance*). In 'The son of Jesse slew Goliath with a sling,' 'of Jesse' and 'Goliath' are complements of 'son' and 'slew,' which would seem incomplete without them; while the less essential 'with a sling' expresses a circumstance of 'slew,' viz. the instrument.

e. A complement is distinguished as *direct* or *indirect*, according to the closeness of its relation. This distinction appears especially in the objects of verbs, which form the most prominent class of complements.

f. Among the most prominent circumstances, are those of *place, time, cause, origin, material, motive, price, manner, means, degree, agency, &c.*

g. There is no line of division between complements and circumstances, or between direct and indirect complements; and many adjuncts may be differently classed, according to the view which the mind takes of them.

h. A MODIFYING CLAUSE performs the office of an *adjective, adverb*, or *substantive* (*appositive* or *adjunct*) in the sentence to which it belongs. See 62 b, h. (i) Hence, all modifiers are *adjective, adverbial*, or *substantive*, in their force; and, as *substantive* modifiers, when they modify other substantives, are akin to the *adjective*, but when they modify verbs, adjectives, or adverbs, to the *adverbial*, ADJECTIVES and ADVERBS may be taken as the *types* of all modifiers.

59. Some words have a *double relation*, which may be termed COMPLEX MODIFICATION. Thus,

a. A word modifying a verb, and thus partaking of an adverbial force (58 i), may also belong as an *adjective, appositive*, or *adjunct*, to the subject or a complement of the verb: 'He is esteemed *wise*.' 'He stood *erect*.' 'They made him *king*.' An adjective, &c., thus predicated of its subject, is termed a *predicate adjective*, &c.; while others, joined without predication, are termed *direct* or *assumed* (393 a, b). An assumed adjective is also called an *epithet*. A verb which can thus connect an appositive to its subject, is termed an *appositional verb*.

b. A clause modifying the predicate is often incorporated in a participial form, and *assumed* of the subject: '*Fearing this* [as he feared this], he fled.' See 62 a, d.

c. When two adjectives belong to the same substantive, one sometimes exerts an *adverbial* force upon the other, or modifies the *substantive taken with the other as a complex whole:* 'Red hot iron'; 'All *good men.*'

d. An adverb modifying a sentence or phrase, often gives a *special emphasis*, or bears a *special relation* to a *particular word* in the sentence or phrase : 'Bless me, *even* ME *also*,' Gen. 27. 34. 'He, HE *surely*, will go.'

60. a. Any element, with all the words which are subordinate to it and aid in expressing its idea, forms a logical part bearing the name of its element, but distinguished by the addition of '*part*'; while the element itself is distinguished, if need be, by the addition of '*word.*' The former is also distinguished as '*logical*,' and the latter as '*grammatical*' (sometimes called the "basis" of the logical part). In 'Good men are wise,' the subject-part, or logical subject (the subject *as thought of*), is 'Good men,' containing the subject-word, or grammatical subject, 'men'; and the predicate-part is 'are wise,' containing the predicate-word, or grammatical predicate (the word that expresses predication, and has the appropriate grammatical form and office) 'are.'

b. The predicate-part may be resolved into the ATTRIBUTE and the COPULA. The ATTRIBUTE (attribūtus, *ascribed*) expresses the action, state, property, &c., ascribed to the subject; as 'wise,' above. The COPULA (Lat. *tie, bond*) is a substantive verb (a verb which simply expresses *being*), uniting the attribute with the subject; as 'are,' above: 'The sun shines [*is* SHINING].' 'He fears [*is* AFRAID].'

II. OFFICES AND RELATIONS OF SENTENCES.

61. A sentence is INTELLECTIVE (intellectus, *understanding*) or VOLITIVE (volo, *to will*), according as it primarily expresses an act of the understanding, or an act of the will.

a. An intellective sentence is DECLARATIVE or INTERROGATIVE, according as it *makes a statement*, or *asks a question:* 'He will go.' 'Will he go?' (b) Interrogation is sometimes used rhetorically for strong statement. (c) A volitive sentence (also termed IMPERATIVE, from its mode) may express *command, entreaty, exhortation, permission*, or even *supposition:* 'Go.' (d) A sentence of any one of these forms is termed EXCLAMATORY, when used for exclamation : 'How fast he goes!' (e) Sentences of all these classes may be either POSITIVE or NEGATIVE ; i. e. they may *affirm* or *deny, require* or *prohibit*, &c. : 'I will go.' 'Do not go.'

f. A declarative or interrogative sentence is ACTUAL, when it has respect to *fact* (what *is*, or *is not*, &c.); but CONTINGENT, when it has respect to *contingency* (what *may be*, or *may not be*, &c.). See 613 s. These sentences may be also named from their modes and time (*indicative*, &c.)

62. Sentences are connected with each other in four ways :

a.) By INCORPORATION, in which the verb of one sentence is incorporated in another sentence as an *infinitive* or *participle* (i. e. as a *substantive* or *adjective*). — Such a sentence, as well as its verb, is termed *incorporated*, while sentences in which the predicate has a distinct form as a finite verb are termed *distinct* or *finite*. See 657 s.

b.) By SUBORDINATION, in which one of the sentences, without losing its distinct form, belongs to the other as a *part* or *circumstance* (*subject, object, condition, reason, result, time*, &c.) ; and is therefore termed *subordinate, dependent*, or *included*, while the other is distinguished as the *chief, principal*, or *leading sentence* or *clause.* — The two together form a COMPLEX SENTENCE : 'Go, *if you wish*'; '*That he went*, is strange.'

§ 63. METHODS OF INDICATION. 103

c.) By COÖRDINATION, in which the sentences are joined by a connective, but neither is subordinate to the other. Sentences so connected are termed *coördinate*, and together form a COMPOUND SENTENCE. See d, e.
d.) By SIMPLE SUCCESSION, in which one sentence directly follows another, without a connective (often referred to ellipsis, 68 d) : 'Luther said this. He sat down.'— This form may be changed to coördination, by supplying a connective ('L. said this, *and* he sat down'); often even to subordination ('*When* L. had said this, he sat down'), or the yet closer form of incorporation ('*Having said* this, L. sat down'). See 657 s, 693.
e. A sentence is termed SIMPLE, if it is neither complex nor compound; and INDEPENDENT, if it is neither incorporated nor subordinate. (f) A sentence which according to its main division is compound, may have complex members, and the converse. (g) Parts of a sentence are also *compound, complex*, or *simple*, according as they consist of portions joined by coördinate conjunctions expressed or understood, of portions joined by subordinate conjunctions, or of neither : '*Asa and Eli* gave *more than ten* dollars to *John*.' A sentence containing a compound or complex part may usually be resolved into two or more clauses, by supplying words.
h. A subordinate clause is usually *declarative* in form. It is termed ADJECTIVE (or *relative*), ADVERBIAL (*final, conditional, concessive, causal*, &c.), or SUBSTANTIVE (*appositive, adjunct*, &c.), according to its office or connective. See 58 h, 66. (i) An incorporated clause, though always substantive or adjective in form, is often *adverbial* in force (665, 674).
j. An independent sentence, whether simple or compound, with all its dependent clauses, forms a PERIOD, which may be further named according to its special character. If a dependent clause expresses a *condition* of the principal, the combination is called a HYPOTHETICAL PERIOD (ὑπόθεσις, *supposition*); the dependent clause being called the *premise, condition*, or *protasis* (προτείνω, *to stretch forth*); and the principal clause, the *conclusion*, or *apodosis* (ἀποδίδωμι, *to give back*).— Some of these terms are also applied to parts of other complex sentences.
k. QUOTATIONS, which form so important a class of substantive sentences, have two forms. In the first and more *dramatic* form, we simply repeat the words of another, without change or incorporation into our own discourse : *He said*, "I will go." This is termed ORATIO RECTA, *Direct Discourse* or *Quotation*. In the second and more *narrative* form, we make such changes and insert such connectives as will render the quotation an integral part of our own discourse : *He said, that he would go*. This is termed ORATIO OBLIQUA, *Indirect Discourse* or *Quotation* (643 s). This distinction likewise applies to the *thoughts* and *feelings* of another.
l. An incorporated clause does not usually require a separate analysis, except where, as in Latin and Greek, an Infinitive takes the place of another mode in Indirect Discourse.

III. METHODS OF INDICATION.

63. The offices and relations of sentences and their parts are indicated in three ways : (A) by the *form of the words;* (B) by the *arrangement;* and (C) by separate words, which act as *signs* or *exponents* of these offices or relations.
A. INDICATION BY FORM. This has four chief objects :
a.) To mark the connection of appositives, adjectives, pronouns, and verbs, with their *subjects* (i. e. the substantives to which they refer), by a *correspondence of form*, termed AGREEMENT or CONCORD. See 76, 492 s.

b.) To mark, by appropriate forms, the offices and relations of *substantives*. This is done, in most languages, through the distinction of *case*. When the form of a substantive is determined by its dependence upon another word, it is said to be *governed* by that word; and the influence exerted upon it is termed GOVERNMENT or REGIMEN. See 76.

c.) To mark, by the form of an adjective or adverb, the *degree* in which its property is possessed (COMPARISON, 29, 256 s).

d.) To mark the offices and relations of *sentences*, through the form of the VERB, the *predicating word*. See 57 c, 30, 265 s.

e. In *agreement*, the words which are connected are regarded, by a species of personification, as *allies;* in *government*, as *ruler* and *ruled*.

(f.) Of *nude adjuncts*, those only which are *complementary* (58 c, d), are usually spoken of as governed. *Prepositional adjuncts* are commonly said to be governed by the prepositions; and are called their *complements*, objects, or, by a happier term, *sequents*.

g. In the development of a language, new forms arise to express more specifically what has been generally expressed by some older form. This older form thus becomes narrowed in its appropriate sphere, and itself more specific in its expression. But habit, which is mighty everywhere, is peculiarly the arbiter of language; —

"Usus,
Quem penes arbitrium est et jus et norma loquendi"; —

and, wherever the new distinction is unimportant, there is a tendency to employ the old and familiar form in its original extent of meaning. The same is true of words and methods of construction. See 70 v.

64. B. ARRANGEMENT. a. Words are arranged for effect upon the *understanding*, the *emotions*, or the *ear:* in other words, the arrangement of a sentence may have for its object, (1) To exhibit the offices and relations of the words; (2) To present the thought in an impressive manner; (3) To produce an agreeable effect upon the ear. — That order which most effectually secures the first object is termed the *logical order;* the second, the *rhetorical order;* the third, the *rhythmical order*.

b. In the LOGICAL ORDER, the *verb* is usually placed after the *subject*, and before the *attribute*, if this is distinct from the verb (60 b); and (c) a word which *is governed* by another is usually placed after it. (d) Words are often spoken of in Syntax, as *following* or *preceding* others, with reference to the logical or usual order, without regard to their actual position.

65. C. USE OF EXPONENTS. These mark the offices or relations (1) of *words* (including *phrases*), or (2) of *sentences*.

1. WORD-EXPONENTS are (a) those which mark the relations of *adjuncts* (58 c), i. e. PREPOSITIONS ("case-links"); (b) CONJUNCTIONS used as in 62 g; (c) INTERJECTIONS marking *address* or *exclamation* (*O, ah*, 484, 73 e); (d) MODAL SIGNS (modus, *manner*), i. e. connective adverbs of manner used elliptically to limit the application of modifiers ('I took him *as* a friend,' 393 c, 711). The last may be parsed as connective adverbs by supplying ellipses, but most conveniently as mere signs uniting modifiers with their principals.

66. 2. SENTENTIAL EXPONENTS are either CONNECTIVE (denoting the connection of sentences), or CHARACTERISTIC (marking their character, without connecting them).

a. The CONNECTIVES may *simply denote the relations* of the sentences (CONJUNCTIONS, "clause-links," 700 s); or (b) they may also *enter into their structure* as pronouns or adverbs (CONNECTIVE PRONOUNS or ADVERBS). A connective pronoun or adverb is either (c) *relative* (referring to an antecedent, 549 s), or (d) *complementary* (introducing a sentence used substantively, 563 s). Thus, (a) *that, if, until, though,* (c) *who* (73 e); (d) *what* (73 d).

Connectives are either (e) *primary* (directly uniting the sentences), or (f) *secondary* (corresponding to the primary, "as the eye to the hook"): 'He (f) *both* reads (e) *and* writes;' '(e) *Though* he feared, (f) *yet* he went.'

g. The CHARACTERISTIC EXPONENTS (marking sentences as *negative, interrogative, contingent,* &c.) may be *adverbs* or *pronouns:* '*Who* was it?' 'It was *not* I.' 'I see *no* man.'

B. FIGURES OF SYNTAX.

67. Those special forms of expression which are termed FIGURES OF SYNTAX, may be referred to four great heads, ELLIPSIS, PLEONASM, ENALLAGE, and HYPERBATON.

a. FIGURES OF SYNTAX are associated and blended with those of RHETORIC; and some of the latter will be mentioned below. Both classes are more common in *poetry* than in *prose;* in *colloquial,* than in *formal* discourse; and in the language of *passion,* than in that of *narrative* or *argument.*

b. The use of *unauthorized constructions* is termed SOLECISM (from Σόλοικοι, *dwellers in Soli,* of Cilicia, famed for their bad Greek); of *unauthorized words,* BARBARISM (βάρβαρος, *barbarian*); of *antique words* or *constructions,* ARCHAISM (ἀρχαῖος, *ancient*). A form of construction specially belonging to a particular language is called an IDIOTISM or IDIOM (ἴδιος, *peculiar*); or, from the name of the language, a *Hebraism, Hellenism* or *Grecism, Latinism, Anglicism,* &c.

68. I. ELLIPSIS (ἔλλειψις, *defect*) is the omission of words which are required for the most complete and regular expression of the sense.

1. These words are said to be *understood.* The omission may take place without any other change in the form of the expression; or it may be attended with other changes, respecting either the words which are employed, or the forms of those words: 'Will you go?' '[I will go] *Certainly*'; or '*Yes*' [= I will go]; or, '*No*' [= not]. See 69 a.

(2) There is a rhetorical figure called *Omission,* in which there is a *pretence* of omitting something, which is thus mentioned and often made more prominent: 'His *crime* and *folly* I forbear to mention.'

3. Ellipsis exhibits a striking paradox. It is generally true, that, the more essential a word is to the grammatical construction of the discourse, the more apt it is to be omitted; for this reason, that it is the more readily supplied from the very necessity of the case. Hence the frequent omission of the word to which another refers as its subject or by which another is governed, of the substantive verb, of the direct object of a transitive verb, &c.; in general, of *words modified* rather than *modifiers,* and of *leading* rather than *subordinate* clauses. See 506, 571 s, 476, 626.

4. To ELLIPSIS are usually referred, by grammarians, all abbreviated and compendious forms of construction, however familiar (though the term *Brachylogy* [*brief expression*] would often apply more properly): as,

a.) Adjectives used *substantively,* and adverbs used *substantively* or *adjectively* (506 s, 526 s): (b) Many forms of *inscription, salutation, exclamation,* &c. (401, 670): (c) The construction of RESPONSIVES (words in the *answer,* corresponding to *interrogatives* in the *question*), and other

forms of reply; as, 'Who saw it?' '*I*' [saw it]: (d) ASYNDETON (ἀσύνδετος, *not bound together*), the omission of a *conjunction* or other connective; often greatly promoting energy and vivacity, as in Cæsar's celebrated despatch, Veni, vidi, vici, *I came — saw — conquered*. See 707.
(e) APOSIOPĒSIS (ἀποσιώπησις, *the becoming silent*), the failure to finish a sentence, whether from design, diversion of thought, overpowering emotion, or any other cause; as, 'If you ever do this again ——' So not unfrequently after a conditional clause (636 s).

f.) Most cases of COMPOUND CONSTRUCTION (60). A word referring to a compound subject has either the form which is required by *all* the substantives in the subject, taken *together*, or that which is required by *one* of them, taken *singly*. In the former construction, named *Syllepsis* (σύλληψις, *taking together*), the word is said to agree with all the substantives; in the latter, named *Zeugma* (ζεῦγμα, *yoking*), it is said to agree with one of the substantives, and to be *understood* with the rest. For 'My heart and my flesh *rejoice*,' Ps. 84. 2, an older version has, 'My heart and my flesh *crieth out*.' See 495 s. (g) The term *zeugma* is used, in general, to denote the connection of a word with a number of words, to a part of which only it is appropriate in meaning, or in form (while, in *syllepsis*, it would suit the whole): 'You are *blind* of ear, mind, and eye' (Soph. O. T. 371). Cf. § 572 b.

69. II. PLEONASM (πλεονασμός, *redundance*) is the use of more words than the sense requires.

a. Pleonasm may consist in the simple repetition or insertion of words, or it may be attended with more important changes in the form of the expression (cf. 68. 1; the limits of both Ellipsis and Pleonasm are very indefinite). (b) One of its common forms is *emphatic repetition*, in the same or in similar words (the latter specially named *Synonymia*): 'Never, never, NEVER!' 'Oh, spare me! pardon and forgive!'

c. Useless repetition is termed *Tautology* (ταυτολογία, *saying the same thing*): (d) a circuitous manner of expression, *Periphrasis* or *Circumlocution* (περίφρασις circumlocutio, *roundabout speaking*); as *loss of life*, for *death*: (e) the expression of *one* thing as though it were *two*, *Hendiadys* (ἓν διὰ δυοῖν, *one thing by two*); as, 'Whose *nature and property* is ever to have mercy': (f) the use of more connectives than are needed, *Polysyndeton* (πολύς, *many*; cf. 68 d); as, 'Whenne that,' for 'when,' *Chauc*.

70. III. ENALLAGE (ἐναλλαγή, *exchange*) is the use of one word or form for another. — 1. As the *use of one word for another*, it has respect either to the *grammatical office* of words, or to their *signification*.

a. The use of one part of speech for another is termed ANTIMERIA (ἀντί, *instead of*, μέρος, *part*): '*Now's* the day,' *Burns*. Cf. 68 a.

b. A figure by which a word is *turned* from its literal sense, is called a TROPE (τρόπος, *turning*). The principal tropes (commonly classed as rhetorical figures, 67 a) are mentioned below. (c) The figurative sense of a word often becomes so familiar that we employ it without intending or being conscious of any figure: 'a *sweet* temper,' 'works of *taste*.' This use, in which the word has *passed over* from its primary to a secondary sense, is hence termed *transitive* (transeo, *to pass over*).

d. In METAPHOR (μεταφορά, *transfer*), a word appropriate to one object is *transferred* to another, by reason of some analogy between them: 'Tell that *fox*,' Lk. 13. 32. (e) *Allegories* are formed by extending and combining metaphors. (f) When inanimate or irrational objects are represented as *persons*, the figure is termed *Prosopopœia* or *Personification* (πρόσωπον persōna, *person*, ποιέω facio, *to make*); (g) when a speaker turns aside in his discourse so to address them (or to address absent persons as if present), it is termed *Apostrophe* (ἀποστρέφω, *to turn from*): 'Sing, O heavens ; and be joyful, O earth !' Is. 49: 13.

h. METONYMY (μετωνυμία, *change of name*) gives to one object the name of another which is *related* to it: as, *crown, throne*, and *sceptre*, for *sovereignty*. (i) An *abstract noun* is often used for a *concrete*, for greater strength of expression, especially in *apposition:* 'He is my *defence*.'

j. SYNECDOCHE (συνεκδοχή, *comprehension*) puts a *part* for the *whole*, or the *whole* for a *part: keel*, for *ship; steel*, for *sword*.

k. IRONY (εἰρωνεία, *dissimulation*) is the use of a word for its opposite: *hero*, for *coward*. (l) A seeming contradiction, termed *Oxymōron* (ὀξύμωρος, *keenly foolish*), is sometimes made by uniting words of opposite signification : *learned ignorance*.

m. A form of expression beyond the truth is termed *Hyperbole* (ὑπερβολή, *throwing beyond*) ; designedly short of it, *Litotes* (λιτότης, *simplicity*) ; more agreeable, *Euphemism* (εὐφημισμός, *use of good words*). (n) A play upon words similar in sound but differing in sense, or upon the same word used in different senses, is termed *Paronomasia* (παρονομασία, *comparison of names, pun*); and (o) an imitation of the sense by the sound, *Onomatopœia* (ὀνοματοποιία, *name-making;* certainly one of the most copious of the original sources of language).

2. ENALLAGE, as the *use of one form for another*, is specially termed,

p.) SYNESIS (σύνεσις, *understanding*), when the construction follows the sense or the conception of the mind, in disregard of grammatical form or of the reality of things (498 s): (q) ATTRACTION (attractio), when a word is drawn from its appropriate form by the influence of another word (500, 552, 71 b): (r) HYPALLAGE (ὑπαλλαγή, *interchange*), when two words interchange constructions (474 a) : (t) ANACOLŪTHON (ἀνακόλουθος, *inconsistent*), when there is a *change of construction*, so that two parts of a sentence do not agree (402, 504 b) : (u) VISION (visio, *seeing*), when the present tense is used in speaking of past or future events, as if they were actually occurring before the eye (609) : (v) RETENTION (retentio), when a form retains from its earlier extent of application a use afterwards assigned to another form (392 a*, 485, 576, 603 s, 651 s): (w) CHANGE OF NUMBER, GENDER, OR PERSON (488 s, 501 s).

71. IV. HYPERBATON *(ὑπερβατός, transposed)* is a disregard of the common laws of arrangement. It is specially termed,

a.) INVERSION, or ANASTROPHE (ἀναστροφή inversio, *inversion*), when words in a clause are *inverted* (chiefly for emphasis, euphony, rhythm, to bring similar or contrasted words nearer together, or to mark the connection of sentences, 719 a, s). — The name *Chiasma* (χίασμα, *imitation of* χ) is applied, when the arrangement in one pair of words or expressions is inverted in a similar pair following.   'Kind ╳ words, but thoughts ╳ unkind.'

b.) PROLEPSIS (πρόληψις, *anticipation*), when a word is placed in a clause earlier than that to which it properly belongs, or is otherwise *anticipated*. This is commonly due to *attraction* (70 q, 474, 657).

c.) PARENTHESIS (παρένθεσις, *insertion*), when one sentence is inserted within another, with which it has no grammatical connection: 'This, *mark me*, is true.' — The term may be likewise applied to any interruption of the sense by the insertion of unessential words or clauses.

d.) HYSTERON PROTERON (ὕστερον πρότερον, *the last first*), when that which follows in the order of occurrence or nature, is placed first: 'I was bred and born,' *Shaks.* (e) CONFUSED ARRANGEMENT, when this term applies. (f) TMESIS, see 388 c.

C. FORMS OF ANALYSIS AND PARSING.

72. 1. FOR SENTENCES.

1. *Describe the Sentence:* as, — It is Simple, Complex, *or* Compound [consisting of the Coörd., *or* Lead'g & Subord. Clauses —]; Pos. *or* Neg.; {Infinitive, incorporated in the sentence — as a Substantive.} {Participial, " " " " " " an Adjective.} } *Remarks.* {Finite, {Intellective, {Declarative, {Actual [Indicative, Past, &c.]; {Interrogative, {Contingent [Subjunctive, &c.]; } fol- {Imperative, expressing *command, entreaty,* exclamatory, &c.;} lowing — by simple succession, *or* connected by ⌒ to — as a Coördinate Sentence, *or* as a Subordinate Clause, performing the office of a Substantive, Adjective, *or* Adverb. *Remarks.*

2. *Analyze the Sentence into its Grammatical or its Logical Parts, or both:*

Subject } Adjective } The Predicate } is —, modified by the Adverb } —, which [is intro- Compellative} Appositive } Adjunct } duced by —, and] is itself modified by —, and this by —, &c.; *or* by the Dependent Clause —, which performs the office of —, and consists of —. [Minor parts independent are the Interjection —, &c.] *Remarks.*

Or, more fully, thus: The Subject-Part } is —, containing the Simple } Predicate-Part, &c.} Comp'd} Subject } —, modified by the Adjective-Part } —, consisting of the Predicate, &c.} Adjunct-Part, &c.} Adjective } —, [introduced by —, and] modified by —, &c. [The Pred- Adjunct, &c.} icate-Part may be resolved into the Copula —, and the Attribute —.]

73. WRITTEN ANALYSIS. It is of great benefit, in the study of other languages, as of English, so to write the analysis of sentences, that the office of each word shall determine its place. Of the several methods that have been proposed for this, the following is suggested as the most simple in use, that is also minute:

a. Write the several sentences under each other, prefixing symbols to mark their general offices and relations, and placing connectives in one column, subject-parts in another, predicate-parts in the third, and independent parts in a fourth. Write all modifiers (or their symbols, in the case of modifying clauses) *under* the words which they modify, but *indented*, that is, with the line beginning farther to the right. Exponents of the use of words are simply written with the words, in the same line. Compound parts, according to convenience, are either written as if simple, or with their elements under each other and connected by a brace (which may be extended below, to meet a common modifier). Words supplied

§ 73. ANALYSIS OF SENTENCES. 109

to complete the grammatical construction are underlined in writing (printed below as Italic, or, in Greek, with smaller type); while parentheses or brackets mark the repetition of a word in the scheme, to show a double office or relation (especially where a word in the subject or predicate part serves also as a connective). In complex modification, the modifier is sometimes repeated; but oftener written only once, in the place which shows its closest connection or is most convenient, its double office being shown, if desired, by a double mark. Space may be gained, if wished, by writing the article in the same line with its noun or with another modifier; and time, by abbreviating words, or simply writing their initials. The article is sometimes even omitted.

b. For sentences, the following symbols may be used: The capitals A, B, C, &c., for independent sentences (sentences of the 1st rank); the numerals 1, 2, 3, &c., for sentences immediately dependent upon these (2d rank); the small letters a, b, c, &c., for sentences dependent upon the latter (3d rank); the Italics *a*, *b*, *c*, &c., for sentences of the 4th rank; the last letters of the alphabet, z, y, x, &c., for those of the 5th rank; these in Italics, for the 6th rank; the middle letters, m, n, o, &c., and *m*, *n*, *o*, &c., for the rare 7th and 8th ranks. If the sentence is interrogative, the sign ? may be added; if imperative, †; if exclamatory, !; if quoted or parenthetic, the usual sign in part, " or). The members of compound sentences, or of those which have prominent parts compound, may be distinguished by the use of accents (unless a separate notation is preferred): as A, A′, A″, &c. (read "A," "A prime," "A second," &c.). The different kinds of modifiers may be distinguished by any convenient marks, or indices. An adjective modifier is marked below with °; an adverbial modifier, with ‵; a substantive modifier, with an angle, the opening turned up for an adjunct (ᵛ), and down for an appositive (^). Judgment will, of course, be exercised in regard to the extent to which, in any exercise, the notation shall be carried.

c. When minute analysis is not desired, some of its most important objects may be rapidly obtained by *symbolizing* a period or paragraph, that is, by writing the symbols of its sentences in the order of occurrence (the symbol being repeated, when a clause is divided), with additional signs above or below to mark the offices of the sentences, and such punctuation as will best suit their connections. The examples below will be first symbolized, and then analyzed more fully, with the proposed arrangement and notation. — d. From *Campbell's* Ode to the Rainbow:

"Triumphal Arch, that fill'st the sky,
When storms prepare to part,
I ask not proud Philosophy
To teach me what thou art."

A 1 a, A 2.
  ° ‵

	CONN.	SUBJ.	PRED.	IND.
A		I	ask	Arch
			not‵	triumphal°
			Philosophyᵛ	(1°)
			proud°	
			to teachᵛ	
			meᵛ	
			(2ᵛ)	
1°	(that)	That	fill'st	
			skyᵛ	
			the°	
			(a‵)	
a‵	(when)	Storms	prepare	
			to partᵛ	
			when‵	
2ᵛ	(what)	Thou	art	
			what^‵	

110 TABLES. — SENTENCES. § 73.

e. How long, men of Athens, will you indulge in this guilty and, alas ! fatal supineness ? The clouds continually gathering and darkening above us, how can you hope that the storm will not at length burst upon the city ? Beware of imagining, my fellow-citizens, that this ambitious prince and warrior, who delights in the severest toil if it may advance his schemes of conquest, will ever rest until he has reached the coveted goal, the subjugation of Attica, — that, having conquered the rest of Greece, he will cry "Enough!" and will offer us terms of honorable friendship. It is only through the strangest infatuation, be assured, that you can expect to escape, ah foolish dreamers ! though all others fall.

A ; B 1 ; C 2 a a, 2 b, 3 c, 3' ; D (E) 4 d.
? ? ᵛ † ᵛ ₒ ' ' ᵛ " † ^'

	CONN.	SUBJ.	PRED.	IND.
A?		You	will indulge long' how' in supineness ᵛ this ° guilty & fatal °	Men of Athens ᵛ alas
B?		You	can hope how' (1 ᵛ)	The clouds [ening ° gathering & dark- continually'
1 ᵛ	that	The storm	will burst not' at length ᵛ upon the city ᵛ	above us ᵛ
C†		Ye	Beware of imagining ᵛ (2 ᵛ, 3 ᵛ)	fellow-citizens my °
2 ᵛ	that	Prince & warrior this ° ambitious ° (a °)	will rest ever' (b')	
a °	(Who)	Who	delights in the toil ᵛ severest ° (a')	
a'	if	It	may advance schemes ᵛ his ᵛ of conquest ᵛ	
b'	until	He	has reached the goal ᵛ coveted ° [tion ^ the subjuga- of Attica ᵛ	
3 ᵛ	that	He having conquered °' the rest ᵛ of Greece ᵛ	{will cry (c") {& will offer us ᵛ terms ᵛ of friendship ᵛ honorable °	

§ 73. WRITTEN ANALYSIS. 111

c"		*It*	*is*	
			enough°'	
D		It	is	
		(4^)	only'	
			through infatuation^v	
			the strangest°	
E†)	that	*Ye*	be assured	ah dreamers
4^		You	can expect	foolish°
			to escape^v	
			(d')	
d'	though	Others	fall	
		all°		

f. Κλέαρχε καὶ Πρόξενε, καὶ οἱ ἄλλοι οἱ παρόντες Ἕλληνες, οὐκ ἴστε, ὅ τι ποιεῖτε. Εἰ γάρ τινα ἀλλήλοις μάχην συνάψετε, νομίζετε, ἐν τῇδε τῇ ἡμέρᾳ ἐμέ τε κατακεκόψεσθαι, καὶ ὑμᾶς οὐ πολὺ ἐμοῦ ὕστερον· κακῶς γὰρ τῶν ἡμετέρων ἐχόντων, πάντες οὗτοι, οὓς ὁρᾶτε, βάρβαροι πολεμιώτεροι ἡμῖν ἔσονται τῶν παρὰ βασιλεῖ ὄντων. "Clearchus and Proxenus, and the other Greeks present, you know not what you are doing. For, if you engage in any battle with each other, consider that this day both I shall be cut down, and you not long after me; for, our affairs going ill, all these barbarians, whom you see, will be worse enemies to us than those with the king." Xen. An. i. 5. 16.

A 1; *a* 2 *a* 2 *a a'*, *b z b*.
      '†'   v '°

	CONN.	SUBJ.	PRED.	IND.
A		Ὑμεῖς	ἴστε	Κλέαρχε καὶ Πρόξενε
			οὐκ'	καὶ Ἕλληνες
			(1^v, 2')	οἱ ἄλλοι°
				οἱ παρόντες°
1^v	(ὅ τι)	Ὑμεῖς	ποιεῖτε	
			ὅ τι^v	
2†'	γάρ	Ὑμεῖς	νομίζετε	
			(a^v)	
a^v	⎧ τέ	ἐμέ	κατακεκόψεσθαι	
	⎨		ἐν τῇ ἡμέρᾳ^v	
	⎩		τῇδε°	
			(a', b')	
a'	καί	ὑμᾶς	(κατακεκόψεσθαι, &c.)	
			ὕστερον'	
			ἐμοῦ^v	
			πολύ'	
			οὐ'	
a'	Εἰ	Ὑμεῖς	συνάψετε	
			μάχην^v	
			τινά°	
			ἀλλήλοις^v	
b'	γάρ	Βάρβαροι	ἔσονται	πραγμάτων
		πάντες°	πολεμιώτεροι°'	τῶν°
		οὗτοι°	ἡμῖν^v	ἡμετέρων°
		(z°)	τῶν βαρβάρων^v	ἐχόντων°
			ὄντων°	κακῶς'
			παρὰ βασιλεῖ^v	
z°	(οὓς)	Ὑμεῖς	ὁρᾶτε	
			οὓς^v	

74. II. For Greek Words.

—— is a {Proper / Common / Collective / Abstract, &c.} Noun, {of the 1 Dec. / " " 2 " / " " 3 " / Irregular, &c.} {Masc. / Fem. / Neut. / Com.}, *(Decline.)* from — — —; [Derived from —, / ed of —,] Stem —, Affix —; the Gen. {Nom. / Gen. / &c.} {Sing. / Plur. / Dual} the subject of —, governed by —, Gen. of —, &c., Rule. *Remarks.*

—— is an Adjective [in the {Pos. / Comp. / Sup.}] Degree, from — — — — *(compare),*] of {1 / 2 / 3} Terminations *(decline);* [Derived from —, / Compounded of —,] Stem —, Affix —; the Gen. {Nom. / Gen. / &c.} {Sing. / Plur. / Dual} {Masc. / Fem. / Neut.}; agreeing with —, used substantively, &c.}, Rule. *Remarks.*

—— is a {Personal / Reflexive / Relative, &c.} Pronoun, [of the {1 / 2 / 3} Pers.], from — — —; *(Decline.)* [Der. —,] [Comp. —,] Stem —, Affix —; the Gen. {Nom. / Gen. / &c.} {Sing. / Plur. / Dual} {Masc. / Fem. / Neut.} the subject of —; agreeing with —, gov'd by —, &c.}, Rule. [It refers to — as its {Subject / Antecedent}, Rule; and connects — to —.] *Remarks.*

—— is a {Transitive Verb, / Deponent " / Contract " / Verb in μι, &c.,} *(Conjugate.)* from — — —; [Der'd from —,] [Comp'd of —,] {Stem — / Stems — —}, [Prefix —,] Affix —; the {Pres. / Impf. / Fut., &c.} {Ind. / Subj. / Opt., &c.} {Act. / Mid. / Pass.} *(vary and inflect);*

{(*if finite*) the 1 Pers. Sing., &c., agreeing with —, / (*if Inf.*) having for its subject —, and {depending on —, subject of —, &c., / (*if Part.*) the Gen. {Nom. / Gen. / &c.} {Sing. / Plur. / Dual} {Masc. / Fem. / Neut.} agreeing with —, used substantively, &c.,} Rule. *Remarks.*

—— is an {Interrogative / Demonstrative / Indefinite, &c.} Adverb of {Manner / Place / Time, &c.}, [in the {Pos. / Comp. / Sup.}] Degree, from — *(compare);* Der. from —, *or* Comp. of —]; modifying —, Rule. [It refers to — as its antecedent, and connects — to —.] *Remarks.*

—— is a Preposition [Der. *or* Comp. —], governing —, and marking its relation to — (a relation of *place, time, agency, cause,* &c.), Rule. *Remarks.*

—— is a {Copulative / Final, &c.} Conjunction, [Der. —,] [Comp. —,] connecting — to —, (and

§ 75.   PARSING OF WORDS.   113

denoting *addition, opposition, comparison, &c.,* or introducing its clause as an *end, condition, &c.,* or as used substantively), Rule. *Remarks.*

—— is an INTERJECTION [Der. *or* Comp. —], (expressing *emotion*, &c.,) and independent of grammatical construction (684). *Remarks.*

75. NOTES. a. When *declension in full* is not desired, give the Nom. and Gen. in Substantives and in Adjectives of 1 Term., and the different forms of the Nom. in Adjectives of 2 or 3 Term. (b) In *conjugating,* give the Theme, with the corresponding Fut. and Perf. if in use (to which it is also well to add the 2 Aor. if used); but sometimes, more fully, the leading tense of each *system* in use. The term "*vary*" is used above in a specific sense, to denote *giving the different modes of a tense*, or, as it is sometimes called, *giving the synopsis of the tense;* and the term "*inflect*," to denote *giving the numbers and persons* (in the Participle, *declension,* of course, takes the place of this). (c) After completing the formula above (which will be done with least danger of omission or delay, if a uniform order is observed), add such *Remarks* as may properly be made upon the *form, signification,* and *use* of the word; as, in respect to contraction, euphonic changes of consonants, literal or figurative sense, the force or use of the number, case, degree, voice, mode, tense, &c.; citing, from the Grammar, the appropriate rule or remark. (d) Some particulars in the forms above, which do not apply to all words, are inclosed in brackets; and some directions or suggestions, in parentheses.

e. It is a very useful exercise to write minute analyses of words; sometimes even marking the offices of the different parts of a flexible ending (12, 33). E. g., the following verbs (mostly in compound forms), and the following compound nouns and adjectives may be written as below: ἐλύσατο, λελύκασιν (37), ὥρισαν (39 d), ἠθέλησεν (311 b), κελευσθείητε (307 b), πεφιλήσομαι (42 f), ἐδεδιδάχειν (50, διδάσκω), γεγονώς (50), τιμησάσθων (42); φιλοσοφίαν (Acc.) *philosophy,* ἄνοπλος (385 a), ἐργολάβου (387 a), ἀγνῶτες (386. 4), πυριγενέσιν (383 a), λιθοβόλῳ (386. 1), νομοθέτας (386. 3), θεσφάτοις *divinely appointed* (383 c).

	PREFIX.			STEM.				AFFIX.			STEM.			AFFIX.		
Preposition.	Augment.	Reduplication.	Preformative.	Root.	Afformative.	Inserted Letter.	Tense-Sign.	Connecting Vowel.	Flexible Ending.	Paragogic ν.	1st Element.	Union Letters.	2d Element.	Afformative.	Connecting Vowel.	Flexible Ending.	Paragogic ν.
ἐξ	ε			λύ			σ	α	το		φιλ	ο	σοφ	ι	α	ν	
ἐξ		λε		λύ			κ	α	νσι	ν	ἀν		οπλ		ο	ς	
	ε			δρ		ιδ	σ	α	ντ		ἐργ	ο	λάβ		ο	ο	
	ἐ		ε	θελ			σ	ε	τ	ν	ἀ		γνο γνῶ	τ		ες	
ἐν				κελ		ευ	θε	[η	τε		πυρ	ι	γεν	ἐ		σι	ν
		φε πε		φιλ		ε ή	σ	ο	μαι		λιθ	ο	βαλ βόλ		ο	ι	
ἐξ	ε	δε	δι	δά	χ		κ	ει	μ		νεμ νομ	ο	θέ	τ	α	m νς m	
ἐν		γε		γα γο	ν		ὀ		τς πνmn		θε	σ	φά	τ	ο	ι ς	
ἐν				τι	μα		σ	ά	σθων								

76. D. CHIEF RULES OF GREEK SYNTAX.

I. An APPOSITIVE agrees in *case* with its *subject*. § 393.
II. The SUBJECT of a FINITE VERB is put in the Nominative. 400.
III. SUBSTANTIVES INDEPENDENT OF GRAMMATICAL CONSTRUCTION are put in the Nominative. 401.
A. General Rule for the Genitive. THE POINT OF DEPARTURE AND THE CAUSE ARE PUT IN THE GENITIVE; or, The GENITIVE is used to express that OF or FROM which something is or is done. 403.
IV. Words of SEPARATION and DISTINCTION govern the Genitive. 404.
V. The COMPARATIVE DEGREE governs the Genitive. 408.
VI. The ORIGIN, SOURCE, and MATERIAL are put in the Genitive. 412.
VII. The THEME of DISCOURSE or of THOUGHT is put in the Gen. 413.
VIII. Words of PLENTY and WANT govern the Genitive. 414.
IX. The WHOLE *of which a part is taken* is put in the Genitive. 415.
X. Words of SHARING, BEGINNING, and TOUCH govern the Genitive. 424.
XI. The MOTIVE, REASON, and END IN VIEW are put in the Gen. 429.
XII. PRICE, VALUE, MERIT, and CRIME are put in the Genitive. 431.
XIII. Words of SENSATION and of MENTAL STATE OR ACTION govern the Genitive. 432.
XIV. The TIME and PLACE *in which* are put in the Genitive. 433.
XV. The AUTHOR, AGENT, and GIVER are put in the Genitive. 434.
XVI. An ADJUNCT DEFINING A THING OR PROPERTY is put in the Genitive; or, A SUBSTANTIVE, ADJECTIVE, or ADVERB, *as such*, governs the Genitive. 435.
  B. A word may govern the Genitive, by virtue of an *included* substantive, adjective, or adverb. 436.
  C. The Compounds of *Alpha Privative* govern the Genitive. 436.
D. General Rule for the Dative Objective. THE OBJECT OF APPROACH OR OF INFLUENCE IS PUT IN THE DATIVE; or, An INDIRECT OBJECT is put in the DATIVE; or, The DATIVE is used to express that TO or FOR which something is or is done. 448.
XVII. Words of NEARNESS and LIKENESS govern the Dative. 449.
XVIII. The OBJECT OF INFLUENCE is put in the Dative. 452.
  E. SUBSTANTIVE VERBS take a Dative of the *possessor*. 459.
F. General Rule for the Dative Residual. AN ATTENDANT THING OR CIRCUMSTANCE, SIMPLY VIEWED AS SUCH, IS PUT IN THE DATIVE. 465.
XIX. The MEANS and MODE are put in the Dative. 466.
XX. The TIME and PLACE *at which* are put in the Dative. 469.
XXI. The DIRECT OBJECT and the EFFECT of an action are put in the Accusative. 472.
  G. An adjunct *simply considered as modifying a verb* is put in the Accusative. 472.
  CAUSATIVES govern the Accusative together with the case of the included verb. 473.
  H. ADVERBS OF SWEARING are followed by the Accusative. 476.
XXII. The Accusative is used in *specifying* to what PART, PROPERTY, &c. a word or expression applies. 481.
XXIII. EXTENT of TIME or SPACE is put in the Accusative. 482.
XXIV. The Accusative is often used ADVERBIALLY, to express *degree, manner, order*, &c. 483.
XXV. The COMPELLATIVE of a sentence is put in the Vocative. 484.
  J. AGREEMENT is commonly *according to form*, but often rather *according to sense*. 493.
XXVI. An ADJECTIVE agrees with its *subject* in *gender, number*, and *case*. 504.
XXVII. A PRONOUN agrees with its *subject* in *gender, number*, and *person*. 505.

§ 76.   RULES OF SYNTAX.   115

The RELATIVE *commonly takes the case of the antecedent*, when the relative clause limits or defines an antecedent in the *Genitive* or *Dative*, and the RELATIVE would properly be an *Accusative depending upon a verb*. 554.

K. The repetition of the RELATIVE is commonly avoided, either by *ellipsis*, or by the substitution of a *personal pronoun* or of a *demonstrative*. 562.

XXVIII. The ARTICLE is prefixed to SUBSTANTIVES, to mark them as *definite*. 520.

XXIX. A VERB agrees with its *subject* in *number* and *person*. 568.

L. The NEUTER PLURAL has regularly its VERB in the *singular*. 569.
M. The uses of the VOICES are sometimes interchanged. 575.

The PASSIVE VOICE has for its SUBJECT a *complement of the Active*, commonly a *direct*, but sometimes an *indirect* complement. Any other word governed by the Act., and not in apposition with this, may *remain unchanged* with the Pass. THE SUBJECT OF THE ACTIVE is commonly expressed, with the Pass., by the *Gen. with a preposition*. 586.

XXX. The DEFINITE TENSES express the action as *doing at* the time; the INDEFINITE, simply as *performed in* the time; and the COMPLETE, as *complete at* the time. In the *Indicative*, this time is marked as PRESENT or FUTURE by the *primary tenses*, and as PAST by the *secondary*; in the *other modes*, it is not marked. 590.

N. The uses of the TENSES are often *interchanged*. 602.

XXXI. The INDICATIVE expresses *fact;* the SUBJUNCTIVE, *present contingency;* and the OPTATIVE, *past contingency*. 613.

O. The SUBJUNCTIVE regularly follows a tense referring to *present* or *future* time; and the OPTATIVE, a tense referring to *past* time. 617.
P. After a FINAL CONJUNCTION, (a) an object of *present forethought* is expressed by the *Subj.*, or (b) in the Future, by the *Ind.;* but (c) an object of *past forethought*, by the *Opt.*, or (d), to mark it as now contrary to fact, by a *prior tense* of the *Ind.* 624.
Q. In prohibitions with μή, the PRESENT is put in the *Imperative*, and the AORIST in the *Subjunctive*. 628.
R. In the HYPOTHETICAL PERIOD, (a, b) if the PREMISE is presented as *already decided in point of fact*, it takes the INDICATIVE; (c) if it is presented as *undecided, but with present expectation of decision*, it takes the SUBJUNCTIVE; (d) otherwise, it takes the OPTATIVE. In the first case, the CONCLUSION is commonly in the *Ind.* or *Imv.;* in the second, in the *Fut. Ind.* or an equivalent; and in the third, in the *Opt.* with ἄν. 631.
S. A RELATIVE CLAUSE commonly uses the modes like other sentences to which it is most nearly akin. 640.
T. The OPTATIVE is the finite mode appropriate to *Indirect Discourse in past time*. 643.
U. The uses of the FINITE MODES are often *interchanged*. 649.

XXXII. The IMPERATIVE is the most direct expression of an *act of the will*. 655.

XXXIII. The INFINITIVE is construed as a *neuter noun*. 663.

XXXIV. The SUBJECT OF THE INFINITIVE is put in the Accusative. 666.

V. The INFINITIVE often forms an elliptical *command, request, counsel, salutation, exclamation*, or *question*. 670.
W. Some CONNECTIVES are followed by the Infinitive; especially ὡς, ὥστε, οἷος, and ὅσος. 671.

XXXV. A PARTICIPLE AND SUBSTANTIVE are put *absolute* in the *Genitive;* an IMPERSONAL PARTICIPLE, in the *Accusative*. 675.

X. A PARTICIPLE is often preceded by ὡς or ὥσπερ, chiefly to mark it as *subjective*. 680.
Y. IMPERSONAL VERBALS in -τέον, or -τέα, (a) govern the same cases as the verbs from which they are derived; and (b) have sometimes the agent in the *Accusative*, instead of the *Dative*. 682.

XXXVI. ADVERBS modify *sentences, phrases,* and *words;* chiefly *verbs, adjectives,* and *other adverbs*. 685.

NEGATION, as *desired, feared,* or *assumed,* uses μή; but otherwise, οὐ. 686.

XXXVII. PREPOSITIONS govern *adjuncts,* and mark their *relations*. 688.

Z. A Preposition *in composition* often governs the same case, as when it stands by itself. 699.

XXXVIII. CONJUNCTIONS connect *sentences* and *like parts* of a sentence. 700.

The uses of the PARTICLES are often *interchanged*. 703.
The INTERJECTION is independent of grammatical construction. 684 b.

IV. PROSODY AND PRONUNCIATION.

77. A. Table of Feet.

The Numeral prefixed to each Class marks the number of Breves in its measure.

1.	[Συλλαβὴ Βραχεῖα,	Short Syllable,	⏑	μέν.]
2.	[Συλλαβὴ Μακρά,	Long Syllable,	–	μήν.]
	Πυρρίχιος,	Pyrrhic,	⏑⏑	μένε.
3.	Ἴαμβος,	Iambus, Iamb,	⏑–	μένω.
	Τροχαῖος, Χορεῖος,	Trochee, Choree,	–⏑	μῆκος.
	Τρίβραχυς,	Tribrach,	⏑⏑⏑	μένομεν.
4.	Δάκτυλος,	Dactyl,	–⏑⏑	δώσετε.
	Ἀνάπαιστος,	Anapæst,	⏑⏑–	ἐθέλω.
	Σπονδεῖος,	Spondee,	– –	σώζω.
	Ἀμφίβραχυς,	Amphibrach,	⏑–⏑	ἔδωκεν.
	Προκελευσματικός,	Proceleusmatic,	⏑⏑⏑⏑	λεγόμενος.
5.	Κρητικός, Ἀμφίμακρος,	Cretic, Amphimacer,	–⏑–	δώσομαι.
	Βακχεῖος,	Bacchīus,	⏑– –	λέγωντai.
	Ἀντιβάκχειος,	Antibacchīus,	– –⏑	σώζωμεν.
	Παίων α΄,	Pæon I.,	–⏑⏑⏑	δωσόμενος.
	Παίων β΄,	Pæon II.,	⏑–⏑⏑	ἐγείρομεν.
	Παίων γ΄,	Pæon III.,	⏑⏑–⏑	ἐθέλητε.
	Παίων δ΄,	Pæon IV.,	⏑⏑⏑–	θεοσεβής.
6.	Χορίαμβος,	Choriamb,	–⏑⏑–	σωζομένων.
	Ἀντίσπαστος,	Antispast,	⏑– –⏑	ἐγείρωμεν.
	Διΐαμβος,	Diiamb,	⏑–⏑–	σοφωτέρων.
	Διτρόχαιος,	Ditrochee,	–⏑–⏑	αἰνέσαιτε.
	Ἰωνικὸς ἀπὸ μείζονος,	Falling Ionic,	– –⏑⏑	βουλεύετε.
	Ἰωνικὸς ἀπ' ἐλάσσονος,	Rising Ionic,	⏑⏑– –	ἐθελήσει.
	Μολοσσός,	Molossus,	– – –	μνηστήρων.
7.	Ἐπίτριτος α΄,	Epitrite I.,	⏑– – –	ἐγείρωνται.
	Ἐπίτριτος β΄,	Epitrite II.,	–⏑– –	εὐπροσώπων.
	Ἐπίτριτος γ΄,	Epitrite III.,	– –⏑–	ἡγουμένων.
	Ἐπίτριτος δ΄,	Epitrite IV.,	– – –⏑	βουλεύσειε.
8.	Δόχμιος,	Dochmius,	⏑– –⏑–	ἐβουλευόμην.
	Δισπόνδειος,	Dispondee,	– – – –	βουλεύσωνται.

78. B. Metrical Description and Analysis.

I. *Give a general description of the Metre in which the Poem is written.*

II. *Describe the particular Verse.*

It is { Dactylic / Iambic, &c. } { Monometer / Dimeter, &c. } { Acatalectic / Catalectic, &c. } { consist- / ' ing of } { 1 / 2, &c. } Feet, which are —. The Cæsura is the { [Masc.] / [Fem.] } { Penthemim, / Hephthemim, / Pastoral, &c., } after —.

III. *Analyze by [Dipodies and] Feet.*

— — is a { Spondee, / Dactyl, &c., } the { 1 / 2, &c. } Syllable { Long / Short } by { Position, / Nature, &c., } Rule.

79. C. Methods of Pronunciation.

[a. The directions here given do not apply to γ before κ, γ, χ, or ξ, where it is regarded as a nasal, having the sound of *ng* in *king*: ἄγγελος, λύγξ. Those for ᾱ, η, and ω apply also to ᾳ, ῃ, and ῳ. See 137 c, 109.

b. Where consonants or the rough breathing are not specially noticed, it will be understood that they have the prevalent sounds of the corresponding letters in English: thus, β, δ, ζ, λ, μ, ν, π, ρ, τ, φ, ψ, ' pronounced like *b, d, z, l, m, n, p, r, t, ph, ps, h*, in *bud, zeal, phantom, rap, hops;* γ, κ, hard, like *g, k*, in *keg;* θ, ξ, σ, sharp, like *th, x, ·s*, in *sixth*. The *smooth breathing* simply marks the absence of the *rough*.

c. To avoid confusion, the terms *protracted* and *abrupt* are used below to mark what are commonly called, in English orthoëpy, *long* and *short sounds;* and the term ICTUS (Lat., *stroke, beat*), to denote that stress of the voice which in English we usually call *accent*. Any *secondary ictus* needed in long words, may commonly be placed as their formation and the ear seem to require.]

1. ANCIENT GREEK METHOD. d. The pronunciation of every language, from the very laws of language, is in a *continual process of change*, more or less rapid. And in respect to the Greek, there is full internal evidence, both that its pronunciation had materially changed before its orthography became fixed, and that it has materially changed since. Therefore, as *there is no art of embalming sounds*, the ancient method can now only be inferred, and, in part, with much uncertainty. For the probable pronunciation of the simple vowels, see 107. (e) In the diphthongs, the sounds of the two elements seem originally to have been simply combined, and uttered with a single impulse of the voice. But the mode of representing Greek words in Latin (92 b) shows that, in some diphthongs, one of these sounds was early lost or became obscure. (f) The consonants seem, in general, to have been pronounced like the corresponding letters in English; χ, however, resembling the German guttural *ch* more than the English *k*, and doubled or combined consonants being both sounded. — For probabilities respecting the details of the Ancient Method, see "History of the Greek Alphabet and Pronunciation," by Professor Sophocles; from whose Romaic Grammars, the following statement of Method 2 has been chiefly condensed. It shows how greatly the Greek, like the English, has been affected by the precession of vowels.

2. MODERN GREEK METHOD. g. *Vowels:* α like *a* in *father;* but after the sound of ι, more like *a* in *peculiarity:* ε or αι a little longer than *e* in *men:* ι, η, ῃ, ει, οι, υ, or υι, like *i* in *machine:* ο or ω nearly as *o* in *obey:* ου like *oo* in *moon*. In αυ, ευ, ηυ, ωυ, the υ has the sound of β before β, γ, δ, ζ, λ, μ, ν, ρ, or a vowel; but otherwise, that of φ: φεύγω, αὐτός, pronounced φέβγω, ἀφτός.

h. *Consonants:* β nearly as *v* (a little softer): γ before the sound of ε or ι, a little stronger than *y* in *yes;* otherwise guttural, very nearly like the German *g* in *Tag:* δ like *th* in *the:* κ like *k* (somewhat softened before the sound of ε or ι); but after the sound of *ng*, like *g* in *go:* λ and ν like *l* and *n;* but before the sound of ι, like *li* in *filial*, and *ni* in *onion;* while final ν in ἄν, ἐάν, ἐν, σύν, or the article, sounds like *ng* before κ or ξ, and like *m* before π or ψ (τὸν καιρόν, σὺν πόλει pron. *tong-gerón*, (*simbóli*) : π, ψ, like *p, ps;* but after the sound of *m*, like *b, bs:* σ like *s* in *so;* but before β, γ, δ, ζ, λ, μ, ν, ρ, like *z* (so even σ final in the article, as τοὺς βασιλεῖς τῆς γῆς, pron. *tooz-vasilís tiz-yís*) : τ like *t*; but after ν, like *d* (so even in initial τ after ἄν, ἐάν, ἐν, σύν, or the article; as ἐν τιμῇ,

pron. *en-dimí*) : φ nearly as *f* (a little softer) : χ like the German *ch*. See a, b. As in English, a consonant doubled is sounded but once.
i. The *rough breathing* is silent ; and the quantity of a vowel is not considered. The *ictus* is placed according to the written accent. A *proclitic* is pronounced as if a part of the word which it precedes ; and an *enclitic*, as if a part of the word which it follows. The accent of an enclitic is only regarded when the preceding word is accented on the antepenult : thus λέλεκταί μοι has a *secondary ictus* on κται.

3. ENGLISH METHOD. j. Modern scholars have pronounced the Greek variously ; commonly according to the analogy of their respective languages. Hence the following method, though not closely approaching the ancient, has been extensively used in England and this country :
k. *Simple Vowels :* η, ν, ω, like *e* in *mete*, *u* in *tube*, *o* in *note* (τυπτήσων): ε, ο, like *e* in *let*, *o* in *dot ;* but before another vowel, or at the end of a word, like *e* in *real* and *o* in *go* (ἐν, λέοντε, τό) : α and ι, in general, like *a* and *i* in English ; when protracted, like *a* in *hate*, *i* in *pine ;* when abrupt, like *a* in *hat*, *i* in *pin*. At the end of a word, ι is always protracted ; but α, except in monosyllables, takes the sound of *a* in *era ;* ἀντί, μία, τά. If α or ι receives the *ictus*, whether primary or secondary, and is followed by a single consonant or ζ, it is protracted in the penult, but abrupt in any preceding syllable (except that α is here protracted, if the next vowel is ε or ι before another vowel) : ἴζω · πατέρα, καταφιλέω · ταμίας. See c. — P affects an abrupt vowel preceding, in the same way as *r* in English : ἅρμα, Ἑρμῆς, ὄρνις.
l. *Diphthongs :* αι like the affirmative *ay ;* ει, *ei* in *height ;* οι, *oi* in *oil ;* υι, *ui* in *quiet ;* αυ, *au* in *haul ;* ευ and ηυ, *eu* in *feud*, *Europe ;* ου and ωυ, ου in *thou :* εἰδυῖαι, φεύγοι, αὑτοῦ, υἱῷ See a.
m. *Consonants :* σ like *s* in *so ;* but in the middle of a word before μ, or at the end after η or ω, like *z* (στήσας · κοσμίως, ἧς) : σ and τ never like *sh :* χ like *ch* in *chaos :* ξ, ψ, like *x, ps*, in *ox, lips ;* but, when initial, like *z, s* (Ξέρξης, ψυχή). Of two initial consonants which cannot both be pronounced with ease, the first is silent ; a consonant doubled is sounded but once ; and ῥ is pronounced like ρ : μνᾶ, πτήσσω, ἔρρω. See a, b.
n. In *dissyllables*, the ICTUS is on the penult ; in *polysyllables*, on the penult if *long* in quantity, but otherwise on the antepenult.

4. "CONTINENTAL METHOD." o. Many of our scholars prefer a method of pronouncing Greek more like that which prevails, though with much variety, upon the *continent* of Europe. This method, in the details of which there is not yet full agreement, appears to be taking, in our country, a form like the following :
p. *Simple Vowels :* ᾱ, ᾰ, like *a* in *father, fast* (nearly as in *man*) ; η, ε, *e* in *fête, men* (or *a* in *machine*) ; ῑ, ῐ, *i* in *machine, pin* (or *direct*) ; ω, ο, *o* in *hope, hop* (or *obey*) ; ῡ, ῠ, *u* in *tube, duet*, or yet closer, like the French *u*. Cf. 107. The distinction between vowels long and short by nature should be carefully observed : πρᾶγμα · δή, δέ · Ἴρις · λόγων · σῦς, σύός.
q. *Diphthongs :* αι like the affirmative *ay* (by some closer, like *ai* in *aisle*) ; ει, *ei* in *height ;* οι, *oi* in *oil ;* υι, *uee* in *queen ;* αυ, *ou* in *loud ;* ευ, ηυ, *eu* in *feud ;* ου, ωυ, *ou* in *soup :* εἰδυῖαι, αὑτοῦ, φεύγοι, υἱῷ See a.
r. *Consonants :* ζ like *z* (by some, like a soft *dz*) : χ, by some, like *ch* in *chaos ;* by others, like the German guttural *ch :* χειμάζω. Every consonant should be pronounced, and with a uniform sound except γ (a) ; the doubling of a consonant should be, at least, slightly marked ; and ῥ should be rougher than ρ : μνᾶ, πτήσσω, βδέλλιον, ἔρρω. See b.
t. The ICTUS is placed according to the written accent.

80. ΠΑΡΑΡΤΗΜΑ ΕΛΛΗΝΙΚΟΝ.

[α. ΟΡΘΟΓΡΑΦΙΑ. Στοιχεία elements, γράμματα letters; επίσημα. Φωνήεντα vowels: βραχέα short, μακρά long, δίχρονα doubtful, δίφθογγοι diphthongs. Σύμφωνα consonants: ἡμίφωνα semivowels, ὑγρά liquids, σύμφωνα διπλᾶ double consonants; ἄφωνα mutes, ψῑλά smooth, μέσα middle, δασέα rough. Συλλαβή syllable; χρόνος quantity.

β. Πνεύματα breathings: δασύ rough, ψιλόν smooth. Προσῳδίαι (τόνοι) accents: ὀξεῖα acute, βαρεῖα grave, περισπωμένη circumflex. Στιγμαί points: τελεία στιγμή period, μέση στιγμή colon, ὑποστιγμή comma.]

γ. ΕΤΥΜΟΛΟΓΙΑ. Τὰ τοῦ λόγου στοιχεῖα λέγονται ὧδε· [κλιτὰ] ἄρθρον, ὄνομα, ἐπίθετον, ἀντωνυμία, ῥῆμα· [ἄκλιτα] ἐπίρρημα, πρόθεσις, σύνδεσμος, ἐπιφώνημα. [Κλίσις, σύγκρισις, συζυγία.]

δ. Τοῦ ὀνόματος αἱ πτώσεις ὀνομάζονται [εὐθεῖαι] ὀρθὴ ἢ ὀνομαστικὴ, κλητικὴ, [πλάγιαι] γενικὴ, δοτικὴ, αἰτιατική (179)· τὰ δὲ τρία γένη (174), ἀρσενικὸν, θηλυκὸν, οὐδέτερον· [τὰ δὲ τρία πρόσωπα, πρῶτον, δεύτερον, τρίτον.] Τριπλοῦς δ' ἐστὶν ὡσαύτως ὁ ἀριθμὸς, δηλαδὴ ἑνικὸς, δυϊκὸς, πληθυντικός (178). Τοῦ ἐπιθέτου οἱ βαθμοὶ λέγονται θετικὸς, συγκριτικὸς, ὑπερθετικός (256).

ε. Τρεῖς ἔχει διαθέσεις τὸ ῥῆμα, ἐνεργητικὴν, μέσην, παθητικήν (266)· καὶ ἐν ἑκάστῃ διαθέσει πέντε διακρίνονται ἐγκλίσεις, ὧν τέσσαρες μὲν παρεμφατικαὶ, ὁριστικὴ, ὑποτακτικὴ, εὐκτικὴ, προστακτικὴ, μία δὲ ἀπαρέμφατος· μέρος δὲ τοῦ ῥήματός ἐστι καὶ ἡ μετοχή (269). Οἱ χρόνοι τοῦ ῥήματος λέγονται ὧδε (267)· ἐνεστὼς, παρατατικὸς, μέλλων, [μετ' ὀλίγον μέλλων,] ἀόριστος, παρακείμενος [ἢ συντελικός], ὑπερσυντελικός. [Αὔξησις συλλαβικὴ καὶ χρονική, ἀναδιπλασιασμός, 277.]

ζ. ΣΥΝΤΑΞΙΣ. Λόγος ὀνομάζεται ἄθροισις λέξεων ἀκέραιον δηλοῦσα διάνοιαν. Ὑποκείμενον λέγεται τὸ περὶ οὗ ὁ λόγος· καὶ κατηγορούμενον ἢ κατηγόρημα, τὸ κατὰ τοῦ ὑποκειμένου λεγόμενον (56 b). Διὰ μόνου τοῦ ῥήματος κατηγορεῖταί τι. — Μεταβατικὰ καλοῦνται τὰ ῥήματα τὰ τοιάνδε ἐνέργειαν δηλοῦντα, ἥτις ἐξ ἀνάγκης εἰς πρόσωπον ἢ πρᾶγμα διάφορον τοῦ ὑποκειμένου, τὸ παρὰ γραμματικοῖς ἀντικείμενον [object] λεγόμενον, μεταβαίνει (58 c).

η. Παρεμφατικοῦ ῥήματος τὸ ὑποκείμενον τίθεται κατ' ὀνομαστικήν (400)· καὶ ταύτῃ συμφωνεῖ τὸ ῥῆμα κατ' ἀριθμόν τε καὶ πρόσωπον (568). — Πλειόνων ὄντων τῶν τοῦ ῥήματος ὑποκειμένων καὶ ἑτεροπροσώπων, τίθεται τὸ ῥῆμα κατὰ τὸ ἐπικρατέστερον· νικᾷ δ' ἀεὶ τὸ πρῶτον τὸ δεύτερον πρόσωπον, καὶ τοῦτο τὸ τρίτον (496 d).

θ. Σχῆμα Ἀττικόν. Εἰώθασι μέντοι οἱ Ἀττικοὶ πληθυντικὴν ὀνομαστικὴν οὐδετέραν ῥήματι ἑνικῷ παρατιθέναι (569).

ι. Τῆς ἀπαρεμφάτου τὸ ὑποκείμενον τίθεται κατ' αἰτιατικήν (670).

κ. Τὸ ἐπίθετον καὶ ἡ μετοχὴ συμφωνοῦσι τοῖς εἰς ἃ ἀναφέρονται ὀνόμασι, κατὰ γένος, ἀριθμὸν, πτῶσιν (504). — Πολλῶν τῶν ὀνομάτων ὄντων, τίθεται τὸ ἐπίθετον ἢ ἡ μετοχὴ πληθυντικῶς· ἐπὶ μὲν ἀψύχων, εἴτε ὁμογενῶν εἴτε ἑτερογενῶν (223 a), κατ' οὐδέτερον γένος· ἐπὶ δὲ ἐμψύχων, τῶν μὲν ὁμογενῶν, κατὰ τὸ τοῖς ὀνόμασι κοινὸν γένος, τῶν δὲ ἑτερογενῶν, κατὰ τὸ ἐπικρατέστερον (496).

λ. Ἡ ἀναφορικὴ λεγομένη ἀντωνυμία συμφωνεῖ τῷ ἑαυτῆς ἡγουμένῳ κατὰ γένος καὶ ἀριθμὸν καὶ πρόσωπον (505). — Τῷ συντακτικῷ δὲ σχήματι ὃ καλεῖται ἔλξις ἢ ἔφελξις, ἕλκεται ἡ ἀντωνυμία εἰς τὴν πτῶσιν τοῦ ἡγουμένου· ἀντιστρόφως δ' ἔσθ' ὅτε καὶ ἡ ἀντωνυμία ἕλκει τὸ ἡγούμενον (554 a, c).

μ. Ὀνόματα, τὰ μὲν πρὸς τὸ αὐτὸ πρόσωπον ἢ πρᾶγμα ἀναφερόμενα, ὁμοιοπτώτως τίθενται· τοῦτο δὲ ὀνομάτων πρόσθεσις καλεῖται (393). Τὰ δὲ πρὸς διάφορα ἄλλῳ ἄλλο ὑποτάσσεται ἐπὶ γενικῆς (435 a).

ν. Γενικῇ συντάσσονται ἐπίθετα καὶ ῥήματα τὰ πληρώσεως (414), μεθέξεως (424), ἐμπειρίας, ἐπιμελείας, μνήμης (432), ἐπιτυχίας (426 s), φειδοῦς (405 b) σημαντικά, καὶ τὰ τούτοις ἐναντία· πρὸς δὲ ἐκ τῶν ἐπιθέτων, τὰ εἰς -ικός λήγοντα (444), τὰ ἐκ τοῦ ἀ- στερητικοῦ σύνθετα (436 b), καὶ τὰ παραθετικὰ (406 s), τὰ συγκριτικὰ δηλαδὴ καὶ ὑπερθετικά, καὶ τούτοις ἀνάλογα· ἐκ δὲ τῶν ῥημάτων, τὰ ἀρχικὰ (407) καὶ ὑπαρκτικὰ (437), τὰ ἐνάρξεως ἢ λήξεως σημαντικὰ (425, 405), καὶ τὰ τῶν αἰσθήσεων, πλὴν τοῦ ὁρῶ (432 a, h).

ξ. Δοτικῇ συντάσσονται ἐπίθετα καὶ ῥήματα, τὰ ὁμοιότητος, ἀναλογίας, προσεγγίσεως, μίξεως, ἐναντιότητος, διηγήσεως, δόσεως σημαντικά, τά τε φιλικὴν ἢ ἐχθρικὴν πρός τινα διάθεσιν δηλοῦντα (450 s).

ο. Αἰτιατικῇ συντάσσονται τὰ ἰδίως ἢ ἀμέσως μεταβατικὰ ῥήματα (472). Διπλῇ αἰτιατικῇ συντάσσονται τὰ ἱκετευτικά, τὰ παιδευτικά, τὰ ἐνδύσεως ἢ ἐκδύσεως σημαντικά, τὰ τὴν ἔννοιαν ἔχοντα τοῦ εὖ ἢ κακῶς λέγειν ἢ ποιεῖν (480 c).

π. Ὁ χρόνος ὁπότε ἢ ἐν ᾧ γίνεται τι, ἐκφέρεται δοτικῇ ἢ γενικῇ, εἴτε ἀπροθέτῳ εἴτε ἐμπροθέτῳ [without or with a preposition, 433, 469, 487].

ρ. Ὁ τόπος { ὅπου ἵσταται ἢ / ὁπόθεν / δι' οὗ / ὁπόσε } κινεῖται τι, ἐκφέρεται διὰ { δοτικῆς (469), / γενικῆς (405), / γενικῆς (433 d), / αἰτιατικῆς (472 g), } { ἐμπροθέτου τε καὶ ἀπροθέτου.

σ. Τὸ αἴτιον — διὰ γενικῆς (410 s); διὰ δοτικῆς (466 a).

Τὸ ὄργανον δι' οὗ γίνεταί τι,
Ὁ τρόπος καθ' ὃν γίνεταί τι,
Τὸ διαφορᾶς μέτρον
Τὸ κατά τι
Τὸ ποσὸν τόπου ἢ χρόνου
Τὸ ποσὸν ἐπὶ ἀνταλλαγῶν
} ἐκφέρεται {
διὰ δοτικῆς (466).
διὰ δοτικῆς (467).
διὰ δοτικῆς (468).
δι' αἰτιατικῆς (481).
δι' αἰτιατικῆς (482).
διὰ γενικῆς (431).

τ. Τῇ ὁριστικῇ, ὡς θετικόν τι καὶ βέβαιον παριστώσῃ, πρέπει τὸ ἀποφατικὸν ΟΥ· ταῖς δὲ λοιπαῖς τῶν ἐγκλίσεων, αἳ οὐκ ὄντως τι ὂν παριστᾶσι, ἀλλά τι ὑποτιθέμενον ἢ προστασσόμενον ἢ εὐκτόν, πρέπει τὸ ΜΗ (731 a).

END OF TABLES.

INTRODUCTION.

81. THE Ancient Greeks were divided into three principal races: the Ionic, of which the Attic was a branch, the Doric, and the Æolic. These races spoke the same general language, but with many dialectic peculiarities.

82. The ANCIENT GREEK LANGUAGE (commonly called simply *the Greek*) has accordingly been divided by grammarians into four principal DIALECTS, the ATTIC, IONIC, DORIC, and ÆOLIC.

Of these the Attic and Ionic were far the most refined, and had far the greatest unity within themselves. The Doric and Æolic were not only much ruder, but, as the dialects of races widely extended and united by no common bond of literature, abounded in local diversities. Some of the varieties of the Doric or Æolic were separated from each other by differences scarcely less marked than those which distinguished them in common from the other dialects. Of the Æolic, the principal varieties were the Lesbian, the Bœotian, and the Thessalian. The Doric, according as it was more or less removed from the Attic and Ionic, was characterized as the *stricter* or the *milder* Doric: the former prevailing in the Laconic, Tarentine, Cretan, Cyrenian, and some other varieties; the latter in the Corinthian, Syracusan, Megarian, Delphian, and some others.

83. The Greek colonies upon the coast of Asia Minor and the adjacent islands, from various causes, took the lead of the mother country in refinement; and the first development of Greek literature which secured permanence for its productions was among the Asiatic Ionians. This development was EPIC POETRY, and we have, doubtless, its choicest strains remaining to us in the still unsurpassed Homeric poems.

The language of these poems, often called *Epic* and *Homeric*, is the old Ionic, with those modifications and additions which a wandering bard would insensibly gather up, as he sang from city to city, and those poetic licenses which are always allowed to early minstrelsy, when as yet the language is unfixed and critics are unknown. The Old Ionic of the Epic poets was followed by the Middle Ionic of the Elegiac poets; and this again by the New Ionic, found in the prose of Herodotus and Hippocrates.

84. The next dialect which attained distinction in literature was the Æolic of Lesbos, in which the lyric strains of Alcæus and Sappho were sung. But its distinction was short-lived, and we have scarce any remains of the dialect except some brief fragments. There arose later among the Æolians of Bœotia another school of Lyric Poetry, of which the most illustrious ornament was Pindar; who is commonly said, however, but loosely, to have written in the Doric.

85. Meanwhile, the Athenians, a branch of the Ionian race, were gradually rising to such political and commercial importance, and to such intellectual pre-eminence among the states of Greece, that their dialect, the Attic, adorned by such dramatists as Æschylus, Sophocles, Euripides, Aristophanes, and Menander, by such historians as Thucydides and Xenophon, by such philosophers as Plato and Aristotle, and by such orators as Lysias, Æschines, and Demosthenes, became at length the standard language of the Greeks, and, as such, was adopted by the educated classes in all the states. It became the general medium of intercourse, and, with a few exceptions, the universal language of composition. Its diffusion was especially promoted by the conquests of the Macedonians, who adopted it as their court language.

a. As its use extended, it naturally lost some of its peculiarities, and received many additions; and thus diffused and modified, it ceased to be regarded as the language of a particular state, and received the appellation of the COMMON DIALECT or LANGUAGE.

b. The pure Attic has been divided into three periods: the *Old*, used by Thucydides, the Tragedians, and Aristophanes; the *Middle*, used by Xenophon, Isocrates, and Plato; and the *New*, used by Demosthenes, and the other Orators of his time, and the later Comedians. The period of the Common dialect may be regarded as commencing with the subjection of Athens to the Macedonians.

c. The exceptions to the universality acquired by the Attic dialect are found almost entirely in poetry. Here the later writers felt constrained to imitate the language of the great early models. The Epic poet never felt at liberty to depart from the dialect of Homer. Indeed, the old Epic language was regarded by subsequent poets in all departments as a sacred tongue, *the language of the gods*, from which they might enrich their several compositions.

d. The culture of the Athenians was so liberal, and their intercourse with other states so extensive, that not only Attic poets, but even prose-writers, felt at liberty to borrow some forms of expression which belonged more strictly to other dialects.

86. Of the Doric dialect, in proportion to its wide extent, we have very scanty remains; and of most of its varieties our knowledge is derived from passages in Attic writers, from monuments, and from the works of grammarians. In Greece itself, it seems scarcely to have been applied to any other branch of literature than Lyric Poetry. In the more refined Dorian colonies of Italy and Sicily, it was employed in Philosophy by the Pythagoreans (Archȳtas, Timæus, &c.), in Mathematics by the great Archimēdes, in Comedy by Epicharmus and his successors, and in Pastoral Poetry (which was confined to this dialect) by Theocritus, Bion, and Moschus.

87. In this grammar, an attempt is made to exhibit first and distinctly, under each head, the language in its standard form, that is, the Attic and the purer Common Greek; and afterwards to specify the important dialectic peculiarities. It will not, however, be understood that everything which is ascribed to one of the dialects prevails in that dialect throughout, or is found in no other.

  a. This applies especially to the Doric and Æolic, which, with great variety within themselves (§ 82), are closely akin to each other. By the term Æolic, as employed by grammarians, is commonly denoted the cultivated Æolic of Lesbos.

  b. Grammar flourished among the Greeks only in the decline of their language, and the Greek grammarians usually treated the dialects with little precision. Whatever they found in the old Ionic of Homer that seemed to them more akin to the later-cultivated Æolic, Doric, or even Attic, than to the new Ionic, they did not hesitate to ascribe to those dialects. Even in the common language, whatever appeared to them irregular or peculiar, they usually referred to one of the old dialects.

88. The wide diffusion of the Greek by the Macedonian conquerors, and subsequently the conquest of the Greek world by the Romans, much affected the purity of the later language, which became especially degenerate in the Byzantine period.

  a. The Macedonians, who had previously spoken a rude and semi-barbarous dialect of the Greek, retained and diffused some of the peculiarities of their native tongue. These are termed *Macedonic*, or, sometimes, from Alexandria, the principal seat of Macedonian, and indeed of later Greek culture, *Alexandrine*. Words and forms borrowed from the language of the Romans are called *Latinisms*.

  b. The Greek, as the common language of the civilized world, was employed in the translation of the Jewish Scriptures, and the composition of the Christian. When so employed by native Jews, it naturally received a strong Hebrew coloring; and, as a Jew speaking Greek was called Ἑλληνιστής (from ἑλληνίζω, *to speak Greek*), this form of the language has been termed the *Hellenistic* (or by some the *Ecclesiastical*) dialect.

89. Since the destruction of the Eastern Empire by the Turks, the fusion of the Byzantine and Ecclesiastical Greek with the popular dialects of the different districts and islands of Greece has produced the MODERN GREEK, or, as it is often called, by a name derived from the Roman Empire in the East, the ROMAÏC. The Greek, therefore, in its various forms, has never ceased to be a living language; and it offers to the student a series of compositions, not only including many of the highest productions of genius, but extending through a period of nearly three thousand years.

BOOK I.

ORTHOGRAPHY AND ORTHOËPY.

'Εξεῦρον αὐτοῖς. Γραμμάτων τε συνθέσεις
Prometheus of Æschylus.

CHAPTER I.

CHARACTERS.

90. THE Greek language is written with *twenty-four letters, two breathings, three accents, four marks of punctuation,* and a few other characters.

I. For the LETTERS (called the Alphabet from Alpha, Beta, just as we speak of "the A, B, C"), see Table, § 1.

REMARKS. 1. DOUBLE FORMS. Sigma *final* is written ς; *not final,* σ: as, στάσις. Many editors, without authority from manuscripts, use the final form at the end of any word compounded with another: as, προσεισφέρεις. The other double forms are used indifferently: as, βῆϑι or βῆθι.

2. LIGATURES. Two or more letters are often united, except in recent editions, into one character, called a *ligature* (ligatūra, *tie*): as, ȣ for ου, ϛ (named στῖ or στίγμα) for στ. See § 3.

91. 3. NUMERAL POWER. To denote numbers under a thousand, the Greeks employed the letters of the alphabet, and three obsolete letters termed *Epīsēma* (ἐπίσημον, *sign, mark*), as shown in § 1, with the mark (´) over them: as, αʹ 1, ιʹ 10, ιβʹ 12, ρκγʹ 123. The first eight letters, with Vau, represented the nine units; the next eight, with Koppa, the nine tens; and the last eight, with San, the nine hundreds. The thousands were denoted by the same letters with the mark *beneath:* as, ͵ε 5, ͵ε 5,000, ͵κγ or ͵κ.γ 23,000.

a. Sometimes the Greek letters, like our own, denote ordinal numbers, according to their own order in the alphabet. In this way the books of Homer are marked: as, Ἰλιάδος Α, Ζ, Ω, *The Iliad, Books* 1, 6, 24.

92. 4. ROMAN LETTERS. By the side of the Greek letters in § 1, are placed the Roman letters which take their place when Greek words are transferred into Latin or English: as, Κύκλωψ Cyclops.

§ 96.   CHARACTERS.   125

  a. The letter γ becomes *n*, when followed by another palatal ; but, otherwise, *g* (137 c) : as, ἄγγελος, Lat. angelus, Eng. *angel*, συγκοπή syncope, λάρυγξ larynx, Αἴγῖνα Ægīna.
  b. The *diphthong* αι becomes *æ* ; οι, *œ* ; ει, *ī* or *ē* (before a consonant almost always *ī*) ; ου, *ū* ; and υι, *yi* : as, Φαῖδρος Phædrus, Βοιωτία Bœotia, Νεῖλος Nīlus, Δαρεῖος Darīus, Μήδεια Medēa, Μοῦσα Mūsa, Εἰλείθυια Ilithyia. A few words ending in -αια and -οια are excepted : as, Μαῖα Maia, Τροία Troia or Troja ; so also Αἴας Ajax. For ᾳ, ῃ, ῳ, see 109.

93. II. The BREATHINGS are the SMOOTH or SOFT (spiritus lenis : '), and the ROUGH (spiritus asper : '), also called the ASPIRATE (aspīro, *to breathe*). The first denotes a gentle emission of the breath, such as is needed before the utterance of any initial vowel, but in most languages is not marked ; the second, a strong emission, such as in English is represented by *h*.

  a. The *rough breathing* becomes, in Latin and English, *h*, while the *smooth* is not written : as, Ἕκτωρ Hector, Ἔρυξ Eryx, Ῥέα Rhea.
  b. One of the breathings is placed over every initial vowel. For its place over a diphthong, see 110.
  c. An *initial* υ has always the rough breathing to assist in its utterance (as in English an initial long *u* is always preceded by the sound of *y* ; thus, ὗς, ὑμεῖς, as, in English, *use*, pronounced *yuse*, *union*) ; except in the Æolic dialect, and in the Epic forms ὕμμες, ὕμμι, ὕμμε.
  d. An *initial* ρ requires, for its proper vibration or rolling, a strong aspiration, and is therefore always marked with the rough breathing : as, ῥέω. When ρ is *doubled*, the first ρ has the smooth breathing, and the second the rough (in Latin *rrh*) : as, Πύῤῥος Pyrrhus. Some excellent editors, however, notwithstanding old usage and Latin analogy, now write ρρ without the breathings : thus, Πύρρος.

94. III. The ACCENTS are the ACUTE (′), the GRAVE (`), and the CIRCUMFLEX (˜ or ˆ). For their use, see Prosody. See also 5.

95. IV. The MARKS OF PUNCTUATION are the COMMA (,); the COLON (·), taking the place of our colon and semicolon ; the PERIOD (.) ; and the NOTE OF INTERROGATION (;), which has the form of ours (?) inverted.
  To these some editors have judiciously added the NOTE OF EXCLAMATION (!).

96. V. OTHER-CHARACTERS.   *a.* CORONIS and APOSTROPHE. The mark ('), which at the *beginning* of a word is the *smooth breathing*, over the *middle* is the CORŌNIS (κορωνίς, *crooked mark*), or *mark of crasis*, and at the *end*, the APOSTROPHE (124 b, 127) : as, ταὐτά for τὰ αὐτά, ἀλλ' ἐγώ for ἀλλὰ ἐγώ.
  b. The HYPHEN, DIÆRESIS, DASH, and MARKS OF PARENTHESIS and QUOTATION are used in printing Greek as in English.
  c. Among the other signs used by critics and editors are BRACKETS [ ], to enclose words of doubtful authenticity ; the OBELISK († or —), to mark verses or words as faulty ; the ASTERISK (*), to denote that some-

thing is wanting in the text; and MARKS OF QUANTITY, viz. (¯), to mark a vowel or syllable as *long;* (˘), as *short;* (˘ or ¯˘), as *either long or short.*

HISTORY OF GREEK ORTHOGRAPHY.

97. That the Greek alphabet was borrowed from the Phœnician is abundantly established both by historical and by internal evidence.

a. According to common tradition, letters were first brought into Greece by Cadmus, a Phœnician, who founded Thebes long before the Trojan war. In illustration, we present in § 2 the common Hebrew alphabet, which is substantially the same with the old Phœnician, placing by the side the corresponding Greek letters, and also the Latin.

98. This borrowed alphabet received in the course of time important modifications.

a. The original Phœnician alphabet had no proper vowels. The Greeks, therefore, employed as such those letters which, as representing various breathings or aspirate sounds, were nearest akin to vowels; viz. A, E, F, H, 1, and O.

b. The aspirate use of E and F still continued for a period, and hence these letters when employed as vowels were distinguished by the term ψῑλόν, *smooth;* thus, Ἔ ψῑλόν, Ὕ ψῑλόν. It will be observed that the last of these letters, when used as a vowel, was somewhat changed in form, and was put at the end of the old alphabet.

c. To the Phœnician alphabet the Greeks added the aspirates Φ and Χ, the double consonant Ψ, and the sign for long *o*, Ω, naturally placing them at the end. In distinction, the short *o* was now termed Ὄ μῑκρόν, *small O;* and the long *o*, Ὦ μέγα, *great O.*

d. In the softening of the language, the labial breathing F, and also Ϙ and ϻ, which were only rougher forms of K and Σ, fell into disuse, and these letters were retained only as numeral characters; F and Ϙ in their proper places in the alphabet, but ϻ at the end. The Latin alphabet, which ours here follows, dropped ϻ, but retained the other two, F and Q, in their proper places.

e. F (also named from its form the *Digamma,* i. e. the double Gamma) is still found upon some inscriptions and coins, and performs an important office in the explanation of the forms of the language. Its restoration by Bentley to the Homeric poems has removed so many apparent hiatuses and irregularities of metre, that we cannot doubt its existence in the time of Homer, though apparently even then beginning to lose its power.

CHAPTER II.

FIGURES AFFECTING LETTERS AND SOUNDS.

99. The letters and sounds in words are subject to many changes, called FIGURES, as affecting the *form* of the word.

a. These changes may be either *euphonic, poetic,* or *dialectic.*

b. Euphonic changes are chiefly to avoid *hiatus* (the succession of distinct vowels without an intervening consonant); to reduce the openness of vowels (107, 114–116); to secure a proper rhythm; and to prevent excessive or undesirable combinations of consonants, and difficult or less agreeable modes of beginning and ending words.

100. In the earliest Greek of which we have traces, the prevalent method of preventing hiatus was by the insertion of consonants; particularly F and Σ (as in Latin *v*, *b*, and *r*), but also Δ, Φ, &c. In the progress of the language, these inserted consonants extensively dropped out, and the more rapid method by contraction prevailed.

101. To give to the discourse a proper flow and rhythm, especially in poetry, syllables are lengthened or shortened, united or resolved.

102. To prevent undesirable combinations of consonants, or modes of beginning and ending words, letters are dropped, added, changed, and transposed.

a. The names below ending in *-thesis* and *-æresis* are derived from compounds of τίθημι, *to put*, and αἱρέω, *to take*.

103. Figures (see § 6). *Addition and Subtraction.* a. Prothesis (πρό, *before;* less properly Prosthesis) *adds* one or more letters at the *beginning* of a word; Epenthesis (ἐπί, *to*, ἐν, *in*), in the *middle;* and Paragōge (παραγωγή, *a bringing beside*), at the *end:* as, χθές ἐχθές, heri, *yesterday;* ἀυρος ἀνδρός (18); εἴκοσι εἴκοσιν, *twenty.*

b. By the *extension* of a vowel is meant its repetition, either in whole or in part, either before or after: as, ἔ ἐέ, *himself,* φῶς φόως, *light.*

c. Aphæresis (ἀπό, *from*) *takes* one or more letters from the *beginning* of a word; Syncope (συγκοπή, *abridgment*), from the *middle;* and Apocope (ἀποκοπή, *a cutting off*), from the *end:* as, λείβω εἴβω, libo, *to pour;* πατέρος πατρός, patris (18); ἀνά ἄν, *up.*

d. One form of Apocope has received the special name of *Apostrophe* or *Elision* (117).

104. *Exchange.* Metathesis (μετά, *among, interchangeably*), or Transposition, *changes the order* of letters; and Antithesis (ἀντί, *instead of*) *substitutes* one letter for another: as, ἔδαρθον ἔδραθον, τάσσω τάττω.

a. When one letter thus becomes the same with an adjoining letter, the change is called *Assimilation:* as, συνλέγω συλλέγω, *to collect.*

105. *Union, &c.* a. Synæresis (σύν, *together*) *unites* two vowels (and thus two syllables) into one; and Diæresis (διά, *apart*), or Resolution, *divides* one vowel into two: as, νόος νοῦς, *mind;* παῖς πάϊς, *boy.*

b. Synæresis is divided into *Contraction, Crasis,* and *Synizesis* (117).

c. Systole (συστολή, *a drawing in*) *shortens* a long vowel; and Diastole (διαστολή, *a drawing out*) *lengthens* a short one: as, ἑταῖρος ἔτᾰρος, *comrade,* ξένος ξεῖνος, *stranger.* For Precession, see 107, 113s.

CHAPTER III.

VOWELS.

106. The Greek has *five simple vowels*, and *seven diphthongs*. Each of the simple vowels may be either long or short, and each of the diphthongs may have either a long or short prepositive, or first vowel.

a. Of three vowels, the short and long sounds are represented by the same letters (ᾰ, ᾱ; ῐ, ῑ; ῠ, ῡ); but of the other two, whose long sounds occur far more frequently, by different letters (ἔ, ῆ; ŏ, ῶ).

b. When speaking of letters, and not of sounds, we say that the Greek has seven vowels; and call ε and ο the *short vowels*, because they always represent short sounds, η and ω the *long vowels*, because they always represent long sounds, and α, ι, and υ the *doubtful vowels*, because their form leaves it doubtful whether the sound is long or short.

107. There is strong evidence, that, in general, these vowels were pronounced nearly as follows: *a* like *a* in *far, fast* (not as in *fate*); η, ε, like *e* in *they, then* (not as in *mete*); ι like *i* in *machine, pin* (not as in *pine*); ω, ο, like *o* in *note, obey;* υ like *u* in *rule, full* (afterwards becoming closer, more like *u* in *tube*, or the still closer French *u* or German *ü*). They may hence be thus placed upon a *scale of precession* or *attenuation*.

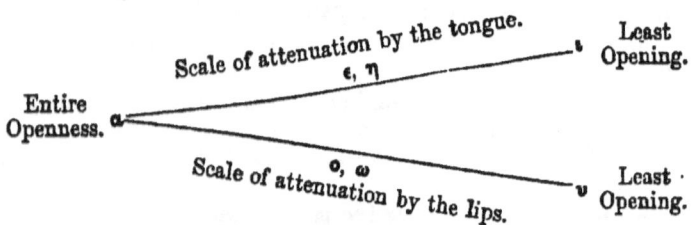

a. In general, ι and υ are termed the *close*, and the others the *open* vowels; but α is more open than ε and ο, and ι is somewhat closer than υ.

b. There is a strong tendency, in the progress of language, towards the attenuation, or closer pronunciation, of the open, especially the long open vowels (99). This change would be represented on the scale above by a moving forward of the vowel from the left to the right; and hence has been called *precession* (præcessio, *going forward*). Thus the open α of the old Greek became η in the refined Ionic; and this again in the Modern Greek has passed (as also υ, ει, ῃ, οι, and υι) into the closer sound of ι.

108. In the Greek diphthongs, the voice always passes from a *more open* to a *closer* sound; and the subjunctive, or last vowel, is always ι or υ.

a. A *short* prepositive left time for the full utterance of the subjunctive vowel, and the diphthong was then termed *proper*, as really combining two sounds; but a *long* prepositive nearly or quite crowded out the sound of the subjunctive, and the diphthong was then termed *improper*, as though diphthongal only in appearance.

109. After α long, η, and ω, the subjunctive ι so lost its sound, that it was at last merely written beneath the prepositive, if this was a small letter, and was then termed *Iota subscript* (subscriptus, *written beneath*). With capitals, it still remains in the line, but is not sounded. It is not represented in Latin, except that, in a few compounds of ᾠδή, ῳ becomes *œ*. Thus, ῍Αιδης or ᾄδης Hādēs, Θρῇσσα Thressa, Ἧι or ᾗ, *where*, Ὠιδή or ᾠδή ōdē, *song;* but τραγῳδία tragœdia, *tragedy*.

a. Editors vary in the use of the ι subscript, from different views of etymology, &c.: as, contract infinitive τιμᾶν or τιμᾷν, adverbial datives ὅπῃ or ὅπη, Ἀθήνῃσι or Ἀθήνησι. So some have improperly written ἔφηνα, πέφηνα (40, as if made directly from φαίνω, instead of the root φαν-), &c.

110. In diphthongs, except the three just mentioned (ᾳ, ῃ, and ῳ), the breathings and accents are written over the second vowel, and thus often mark the union of the two vowels: as, αὐτή *herself,* but ἀϋτή *cry;* ηὖδα *he spoke,* but ἤϋσε *he shouted;* Αἵμων (ᾰ) Hæmon, but ῍Αιδης (ᾱ).

a. If two vowels which might form a diphthong are pronounced separately, the second is commonly marked, as above, with a diæresis; though the place of a breathing, accent, or ι often renders this needless, and it is then omitted by some: as in ἀϋτή, ἰχθύϊ, ληϊζοίμην (109).

b. In the table (4), the vowels, simple and compound, are divided into *classes*, according to the simple sound which is their sole or leading element, as *A sounds*, &c.; and into *orders*, according to the length of this sound, or its combination with other sounds, as *short vowels*, &c. Vowels of the same class are termed *cognate;* and those of the same order, *coordinate*.

111. SYLLABICATION. In Greek, a word has as many syllables as it has simple vowels or diphthongs: ποιέεαι has four.

a. The last syllable in a word is termed the *ultima* (ultimus, *last*); the last but one, the *penultima* or *penult* (pene, *almost*); and the last but two, the *antepenultima* or *antepenult* (ante, *before*).

b. In the syllabication of a word, any consonant between two vowels is now joined by most editors with the latter; and so even two or more consonants, — unless the first is a liquid, or the same with the second, or a smooth mute before its cognate rough, when it is joined with the former vowel (except in the case of μν): as, ἐ-ψη-φί-σμε-θα, ἀ-στρά-πτω, ἐ-μνή-σθην · but ἔρ-γον, ἄν-τρον, ἄγ-χι (137 c), ἵππος, τάσ-σω, Βάκ-χος.

c. Words joined by crasis or elision are here regarded as a single word:

as, ἀλ-λ' οἶ-δ' ὅ-τι · so, in composition, ἐ-πά-νειμι (ἐπί, ἀνά, εἶμι). But the elements of a compound word not so joined are here treated as separate words : as, συν-εἰσ-ειμι.

112. A vowel preceded by a consonant is said to be *impure* (impūrus, *mixed*, sc. with the consonant sound); otherwise, it is said to be *pure*.

a. The same distinction is made in affixes beginning with a vowel; and even the word itself and its stem are termed pure or impure, according as these affixes are preceded by a vowel or consonant. Thus, in συός (14) the o and affix ος are pure, and the same term, by an extension of its use, is applied to the word and its stem συ- ; while in γυπός (17) the o and ος are impure, and the word itself and its stem γυπ- are so termed.

113. The Greek vowels are subject to a great number of EUPHONIC CHANGES, which may be referred, for the most part, to two great heads, the PRECESSION OF VOWELS, and the UNION OF SYLLABLES.

I. PRECESSION OF VOWELS.

114. The great tendency in Greek to the attenuation of vowel sounds shows itself,

1.) In the interchange of vowels.

a. Precession especially affects α, as the most open of the vowels, changing it, when short, to ε and o ; and, when long, to η, and sometimes to ω.

b. Hence, these three vowels may be regarded as *kindred*, and are often interchanged in the formation and inflection of words. Thus, in the verbs τρέπω *to turn*, στρέφω *to twist*, we find the stem in three forms, τραπ- τρεπ- τροπ-, στραφ- στρεφ- στροφ-, as in the Eng. *speak*, *spake*, *spoken*, or in the equivalent Germ., where precession is carried still further, *spreche*, *spricht*, *sprach*, *gesprochen ;* and in ῥήγνυμι *to break*, we find the forms ῥαγ- ῥηγ- ῥωγ- (cf. frango, fregi). The change extends to diphthongs : thus, in πείθω *to persuade*, the forms πειθ- and ποιθ- ; σπεύδω *to hasten*, σπουδή *haste ;* μεσόγαια and μεσόγεια, *interior*.

c. This interchange is also illustrated by the connecting vowels inserted in the inflection of words. Thus, in Dec. 1, the connecting vowel is α, but in Dec. 2, ο, for which in one case ε appears (12). In the Indicative active, the connecting vowel in the Aorist and Perfect is α (passing, however, into ε in the 3d pers. sing. ; compare the Imperative λῦσον) ; while in the Present, Imperfect, and Future, it is o before a liquid, but otherwise ε. So, in the Aor. optative, we find both αι and εια. See 35.

d. The change of ε to the closer ι abounds especially in stems of the third declension : as, πολε- πόλις, *city*. Cf. ἥκω and poet. ἵκω, *to come*. The use of υ for ο or ω is especially Æolic : as, ὄνομα ὄνυμα, *name*, χελώνη χελύνη, *tortoise*.

115. 2.) In the lengthening of the short vowels, and in the general laws of contraction. Thus,

a. The long vowel is regarded as the short vowel doubled; that is, ā, η, ω, ῡ, ῑ = ăă, εε, οο, ὔὔ, ῐῐ. In the formation of words, therefore, the lengthening of a short vowel, or the union of two short vowels of the same class, should produce the cognate long. The close vowels obey this law: as, Χιῖος Χῖος, *a Chian*, μαγάδ⟨ῐῐ⟩ῑ vii. 3. 32, (ὔὔ)ὕβρικα, *I have insulted*. Cf. Lat. otii oti, curruum currûm. But through precession, which especially affects the long open vowels, ᾰ, unless it follows ε, ι, ρ, or ρο, is usually lengthened, not to ā, but to the closer η; and εε and οο commonly form, not η and ω, but the closer diphthongs ει and ου, which are hence termed the *corresponding diphthongs* of ε and ο. Cf. Lat. amaam amem (43).

116. In Latin inflection, through precession and the interchange of kindred vowels, *e* takes extensively the place of α; *i* of ε, ει, ο, οι, αι, and even α; and *u* of ο and ω; and they are often similarly contracted. This must be kept in mind, in comparing affixes and contractions. Thus, -ας -es, -ος -is, -ων -um, Dec. 3; -αις -is, Dec. 1; -οι -i, -οις -is, -ος -us, -ον um, Dec. 2; and in verbs, -εις, -ει (Bœot. -ις, -ι), -is, -it, -ομεν (Dor. -ομες) -imus, -ετε -itis, -εται -itur, -ονται -untur, -α (in Perf. and Aor.) -i, -ασθα -isti. See 13, 36.

II. UNION OF SYLLABLES.

117. The most important changes belonging to this head are, A. CONTRACTION, which unites two successive vowels in the same word; B. CRASIS (κρᾶσις, *mingling*), which unites the *final* and *initial* vowels of successive and closely connected words; and C. APOSTROPHE or ELISION, which simply *drops* a final vowel before a word beginning with a vowel.

a. All these forms may occur in the composition of words.

b. In poetry, two vowels are often united in pronunciation, which are written separately. This union is termed *synizēsis* (συνίζησις, *placing together*), or *synecphonēsis* (συνεκφώνησις, *pronouncing together*). Here, the first vowel (which may have commonly had a kind of semivowel force, like our *y* and *w*) is in most instances an *E* vowel; more rarely ι, α, &c. E. g. (using a mark employed by grammarians) πόλεως (as if pron. *polyōs*).

A. CONTRACTION.

118. Contraction takes place in three ways; (a) by *simple union*, when ι or υ simply unites with the preceding vowel to form a diphthong, as οἶ οι ; (b) by *union with precession,* when the second vowel passes into ι or υ, and then forms a diphthong with the preceding, as εε ει, οο ου ; and (c) by *absorption,* when one vowel is simply lost in the other, which, if before short, now of course becomes long (including the case in which both vowels are of the same class, 115 a), as εᾰ η, οᾰ ω, ᾰᾰ ᾱ.

d. In the following general rules, α, ε, and η are regarded as including the cognate diphthongs in ι. For the mode of writing ι, when contracted with α long, η, or ω, or absorbed in these, see 109.

e. In the examples below, and in others similarly printed, the letters or syllables which receive the change are inclosed in parentheses, and the result of the change follows in full-face type ; so that, in reading the forms of the word before and after the change, we first omit the full-face letters, and then the letters in the parentheses ; thus, ῥ(άϊ)**ᾷ**στος is an abridged mode of representing that "άϊ becomes ᾷ, as ῥάϊστος ῥᾷστος."

119. GENERAL RULES. I. Two vowels which can form a diphthong unite without further change: as,

γέν(εἴ)**ει**, ἠχ(όϊ)**οῖ** (19) ; ῥ(άϊ)**ᾷ**στος *easiest,* Θρ(ήϊ)**ῇ**σσα, λ(ώϊ)**ῷ**στος *best,* νέκ(υϊ)**υι** (Epic), γήρ(άϊ)**αι** (so Thiersch, Bekker, Kühner in his latest grammar, &c., while others have written γήρᾳ, as if ι were absorbed).

120. II. (a) α, before an *E* sound (§ 4), absorbs it ; but, (b) after an *E* or another *A* sound, is itself absorbed. (c) α, or (d) η, with an *O* sound, forms ω. Thus,

(a) τίμ(αε)**ᾱ**, τιμ(άει)**ᾷ**, τιμ(άη)**ᾷτε**, τιμ(άῃ)**ᾷ** (42) ; (b) γέν(εα)**η**, γέρ(αα)**ᾱ** (19), λύ(εαι)**ῃ**, λύ(ηαι)**ῃ** (37) ; (c) τιμ(άο)**ῶμεν**, τιμ(άω)**ω**, τιμ(άοι)**ῷ**, τιμ(άου)**ῶ** (42), ἠχ(όα)**ώ**, ἤρ(ωα)**ω** (19), (οὐα)**ὠτός** (17 ; while, in the Nom. sing., οὔας becomes οὖς by an absorption of the α, or by precession from the Dor. ὦς) ; (d) δηλ(όη)**ῶτε** (42), διδ(όη)**ῷ** (45), ν(ηο)**ωδύς** *toothless.* Cf. Lat. lyr(ăē)**ā**, am(ăē)**āre**, am(ao)**o**, c(ŏā)**ō**go, am(aī)**āte** (116).

e. In Dec. 1, and the plural and dual of the common Dec. 2, contraction imitates the forms of uncontracted words ; but in the Attic Dec. 2 (200), it has ω throughout : as, χρυσ(έα)**ῆ** and διπλ(όη)**ῆ**, -**ῆς**, -**ῇ**, -**ῆν**, -**αῖ**, &c. (23 ; cf. ᾠδή, 15) ; ὀστ(έα)**ᾶ** (16) ; ἀγήρ(αα)**ω** (22).

f. After a vowel, εα commonly becomes **α** ; as Πειραι(έα)**ᾶ** (220 e), Ἡρακλέ(εα)**ᾶ** (19) ; but adjectives in -ιής and -υής vary in the neuter pl. : as, from ὑγιής *sound,* εὐφυής *clever,* ὑγι(έα)**ᾶ** and -**ῆ**, εὐφυ(έα)**ᾶ** and -**ῆ**.

g. In the purer Attic, η takes the place of ᾱ in the contract forms of four *every-day* verbs : **πεινάω** *to hunger,* **διψάω** *to thirst,* **χράω** *to supply need,* and **ζάω** *to live :* as, πειν(άει)**ῇ**, χρ(άε)**ῆ**σθαι. Add κνάω *to scratch,* σμάω *to smear,* and ψάω *to rub.*

h. In the liquid Aorist, and in the Subjunctive and Imperative of verbs in -μι, αε and αη commonly become **η**, unless ι or ρ precedes : as, ἔφηνα, ἐπιᾱνα (152) ; ἱστ(άη)**ῇ**, δρ(άη)**ᾷ**, ἱστ(αε)η (45).

i. When **α** long is contracted with an *O* sound, there is usually inserted before the ω an ε, which, however, is not treated in the accentuation as a distinct syllable (cf. 117 b) : as, νᾱός (νως) νεώς (16), Ἀτρείδ(ᾱο)εω (197 c). So sometimes, chiefly in the Ion. (135 a, 322), when the α is short.

§ 124. CRASIS. 133

121. III. (a) εε becomes ει. (b) ε or ο, with ο, forms ου; but (c) with other Ο sounds is absorbed. (d) In other combinations not already given (119, 120), ε is absorbed. Thus,

(a) φιλ(εε)ει, φιλ(έει)εῖ (42), πόλ(εες)εις (19), κλ(εῖες)εῖς (207); (b) φι-λ(έο)οῦμαι, δηλ(οε)ου (42), Ὀπ(όεις)οῦς (17), ν(όος)ους (16); (c) φιλ(έω)ῶ, φιλ(έοι)οῖ, φιλ(έου)οῦ, δηλ(όω)ῶ, δηλ(όοι)οι, δηλ(όου)οῦ (42), ὀστ(έῳ)ῳ, ν(όῳ)ῳ (16); (d) φιλ(έη)ῆτε, φιλ(έῃ)ῇ (42), τιμ(ήεις)ῇς, τιμ(ῆεν)ῆν (207 c), ἰχθ(ύε)ῦ (19), (ἑαυ)αὑτοῦ (27).

e. In the *dual* of Dec. 3, εε becomes η : as, γέν(εε)η (19). So, in the older Attic writers, in the Nom. plur. of nouns in -ευς : as, ἱππέες ἱππῆς (by some incorrectly written -ῆς, 109 a) Th. 6. 68, instead of the common ἱππεῖς. Cf. Lat. rĕĕ rē, mon(ĕĕ)ēre. For (οε) υι, see 233 c.

122. SPECIAL RULES. 1. *a*, taking the place of ν before σ (156) is contracted like ε : as, in the affixes of the Accusative pl., (-ονς -οας) -ους, (-ανς -αας) -ᾱς (13 ; cf. Lat. -oms -ōs, -ams -ās). Hence, in Dec. 3, the contract Nom. and Acc. pl. agree in form : as, πόλεες and πόλεας πόλεις, ἰχθύες and ἰχθύας ἰχθῦς (19), μείζους (22) ; cf. Acc. βόας βοῦς, οἴας οἷς (19). So, in Lat., Nom. and Acc. pl. sues, fructus, res. See 156.

a. By a similar contraction with βόας βοῦς, we find also νᾶας ναῦς (19), γρᾶας γραῦς ; and in late writers, even Nom. pl. ναῦς. For χοέᾱς χοᾶς, see 220 e.

123. 2. In a few cases, the first vowel of a diphthong in ι is absorbed, and the ι retained. Thus, (a) in verbs in -όω (not -ωμι), οει and οη become οι : as, δηλόει δηλοῖ, δηλόῃ δηλοῖ (42). (b) In the 2d pers. sing., the affix -εαι becomes not only -ῃ (120 b), but, as a special Attic form, -ει : as, λύεαι λύῃ and λύει (37). (c) In a very few roots, αει becomes αι, as ἀεικής αἰκής, *unseemly*.

d. For special contractions in the affixes of declension, see 7, 13 ; in the augment and reduplication, 7, 278 s.

e. REMARK. Contraction is omitted in many words in which it might take place according to the preceding rules, particularly in nouns of the third declension, and in dissyllabic verbs in -έω ; and other forms of contraction occur in the dialects, or rarely in the common language.

B. CRASIS.

124. Crasis (1), for the most part, follows the laws of contraction, disregarding however an ι *final*, which according to the best usage is not even subscribed. But often (2), without respect to these laws, a final, or (3) an initial vowel is entirely absorbed.

a. See examples below of these three forms, chiefly marked with corresponding numbers. The first word, as the less important, is commonly most affected. Hence the rule above respecting ι.

b. Crasis prevails most in Attic poetry. It is commonly indicated (96) by the coronis ('), except when this mark is excluded by the rough breathing : as, τἀμά, οὑμοί. When an initial vowel has been simply absorbed, the words are more frequently separated in writing: as, οἱ 'μοί. The same is sometimes done, when a final vowel has been absorbed. Hence, cases are often referred to *aphaeresis* and *apostrophe*, which properly belong to crasis. For the change of a smooth mute to its cognate rough, when the second word is aspirated, see 161. For the accent, see Prosody, 773.

125. The principal words in which the final vowel is subject to crasis are the following :

a.) The *article ;* in which (as in the particle τοί, 126 γ) the second form prevails before a : as,

(1) ὁ ἐκ, becoming by crasis οὐκ· ὁ ἐπί, οὑπί· οἱ ἐμοί, οὑμοί· ὁ ὄρνις, οὕρνις· τῇ ἐμῇ, τἠμῇ. (2) ὁ ἀνήρ, ἁνήρ (less Att. ὡνήρ)· τῷ ἀνδρί, τἀνδρί· ἡ ἀρετή, ἁρετή· αἱ ἀγαθαί, ἁγαθαί· τοῦ αὐτοῦ, ταὐτοῦ· τοῦ ἡμετέρου, θἠμετέρου. (3) ὁ οἶνος, ᾧνος· οἱ ἐμοί, οἱ 'μοί· τοῦ ὕδατος, θοὔδατος.

a. The *neuter forms* τό and τά are especially subject to crasis : as (1) τὸ ἐναντίον, τοὐναντίον· τὸ ἱμάτιον, θοἰμάτιον· τὸ ὕδωρ, θοὔδωρ· τὰ ὅπλα, θὤπλα. (2) τὸ ἀληθές, τἀληθές. (3) τὰ αἰσχρά, τᾀσχρά.

b. In crasis with the article, ἕτερος, *other,* retains the old form ἅτερος : as, (2) ὁ ἕτερος, ἅτερος· τὸ ἕτερον, θάτερον· τοῦ ἑτέρου, θατέρου.

126. β.) The *conjunction* καί, *and :* as,

(1) καὶ ἄν, κἄν· καὶ ἐν, κἀν· καὶ ἕτερος, χἄτερος· καὶ εἶτα, κᾆτα· καὶ ὁ, χὠ· καὶ οἱ, χοἰ (2) καὶ εἰ, κεἰ· καὶ οὐ, κοὐ. (2, 3) καὶ ἡ ἄγχουσα, χἤγχουσα.

γ.) The *preposition* πρό (chiefly in composition before ε and ο unaspirated); the *interjection* ὦ (especially before a) ; and a few other *particles :* as,

προέδωκα προὔδωκα, πρόοπτος προὖπτος (ἐ-, ὀπ-)· πρὸ ἔργου, προὔργου· ὦ ἀγαθέ, ὠ'γαθέ· ὦ ἄνθρωπε, ὤνθρωπε· ἤτοι ἄρα, ἦτἄρα· μέντοι ἄν, μεντἄν· οὔτοι ἄρα, οὔτἄρα· εἰ μὴ ἔχοιμι, εἰ μὴ 'χοιμι· μὴ εὕρω, μὴ 'ὕρω.

δ.) Some forms of the *pronouns :* as,

ἐγὼ οἶδα, ἐγῷδα· ἐγὼ οἶμαι, ἐγῷμαι· μοι ἐδόκει, μοὐδόκει· σοί ἐστιν, σοὔστιν· ὁ ἐφόρει, οὐφόρει· οὗ ἕνεκα, οὕνεκα· ὅτου ἕνεκα, ὀθούνεκα· ἃ ἄν, ἄν· ἃ ἐμέ, ἀμέ.

C. Apostrophe, or Elision.

127. Apostrophe affects the short vowels ἄ, ε, ῐ, and ο (in monosyllables only ε) ; and sometimes, in poetry, αι in verbal affixes (chiefly passive) where it is treated as short in accentuation : as,

Τόδ' ἔστ' ἐκείν' αἴνιγμ' ὃ προσπόλου κλύω Eur. Hel. 788. Κλαύσετ' ἄρα (κλαύσεται ἄρα) Ar. Th. 916. Ἔρχεθ' ὡς (ἔρχεται, 161) Ib. 1178. Κολάσ' ἔξεστι (κολάσαι, Inf. act.) Nub. 7. In Tragic dialogue, the elision of αι is rare : Λειφθήσομ' ἤδη Soph. Ph. 1071.

a. For the sign of apostrophe ('), which has the same name with the figure, see 96. For the accentuation, see Prosody.

128. Elision is most common,

a. In the prepositions, and other particles of constant use: as, ἀφ' ἑαυτοῦ (ἀπό, 161), ἐπ' ἐκεῖνον, κατ' ἐμέ, ἀλλ' ἐγώ, ἆρ' οὖν, γ' οὐδέν, μάλ' ἄν, ὅθ' ὁ (ὅτε ὁ), τάχ' ἄν. So, in composition (where the sign ' is omitted), ἀνέρχομαι, διελαύνω, πάρειμι, ὅταν.

b. In a few pronouns, and in some phrases of frequent occurrence: as, τοῦτ' ἄλλο, ταῦτ' ἤδη · γένοιτ' ἄν, ἔσθ' ὅπου (ἔστι), λέγοιμ' ἄν, οἶδ' ὅτι, φήμ' ἐγώ.

129. a. Elision is less frequent in ι, than in the other short vowels above mentioned. Particularly, it is not elided by the Attics in περί, ἄχρι, μέχρι (§ 164), or ὅτι (which might then be confounded with ὅτε); or, except rarely in poetry, in the Dat. sing., which might then be confounded with the Acc. The forms which take ν *paragogic* (163) are not elided in prose, except ἐστί · and in the Dat. pl., not even in Attic poetry.

b. Elision is least frequent in Ionic prose. In Attic prose, it is found chiefly in a few words, but these often recurring. In poetry, where hiatus is more carefully avoided and the metre so governs, its use is far more extended; and here an especial freedom belongs to Comic and Epic verse.

c. On some points in crasis and elision, critics differ. Thus, some regard the enclitics μοί, σοί, and τοί, and the possessive pronoun σά, as affected by elision in Attic poetry; but others, only by crasis.

d. Both elision and the absorption of a vowel by crasis may occur at those minor punctuation-marks which the voice disregards; and in poetry, are sometimes permitted at the more important marks, even where the speaker is changed: as, νὴ Δί', ἔφη Mem. 2. 7. 4; ἥξω · 'πὶ τούτοις Eur. Rh. 157; τοὔπ' ἐμ'. El. ὦ Id. Or. 1345.

DIALECTIC VARIATIONS.

130. The dialectic variations in the vowels may be mostly referred to the heads of PRECESSION, UNION or RESOLUTION, QUANTITY, and INSERTION or OMISSION.

I. PRECESSION prevailed most in the soft Ionic, and least in the rough Doric and Æolic; while the Attic, which blended strength and refinement, held a middle place. E. g.

a. Long α, for the most part, is retained in the Dor. and Æol., but in the Ion. passes into η; while the Att. preserves a mean: as, Dor. 'ἀμέρα, Att. ἡμέρᾱ, Ion. ἡμέρη · Dor. δᾶμος, πᾶγά, ὠκύτᾱς, Att. and Ion. δῆμος, πηγή, ὠκύτης · Dor. and Att. σοφίᾱ, πρᾶγμα, Ion. σοφίη, πρῆγμα. So, even in diphthongs, Ion. νηῦς, γρηῦς, for ναῦς, γραῦς, and in Dat. pl. of Dec. 1, -ῃσι, -ῃς, for -αισι, -αις. The use of long α produced, in great measure, the Dor. feature called πλατειασμός, *broad pronunciation*, which was imitated by the Attics in the lyric parts of their drama.

b. Short α is retained by the Dor. and Æol. in some words, where, in the Att., it passes into ε; and in some (particularly verbs in -άω) by the Att., where it becomes ε in the Ion. Thus, Dor. τράφω, φράσί, ὅκά, γά, Att. τρέφω, φρεσί, ὅτε, γέ · Att. ὁράω, ἄρσην, Ion. ὁρέω, ἔρσην.

c. As the long of ε and ο, or the contraction of εε and οο or οε, the stricter Dor. prefers the long vowels η and ω to the closer diphthongs ει and ου; while, on the other hand, the Ion. is particularly fond of protracting ε to ει, and ο to ου or οι. Thus, Dor. χήρ, δῶλος · Gen. of Dec. 2, τῶ ὠρανῶ · Inf. εὑρῆν, ὑπνῶν · for χείρ, δοῦλος, τοῦ οὐρανοῦ, εὑρεῖν, ὑπνοῦν. Ion. ξεῖνος, μοῦνος, ποίη, for ξένος, μόνος, πόα.

d. Other examples of precession or the interchange of kindred vowels (114) are the following; in some of which, contrary to the general law of the dialects, the Ion. has a more open sound than the Att., or the Att. than the Dor. or Æol.: Att. ἀεί, ἀετός, ἐστιά, θᾶκος, Ion. αἰεί, αἰετός, ἰστίη, θῶκος · Old Att. κάω, κλάω, Ion. and Com. καίω, κλαίω · Ion. τράπω, μέγαθος, μεσαμβρίη, ἀρρωδέω, Att. τρέπω, μέγεθος, μεσημβρία, ὀρρωδέω · Dor. and Ep. αἰ, Att. εἰ · Dor. θνάσκω, Ion. and Att. θνήσκω, Æol. θναίσκω · Att. στρατός, ἑρπετόν, στόμα, Æol. στροτός, ὄρπετον, στύμα.

131. II. Union or Resolution. A. The Contraction of vowels prevailed most in the vivacious Attic, and least in the luxurious Ionic. By the poets, it is often employed or omitted according to the demands of the metre. There are also dialectic differences in the mode of contraction, which, for the most part, may be explained by precession. E. g.

a. In contracting α with an Ο sound, the Dor. often prefers ᾱ to the closer ω; in Dec. 1, regularly. Thus, Dor. Ἀτρείδᾱ, τᾶν θυρᾶν (20 a), Ποτειδάν, πεινᾶντι, πρᾶτος, Μενέλᾱς, for Ἀτρείδου (uncontracted -άο), τῶν θυρῶν (-άων), Ποσειδῶν (-άων), πεινῶντι (-άοντι), πρῶτος, Μενέλεως (-άος).

b. For the contraction of εε, and οο or οε, see 130 c. With the Ionics and some of the Dorics, the favorite contraction of εο and εου is into ευ, instead of ου. This use of ευ for ου sometimes extends to cases where this diphthong results from a different contraction. Thus, φιλεῦμεν, φιλεῦ, ἐμεῦ, θέρευς, for φιλοῦμεν (-έομεν), φιλοῦ (-έου), ἐμοῦ (-έο), θέρους (-εος) · ἐδικαίεν, ἐδικαίευν, δικαιεῦσι, in Hdt. for ἐδικαίου (-οε), ἐδικαίοιν (-οον).

c. The Dorics (but not Pindar), contrary to the general law of the dialect, commonly contract α with an Ε sound following, into η: as, ἐρώτη, σιγῆν, λῇς, from ἐρώταε, σιγάειν, λάῃς. Cf. 120 g.

d. In the contractions which follow the change of ν before σ (156), the Æol. often employs αι and οι for ᾱ and ου: as, Acc. pl. ταῖς τιμαῖς, τοῖς νόμοις, for τὰς τιμάς, τοὺς νόμους · Nom. sing. of adj. and part. μέλαις, τύψαις, ἔχοισα, for μέλᾱς, τύψᾱς, ἔχουσα · 3d pers. pl. of verbs, φαισί, κρύπτοισι, for φᾱσί, κρύπτουσι. The Dor. has here great variety, both employing the simple long vowels, the short vowels (as though ν were simply dropped before σ), the common diphthongs of contraction (122), and the Æol. diphthongs: thus, Acc. pl. τέχνᾱς and τέχνα̍ς Theoc. 21. 1; τοὺς λύκους and τὼς λύκος Theoc. 4. 11; εἶς and ἦς, one.

e. The Ion. use of ωυ (written by some ωϋ) for αυ in a few words, appears, at least in some of them, to have arisen from a union of ο and α to form ω: thus, for ταὐτό, ἐμαυτοῦ, Ion. τωὐτό, ἐμεωυτοῦ, from τὸ αὐτό, ἐμέο αὐτοῦ. Also Ion. θωῦμα, τρωῦμα (yet better τρῶμα), for θαῦμα, τραῦμα.

f. The Ion. in a few cases employs contraction where the Att. omits it, particularly of οη into ω: as, ἰρός, ἔβωσα, for ἱερός, ἐβόησα.

132. B. Vowels which appear only as diphthongs in the Attic are often RESOLVED in the other dialects, especially the Ionic and Æolic, into separate sounds: as, εὖ, Ep. ἐΰ, well. In the Ionic, the resolution of ει, with ε prolonged, into ηι, is especially common: as, βασιληίη, κληίς, for βασιλεία, κλείς.

a. The fondness of the Ion. for a concurrence of vowels leads it, in some cases, to change ν to α (138) after a vowel (which, if previously α, now becomes ε): as, Ἀρισταγόρεα, ἐδυνέατο, for Ἀρισταγόραν, ἐδύναντο.

133. C. In CRASIS, the Doric and Ionic often differ from the Attic by uniting the ο of the article with α and αι initial, to form ω and ῳ: as, τὸ ἀληθές, τὠληθές · οἱ αἰπόλοι, ᾠπόλοι.

a. A few crases in Hom. and Hdt. are written by most editors with the coronis or the smooth breathing in place of the rough: as, ὁ ἄριστος, ὥριστος Λ. 288; ὁ αὐτός, ωὑτός Ε. 396; οἱ ἄλλοι, ὧλλοι · ὁ ἄνθρωπος, ὤνθρωπος.

b. The concurrence of vowels in Hom. is often only apparent, as they were once separated by a Digamma; which, of course, forbade either contraction, crasis, or elision.

134. III. QUANTITY. For a short vowel in the Attic, the other dialects often employ a long vowel or diphthong, and the converse: as, Ion. διπλήσιος for διπλάσιος · Ion. εὑρέη, ἀπόδεξις, μέζων, ἔσσων, for εὑρεῖα, ἀπόδειξις, μείζων, ἥσσων · Dor. and Ep. ἕτᾰρος for ἑταῖρος · Æol. Ἀλκᾰος, ἀρχᾰος, for Ἀλκαῖος, ἀρχαῖος.

a. The poets, especially the Epic, often lengthen or shorten a vowel according to the metre. A short vowel, when lengthened in Epic verse, usually passes into a cognate diphthong: as, εἰλήλουθας Λ. 202, παραί Β. 711, πνοιή Ε. 697, εἰν α. 162, for ἐλήλυθας, παρά, πνοή, ἐν.

135. IV. ADDITION OR OMISSION. Vowels are often employed in one dialect which are omitted in another; and here, as elsewhere, a peculiar freedom belongs to the poets, especially the Epic. These often add or drop a vowel, and often double a vowel or insert the half of it (the *short* for the *long*), for the sake of the metre, particularly in *contract verbs*: as,

ἐνί and εἰνί for ἐν · ἠλέ Ο. 128, for ἠλεέ β. 243; κρήηνον ἔελδωρ, for κρῆνον ἔλδωρ, Α. 41, φάανθεν, ἡβώωσα, ὁρόω, ὁράᾳς, γελώοντες, φόως, ἐέ, ἐείκοσι, ἠέ, for φάνθεν, ἡβῶσα, ὁρῶ, ὁρᾷς, γελῶντες, φῶς, ἔ, εἴκοσι, ἤ.

a. The Ion. is especially fond of the insertion of ε: as, Gen. pl. ἀνδρέων, αὐτέων, for ἀνδρῶν, &c.; 2 Aor. inf. εὑρέειν, for εὑρεῖν.

b. The use of elision is extended in the dialects: as, in Hom., to the enclitics μοί, σοί, τοί, ῥά (by aphaeresis for ἄρα); to ι in ὅτι and in the Dat., both sing. and pl.; to the affix of declension -αι in ὀξεῖ᾽ ὀδύναι Λ. 272; and, as some think, to καί (χ᾽ ὁπόσα occurs Anac. 43. 7).

136. In the Dor., Æol., and Ep., a particle often omits its final vowel before a consonant, with such assimilation of the preceding consonant as euphony may require: chiefly ἄρα, ἀνά, κατά, παρά, and ποτί · rarely ἀπό, ὑπό, and (in Æol.) περί · as,

ἄρ σφωε, ἄμ βωμοῖσι, ἄγκρισις, ἀνστάς (166 a), κἀδ δύναμιν, κὰπ φάλαρα (159 f), κἀκ κεφαλῆς, κὰγ γόνυ, κακχεῦαι, κὰρ ῥόον, κάλλιπον, καμμίξας, πὰρ Ζηνί, πὸτ τόν, ἀππέμψει, ὑββάλλειν, πὲρ σῷ.

a. When three consonants are thus brought together, the first is sometimes rejected: as, κάκτανε, ἀμνάσει, for κάκκτανε, ἀμμνάσει.

b. In some of these words, the final vowel was probably a euphonic addition to the original form (102). Compare ἀπό and ὑπό (which has also the poetic form ὑπαί) with the Lat. *ab* and *sub*. The old form πρότ, in accordance with the rule (160), became πρός and προτί, whence the Dor. and Ep. ποτί.

c. From the close connection of the preposition with the following word, these cases are not regarded as making any exception to the rule in 160. Compare 165 d. The two words are often written together, even when there is no composition: as, καδδύναμιν, ποττόν.

d. Some of these forms even passed into the Att. and into Ion. prose: as, κατθάνῃς Eur. Or. 308, ἀμβατῶν Mem. 3. 3. 2, ἀμπαύονται Hdt. 1. 181.

CHAPTER IV.

CONSONANTS.

137. The Greek has eighteen CONSONANTS, represented by seventeen letters.

a. In § 4, these consonants are arranged in CLASSES according to the organs which give them their distinctive character, as LABIALS, or lip-consonants, PALATALS, or palate-consonants, and LINGUALS, or tongue-consonants. They are also arranged in ORDERS, according to the method in which they are made by these and assisting organs, as SMOOTH MUTES, made by a simple closure of the organs; MIDDLE MUTES, so called as intermediate between the smooth and rough; ROUGH MUTES, or ASPIRATES, in which the breath is sent strongly through the organs partially closed; SPIRANTS (spirans, *breathing*), similarly formed, but with the organs more open, — one of these specially called a *sibilant*, from its hissing sound; DOUBLE CONSONANTS, or *compound sibilants*, so named as combining a mute and simple sibilant; NASALS, in which the passage through the mouth is closed, and the voice is sent through the nose; and FLUENTS (fluens, *flowing*), so named from their flowing so easily with other consonant sounds; while the nasals and fluents, all *flowing* sounds of various kind and degree, are classed together as LIQUIDS; and all the consonants, except the MUTES (*dumb* in comparison with the others), are called SEMIVOWELS, as *intermediate* in vocality between the vowels and mutes.

b. Consonants of the same class are termed *cognate;* and those of the same order, *co-ordinate*. The classes are sometimes named from the letters standing at the head: as, the π class, &c.; so, π, κ, and τ *mutes*. Some use the term *guttural* instead of *palatal*, and *dental* instead of *lingual*. Euphonic, dialectic, and other interchanges of consonants are most frequent in cognates; and then, in co-ordinates.

c. The letter γ performs a double office. When followed by another palatal, it is a *nasal;* otherwise, a *middle mute*. As a nasal it has *n* for its corresponding Roman letter; as a middle mute, *g* (92 a).

d. The double consonants were formed by the union of a mute with σ; in ψ and ξ the mute preceding, and in ζ the σ: as, γυπς γύψ, κορακς κόραξ (17), Θήβασδε Θήβαζε, *to Thebes*.

§ 142.   OLD SEMIVOWELS.   139

138. The early Greek speech appears to have had four semivowels which were not yet as fixed in their character as the consonants afterwards became, and which had corresponding vowels into which they often passed when the later laws of euphony forbade their use : viz., Σ, corresponding to ε ; N, corresponding to α ; F, corresponding to υ, as *v* in Latin and *w* in English to *u ;* and a palatal spirant corresponding to ι, as *j* in Latin and *y* in English to *i*, yet partaking perhaps, somewhat more than these consonants, of the nature of a sibilant.

a. The last seems to have had no character distinct from that of the vowel ι (cf. 98 a), just as in the old Latin alphabet *i* and *j* were written alike, and *u* and *v*. It will here be distinguished, so far as this seems important, by the use of the capital I, which should then be pronounced nearly like the semivowel *y*, or *i* in *valiant*. It may be distinguished, in speaking, as the *consonant, spirant,* or *semivowel* I. Capitals are also sometimes used to distinguish other consonants in an early unfixed state.

139. In the progress of the language, these old semivowels met with various fortunes :

1.) They became fixed as *consonants :* the old Σ as σ (Lat. *s ;* yet in Lat. formation extensively represented by *r*) ; the old N as ν (often in Lat. as *m*, which, however, ecthlipsis shows to have been a very weak consonant) ; F, especially in the older or less refined dialects, as β or φ (in Lat. as *v, f,* or *b ;* sometimes also in Eng. as *w*) : as, σῦς sus, SWINE (cf. 141), λύραν lyram, LYRE, βρόδων Æol. for ῥόδων, *of* ROSES, Sap. 69 [19].

a. Cf. βούλομαι volo, *to* WILL, ἴς and βία vis, *force*, βιόω vivo, *to live*, φέρω fero, *to* BEAR, φάναι fari, *to say*, φώρ fur, *thief*.

140.   2.) They were simply *dropped :* as, between two vowels, F regularly, Σ often, and N and I sometimes : as, ὠϝον ὠόν ovum, *egg*, βοϝας βόας boves, γενεσος γένεος generis, λυεσαι λύεαι lueris *or* luere, ἐλάσω ἐλάω, μείζονα μείζοα, πλείων πλέων *more*.

a. So τ in a few, and δ in many words, of Dec. 3. See 207, 217.

b. The two vowels were then often contracted : as, βοῦς, γένους (19), λύῃ or λύει (37), ἑλῶ (42), μείζω (22).

141.   3.) They were changed into *common breathings.* So, before an initial vowel, F regularly, and Σ in some words : as, ϝεσπερα ἑσπέρα vespera, *evening*, ϝιδειν ἰδειν video, *to see*, ϝοινος οἶνος vinum, WINE, ϝεαρ ἔαρ ver, *Spring ;* σῦς and ὗς sus, SWINE, σιστημι ἵστημι sisto, *to* STAND, ἕξ sex, SIX, ἑπτά septem, SEVEN, ἅλς sal, SALT, ὑπέρ super, OVER. Also F before initial ρ: as, ϝρηγνυμι ῥήγνυμι frango, *to* BREAK.

142.   4.) They were changed into their *corresponding vowels*. So F regularly, except as above ; and the others in many formations : as, ναϝς ναῦς navis, *ship*, βοϝ βοῦ (19) ; γυπν γῦπα (160 e) ; φανσω φανέω φανῶ (152) ; ἡδιων ἡδίων, πλειων πλείων (260 s).

a. Here contraction often takes place, as in most of the examples above ; and, after a liquid, ε and ι are sometimes transposed and contracted with the preceding vowel : as, ἠγγελσα ἤγγειλα (152 b), ῥητορς ῥήτωρ (153) ; χερΙων χείρων, ἀμενΙων ἀμείνων (261), μελανΙα μέλαινα (233).

143. The PALATAL SPIRANT, or *consonant* I, with a consonant preceding, received yet other changes: thus,

a.) With λ, it was assimilated: as, μαλΙον μᾶλλον *more*. Cf. Lat. melius; and also ἄλλος alius, *other*, ἄλλομαι salio, *to leap*.

b.) It united with τ to form σ or σι: as, παντΙα πανσα πᾶσα (233), πλουτΙος πλούσιος *rich*, ἀθανασία (from ἀθάνατος) *immortality*. Hence, we often find σ for τ before ι.

c.) It united with a palatal or lingual mute (or, rarely, with a labial mute or a double palatal) to form σσ (in later Attic ττ) or ζ: as, ἡκΙων ἥσσων or ἥττων, ταγΙω τάσσω, κορυθΙω κορύσσω, πεπΙω πέσσω, ἀγχΙον ἆσσον· ὀλιγΙων ὀλίζων, ἐλπιδΙω ἐλπίζω. See 233, 261 b, 349.

144. LIQUIDS, from their flowing, semivowel character, often affect or are affected by adjoining vowels:

1. *Syncope.* In some stems, the adjoining vowel is syncopated: as, μητέρος μητρός (210), μιμενω μίμνω *to remain*, ἤλυθον ἦλθον *I came*, κεκαληκα κέκληκα *I have called*. See also 140 for the syncope of the liquid.

145. 2. *Metathesis.* In some cases, a liquid is transposed with a vowel, which is then often contracted with another vowel, or otherwise changed. In some of these, the liquid is evidently fleeing from combination with a following consonant. Thus, θάρσος θράσος *boldness*, βέβληκα (stem βαλ- βλα-) *I have thrown*. See also 142 a.

a. In the Dat. pl. of syncopated liquids of Dec. 3, and of ἀστήρ *star*, ε is transposed with ρ or ν, and changed to α: as, πατερσι πατράσι (18).

146. 3. *Epenthesis, &c.* a. When a *simple vowel* is brought by inflection or composition before an *initial* ρ, a smooth ρ is inserted: as, ἔρρωσα, ἄρρωστος, ἐπιρρώννυμι, from ῥώννυμι *to strengthen* (ἐ-, ἀ-, and ἐπί prefixed); but εὔρωστος (the *diphthong* εὖ prefixed).

b. When, by syncope or metathesis, a nasal is brought before λ or ρ, the cognate middle mute is inserted or substituted: as, ἀνέρος (ἀνρος) ἀνδρός (18), μεσημερια μεσημβρία *midday*; βλώσκω (s. μολ- μλο- βλο-) *to go*, βροτός (s. μορτ- μροτ- βροτ-) mortalis, MORTAL.

147. The following laws, mostly euphonic, are observed in the formation and connection of words.

A. IN THE FORMATION OF WORDS.

I. Before a LINGUAL MUTE, a *labial* or *palatal* mute becomes *co-ordinate* (137 b); and a *lingual* mute, σ: as,

τέτρι(βτ)πται, τέτα(γτ)κται, πέπει(θτ)σται, κομι(δτ)στός (39); γρα-(φτ)πτός *written*, τυ(χτ)κτός *made*, ψεύ(δτ)στης *liar*; ἕ(πδ)βδομος *seventh*, ὄ(κδ)γδοος *eighth*, γρά(φδ)βδην, βρύ(χδ)γδην · ἐτρί(βθ)φθην, ἐτά(γθ)χθην, ἐπεί(θθ)σθην, ἐκομί(δθ)σθην (39); ἐδεί(κθ)χθην (45), ἐλεί(πθ)φθην, ὠνομά-(τθ)σθην. Cf. Lat. scri(bt)*pt*us, re(gt)*ct*us, tra(ht)*ct*us, clau(dt)*str*um.

§ 152.   EUPHONIC CHANGES.   141

a. Two lingual mutes may remain together, if both belong to the stem: as, τάττω *to arrange,* Ἀτθίς *Attic.*

148. II. Before μ, a *labial mute* becomes μ; a *palatal mute,* γ; and a *lingual mute,* σ: as,

τέτρι(βμ)μμαι, πέπει(θμ)σμαι, κεκόμι(δμ)σμαι (39) ; δέδει(κμ)γμαι (45); γρά(φμ)μμα *letter,* τέτυ(χμ)γμαι, ὠνόμα(τμ)σμαι. Cf. Lat. se(cm)gmen.
a. If two μ's or two γ's are thus brought before μ, one of them is dropped: as, πέπε(μπμ, μμμ)μμαι, ἐλήλε(γχμ, γγμ)γμαι (41).
b. This rule has exceptions, when the μ does not belong to an affix of inflection, as ἀκμή *point,* ACME, δραχμή drachma, *drachm,* ἀτμός *vapor,* ῥυθμός *rhythm;* and in the dialects, even when it does so belong, as in Hom. ἴδμεν *we know,* ἐπέπιθμεν, κεκορυθμένος, ἀκαχμένος.

149. III. Before the *tense-sign* κ, a *labial* or *palatal mute* unites with it in the cognate *rough,* and a *lingual mute* is dropped: as,

τέτρι(βκα)φα, τέτα(γκα)χα, πέπει(θκα)κα, κεκόμι(δκα)κα (39) ; δέδει(κκα)χα (45), κέκο(πκα)φα, γέγρα(φκα)φα, δεδίδα(χκα)χα, ὠνόμα(τκα)κα.

150. IV. ν, before a (a) *labial* or (b) *palatal,* is changed into the *cognate nasal* (4, 137 b); and (c) before a *liquid,* is *assimilated* (104 a): as,

(a) συ(νπ)μπάσχω, ἐ(νβ)μβάλλω, συ(νφ)μφέρω, ἐ(νμ)μμένω, ἔ(νψ)μψῦχος· (b) ἐ(νκ)γκαλέω, συ(νγ)γγενής, συ(νχ)γχαίρω, ἐ(νξ)γξέω· (c) ἔ(νλ)λλογος, συ(νρ)ρράπτω. Cf. Lat. i(np)mpello, imbibo, co(nl)lloco, corrumpo.
d. Before μ in the Perfect passive, ν commonly becomes σ or is omitted: as, πέφα(νμ)σμαι (40), κέκλιμαι (Pf. of κλίνω *to bend*).
e. Before κ in the Perfect active, ν was commonly omitted, or the form avoided, except by later writers: as, κέκρικα (Pf. of κρίνω *to judge*) ; πέφαγκα, Dinarch. 92. 4.
f. In applying Rule IV., enclitics are regarded as distinct words: thus, ὅνπερ, τόνγε.

151. V. *No consonant should stand before* σ, except σ *itself.* This principle, from the great use of σ in formation, requires many changes:

1.) Before σ, a *labial* or *palatal mute* unites with it in the cognate double consonant; and a *lingual mute* is dropped: as,

γύ(πς)ψ, φλέ(βς)ψ, κόρα(κς)ξ, αἴ(γς)ξ, θρί(χς)ξ, σώμα(τσι)σι, ἐλπί(δς)s, κόρυ(θς)s (17) ; γρά(φσω)ψω. Cf. Lat. du(cs)x, re(gs)x, ar(ts)s, lapi(ds)s.
a. It will be seen that some of these changes are simply orthographic.

152. 2.) In the *Future* and *Aorist* of *liquid verbs,* the tense-sign σ is changed into ε; which (a) in the *Future* is contracted with the following vowel, but (b) in the *Aorist* is transposed and contracted with the preceding vowel. See 142 a.

Thus, in the Fut. and Aor. of ἀγγέλλω *to announce,* νέμω *to distribute,* κρίνω *to judge,* πλύνω *to wash,* and δέρω *to flay,* —

(a) ἀγγελ(σω, ἐω)ῶ, νεμ(σω, ἐω)ῶ, κριν(σω, ἐω)ῶ, πλυν(σω, ἐω)ῶ, δερ(σω, ἐω)ῶ '
(b) ἤγγ(ελσα, εελα)ειλα, ἔν(εμσα, εεμα)ειμα, ἔκρ(ινσα, ιενα)ῖνα, ἔπλ(υνσα, υενα)
ῦνα, ἔδ(ερσα, εερα)ειρα.

c. Here αε commonly passes into η, unless ι or ρ precedes (120 h) : as, φαίνω to show, σφάλλω to trip, πιαίνω to fatten, περαίνω to complete (s. φαν-, σφαλ-, πιαν-, περαν-); Aor. ἔφηνα (not ἔφηνα, 109 a), ἔσφηλα, ἐπίανα, ἐπέρᾱνα. But ἰσχναίνω to make lean, κερδαίνω to gain, κοιλαίνω to hollow out, λευκαίνω to whiten, ὀργαίνω, to enrage, πεταίνω to ripen, αἴρω to raise, and ἅλλομαι to leap, have here ᾱ (in the two last becoming η in the Ind. through the augment : ἦρα, Subj. ᾄρω) ; τετραίνω, to bore, has η ; and σημαίνω to give a signal, μιαίνω to stain, and καθαίρω to purify, both η and ᾱ. The use of ᾱ in the liquid Aor. increased in the later Greek.

d. A few poetic verbs retain the old forms with σ : as, κέλλω to land, κύρω to meet, ὀρνῦμι to rouse, φύρω to knead, F. and A. κέλσω, ἔκελσα, ὄρσω, ὦρσα, &c. Add these forms, mostly from Hom., ἦρσα, ἔλσα, ἔρσα, θέρσομαι, κέρσω, ἔκερσα, διαφθέρσω, ἤερσα.

153. 3.) In the *Nominative*, the affix -s after ρ, and sometimes after ν, is transposed as ε, and *absorbed* (118 c) by the preceding vowel : as,

ψ(αρs, αερ)άρ starling; πατ(ερs, εερ)ήρ, ῥήτ(ορs, οερ)ωρ (18) ; παι(ανs, αεν)άν paean ; λιμ(ενs, εεν)ήν, δαίμ(ονs, οεν)ών (18). Cf. Lat. fu(rs)r, pate(rs)r, orāto(rs)r ; lie(ns)n, dœmo(ns)n.

a. Except in δάμαρ *wife*, where σ is simply dropped.

154. 4.) In liquids of Dec. 3, ν is simply *dropped* before -σι in the Dative plural : as,

μέλα(νσι)σι (23) ; λιμέ(νσι)σι, δαίμο(νσι)σι, ῥι(νσι)σί (18). For the Dat. pl. of syncopated liquids and ἀστήρ, see 145 a.

155. 5.) In *adjectives* (not participles) in εις, ν becomes σ before σ in the feminine, and is simply dropped before σι in the Dat. pl. : as, χαριενσα χαρίεσσα, χαριεντσι χαρίεσι (23).

156. 6.) Otherwise, ν before σ is changed into α, which is then *contracted* with the preceding vowel (142, 122) : as,

Nom. Sing. Masc. and Fem., and Dat. Pl. μέλ(ανs, αas)ᾶs, π(αντs, ανs, 151. 1, αas)ᾶs, π(ανσα, 233, αασα)ᾶσα, π(αντσι, ανσι, αασι)ᾶσι (23) ; θ(εντs, ενs, εαs)είς, θ(ενσα, εασα)εῖσα, θ(εντσι)εῖσι, δ(οντs)ούς, δ(ονσα)οῦσα, δ(οντσι)οῦσι, δ(υντs)ύς, δῦσα, δῦσι (26) ; ῥ(ινs)ῥίς (18) : Verbs in 3d Pers. Pl. ἱστ(ανσι, αασι)ᾶσι, τιθ(ενσι)εᾶσι τιθεῖσι, διδ(ονσι)οῦσι διδοῦσι, δεικν(υνσι)ύᾶσι δεικνῦσι, ἱ(νσι)ᾶσι (45) : Fut. σπ(ενδσω, εασω)είσω, π(ενθσ, εασ)είσομαι.

a. The forms τιθέᾱσι, διδόᾱσι, and δεικνύᾱσι were used by the Attics for the most part, and ἱᾶσι uniformly, without contraction.

b. In nouns, if νθ precede σ, the ν is retained : as, (ἐλμινθs) ἔλμυνs *worm*, ἔλμι(νθσι)νσι (yet others, ἔλμῖσι). It is also retained in some forms in -σαι and derivatives in -σις, from verbs in -νω, as πέφανσαι from φαίνω (40), ἄδρυνσις from ἀδρύνω *to ripen*. Add the Homeric κένσαι, Ψ. 337. For ἐν, σύν, πάλιν, and πᾶν, see 166.

157. 7.) In cases not mentioned above, the combinations λσ and ρσ were permitted to stand ; except as σ radical after ρ was softened in the later Attic to ρ : as, ἅλs SALT, sea ; ἄρσην *male*, θάρσος *boldness*, New Att. ἄρρην, θάρρος.

158. VI. Between two consonants, σ *inflective* is dropped, and ν is changed to α (102): as,

τετρί(βσθ)φθαι, τέτριφθε, τετά(γσθ)χθαι (39, 147); ἐφθά(ρντ)ραται (142). This rule applies to cases where the first consonant is not removed by previous rules.

159. VII. If *rough mutes* begin two successive syllables, the *first* is often changed into its cognate *smooth*, especially (a) in *reduplications*, or (b) when both letters are *radical*; but (c) in the *second person singular* of the Aorist imperative passive, the *second* rough mute is changed: as,

(a) (φεφ)πεφίληκα (42); (χεχ)κέχρημαι· (θεθ)τέθυκα (44); (θιθ)τίθημι (45); (b) (θριχ)τριχός (17); (θαχ)ταχύς *swift*, (θρεχ)τρέχω *to run*, (θρεφ)τρέφω *to nourish*; (c) λύ(θηθι)θητι (37).

d. So ἀμπέχω (ἀμφὶ ἔχω) *to cover*: and in Aor. pass., ἐτέθην (45), ἐτύθην (44); but here in most words the aspiration remains, as even ἐθρέφθην.

e. Upon the same principle, ἔχω becomes ἔχω· and whenever ῥ is reduplicated, the first ῥ becomes *smooth*, and, as it then cannot stand at the beginning of a word (93 d), is transposed: as, ῥέρῖρα ἐρρῖρα. Yet we find, by a softening of the second ρ, ῥερυπωμένα ζ. 59.

f. So, to avoid excessive aspiration, a rough mute is never preceded by the same rough mute, but, instead of it, by the cognate smooth: as, Σαπφώ Sappho, Βάκχος Bacchus, Ἀτθίς (147 a); and, upon the same principle, Πύρρος (93 d). See also the Epic κὰπ φάλαρα, κακχεῦαι (136).

g. Aspiration is sometimes transferred: as, παθσκω πάσχω *to suffer*.

160. VIII. The semivowels ν, ρ, and ς are the only consonants that may end a word. Any other consonant, therefore, falling at the end of a word, is either (a) *dropped*, or (b) *changed* into one of these, or (c) *assumes a vowel:* as

σῶμ(ατ)α, ἦπ(ατ)αρ, κέρ(ατ)ας (17); ἔλυ(ομ)ον, λύ(οιμ)οιμι, ἔλυ(ετ)ε, ἔλυ(οντ)ον, λῦ(οντ)ον, λῦ(εθ)ε (37); τίθ(ημ)ημι, ἐτίθ(ημ)ην, ἐδίδ(ωτ)ω, στ(ηθ)ῆθι, δ(οθ)ός (45); μέλ(ιτ)ι mel, *honey*, γάλ(ακτ)α lac, *milk*; φ(ωτ)ῶς *light*; Voc. π(αιδ)αῖ, *boy*! γύν(αικ)αι, *woman*! Cf. Lat. co(rd)r.

d. Both the assumption and the change appear in -σι for -τ, and -νσι for -ντ, in the 3d pers. of verbs: as, ἰστ(ηντ)ησι, ἰστ(αντ)ᾶσι (45, 143 b, 156). In applying this rule and the note below, ξ and ψ are considered as combinations ending with ς (137 d).

e. A word can end with two consonants, only when the last is σ: as, ἅλς· γύψ (γυπς), αἴξ (αἴγς), κόραξ (17). Hence the *formative* ν of the Accusative is changed into α (142) after a consonant, except in a few cases, in which a lingual mute preceding ν is dropped: as,

γύ(πν)πα, κόρα(κν)κα, πό(δν)δα· κλεῖ(δν)ν and -δα, κόρυ(θν)ν and -θα (17).

f. As final μ and τ or θ so extensively pass into ν and ς, they may be considered as having the same corresponding vowels : viz. α corresponding to final μ, and ε to final τ or θ (138).

B. In the Connection of Words.

161. I. When a *smooth mute* is brought by (a) *crasis* or (b) *elision* before the *rough breathing*, it unites with it to form the cognate *rough :* as,

(a) καὶ ὁ, χὠ · καὶ οἱ, χῴ · τὸ ἱμάτιον, θοἰμάτιον · τοῦ ἑτέρου, θατέρου · ὅτου ἕνεκα, ὁθοὔνεκα · (b) ἀπὸ οὗ, ἀφ' οὗ · νύκτα ὅλην, νύχθ' ὅλην · and in composition, ἀφίημι (ἀπό, ἵημι), δεχήμερος (δέκα, ἡμέρα), ἐφθήμερος (ἑπτά, ἡμέρα).

162. II. Some words and forms end either *with* or *without* a *final consonant* according to euphony, emphasis, or rhythm.

a. Such consonants are termed *movable;* and in grammars and lexicons are often marked thus : εἶπε(ν), or εἶπε(ν. Before the digamma, they were of course not needed to prevent hiatus : δαΐε Ϝοι E. 4 ; οὐ Ϝέθεν A. 114.

163. 1.) *Datives plural in* ι, and *verbs of the third person in* ε or simple ι, assume ν at the end of a sentence, or when the next word begins with a vowel : as,

Πᾶσι γὰρ εἶπε τοῦτο · but, Εἶπεν αὐτὸ πᾶσιν.
Πᾶσι λέγουσι τοῦτο · but, Πᾶσιν αὐτὸ λέγουσιν.

a. So, likewise, *adverbs of place in* -σι (properly datives plural), the adverb πέρυσι, *last year*, the numeral εἴκοσι (commonly), the demonstrative -ι preceded by σ (sometimes), the Epic case-ending -φι, and the Epic particles κέ, νύ, and νόσφι · as, ἡ Πλαταιᾶσιν ἡγεμονία · εἴκοσιν ἔτη.

b. So, also, in a few instances, chiefly poetic, the Plup. and Impf. 3d Pers. in -ει (contracted from -εε) : as, ᾔδειν · ἐν Eur. Ion 1187, 'πεποίθειν, οὐκ Ar. Nub. 1347, βεβλήκειν ὑπέρ Ξ. 412 ; προσῄειν ; Οὐδέπω Ar. Pl. 696, ᾔσκειν εἷρια Γ. 388. The form with ν became the common form in the Impf. 3d Pers. ἦν, *was*, and ἐχρῆν or χρῆν, *ought*, even before a consonant : as, ἦν δε i. 2. 3, ἐχρῆν ταῦτα Cyr. 5. 5. 9.

c. The ν thus assumed is often called ν *paragogic* (in Greek, ν ἐφελκυστικόν, *attached*). It is sometimes employed by the poets before a consonant to make a syllable long by position ; and in most kinds of verse, is used at the end of a line. In Ionic prose it is generally neglected ; but in Attic prose it is sometimes found even before a consonant in the middle of a sentence, while, on the other hand, it is sometimes omitted in closely connected discourse, even where we point with a period.

164. 2.) The adverb οὕτως, *thus*, commonly loses σ before a consonant ; and ἄχρι and μέχρι, *until*, often assume it before a vowel : as οὕτω φησίν · μέχρις οὗ.

a. Some other words have poetic or dialectic forms, in which a final ν or ς is dropped or assumed : as, local adverbs in -θεν (poet., chiefly Ep., -θε), numeral adverbs in -κις (Ion. -κι), ἀμφίς, ἄντικρυς, ἀτρέμας, αὖθις, ἔμπας, πάλιν, ἀφνω(ς, ἐγώ(ν, εὐθύ(ς, ἰθύ(ς, μεσηγύ(ς.

C. Special Rules.

165. a. The preposition ἐξ, *out of*, has the form ἐκ before any consonant : as, ἐκ κακῶν, ἐκσεύω, ἐκγελάω, ἔκθετος, ἐκμάσσω.

b. So in Hom. the compounds ἀπέξ, διέξ, ὑπέξ, and commonly παρέξ · but not πάρεξ in Hdt. : as, ὑπὲκ κακοῦ N. 89 ; but πάρεξ δέ Hdt. 1. 14.

c. The adverb οὐ, *not*, before a vowel, has the form οὐκ, which becomes οὐχ before the rough breathing : as, οὔ φησιν, οὐκ ἔνεστιν, οὐχ ὕει, οὐκέτι (imitated by μή, *not*, in μηκέτι).

d. In these words, ἐκ and οὐκ may perhaps be regarded as the original forms. That in certain situations these forms are retained is owing to their close connection as proclitics, or in composition, with the following word, and therefore forms no real exception to the rule in 160. When orthotone, they conform to the rule, the one by assuming s, and the other by dropping κ, except as it also takes the form οὐχί.

166. In composition, the preposition ἐν, *in*, regularly retains its ν before ρ and σ ; σύν, *with*, drops its ν before σ followed by another consonant, and before ζ ; but before σ followed by a vowel, changes ν to σ ; while πάλιν, *again*, and πᾶν, *all*, vary in their forms : as, ἐνράπτω, ἐνσείω, ἔνρυθμος, yet also ἔρρυθμος · σύστημα (for σύνστημα), συζυγία · συσσεύω (for συνσεύω), συσσιτία · παλίνσκιος and παλίσκιος, πάνσοφος and πάσσοφος.

a. The Epic ἄν for ἀνά (136) here imitates ἐν · as, ἀνστάς, ἄνσχετος.

DIALECTIC VARIATIONS.

167. A. The dialects often *interchange* consonants : chiefly,

1. COGNATE MUTES (137 b) : as, Ion. αὖτις, δέκομαι, for αὖθις, δέχομαι · Æol. ἀμπί for ἀμφί. Compare ἀμφω and ambo, *both*, ἄγχω and ango, *to choke*, κύκνος and cygnus, *swan*, μίσγω and misceo, *to mix*.

a. The Æol. and Ion. were both far less inclined than the Att. to aspiration (cf. 93 c). In the new Ion. the smooth mute remains before the rough breathing (161, 165 c) : as, ἀπ' οὗ, δεκήμερος, οὐκ ὕει. In some compounds, this passed into the Att. : as, ἀπηλιώτης (ἀπό, ἥλιος).

b. Aspiration is sometimes *transposed* : as, Ion. κιθών, ἐνθαῦτα, ἐνθεῦτεν, Καλχηδών, for χιτών, ἐνταῦθα, ἐντεῦθεν, Χαλκηδών.

c. The dialects also varied in the use of the breathings. In place of the rough, the Æolic seems commonly, and the Epic often, to have used the smooth breathing or the digamma. In Homer we find the smooth for the rough particularly in words which are strengthened in some other way : as, εὔκηλος, οὖλος, ἠέλιος, ὔμμες, for ἕκηλος, ὅλος, ἥλιος, ὑμεῖς.

168. 2.) CO-ORDINATE MUTES (137 b) : as, Ion. κ for π in *interrogative* and *indefinite pronouns* and *adverbs* : thus, κοῖος, κοῦ, κοτέ, for ποῖος, ποῦ, ποτέ · Dor., κ for τ in πόκα, ὄκα, τόκα, for πότε, ὅτε, τότε, and in similar *adverbs of time* ; Æol. πέμπε for πέντε quinque, *five*, φήρ for θήρ fera, *wild beast* ; Dor. γλέφαρον for βλέφαρον, δᾶ for γῆ, ὀδελός for ὀβελός, ὀριῖχος for ὀριῖθος. Compare λύκος and lupus, *wolf*, γλυκύς and dulcis, *sweet*, τίς and quis, *who?* and Lat. bis, bellum, fr. duis, duellum.

3.) LIQUIDS : as, Dor. ἤνθον, βέντιστος, φίντατος, for ἦλθον, βέλτιστος, φίλτατος · Ion. and Att. πλεύμων for πνεύμων pulmo, *lung ;* Ion. μίν, Dor. νίν. Cf. λείριον lilium, LILY.

a. The interchange of λ with another lingual appears in 'Οδυσσεύς Ulixes, δάκρυον lacrima.

169. 4.) σ with other letters. E. g.

a. The Dor., Ion., and Old Att. σσ passes, for the most part, in the later Att., into ττ: as, τάσσω τάττω (39), γλῶσσα γλῶττα, *tongue.* So τ Att. for initial σ in a few words : as, σήμερον τήμερον, *to-day.*

b. Dor. τ for σ : as, Ποτειδάν, ἔπετον, εἴκατι, for Ποσειδῶν, ἔπεσον, εἴκοσι. This appears especially in the 2d personal pronoun, and in the 3d pers. of verbs : as, τύ, τέ, for σύ, σέ (Lat. *tu, te*) ; φατί, φαντί, φέροντι, for φησί, φασί, φέρουσι (Lat. *ferunt*). See 160 d.

c. Dor. σ for ν, and ν for σ : as, ἔνδος for ἔνδον intus, *within,* ἐντί for ἐστί est, *is ;* and in the verb-ending of 1st pers. pl. -μες for -μεν (Lat. -*mus*), as λέγομες for λέγόμεν (Lat. *legimus*).

d. The Laconic often changes θ to σ, and final ς to ρ : as, παλεόρ Ar. Lys. 988, σιόρ, σέλω, for παλαιός, θεός, θέλω · πόιρ for παῖς (Lat. *puer*, cf. *Marcipor*). Compare the marked correspondence of σ and the Lat. *r ;* and in Lat., arbos and arbor, honos and honor.

170. 5.) The DOUBLE CONSONANTS with other letters : as, old ξύν, later and common σύν (in the Lat. *cum* the σ has been omitted instead of the κ) ; Æol. Ψαπφώ for Σαπφώ · Æol. σκένος, σκίφος, for ξένος, ξίφος · Dor. ψέ, ψίν, for σφέ, σφίν · Ion. διξός, τριξός, for δισσός, τρισσός.

a. For ζ, we find, in the Æol. and Dor., σδ, δδ, and δ : as, ὕσδος, μελίσδω (137 d), παίσδω, μᾶδδα, Δεύς, for ὄζος, μελίζω, παίζω, μᾶζα, Ζεύς.

b. Interchanges of consonants are sometimes poetic rather than dialectic, or simply took place in the progress of the language.

171. B. Consonants are often *doubled, inserted, omitted,* and *transposed* by the poets, especially the Epic, for the sake of the metre : as,

ἔλλαβον, φράσσομαι, νέκυσσι, ὅσσος, ὅππως, ἔδδεισε, for ἔλαβον, &c. ; πτόλεμος, πτόλις, διχθά, νώνυμνος, ἀπάλαμνος, for πόλεμος, πόλις, δίχα, νώνυμος, ἀπάλαμος · ἔρεξον, 'Οδυσεύς, 'Αχιλεύς, φάρυγος, for ἔρρεξον, 'Οδυσσεύς, 'Αχιλλεύς, φάρυγγος · κραδίη, κάρτιστος, βάρδιστος, ἀταρπός, for καρδία, κράτιστος, βράδιστος, ἀτραπός.

a. Similar changes are also dialectic, or took place in the progress of the language. E. g., the Æolic, instead of lengthening a vowel before a liquid, often made the syllable long by doubling the liquid : as, ἔμμι for εἰμί *to be,* σπέρρω for σπείρω *to sow,* κρίννω for κρίνω *to judge,* ἔστελλα for Aor. ἔστειλα. Not unfrequently, that which is poetic in one dialect is used in the prose of another.

BOOK II.

ETYMOLOGY.

Ἔπεα πτερόεντα.
Homer.

172. Etymology treats of the INFLECTION and FORMATION OF WORDS: the former including DECLENSION, COMPARISON, and CONJUGATION; and the latter, DERIVATION and COMPOSITION.

a. INFLECTION is variation in the form of a word to distinguish its different offices or relations (inflecto, *to bend to, change*). A word which is inflected has two parts: the one constituting its *essence*, and receiving no change except as euphony or emphasis may require; the other *circumstantial*, and varying according to its different offices and connections. The former is called the *essential part*, or, by a botanical figure, the STEM or ROOT; and the latter, from its producing the various forms of inflection, the *inflective part*.

b. It is now common to limit the term *root* to primitive elements in the formation of words, while the term *stem* is not thus limited. Syllables or letters belonging to the root are termed *radical*; and others, *formative*.

c. Syllables or letters belonging to the stem are called *essential*; and others, *inflective*. Of the latter, those which precede the stem are termed PREFIXES; and those which follow it, AFFIXES. Affixes are of two kinds: *open*, or *vowel affixes*, those which begin with a vowel; and *close*, or *consonant affixes*, those which begin with a consonant.

d. The last letter, or sometimes letters, of the stem, as *marking* its *character*, are called the STEM-MARK or CHARACTERISTIC; and from this, words and stems are named *mute, liquid, double-consonant, labial, pure* (112 a), &c.

e. By the THEME of a word, is meant that form which is first given in grammatical inflection: as commonly, in declension, the Nominative singular, and, if the word has the different genders, the masculine; in comparison, the Positive; in conjugation, the first person singular of the Present indicative active, or, if the verb is deponent, middle (though some prefer the Present infinitive).

CHAPTER I.

PRINCIPLES OF DECLENSION.

173. The two classes of SUBSTANTIVES (including Nouns and Substantive Pronouns) and ADJECTIVES (including the Article, Adjectives commonly so called, Adjective Pronouns, and Participles) are declined to mark three distinctions, GENDER, NUMBER, and CASE.

a. Adjectives receive these distinctions merely for the sake of conforming to the substantives to which they belong.

b. In grammars and lexicons, these distinctions are often marked by the appropriate forms of the article (with the interjection ὦ for the Vocative): thus, in ὁ ταμίας, or ταμίας, ὁ, *steward*, the noun is marked as masculine and in the Nom. sing.; while in ὁ, ἡ τροφός, *nurse*, it is marked as of the common gender, and in τὰ σῦκα, *figs*, as neuter.

174. A. GENDER. The Greek has three genders; the MASCULINE, FEMININE, and NEUTER.

a. Nouns which are both masculine and feminine are said to be of the *common gender*. In the case of most animals, it is seldom important to distinguish the gender. Hence in Greek, for the most part, the names of animals, instead of being common, have but a single gender, which is used indifferently for both sexes. Such nouns are termed *epicene* (ἐπίκοινος, *promiscuous*). Thus, ὁ λύκος *wolf*, ἡ ἀλώπηξ *fox*, whether the male or the female is spoken of.

b. In words in which the feminine may either have a *common* form with the masculine or a *distinct* form, the *Attic* sometimes prefers the common form, where the *Ionic* and *Common* dialects prefer the distinct form: as, ὁ, ἡ θεός, *god, goddess*, and ἡ θεά or θέαινα, *goddess*. So, likewise, in adjectives.

175. The masculine gender belongs properly to words denoting *males*; the feminine, to words denoting *females*; and the neuter, to words denoting *neither* males nor females. In Greek, however, the names of most things without life are masculine or feminine, either from the real or fancied possession of masculine or feminine qualities, or from a similarity in their formation to other nouns of these genders.

Thus, for the most part, the names of *winds* and *rivers* (from their power and violence), and also of the *months*, are *masculine*; and the names of *trees, plants, countries, islands,* and *cities* (regarded as mothers of their products or inhabitants) are *feminine;* while nouns denoting mere *products*, or implying *inferiority* (even though names of persons), especially *diminutives*, are *neuter:* as,

ὁ ἄνεμος *wind*, ὁ Βορρᾶς *Boreas*, ὁ ποταμός *river*, ὁ Νεῖλος *the Nile*, ὁ μήν *month*, ὁ Ἑκατομβαιών *June – July;* ἡ συκῆ *fig-tree*, ἡ μηλέα *apple-tree*, ἡ ἄμπελος *vine*, ἡ βύβλος *papyrus*, ἡ χώρα *country*, ἡ Αἴγυπτος *Egypt*, ἡ νῆσος *island*, ἡ Σάμος *Samos*, ἡ πόλις *city*, ἡ Λακεδαίμων *Lacedæmon;* τὸ σῦκον *fig*, τὸ μῆλον *apple*, τὸ τέκνον *child*, τὸ ἀνδράποδον *slave*, τὸ γύναιον, dim. of γυνή *woman*, τὸ παιδίον *little boy* or *girl*.

176. The gender of nouns, when not determined by the signification, may be, for the most part, inferred from the form of the theme or stem, according to the following rules:

I. In the FIRST DECLENSION (15), all words in -ας and -ης are *masculine;* and all in -α and -η, *feminine:* as, ὁ ταμίας, ὁ ποιητής· ἡ τράπεζα, ἡ τιμή.

II. In the SECOND DECLENSION (16), most words in -ος and -ως are *masculine*, but some are *feminine* or *common;* words in -ον and -ων are *neuter:* as, ὁ χορός, ὁ νεώς· ἡ νῆσος, ἡ ἔως *dawn;* ὁ, ἡ θεός *god*, ὁ, ἡ ἄρκτος *bear;* τὸ ᾠόν, τὸ ἀνώγεων *chamber*.

a. Except when the diminutive form in -ον is given to feminine proper names: as, ἡ Λεόντιον, ἡ Γλυκέριον.

177. III. In the THIRD DECLENSION (17 s),

a.) All words in -ευς are *masculine;* all in -ω and -αυς, *feminine;* and all in -α, -ι, -υ, -ος, and -ορ, *neuter:* as, ὁ ἱππεύς, ὁ ἀμφορεύς *amphora;* ἡ ἠχώ, ἡ ναῦς· τὸ σῶμα, τὸ μέλι *honey*, τὸ ἄστυ, τὸ γένος, τὸ ἦτορ *heart.*

b.) All *abstracts* in -της and -ις, and most other words in -ις are *feminine:* as, ἡ γλυκύτης *sweetness*, ἡ δύναμις *power*, ἡ ποίησις *poesy*, ἡ ῥίς, ἡ πόλις.

c.) All *labials* and *palatals*, and all *liquids* (except a few in which ρ is the stem-mark) are either *masculine* or *feminine.* Except palatals, they are more frequently masculine.

d.) Nouns in which the stem ends

1.) in -ωτ-, -αν-, -εν-, or -ντ-, are *masculine:* as, ὁ γέλως, -ωτος, *laughter;* ὁ παιάν, -ᾶνος, *pæan;* ὁ λιμήν, -ένος· ὁ λέων, -οντος, ὁ ὀδούς, ὁ γίγας, ὁ ἱμάς, -άντος, *thong.* Except τὸ οὖς, ὠτός, *ear*, τὸ φῶς, φωτός, *light* (both contracts), ἡ φρήν, φρενός, *mind*, ὁ, ἡ ἀδήν, -ένος, *gland;* and a few names of cities (175): as, ἡ Ῥαμνοῦς, -οῦντος, *Rhamnus.*

2.) in -δ-, -θ-, or two palatals, *feminine:* as, ἡ λαμπάς, -άδος, *torch*, ἡ ἔρις, -ιδος, *strife*, ἡ χλαμύς, -ύδος, *cloak;* ἡ κόρυς, -υθος, *helmet;* ἡ σάλπιγξ, -ιγγος, *trumpet.* Except ὁ, ἡ παῖς, παιδός, *child*, ὁ πούς, ποδός, *foot;* ὁ, ἡ ὄρνις, -ιθος, *bird;* ὁ λύγξ, λυγκός, *lynx*, and a few other double palatals.

3.) in -ατ-, or -ᾰ-, *neuter:* as, τὸ ἧπαρ, -ατος, τὸ κέρας, -ᾰτος, τὸ γέρας, -ᾰος.

178. B. Number. The Greek has three numbers; the Singular, denoting *one;* the Plural, denoting *more than one;* and the Dual (duālis, from duo, *two*), a variety of the plural, which may be employed when only *two* are spoken of.

Thus, the singular ἄνθρωπος signifies *man,* the plural ἄνθρωποι, *men* (whether two or more), and the dual ἀνθρώπω, *two men.*

a. The dual is most used in the Attic and Homeric Greek. The Æolic dialect (as the Latin, which it approaches the most nearly of the Greek dialects) and the Hellenistic Greek show scarce a trace of the dual (the New Testament, like the Modern Greek, none), except in δύο, *two,* and ἄμφω, *both* (Lat. *duo, ambo*).

179. C. Case. The Greek has five cases: the Nominative, Genitive, Dative, Accusative, and Vocative.

a. From the general character of the relations which they denote, the Nominative, Accusative, and Vocative are termed the *direct,* and the Genitive and Dative, the *indirect* cases. The cases are also distinguished as *subjective, objective,* and *residual.* See 10, 14, and Syntax.

b. The Nominative and Vocative are also termed *casus recti, the right cases,* and the other three, *casus oblīqui, the oblique cases.*

180. D. Methods of Declension. Words are declined, in Greek, by annexing to the stem certain Affixes (172 a, c), which mark the distinctions of gender, number, and case. There are three sets of these affixes; and hence arise three distinct methods of declining words, called the First, Second, and Third Declensions.

a. The first of these methods applies only to masculine and feminine words; but the second and third, to words of all the genders. In some of the cases, however, the affixes vary, in the same declension, according to the gender; so that, to know how a word is declined, it is necessary to ascertain three things: 1. its *stem;* 2. the *declension* to which it belongs; and 3. its *gender* (173 b, 174 s).

b. If the theme (172 e) and gender do not determine the stem and declension, these are commonly shown, as in Latin, by adding the Genitive singular, or its ending. *If the Genitive singular ends in* -ας *or* -ης, *or in* -ου *from a theme in* -ας *or* -ης, *the word is of the first declension; if it ends in* -ου *from a theme in* -ος *or* -ον, *the word is of the second declension; if it ends in* -ος, *the word is of the third declension. The stem is obtained by throwing off the affix of the Genitive;* or it may be obtained by throwing off any open affix (172 c).

Thus the nouns, ὁ ταμίας *steward*, ἡ οἰκία *house*, ἡ γλῶσσα *tongue*, ὁ δῆμος *people*, and ὁ Ἄραψ *Arab*, make in the Gen. ταμίου, οἰκίας, γλώσσης, δήμου, and Ἄραβος. From these genitives we ascertain that ταμίας, οἰκία, and γλῶσσα belong to Dec. 1, δῆμος to Dec. 2, and Ἄραψ to Dec. 3. By throwing off the affixes -ου, -ας, -ης, and -ος, we obtain the stems ταμι-, οἰκι-, γλωσσ-, δημ-, and Ἀραβ-. The words are then declined by annexing to these stems the affixes in § 11.

181. Each declension observes the following
GENERAL RULES. 1. The masculine and feminine affixes are the same, except in the *Nominative* and *Genitive singular* of the *first* declension. The neuter has also the same affixes, except in the *direct* cases, *singular* and *plural*.

2. In *neuters*, the three *direct* cases have the same form, and in the plural always end in ᾰ.

3. The dual has but two forms : one for the *direct*, and the other for the *indirect* cases.

4. In the *feminine singular* of the *first* declension, and in the *plural* of all words, the *Vocative* has the same form with the Nominative.

182. a. The use of the Voc. as a distinct form is still further limited. Few substantives or adjectives, except proper names and personal appellatives or epithets, are sufficiently employed in address to require a separate form for this purpose. Hence a distinct Voc. is scarce found in the *participle, pronoun, article*, or *numeral*. In respect to other words :
b. *Masculines* of Dec. 1 are commonly names or epithets of persons, and therefore form the Voc. sing.
c. In Dec. 2, the distinct form of the Voc. is commonly used, except for euphony or rhythm : as, Ὦ φίλος, ὦ φίλος, *my friend! my friend!* Ar. Nub. 1167. Φίλος ὦ Μενέλαε Δ. 189. Ἥλιός τε Γ. 277. To avoid the double ε, θεός, *god* (like *deus* in Latin), has, in classic writers, no distinct Voc. ; yet Θεέ St. Mat. 27. 46.
d. In Dec. 3, few words, except proper names and personal appellatives and epithets, have a distinct Voc. ; and even in those which have, the Nom. is sometimes employed in its stead, especially by Att. writers : thus, Ὦ πᾶσα πόλι Ar. Ach. 971 ; but Ὦ πόλις Soph. Phil. 1213.

183. The Table (12) exhibits the affixes as resolved into their two classes of ELEMENTS : I. FLEXIBLE ENDINGS, which are *significant* additions, marking distinctions of number, case, and gender ; and II. CONNECTING VOWELS, which are chiefly *euphonic* in their origin, and serve to unite the flexible endings with the stem.

a. These elements, when there is no danger of mistake, may be more briefly called *Flexives* and *Connectives*. The affixes are termed *euphonic*, when they have connecting vowels, and *nude* (nudus, *naked*), when they want them. Where the connectives were followed by other vowels, contraction took place in one or another of its forms, though not always according to the common laws. See 7, 13.

184. The tables (11 s) show, that, in regular declension,

a.) The flexive of the Nom. sing. masc. and (except in Dec. 1) fem. is always ς.

b.) The Dat. has always ι : in the sing., ending with this vowel ; in the plur., joining it with σ, and in the dual, with ν.

c.) The Acc. sing. (except in neuters of Dec. 3) always ends in ν, or its corresponding vowel α (138) ; and the Acc. pl. masc. and fem. is always formed by adding ς to the Acc. sing. (122, 156).

d.) The Gen. pl. and dual always ends in ν ; which, in the plur., is preceded by ω, and in the dual by an ι diphthong.

e.) In Dec. 1 and 2, the affixes are all *open* (172 c) and constitute a distinct syllable. In Dec. 3, three of the affixes, σ, ν, and σι, are *close*.

f.) In the singular of Dec. 3, the direct cases neut., and the Voc. masc. and fem., have no affixes.

185. The three Greek and first three Latin declensions correspond. The fourth and fifth declensions in Latin are contract varieties of the third.

186. E. HISTORIC VIEW. a. The following view has much evidence in its support, though, from the very nature of the case, it cannot be established by direct testimony : (b, c) The Greek cases were at first only two, a *Direct* and an *Indirect Case;* and these only singular and plural. (d) From the Direct Case, in the masculine and feminine genders, the *Nominative* and *Accusative* were formed by significant affixes, to distinguish the *subject* and *direct object* of an action. (e, f) To mark *indirect subjective relations*, the *Genitive* was separated from the old Indirect Case, which then remained as a *Dative*. The different forms of the Gen. sing. point to θ, or, with a euphonic vowel, oθ, as its original affix. As, by the laws of euphony which afterwards prevailed, θ could not end a word (160), it was dropped, or became ς, or assumed ε (commonly written with ν paragogic, 164 a). (g) After the formation of a new and enlarged plural, the old plural with its two case-forms was restricted to a *dual* sense ; while the old Direct Case singular, in which the stem received no affix, was now left simply as a Vocative.

187. a. To the primitive nude declension, now called the *third*, two others were afterwards added, having connecting vowels. (b) In the Nom. and Acc. sing. of these declensions, the primitive direct form, without ς or ν appended, was sometimes retained (197 b, 199).

188. *Neuters*, as denoting things without life, which can have no voluntary action, and therefore require less the distinction of subject and object, remained content with the single Direct Case. In the singular, this was the simple stem in Dec. 3 ; and in Dec. 2, took the Acc. form, which suited the *objective* character of the gender. In the plural, instead of the old affix -ε, it took the more *objective* -ἄ, and with no connecting vowel. Observe here the striking analogy of the Latin throughout.

189. a. The *first declension* appears to have arisen in the effort to obtain a distinct form for the *feminine*, with an appropriate connecting vowel. This vowel was commonly lengthened, unless contracted with a vowel following. (b) The feminine is distinguished from the masculine words admitted into this declension by the want of the strong flexive -ς in the Nom. sing., and by the affix -ος, instead of -ο in the Genitive.

190. The prevention of hiatus by the insertion of aspirate consonants (the successors of the digamma or used like it), and by different modes of contraction (100), has given an especial variety of form, in the *first* and *second declensions*, to the *Dative singular*, which, as the primitive Indirect Case (186 c), originally performed the offices of both the Genitive and the Dative. Thus, we find,

1.) The ι appended with the insertion of φ, a natural successor of the digamma. This form is Epic, and from its being used as both Gen. and Dat., and in Dec. 2 even as plural, is evidently of great antiquity. It does not occur in names of persons, and is chiefly used where local relations are spoken of. E. g.

Dec. 1. ἐξ εὐνῆφι, *from the bed*, γ. 405; ἀπὸ νευρῆφιν (163 a) Θ. 300; ἧφι βίηφι πιθήσας, *trusting to his strength*, X. 107; κεφαλῆφιν ἐπεὶ λάβεν Il. 762; ὡς φρήτρη φρήτρηφιν ἀρήγῃ B. 363; χερσίν τε βίηφί τε μ. 246; ἅμ᾽ ἠοῖ φαινομένηφιν I. 618, 682; κρατερῆφι βίηφιν Φ. 501; ἑτέρηφι Π. 734; θύρηφιν ι. 238.

Dec. 2. Ἰλιόφι κλυτὰ τείχεα, *the famed walls of* (or *at*) *Troy*, Φ. 295; ἐκ ποντόφιν ω. 83; ἀπὸ πλατέος πτυόφιν N. 588; ἐπὶ δεξιόφιν N. 308; δακρυόφι πλῆσθεν, *were filled with tears*, P. 696; ἀπὸ πασσαλόφι, Ω. 268; παρ᾽ αὐτόφι μ. 302; ἀμφ᾽ ὀστεόφιν μ. 45; θεόφιν μήστωρ ἀτάλαντος H. 366. So ἐσχαρόφιν ε. 59, and κοτυληδονόφιν ε. 433, as of Dec. 2, while the themes in use are ἐσχάρη of Dec. 1, and κοτυληδών of Dec. 3.

a. The φ is likewise inserted in the *Dative plural* of a few words of Dec. 3, chiefly neuters in -ος; and here serves to lengthen the preceding syllable. These forms were also used as both Gen. and Dat., and sometimes with the force of the singular: as, κατ᾽ ὄρεσφι, *down the mountains*, Δ. 452; ἀπὸ στήθεσφιν, *from the breast*, Ξ. 214; πρόσθ᾽ ἵπποιιν καὶ ὀχεσφιν E. 107; σὺν ὄχεσφι Π. 811; ὄρεσφι Λ. 474 (cf. Λ. 479); ὑπὸ κράτεσφι, *under the head*, K. 156; Ἐρέβεσφιν (probably the correct form for Ἐρεβευσφιν I. 572, &c.); ἀπὸ ναῦφι (σ here dropped), *from the ships*, II. 246.

191. 2.) The ι appended with the insertion of θ. This form became adverbial (chiefly poetic), denoting the *place where*: as, οἴκοθι *at home*, ἄλλοθι *elsewhere*, αὐτόθι, ὅθι, Κορινθόθι. It was mostly confined to Dec. 2; and, in the few instances in which it was made from nouns of other declensions, it still imitated the forms of this. Traces of its old use as the Indirect Case still remain in Homer: thus, Gen. Ἰλιόθι πρό, *before Troy*, Θ. 561, οὐρανόθι πρό Γ. 3, ἠῶθι πρό ζ. 36; Dat. κηρόθι I. 300.

3.) The ι appended with the insertion of χ. This appears in the Epic ἧχι for the adverbial Dative ᾗ, *where*, A. 607.

4.) The ι contracted with the preceding vowel into αι or οι (119). This simpler mode of contraction now scarcely appears except in adverbial Datives: as, χαμαί humi, *on the ground*, οἴκοι *at home* (but οἴκῳ *to a house*; cf. Lat. *domi* and *domus*), πέδοι, Ἰσθμοῖ, οἷ, ὅποι. Yet ἐν Ἰσθμοῖ Simon. Fr. 209; ἐν Πριανσιοῖ Insc. Cret.; τοῖ δάμοι Insc. Bœot.

5.) The common form, in which the ι is absorbed by the preceding vowel: as, λύρ(α-ι)ᾳ, οἰκ(ο-ι)ῳ, Ἰσθμῷ, τῷ δήμῳ.

192. The forms of the Genitive in -οθεν or -θεν (186 e) remained in the common language only as adverbs, denoting the *place whence*: as, οἴκοθεν *from home*, ἄλλοθεν, αὐτόθεν, Ἀθήνηθεν. As examples of their use as decided Genitives, may be cited ἀπ᾽ οὐρανόθεν, *from heaven*, Θ. 365, ἐξ Αἰσύμηθεν Θ. 304, ἐξ ἁλόθεν Φ. 335, Διόθεν O. 489; and the pronominal forms ἐμέθεν, σέθεν, ἕθεν (27), which even occur in Attic poets.

CHAPTER II.

DECLENSION OF NOUNS.

193. The declension of adjectives is also here treated, so far as it corresponds with the declension of nouns. See 229.

I. THE FIRST DECLENSION.

(For the affixes and paradigms, see 11–15, 20; for the gender, 176.)

194. The original affixes of Dec. 1 all had *a* as a connecting vowel (187, 189). In most of these, the *a*, if not contracted with a vowel following (183 a), was itself made long. Short *a*, however, remained in the *singular*,

1.) In the *direct cases* of *feminines* whose stem ended in σ, a double consonant, λλ, or αιν : as, μοῦσᾰ, μοῦσᾰν, τράπεζᾰ (15), γλῶσσᾰ (or γλῶττᾰ, 169 a) *tongue*, ἅμιλλᾰ *contest*, λέαινᾰ *lioness*.

a. Add a few others in -λα and -να ; as, παῦλᾰ *rest*, ἔχιδνᾰ *viper*, μέριμνᾰ *care*, δέσποινᾰ *mistress:* and a very few in which μ or a mute precedes α ; as, τόλμᾰ *courage*, ἄκανθᾰ *thorn*, δίαιτᾰ *mode of life*.
b. Add many feminines in -α pure and -ρα, mostly having a diphthong in the penult, and easily recognized by the accent. The principal classes are, (α) Polysyllables in -εια and -οια, except abstracts in -εια from verbs in -ευω ; as, ἀλήθειᾰ *truth*, εὔνοιᾰ *good-will*, βασίλειᾰ *queen*, but βασιλείᾱ *reign*, from βασιλεύω · (β) Female designations in -τρια ; as, ψάλτριᾰ *female musician:* (γ) Dissyllables and some polysyllabic names of places in -αια ; as, μαῖᾰ *good mother*, Ἑστιαῖᾰ · (δ) Words in -υια ; as, μυῖᾰ *fly:* (ε) Most words in -ρα, whose penult is lengthened by a diphthong (except αυ), by ῡ, or by ῥῥ ; as, μάχαιρᾰ *sword*, γέφυρᾰ *bridge*.
c. The accent commonly shows the quantity of final **α** in the theme. Thus, in all *proparoxytones* and *properispomes* it must be *short* by the general laws of accent ; while, by a special law of the declension, it is *long* in all *oxytones*, and in all *paroxytones* in -α, Gen. -ας, except the proper names Κίρρᾰ, Πύρρᾰ (b. ε), and the numeral μίᾰ *one*.

2.) In the *Vocative* of nouns in -της, and of *gentiles* and compound verbals in -ης : as, ναύτης (14), Πέρσης *Persian*, μυροπώλης (μύρον *perfume*, πωλέω *to sell*) *perfumer;* Voc. ναῦτᾰ, Πέρσᾰ (but Πέρσης *Perses*, a man's name, Voc. Πέρση), μυροπῶλᾰ.

195. In the singular, long *α* passed, by precession, into η, unless preceded by ε, ι, ρ, or ρο (115 a): as, ναύτης, ναύτῃ, Ἀτρείδη, μούσης, μούσῃ, ᾠδή, ᾠδήν · but ταμίᾱς, ταμίᾳ, θεά, θεᾶς, λύρᾱ, λύρᾱν (14, 15), ἰδέᾱ *idea*, χρείᾱ *need*, χρόᾱ *color*.

a. Long α likewise remains in the pures, πόᾱ *grass*, στοά *porch*, γύᾱ *field*, σικύᾱ *gourd*, καρύᾱ *walnut-tree*, ἐλάᾱ *olive-tree*, Ναυσικάᾱ; in ἀλαλά *war-cry*, ἐπίβδᾱ, σκανδάλᾱ, γεννάδᾱς; and in some proper names, particularly those which are Doric or foreign, as, Λήδᾱ, Φιλομήλᾱ, Λεωνίδᾱς, Σύλλᾱς· and it became η after ρ or ρο in the words δέρη *neck*, κόρη *maiden*, κόρρη (Ion. and Old Att. κόρση, 157) *cheek*, ἀθάρη *pap*, αἴθρη *clear sky*, ῥοή *stream*; in some proper names, as Τήρης· and in compounds of μετρέω, as γεωμέτρης *land-measurer, geometer*. In some words, usage fluctuates between long or short α and η : as, πρύμνᾱ and πρύμνη, *stern*.

196. CONTRACTS. A few nouns, in which the stem ends in α or ε, and feminine adjectives in -εα and -οη, are contracted : as, μνάα μνᾶ, Ἑρμέας Ἑρμῆς, βορέας βορρᾶς (ρ doubled), συκέα συκῆ, *fig-tree*; χρυσέα χρυσῆ, διπλόη διπλῆ. See 15, 23, 120 e.

DIALECTIC FORMS.

197. a. In the affixes of this declension, the *Doric* dialect retains throughout the original α; while, in the singular, the *Ionic* has η in most of those words in which the *Attic* and *Common* dialects have long α, and even in some in which they have short α, particularly derivatives in -ειᾰ and -οιᾰ (130): as, Dor. ᾠδά, ᾠδᾶς, ᾠδᾷ, ᾠδάν· Ion. λύρη, λύρης, λύρῃ, λύρην, ταμίης (yet Hom. has θεά)· Ep. ἀληθείη, εὐπλοίη, New Ion. ἀληθηίη, μίη, for ἀλήθειᾰ, εὔπλοιᾰ, μίᾰ.

b. In words in -ης, the *primitive Direct Case* in -ᾰ is sometimes retained by Hom. and some of the other poets as Nom. (187 b), for the sake of the metre or euphony: as, ὁ αὖτε Θυέστᾰ B. 107; ἱππότᾰ Νέστωρ B. 336; εὐρύοπα Ζεύς β. 146; βαθυμῆτα Χείρων Pind. N. 3. 92. Compare Lat. *nauta, scriba*. So in feminines in -η, the poets sometimes retain the old short α in the Voc.: as, νύμφᾰ φίλη Γ. 130; Ὦ Δίκᾰ, Sapph.

c. The old Gen. affixes, -ᾱο and ᾱων, which often occur in the Epic writers, were contracted as follows: (1) In the Ion., they were regularly contracted into -ω and -ων, with the insertion of ε after a consonant, but commonly in the poets with synizesis (120 i, 117 b): as, Ἀτρείδ(αο, ω)εω, Ἀτρείδ(άων, ῶν)έων· Βορέαο Βορέω, Ἑρμείω O. 214, εὐμμελίω Δ. 47. (2) In the Dor., ᾱ absorbed the following vowel, and the affixes became ᾱ and ᾶν (131 a): as, Ἀτρείδ(αο)ᾱ, Ἀτρείδ(άων)ᾶν. (3) In the Att., ᾱο and ᾱων were contracted into ου (by precession from ω, 115) and ῶν: as, Ἀτρείδ(αο, ω)ου, Ἀτρείδ(άων)ῶν.

d. In some *masculines*, chiefly proper names, the later Ion. has εᾰ in the Acc. for ην: as Λεωνίδεα Hdt. 8. 15 (-ην Id. 7. 206), δεσπότεᾰ Id. 1. 11.

198. a. The Dat. pl. in Hom. commonly ends in -ῃσι or -ῃς before a vowel (which may be referred to apostrophe): as θεῇσιν Λ. 638, θεῇς εἰς Γ. 158. In a few instances, -ῃς precedes a consonant: as, σῇς καί A. 179, πέτρῃς πρός η. 279. We even find θεαῖς ε. 119, ἀκταῖς M. 284.

b. Antique, Ion., and Dor. forms are sometimes found in Att. writers:

1.) The Dor. Gen. in -ᾱ, from some nouns in -ας, mostly proper names: as, ὀρνιθοθήρας, *fowler*, Γωβρύας, Καλλίας· G. ὀρνιθοθήρα, Γωβρύα Cyr. 5. 2. 14 (Γωβρύου Ib. 2). So all contracts in -ᾶς: as, βορρᾶς, G. βορρᾶ.

2.) The Ion. Gen. in -εω, from a few proper names in -ης: as Τήρης, Καμβύσης· G. Τήρεω Th. 2. 29, Καμβύσεω Cyr. 1. 2. 1.

3). The old Dat. pl. in -αισι, which is frequent in the poets. So, in Plato, τέχναισι Leg. 920 e, ἡμέραισι Phaedr. 276 b.

II. THE SECOND DECLENSION.

(For the affixes and paradigms, see 11-14, 16, 20; for the gender, 176.)

199. The flexible endings of the Nominative and Accusative singular are wanting (187 b),

1.) In the *theme* of the *article:* thus, ὁ for ὅς.

2.) In the *neuter* of the *article* and of the *pronouns* ἄλλος, αὐτός, ἐκεῖνος, and ὅς · thus, τό, ἄλλο, αὐτό, ἐκεῖνο, ὅ, for τόν, &c.

  a. In crasis with the article (125), and in composition with the definitives τοῖος, τόσος, τηλίκος, and τύννος, the neuter αὐτό more frequently becomes αὐτόν · thus, ταὐτόν and ταὐτό, for τὸ αὐτό · τοιοῦτον and τοιοῦτο.

3.) Frequently in the *Accusative* of the *Attic declension* (200), particularly in ἡ ἕως *dawn*, ἡ ἅλως *threshing-floor*, ὁ λάγως *hare*, ἡ Κέως, ἡ Κῶς, ἡ Τέως, ὁ Ἄθως · thus, Acc. ἕω (only), λάγων and λάγω, Ἄθω. So, in the adjectives ἀγήρως (22), ἀνάπλεως *full*, ἀξιόχρεως *competent*.

200. CONTRACTS. If the stem-mark (172 d) is α, ε, or ο, it may be contracted with the affix. See ἀγήραος (22), ὀστέον, νόος (16); and also 120 c, e, i, 121. The contract declension in -ως and -ων, from -αος and -αον, is termed by grammarians the *Attic Declension* from its prevalence among Attic writers, although it is far from being peculiar to them (87 b).

  a. If the stem-mark is long α, ε is inserted after the contraction (120 i): as, νᾱῦς (νως) νεώς (16), ναοῦ (νω) νεώ, ναῷ (νῳ) νε ᾳ, ναόν (νων) νεών.
  b. The number of words belonging to the Attic declension is small. In some of them, the uncontracted form does not occur, or occurs only with some change. Thus εὔγεως, *fertile*, is the contract form of εὔγαος (fr. (γαα)γῆ, poet. γαῖα, *earth*), in place of which we find the protracted εὔγαιος and εὔγειος.

Dialectic Forms.

201. a. The affix of the Gen. sing. -ο-ο (13), which was commonly contracted to -ου, or, in the Æol. and stricter Dor., to -ω (130 c), was often prolonged by the poets, especially the Epic (sometimes even by the Tragic in lyric portions), to -οιο (called the *Thessalian* form, and not receiving elision): thus, πόντου Ἰκαρίοιο Β. 145; δόμου ὑψηλοῖο a. 126; οἷο δόμοιο a. 330; ποταμοῖο ... Ἀνάπω Theoc. 1. 68; μαλακῷ χόρτοιο Id. 4. 18.

  b. A single contraction, with the insertion of ε (120 i), gives the Epic genitives Πετ(άοο)έωο Δ. 327, Πενελ(άοο)έωο (v. 1. -έοιο) Ξ. 489. The poetic doubling of ι gives the Epic *dual* form in -οιϊν (so always in Hom.).

  c. The new Ion. has Gen. forms with ε inserted: as, πυρέων Hdt. 2. 36, Σουσέων Id. 5. 35. In some proper names in -ος, these imitate Dec. 1: as, Κροῖσος, Κροίσεω Hdt. 8. 122 (Κροίσου 1. 6); Βάττεω, Κλεομβρότεω, Id. 4. 160; 5. 32.

  d. The old Dat. pl. in -οισι is common in the poets of all classes, and in Ion. prose. So, even in Plato, θεοῖσι Leg. 955 e.

III. THE THIRD DECLENSION.

(For the affixes and paradigms, see 11-14, 17-21; for the gender, 177.)

202. In this declension, the Nominative, though regarded as the theme of the word, seldom exhibits the stem in its simple distinct form. This form must therefore be learned from the Genitive, or some case which has an open affix (172 c).

a. Special attention must be given to the euphonic changes which occur in those cases which have either *close* affixes, or *no* affixes; that is, in the Nom. and Voc. sing., in the Acc. sing. in -ν (where the stem receives the same changes as in the theme), and in the Dat. pl.

b. The change of ν, the original flexive of the Acc. sing., into α, was so extensively required in this declension by the rule (160 e), that α became the prevailing affix, and was often used even after a vowel. It will therefore be understood that the affix is α, if not stated otherwise.

Words of Dec. 3 are divided, according to the stem-mark, or characteristic, into MUTES, LIQUIDS, and PURES (172 d).

A. MUTES (17).

203. LABIALS AND PALATALS. These are all masculine or feminine (177 c). Except in the irregular γυνή, the theme ends in ψ or ξ (151), and the Voc. has no distinct form.

a. Γυνή, *woman, wife*, which has its theme after the form of Dec. 1, and is accented as if dissyllabic throughout, is thus declined: S. N. γυνή, G. γυναικός (accented as if pronounced γ'ναικός), D. γυναικί, A. γυναῖκα, V. γύναι· P. N. γυναῖκες, G. γυναικῶν, D. γυναιξί, A. γυναῖκας· &c.

b. In the stem θριχ-, θ becomes τ, except where χ is changed (159 b). In ἡ ἀλώπηξ, -εκος, *fox*, the ε of the stem is lengthened in the theme.

204. LINGUALS. In these, the characteristic lingual cannot remain in any case which has either a *close affix* or *no affix* (202 a); and if another consonant is thus brought before σ or to the end of a word, further change may be required: as,

ἐλπί(δs)s, κόρυ(θs)s, παι(δσι)σί, κλεῖ(δν)ν, (παιδ)παῖ, σῶμ(ατ)α, λέο(ντ)ν (17); ἔλμι(νθs)νs (156 b); φῶ(τ)s, ἧπα(τ)ρ (17): ἄνα(κτs, κs)ξ, ἄν(ακτ)α, δάμα(ρτs)ρ, λέ(οντs, ονs, οεν)ων, λέ(οντσι)ουσι (17). Cf. Lat. æta(ts)s.

a. *Barytones* in -ις and -υς form the Acc. sing. both in -ν and less frequently in -α: as, ἔρις, κόρυς (17), ὁ, ἡ ὄρνις *bird*, ἡ χάρις *grace*; Acc. ἔριν, ὄρνιν (160 e), and poet. ἔριδα, ὀρνῖθα, commonly Χάριτα as the name of a goddess, but otherwise χάριν. So κλείς (17), ὁ γέλως *laughter*, and the compounds of πούς *foot*, have both forms: κλεῖν and κλεῖδα, γέλωτα and γέλων; see Οἰδίπους, δίπους (21, 22).

b. If a distinct Voc. is needed, linguals obtain this by dropping the stem-mark (160 a): as, παῖ, λέον (17); Ἄρτεμις *Diana*, νεᾶνις *girl*, τυραννίς *sovereignty*, V. Ἄρτεμι, νεᾶνι, τυραννί Soph. O. T. 380. A few proper names in -ᾱς, -αντος, then change ν as in the theme: as, Ἄτλᾱς, Πολυδάμᾱς, V. Ἄτλ(αντ, αν, αα)ᾱ, Πολυδάμᾱ Hel. 6. 1. 5. The Voc. form ἄνα is used only in addressing a god, as Ζεῦ ἄνα Γ. 351, Soph. O. C. 1485.

205. STEMS IN -ντ-. When, by the dropping of τ, ν is brought before ς in the theme, the ς is changed, if an O vowel precedes; but otherwise the ν: as, λέ(οντς, ονς, οεν)ων, γίγ(αντς, αντς, αας)ᾶς (17, 153, 156); λύ(οντς)ων, θ(εντς)εῖς, λύσας, δύς (26).

a. Except ὀδούς (17), and participles from verbs in -ωμι: as, δίδους, δούς, fr. δίδωμι (45). Yet Ion. ὀδών Hdt. 6. 107.

206. NEUTER LINGUALS. In these the stem-mark is always τ, which, in the theme, is commonly dropped after μα, but otherwise gives place to ς or ρ (160): as, σῶμ(ατ)α, φ(ωτ)ῶς, ἦπ(ατ)αρ (17); εἰδ(οτ)ός (26). Cf. Lat. poēm(at)a, co(rd)r.

a. The τ is also omitted in μέλ(ιτ)ι mel, honey; in γάλ(ακτ)α lac, milk, which also drops κ; and in γόν(ατ)υ genu, knee, and δόρ(ατ)υ spear, which have also υ in place of α (cf. 224 c). In the poet. ἦμ(ατ)αρ day, ρ takes the place of τ after μα; and in ὕδ(ατ)ωρ water, σκ(ατ)ώρ filth, ωρ takes the place of ατ.

207. CONTRACT LINGUALS. a. A few linguals drop the stem-mark (140 a) before some or all of the open affixes, and are then contracted: as, κλεῖδας (κλεῖας) κλεῖς· κέρ(ᾱτος, αος)ως (17); τὸ τέρας, prodigy, P. N. τέρᾱτα τέρᾱ, G. τεράτων τερῶν· ὁ χρώς, skin, S. D. χρ(ωτί, ωϊ)ῷ (in the phrase ἐν χρῷ). So, in Hom., from ὁ ἱδρώς sudor, sweat, ὁ γέλως laughter, ὁ ἔρως love, S. D. ἱδρ(ῶτι)ῷ, γέλῳ, ἔρῳ· A. ἱδρ(ῶτα, ωα)ῶ, γέλω.

b. These neuters are contracted in the stem: οὖς, ὠτός, ear, fr. the old οὖας, οὔατος (17); στέαρ στήρ, tallow, G. στέᾱτος στητός· φρέαρ well, G. φρέατος (ᾰ) φρητός. See 120 b, c.

c. So, usually, nouns and adjectives in -εις, -εντος, preceded by ο or η: as, Ὀπ(οεντς, ὀεις)οῦς, -(όε)οῦντος (17), ὁ πλακ(όεις)οῦς cake; τιμ(ήεις)ῆς or ἧς (109 a), τιμ(ήε)ῆσσα, τιμ(ῆεν)ῆν, honored. Add some in -ις, -ιδος: as, ἡ δαΐς δᾴς torch, παρηΐς παρῄς cheek, φωΐς φῴς blister.

B. LIQUIDS (18).

208. MASCULINE AND FEMININE LIQUIDS. In these the stem always ends in ν or ρ, except in ἅλς (ὁ sal, salt, ἡ sea), of which the singular is rare in Attic prose. For the euphonic changes in the theme and Dat. pl., see 153, 154, 156, 145 a. In -νς of the theme, (a) the ς is changed after an E or O vowel; (b) the ν, after ι or υ; and (c) after a, in nouns the ς, but in adjectives the ν: as,

(a) λιμ(ενς, εεν)ήν, δαίμ(ονς)ων (18); ὁ αἰ(ωνς)ών ævum, age, ὁ μ(ηνς)ήν mensis, MONTH; (b) ῥ(ινς, ιας)ίς (18), ὁ Φόρκ(ῡνς)ῡς Phorcys; (c) παι(ανς)ᾱν (18), μέλ(ανς)ᾱς (23).

d. Except ὁ κτείς, κτενός, comb; εἷς, ἑνός, one (25); the Ion. ὁ μείς (as fr. s. μεν-, yet G. μηνός) for μήν month, Hdt. 2. 82; and ὁ μόσσυν, -ῡνος, wooden tower. In the pronoun τίς (28), ν is simply omitted in the theme.

e. Most words in -ις and -υς have a second, but less classic form, in -ιν and -υν: as, ῥίς and ῥίν, Φόρκυς and Φόρκυν, ὁ δελφίς and δελφίν.

f. In the Voc. of Ἀπόλλων, -ωνος, Apollo, Ποσειδῶν, -ῶνος, Neptune, ὁ σωτήρ, -ῆρος, savior, δᾱήρ, -έρος, brother-in-law, and of the personal words in 210, the natural tone of address has thrown back the accent as far as possible, and shortened the last syllable of the stem if long : Ἄπολ-λον, Πόσειδον, σῶτερ, δᾶερ, ἄνερ, πάτερ, θύγατερ, Δήμητερ. If the accent is not thrown back, oxytone nouns retaining ν or ρ in the theme have no distinct Voc. : as, λιμήν, ὁ, ἡ αἰθήρ, -έρος, ETHER.

209. NEUTER LIQUIDS. A few nouns in which the stem ends in ρ are neuter. They are, for the most part, confined to the singular; and require, in their declension, no euphonic changes of letters. E. g. πῦρ, πῠρός (14 ; υ lengthened in the monosyllabic stem), νέκτᾰρ, -ᾰρος, *nectar*.

  a. In ἔαρ (Ϝεαρ) ver, *spring*, and the poetic κέαρ cor, *heart*, contraction takes place in the stem : N. ἔαρ, poet. ἦρ, G. and D. ἔαρος, ἔαρι, oftener ἦρος, ἦρι · N. κέαρ, in Hom. always κῆρ, D. κῆρι.

210. SYNCOPATED LIQUIDS. I. In a few familiar liquids, a short vowel is syncopated before the stem-mark : viz.,

  a. In these three, the syncope takes place *before all the open affixes:* ἀνήρ (s. ἀνερ-, sync. ἀνρ-, ἀνδρ-, 146 b) *man;* κύων (s. κυον, sync. κυν-) canis, *dog*, also syncopated in Dat. pl. ; ἀρνός (s. ἀρεν-, sync. ἀρν-) *lamb's*, of which the Nom. sing. is not used, but in its place, ἀμνός agnus, of Dec. 2. See 18.

  b. These five are syncopated *in the Gen. and Dat. sing.* : πᾰτήρ (18 ; s. πατερ-, πατρ-) FATHER ; μήτηρ MOTHER, G. μητέρος μητρός, D. μητέρι μητρί ; θῠγάτηρ DAUGHTER, θυγα(τέρος)τρός, θυγα(τέρι)τρί · ἡ γαστήρ *stomach*, γασ(τέρος)τρός, γασ(τέρι)τρί · ἡ Δημήτηρ Ceres, Δήμη(τερος)τρος, Δήμη(τερι)τρι, also Acc. Δήμη(τερα)τρα.

  c. In these words, the poets sometimes neglect the syncope, and sometimes employ it in other cases than those which are specified.

  d. Compare Lat. păter, pa(ter)*tris* ; māter, ma(ter)*tris* ; caro, carnis.

211. Comparatives in -ων often drop the ν before α and ε in the sing. and pl., and are then contracted (140 b) : as,

μείζονα μείζ(οα)ω, μείζονες μείζ(οες)ους, μείζονας μείζους (22). Both forms are freely used, and even together : as, ἀμείνονας καὶ κρείττους i. 7. 3.

  a. A like contraction occurs in a few other words, particularly in the Acc. of Ἀπόλλων and Ποσειδῶν (itself contr. fr. Ποσειδάων, 131 a) : Ἀπόλ-λωνα Ἀπόλλ(ωα)ω (iii. 1. 6), Ποσειδῶνα Ποσειδῶ. See for both forms, of which the shorter is especially used with the article, Pl. Crat. 402 d, e, 404 d, 405 d. So, likewise, ὁ κυκεών *mixed drink*, Acc. κυκεῶνα, and poet. κυκεῶ (κ. 316, κυκειῶ Λ. 624) ; ἡ γλήχων *pennyroyal*, A. γλήχωνα, γλήχω.

C. PURES (19).

212. The euphonic changes in the declension of pures may be mostly referred, (I.) to a special law of Greek declension, and (II.) to contraction.

I. SPECIAL LAW OF GREEK DECLENSION. *The short vowels, ε and ο, can never remain in the stem, either before the affixes -ς and -ν, or at the end of a word.* Hence,

213. A.) Before the affixes -ς and -ν, ε becomes η, ι, υ, or ευ; and ο becomes ω or ου: thus,

1.)˙ a. In *masculine nouns*, ε becomes ευ in *simple*, and η in *compound* words: as,

Simple, ὁ ἱππεύς, -έως (19; stem ἱππε-), βασιλεύς *king*, Θησεύς *Theseus;* *compound*, Σωκράτης, -εος (19; fr. σῶς *entire*, and κράτος *strength*), Ἀριστοτέλης, Δημοσθένης (observe the difference in accentuation).

EXCEPT the simples Ἄρης, -εος, *Mars*, ὁ σής, σεός, *moth;* and the following, in which ε becomes υ or ι, ὁ πῆχυς, -εως, A. πῆχυν (19), ὁ πέλεκυς *axe*, ὁ πρέσβυς *elder* (properly an adj.); ὁ ἔχις, -εως, *viper*, ὁ ὄφις *serpent*, πρύτανις *president*, and also κόπις, κόρις, μάρις, and ὄρχις.

b. In *feminine* and *common nouns*, ε becomes ι: as, ἡ πόλις, -εως, A. πόλιν (19), ἡ δύναμις *power;* ὁ, ἡ μάντις *prophet.*

c. In *adjectives*, ε becomes˙ υ in *simple*, and η in *compound* words: as, ·

Simple, ἡδύς, -έος, A. ἡδύν (23), γλυκύς *sweet*, ὀξύς *sharp;* *compound*, ἀκρατής, έος (ἀ *not*, κράτος *strength*), *weak*, τριήρης *having three banks of oars*, or, as a substantive (ναῦς, *vessel*, being understood), *trireme.*

EXCEPT a few simple adjectives, in which ε becomes η: as, σαφής, -έος (22), πλήρης *full*, ὑγιής *healthy*, ψευδής *false.*

d. If the last element of a compound ends in -ευς, -ις, or -υς, its form is commonly retained: as in ἀρχ-ιερεύς *high-priest*, φιλό-πολις (Gen. -εως, -ιδος, or -ιος, 218) *patriotic*, δί-πηχυς *two cubits long* (yet contracted in neut. pl., as if formed in -ης, 219: διπήχ(εα)η iv. 2. 28).

214. 2.) In *monosyllables*, ο becomes ου; otherwise ω: as, βοῦς, βοός, A. βοῦν (19); but ἡ αἰδώς, -όος, *shame.*

a. This rule applies also to *linguals* in which ο precedes the stem-mark: as, πούς, ποδός (17), and its compounds; but εἰδώς, -ότος (26).

b. In feminine nouns of more than one syllable, in which the stem ends in ο, the affix ς is absorbed, as if ε (142 a). Thus from the stem ἠχο- is formed the theme ἠχ(ος, οε)ώ (19). So ἡ πειθώ, -όος, *persuasion*, ἡ Λητώ, -όος, *Latona*, &c. Except, as above, αἰδώς, and the Ionic ἡ ἠώς *dawn.* In these words in -ώ and -ώς, the plural and dual are very rare, and only formed according to Dec. 2: as, λεχώ, N. pl. λεχοί; εἰκούς, (224 a).

215. B.) In cases which have *no affix*, ε characteristic becomes ι, υ, or ευ, or else assumes a euphonic ς; and ο *characteristic* becomes οι or ου: thus,

a.) If the theme ends in -ης, ε becomes ες; but, otherwise, is changed as in the theme: thus, Nom. neut. and Voc. σαφές (22), ἡδύ (23); Voc. Σώκρατες, πόλι, πῆχυ, ἱππεῦ (19).

b.) In the theme of *neuter nouns*, ε assumes ς, becoming itself ο (114 b): as, τὸ γένος, -εος (19), τὸ τεῖχος, -εος, *wall.*

EXCEPT τὸ ἄστυ, -εος, *town* (19), the Epic τὸ πῶϋ, -εος, *flock*, and a few foreign names of natural productions in -ι, as τὸ πέπερι, -εως, PEPPER.

§ 217. CHANGES OF STEM-MARK. 161

c.) In the *Vocative*, o becomes οἶ, if the theme ends in ώ or -ώς; but ου, if it ends in -ους: as, ἠχοῖ (19), αἰδοῖ (fr. αἰδώς, 214); βοῦ (19); and in like manner, Οἰδίπου (21, 214 a).

216. a. After the analogy of ε and ο, *a characteristic* becomes αυ in ἡ ναῦς (s. *να*-) *ship*, ἡ γραῦς, γραῦς, *old woman;* and assumes **s** in the theme of *neuters:* as, τὸ γέρας, -αος (19).

For the declension of ναῦς, see 19, 21, 222 f. That of γραῦς agrees with the Dor. forms of ναῦς, as first given, contracting γράας into γραῦς (122 a).

b. In the *Accusative singular* of pures, the inflective **ν** becomes *a* (202 b), except when the theme ends in -ας, -ις, -υς, -αυς, or -ους: as, ἥρωα, ἠχόα, ἱππέα (19); σαφέα (22); but from ὁ λᾶς, *stone*, κίς, οἶς (contracted from ὄϊς), πόλις, ἰχθύς, πῆχυς, ναῦς, βοῦς, Acc. λᾶν; κίν, οἶν, πόλιν, ἰχθύν, πῆχυν, ναῦν, βοῦν (19).

c. Proper names in -ης, -εος, for the most part, admit both forms of the Acc.: as, Σωκράτης (19), Α. Σωκράτη (Plat.), Σωκράτην (Xen.); ὁ Ἄρης, *Mars*, Α. Ἄρη and Ἄρην. So ἥρως, Α. ἥρων Hdt. 1. 167 (ἥρωα 2. 143).

d. When the stem-mark is changed to a *diphthong* before -**s** in the theme, the same change is made before -σι in the *Dative plural:* as, ἱππεῦσι, βουσί, ναυσί (19).

217. These changes in pures indicate the use of certain consonants, as F, Σ, Δ, in their early inflection, to prevent hiatus (100). Of these, F and Σ were afterwards (a) *simply dropped between two vowels* (140; hence, except as above, 216 d, in the Dat. pl., originally ending in -εσι, 12); but otherwise (b) the F, as **ν** (142), *formed a diphthong* with the preceding vowel or (c) *was absorbed* by it; while the Σ (d) *remained* where there was *no affix*, but (e) before the *affixes* -**s** and -**ν** was absorbed, as if ε, by the preceding vowel. If the old stem ended in -εΔ-, three forms afterwards arose: (f) the Δ remained, and the ε became ι throughout by precession (114 d); (g) the Δ was dropped, and ε became ι in the *Nom., Acc.*, *and Voc. sing.;* (h) the Δ was dropped, and ε became ι *throughout*. Thus,

(a) βοFoς βοός *bovis*, ἰχθ(υFoς)ύος, ἱππ(εFες)έες · γέν(εΣος)εος (fr. γένος; cf. Lat. *gĕnŭs, genĕris*, 139), γέρ(αΣος)αος (19); ΔιFος Διός (21; cf. Lat. *divus* and *dīus*, and *boum* for *bovum*), ἠδ(εFος)έος (23); σαφ(εΣος)έος (22).

(b) βοFς βοῦς, βοFν βοῦν, βοF βοῦ, ἱππ(εFς)εύς, ἱππ(εF)εῦ, ἱππεῦσι, ναFς ναῦς *navis*, ναυσί (19). In adjectives, and in a few masculine and neuter nouns, short **υ** takes the place of ευ: as, ἠδεFς ἠδύς, ἠδ(εF)ύ (23); πῆχ(εFς)ὑς, πῆχυν, πῆχυ, ἀστ(εF)υ (19).

(c) ἰχθυFς ἰχθύς, ἰχθ(υF)ύ, but Dat. pl. ἰχθύσι; κιFς (or κιἸς, Kühn.) κῖς (19).

(d) Nom. neut. σαφεΣ σαφές (22), γέν(εΣ)ος (ε passing into a kindred vowel, 114 b), γέρ(αΣ)ας (19); Voc. Σώκρατ(εΣ)ες (19). The peculiar form of the Voc. of ἠχώ and αἰδώς (215 c) may have arisen from the change of **s** to its corresponding ε, and then contraction with precession (142, 118 b); thus, ἠχ(οΣ, οε)οῖ (cf. 214 b).

(e) σαφεΣς σαφής (22), Σωκράτ(εΣς)ης (19), αἰδ(οΣς)ώς (214), ὁ μυΣς μῦς mūs, *mouse*, G. μυΣός μυός mūris (a). For ἠχώ, see 214 b; cf. ἠχοῖ (d).

(f) Μεγαρε-, *Megarian*, had two forms, ΜεγαρεF- masc., and with precession ΜεγαριΔ- fem.; from the former we have Μεγαρεύς, -έως, *Megarian man*, and from the latter (Δ retained and becoming the stem-mark), Μεγαρίς, -ίδος, *Megarian woman* or *land.* This became the prevalent mode of

COMP. GR. K

declining feminines in -ις, if we except abstract nouns in -σις. Especially many fem. adjectives, or words which are properly such, are thus declined.

(g) πόλ(εΔs)ις, πόλ(εΔos)εως, πόλει, πόλιν, πόλι · πόλεις, &c. (19). This became the usual form of fem. pures in -ις, in the Att. and Comm. Greek.

(h) This became the regular form of feminine pures in -ις in the Ionic (130) : thus, Ion. N. -ις, G. -ιος, D. -ιι, commonly contracted into -ῑ, A. -ιν, V. -ι ; Pl. N. -ιες, sometimes contr. into -ῑς, G. -ιων, D. -ισι, A. -ιας, commonly contr. into -ῑς : as, πόλις, πόλιος, πόλῑ, πόλιν · πόλιες, -ιων, πόλισι, πόλιας, -ῑς. The ι was also the prevalent vowel in the Doric.

218. As might have been expected, the three last forms (f, g, h) are far from being kept entirely separate ; and are not wholly restricted to feminines (213 a, b, 215 b). Thus,

1.) Some words exhibit both the lingual and the pure inflection, the latter especially in the Ionic and Doric, which were less averse than the Attic to hiatus (131 s): as, ἡ τρόπις *keel*, G. τρόπεως, τρόπιος, and τροπιδος · particularly proper names, as Ἴσις, G. -ιδος, -ιος Hdt. 2. 41, D. -ιδι, Ἰσῑ Ib. 59 ; Θέτις, G. Θέτιδος Θ. 370, D. Θέτῑ Σ. 407. Compare 207, 211.

2.) In some pures in -ις, the Attic adopts, in whole or in part (particularly in the Gen. sing.), the Ionic forms: as, ἡ τύρσις *turris, tower*, G. τύρσιος vii. 8. 12, but Pl. N. τύρσεις iv. 4. 2, τύρσεων Hel. 4. 7. 6, τύρσεσι Cyr. 7. 5. 10 ; ὁ πόσις *spouse*, G. -ιος, D. -ει · ἡ μάγαδις, -ιος, *a kind of harp*, D. μαγάδῑ vii. 3. 32 ; ὁ, ἡ τίγρις *tigris, tiger*, G. τίγριος, and in later writers τίγριδος, Pl. N. τίγρεις, G. τίγρεων · some proper names, as ὁ Συέννεσις, G. -ιος, i. 2. 12, ὁ Ἴρις, G. -ιος vi. 2. 1 ; and the adjectives ἴδρις *intelligent*, νῆστις *abstemious*. In like manner, ἡ, ὁ ἔγχελυς (217 b) *anguilla, eel*, G. ἐγχέλυος, Pl. N. ἐγχέλεις, G. ἐγχέλεων · τὸ πέπερι (215 b), G. -εως and -ιος.

219. II. CONTRACTION. Most pures in -ας, -ης, -ος, and -ω are contracted in *all* the cases that have *open affixes;* but others, for the most part, only in the *Nom. and Acc. pl.* and *Dat. sing.;* and some, if at all, only in the *Acc. pl.*

a. See 19, and also σαφής (which ἡ τριήρης and like words, properly adjectives, follow, 213 c), ὑγιής, and ἡδύς (22, 23). The common contractions are given in the tables ; and also some in brackets which are rare or doubtful. The contractions there shown are sometimes omitted, and others sometimes occur ; especially in the poets.

b. Of nouns in -ω, the uncontracted form scarcely occurs, even in the poets and dialects. So, in αἰδώς and ἠώς (214 b) : G. -(οοs)οῦς, D. -οῖ, A. -ῶ, V. -οῖ. Cf., in Lat., Dīdō, G. -dūs (92 b), D. A. V. -dō.

c. In proper names in -κλέης, cont. -κλῆς (fr. κλέος *renown*), the Dat. and sometimes Acc. sing. are *doubly* contracted. See Ἡρακλέης (19) ; and for its Attic forms, Mem. 2. 1. 21 – 26. For the later Voc. Ἡρακλες, used in exclamations, cf. 208 f.

d. For the contraction of the Nom. pl. of nouns in -ευς into ῆς, see 121.

e. It is not as often that we wish to pass rapidly over a noun which is the *subject* of a sentence, as over one which is a mere *object*. Hence, as we observe from the tables, the Nominative plural is less frequently contracted than the Accusative.

f. Compare the contracts in -υς, -υος, with the Lat. Dec. 4 :

ἀρκῦς, *net*, -ῠος, -υΐ, -ῠν· Pl. -(υες)ῦς, -ύων, -υσι, -(υας)ῦς.
arcūs, *bow*, -(ŭis)ūs, -uī, -ŭm; Pl. -(ues)ūs, -uum, -ubus, -(ues)ūs.

220. In the Attic and Common Greek, the endings -εος, -εα, and -εας, instead of the common contraction, receive in certain words a peculiar change, which lengthens the last vowel. This change takes place,

a.) In the Gen. sing. of nouns in -ις, -υς and -ευς, and sometimes of nouns in -ι and -υ: as, πόλις, G. πόλεος πόλεως, πῆχυς, -εως, ἱππεύς, -έως, ἄστυ, -εος and -εως (19); πέπερι, -εως (215 b). Also ὁ Ἄρης (213 a), G. Ἄρεος and Ἄρεως.

b.) In the Acc. sing. and pl. of nouns in -ευς: as, ἱππεύς, Acc. sing. ἱππέᾰ ἱππέᾱ, pl. ἱππέᾰς ἱππέᾱς.

c. This change appears to be simply a less perfect and an earlier mode of contraction. From the accentuation of such words as πόλεως, it is evident that the ε (as in Μενέλεως, 120 i) has not the full force of a distinct syllable. We may infer that it commonly united as a species of semivowel (cf. 117 b) with the vowel following, and thus lengthened it.

d. The poets sometimes complete the contraction by synizesis: as, βασιλέως Eur. Alc. 240, Ἀχιλλέα Id. Iph. A. 1341. Instances also occur, in the Attic poets, of the unchanged Gen. in -εος, of the Acc. in -εᾰ and -εᾰς, and of the Acc. sing. regularly contracted into ῇ: as, Νηρέος Eur. Ion 1082, πόλεος Id. Hec. 866; φονέᾱ Ib. 882; ξυγγραφῇ Ar. Ach. 1150, Ὀδυσσῇ Eur. Rh. 708, and even ἱερῇ Id. Alc. 25. The regularly contracted Acc. pl. in -εις, instead of -εᾱς, is sometimes found in Attic writers, and later became the common form: βασιλεῖς Mem. 3. 9. 10.

e. If another vowel precedes, the ε is commonly absorbed by the -ως, -ᾱ, and -ᾱς: as, Πειραιεύς Piraeus, G. Πειρ(αιέως)αιῶς, A. Πειρ(αιέα)αιᾱ.

f. Grammarians give the name *Attic Genitive* to the form in -εως; and also to the Gen. pl. in -εων when accented upon the antepenult, the accent then showing a like use of ε; as, πόλεων (19). The regularly contracted πηχῶν occurs iv. 7. 16.

g. The Gen. in -εως is also found in a few adjectives in -ις (213 d); in ἥμισυς, *half* (G. -εος; later -εως and -ους, and also Neut. pl. -(εα)η); and, in later writers, in other adjectives in -υς (thus, βραχέως Plut.).

DIALECTIC FORMS.

221. (A.) Dialectic changes affecting the AFFIX.

a. In the poets, especially the Epic, the Acc. sing. sometimes ends in -α, in words in which it has commonly -ν; as, εὐρέα Z. 291, νῆα or νέα, πόληα, for εὐρύν, ναῦν, πόλιν· ἰχθύα Theoc. 21. 45. On the other hand, the New Ion. often forms the Acc. of nouns in -ώ or -ώς, -όος, in -οῦν (in the Æol. and stricter Dor. -ων, 130 c): as, Ἰώ Io, ἠώς dawn, A. Ἰοῦν, ἠοῦν.

b. In the Gen. pl., the Ion. sometimes changes -ων to -εων (135 a, cf. 201 c): as, χηνέων Hdt. 2. 45, μυριαδέων, for χηνῶν, μυριάδων.

c. In the Dat. pl., for the common affix -σι(ν, the poets often employ the old or prolonged forms -εσι, -εσσι, and -σσι (186 f, h, 171). Hom. uses the four forms, though -εσι rarely. The forms -εσσι and -εσι are also common in Dor. and Æol. prose; and -εσι is used in Ion. prose after the stem-mark ν. Thus, χερσίν A. 14, χείρεσσι Γ. 271, χείρεσι Τ. 468;

ποσί Ε. 745, ποσσί Β. 44, πόδεσσιν Γ. 407 ; ἔπεσιν Β. 73, ἔπεσσι δ. 597, ἐπέεσσιν Β. 75 ; δαιτυμόνεσι Hdt. 6. 57. So, F dropped between two vowels (217 a), βόεσσι Β. 481, νάεσσι Pind. P. 4. 98, ἀριστήεσσι Α. 227.

d. In the Dual, the Epic prolongs -οιν (as in Dec. 2, 201 b) to -οιῖν : thus, ποδοιῖν Ξ. 228, Σειρήνοιῖν μ. 52.

222. (B.) Dialectic changes affecting the STEM, either simply or in connection with the affix.

a. Many changes result from dialectic preferences of vowels (130 s) : as, Ion. θώρηξ, νηῦς, γρηῦς, for θώραξ, &c. : Dor. ποιμάν, ὠκύτᾶς, νᾶες, for ποιμήν, &c. ; χήρ for χείρ ; ὡς, βῶς, ἀχῶς, for οὗς, βοῦς, ἠ;ώ;ς ; for κλείς key, Dor. (κλᾶFις clāvis) κλᾶῖς, Ion. κληῖς, Old Att. κλῂς.

b. The dialects and poets vary greatly in the extent to which they employ contraction, and in the mode of contraction (131). The Epic has here especial license. In the poets, contractions are often made by synizesis (117 b), which are not written. In respect to the usage of Homer, we remark as follows : (1) In the Gen. sing., contraction is commonly omitted, except in nouns in -ώ and -ώς, G. -όος. In a few instances, -εος is contracted into -ευς (131 b), or synizesis occurs : as, Ἐρέβευς Θ. 368, θέρευς η. 118 ; Πηλέος Α. 489, πόλῖος Β. 811. (2) In the Dat. sing., both the contracted and uncontracted forms are freely used in most words : as, γήραϊ and γήραι or γήρᾳ (119), τείχεϊ and τείχει, ἥρωϊ and ἥρῳ Η. 453. See 21. The endings -υι, -νι, and -οι are almost always contracted : as, κνήστι Λ. 640, νέκυι Π. 526, ἠοῖ Ι. 618. (3) The endings -εα, -εων, and -εας are commonly uncontracted, except by synizesis : as, θεοειδέ'α Γ. 27, ἄλγεα Ω. 7, νέα ι. 283; στηθέων Κ. 95 ; πολέας Α. 559. So πόλῖας θ. 560 ; but Τυδῆ Δ. 384, Ὀδυσῆ τ. 136 (21 ; so βασιλῆ Oracle in Hdt. 7. 220). (4) The ending -εες is used both with and, oftener, without contraction : as, πρωτοπαγεῖς νεοτευχέες Ε. 194. (5) The neut. plur. ending -αα, with scarce an exception, is contracted or drops one α (cf. d) : as, κέρα, δέπα, γέρα Β. 237. The form with the single short α sometimes occurs in the Attic poets : as, κρέα Ar. Pax 192.

c. In *common nouns in* -εύς, the characteristic εF before a vowel regularly becomes η, in the Epic : as, ἱππῆος, ἱππῆες (21 ; ἱππεῖς Α. 151, and βασιλεῖς Hes. Op. 246, are doubtful). Doubtful examples of this change appear in Hdt. (βασιλῆος, βασιλῆα, 7. 137, &c.) ; while the regular inflection of these nouns in Ion. prose, and in the Dor., is in -έος, &c. In proper names in -εύς, the Epic has much freedom in using the long or short vowel according to the metre. So in Ἄρης and πόλις (21). These Ep. and Ion. forms are not wholly unknown to Att. poetry, or even prose.

d. In words whose root ends in εε-, the Epic often unites these vowels into η (as regularly in proper names in -κλέης), or into ει ; but sometimes protracts the first ε into ει or η. In many instances, the root is shortened by the poets, or in dialectic prose, by dropping one ε. E. g., forms of κλέος, *fame*, and of its compounds in -εης, κλεῖα Hes. Th. 100, κλέα Ι. 189, ἐϋκλείας Κ. 281, εὐκλέας Pind. O. 2. 163, ἀκληεῖς Μ. 318, ἀγακλῆος Π. 738, δυσκλέα Β. 115 (so εὐρρεῖος Ζ. 508, ὑπερδέα P. 330, but ἐπιδεέες Hdt. 4. 130 ; see σπέος and Πάτροκλος, 21).

e. In κέρας and τέρας (207), the τ is commonly omitted in dialectic Greek ; and then in these, as in other neuters in -ας, -αος, the later Ionic often changes α into ε except in the theme : as, κέρεος, γέρεα, Hdt.

f. In ναῦς (ναFς, nāvis, 217 b, 19, 21), the original α remains throughout in the Dor. ; but in the Ion. passes by precession either into η, or with short quantity, especially in the later Ion., into ε. The Att. retains the α in the diphthong αυ, but has otherwise η or ε (the latter having apparently been inserted in the Gen. sing. and pl. after the contraction of ᾶο and ᾶω, 120 i; and the Gen. dual having followed the analogy of the other numbers). In the Att. poets, the Ion. forms occur rarely, the Dor. oftener: as, νηός Eur. Iph. T. 1385, ναός Soph. Ant. 715.

IV. IRREGULAR NOUNS.

223. Irregularities in the declension of nouns, which have not been already noticed, may be chiefly referred to two heads: *variety of declension*, and *defect of declension*.

A. VARIETY OF DECLENSION.

a. A noun may vary, (1.) in its *stem*; (2.) in its *method* of declension; and (3.) in its *gender* (180). In the first case, it is termed a *metaplast* (μεταπλαστός, *transformed*); in the second, a *heteroclite* (ἑτερόκλιτος, *of different declensions*); in the third, *heterogeneous* (ἑτερογενής, *of different genders*).

b. Words which have distinct double forms, either throughout or in part, are termed *redundant*. Those, on the other hand, that want some of the usual forms, are termed *defective*.

224. 1. METAPLASTS.

Metaplasm has mostly arisen from a change of the stem, in the progress of the language, for the sake of euphony or emphasis, chiefly by the precession of an open vowel, or the addition of a consonant to prevent hiatus; while, at the same time, forms have remained from the old stem, especially in the poets and in the dialects. The double stem may be,

a.) In ον- and in ο- (cf. 140, 211): ἡ ἀηδών, -όνος, *nightingale;* from the stem ἀηδο-, G. ἀηδοῦς Soph. Aj. 629, D. ἀηδοῖ Ar. Av. 679: ἡ εἰκών, -όνος, *image;* (s. εἰκο-) G. εἰκοῦς Eur. Hel. 77, A. εἰκώ Hdt. 7. 69; Pl. A. εἰκούς Ar. Nub. 559: ἡ χελῑδών, -όνος, *swallow;* (s. χελιδο-) V. χελιδοῖ.

b.) In α- and in -ε (ε- esp. Ion., 222 c): τὸ βρέτας, -εος, *wooden image,* poet.: τὸ κνέφας, *darkness*, G. Ep. κνέφαος, Att. κνέφους Ar. Eccl. 291.

c.) In F- and Fατ-: τὸ γόνυ, γόνατος, genu, KNEE, and τὸ δόρυ, -ατος (s. δορF-, δορ- 140, δορυ- 142, δουρ- 145, δορFατ-, δορατ-, δουρατ-), *spear*. For the forms of δόρυ, see 21. Those which occur of γόνυ correspond: Ion. and poet. γούνατος, -ατα, -άτων, -ασι; also poet. γουνός, γοῦνα, &c.

d.) With and without α- final: ὁ κάλως, *cable*, (s. καλα-, Att. Dec. 2), G. κάλω · Ion. κάλος, -ου, ε. 260 and Hdt.; in later Ep., Pl. κάλωες, &c.

e. Lingual and Pure: ὁ, ἡ ὄρνῑς, *bird*, G. ὄρνιθος (Dor. ὄρνῑχος, 168), D. ὄρνῑθι, A. ὄρνῑν and ὄρνῑθα · Pl. ὄρνῑθες, &c.; (s. ὀρνε-) N. ὄρνῑς, A. ὄρνῑν, Pl. N. ὄρνεις, G. ὄρνεων, A. ὄρνεις and ὄρνῑς (218); also τὸ ὄρνεον, -ου: ὁ σής, *moth*, G. σεός and later σητός: ὁ χρώς, *skin, surface*, -ωτός, -ωτί (χρῴ, 207 a), &c.; Ion. and poet. G. χροός, D. χροΐ, A. χρόα.

f.) Variously Double: δορυξ(όος)οῦς and -ξός Ar. Pax 447, -οῦ, *spear-maker:* Ζεύς (s. ΖεF-, ΔιF-, Ζαν-); see 21, and cf. Lat. Jupiter (Ζεῦ πάτερ Γ. 276), Jovis, divus: ὁ θεράπων, -οντος, *attendant;* poet. A. θέραπα, N. pl. θέραπες Eur. Ion 94: τὸ φάος, -εος -ους Cyr. 4. 2. 26, *light*, poet.; contr. φῶς, φωτός: ὁ, ἡ φάρυγξ, -υγγος, poet. -ύγος ι. 373, *throat:* ὁ Φόρκυς, -ῠος and -ῡνος, Phorcys: ἡ χείρ, *hand*, G. χειρός and χερός, &c. (for the common forms, see 18; for the rest, the poets and Ion. prose).

g. ἡ Θέμις, *Themis*, as a common noun, *right*, *law*, G. Θέμιδος, Ep. Θέμιστος β. 68, Ion. Θέμιος Hdt. 2. 50, Dor. Θέμιτος Pind. O. 13. 11, also Pl. Rep. 380 a. In the Attic, θέμις occurs mostly in certain forms of expression, where it is used without declension, as an adjective or neuter noun : thus, θέμις ἐστί, *it is lawful;* φασί . . . θέμις εἶναι, *they say that it is lawful*, Pl. Gorg. 505 d ; τὸ μὴ θέμις, *that which is not lawful*, Æsch.

h. ἡ πνύξ (s. πυκν-, as in adj. πυκνός, *crowded;* by met., from the difficulty of appending ς in the theme, πνυκ-), G. πυκνός and later πνυκός.

i. Poetic, mostly Epic, forms (with the themes to which they are referred or allied, in parentheses) : A. pl. Αἰθιοπῆας A. 423 (ὁ Αἰθίοψ, -οπος, *Ethiopian*) ; ἡ δώς Hes. Op. 354 (δόσις *gift*) ; G. λιβός Æsch. Ch. 292, A. λίβα Id. Fr. 49 (ἡ λιβάς *libation*) ; ὁ λῖς O. 275 (λέων *lion*).

j. Many prolonged forms are used in poetry or dialectic prose : as, Ἀθηναία, σεληναία, Πηνελόπεια, for Ἀθηνᾶ Minerva, σελήνη *moon*, Πηνελόπη.

225. 2. HETEROCLITES.

a. Of the FIRST and SECOND DECLENSIONS. Some *personal nouns* have forms both in -ος and in -ης or -ας, particularly compounds of ἄρχω (where the form in -ος is usually more Att.) : as, ὁ γυμνασίαρχος and -άρχης, *gymnasiarch;* ὁ ἀδολέσχης and -ος, *prater*.

b. Of the FIRST and THIRD DECLENSIONS : ὁ Ἅιδης, -ου, poet. Ἀΐδης, *Hades;* Dec. 3, Ep. G. Ἄϊδος, D. Ἄϊδι · also poet. Ἀϊδωνεύς, -έως, Ion. -ῆος : ἡ γυνή (203 a) : ὁ λᾶας, contr. λᾶς, *lapis, stone*, G. λᾶος M. 462, and λάου Soph. O. C. 196, D. λᾶϊ, A. λᾶαν, λᾶν, and λᾶα, Pl. N. λᾶες, &c.

c. Some *personal derivatives* have double forms in -της, -του, and in -τήρ, -τῆρος, or -τωρ, -τορος : as, οἰκητής, οἰκητήρ, and οἰκήτωρ, *dweller*.

d. Add some *proper names*, mostly in -ης, of which a part admit a double formation throughout, as Θαλῆς, Θάλεω (198. 2 ; late -οῦ) and Θάλητος · but others only in part : as, Τισσαφέρνης, -ους, but ὦ Τισσαφέρνη ii. 5. 3 ; Στρεψιάδης, -ου, but ὦ Στρεψιάδες Ar. Nub. 1206.

e. Add, also, the Epic D. pl. ἀγκαλίδεσσι Σ. 555 (ἡ ἀγκάλη *arm*) ; D. ἀλκί (always in the phrase ἀλκὶ πεποιθώς) E. 299 (ἀλκή *might*) ; ἡ ἅρπαξ Hes. Op. 354 (ἁρπαγή *robbery*) ; D. ὑσμῖνι Θ. 56 (ὑσμίνη *battle*) ; A. φύγα (only in φύγαδε, *to flight*) Θ. 157 (ἡ φυγή *flight*).

f. Of the SECOND and THIRD DECLENSIONS : τὸ δάκρυον and poet. δάκρυ (14), *lacrima* (168 a), *tear*, G. δακρύου, D. δακρύῳ · Pl. N. δάκρυα, G. δακρύων, D. δακρύοις and δάκρυσι Th. 7. 75 : τὸ δένδρος, -ου, and Ion. δένδρεον, *tree;* Dec. 3, D. δένδρει, A. δένδρος Hdt. 6. 79 ; Pl. N. δένδρη, D. more Attic form δένδρεσι iv. 8. 2, Th. 2. 75, but δένδροις iv. 7. 9 : ὁ μόσσυν, -υνος, *wooden tower*, D. μόσσυνι v. 4. 26 ; Dec. 2, D. pl. μοσσύνοις Ib.: ὁ ὄνειρος and τὸ ὄνειρον, *dream* (fr. ὄναρ, 228 a), G. ὀνείρου and ὀνείρατος · Pl. ὀνείρατα and sometimes ὄνειρα : Πάτροκλος (21) : τὸ πῦρ, πυρός (14), *fire;* Dec. 2, Pl. N. πυρά, *watch-fires*, D. πυροῖς vii. 2. 18.

g. Some *contracts in -ους* of Dec. 2 have also forms, mostly late, like those of βοῦς (19) : as, ὁ νοῦς *mind*, ὁ πλοῦς *voyage*, G. νοός, 1 Cor. 14. 19, πλοός Acts 27. 9, D. νοΐ Rom. 7. 25 ; ἡ πρόχους *ewer*, D. pl. πρόχουσι Ar.

h. Some *verbals* have double forms in -ος, -ον, and -εύς, -έως, or -τήρ, -τῆρος : as, ὁ πομπός and πομπεύς, *guide*, ὁ ἰατρός and poet. ἰατήρ, *healer*.

i. Add the poetic D. pl. ἀνδραπόδεσσι H. 475 (τὸ ἀνδράποδον *slave*) ; ὁ ἔρος Ξ. 315, A. ἔρον I. 92 (ἔρως, -ωτος, *love*) ; A. οἶκα, only in οἴκαδε, *homeward*, Hom., and even in Att. prose, vii. 7. 57 (ὁ οἶκος *house*).

j. Of the ATTIC SECOND and THIRD DECLENSIONS : ἡ ἅλως *threshing-floor*, G. ἅλω, ἅλωνος, and poet. ἅλωος · also Ep. ἡ ἀλωή · ἡ ἕως *dawn* (s. ἀ-), G. ἕω, D. ἕῳ, A. ἕω (199) ; Dor. ἀώς (s. ἀο-), G. ἀ(όος)οῦς · Ion. ἠώς, G. ἠοῦς, D. ἠοῖ, A. ἠῶ and ἠοῦν (221 a) ; ὁ Μίνως, -ω and -ωος, *Minos*.

226. 3. Heterogeneous Nouns.

The names of things without life naturally vary in gender, according to the conceptions formed by the mind (175). Hence there are many words in which two genders are associated, either throughout or in part; chiefly the neuter, as the natural gender of things without life, with the masculine or feminine, the genders of personification. E. g.

a. Of Dec. I. ἡ τιάρα or ὁ τιάρας Hdt. 1. 132, tiāra *or* tiāras, *turban*.

b. Of Dec. II. ὁ δεσμός *band*, Pl. τὰ δεσμά, οἱ δεσμοί, and poet. τὰ δέσματα · τὸ ζυγόν and ὁ ζυγός, *yoke*, Pl. τὰ ζυγά · ὁ σῖτος *corn*, Pl. τὰ σῖτα · τὸ στάδιον *stadium*, Pl. τὰ στάδια and οἱ στάδιοι · ὁ σταθμός *station, balance*, Pl. οἱ σταθμοί and τὰ σταθμά *stations*, τὰ σταθμά *balances*: ὁ Τάρταρος (ἡ Pind. P. 1. 29), Pl. τὰ Τάρταρα, Tartarus, Tartara.

c. Things, when viewed *collectively*, seem least akin to persons; and other masculines and feminines occur with which a neuter pl. is associated (chiefly in the poets and dialects): ὁ δρυμός *thicket*, ὁ ἔπαυλος *stall*, ὁ ἰός *arrow*, ἡ κέλευθος *way*, ὁ κύκλος *circle*, ὁ ῥύπος *filth*, and others.

d. Of Dec. III. τὸ ἄορ, ἄορος, poet., *sword*; A. pl. ἄορας ? *p.* 222: τὸ πλῆθος, -εος, and less common ἡ πληθύς, -ύος, *fulness*: τὸ κάρα and (Soph. Ph. 1457) κράτα, *head*, poet., G. κρατός (τῆς, Eur. El. 140), D. κρᾶτί and κάρᾳ Soph. El. 445, A. like N. and also masc. κρᾶτα Soph. Ph. 1207, pl. κρᾶτας Eur. Ph. 1149. The following forms are found in Homer:

S. N. A. κάρη, κάρ Π. 392,
G. κάρητος   καρήατος κρᾶτός   κράατος κρήθεν λ. 588 κάρηνου
D. κάρητι O. 75 καρήατι κρᾶτί μ. 99   κράατι χ. 218   Mar. 12
P. N. A. κάρᾱ Cer. 12 καρήατα κρᾶτα θ. 92 κράατα T. 93   κάρηνα
G.   P. 437   κρᾶτων χ. 309   καρήνων
D.   κρᾶσί, κράτεσφι, K. 152, 156   A. 44

e. Of Dec. I. and II. τὸ δρέπανον and ἡ δρεπάνη, *sickle*; ἡ ἑσπέρα, Ep. ὁ ἕσπερος, vespera and vesper, *evening* (also τὰ ἕσπερα *p.* 191): ἡ πλάνη and ὁ πλάνος, *error*; ἡ πλευρά and τὸ πλευρόν, *rib*.

f. Of Dec. I. and III. ἡ βλάβη and τὸ βλάβος, -εος, *injury*; ἡ δίψα and τὸ δίψος, *thirst*; ἡ νάπη and τὸ νάπος, *dell*; ἡ στέγη and τὸ στέγος, *roof*.

g. Of Dec. II. and III. ὁ ἀστήρ, -ερος, and τὸ ἄστρον, astrum, STAR; ὁ and τὸ σκότος (also ἡ σκοτία), *darkness*; ὁ and τὸ σκύφος, *cup*.

B. Defect of Declension.

227. a. Some nouns receive *no declension*, as the names of the letters, some foreign proper names, and a few other words, chiefly foreign: thus, τό, τοῦ, τῷ ἄλφα · ὁ, τοῦ, τῷ, τὸν Ἀβραάμ · τό, τοῦ, τῷ πάσχα, *passover*. A word of this kind is termed *indeclinable*, or an *aptote* (ἄπτωτος, *without cases*).

b. A few shortened or foreign proper names, whose stem ends with a vowel, receive ς in the Nom., ν in the Acc., and, if the vowel admits it, an iota subscript in the Dat., but have no further declension: as,

Γλοῦς (21) ii. 1. 3; ὁ Διονῦς (fr. Διόνυσος, *Bacchus*), A. Διονῦν, G. D. V. Διονῦ · ὁ Μηνᾶς (fr. Μηνόδωρος) Th. 5. 19, D. Μηνᾷ, A. Μηνᾶν, G. V. Μηνᾶ · ὁ Μάσκας, D. Μάσκᾳ, A. Μάσκαν, G. V. Μάσκα, i. 5. 4.

c. Many nouns are defective in *number*. Thus,

1. Many nouns, from their signification, want the *plural:* as, ὁ, ἡ αἰθήρ, æther, τὸ ἔλαιον oleum, OIL, ἡ ταχυτής, *swiftness*. Proper and abstract nouns do not require a plural, except when employed as common nouns.

2. The names of *festivals*, some names of *cities*, and a few other words want the *singular*: as, τὰ Διονύσια *the feast of Bacchus*, αἱ Ἀθῆναι Athēnæ, *Athens*, οἱ Δελφοί Delphi, οἱ ἐτησίαι *the trade-winds*.

228. Some nouns are employed only in particular *cases*, and these, it may be, occurring only in certain forms of expression: as,

a. Neut. Nom. and Acc.: **ὄναρ** *sleep, dream*, **ὕπαρ** *waking, reality;* **ὄφελος** *advantage;* **τέκμαρ** and Ep. τέκμωρ, *mark:* Poet., **δέμας** instar, *body, form;* **ἦδος** *pleasure;* **δῶ** (s. δωμ-, 160) A. 426 (τὸ δῶμα domus, *house*), pl. Hes. Th. 933; **κρῖ** (s. κριθ-, cf. βρῖ, ῥᾷ, 238 b) Θ. 564 (ἡ κρῖθή *barley*).

b. Neut. **λίπα** *with oil*, indecl., chiefly as Dat. ς. 227; Du. N. and A. **ὄσσε** *eyes*, poet., M. 466, Pl. ὄσσων, ὄσσοις, Eur. Hec. 915, 1105.

c. Fem. G. **μάλης** (μασχάλη, ala, axilla, *arm-pit*), in the phrase ὑπὸ μάλης, *under the arm, secretly*, Hel. 2. 3. 23; D. **δαῖ** (ῖ) *battle*, Ep., N. 286.

d. Dat. **λιτί**, Ep., Σ. 352, A. sing. or pl. λῖτα Θ. 441 (τὸ λίνον linum, LINEN); Voc. masc. and fem. **ὦ μέλε**, *my friend*, in familiar address, Ar. Lys. 157; Voc. **ὦ τάν** or τᾶν (also written ὦ 'ταν or ὦταν), *my good sir* (ὁ ἔτης, -ου, *comrade*), Attic, Pl. Apol. 25 c.

e. A word which is only employed in a *single* case, is termed a *monoptote* (μόνος *single*, πτῶσις *case*); in *two* cases, a *diptote;* in *three,* a *triptote;* in *four*, a *tetraptote*.

CHAPTER III.

DECLENSION OF ADJECTIVES.

(For paradigms, see 22 – 26, 28.)

229. Adjectives are declined like substantives, except so far as they vary their form to denote variation of gender (173 s). In this respect, they are divided into three classes, *adjectives of one, of two*, and *of three terminations*.

a. In adjectives of more than one termination, the *masculine* is regarded as the primary gender, and the stem, theme, and declension of the masculine, as the general stem, theme, and declension of the word. The mode of declining an adjective is commonly marked by subjoining to the theme the other forms of the Nom. sing., or their endings; and, if necessary, the form of the Gen. sing. Thus, **ἄδικος**, -ον · σαφής, -ές · μῶρος, -ᾱ, -ον · ὁ, ἡ δίπους, -οδος, τὸ δίπουν.

230. I. ADJECTIVES OF ONE TERMINATION are declined precisely like nouns, and therefore require no separate rules or paradigms. They are chiefly confined to the masculine and feminine genders, or even to one of these. E. g.

Dec. 1, ὁ γεννάδας, -ου, *noble*, ὁ μονίας, -ου, *solitary*, ὁ ἐθελοντής, -οῦ, *voluntary*: Dec. 3, ὁ γυμνής, -ῆτος, *light-armed;* ἡ μανιάς, -άδος, *frantic*, ὁ, ἡ ἄπαις, -αιδος, *childless*, ὁ, ἡ δρομάς, -άδος, *running*, ὁ, ἡ ἧλιξ, -ικος, *of the same age*, ὁ, ἡ ἡμιθνής, -ῆτος, *half dead*.

a. In indirect cases of Dec. 3, where all the genders have the same form, such adjectives are sometimes employed in poetry (rarely in prose) as neuter: as, μανιάσιν λυσσήμασιν, *with frantic ravings*, Eur. Or. 270; δρομάδι κώλῳ, *with swift limb*. A neuter is sometimes supplied from a kindred or derived root: as, ὁ, ἡ ἅρπαξ, -αγος, *rapacious*, τὸ ἁρπακτικόν.

231. II. In ADJECTIVES OF TWO TERMINATIONS (22), the *masculine* and *feminine* agree, but the *neuter* differs in those cases which have special neuter affixes.

a. It is only in Dec. 2 and 3 that adjectives can have a neuter (176 s); and in Dec. 3, labials and palatals do not form it, on account of the maiming of the stem which this would require (160).

b. The neuter must have *two distinct forms*, and can have only two, one for the direct cases sing., and the other for the direct cases pl. (181). Hence, every complete adjective must have two terminations. A neut. pl. is sometimes given, though rarely, to adjectives which do not form the neut. sing.: as, τέκεα πατρὸς ἀπάτορα, 'fatherless,' Eur. Herc. 114.

c. In δίπους (22), and similar compounds of πούς, *foot*, the neut. sing., on account of the difficulty of forming it from the stem, is formed from the theme, after the analogy of contracts of Dec. 2 (23): thus, ὁ, ἡ τρίπους, -οδος, *three-footed*, τὸ τρίπουν. Some of these compounds have secondary, chiefly poetic, forms in Dec. 2: as, τρίπος X. 164, Ἶρις ἀελλόπος.

232. III. ADJECTIVES OF THREE TERMINATIONS (23 s) differ from those of two in having a distinct form for the *feminine*. It is only in Dec. 1 that the feminine has a separate form. These adjectives, therefore, are of two declensions, adding the *feminine* forms of the *first* to the *masculine* and *neuter* of the *second* or *third;* as follows:

RULE I. If the theme belongs to the *second declension*, the feminine affixes of the first are annexed to the *simple stem*.

a. If the stem ends in ε, ι, ρ, or ρο, the feminine is declined like θεά· otherwise, like ᾠδή (15): as, μῶρᾱ, μωρᾶς· σοφή, σοφῆς· χρυσέᾱ, διπλοή (23); φίλιος, -ᾱ, -ον, *friendly*, ἀθρόος, -ᾱ, -ον, *dense;* καλός, -ή, -όν, *beautiful;* δῖος dīvus, *divine*, F. δίᾱ, Ep. and Lyr. δίᾰ.

233. RULE II. If the theme belongs to the *third declension*, the feminine affixes of the first are annexed to the *stem modified by the consonant I*:

a. After ε or a liquid, I became ι, which was contracted, either directly or through transposition, with the preceding vowel (142 a): as, ἡδε- (ἡδεI-) ἡδεῖα, μελαν- (μελανI-) μέλαινα (23).

b. The ι united with a preceding τ to form σ (143 b) : as, παντ- (παντἰ- πανσ-) πᾶσα, χαριεντ- (χαριεντἰ- χαριενσ-) χαρίεσσα (23, 155, 156) ; λυοντ- (λυονσ-) λύουσα, θεντ- (θενσ-) θεῖσα (26).

c. In *perfect participles*, this σ united, as ε, with a preceding ο, to form υι : as, εἰδοτ- (εἰδοτἰ- εἰδοσ- εἰδοε-, 142) εἰδυῖα (26).

a. The σ remained, if the ο had already been contracted with another vowel : as, ἑσταοτ- ἑστωτ- ἑστῶσα (26). Here the neuter has not only the contracted ἐστ(αός)ώς, but also the syncopated ἐστός.

d. If the stem, after these changes, ends in ι or ρ, the feminine is declined like μυῖα · but, if it ends in σ or ν, like μοῦσα or τράπεζα : as, ἡδεῖᾰ, ἡδείᾱς · πᾶσᾰ, πάσης · μέλαινᾰ, μελαίνης (23).

e. For the fem. termination -ειᾰ, the shorter -ἐᾰ (a added to the simple stem) is commonly used in Ion. prose, and sometimes in Ep. and other poetry (sometimes Ion. -ἰη, especially in Hipp.) : as, βαθέα, εὑρέα Hdt. 1. 178, βαθέην Ib. 75, βαθέης E. 147. The poets, in a few instances, prolong -ἐα of the neut. pl. to -εῖα for the sake of the metre (134 a) : as, ὀξεῖα Hes. Sc. 348, ἀδεῖα Soph. Tr. 122 (so σκιόειν for σκιόεν, Ap. Rh. 2. 404).

234. Of those words which belong to the general class of ADJECTIVES (173), the following have three terminations :

1.) All *participles* : as, λύων, θείς, λύσας, εἰδώς (26).

a. In *participles*, which partake of the verb and the *adjective*, a distinction must be made between the *stem*, *affix*, *connecting vowel*, and *flexible ending* of *conjugation*, and those of *declension* : thus, in Gen. λύοντος, the stem of conjugation is λυ-, and the affix -οντος · while the stem of declension is λυοντ-, and the affix -ος.

2.) All *comparatives and superlatives in* -ος : as, σοφώτερος, -ᾱ, -ον, *wiser ;* σοφώτατος, -η, -ον, *wisest*.

3.) All *numerals*, except cardinals from 2 to 100 inclusive : as, διακόσιοι, -αι, -α, *two hundred*, τρίτος, -η, -ον, *third*.

4.) The *article* and *adjective pronouns* (28), except τίς (τἰς).

5.) Of adjectives commonly so called, *simples in* -ος, -εις, and -υς, with some others : as, μῶρος, σοφός, χαρίεις, ἡδύς, πᾶς, μέλας (23) ; ἑκών, -οῦσα, -όν, *willing ;* τάλας, -αινα, -αν, *wretched*.

b. For the most part, *simples* in -ος have *three* terminations, and *compounds*, but *two*. Yet some compounds have three, and many simples, particularly derivatives in -ειος, -ιος, and -ιμος, have but two. Derivatives from compound verbs, as being themselves uncompounded, especially those in -ικός, -τός, and -τέος, have more commonly three terminations. A distinct fem. is most found in oxytones, and least in proparoxytones. In many words, usage is variable (d, e, f).

c. Adjectives in -ως, of the Attic Dec. 2, have but two terminations : as, ἀγήρως (22), ὁ, ἡ εὔγεως, τὸ εὔγεων, *fertile*. For πλέως, see 236.

d. In words in which the fem. has commonly a distinct form, the form of the masc. is sometimes employed in its stead : as, Adjectives in -ος (particularly in Att. writers, 174 b), δῆλος Eur. Med. 1197, ἀναγκαῖον Th. 1. 2 ; Adjectives in -υς and -εις (chiefly in the poets), ἡδύς μ. 369, γενεὰν θηλύν, *female sex*, Eur. Med. 1083 ; Comparatives, Superlatives, Participles, and Pronouns (all rarely, except in the dual, e), ἀπορώτερος Th. 5. 110, ὀλοώτατος δ. 442, τιθέντες Æsch. Ag. 560.

§ 236. IRREGULAR DECLENSION. 171

e. This use of the masc. form for the fem. is particularly frequent in the *dual*, in which, from its limited use, the distinction of gender is least important : as, τὼ χεῖρε, *the two hands*, vi. 1. 8 (the fem. form τά is especially rare, Soph. Ant. 769) ; τούτω τὼ ἡμέρᾳ, *these two days*, Cyr. 1. 2. 11 ; ἰδόντε καὶ παθοῦσα Soph. O. C. 1676 ; πληγέντε Θ. 455.

f. On the other hand, a distinct form is sometimes given to the fem. in words in which it is commonly the same with the masc. : as, ἀθανάτη K. 404, αὐτόμαται iv. 3. 8. This use is especially Epic and Lyric.

235. To some adjectives, feminine forms are supplied from a kindred or derived stem. These forms may be either required to complete the adjective, or they may be only special feminines, used (particularly in poetry and the dialects) by the side of forms of the common gender (174 b). The feminines thus supplied most frequently end in -ις, G. -ιδος (217 f), but also in -ας, G. -αδος, in -εια, -ειρα, &c. Thus,

a. Masculines in -ης of Dec. 1, and in -εύς of Dec. 3, have often corresponding feminines in -ις, -ιδος. These words are chiefly patrials and gentiles, or other personal designations, and are commonly used as substantives. Thus, ὁ πολίτης, -ου, *belonging to a city* (θεοὶ πολῖται Æsch. Th. 253), *citizen*, ἡ πολῖτις, -ιδος · ὁ Μεγαρεύς, -έως, ἡ Μεγαρίς, *Megarian*.

b. The compounds of **ἔτος** *year* (in -ης, -ες of Dec. 3, but sometimes in -ης, G. -ου of Dec. 1), have often a special fem. in -ις, -ιδος : as, ὁ, ἡ ἑπτέτης, τὸ ἑπτέτες, *seven years old*, and ἡ ἑπτέτις, -ιδος.

c. Some compounds in -της, -ες have a poetic (particularly Epic) fem. in -εια : as, ἠριγενής, -ές, *early-born*, ἡ ἠριγένεια A. 477 ; ἡδυέπεια, Hes. Th.

d. Add ὁ, ἡ πίων, and ἡ πίειρα, τὸ πῖον, *fat* ; ὁ πρέσβυς, *old, venerable*, fem., chiefly poet., πρέσβα, πρέσβειρα, and πρεσβηΐς · ὁ, ἡ μάκαρ, and ἡ μάκαιρα, *blessed*, poet. ; and some others.

236. IRREGULAR ADJECTIVES. Among the adjectives which deserve special notice are the following :

a. μέγας *great*, and πολύς *much* (24). In these adjectives, the Nom. and Acc. sing. masc. and neut. are formed from the stems μεγα- and πολε-, according to Dec. 3. The other cases are formed from the stems μεγαλ- and πολλ-, according to Dec. 1 and 2. The Voc. μεγάλε occurs once, Æsch. Th. 822. From its signification, πολύς has no dual. In Hdt., the forms from πολλός prevail throughout, yet not exclusively.

b. ὁ πλέως, ἡ πλέα, τὸ πλέων, *full*. The masc. and neut. are formed from s. πλα-, according to the Attic Dec. 2 (200) ; the fem. is formed from s. πλε- (with Nom. pl. πλέα in imitation of masc., according to some editors, Soph. El. 1405). Ion. πλέος plenus, Ep. πλεῖος, -η, -ον. So, likewise, in Att. writers, the neut. pl. πλέα Cyr. 7. 4. 6, and the pl. compounds ἔμπλεοι, ἔκπλεα. In like manner ἵλεα N. pl. from ἵλεως.

c. ὁ πρᾶος (24 ; by some written πρᾷος, 109 a), *mild*, borrows fem. and plur. forms from πρᾶΰς, which occurs Pind. Py. 3. 125.

d. ὁ, ἡ σῶς, τὸ σῶν, *safe*. In this adj., contract forms from s. σα- are blended with forms from s. σω- (contr. from σαο-), belonging partly to Dec. 2, and partly to Dec. 3. Thus,

	ὁ, ἡ		τὸ	
S. N.	(σαος)σῶς Ar.	σῶος iii. 1. 32	σῶα Hel.	(σαον)σῶν vii. 6.
A.	(σαον)σῶν Th.	σῶον Lys. 109. 3	σῶαν Dem.	σῶον Hdt. [32.
P. N.	ii. 2. 21 σῶοι,	(σῶες) σῶς Dem.	σῶαι Hdt.	(σαα)σᾶ Eur.
A.	Luc. σώους, (σῶας) σῶς Dem. 93. 24.			σῶα Hel. 1.1.24.

In Hom., forms from σόος prevail, τ. 300. With the above may be compared the Homeric (ζαος) ζώς E. 87, Acc. ζώ/ II. 445, = ζωός, ζωόν, *living* (iii. 4. 5).

237. a. Some adjectives vary in the mode of declension from the same stem: as,

Dec. 1 and 3, κελαινώπαν Soph. Aj. 954, and κελαινώπεσσι Pind. P. 4. 377, *dark*; Dec. 2 and 3, ἀλάστωρ *accursed*, ἀλαστόροισιν Soph. Ant. 974.

b. In compounds of **γέλως** *laughter*, and **κέρας** *horn*, we find both the Att. Dec. 2 and Dec. 3: as, φιλόγελως, -ων, G. -ω and -ωτος, *laughter-loving*, βούκερω παρθένου, 'heifer-horned,' Æsch. Pr. 588. Shorter forms also occur, according to the common Dec. 2: as, νήκεροι *hornless*, Hes. Op. 527.

c. Adjectives in -ις vary in declension like substantives (118).

d. Among other examples of *varied inflection*, we notice the Homeric ὁ ἐΰς B. 819, and ἠΰς II. 464, *good, brave*, τὸ ἐΰ, εὖ, and ἠΰ, G. ἐῆος A. 393 (cf. 222 c), A. ἐΰν and ἠΰν, G. pl. neuter ἐάων Ω. 528; ὁ **ἐρίηρος** Δ. 266, *trusty*, Pl. ἐρίηρες, ἐρίηρας, Γ. 47, 378; ὁ **πολύρρηνος** λ. 257, *rich in sheep*, Pl. πολύρρηνες I. 154 (cf. πολύαρνι, 238 d); **αἰπύς ὄλεθρος** N. 773, Ἴλιον αἰπύ O. 71, Ἴλιος αἰπεινή N. 773, πόλιν αἰπήν N. 625, αἰπὰ ῥέεθρα Θ. 369, Πήδασον αἰπήεσσαν Φ. 87; **ἀργῆτι** Γ. 419, ἀργέτι Λ. 818, ἀργῆτα and ἀργέτα; **ἀργύφεον** Σ. 50, ἀργυφον Ω. 621; πόλιν... εὐτείχεον A. 129, πόλιν εὐτείχεα II. 57; Τροίην ἐριβώλακα Γ. 74, Τροίην ἐριβωλον I. 329; **πολύτλας** ε. 171, πολυτλήμων σ. 319, πολύτλητοι λ. 38.

238. Among DEFECTIVE ADJECTIVES, we notice,

a.) The following, chiefly poetic: ὁ, ἡ **ἄδακρυς**, τὸ ἄδακρυ, *tearless*, Acc. ἄδακρυν (the other cases supplied by ἀδάκρυτος, -ον); so **πολύδακρυς** *tearful*; ὁ **πρέσβυς** (for fem. see 235 d) *old*, as subst. *elder*, *ambassador* (in the last sense G. πρέσβεως Ar. Ach. 93), A. πρέσβυν, V. πρέσβυ · Pl. πρέσβεις, πρεσβῆες Hes. Sc. 245, *elders, ambassadors*, G. πρέσβεων, D. πρέσβεσι, πρεσβεῦσιν Lyc. 1056, A. πρέσβεις, Du. πρέσβη Ar. Fr. 495 (the plur. in the sense of *ambassadors* was in common use; otherwise, the word was almost exclusively poetic, and its place supplied by ὁ πρεσβύτης, *old man*, and ὁ πρεσβευτής, *ambassador*); **φροῦδος**, -η, -ον, *gone*, which, with the Nom. throughout, has the Gen. φρούδου Soph. Aj. 264.

b.) Poetic *feminines* and *neuters*, which have no corresponding masc.: as, ἡ **πότνια** A. 357 (sometimes πότνᾰ υ. 61) *revered*, τὴν πότνιαν, αἱ πότνιαι (yet πότνιε Orph. H. 10. 20); ἡ **θάλεια** *rich*, H. 475; **ἀνδρολέτειρα** *man-destroying*, Æsch. Th. 314; **κυδιάνειρα** *ennobling*, Δ. 225; **εὐρυάγυια** *wide-streeted*, Δ. 52; εὐρυοδείης λ. 52; **ἱπποδάσεια** *crested*, P. 295; ἀμφιδάσειαν O. 309; ἡ **λίς** and λισσή, μ. 79, γ. 293 (akin to λεῖος *smooth*); τὸ **βρῖ** (s. βριθ-) Hes. ap. Strab. 364 (βριθύς *heavy*); τὸ **ῥά** (s. ῥαδ-) Soph. Fr. 932 (ῥᾴδιος *easy*; cf. δῶ, κρῖ, 228 a); τὰ **ἦρα** and ἐπίηρα, *pleasing*, γ. 164, A. 572.

c.) Poetic *plurals* which have no corresponding sing.: as, οἱ **θαμέες** K. 264, and **ταρφέες** Λ. 387 (yet ταρφύς Æsch. Th. 535), -εῖαι, -έα, *thick, frequent*; **ἰρυσάρματες**... ἵπποι II. 370; οἱ **πλέες** Λ. 395, τοὺς πλέας B. 129 = πλέονες, πλέονας, *more*.

d.) Poetic *oblique cases* which have no corresponding Nom.: as, τοῦ **δυσδάμαρτος** *unhappily wedded*, Æsch. Ag. 1319; **καλλιγύναικος** *having beautiful women*, Sapph. (135), Ἑλλάδα καλλιγύναικα B. 683; **πολυάρνι** Θυέστῃ B. 106; **πολυδένδρεσσιν** Eur. Bac. 560; **ὑψικέρατα** πέτραν Ar. Nub. 597; χέρηϊ, χέρηα, also Pl. χέρηες, χέρηα or χέρεια, A. 80, Δ. 400, &c. (as fr. χερ- *hand*, 224 f; *under the hand of, subject), inferior, worse*.

CHAPTER IV.

NUMERALS.

239. I. NUMERAL ADJECTIVES. Of numeral adjectives, the principal are, (1) the CARDINAL, answering the question, πόσοι; *how many?* (2) the ORDINAL, answering the question, πόστος; *which in order?* or, *one of how many?* (3) the TEMPORAL, answering the question, ποσταῖος; *on what day?* or, *in how many days?* (4) the MULTIPLE (multiplex, *having many folds*), showing to what extent anything is *complicated*; and (5) the PROPORTIONAL, showing the *proportion* which one thing bears to another.

240. 1. CARDINAL. The first four cardinals (25), and those above 100 are declined; the latter as adjectives of Dec. 2 and 1. The rest are indeclinable. Cf. the Lat. cardinals.

a. Εἷς, from its signification, is used only in the sing.; δύω, only in the dual and pl.; and the other cardinals only in the pl., except with collective nouns in such expressions as ἀσπὶς μυρία καὶ τετρακοσία, 10,400 *infantry*, i. 7. 10, ἵππον ὀκτακισχιλίην, 8,000 *horse*, Hdt. 7. 85.

b. Εἷς has two stems, ἑν- and μι-. Its compounds οὐδείς and μηδείς (written, with more strength, οὐδὲ εἷς, μηδὲ εἷς) have a masc. plural.

c. The common form of the second cardinal is δύο, shortened from the regular δύω. The Dat. pl. δυσί, found in late writers and Hipp., also occurs (?) Th. 8. 101. Both δύο (δύω) and ἄμφω, *both* (which is placed in 25, as partaking of the nature of a *numeral*, with that of an emphatic pronoun), are sometimes indecl. (in Hom. never otherwise) : as, δύο πλέθρων i. 2. 23, δύω κανόνεσσι N. 407, χερσὶν ἅμ' ἄμφω Hom. Cer. 15.

d. In the derivatives from ἐννέα, ἐννα-, for ἑνα-, is a less classic form.

e. In τεσσαρεσκαίδεκα, and the later δεκατέσσαρες, δεκατρεῖς, the τρεῖς and τέσσαρες are declined: δεκατρεῖς, δεκατρία, δεκατριῶν· τοῖς τεσσαρσικαίδεκα. Yet we sometimes find τεσσαρεσκαίδεκα, and later even τεσσαρακαίδεκα used as indeclinable; as in Hdt. 1. 86, Mem. 2. 7. 2. The compounds from 13 to 19, both cardinal and ordinal, are often written separately: as, τρεῖς καὶ δέκα i. 5. 5, τρία καὶ δέκα Hdt. 1. 119, τέσσαρες καὶ δέκα · τρίτον καὶ δέκατον Th. 5. 56, τέταρτον καὶ δέκατον, Ib. 81, πέντε ἢ ἑκκαίδεκα Cyr. 1. 4. 16, πέμπτῃ ἢ ἕκτῃ καὶ δεκάτῃ Hel. 4. 6. 6; also ἓν καὶ εἰκοστόν Th. 8. 109.

f. The cardinals become *collective* or *distributive* by composition with σύν · as, σύνδυο bini, *two together*, or *two at a time*, vi. 3. 2, σύντρεις terni, ι. 429, συνδώδεκα duodēni, Eur. Tro. 1076. The distributive sense is also expressed by means of the prepositions ἀνά, κατά, and, in some connections, εἰς and ἐπί · as, ἐξ λόχους ἀνὰ ἑκατὸν ἄνδρας, *6 companies, each 100 men*, iii. 4. 21; κατὰ τετρακισχιλίους, *4,000 at a time*, iii. 5. 8; εἰς ἑκατόν, *100 deep*, Cyr. 6. 3. 23; ἐπὶ τεττάρων, *4 deep*, i. 2. 15.

2. The ORDINAL NUMBERS are all derived from the cardinal, except πρῶτος, and are all of Dec. 2 and 1. They all end in -τος (Eng.

-*th*), except δεύτερος, ἕβδομος, and ὄγδοος · and those from 20, upwards, all end in -οστός (Lat. -*esimus*).

3. The TEMPORAL NUMBERS are formed from the ordinals by changing the final -ος into -αῖος, -ᾱ, -ον: as, τρίτος τριταῖος, v. 3. 2.

4. The MULTIPLE NUMBERS end in -πλόος, contracted -πλοῦς (Lat. -*plex*), and are declined like διπλόος, διπλοῦς (23).

5. The PROPORTIONAL NUMBERS have double forms, in -πλάσιος, -ᾱ, -ον (Lat. -*plus*), and, more rarely, -πλασίων, -ον, G. -ονος. Thus the ratio of 2 to 1 is expressed by διπλάσιος duplus, or διπλασίων.

241. II. NUMERAL ADVERBS. a. The numeral adverbs which reply to the interrogative ποσάκις; *how many times?* all end in -άκις (Lat. -*ies*), except the three first: as, δεκάκις decies, *ten times*, ἐννεακαιεικοσικαιεπτακοσιοπλασιάκις 729 *times*, Pl. Rep. 578 c.

b. These adverbs are employed in the formation of the higher cardinal and ordinal numbers: as, δισχίλιοι bis mille, 2,000, πεντακισχιλιοστός.

c. Other numeral adverbs relate to *division, order, place, manner*, &c.: as, δίχα or διχῇ, poet. διχθά, *in two divisions*, τρίχα, -χῇ, or -χθά, *in 3 divisions;* δεύτερον *secondly*, τρίτον *thirdly;* τριχοῦ *in 3 places*.

III. NUMERAL SUBSTANTIVES. These, for the most part, end in -άς, -άδος, and are employed both as abstract and as collective nouns. Thus, ἡ μυριάς may signify, either the number 10,000, considered abstractly, or a collection of 10,000. These numerals often take the place of the cardinals, particularly in the expression of the higher numbers: as, δέκα μυριάδες, *ten myriads* = 100,000, i. 7. 10.

242. a. When numerals are combined, the less commonly precedes with καί · but often the greater with or without καί: as,

πέντε καὶ εἴκοσιν, *five and twenty*, i. 4. 2; τριάκοντα καὶ πέντε, *thirty and five*, Ib.; τετταράκοντα πέντε, *forty-five*, v. 5. 5; σταθμοὶ τρεῖς καὶ ἐνενήκοντα, παρασάγγαι πέντε καὶ τριάκοντα καὶ πεντακόσιοι, στάδιοι πεντήκοντα καὶ ἑξακισχίλιοι καὶ μύριοι, ii. 2. 6; σταθμοὶ διακόσιοι δεκαπέντε, παρασάγγαι χίλιοι ἑκατὸν πεντήκοντα πέντε, στάδια τρισμύρια τετρακισχίλια ἑξακόσια πεντήκοντα, vii. 8. 26. See v. 5. 4, and § 240 e.

b. From the division of the Greek month into *decades*, the days were often designated as follows: μηνὸς βοηδρομιῶνος ἕκτῃ ἐπὶ δέκα, *upon the* [6*th after* 10] 16*th of the month Boëdromion*, Dem. 261. 12; ἀνθεστηριῶνος ἕκτῃ ἐπὶ δεκάτῃ, Id. 279. 17; βοηδρομιῶνος ἕκτῃ μετ᾽ εἰκάδα, 'the 26th,' Id.

c. Instead of adding eight or nine, *subtraction* is often employed: as, νῆες ... μιᾶς δέουσαι τεσσαράκοντα, *forty ships wanting one* [40 − 1 = 39], Th. 8. 7; ναυσὶ δυοῖν δεούσαις πεντήκοντα [50 − 2 = 48] Ib. 25.

d. In fractions, the denominator may be expressed; or, if it is only greater by one than the numerator, it may be understood: as, τῶν πέντε τὰς δύο μοίρας, $\frac{2}{5}$, Th. 1. 10, τῶν δύο μερῶν, *of* $\frac{2}{3}$, Ib. 104, τὰ πέντε μέρη, $\frac{5}{6}$.

e. The combinations of *fractions* with whole numbers are variously expressed: thus, (α) τρία ἡμιδαρεικά, *three half-darics*, i. e. 1$\frac{1}{2}$ *darics*, i. 3. 21: (β) Particularly in Herodotus, τρίτον ἡμιτάλαντον, *the third talent a half one*, i. e. 2$\frac{1}{2}$ *talents* (so Germ. *dritthalb*), Hdt. 1. 50; ἕβδομον ἡμιτάλαντον + τέταρτον ἡμιτάλαντον = τάλαντα δέκα, 6$\frac{1}{2}$ + 3$\frac{1}{2}$ = 10, Ib. (cf. Lat. *sestertius*, fr. *semis-tertius*: (γ) Less classic, δύο καὶ ἡμίσειαν μνᾶν, δύω καὶ ἥμισυν δραχμαί, Poll. 9. 56, 62 : (δ) ἐπίτριτον, *a third in addition*, i. e. 1$\frac{1}{3}$, Vect. 3. 9; ἐπίπεμπτον, 1$\frac{1}{5}$, Ib. : (ε) ἡμιόλιον, *half as much again*, i. e. 1$\frac{1}{2}$, i. 3. 21.

CHAPTER V.

PRONOUNS.

I. SUBSTANTIVE (27).

243. 1. PERSONAL, ἐγώ, σύ, οὗ. These pronouns have special laws of declension.

  a. The analysis of these pronouns (27 c) shows that the numbers vary in the *stem;* that the connective is ε in the sing. and pl., and ω in the dual; that the Acc. sing. has no flexive (the primitive Direct Case remaining as Acc., while the Nom., in the 1st and 2d Persons, has the peculiar forms ἐγώ and σύ, and in the 3d, from its reflexive use, early disappeared; compare the Latin); that the Dat. pl. has the flexive of the old Indirect Case (186 c), except in the form σφίσι, where the connective ε, in imitation of other forms of this case, becomes ι; and that, in the contraction of the connectives and flexives, ε passes into its kindred ο in the Dat. sing. (114 b). The dual of the 3d Pers. was distinguished from that of the 2d, by the accent, and by remaining uncontracted.

  b. The pronoun οὗ is used both as a simple personal pronoun, and as a reflexive; but in the common language not greatly in either sense. See Syntax. To complete its inflection, the Ep. σφωέ and σφωΐν, and the Ion. σφέα are added in 27 a.

244. 2. REFLEXIVE, ἐμαυτοῦ, σεαυτοῦ, ἑαυτοῦ. These pronouns, from their nature, want the Nom., and the two first also the neuter. They are formed by joining the personal pronouns with αὐτός.

  a. In the plur. of the 1st and 2d Persons, and often of the 3d, the two elements remain distinct: ἡμῶν αὐτῶν. Otherwise, the old Direct Case of the personal pronoun unites with the forms of αὐτός; while, in the 1st Pers., and often in the other two, contraction takes place: (ἐμε-αυτοῦ) ἐμαυτοῦ, σε-αυτοῦ σαυτοῦ, ἑ-αυτοῦ αὑτοῦ.

  3. RECIPROCAL. This pronoun is formed by doubling ἄλλος, *other:* ἀλλήλων, for ἀλλάλλων. From its nature, it wants the Nom. and the sing., and is not common in the dual.

245. 4. INDEFINITE, ὁ δεῖνα. This pronoun may be termed, with almost equal propriety, *definite* and *indefinite.*

  a. It is used to designate a particular person or thing, which the speaker either cannot, or does not care to name; in the language of Matthiæ, it "indefinitely expresses a definite person or thing": Τὸν δεῖνα γιγνώσκεις; *Do you know Mr. So and So?* Ar. Th. 620. Ὁ δεῖνα τοῦ δεῖνος τὸν δεῖνα εἰσαγγέλλει, *A. B., the son of C. D., impeaches E. F.,* Dem. 167. 24. In the sing. this pronoun is of the three genders; in the plur. it is masc. only, and wants the Dat. It is sometimes indecl.: τοῦ δεῖνα Ar. Th. 262.

  b. The article is an essential part of this pronoun; and it were better written as a single word, ὁδεῖνα. It appears to be simply an extension of the demonstrative ὅδε, by adding -ιν- or -ινα, which gives to it an indefinite force (cf. 253 b), making it a *demonstrative indefinite*. It belongs properly to the colloquial Attic, and first appears in Aristophanes.

246. HISTORY. a. The distinction of *person*, like those of *case* and *number* (186 b, c), appears to have been at first only twofold, merely separating the person speaking from all others, whether spoken to or of.

b. To denote ourselves, we naturally *keep the voice at home* as much as is consistent with enunciation; while we denote another by a *forcible emission* of it, a *pointing*, as it were, of the voice towards the person. The former of these is accomplished by closing the lips and murmuring within, that is, by uttering *m*, which hence became the great root of the 1st personal pronouns. The latter is accomplished by sending the voice out forcibly through a narrow aperture. This, according to the place of the aperture, and the mode of emission, may produce either a *sibilant*, a *lingual*, or a *strong breathing*. Hence we find all these as roots of the 2d and 3d personal pronouns.

c. The μ- of the 1st Pers. passed in the old plur. (which afterwards became the dual, 186 g) into the kindred ν- (cf. Lat. *nos*); and in the sing., when pronounced with emphasis, assumed an initial ἄ which passed by precession into ε. In the new plur., the idea of plurality was conveyed by doubling the μ (ἀμμ-); or more commonly by doubling the ἄ to η (115 a), pronounced with the rough breathing (ἡμ-).

d. From this the new plur. of the 2d Pers. appears to have been formed, by changing α, the deepest of the vowels, into υ, the most protrusive (ὑμμ-, ὑμ-). With the exception of this imitative plural, the plur. and dual of the 2d and 3d Persons have the same root, in which plurality is expressed by joining two of the signs of these persons (σφ- = σ + F, the latter remaining in the Lat. *vos*). In the separation of the two persons, the sign σ- became appropriated to the pronoun of the 2d Pers. (but in the Dor., τ-, as in the Lat., and also in the verb-endings -τε, -τον, -*tis*); and the rough breathing to that of the 3d Pers. (in an early state of the language, this was F-, 247 a; in Lat. it became *s-*; while in the article we find both the rough breathing and τ-, and in verb-endings of the 3d Pers. both σ, and more frequently τ).

e. In the Nom. sing., the subjective force appears to have been expressed by peculiar modes of strengthening; in the 1st Pers. by a double prefix to the μ, thus, ἐ-γ-ο-μ (the γ being inserted simply to prevent hiatus), which passed into (ἔγοα, 160 f) ἐγώ; in the 2d Pers. by affixing F, which with the preceding ε passed into ὔ (cf. 217 b); in the 3d Pers. perhaps by affixing Δ, before which precession took place (217 f), so that the form became (FιΔ, ἰΔ or ἰΔ, d, 160) ἴ or ἱ (an obsolete Nom. cited by Apollonius). With this Nom. there appears to have been associated an Acc. ἰν or ἱν, of which μίν and νίν are strengthened forms.

247. DIALECTS. The dialectic forms of the PERSONAL PRONOUNS arise chiefly,

a.) From *variation of stem:* as, Dor. and Æol. τ- for σ- (169 b; sometimes Ep., or even Ion.), τύ tu, Sap. 1. 13, τέ te, Theoc. 1. 5, τοί A. 28, Hdt. 1. 9; Æol. and Ep. F- for the rough breathing, Fέ Alc. 56 [84], Foῖ Sap. 2. 1 (so originally in Hom., 98 c, 162 a); Dor. ἅμ-, ὑμμ-, Æol. and Ep. ἀμμ-, ὑμμ- (130 a, 167 c), for ἡμ-, ὑμ-, ἀμῶν, ἀμίν Theoc. (d, e).

b.) From *want of contraction*, or from *peculiar contraction* (131 b): ἐμέο K. 124, σέο Hdt. 1. 8, σφωέ A. 8; (with precession, in imitation of the Gen.) νῶϊ Δ. 418; σφωΐν A. 338: μεῦ Hdt. 7. 209, σεῦ Id. 1. 9, εὖ T. 464.

c.) From *lengthening* or *repeating the connective* (134 a, 135) : ἐμεῖο Α. 174, σφεῖας ν. 213 : ἓξ Τ. 171, ἑοῖ Ν. 495, τεείο (v. l. τεοῖο) Θ. 37.

d.) From *want of a connective :* ἀμές Alcm. 58, ἄμμες Φ. 432, ὑμές Ar.

e.) From the retention of *primitive forms having no flexive :* ἀμέ, ὑμέ, ὔμμε, Ar. Lys. 95, 87, 1076, ἄμμε Α. 59, ὔμμε Ψ. 412, σφέ Λ. 111.

f.) From the use of *different endings :* as, Gen. Ep. -θεν (192), ἐμέθεν, σέθεν, ἔθεν, Α. 525 ; Acc. sing. -ν, μίν Α. 29, νίν Pind. Ο. 1. 40 (246 c).

g.) From the *retraction of the accent,* or *shortening the last syllable,* or both ; and also from an extension of *enclitic use :* ἡμῖν (v. l. ἥμιν) Α. 147, ἥμιν (v. l. ἥμῑν) λ. 344, ἥμας (v. l. ἥμᾱς) π. 372 ; σφεων Σ. 311. Cf. i.

h.) Add the strengthened Nom. forms ἐγών Α. 76 (in Hom. only before a vowel), τύνη Ε. 485 ; and the Ion. Acc. neut. pl. σφέα Hdt. 1. 46.

i. Some of these forms are also found in the Attic poets : as, ἐγών Æsch. Pers. 931 ; ἐμέθεν Eur. Or. 986, σέθεν Id. Alc. 51, ἔθεν Æsch. Sup. 66 ; νίν (often, and without distinction of number or gender) Id. Pr. 55, Soph. El. 436, μίν (rarely) Æsch. Th. 453, Soph. Tr. 388, σφέ (often ; also in sing.) Id. Ant. 44 ; ὔμμε Ib. 846, ἀμίν Æsch. Eum. 347 ; ἡμίν or ἥμιν Soph. El. 17, 41, ὑμίν or ὔμιν Id. Ant. 308, σφας Ib. 839. This retraction of the accent belongs especially to Sophocles.

248. REFLEXIVE PRONOUNS. In these the New Ionic compounds the *Genitive* of the personal pronouns with the forms of αὐτός, contracting οαυ into ωυ (131 c) : ἐμε(ο-αυ)ωυτοῦ, ἐμεωυτῆς, ἐμεωυτῷ. In Hom., the elements are always distinct : as, ἔμ' αὐτόν Α. 271, σοὶ αὐτῷ Γ. 51, ἓ αὐτήν.

II. ADJECTIVE (28).

249. All the pronouns which are declined in 28, may be traced back to a common foundation in an old DEFINITIVE, which had two roots, the *rough breathing* and *τ-* (cf. 246 b, d), and which performed the offices both of an *article* and of a *demonstrative, personal,* and *relative pronoun.*

a. To this definitive the Greeks gave the name ἄρθρον, artus, *joint,* from its giving connection to discourse, by marking the person or thing spoken of as one which had been spoken of before, or which was about to be spoken of further, or which was familiar to the mind. The Greek name ἄρθρον became, in Latin, ARTICULUS, *small joint,* from which has come the English name, *article.*

b. This definitive, when used as a *demonstrative,* or simply as the *definite article,* naturally *precedes* the name of the person or thing spoken of ; but when used as a *relative,* usually *follows* it : as, οὗτός ἐστιν ὁ ἀνήρ ὃν εἶδες, *this is THE man WHOM you saw ;* τὸ ῥόδον ὃ ἀνθεῖ, *THE rose WHICH blooms.* Hence, in the former use, it was termed the *prepositive,* and in the latter, the *postpositive article.* When prepositive, it was so closely connected with the following word that its aspirated forms became proclitic. Compare the different uses of the Germ. *der,* the Anglo-Saxon *se,* the Eng. *that,* &c.

c. In the progress of the language, the forms of this old DEFINITIVE became specially appropriated, though with many exceptions in the dialects and poets, and some even in Attic prose (see Syntax) ; and other pronouns arose from it by derivation and composition. The forms τός and τή of the Nom. sing. became obsolete. Special care is required in distinguishing the forms of ὁ, ὅς, οὗ, τίς, and τις. Forms which have the same letters may be often distinguished by the accentuation.

A. Definite.

250. 1. ARTICLE, ὁ, ἡ, τό. The *prepositive article*, or, as it is commonly termed simply, the *article*, unites the *proclitic aspirated forms* of the old definitive, ὁ, ἡ, οἱ, αἱ, with the *τ-forms* of the *neuter*, the *oblique cases*, and the *dual*.

2. RELATIVE, ὅς, ἥ, ὅ. The *postpositive article*, or, as it is now commonly termed, the *relative pronoun*, has the *orthotone aspirated forms* of the old definitive. See 786, 788 g.

251. 3. ITERATIVE, αὐτός, -ή, -ό. This pronoun appears to be compounded of the particle αὖ, *again, back*, and the *old definitive τός* (249 c). It is hence a PRONOUN OF RETURN (or, as it may be termed, an *iterative* pronoun), marking the return of the mind to the same person or thing.

a. The article and αὐτός are often united by crasis (125) : as, αὑτός, *the same*, ταὐτόν (199 a) or ταὐτό (Ion. τωὐτό Hdt. 1. 53, § 131 c), ταὐτοῦ, ταὐτά, for ὁ αὐτός, τὸ αὐτό, τοῦ αὐτοῦ, τὰ αὐτά.

252. 4. DEMONSTRATIVE. The primary demonstratives are οὗτος, *this*, compounded of the article and αὐτός · ὅδε, *this*, compounded of the article (declined as usual) and δε, an inseparable particle marking *direction towards;* and ἐκεῖνος, *that*, derived from ἐκεῖ, *there* (28 l).

a. The definitives of *quality, quantity*, and *age*, τοῖος talis, *such*, τόσος tantus, *so much*, τηλίκος *so old*, and τύννος tantulus, *so small*, are strengthened, in the same manner as the article, by composition with αὐτός and δέ · thus, τοιοῦτος and τοιόσδε, *just such*, τοσοῦτος and τοσόσδε, *just so much*, τηλικοῦτος and τηλικόσδε, τυννοῦτος. These compound pronouns are commonly employed, instead of the simple (which are chiefly poetic), even when there is no special emphasis.

b. In these compounds with αὐτός, *if the affix of the first element has an O vowel, it unites with* αὐ- *to form* ου *; but otherwise, it is absorbed:* as, (ὁ αὐτός) οὗτος, (ἡ αὐτή) αὕτη, (τοῦ αὐτοῦ) τούτου, (τῆς αὐτῆς) ταύτης, (οἱ αὐτοί) οὗτοι, (αἱ αὐταί) αὗται, (τῶν αὐτῶν) τούτων · (τόσος αὐτός) τοσοῦτος, (τόσῃ αὐτῇ) τοσαύτη.

c. To demonstratives, for the sake of stronger expression, an ι is affixed, which is always long and acute, and before which a short vowel is dropped, and a long vowel or diphthong regarded as short: as, οὑτοσί, αὑτηΐ, τουτί, hicce, Fr. *celui-ci, this here* (28) ; ἐκεινοσί illic, Fr. *celui-là, that there;* ὁδί, τοσουτοσί.

d. This ι *paragogic* is Attic, and belongs especially to the style of conversation and popular discourse. It was also affixed to adverbs : as, οὑτωσί, ὡδί, νυνί, ἐνταυθί, ἐντευθενί. So, in comic language, even with an inserted particle, νυνμενί Ar. Av. 448, ἐνγεταυθί Id. Th. 646, ἐνμεντευθενί.

5. POSSESSIVE. The possessive pronouns are derived in Greek, as in other languages, from the personal; and are arranged in 28 according to the person and number of the pronouns from which they are formed.

B. Indefinite.

253. 1. The SIMPLE INDEFINITE is τὶς, which has two stems: τιν-, declined throughout after Dec. 3; and τε-, declined in the Gen. and Dat. only, after Dec. 2 (except that the Gen. sing. imitates the personal pronouns) with contraction: thus,

τὶς, τὶ (the ν omitted as in the theme, 208 d), τινός, &c. : G. τέο του Cyr. 8. 5. 7, τοῦ; Soph. O. T. 1435, D. τέῳ τῳ A. 299, i. 9. 7, τῷ; Soph. El. 679; and, in the compound, ὅτου i. 9. 21, Æsch. Pr. 170, ὅτῳ ii. 6. 23, Pl. G. ὅτεων ὅτων vii. 6. 24, D. ὀτέοις ὅτοις Soph. Tr. 1119, ὅτοισι Ar. Eq. 758 (so, rarely, τοῖσι; Soph. Tr. 984). See c, and 254 b.

2. The INTERROGATIVES in Greek are simply the *indefinites with a change of accent.* See Syntax, 563 s.

a. Thus, the forms of the indefinite τὶς (except the peculiar ἄττα, which is rarely used except in connection with an adjective, and which is never used interrogatively) are *enclitic;* while those of the interrogative τίς are *orthotone,* and never take the grave accent. In lexicons and grammars, for the sake of distinction, the forms τὶς and τὶ of the indefinite are written with the *grave* accent, or *without* an accent. See 784 a, 787 b.

b. The stems τε- and τιν- may be traced back to the great pronominal root τ-, here rendered indefinite by the additions made.

c. The short ι of τὶς, and the omission of ν in τὶ, suggest an intermediate root τι-, formed from τε- by precession, and afterwards increased by ν (cf. 218). To this intermediate root may be referred, according to Dec. 2, the Æol. τίῳ; and Dor. neut. pl. (τια) σά (cf. 143 b) Ar. Ach. 757.

254. 3. The composition of ὅς with τὶς forms the RELATIVE INDEFINITE ὅστις, *whoever,* of which both parts are declined in those forms which have the root τιν-, but the latter only in those which have the root τε-; thus, οὕτινος, but ὅτεο ὅτου.

a. Of the double forms of the Gen. and Dat., the longer prevail in Attic prose, and the shorter in Attic poetry.

b. The form ἅσσα, Att. ἅττα (169 a) appears to be compounded of ἅ and the Dor. σά (253 c). In certain connections, it passed into a simple indefinite, and then, by a softer pronunciation, became ἅσσα, ἅττα.

c. In ὅ τι a space is used to distinguish it from the conjunction ὅτι.

255. DIALECTIC FORMS. a. *Article* (28 i, j). With οἱ and αἱ of the Nom. pl., the old forms τοί and ταί are also used, especially for the sake of metre, euphony, or emphasis, in the Dor. and Ion. (chiefly the Ep.); and, rarely, even in Att. poetry.

b. *Iterative.* The New Ion. often inserts ε in αὐτός and its compounds, before a long vowel in the affix (135 a, 28 l): αὐτέων τουτέων Hdt. 2. 3.

c. *Demonstrative* (28 l, m). The shorter κεῖνος is also used by the Att. poets for the sake of the metre; and, according to some, even occurs in Att. prose, as Hel. 2. 3. 48.

d. *Possessive.* Some of the forms in 28 n also occur in Att. poetry: as, ὅς, τεός, ἁμός or ἀμός (sometimes used for ἐμός, as in Eng. *our* for *my*).

e. *Indefinite.* For dialectic forms, see 28 o, 253 c. Hom. and Hdt. have also regular forms from ὅστις. Some references are added: ὅτις (= ὅστις, but the first part undeclined) Γ. 279 (ὅστις Γ. 167), ὅ ττι (171) Θ. 408, τεο Hdt. 1. 58, τευ (131 b) B. 388, τέο; B. 225, τεῦ; Hdt. 5. 106, τέοισι; Id. 1. 37, ὀτέοισιν O. 491, ὀτέῳσιν Hdt. 2.66 v. 1., ἅσσα τ. 218, ὅτινας O. 492 (οὕστινας Δ. 240), ἅσσα Hdt. 1. 138.

CHAPTER VI.

COMPARISON.

256. ADJECTIVES and ADVERBS have, in Greek, three degrees of comparison, the POSITIVE, COMPARATIVE, and SUPERLATIVE.

a. Comparative and superlative forms may be analyzed into the BASE, which is commonly the stem of the positive; the CONNECTIVE, which varies according to euphony, metre, and other influences; and the DEGREE-SIGN, to which, in the adjective, are also attached the AFFIXES OF DECLENSION. See 29.

I. COMPARISON OF ADJECTIVES.

A. By -τερος, -τατος.

257. In adjectives, the *comparative* is usually formed in -τερος, -ᾱ, -ον, and the *superlative* in -τατος, -η, -ον. In receiving these affixes, the endings of the theme are changed as follows:

1.) -ος, preceded by a long syllable, becomes -ο-; by a short syllable, -ω-: as,

κοῦφος *light*,   κουφότερος, -ᾱ, -ον,   κουφότατος, -η, -ον.
σοφός *wise*,   σοφώτερος *wiser*,   σοφώτατος *wisest*.

a. A syllable before a mute and liquid is here regarded as long: as, σφοδρός *vehement*, σφοδρότερος, -ότατος.
b. The change to -ω- takes place to avoid the succession of too many short syllables. Epic verse admits only two short syllables in succession. Some exceptions to the rule occur in the poets for the sake of the metre: as, κακοξεινώτερος v. 376, εὐτεκνώτατε Eur. Hec. 620.
c. Adjectives contracted in the theme are commonly contracted in the Comp. and Sup.: as, πορφύρεος πορφυροῦς, *purple*, πορφυρ(εώ)ώτερος.
d. In a few words, -ος is dropped; and, in a few, it becomes -αι-, -εσ-, or -ισ-: as, commonly,

παλαιός *ancient*, παλαίτερος, -αίτατος · φίλος *dear*, φίλτερος, φίλτατος · (-ος -αι-) φίλος *friendly*, φιλαίτερος, -αίτατος · (-ος -εσ-) ἐρρωμένος *strong*, ἐρρωμενέστερος, -έστατος · so most contracts in -οος, as ἁπλ(όος)οῦς *simple*, ἁπλ(οέσ)ούστερος · (-ος -ισ-) λάλος *talkative*, λαλίστερος, -ίστατος.

e. **Μέσος** *middle*, and **νέος** *new*, have old superlatives of limited and chiefly poetic use in **-ατος**: μέσατος *midmost*, Ar. Vesp. 1502, Ep. μέσσατος Θ. 223, νέατος novissimus, *last*, Λ. 712, Soph. Ant. 627. Cf. ἔσχατος, (πρόατος) πρῶτος, ὕπατος (262 d); and Poet. μύχατος *inmost*, πύματος *last*.

258. 2.) -εις, and -ης of Dec. 3, become -εσ-; and -υς becomes -υ-: as,

§ 261. SECOND FORM. 181

χαρίεις *agreeable*, χαριέστερος, -έστατος · τολμ(ήεις)ῆς *daring*, τολμ(ήέσ)ήστατος (207 c) Soph. Ph. 984 ; σαφής *evident*, σαφέστερος, -έστατος · πένης *poor*, πενέστερος, -έστατος · ὀξύς *sharp*, ὀξύτερος, -ύτατος.

a. In adjectives of Dec. 1, -ης becomes -ισ- : as, πλεονέκτης, -ου, *covetous*, πλεονεκτίστατος.

259. 4.) In adjectives of other endings, -τερος and -τατος are either added to the simple stem, or to the stem increased by -εσ-, -ισ-, -ο-, or -ω- : as, τάλας, -ανος, *wretched*, ταλάντερος, -τατος · so μέλας *black*, μάκαρ, *blessed*, μακάρτατος · (-εσ-) σώφρων, -ονος, *discreet*, σωφρονέστερος, -έστατος · so most adjectives in -ων · (-ισ-) ἅρπαξ, -αγος, rapax, *rapacious*, ἁρπαγίστατος · (-ω-) ἐπίχαρις, -ιτος, *pleasing*, ἐπιχαριτώτερος, -ώτατος.

a. No part of inflection is less strictly bound by rule than comparison (while the poets have here, as elsewhere, especial freedom) ; and the forms above stated are sometimes interchanged or varied from regard to metre, euphony, brevity, &c. : as, πτωχός *poor*, -ότερος and -ίστερος, Ar. Ach. 425 ; ὑβριστής *insolent*, -τότερος, -τότατος, v. 8. 3, 22 ; ἐπιλήσμων *forgetful*, ἐπιλησμότατος, Ar. Nub. 790 ; πέπων *ripe*, πεπαίτερος Æsch. Fr. 244 ; ἄχαρις *disagreeable*, ἀχαρίστερος v. 392 ; ἰθύς *straight*, ἰθύντατα, for the sake of the metre, Σ. 508 ; φαεινός, *shining*, φαάντατος v. 93.

B. By -ίων, -ιστος.

260. A few adjectives are compared by -ίων and -ιστος, commonly adding these to the *root* of the word.

a. In adducing examples, a noun or verb will sometimes be introduced, as showing well the base : **κακός** *bad*, **κακίων**, **κάκιστος** · **ἡδύς** *pleasant* (ἥδω *to please*), ἡδίων, -ιστος · **αἰσχρός** *shameful* (**αἶσχος** *shame*), αἰσχίων, -χιστος · so ἐχθρός *hostile*, κυδρός *glorious*, poet., and in Sup. οἰκτρός *pitiable* (ἔχθος *hatred*, κῦδος *glory*, οἶκτος *pity*), ἐχθίων, κυδίων, οἴκτιστος · **ἀλγεινός** painful (**ἄλγος** *pain*), ἀλγίων, -γιστος · **κερδαλέος** *gainful* (**κέρδος** gain), poet. κερδίων, -διστος · **καλός** *beautiful* (**κάλλος** *beauty*), καλλίων, -ιστος · (**βελτ-**, akin to βέλος, *weapon ?*), βελτίων *better*, βέλτιστος *best*.

b. This was an early method of comparison, retained in a few common words, and in poetic forms of some others. For the declension of comparatives in -ων, see 22, 211. The ι in -ίων is regularly long in the Att. poets, but short in the Epic and Doric. Yet ἥδιον Eur. Sup. 1101.

261. The different forms of the Comp. in -ων are well explained by reference to -Ιων as their common origin, and to the various changes of the *consonant* Ι. Thus, we notice, besides the use of the corresponding vowel ι,

a.) Contraction (sometimes with transposition), or omission between two vowels (142, 140) : as, **πολύς** *much* (base πολε-, sync. πλε-), πλείων or πλέων *more*, πλεῖστος *most*, Lat. plus, plurimus ; **μικρός** *small* (με-) μείων minor, rare poet. μεῖστος minimus ; **ῥᾴδιος** *easy* (ῥᾰ-) ῥάων, ῥᾷστος (Ion. ῥηίων, ῥήιστος, δ. 565) ; (λω-, akin to Dor. λῶ *to desire*, neut. pl. λῶϊα *desirable*, Theoc. 26. 32) λωίων, β. 169, Att. λῴων, vi. 2. 15, λῷστος ; (**ἀρ-, ἀρε-**, in ἀρετή *virtus, valor, virtue*) ἀρείων poet., *braver, better*, ἄριστος *best ;* (**ἀμεν-**, cf. amoenus) ἀμείνων *better* ; (**χερ-** or **χειρ-**, 238 d) χείρων (Ep. χερείων A. 114) *inferior, worse*, χείριστος.

b.) The change into σσ (ττ) or ξ (143 c), the preceding vowel, if short, now becoming long by nature: as, **τᾰχύς** *swift*, (θαχ-, 159 b; θαχlων) **θάσσων** or θάττων, τάχιστος· **ἐλαχύς** Ep., *small*, ἐλάσσων, ἐλάχιστος· **μακρός** *long* (μᾰκ-, μηκ-), μάσσων poet., μήκιστος· **κρατύς** Ep., *strong*, (κρατIων) κρείσσων, κράτιστος (κρέσσων, Hdt. 1. 66, κάρτιστος, A. 266, § 134, 171); **ὀλίγος** *little*, ὀλίζων Ep., ὀλίγιστος· **μέγας** magnus, *great*, μείζων major (Ion. μέζων Hdt. 1. 202), μέγιστος maximus.

c. Some Comparatives have a double form in -ίων and -σσων· as, βραδύς bardus, *slow*, βραδίων, Hes. Op. 526, βράσσων K. 226.

d. Of the Comp. forms **πλείων** and **πλέων**, the Attic uses more the former, especially in the contracted cases; but in the neut. sing., prefers πλέον, especially as an adverb. It sometimes syncopates πλεῖον to πλεῖν, but only in such phrases as πλεῖν ἢ μύριοι, *more than* 10,000. Hdt. prefers πλέων, often contracting εο to ευ: as, πλεῦν, πλεῦνος. The Epic varies according to the metre.

e. Most adjectives compared by -ων, -ιστος, have also forms, often more common, in -τερος, -τατος· as, ἀλγεινός, μακρός, μικρός, -ότερος, -ότατος· βραδύς, παχύς, ταχύς, -ύτερος, -ύτατος· βέλτερος and βέλτατος, Æsch.; φίλος, φίλτατος, Cyr. 4. 3. 2, φιλαίτερος, i. 9. 29, φιλώτερος, Mem. 3. 11. 18; φιλίων τ. 351, φίλιστος, Soph. Aj. 842. Other adjectives compared in both ways are αἰσχρός, ἐχθρός, οἰκτρός, βαθύς *deep*, βραχύς *short*, &c.

f. New poetic or late comparatives are made by changing -ων into -ότερος or -τερος· as, χείρων χειρότερος, μειότερος, μειζότερος· λωίτερος.

C. Irregular Comparison.

262. Many adjectives (a) are *defective* or *redundant* in comparison; and some comparatives and superlatives are formed (b) from *positives which are not in use*, (c) from words which are themselves *comparatives* or *superlatives*, or (d) from *other parts of speech*. Some of these are usually referred to positives in use, which have a similar signification. Thus,

(a) Only those words which express properties that may exist in different degrees, are compared; except in a *modified sense*, for *hyperbole*, or for *comic effect*: as, μόνος *alone*, μονώτατος *alonest*, most emphatically *alone*, Ar. Pl. 182. See c and d.

(b) Several forms, not strictly synonymous, are commonly referred to ἀγαθός, *good*: thus, **ἀγαθός**, ἀμείνων, ἄριστος· βελτίων, βέλτιστος· κρείσσων, κράτιστος· λῴων, λῷστος· poet. φέρτερος, φέρτατος and φέριστος (late ἀγαθώτατος, Diod. 16. 85). So, χείρων and χείριστος are referred to **κακός**· ἥσσων, ἥκιστος, to **κακός** or **μικρός**· ἐλάσσων, ἐλάχιστος, to **μικρός** or **ὀλίγος**. See 260 a, 261 a, b.

(c) *Double Comparison*. **ἔσχατος** *last, extreme*, ἐσχατώτερος (Οὔτε γὰρ τοῦ ἐσχάτου ἐσχατώτερον εἴη ἄν τι Aristl. Metaph. 10. 4), ἐσχατώτατος, Hel. 2. 3. 49; **ἐλάχιστος** *least*, ἐλαχιστότερος *less than the least*, Ephes. 3. 8; **πρῶτος** *first*, πρώτιστος *first of all*, B. 228.

(d) *Comparatives and Superlatives from other parts of speech*. **βασιλεύς** *king*, βασιλεύτερος *more kingly*, *a greater king*, I. 160, βασιλεύτατος *the greatest king*, I. 69; **κλέπτης** *thief*, κλεπτίστατος *most adroit thief*; **κύων** *dog*, κύντερος *more dog-like*, *more impudent*, Θ. 483, κύντατος K. 503; **αὐτός** *himself*, αὐτότερος Epich. 2 (1), αὐτότατος (*ipsissimus* Plaut. Trin. 4. 2) *his very self*, Ar. Plut. 83; **ἄγχι** or **ἄγχου** *near*, ἀγχότερος *nearer*, Hdt. 7. 175, ἄγχιστος Soph. O. T. 919; **ἄνω** *up*, ἀνώτερος *upper*, ἀνώτατος *uppermost*, Hdt. 2. 125; **ἠρέμα** *quietly*, ἠρεμέστερος *more quiet*, Cyr. 7. 5.

63 ; **προὔργου** *of importance,* **προυργιαίτερος** *more important,* Pl. Gorg. 458 c, **προυργιαίτατος·** **ἐξ** ex, *out of,* **ἔσχατος** (104) extrēmus, *uttermost;* **πρό** præ, *before,* **πρότερος** prior, *former,* **πρῶτος** (257 e) primus, *first;* **ὑπέρ** super, OVER, **ὑπέρτερος** superior, **ὑπέρτατος** and **ὕπατος** suprēmus, *highest;* **ὑπό** (?) sub, sus-, *below,* **ὕστερος** *later,* **ὕστατος** *last.*

II. COMPARISON OF ADVERBS.

263. Adverbs derived from adjectives are commonly compared by taking the *neuter singular comparative*, and the *neuter plural superlative* of these adjectives; but other adverbs by -τέρω and -τάτω:

σοφῶς (fr. **σοφός**, 257) *wisely,* **σοφώτερον** *more wisely,* **σοφώτατα** *most wisely;* **ταχέως** (**ταχύς**, 261 b) *quickly,* **θᾶσσον, θᾶττον, τάχιστα·** **ἄνω** *up,* **ἀνωτέρω, ἀνωτάτω·** **ἑκάς** *afar,* poet. and Ion. **ἑκαστέρω, ἑκαστάτω.**

a. Adverbs from which adjectives are formed are sometimes compared in the first method : as, **ὀψέ** *late,* **πρωΐ** *early,* **ὀψίαίτερον, -τατα,** &c. (257 d). So **μάλα** *very,* **μᾶλλον** (143 a), **μάλιστα.**

b. The adverbial Sup. has sometimes the neut. sing. form, chiefly when denoting time or place : as, **πρῶτον καὶ ὕστατον,** *first and last,* Pl. Menex.

c. The adverbial termination **-ως** is sometimes given to the Comp. ; and, rarely, to the Sup.: as, **χαλεπωτέρως** *more severely,* Th. 2. 50, **μειζόνως** Th. 4. 19, **ξυντομωτάτως** *most concisely,* Soph. O. C. 1579.

d. Some adverbs vary in their comparison : as, **ἐγγύς** *near,* **ἐγγυτέρω, ἐγγυτάτω· ἐγγύτερον, ἐγγύτατα·** less Att. **ἔγγιον, ἔγγιστα· ἄγχι** or **ἀγχοῦ** poet. and Ion., *near,* **ἆσσον** A. 335 (143 c), **ἄγχιστα** Æsch. Sup. 1036, **ἀσσοτέρω** (cf. 261 f) ρ. 572, **ἀγχοτάτω** Hdt. 2. 24.

264. HISTORY OF COMPARISON. a. So far as we can trace comparison in the Greek, it appears to have commenced with an *emphatic* annexation of the old article, in its strong form **τος**, to the stem of the positive, with a connecting vowel where needed : as, **νέ-α-τος,** THE *new one,* i. e. *the newest;* **μέσ-α-τος,** THE *middle one* (257 e). So, in numerals, **τρί-τος λόγος,** THE *No.* 3 *book.*

b. This form was then strengthened by doubling the root of the article : **-ττ-ος.** And now two forms arose. The first **τ** became **σ** : **-στ-ος** (147) ; or a euphonic vowel was inserted : **-τατ-ος.** Connectives were also prefixed according to need or preference. Thus from **φίλος**, **φίλιστος,** and **φίλτατος** or **φιλαίτατος·** among ordinals, **χιλιοστός.**

c. The comparative *distinguishes* or *separates* one person or thing from another in respect to the possession of some quality ; and this separation has been extensively expressed by a *liquid prolongation* of the adjective. In Greek, both **ν** and **ρ** were used for this purpose, with a connecting vowel, viz. **ο** before **ν** (cf. 114 c), and **ε** before **ρ**. After the analogy of the superlative, I (or **ι**) was prefixed to **-ον-** ; and **τ**, with the preceding connective, to **-ερ-** : **φιλίων, φίλτερος, φιλαίτερος.** The two Greek forms are mingled in the Lat. *-ior;* and the **τ** appears also in the Germ. and Eng. : long*ior*, läng*er*, long*er*. The Sanskrit has analogies to the forms of both Greek and Lat. comparison. Its prevalent form is Comp. *-taras* (**-τερος**), Sup. *-tamas* (**-τα-τος,** *-i-mus*).

CHAPTER VII.

GENERAL PRINCIPLES OF CONJUGATION.

265. Verbs are conjugated, in Greek, to mark five distinctions: VOICE, TENSE, MODE, NUMBER, and PERSON. Of these distinctions, the first shows how the *action* of a verb is related to its *subject;* the second, how it is related to *time;* and the third, how it is related to the *mind of the speaker*, or to *some other action*. The two remaining distinctions merely show the number and person of the subject.

a. These distinctions are marked by PREFIXES, by AFFIXES, and also, to some extent, by CHANGES IN THE STEM. See 30 s, 49.

266. A. VOICE. The Greek has three voices: the ACTIVE, MIDDLE, and PASSIVE (30 a).

a. The Middle is so called as *intermediate* between the Active and Passive, representing the subject of the verb not only as *acting*, but also as, more or less directly, *acted upon:* as, from λούω, *to wash*, ἐλουσάμην *I washed myself, I bathed*.

b. The *middle* and *passive* voices have a common form, except in the *Future* and *Aorist*. In Etymology, this form is usually spoken of simply as *passive*, or as *middle*. Even in the Future and Aorist, the distinction in sense between the two voices is not always preserved.

c. The reflexive sense of the *middle* voice often becomes so indistinct, that this voice does not differ from the *active* in its use. Hence, in many verbs, either wholly or in part, the middle voice takes the place of the active. This is particularly frequent in the *Future*. When it occurs in the *theme* (172 c), the verb is termed *deponent* (depōnens, as if *putting off* its proper sense to take that of another voice). E. g.

1.) Verbs, in which the *theme* has the *active*, and the *Future* has the *middle* form: ἀκούω *to hear*, ἀκούσομαι · βαίνω *go*, βήσομαι · γιγνώσκω *know*, γνώσομαι · εἰμί *be*, ἔσομαι · μανθάνω *learn*, μαθήσομαι.

2.) Deponent Verbs: αἰσθάνομαι *to perceive*, βούλομαι *will*, γίγνομαι *become*, δέχομαι *receive*, δύναμαι *be able*, ἥδομαι *rejoice*, οἴομαι *think*.

d. A Deponent Verb is termed *deponent middle*, or *deponent passive*, according as its Aorist has the middle or the passive form.

267. B. Tense. The Greek has seven tenses: the Present, Imperfect, Future, Aorist, Perfect, Pluperfect, and Future Perfect.

a. Tenses may be classified in two ways : I. with respect to the *time* which is spoken of; II. with respect to the *relation* which the action bears to this time.

b. I. The *time* which is spoken of is either, 1. *present*, 2. *future*, or 3. *past*. The reference to time is most distinct in the Indicative. In this mode, those tenses which refer to *present* or *future* time are termed primary or chief tenses; and those which refer to *past* time, secondary or historical tenses.

c. II. The action is *related to the time*, either, 1. as *doing at* the time, 2. as *done in* the time, or 3. as *complete at* the time. The tenses which denote the first of these relations are termed definite; the second, indefinite; and the third, complete. These constitute three great formations, or classes of forms, in the Greek verb.

d. The Aorist (ἀόριστος *indefinite*) represents an action simply as *performed*. Its place is chiefly supplied in the Latin by the Perfect. Thus ἔγραψα scripsi, *I wrote*.

e. Of the *Future Perfect* (also called the *Third Future*, and in old grammars the *Paulo-post Future*), the simple form is found in only a few verbs ; and, with this exception, this tense and those which are marked in 30 as wanting, viz. the *indefinite present* and the *definite future*, are supplied by forms belonging to other tenses, or by participles combined with auxiliary verbs.

f. For the general formation of the Greek tenses, see 31. In respect to the details of formation, they are naturally associated in six systems : 1. the *Present*, or *Definite System*, including the Pres. and Impf. ; 2. the *Future System*, including the Fut. Act. and Mid.; 3. the *Aorist System*, including the Aor. Act. and Mid. ; 4. the *Perfect* (or *Perf. Act.*) *System*, including the Perf. and Plup. Act. ; 5. the *Perfect Passive System*, including the Perf. and Plup. Pass. and Mid., and the Fut. Perf.; and 6. the *Compound System*, including the Aor. and Fut. Pass., which are formed with an auxiliary (274). Of these systems, the 1st belongs to the great definite formation ; the 2d, 3d, and 6th, to the indefinite ; and the 4th and 5th, to the complete. For the so-called *second systems*, see 289 b.

268. In some verbs the sense of the complete tenses, by a natural transition, passes into that of other tenses; and the PERFECT becomes, in signification, a *Present;* the PLUPERFECT, an *Imperfect* or *Aorist;* and the FUTURE PERFECT, a common *Future.* Thus, ἵστημι (45) *to station,* Perf. ἕστηκα (*I have stationed myself*) *I stand,* Plup. ἑστήκειν *I stood,* Fut. Perf. ἑστήξω *I shall stand;* μιμνήσκω *to remind,* Perf. Pass. μέμνημαι (*I have been reminded*) *I remember,* Plup. ἐμεμνήμην *I remembered,* Fut. Perf. μεμνήσομαι *I shall remember.*

a. In a few of these verbs, the Pres. is not used, and the PERF. is regarded as the *theme.* Such verbs, as having a preterite tense for the theme, are termed PRETERITIVE. In like manner, those Perfect systems in which the Perf. is used in the sense of the Pres. may be termed, for convenience, *preteritive systems;* and even a Perf. so used, a *Preteritive.*

269. C. MODE. The Greek has six modes: the INDICATIVE, SUBJUNCTIVE, OPTATIVE, IMPERATIVE, INFINITIVE, and PARTICIPLE.

a. For a table of these modes, classified according to the character of the sentences which they form, see 30 c.

b. In the regular inflection of the Greek verb, the Pres. and Aor. have all the modes; but the Fut. and the Fut. Perf. want the Subjunctive and Imperative; and the Perf., for the most part, wants the Subjunctive and Optative, except as supplied by compound forms, and likewise, in the active voice, the Imperative.

c. The tenses of the Subjunctive and Optative are related to each other as *present* and *past,* or as *primary* and *secondary,* tenses (267 b); and some have therefore chosen to consider them as only different tenses of a *general conjunctive,* or *contingent* mode, calling the Pres. and Perf. Opt. the *Imperfect* and *Pluperfect Conjunctive.* With this change, the number and general offices of the Greek modes are the same with those of the Latin, and the correspondence between the Greek conjunctive and the English potential modes becomes more obvious. In the Infinitive and Participle, the forms called *Present* and *Perfect* belong also to the Imperfect and Pluperfect. Without changing familiar names, the relations of the modes and tenses are illustrated by the arrangement in 37. The Imperative, from its very signification, cannot belong to a past tense.

d. The passive verbal adjectives in -τός and -τέος (Lat. -tus and -ndus), as closely akin to participles, are often included in tables of inflection. In the form of the stem, they commonly agree with the Aor. in -θην, except as a preceding mute is changed before τ (147): as, θρεπτέος, fr. τρέφω *to nourish,* Aor. ἐθρέφθην.

270. D. NUMBER AND PERSON. The numbers and persons of verbs correspond to those of nouns and pronouns (265).

a. The Imperative, from its signification, wants the *first person;* the Infinitive, from its character as partaking of the nature of an abstract noun, wants the distinctions of number and person altogether; and the Participle, as partaking of the nature of an adjective, has the distinctions of *gender* and *case,* instead of person.

b. The 1*st Pers. sing.* of the *Pres. ind.,* is commonly regarded as the THEME of a verb (172 e); while, in adding its meaning, the Eng. Inf. is more frequently used: as, λύω *to loose* (yet also, *I loose,* or simply, *loose*). The STEM is obtained by *throwing off the affix of the theme,* or it may be obtained from any form of the verb, by throwing off the prefix and affix, and allowing for euphonic changes. A verb is conjugated by *adding to the stem the prefixes and affixes in* 35 and 36.

c. Verbs are divided, according to the *stem-mark,* or *characteristic,* into MUTE, LIQUID, DOUBLE CONSONANT, and PURE VERBS; and, according to the *affix in the theme,* into VERBS IN -ω, and VERBS IN -μι. For a full paradigm of *regular conjugation,* see λύω (37); for shorter paradigms of the *several classes of verbs,* see 39 s.

d. In λύω, the υ is short in the Perf., the Plup., and the Compound System; but otherwise, long in the common language. In Homer, it is commonly short in the Pres. and Impf.

271. E. HISTORIC VIEW. a. The following view is offered as one which has much in its support, and serves to explain the general phenomena of the Greek verb: (b) The distinction of person was at first only twofold, μ being affixed for the 1st pers., and a lingual or sibilant for the other two (246, 249); and there were only two numbers, sing. and plur. (c) The 2d and 3d persons were then separated, the 2d taking in the sing. the affix s (sometimes θ or σθ), and the 3d, τ; while they took new plur. forms in -τε and -ντ, the old plural now remaining as dual (cf. 186 g).

d. A *secondary tense* was formed by prefixing ε to denote *past* time, while the original form now became a *primary tense,* expressing *present* and *future* time (267 b, 277). (e) An *objective voice* was formed, chiefly by adding αι or ο, or by inserting θ (-τθ- becoming -σθ-, 147; and -μεν commonly becoming -μεθα, 142); and the older form now became *subjective,* or *active* (30, 285). (f) For euphony, a connecting vowel was used in attaching the affixes to stems ending with consonants, and this became the common mode of inflection even when the stem ended with a vowel.

272. a. The *Infinitive,* which is *substantive* in its use and commonly expresses either a direct or oftener an indirect object, took the objective endings of nouns, -ν or -ι, or uniting these, -ναι, which became in the Pass. -(ν-σθ-αι)σθαι (cf. 271 e, 154 s). (b, c) The *Participle,* which is *adjective* in its use, took the adjective endings -ντς in the Act., and -μενος (or in an older form, afterwards used rather as a verbal adjective, -τος) in the objective voice. (d) From the original mode (which now became *Indicative*), the *Subjunctive* was formed by using ω and η as connectives, to express *present contingence;* and the *Optative,* by protracting a simple vowel to a diphthong in ι, to express *past contingence.* (e) An *Imperative* was also formed, naturally preferring short forms in the 2 Pers., but prolonging the forms of the 3 Pers., through the use of ω.

273. a. A few verbs formed only the old Primary and Secondary Tenses; (b, c) but, in most verbs, a *Future* and *Aorist* were formed by adding σ to the stem, the older tenses now becoming *Present* and *Im-*

perfect. The Aor. was marked by the use of α as a connecting vowel, while the Fut. took the connectives of the Pres. (d) In many verbs, a new Pres. and Impf. were formed from a new stem ; and in some of these verbs. the old Secondary Tense remained as an Aor. (2 Aor., 289 a) ; and in a few, the old Primary (305 f), as a Future. (e) Three reduplicated tenses were formed to mark an action as *completed :* the *Perfect,* having, in the Act., its Ind. in -α, its Inf. in -εναι, its Part. in -ως, and Pres. affixes in the other modes ; the *Pluperfect,* having, in the Act., the connective εα, cont. η, by precession ει (while, in both these tenses, the objective affixes are nude) ; and the *Future Perfect,* having the affixes of the common Future.

274. a. A special *Aor. and Fut. passive* were formed by compounding the past and future tenses of εἰμί, *to be,* with the old passive participle in -τος (τ becoming θ), or in some verbs with an early stem (2 Aor. and Fut., 289). (b). The old objective Aor. and Fut. now became *middle,* and the two voices were so far distinct in form.

275. Subsequent modifications were chiefly euphonic :
a. By a law which became so established in the language as not to allow exception (160), and which strikingly distinguishes Greek from Latin inflection, the endings μ, τ, and θ could not remain. They were, therefore, either *dropped, changed, prolonged,* or *both changed and prolonged :* as, ἔλυετ ἔλυε, λυομ (-οα, 160 f, 120) λύω, λύοιμ λύοιμι, φατ φησί (45 u, 143 b). See 296 s.
b. In some forms, σ fell out between two vowels, which were then usually contracted (140) : as, ἐλέγ(εσο, εο)ου, λέγ(οισο)οιο.
c. A new form of the 3 Pers. plur. secondary was formed by changing -τ of the sing. into -σαν (i. e. by changing τ final into σ, 160), and then affixing the plural sign ν, instead of prefixing it, with the needed union-vowel, which here, as after σ in the Aor., was α, 160, 273 b) : thus, 3 Sing. ἔφατ, Pl. ἔφασαν. Cf. the form in *-erunt,* in the Lat. Perf. (139).
d. In the Greek verb, there is a great tendency to lengthen a short vowel before an affix beginning with a single consonant (it being already long by position before those beginning with two consonants). It is natural that this should appear especially in the shorter forms ; hence, in the subjective more than in the objective, and in the sing. more than in the plur. or dual : thus, φαμ φαμι φημί, φας φής, φατ φησί (a) ; but Pl. φάμέν · ἔφην, ἐφάμεν · φάμενος (45 u).

276. a. We observe THREE CORRESPONDING PERIODS in *declension* and in *conjugation.* The oldest inflection in both, that of Dec. 3, and of the nude Pres. and Impf. (followed by the Perf. and Plup. pass.), was without connecting vowels. The next in order, that of Dec. 2, and of the euphonic Pres. and Impf. (followed by the Fut.), took the connecting vowels ο and ε (Lat. *o* and *u, e* and *i*) ; while the latest form of simple inflection, that of Dec. 1, and of the Aor. and Perf. act. systems, made use of α (Lat. *a* or *i*) as a connective.
b. In the Perf. and Plup. act., we find a series of euphonic devices, to meet the alternate demands of pure and impure stems ; and, as the result, four successive formations : 1. the *primitive nude formation ;* 2. the *formation in -α, -ειν ;* 3. the *formation in -κα, -κειν after a vowel ;* 4. the *formation in -κα, -κειν after a consonant* (after a *labial or palatal mute,* softened to -ά, -εἱν, 149). The last formation nowhere appears in Hom., and the third only in a few words. See 289, 317 s.

CHAPTER VIII.

PREFIXES OF CONJUGATION.

277. The Greek verb has two prefixes: the AUGMENT and the REDUPLICATION (32).

I. The AUGMENT (augmentum, *increase*) prefixes ε- in the SECONDARY TENSES of the *Indicative*, to denote *past time* (271 d).

a. If the verb begins with a *consonant*, the ε- constitutes a distinct syllable, and the augment is termed SYLLABIC: as, λύω *to loose*, γνωρίζω *recognize*, ῥίπτω *throw;* Impf. ἔλυον, ἐγνώριζον, ἔρριπτον (146); Aor. ἔλυσα, ἐγνώρισα, ἔρριψα.

b. If the verb begins with a *vowel*, the ε- unites with it, and the augment is termed TEMPORAL.

c. The *syllabic augment* is so named, because it increases the number of *syllables;* the *temporal* (temporālis, from tempus, *time*), because it increases the *time*, or *quantity*, of an initial short vowel. For the syllabic augment before a vowel, see 279 b. The *breathing of an initial vowel* remains the same after the augment.

278. RULES FOR THE TEMPORAL AUGMENT (7). a. The prefix ε- unites with α to form η, and with the other vowels, if short, to form the cognate long vowels: as,

ἀδικέω *to injure,* ἀθλέω *contend,* ἐλπίζω *hope,* ἱκετεύω *supplicate,* ὀρθόω *erect,* ὑβρίζω *insult;* Impf. (ἐα)ἠδίκουν, ἤθλουν, (ἐε)ἤλπιζον, (ἐϊ)ἱκέτευον, (ἐο)ὤρθουν, (ἐυ)ὕβριζον · Aor. ἠδίκησα, ἤθλησα, ἤλπισα, ἱκέτευσα, &c.

b. In like manner, the ε- unites with the prepositive of the diphthong αι, and also of αυ and οι not followed by a vowel in the stem: as,

αἰτέω *to ask,* αὐξάνω *increase,* οἰκτίζω *pity,* οἴομαι *think;* Impf. (ἔαι) ᾔτουν (109), ηὔξανον, ᾤκτιζον, ᾠόμην · Aor. ᾔτησα, ηὔξησα, ᾤκτισα, ᾠήθην.

c. In other cases, the ε- is absorbed by the initial vowel or diphthong, without producing any change: as,

ἡγέομαι *to lead,* ὠφελέω *profit,* εἴκω *yield,* οἰωνίζομαι *augur,* οὐτάζω *wound;* Impf. (ἐη)ἡγούμην, ὠφέλουν, εἶκον, οἰωνιζόμην, οὔταζον · Aor. ἡγησάμην, ὠφέλησα, εἶξα, οἰωνισάμην, οὔτασα.

d. But in verbs beginning with ευ, a few beginning with οι, εἰκάζω *to conjecture,* and ἀυαίνω *to dry,* usage is variable: as, εἴκαζον and in Att. also ᾔκαζον, αὐάνθην and ηὐάνθην · εὔχομαι *pray,* εὐξάμην and ηὐξάμην · οἰστράω *goad,* οἴστρησα or ᾤστρησα Eur. Bac. 32. Ει is also changed in ᾔειν and ᾔδειν (45 m, 46 a).

279. **a.** The verbs βούλομαι *to will*, δύναμαι *to be able*, and μέλλω *to purpose*, sometimes add the temporal to the syllabic augment, particularly in the later Attic : as,

ἐβουλόμην and ἠβουλόμην, ἐδυνήθην and ἠδυνήθην, ἔμελλον and ἤμελλον. Like forms are found from ἀπολαύω *enjoy*, and παρανομέω *transgress*.

b. In a few verbs beginning with a vowel, the ε- constitutes a distinct syllable, with, sometimes, a double augment: as,

ἄγνῡμι *to break*, ἔαξα· ἀνοίγω *to open*, ἀνέῳγον (278 b), ἀνέῳξα. Add ἁλίσκομαι *to be captured*, ἀνδάνω (Ion. and poet.) *please*, ὁράω *see*, οὐρέω mingo, ὠθέω *push*, ὠνέομαι *buy*, and some poetic, chiefly Epic, forms: as, ἐῳνοχόει Δ. 3.

c. In a few verbs beginning with ε, the usual contraction of εε into ει takes place (121): as,

ἐάω *to permit*, εἴων, εἴᾱσα. Add ἐθίζω *to accustom*, ἑλίσσω *roll*, ἕλκω *draw*, ἕπω *be occupied with*, ἐργάζομαι *work*, ἕρπω and ἑρπύζω serpo, *creep*, ἑστιάω *entertain*, ἔχω *have*; the Aorists εἷλον *took*, εἷσα (Ion. and poet.) *set*, εἷμεν, εἵμην, εἵθην (45 k, n); and the Plup. εἱστήκειν fr. Perf. ἕστηκα (45 f) *stand*. So εἰ from ἐΐ (119) in the Aor. εἶδον, εἰδόμην (s. ἰδ-, 50), *I saw*.

d. An initial ε followed by ο unites with this vowel, instead of uniting with the augment: as, ἑορτάζω *to celebrate a feast*, (ἐεο)ἑώρταζον. So, in the Plup., ἑῴκειν, and the poet. ἑώλπειν, ἑώργειν, fr. Perf. ἔοικα *seem*, ἔολπα *hope*, ἔοργα *have wrought*.

e. The forms in b, c, and d are to be referred, in part at least, to an original digamma or σ (140): as, ἔϝαξαν ἔαξαν γ. 298, iv. 2. 20; (ἐϝα) ἔανδανε Hdt. 9. 5; ἔσερπον (εἑ)εἷρπον Soph. O. C. 147, (ἐσεσ)εἱστήκειν (cf. 141). In a very few cases, a form resembling the augmented is found out of the Indicative: as, Part. κατ-εάξας Lys. 100. 5.

f. An initial α, chiefly when followed by a vowel, remains in the augmented tenses of a very few verbs, mostly poetic: as, ἀΐω *to hear*, ἄϊον (yet ἐπήϊσε Hdt. 9. 93). See ἀναλίσκω (50). So ἑλληνίσθην (that the word Ἕλλην may not be disguised), Th. 2. 68, and in poetry ἐζόμην, καθεζόμην, Æsch. Eum. 3, Pr. 229. In these words ε is long by position.

280. II. The REDUPLICATION (reduplĭco, *to redouble*) doubles the initial letter of the COMPLETE TENSES *in all the modes*, to denote *completed action*.

a. RULE. If the verb begins with a *single consonant*, or with a *mute* and *liquid* (except γν), the initial consonant is repeated, with the insertion of ε; but otherwise, the reduplication has the same form with the augment. In the PLUPERFECT, the *augment is prefixed* to the reduplication, except when this has the same form with the augment. Thus,

λύω *to loose*, Perf. λέλυκα, Plup. ἐλελύκειν· γράφω *write*, γέγραφα, ἐγεγράφειν· φιλέω *love*, πεφίληκα (159 a), ἐπεφιλήκειν· ῥαψῳδέω *prate*, ἐρραψῴδηκα (159 e), ἐρραψῳδήκειν· γνωρίζω (277 a), ἐγνώρικα, ἐγνωρίκειν· ζηλόω *emulate*, ἐζήλωκα· ψεύδομαι *lie*, ἔψευσμαι· ἀδικέω (278 a), ἠδίκηκα, ἠδικήκειν· αὐξάνω (278 b), ηὔξημαι· ἡγέομαι (278 c), ἥγημαι· ὁράω (279 b), ἑώρᾱκα, ἑωράκειν· ἐργάζομαι (279 c), εἴργασμαι· εἶκα, εἴκειν (45 k).

b. In a few cases, the first of two other consonants is repeated, especially if there has been syncope : as, πετάννῦμι *to spread* (s. πετα-, πτα-) πέπταμαι· μιμνήσκω *remind*, μέμνημαι· κτάομαι *acquire*, κέκτημαι, i. 7. 3, but also ἔκτημαι (properly Ion., as Hdt. 2. 42, yet Pl. Prot. 340 d, e).

c. Verbs beginning with βλ, γλ, and a few others vary : as, βλαστάνω *to bud*, βεβλάστηκα and ἐβλάστηκα · γλύφω *carve*, γέγλυμμαι and ἔγλυμμαι. For ἔοικα, ἔολπα, ἔοργα, cf. 279 b, d ; and for the Pret. οἶδα *know*, 278 d.

281. a. In five verbs beginning with a liquid, εἰ- or ἐι- commonly takes the place of the regular reduplication, through euphonic change :

λαγχάνω *to obtain by lot*, εἴληχα and λέλογχα, εἴληγμαι· λαμβάνω *take*, εἴληφα, εἴλημμαι and λέλημμαι· λέγω *collect*, εἴλοχα, εἴλεγμαι and λέλεγμαι· μείρομαι *share*, εἵμαρμαι, εἱμάρμην · s. ῥε- *say*, εἴρηκα, εἴρημαι.

b. Some of these forms seem to have arisen from an omitted consonant (the rough breathing in εἵμαρμαι, as in ἕστηκα, pointing to an original σ ; cf. 141, 279 e). They were sometimes imitated by late writers in the Aor. Pass.: παρειλήφθησαν Dion. H. 168. 3.

c. Some verbs which begin with ἀ, ε, or ο, followed by a single consonant, prefix to the usual reduplication the two first letters of the root : as, ἀλείφω *to anoint*, ἀλήλιφα, ἀληλίφειν, ἀλήλιμμαι· ἐλαύνω *drive*, ἐλήλακα, ἐλήλακειν· ὀρύσσω *dig*, ὀρώρυχα.

d. This prefix is termed by grammarians, though not very appropriately (87 b), the *Attic Reduplication*. It seldom receives an augment in the Plup. (c), except in the verb ἀκούω *to hear*: ἀκήκοα, commonly ἠκηκόειν (Hdt. ἀκηκόειν) ; so ὠρώρυκτο vii. 8. 14. This reduplication prefers a short vowel in the penult : as, ἀλήλιφα, though ἤλειφα · ἐλήλυθα, Pf. of ἔρχομαι (50). In ἐγρήγορα (ἐγείρω *wake*), v. 7. 10, the second consonant is also prefixed ; and in the Ep. ἐμνήμῦκε (ἠμύω *bow*) X. 491, ε lengthened by an inserted consonant is used, instead of repeating ἡ.

282. III. PREFIXES IN COMPOSITION. 1. Verbs compounded with a *preposition*, receive the augment and reduplication *after* the preposition : thus, προσγράφω *to ascribe*, προσέγραφον, προσγέγραφα· ἐξελαύνω *drive out*, ἐξήλαυνον, ἐξελήλακα.

a. Before the prefix ε-, prepositions ending in a consonant which is changed in the theme, resume that consonant ; and those ending in a vowel, except περί and πρό, regularly suffer elision (128). The final vowel of πρό often unites with the ε- by crasis (126 γ). Thus, ἐμβάλλω *to throw in* (150), ἐνέβαλλον· ἐκβάλλω *throw out* (165), ἐξέβαλλον· ἀποβάλλω *throw away*, ἀπέβαλλον· περιβάλλω *throw around*, περιέβαλλον· προβάλλω *throw before*, προέβαλλον and προὔβαλλον.

b. A few verbs receive their prefixes *before* the preposition ; a few receive them both *before* and *after ;* and a few are *variable :* as, ἐπίσταμαι *to understand*, ἠπιστάμην· ἐνοχλέω *trouble*, ἠνώχλουν, ἠνώχληκα· καθεύδω *sleep*, ἐκάθευδον, καθηῦδον, and καθεῦδον (278 d). These exceptions to the rule are chiefly in those compounds in which the simple verb is not in common use, so that the composition is lost sight of.

c. Some derivative verbs, resembling compounds in their form, follow the same analogy : as, διαιτάω *to regulate* (from δίαιτα *mode of life*), διῄτησα and ἐδιῄτησα, δεδιῄτηκα· ἐκκλησιάζω *hold an assembly* (ἐκκλησία), ἐξεκκλησίαζον, ἠκκλησίαζον, and ἐκκλησίαζον (ἐξεκκλησίασαν v. 1. Th. 8. 93) ; ἐπιστατέω *command* (ἐπιστάτης), ἐπεστάτει ii. 3. 11.

283. 2. Verbs in which δυσ-, *ill*, precedes a vowel which the augment changes (§ 278), commonly receive their prefixes *after* this particle : as, δυσαρεστέω *to be displeased*, δυσηρέστουν. So, sometimes, with εὖ, *well*: εὐεργετέω *benefit*, εὐεργέτουν and εὐηργέτουν.

3. Other verbs in which there is composition, receive the augment and reduplication at the *beginning*: as, λογοποιέω *to fable*, ἐλογοποίουν · δυστυχέω *fare ill*, ἐδυστύχησα, δεδυστύχηκα · εὐτυχέω *prosper*, εὐτύχουν or ηὐτύχουν (278 d).

a. With, however, doubtful or rare variations ; as in some compounds of ποιέω : ὡδοπεποιημένη (v. l. ὡδοποιημένη) v. 3. 1.

DIALECTIC USE.

284. a. It was long before the use of the augment as the sign of past time became fully established in the Greek. In the old poets it appears as a kind of *optional sign*, which might be used or omitted at pleasure : thus, ἔθηκεν, θῆκε, Α. 2, 55 ; ὡς ἔφατο, ὡς φάτο, Α. 33, 188 ; ἔβαλε, βάλε, Δ. 473, 480 ; ὁρώρει, ὠρώρει, Σ. 493, 498. Hom. regularly omits it with the dual in -την. The omission of the reduplication is rare in Hom., chiefly found in some preteritive forms : as, ἄνωγα *command*, a. 269 (so retained in Hdt. and Att. poets), ἕσμαι *wear*, ω. 250, ἔρχαται II. 481. But in the Att. redupl., he does not always lengthen the second vowel : as, ἀλάλημαι Ψ. 74, ἀλάλυκτημαι Κ. 94.

b. This license continued in Ionic prose in respect to the *temporal augment*, and the *augment of the Plup.*, and was even extended to the reduplication when it had the same form with the temporal augment : as, ἄγον, ἦγον, Hdt. 1. 70, 3. 47 ; δέδοκτο Id. 5. 96 ; ἄφθη, ἄψατο, ἀμμένης, ἐργάζοντο, κατέργαστο, κατειργασμένου Id. 1. 19, 86, 66, 123. So, more rarely, in respect to the *syllabic augment*, and the reduplication having the same form : as, νόεε or ἐνόεε Hdt. 1. 155 ; παρεσκευάδατο, παρασκευάδατο Id. 7. 218, 219 ; and even, for euphony's sake, ἐπαλιλλόγητο Id. 1. 118.

c. In respect to the *augment of the Pluperfect*, and of the impersonal ἐχρῆν, this freedom remained even in Attic prose : as, ἤδη τετελευτήκει; ἀποδεδράκει, vi. 4. 11, 13, διαβεβήκει vii. 3. 20 (this omission of the augment occurs chiefly after a vowel) ; ἐχρῆν Cyr. 8. 1. 1, oftener χρῆν Rep. A. 3. 6. Of the poets, the lyric approached the nearest to the freedom of the old Epic, while the dramatic, in the iambic trimeter, were confined the most closely to the usage of Attic prose.

d. For such forms as ἔρεξεν B. 274, ἔδδεισεν A. 33, δείδοικα A. 555, see 171, 134 n. For Perf. εἶμαι τ. 72, 'άδηκώς, K. 98, 'άρημένος ζ. 2, cf. 279 c, f. For ῥερυπωμένα, &c., see 159 e. On the other hand, we find, after the analogy of verbs beginning with ῥ, ἔμμορε A. 278, ἔσσυμαι N. 79.

e. In the Epic language, the 2 *Aor. act. and mid.* often receives the reduplication, which remains through all the modes, while the Ind. admits the augment in addition (especially in case of the Att. redupl.) : as, δέδαε θ. 448, κεκάμω A. 168, κεκύθωσι ζ. 303, λελάχωσι H. 80, λελαβέσθαι δ. 388 ; with the augment sometimes added, κέκλετο Δ. 508, ἐκέκλετο Ζ. 66, πέφραδε Ξ. 500, ἐπέφραδον K. 127, πέφνε N. 363, ἔπεφνε Δ. 397 ; Att. Redupl. ἤγαγεν Δ. 179, ἠγάγετο Χ. 116, ἄραρον Μ. 105, ἤραρε Δ. 110, ὤρορε Β. 146. These are reduplicated at the *end* of the stem : ἠνίπαπ-ον from s. ἐνιπ-, Β. 245, and ἠρύκακ-ον from ἐρυκ-, Ε. 321.

§ 287. AFFIXES OF CONJUGATION. 193

f. With some of these 2 Aor. forms, *reduplicated Futures* are associated: as, κεκαδών Λ. 334, κεκαδήσει φ. 153 ; πεπίθοιμεν A. 100, πεπίθοιτο K. 204, πεπιθήσω X. 223 ; πεφιδοίμην ι. 277, πεφιδήσεται O. 215.

g. Some of these reduplicated forms occur in Attic poetry : as, ἀράρεν Soph. El. 147, τετορήσω Ar. Pax 381. Ἤγαγον, and, less frequent, ἠγαγόμην remained even in Attic prose: as, i. 3. 17, Eq. 4. 1.

CHAPTER IX.

AFFIXES OF CONJUGATION.

I. CLASSIFICATION AND ANALYSIS.

285. The AFFIXES of the Greek verb may be divided into two great CLASSES (35 s) :

I. The SUBJECTIVE, belonging to all the tenses of the ACTIVE VOICE, and to the *Aorist passive.*

II. The OBJECTIVE, belonging to all the tenses of the MIDDLE VOICE, and to the *Future passive.*

a. The affixes of the Aor. pass. are subjective, as derived from the Impf. of the verb εἰμί, *to be;* and those of the Fut. pass. are objective, as derived from the Fut. of this verb (274). Of the affixes which are not thus derived, the *subjective* represent the *subject* of the verb as the *doer* of the action, and the *objective*, as, more or less directly, its *object* (30 a).

286. The affixes of the verb may likewise be divided into the following ORDERS :

1. The PRIMARY, belonging to the *primary tenses* of the Indicative mode, and to *all the tenses* of the Subjunctive.

2. The SECONDARY, belonging to the *secondary tenses* of the Indicative, and to *all the tenses* of the Optative (267 b, 269 c).

3. The IMPERATIVE, belonging to the Imperative mode.

4. The INFINITIVE, belonging to the Infinitive mode.

5. The PARTICIPIAL, belonging to the Participle.

287. These affixes may be resolved into the following ELEMENTS : A. TENSE-SIGNS, B. CONNECTING VOWELS, and C. FLEXIBLE ENDINGS.

a. See 32. When there is no danger of mistake, these elements may be simply called *signs, connectives,* and *flexives* or *endings.*

A. Tense-Signs (32 g).

288. The *tense-signs* are letters or syllables which are added to the stem in *particular tenses*, and to which the flexible endings are appended, either immediately or with connecting vowels.

In the *Fut.* and *Aor.*, act. and mid., and in the *Fut. Perf.*, the tense-sign is -σ- ; * in the *Perf.* and *Plup. act.*, it is -κ- ; in the *Aor. pass.*, it is -θε- ; in the *Fut. pass.*, it is -θησ- ; in the *other tenses*, it is *wanting* :

λύ-σ-ω, ἐλυ-σ-άμην, λελύ-σ-ομαι · λέλυ-κ-α, ἐλελύ-κ-ειν · λυ-θε-ίην · λυ-θήσ-ομαι · λύ-ω, ἐλυ-όμην, λέλυ-μαι, ἐλελύ-μην (37).

a. The sign -θε-, before a vowel, is contracted with it ; otherwise, except before ντ, it becomes -θη- (275 d) : λυ(θέ ω)θῶ, λυ(θε-ίην)θείην · λυ-θέ-ντων, λυ(θε-ντς)θείς · ἐλύ-θη-ν, λύ-θη-τι.

289. The letters κ and θ, of the tense-signs, are sometimes *omitted*. Tenses wanting these letters are termed *second ;* and, in distinction, tenses which have them, though commonly later forms, are termed *first :* as, 1 Perf. πέπεικα, 2 Perf. πέποιθα · 1 Plup. ἐπεπείκειν, 2 Plup. ἐπεποίθειν (39) ; 1 Aor. pass. ἠγγέλθην, 2 Aor. pass. ἠγγέλην · 1 Fut. pass. ἀγγελθήσομαι, 2 Fut. pass. ἀγγελήσομαι (40). See § 274, 276 b.

a. The tense in the *active* and *middle voices*, which is termed the *Second Aorist*, is simply an old Present System retained (except the Pres. ind.) in an aorist sense, after the formation of a new Present System from a later form of the stem (273 d) : thus, ἔλιπον and ἐλιπόμην (38) are formed from the old stem λιπ-, in precisely the same way as ἔλειπον and ἐλειπόμην from the new stem λειπ-.

b. We have thus, in the three voices, six additional tense-forms, constituting three systems : viz. (distinguishing the systems in the same way as their tenses), the Second Aorist System, the Second Perfect System, and the Second Compound System.

c. The regular or *first* tenses will be usually spoken of, where no distinction is required, simply as the *Aorist*, the *Perfect*, &c. ; and their systems, as the *Aorist System*, the *Perfect System*, &c.

d. In each system, the form first presented in the tables and rules of inflection is regarded as the *leading form :* and whatever appears in this form of any verb in respect to the *stem*, or the *tense-sign*, or the *union of the affix with the stem*, will be understood as belonging also to the other forms of the system, if nothing appears to the contrary.

e. In each tense, the stem, with the tense-sign and reduplication, if these are present, is termed the *base* of the tense, or the *tense-stem ;* as in the Pres. of λύω, λυ- ; in the Fut., λυσ- ; in the Perf. act., λελυκ-.

f. The regular additions which are made to the base in the Fut. and Fut. Perf. throughout, and in the Subjunctive of every tense, are the same as in the Pres. : as, λύ-ω λύσ-ω, λύ-εις λύσ-εις · λύ-ομαι λύσ-ομαι λυθήσ-ομαι λελύσ-ομαι · Subj. λύ-ω λύσ-ω λελύκ-ω.

B. Connecting Vowels (32 h).

290. The *connecting vowels* serve to unite the flexible endings with the stem or tense-sign, and assist in marking the distinctions of *mode* and *tense*.

a. The *Aor.*, *Perf.*, and *Plup. pass.* have no connecting vowel in the Ind., Imv., Inf., and Part. With this exception, the regular formation is according to the following rules. But wherever these admit *either* an *A* vowel or another vowel, it will be understood that the *A* vowel belongs to the *Aorist* (273 b, c), and the other vowel to the remaining tenses ; and that, wherever they admit *either* an *O* or an *E* vowel, the *O* vowel is used before a liquid, and the *E* vowel before other letters (114 c).

b. The connective is regularly contracted with an α, ε, or ο preceding ; and also with the flexives -ι, -αι, and -ο, except in the Optative.

291. 1. In the Indicative, the connective is -α- in the Aor. and Perf., -ει- in the Plup., and -ο- or -ε- in the other tenses : Aor. ἐλύσ-α-μεν, ἐλυσ-ά-μην · Pf. λελύκ-α-τε · Plup. ἐλελύκ-ει-ν · Pr. λύ-ο-μεν, λύ-ε-τε · Impf. ἔλυ-ο-ν, ἔλυ-ε-ς · Fut. λύσ-ο-μαι, λύσ-ε-ται.

a. In the sing. of the Pres. and Fut. act., the connectives, by simple protraction or the absorption of the flexives, became -ω- and -ει- : λύ(ο-μ, ο-α)ω, λύσω, λύ(ε-s)εις, λύσεις, λύ(ε-τ, ε-ε)ει, λύσει. See 275 a, d, 160 f.

b. In the 3 Sing. of the Aor. and Perf. act., -ε- takes the place of -α- : and in the 3 Plur. of the Plup., it commonly takes the place of -ει- : ἔλυσ-ε, λέλυκ-ε · λελύκ-ε-σαν or λελύκ-ει-σαν.

c. The original connective of the Plup. was -εα-, which remained in the Ion. (273 c) : as, ᾔδεα Ξ. 71, ἐγεγόνεε Hdt. 1. 11. An early contraction into -η- is especially old Att., but also occurs in the Ep. and Dor.: as, 1 Sing. ᾔδη Soph. Ant. 18 ; 2 S. ᾔδης Ib. 447 ; 3 S. ᾔδη Α. 70. By precession (114 s) -η- passed into -ει-, which became the common connective, and in the 3 Sing. is already found in Hom. (fr. -εε) : as, ἑστήκει Σ. 557.

292. 2. The Subjunctive takes the connectives of the Pres. ind., lengthening -ο- to -ω- and -ε- to -η- (§ 272 d) : Ind. and Subj. λύ-ω, λύσ-ω · λύ-ει-ς λύ-η-ς, λύ-ει λύ-η, λύ-ο μεν λύ-ω-μεν, λύ ε-τε λύ-η-τε, λύ(ο-νσι)ουσι λύ(ω-νσι)ωσι · λύσ-ε-ται λύσ-η-ται.

293. 3. The Optative has, for its connective, ι (the general sign of the mode, 272 d), either alone or with other vowels.

Rule. If the tense has no connecting vowel in the Ind., and its base ends in α, ε, or ο, then the Opt. has -ιη- in the *subjective* forms, and simply -ι- in the *objective ;* in other cases, it has -αι- or -οι- : λυθε-ίη-ν (37) : ἰστα-ίη-ν, ἰστα-ί-μην, τιθε-ίη-ν, τιθε-ί-μην, διδο-ίη-ν, διδο ί-μην (45) ; λύσ-αι-μι, λυσ-αί-μην · λύ-οι-μι, λυ-οί-μην, λύσ-οι-μι, λελυσ-οί-μην · ἵ-οι-μι, δεικνύ οι-μι, δεικνυ οί-μην (45 a, c, m).

a. In Optatives in -ίην, the η is often omitted in the plural and dual, especially in the 3 Plur., where the longer form is much less used in classic Greek : ἰσταῖμεν, τιθεῖτε, διδοῖεν, ἰσταῖτον (45) ; λυθεῖεν (37) ; but παραδοίησαν ii. 1. 10, σωθείησαν Cyr. 8. 1. 2.

b. In *contract active forms*, the connective -οι- often assumes η in the Pres., and sometimes in the Fut.: φιλέ-οι-μι, contr. φιλοῖ-μι or φιλοίη-ν (42); φανοῖμι or φανοίην (40).

c. The form of the Opt. in -οίην, for -οιμι, is called the *Attic Optative*, as especially used by Att. writers, though not confined to them: ἐνωρῴη Hdt. 1. 89, οἰκοίητε Theoc. 12. 28. It is most employed in the sing., where it is the common form in contracts in -έω and -όω, and still more in those in -άω. In the 3 Plur. it is very rare. It is also found in the 2 Perf., as πεποιθοίη (38) Ar. Ach. 940, and in the 2 Aor. of the simple verb ἔχω *to have*, though its compounds have commonly the form in -οιμι· σχοίη Cyr. 7. 1. 36, κατάσχοις Mem. 3. 11. 11. So λοίην (45 m).

d. The Aor. opt. act. has, in the 2 and 3 Sing. and the 3 Plural, a second and far more common form, in which the connective is that of the Ind. with ει prefixed: as, λύσ-εια-ς, λύσ-ειε, λύσ-εια-ν.

e. This form, like many other remains of old usage, was termed by grammarians *Æolic*. It was little used in the Dor. It greatly prevailed in the Att. and Ion., but not exclusively: μείνειας Γ. 52, ψαύσειε Hdt. 3. 30, ἄρξειαν Th. 6. 11; λέξαι Æsch. Ag. 170, ἀποδέξαιεν Hdt. 8. 35.

f. The Opt. avoided the immediate attachment of the short flexives -ν and -ντ to ι, and in various ways. See above, and 296, 300.

294. 4. In the IMPERATIVE, the connective is -α-, -ε-, or -ο-; in the INFINITIVE, it is -α- or -ε-; in the PARTICIPLE, it is -α- or -ο-: λυσ-ά-τω, λυσ-ά-σθων, λυ-έ-τω, λύ-ε-σθε, λυ-ό-ντων· λύσ-α-σθαι, λῦσ-α-ι, λύ-ε-σθαι, λελυκ-έ-ναι · λυσ-ά-μενος, λυσ-ό-μενος, λύ(ο-ντς)ων.

a. In the Imv., -α- passes into the kindred -ο- before the flexive -ν (114 b, c, 297 c): λῦς(αθ, αν)ον.

b. In the Inf. of the *Pres. and Fut. act.*, -ε- is lengthened to -ει- (275 d): λύ(ε-ν)ει-ν, λύσ-ει-ν.

C. FLEXIBLE ENDINGS.

295. The *flexible endings* (flexibĭlis, *changeable*) are the chief instruments of conjugation, marking by their changes the distinctions of *person, number, voice*, and, in part, of *tense* and *mode*.

a. In the finite modes they are essentially *pronouns, affixed* instead of being, as in English, *prefixed* (271 b). They are exhibited in 32 i.

b. Where the secondary endings differ from the primary, they are usually shorter, on account of the augment.

296. 1 SING.: -μ (μι, ν, *); -μαι, -μην. The flexive -μ, after -α- *connective*, and, in *primary* forms, after -ο- and -ω- *connective*, is *wanting;* after -οι- and -αι-, and in the *nude Present* (303 a), it becomes -μι; in other cases, it becomes ν (275 a):

ἔλῡσ-α, λελύκ-α, ᾔδ-εα ᾔδη (46 a); λύ(ο-μ)ω, λύ(ω-μ)ω · λύσ-οι-μι, λύσ-αι-μι (293 f), ἵστη-μι (45); ἔλῡ-ο-ν, ἐλελύκ-ει-ν (273 e), ἐλύθην-ν, λυθείη-ν · φιλοίη-ν, φανοίη-ν (293 b); ἵστην, ἱσταίην (45). Cf. Lat. *lu*(o-m)*o, lui*.

§ 299.   FLEXIBLE ENDINGS.   197

a. In those cases in which the flexive -μ is usually said to be wanting, it may still be regarded as virtually present in a vowel into which it has been changed or absorbed ; and so, in some cases, the flexive -τ of the 3 Pers. (μ having passed into α, and τ into ε, 160 f, 291 a).

297. 2 Sing. : -σ (σθα), -θ (θι, ς, ε, ν, *) ; -σαι, -σο.   a. For -ς, a *stronger form* was -σθα (271 c ; cf. Lat. *-sti* and Eng. *-st*).

b. This was retained as the common form in ἦσθα, ἔφησθα (45 l, u), and οἶσθα (46 a) ; and was good Attic in ᾔδεισθα, ᾔδησθα (46 a), and ᾔεισθα (45 m). Other examples are furnished by the poets (particularly in the Subj., by Hom.) : as, ἐθέλῃσθα A. 554, εἴπῃσθα Υ. 250 ; βάλοισθα Ο. 571, κλαίοισθα Ω. 619 ; τίθησθα ι. 404, διδοῖσθα Τ. 270 ; ἔχεισθα, φίλεισθα, Sap.

c. The Imv. flexive -θ is *dropped* after -ε- *connective;* with -α- *connective*, it becomes -ον ; after a *short vowel in the stem*, it becomes -ς in the 2 Aor., but in the *Pres.* unites as ε with the preceding vowel ; in other cases, it becomes -θι (275 a, 160 f) :

λῦ(ε-θ)ε (cf. Lat. *lue*) ; λῦσ(α-θ)ον (294 a ; cf. 169 c) ; θές, δός, ἔς (45 h) ; ἵστ(α-θ, α-ε, 120 h)η, τίθ(ε-ε)ει, δίδ(ο-ε)ου, δείκν(υ-ε)υ (45 a) ; τρίβη-θι (38), λύθη-τι (159 c) ; γνῶθι, δρᾶθι (45 h) ; ἴσθι, δέδιθι (46).

d. Φημί and εἰμί form the Pres. imv. in -θι : φάθί, ἴθι. The poets and late writers sometimes give this form to yet other Presents in -μι ; and they sometimes shorten βῆθι and στῆθι, in composition, to βᾱ and στᾱ : ὄρνῡθι *rouse*, Z. 363, ἵλᾱθι *be gracious;* κατάβα *descend*, Ar. Ran. 35.

e. In the flexives -σαι and -σο, σ is *dropped between two vowels*, except in the *Perf. and Plup. pass.*, and sometimes the *nude Pres. and Impf.* (275 b) : as,

λύ(ε-σαι, ε-αι)ῃ or λύει (123 b) ; λύ(ε-ο)ου, ἐλύ(ε-ο)ου, ἐλύσ(α-ο)ω (120 s) ; λύ-σοι-ο, λύσ-αι-ο · λέλυ-σαι, λέλυ-σο, ἐλέλυ-σο · ἵστα-σαι, ἵστα-σο and ἱστ(α-ο)ω, τίθε-σαι and τίθ(ε-αι)ῃ, δίδο-σο and δίδ(ο-ο)ου, δ(ο-ο)οῦ (45 c, d, i).

f. The contraction of -εαι into -ει is a special Attic form, which was much used by pure writers, especially the more colloquial, and which, after yielding in other words to the common contraction into -ῃ, remained in βούλει, οἴει, and ὄψει, as the only good Attic.

g. The use of -αι for -α-ο in the Aor. imv. seems to be an irregular contraction with precession (118 b) : λῦσ(α-σο, α-ο)αι.

h. In *verbs in* -μι, -σαι remained more frequently than -σο. Exceptional cases occur, both of the retention and omission of the σ, esp. in the poets.

298. 3 Sing. : -τ (σι, *) -τω ; -ται, -το, -σθω. The flexive -τ becomes -σι in the *nude Pres.*, but elsewhere is *omitted:* as,

ἱστ(η-τ)ησι, ἵστη, δίδωσι, ἐδίδω (45 a, b) ; ἔλυ(ε-τ)ε, λύ(ε-τ, ε-ε)ει, ἔλυσε. See 275 a, 296 a.

a. In ἐστί (45 l), -τι is naturally preferred to -σι after σ.

299. 1 and 2 Plur., with the Dual : -μεν, -μεθα (μεσθα); -τε, -σθε ; -τον, -σθον ; -την, -σθην ; -των, -σθων. a. The 1 Pers. is the same in the plur. and dual, having, for its *subjective* ending, -μεν, and for its *objective*, -μεθα (271e ; poet. -μεσθα) : λύο-μεν, λυό-μεθα or, for the sake of the metre, λυό-μεσθα.

b. The 1 *Dual primary* had a special form in -μεθον, of which only three classical examples have been found, all in poetry before a vowel : περιδώμεθον Ψ. 485, λελείμμεθον Soph. El. 950, ὁρμώμεθον Id. Ph. 1079.

c. The 2 Plur. always ends in -ε. The 2 Dual is obtained by changing this vowel into -ον; and the 3 Dual, by changing it into -ον in the *primary* inflection, into -ην in the *secondary*, and into -ων in the *imperative:* 2 Pl. λύε-τε, ἐλύε-τε · 2 Du. λύε-τον, ἐλύε-τον · 3 Du. λυέτον, ἐλυέτην, λυέτων.

d. The 2 and 3 *Dual secondary* were not always distinct in form : as, in Hom. 3 Pers. ἐτεύχετον N. 346, θωρήσσεσθον N. 301 ; in Attic, 2 Pers. εἰχέτην Soph. O. T. 1511, ἠλλαξέτην Eur. Alc., εὑρέτην, ἐπεδημησάτην Pl.

300. 3 PLUR. : -ντ (νσι, ν, εν, σαν), -ντων or -τωσαν; -νται, -ντο, -σθων or -σθωσαν. a. The flexive -ντ, in the *primary tenses,* becomes -νσι. In the *secondary,* after -ο- or -α- *connective,* it becomes -ν; after a diphthong in the Opt., -εν; but, otherwise, -σαν (275 a, c).

λύ(ο-νσι, ο-ασι)ουσι, λύσουσι, λελύκ(α-νσι)ᾶσι, λύωσι · ἱστᾶσι, τιθεῖσι (45 a) ; ἔλῦ-ο-ν, ἔλῦσ-α-ν · λύοι-εν, λύσαι-εν, λυθεί-εν · ἐλελύκε-σαν, ἐλύθη-σαν, ἵστα-σαν, ἔστησαν, ἔθε-σαν (45 b, h). See 160, 143 b, 156, 293 f.

b. In the Perf. and Plup. pass. of *impure verbs,* the 3d Pers. pl. is either formed in -αται and -ατο (158) or, more commonly, supplied by the Part. with εἰσί and ἦσαν (45 l) : as, ἐφθάρ-αται Th. 3. 13, from φθείρω (s. φθαρ-) *to waste,* τετριμμένοι εἰσί (39).

c. The forms in -αται and -ατο are termed *Ionic.* Before these endings, a labial or palatal mute must be *rough* (φ, χ), and a lingual, *middle* (δ) : as, from τρέπω (s. τραπ-) *to turn,* (τετραπ-νται) τετράφαται Pl. Rep. 533 b; from τάσσω (39 ; τεταγ-νται) τετάχαται iv. 8. 5, ἐτετάχατο Th. 7. 4.

d. In the Imv., the older and shorter forms in -ντων and -σθων (termed *Attic,* 87 b), are the more common.

e. The forms in -ωσαν do not occur in Hom., and scarcely in Hdt. or the Dramatists : ἔστωσαν Hdt. 1. 147. They may have been later preferred, as distinct in form from the Part. and 3 Du. In the less frequent ἔστων Cyr. 4. 6. 10, and ἴτων Æsch. Eum. 32 (45 l, m), the old plural form (afterwards the dual, cf. 186 g, 271 c) remained without change.

301. INFINITIVE : -ν, -ναι, -ι ; -σθαι. The *subjective* ending, after -ει- *connective,* is -ν; after -α- *connective,* -ι ; but otherwise, -ναι : λύ-ει-ν, λύσ-ει-ν · λῦσ-α-ι (290 b) ; λελυκέ-ναι, λυθῆ-ναι · ἱστά-ναι, δεικνύ-ναι, θεῖ-ναι, δοῦ-ναι (45).

a. In the Pres. and Fut. act., the old form of the Inf. in -ε-ν prevailed, and obtained an ι in the prolonged connective, in lieu of the Dat. sign ι annexed in other forms. See 272 a.

302. PARTICIPLE : -ντ-ς (τ-ς) ; -μεν-ος. In the Perf. act., ν (passing into α, and then by precession into ο, 142, 114) became a connecting vowel : -ο-τς, for ντς. For the *declension* of the Part., see 26, 232 s ; for the Verbals in -τός and -τέος, 269 d, 272 c.

303. REMARKS. a. Affixes and forms which have no connecting vowel are termed *nude;* and others *euphonic* (183 a). Tenses are so

§ 305.   UNION OF STEM AND AFFIXES.   199

termed according to the *affixes of the Ind*. The REGULAR AFFIXES of the verb are those which are assigned to the tenses in 35 and 36, the *nude Pres. and Impf.* and the *Second Tenses* excepted. These affixes are *open* in the Pres. and Impf., and *close* in the other tenses (172 c). The 2 Aor. act. and mid. has the affixes of the Impf. ind., and of the Pres. in the other modes (289 a), with some variation of accent and, in the nude form, of euphonic change (38, 297 c). The other *Second Tenses* have the affixes of the *First*, with the omission noted in 35, 36, 289.

b. In the study of the Greek verb, the forms should be analyzed throughout, and the force of their parts carefully observed. The inflection should be repeated, not by a simple act of memory, but by an intelligent combination of the elements; which, few in number, produce a great and beautiful variety of forms.

c. Besides the full paradigm in 37, a briefer paradigm of strictly regular conjugation is presented in παύω (34), though less approved forms with an inserted σ also occur (307 e). The leading forms of translation are added, which the student will apply, with the requisite changes, to other verbs, while the details will appear more fully in Syntax.

II. UNION WITH THE STEM.

A. CONSONANT CHANGES.

304. 1. When the *close affixes follow a consonant*, changes are often required by general laws: as,

τρί(β-σω)ψω, ἔτα(γ-σα)ξα, πέπει(θ-σαι)σαι (151); τρί(β-τος)πτός (147); ἐτετρί(β-μην)μμην (148); ἐτετά(γ-κειν)χειν (149); ἐπεφά(ν-κειν)γκειν (150); φα(ν-σω)νῶ, ἔφ(αν-σα)ηνα (152). See 39 s.

a. In the *liquid verbs* κλίνω *to bend*, κρίνω *to judge*, κτείνω *to slay*, τείνω *to stretch*, and πλύνω *to wash*, ν is omitted before the affixes which remain close (152); except sometimes in poetry for the sake of the metre, and in late writers: κέκλιμαι, ἐκλίθην (ἐκλίνθη Z. 468); κέκρικα, ἐκρίθην.

b. In other verbs, ν *characteristic*, before μ, more frequently becomes σ, but sometimes becomes μ or is dropped: as, πέφασμαι (40); ξηραίνω *to dry*, ἐξήρασμαι, ἐξήραμμαι, and late ἐξήραμαι.

305. 2. FUTURE TENSE-SIGN, -σ-. In the FUTURE ACTIVE and MIDDLE, changes affecting the tense-sign often bring together two vowels, which are then *contracted*:

a. ATTIC FUTURE. In Futures in -ίσω from verbs in -ίζω of more than two syllables, the -σ- becomes -ε-: as,

κομ(ι-σω, ι-εω)ιῶ, κομ(ι-σο, ι-εο)ιοῦμαι, κομ(ι-σε, ι-εε)ιεῖσθαι, κομ(ι-σων)ιῶν (39 d); καθιεῖν ii. 1. 4. So in καθέξομαι *to sit*, Fut. (s. ἐδ-) καθε(δ-σο, δ-εο)δοῦμαι · and a few poet. or later forms: as, τε(κ-σε)κεῖσθαι Hom. Ven.

b. Some Futures in -άσω and -έσω drop the -σ-: as,

ἐλαύνω or ἐλάω *to drive*, F. ἐλ(ά-σω, ά-ω)ῶ, ἐλ(άσεις)ᾷς, ἐλ(άσεω)ᾶν or ἐλᾶν, ἐλ(άσων)ῶν · τελ(έ-σω, έ-ω)ῶ, τελ(έσει)εῖ, τελ(έ-σο, έ-ο)οῦμαι (42 g);

χέω *pour*, F. χ(έσω)έω, χ(έσεις, έεις)εῖς, χ(έσο)έομαι (cf. 309 b). So in καλέω CALL, μάχομαι *fight*, ἀμφιέννῦμι *clothe;* in all verbs in -άννῦμι, as σκεδάννῦμι *scatter;* and sometimes in verbs in -άζω, βιβάζω *make go*.

c. This form of Futures in -άσω, -έσω, and -ίσω, is termed the *Attic Future*, from its prevalence in Attic writers. It is not, however, confined to them ; nor do they employ it without exception : κτεριῶ Σ. 334 ; καταγιεῖν, δικᾶν, Hdt. 1. 86, 97 ; ἐλάσονταs vii. 7. 55, τελέσουσιν Cyr. 8. 6. 3, κομίσω Ar. Pl. 768. It is rare in the Opt. : βαδιοίμην Ar. Pl. 90.

d. DORIC FUTURE. A few verbs, in the *Fut. mid.* with an active sense, sometimes add ε to -σ-, after the Dor. form (325 b) :

πλέω *to sail*, F. πλεύσομαι and πλευ(σεο)σοῦμαι · φεύγω *flee*, φεύξομαι and φευξοῦμαι. Other Att. examples are κλαίω *weep*, νέω *no, swim*, παίζω *sport*, πίπτω *fall*, πνέω *blow*, πυνθάνομαι *inquire*. So ἐσσεῖται B. 393.

e. The Liquid, Att., and Dor. Futures, from their formation, are inflected like the contract Pres. (42). In a few verbs, the Pres. and Att. Fut. have the same form : ἐλῶ, τελῶ, καλῶ.

f. In a few verbs, the *old Pres.* remained as a Fut., after the formation of a new Pres.; or the poets used the same form as both Pres. and Fut. (273 a, d) : as, ἐσθίω *to eat*, F. ἔδομαι, Ar. Nub. 121 ; πίνω *drink*, F. πίομαι Cyr. 1. 3. 9 ; ἀνύω *accomplish*, ἐρύω *draw*, τανύω *stretch*, also as Fut. Λ. 365, 454, φ. 174. For χεύω as Fut., β. 222, see 50.

306. 3. AORIST TENSE-SIGN. a. The sign of the Aor. is omitted in εἶπα *said*, ἤνεγκα *bore*, ἔχεα *poured*, ἔκεα poet., *burned;* and in a few Epic forms, as ἔσσενα E. 208. See φημί, φέρω, χέω, καίω, σεύω, ἀλεύω, δατέομαι, in 50. For the Liq. Aor., see 152.

b. The Aor. borrows the Perf. tense-sign in ἔθηκα, ἔδωκα, and ἧκα (45).

These Aorists are used by classic writers only in the Ind., and chiefly in the Sing. and 3 Plur., the other forms being supplied by the 2 Aor. : ἐδώκατε vii. 7. 10. In the Middle, the Att. has only the Ind. ἠκάμην, (Eur. El. 622) ; while other dialects add ἐθηκάμην, K. 31, θηκάμενος Pind. P. 4. 52. Late writers extend the use of forms with κ in these verbs, and sometimes substitute forms with σ : Subj. δώκωσι Æsop. 78 ; δώσῃ Jn.

c. These peculiar forms in -κα, called 1 Aor. from the connective α, are *euphonic extensions* of the 2 Aor., after the analogy of the Perf. The flexive -μ passed into α, which became a connecting vowel ; and then κ was inserted to prevent hiatus (cf. 276 b, 320) : ἔθ(η-ν, η-α)η-κ-α, ἔθηκας.

307. 4. INSERTION OF σ. In many pure verbs, σ is inserted before the *regular passive affixes* beginning with μ, τ, or θ.

a. This insertion is usual after a *short vowel*, and (b) frequent after a *diphthong;* but (c) not after a *simple long vowel.* (d) Exceptions, however, occur both ways ; and (e) some verbs are *variable*. Thus,

(a) σπάω *to draw*, Pass. Pf. ἔσπα-σ-μαι, ἔσπασαι, ἔσπα-σ-ται, ἐσπά-σ-μεθα, ἐσπα-σ-μένος, Λ. ἐσπά-σ-θην, F. σπα-σ-θήσομαι · τετέλε-σ-μαι, ἐτελέσθην, τελεστέος (42 g) ; (b) σέσει-σ-μαι, ἐσείσθην, σειστός (44) ; ἐπεπλεύ-σ-μην (42 g) ; κελεύω *command*, κεκέλευ-σ-μαι, κεκέλευσται, ἐκελεύσθην ·

§ 310.   METATHESIS. VOWEL CHANGES.   201

(c) τετίμημαι, φιλητός, ἐδηλώθην (42 f); (d) λέλυμαι, ἐλύθην (37); βεβούλευμαι, ἐβουλεύθην (44); χόω *heap*, κέχω-σ-μαι, ἐχώσθην; (e) **δράω** *do*, δέδραμαι, rarely δέδρασμαι, ἐδράσθην · κλείω *shut*, κέκλειμαι and κέκλεισμαι, ἐκλείσθην · **μέμνημαι** *remember*, ἐμνήσθην · **χράομαι** *use*, κέχρημαι, ἐχρήσθην.

f. The σ is attracted most strongly by θ. When σ is thus inserted in the Perf. or Plup., the 3 Plur. wants the simple form (300 b): ἐσπασμένοι εἰσί, σεσεισμένοι ἦσαν.

308. 5. METATHESIS. In a few liquid verbs, the concurrence of consonants is avoided by transposing the stem-mark (145; cf. 152): as, βάλλω *to throw*, κάμνω *labor*, τέμνω *cut*; Pf. βέβληκα, κέκμηκα, τέτμηκα, for βέβαλκα, &c.; βέβλημαι, ἐτμήθην.

B. VOWEL CHANGES.

309. 1. CONTRACTION. The *regular open affixes* are contracted with *a*, *ε*, or *o* preceding.

a. Verbs in which this contraction takes place are termed CONTRACT VERBS or, from the accent of the theme, *Perispomena*. In distinction, other verbs are termed *Barytone Verbs* (768).

b. The verbs **κάω** *to burn*, and **κλάω** *weep*, which have likewise the forms καίω and κλαίω, are not contracted. Dissyllabic Verbs in -έω admit only the contractions into ει: as, **πλέω** *sail*, πλέεις πλεῖς, πλέει πλεῖ, πλέομεν, πλέετε πλεῖτε, πλέουσι. Except **δέω** *bind* (thus distinguished from δέω *need*), τὸ δοῦν, τῷ δοῦντι Pl. Crat. 419a, b; and a few rare cases.

c. The Inf. is now commonly regarded as contracted from the old form in -εν (301 a): τιμ(α-εν)ᾶν, rather than τιμ(α-ειν)ᾶν, φιλ(ε-εν)εῖν, δηλ(ο-εν)οῦν. See 109 a. The contract Ind. and Subj. of verbs in -άω agree in form.

310. 2. VOWEL LENGTHENED. Before the *regular close affixes*, a *short* vowel is commonly lengthened (ἄ becoming η, unless preceded by ε, ι, ρ, or ρο, 115 a): as,

τιμάω, τιμήσω, τετίμηκα, ἐτιμήθην · **φιλέω**, ἐφίλησα, φιλήσομαι, πεφίλημαι, πεφιλήσομαι · **δηλόω**, ἐδηλωσάμην, ἐδεδηλώμην (42); τίω *honor*, poet., τίσω, ἔτισα · **φύω** *produce*, φύσω, πέφυκα · **ἐάω**, ἐάσω, εἴασα · ἐστιάω, εἱστίακα (279 c); **θηράω**, ἐθηράθην (42 g); ἀκροάομαι *hear*, ἀκροάσομαι.

a. A few verbs vary from the rule in respect to the use of ᾱ or η: thus, ἄ becomes η, in **τιτράω** *bore*, and tenses from χρα- *to supply need* (F. τρήσω, χρήσω, χρήσομαι); ᾱ, in **ποινάομαι** *avenge one's self*, **πα-** *acquire* (ποινάσομαι, πέπᾱμαι); ᾱ and η, in **θοινάω** *feast*, **πορπάω** *fasten*, and **ἀλοάω** *thresh*: θοινάσομαι Eur. Cycl. 550, ἐκθοινήσομαι Æsch. Pr. 1025.

b. In the Perf. of **τίθημι** and **ἵημι**, ε becomes ει · τέθεικα, εἷκα, εἷμαι (45).

c. In some verbs, the short vowel is *retained;* and (d) some are *variable:* as,

(c) **σπάω** *to draw*, σπάσω, ἔσπακα · τελέω, ἐτέλεσα, τετέλεσμαι (42 g); ἀρόω *plow*, ἀρόσω, ἠρόθην · (d) **δέω** *bind*, δήσω, ἔδησα, δέδεκα, δέδεμαι · **θύω**, θύσω, τέθυκα (44); **λύω** (37); **δύω** *sink*, δύσω, δέδυκα, ἐδύθην.

COMP. GR. 9*

e. Verbs in -άννῦμι and -έννῦμι, and stems in λα-, or in υ- after a short syllable, for the most part retain the short vowel : as, σκεδάννῦμι *scatter*, σκεδ(ἄσω, 305 b)ῶ, ἐσκέδᾰσα · κορέννῦμι *satiate*, ἐκόρεσα, κεκόρεσμαι · γελάω *laugh*, γελάσομαι, ἐγελάσθην · 'ἀνύω *accomplish*, ἀνύσω, ἤνῠκα.

f. The short vowel is least retained before σ in the tense-sign, and most before θ.

311. 3. Vowel Inserted. The *regular close affixes* are annexed with the *insertion of* η,

a.) To *double consonant* stems, except those which end in a *labial* or *palatal mute not preceded by* σ, and those which end in a *lingual mute preceded by a liquid*: as,

αὔξω, αὐξ-ή-σω, ηὔξ-η-μαι, ηὐξ-ή-θην · ἕψω *to boil*, ἥψ-η-σα · ἕρρω *go away*, ἤρρηκα · μέλλω *delay*, μελλήσω (41); ὄζω *smell*, ὤζησα · βόσκω *feed*, βοσκήσω · but πέμπω, πέμψω · ἄρχω, ἦρξα · σπένδω, σπείσω (41).

b.) To *liquid stems* in which a *diphthong* precedes the stem-mark ; and to a few in which ε precedes : as,

βούλομαι *to will*, βουλ-ή-σομαι, βεβούλ-η-μαι · χαίρω *rejoice*, χαιρήσω · ἐθέλω or θέλω *wish*, ἐθελήσω or θελήσω · μέλω *concern*, ἐμέλησα, ἐμελήθην · ἐρ- *inquire*, ἐρήσομαι · μένω *remain*, F. μενῶ, but Pf. μεμένηκα (cf. 150 e).

c.) To a few other stems : as,

δέω *to need*, δε-ή-σω, δεδέ-η-κα · εὕδω *sleep*, εὑδήσω · οἴομαι *think*, οἰήσομαι, ᾠήθην · οἴχομαι *depart*, οἰχήσομαι.

d. In a few verbs, ε is inserted instead of η (cf. 310 c) : as, ἄχθομαι *to be vexed*, ἀχθ-έ-σομαι, ἠχθέσ-θην · μάχομαι *fight*, μαχ(έσο)οῦμαι (305 b), ἐμαχεσάμην, μεμάχημαι.

e. In most of these cases, the vowel is obviously inserted for the sake of euphony, to prevent undesired combinations of consonants. That the vowel should be commonly η, rather than ε, results from 310.

312. 4. In the Second Perfect System, the common affixes are annexed with these changes in the preceding syllable :

a.) Short a, ι, or υ, before a single consonant, is *lengthened* (a commonly becoming η, unless preceded by ε or ρ, 115 a) :

φαίνω, (s. φᾰν-) πέφηνα, ἐπεφήνειν (40) ; θάλλω *to bloom*, τέθηλα · but κράζω *cry out*, (κρᾰγ-) κέκρᾱγα · κρίζω *creak*, (κρῐγ-) κέκρῑγα · μυκάομαι *bellow*, (μῠκ-) μέμῡκα. After the Att. reduplication, the short vowel commonly remains : as, ἐλήλυθα (281 d, 134 a).

b.) ε becomes ο, and ει (lengthened from ῐ) becomes οι : as, κτείνω *to kill*, (κτεν-) ἔκτονα · δέρκομαι *see*, poet., δέδορκα · λείπω (λῐπ-, λειπ-) *leave*, λέλοιπα, πέποιθα (39) ; ἔολπα, ἔοικα, οἶδα (280 c).

c. This change of an *E* to an *O vowel* is also found in ῥήγνῡμι *to break*, 2 Pf. ἔρρωγα ; and in the 1 Perf. System of a few verbs : as, τρέπω *to turn*, τέτροφα · κλέπτω *steal*, κέκλοφα · πέμπω, πέπομφα (41) ; δέδοικα (46 h).

d. A few Perfects obtain an *O vowel* in the penult by a less simple change or by insertion ; and in a few dialectic forms, the change or insertion appears in the Pass. : as, ἄγω *to lead*, Pf. ἦχα, later ἀγή-ο-χα · ἐσθίω,

§ 315. —MI FORM. 203

poet. ἔδω, eat, ἐδήδ-ο-κα, Ep. ἐδήδομαι· οἴχομαι (311 c), οἴχ-ω-κα or ᾤχωκα (278 d) ; (ἐθ-) εἴωθα *I am wont*, pret. ; Pass. ἄωρτο γ. 272, for ἤερτο, ἐπώχατο M. 340, ἀφέωνται Mat. 9. 2 (see ἀείρω, ἐπέχω, ἵημι, 50).

C. —MI FORM (45).

313. In some verbs, chiefly *pure with a short stem-mark*, the Present and Imperfect are *nude* (303).

a. From the affix in the theme, these verbs are named VERBS IN -μι (270 c); and this mode of inflection is called *the -μι form*, a name extended to the nude inflection of all tenses which have regularly a connecting vowel.

b. The 2 Aorist from a pure stem commonly retains the primitive nude form, whatever may be the form of the theme : as, ἔβην, ἔδρᾶν, ἔγνων, ἔδυν (45 h).

c. If a stem in ι- otherwise takes this form, it has commonly a connective before a flexive beginning with ν : ἰ-ό-ντων, ἰ-έ-ναι, ἰών (45 m).

d. The verbs in -μι are few in number, but include some of the most common words in the language. They are subject to many defects and irregularities. The most complete are ἵστημι, τίθημι, ἵημι, and δίδωμι (45).

e. For the 1 Sing. οἴομαι *I think*, Impf. ᾠόμην, the nude forms οἶμαι, ᾤμην, are commonly used, especially when the verb is parenthetic : μάλ', οἶμαι, ἐρῶντες τούτου, *greatly desiring this, methinks*, iii. 1. 29.

314. Before the *nude affixes*, the *short stem-mark is lengthened* (ᾰ becoming η, unless preceded by ρ, 115; and ῐ, ε),

a.) In the *Indicative sing.* of the *Pres.* and *Impf. act.*: as,
ἵστημι, τίθης, δίδωσι, δείκνῡμι (s. ἱστᾰ-, τιθε-, διδο-, δεικνῠ-); ἵστην, ἐτίθην, ἐδίδως, ἐδείκνῡ· εἶμι (s. ῐ-), εἶ, εἶσι (45 a, b, m).

b.) In a few *Middle* forms, mostly poetic : as,
δίζημαι *to seek*, throughout ; ὠνήμην, 2 A. of ὀνίνημι *benefit*.

c.) In the 2 *Aor. act.* throughout, except before ντ (275 d) :
ἔστην, ἔδρᾶν, ἔγνων, ἔδῦν (s. στᾰ-, δρᾰ-, γνο-, δῠ-) ; ἔστημεν, στῆθι, στῆναι, δρᾶναι, ἔγνωσαν, γνῶθι, δῦναι ; στάντων, γνόντων, γν(οντς)ούς (45 h).

d. Exc. The short vowel remains in the 2 Aor. of τίθημι, δίδωμι, and ἵημι, except in the Inf., where it is changed to its corresponding diphthong (115 a) : ἔθεμεν, ἔδομεν, εἷμεν (s. θε-, δο-, ἑ-, augmented εἱ-, 279 c ; for the sing., see 306 c) ; θές, δός, ἕς · (θεντς) θείς · θεῖναι, δοῦναι, εἷναι (45 h, k). Except, also, the poet. ἔκτᾰν *slew*, and Ep. οὖτᾰν *wounded*.

315. The *forms of verbs in* -ω sometimes take the place of the -μι *forms* : particularly,

a.) In *verbs in* -υμι, which may be regarded as having a second but less Attic theme in -ύω : ὀμνύω, δεικνύουσι (a frequent form in the 3 Plur. Pres.), vi. 1. 31, 2. 2, δεικνύει Cyr. 6. 1. 7, δείκνυε Pl. Phædr. 228 e, δεικνύων Mem. 1. 3. 1 ; so Impf., chiefly in Sing. and 3 Plur. (ὤμνυον Th. 5. 19). This form was rare in the Pass. and Mid.: κατεμιγνύοντο vii. 2. 3.

b.) In the *sing. of the Impf. act.*, if the stem-mark is ε or ο. The contract forms in 45 b are the more common, except ἐτίθουν. So ἴεις, ἴει (45 k). We even find by imitation (or precession from ἵην, 115), 1 Sing. ἵεν (ἠφίειν Pl. Euthyd. 293 a) ; also 3 Plur. ἠφίουν Isæ. 60. 19, ἀπεδίδουν.

c.) In the *Opt. mid.*, by the frequent use of -οι- for -ει- when not in the initial syllable : τιθοίμην, λοίμην (45 c, n) ; and, in composition, 2 Aor. συνθοῖτο, προοῖτο, i. 9. 7, 10. So Opt. act. ἀφίοιτε Pl. Apol. 29 d (45 k).

316. a. The Subj. of verbs in -μι agrees with the common form, except in contracting αη into η, and οη into ῳ (120 h, 123 a) : as,

ἱστ(ά-ω)ῶ, ἱστ(ά-ης)ῇς, ἱστ(ά-η)ῇτε, ἱστ(ά-ω)ῶμαι, ἱστ(ά-η)ῇ · τιθ(έ-ω)ῶ, τιθ(έ-ης)ῇς · διδ(ό-ω)ῶ, διδ(ό-ης)ῷς, δ(ό-ω)ῶμαι, δ(ό-η)ῷ.

b. In like manner, ῳη is sometimes found in the Opt. for οιη ; chiefly, but not wholly, in the later Greek : as, ἀλῴη ξ. 183 (ἀλοίην X. 253), βιῴην (2 Aor., thus distinguished from the Att. Pres., 293 c) Ar. Ran.

c. In a few instances, the Subj. and Opt. of verbs in -νυμι are irregularly formed, or supplied by the Ind. : thus, used as Subj., διασκεδάννῦσι, διασκεδάννυται Pl. Phæd. 77 d, b, ζώννυνται ω. 89 ; Opt. (having the common -μι form, with ι absorbed, 293) δ(ν-ι)ύην (45 h), δύη σ. 348, φύη Theoc. 15. 94, ἐκδῦμεν Π. 99, πήγν(υ-ι)ῦτο Pl. Phæd. 118 a, δαινῦτο Ω. 665, δαινύατο (for -ῦντο) σ. 248. So φθίμην (as for φθιμίην) κ. 51, φθῖτο λ. 330.

d. In the Opt. act., the forms without η (293 a) naturally prevail more in the longer Pres., than in the shorter 2 Aor.

D. Complete Tenses.

317. The complete tenses are wholly wanting in many verbs. They are more used in the *passive* than in the *active* system, and more by *later* than by *earlier* writers. The use of their simple forms is chiefly limited, except in preteritive systems (268), to the Perf. and Plup. indic., inf., and part., other needed forms being commonly supplied by the Perf. part. *with the auxiliary* εἰμί.

a. The Perf. subj. and opt. are chiefly so supplied : Subj. λελυκὼς ὦ, λελυμένος ὦ · Opt. λελυκὼς εἴην, λελυμένος εἴην.

b. The *Perf. act.* may also form these modes by inflection, especially when used as a *Prës.:* as, ἐστήκω, vi. 5. 10, ἐστῶ, Pl. Gorg. 468 b, ἑσταίην, ψ. 101, δεδίω, Rep. A. 1. 11 (46 d, b), πεποιθοίην (293 c) ; εἰλήφωσιν Pl. Pol. 269 c, πεπτώκοι v. 7. 26, πεποίηκοι Th., βεβλήκοιεν Id.

c. In the *Perf. pass.*, these modes have a simple form in only a *few pure verbs:* as, κτάομαι *to acquire*, μιμνήσκω *remind*, καλέω *call ;* Pf. P. or M. κέκτημαι *I have acquired, I possess*, μέμνημαι *I remember*, κέκλημαι *I have been called, I am named* (268) ; Subj. κεκτ(η-ω)ῶμαι, κεκτῇ, κεκτῆται Symp. 1. 8, μεμνώμαι, Pl. Phil. 31 a ; *Opt.* κεκτ(η-ι)ῄμην, κεκτῇτο Pl. Leg. 731 c, μεμνῴμην Ω. 745, μεμνῇτο Ar. Pl. 991, κεκλῄμην, κεκλῇο Soph. Ph. 119 (292, 293) ; also κεκτ(η-οι)ῴμην, κεκτῴμεθα Eur. Heracl. 282, μεμνῴμην, μεμνῴο i. 7. 5 (v. l. μεμνῇο, μέμνοιο), μεμνῇτο Cyr. 1. 6. 3 (cf. 315 c). So *Subj.* (ϝαλ-, βλα-) βεβλῆσθε Audoc.; *Opt.* λελ(υ-ι)ῦντο σ. 238.

§ 320. COMPLETE TENSES. 205

318. The Perf., in its proper sense, may have the IMPERATIVE in the 3 Pers.; but otherwise, this mode belongs only to those Perfects which are used in a *Present sense* (268, 46).

a. In the *active voice*, the Perf. imv. is very rare, except in the nude form of the 2 Perf. (320) : ἄνωγε, κεκράγετε (320 f), γέγωνε Eur. Or. 1220, βεβηκέτω Luc. Hist. Sc. 45, ἐοικέτω Ib. 49. The Imv. act. λέλυκε is inserted in 37, not as itself used, but to represent such forms as these.

319. The simple form of the FUTURE PERFECT is found in only a small number of verbs; and is especially rare in liquids, in verbs beginning with a vowel, in verbs in -μι, and in those which form the Perf. pass. in -σμαι: πεφύρσεσθαι Pind. N. 1. 104, εἰρήσεται Cyr. 7. 1. 9, λελήσεται (Pf. λέλησμαι) Eur. Alc.

a. The Fut. Perf. is frequent in those verbs only in which it is used as a common Future (268). Its Participle is scarcely found in classic Greek.

b. Of the *active form*, only two examples belong to Attic prose, both formed from preteritives, and both giving rise to equivalent *middle* forms : Pf. ἕστηκα *I stand*, τέθνηκα *I am dead*, Fut. Pf. ἑστήξω and ἑστήξομαι *I shall stand*, τεθνήξω and τεθνήξομαι. Other examples of the Fut. Pf. mid. with the Perf. act. are κέκλαγγα.*I scream*, κεκλάγξομαι Ar. Vesp. 930, κέκραγα *I cry*, κεκράξομαι Ar. Ran. 265. See 284 f, g.

c. The Fut. Perf. unites the *base of the Perf.* with *Future affixes;* and a vowel lengthened before the tense-sign -σ- in the Fut. is also lengthened in the Fut. Perf. : as, δέω *bind*, δήσω, δέδεμαι, δεδήσομαι.

320. NUDE FORMS. a. In the 2 PERF. and PLUP., the connecting vowel is sometimes omitted in the *Ind. plur.* and *dual* (276 b). When this omission takes place, then commonly, (b) the Ind. sing. is supplied by forms from a *longer base* (cf. 306 c); which forms likewise occur in the plur. and dual, but less frequently; (c) the Subj., Opt., Imp., and Inf. are formed after the analogy of *verbs in* -μι; (d) the Part. is *contracted*, if the characteristic is *a* or *o*. Thus,

(a) ἕστα-μεν, δέδι-μεν, (ἴδ-μεν, 148) ἴσμεν ii. 4. 6, (ἴδ-τε, 147) ἴστε, (ἴδ-νσι, δ becoming σ in imitation of the other persons) ἴσασι · (b) ἕστηκα, ἑστήκειν, δέδοικα, οἶδα (bases ἑστα-, ἑστηκ-; δεδι-, δεδοικ-; ἰδ-, οἰδ-, εἰδε-); ἑστήκασιν Δ. 434, ἑστήκεσαν ... ἕστασαν Cyr. 8. 3. 9, ἐδεδοίκεσαν iii. 5. 18, οἴδαμεν Pl. Alc. 141 c ; (c) ἑστῶ · ἑσταίην, εἰδείην · ἕσταθι, δέδιθι, ἴσθι ii. 1. 13 ; ἑστάναι iv. 5. 7, δεδιέναι (313 c), εἰδέναι · (d) ἑστ(α-ώς)ώς i. 3. 2, βεβρ(ο-ως)ώς, 2 Pf. Pt. of βιβρώσκω *eat*. See 46.

e. The Perfects of θνήσκω *to die*, βαίνω *go*, and τλα- *bear*, τέθνηκα, βέβηκα, and τέτληκα have associated nude forms, partly poet., closely akin to those of ἕστηκα. So γέγονα, 2 Pf. of γίγνομαι *to become*, and μέμονα *I am eager*, have nude poet. forms from the shorter bases γεγα-, μεμα-.

f. In a few nude poet. forms of impure verbs, τ passes into θ : ἄνωγα *I command*, pret., Imv. ἄνωγε Eur. Or. 119, and ἄνωχθι Id. Alc. 1044, ἀνωγέτω β. 195, and ἀνώ(γ-τω)χθω Λ. 189, ἀνώγετε ψ. 132, and ἄνωχθε Eur. Rh. 987 ; κέκραγα (319 b), Imv. κέκραχθι Ar. Vesp. 198, κεκράγετε Ib. 415, and κέκρα(γ-τε)χθε Ar. Ach. 335 ; ἐγείρω *rouse*, 2 Pf. ἐγρήγορα *I am awake*, Imv. 2 pl. ἐγρήγορθε Σ. 299 ; πάσχω *suffer*, 2 Pf. πέπονθα, 2 pl. πέπ(ονθ-τε, ονσθε, 147, 159 g, 151 s)οσθε Γ. 99. See 274 a.

DIALECTIC FORMS (48).

A. Contraction.

321. Forms which are *contracted* in the Attic (and which are also commonly contracted in the Doric, but often with a different vowel of contraction) more frequently remain *uncontracted* in Ionic prose, while the Epic has great freedom in the employment of either *uncontracted, contracted,* or *variously protracted forms.*

a. Here belong, particularly, Contract Verbs in -άω, -έω, and -όω (309), the Liquid, Att., and Dor. Fut. (305), the Aor. Pass. Subj. (288 a), the Subj. of Verbs in -μι (316), and the 2 Sing. in -αι and -ο (297 e). In these forms, the first vowel is commonly either (I.) α, (II.) ε, or (III.) ο.

322. I. THE FIRST VOWEL α. a. In the IONIC, the α is commonly contracted or changed into ε (a change sometimes found in the Dor., 130 b, d); and when α with an O vowel is contracted into ω, ε is often inserted (135, 120 i). Thus we find, as various readings, ὁρῶντες, ὁρέοντες, and ὁρέωντες, Hdt. 1. 82, 99. So ὠρέομεν, χρέεσθαι, χρᾶσθαι, ἐχρέωντο, ἐχρέοντο, χρέω, Id. Subj. of Verbs in -μι, δυνεώμεθα Hdt. 4. 97, 2 Aor. στέωσι Id. 3. 15, βέωμεν 7. 50, κτέωμεν χ. 216. See c. (b) In the 2 Sing., the termination -αο commonly remains : as, ἐχρήσαο Hdt. 1. 117, ἐπίστao 7. 209.

c. In the EPIC, extended forms are made by doubling the vowel of contraction, either in whole, or in part (i. e. by inserting one of its elements, or its corresponding short vowel, commonly ο with ω, and ᾰ with ᾱ, 135) ; and sometimes by prolonging a short vowel, particularly ε used for α to ει : as, ὁράω, contr. ὁρῶ Γ. 234, extended ὁρόω E. 244, ὁρόωτε Δ. 347, ὁρόωσαι Δ. 9, ὁρ(δεις)ᾷς Λ. 202, ὁράᾳς H. 448, ἐμνώοντο B. 686 ; μνάεσθαι α. 39, δρώωσι ο. 324 ; δρώοιμι 317 ; Att. Fut. (305 b) ἐλόωσι N. 315, ἐλάαν ε. 290, κρεμόω H. 83 : 2 Aor. Subj. of Verbs in -μι, στῇ σ. 334, στήῃ E. 598, στείομεν O. 297, στήετον σ. 183, βείω Z. 113. (d) So in Ion. prose, in imitation of the Ep., κομόωσι Hdt. 4. 191; Dor. κομόωντι Theoc. 4. 57. (e) If the flexive begins with τ, α is not prefixed : as in ὁρᾶ-τε, ὁρᾶ-ται.

f. The DORIC sometimes contracts α with an O sound following into ᾱ; and commonly α with an E sound following into η (131 a, c) : as, πεινᾶντι Theoc. 15, 148 ; 1 Aor. 2 sing. ἐπάξα Theoc. 4. 28, for ἐπήξαο, -ω ; τολμῇς Id. 5. 35, ὁρῆτε 110. The latter contraction appears in some Ion. prose-writers ; and in some Ep. Du. forms, as συλήτην N. 202.

323. II. THE FIRST VOWEL ε. a. In IONIC PROSE, contraction is commonly omitted, except as εο and εου often become ευ: as, ποιέω Hdt. 1. 38, ποιέεις 39, ἐποίεε 22, ποιεόμενος 73, ποιεύμενος 68, ποιεῦσι 131; Fut. σημανέω Id. 1. 75, ἀμυνεῦσι 9. 6 ; Aor. Subj. ἀπαιρεθέω Id. 3. 65, θέωσι 4. 71 (316 a) ; 2 Sing. βούλεαι, τεύξεαι, Id. 1. 90, ἐγένεο 35, ἔθευ 7. 209. (b) In like manner, εο, used for αο (322 a), may become ευ : as, εἰρώτευν Hdt. 3. 140. So in the Dor., ἠρώτευν Theoc. 1. 81 ; γελεῦντι 90.

c. The EPIC commonly omits contraction, if the last vowel is ω, ῳ, οι, η, or ῃ (except in the Aor. pass. subj., and in the Perf. subj. εἰδῶ) ; but otherwise employs or omits it according to the metre (εο and εου, when contracted, regularly becoming ευ. Synizesis is frequent when ε precedes a long O vowel, and sometimes occurs in εου, and even in εαι. The Ep., also, often protracts ε to ει, and sometimes doubles the vowel of contrac-

§ 326. CONTRACTION. TENSE-SIGNS. CONNECTING VOWELS. 207

tion η. Thus, φιλέοι ο. 305, φιλέωμεν θ. 42, φιλέησιν ο. 70, πειρηθώμεν Χ. 381, είδώ Α. 515 ; φιλεί Β. 197, φιλέει I. 342, έρρει Ρ. 86, έρρεε Ν. 539, έση τ. 2)4, έσεαι Α. 563, έσσέαι ζ. 33 ; φράξεο Ε. 440, φράξευ δ. 395, κάλεον θ. 5J0, καλεύντο Β. 684 ; νεικείω Δ. 359, έτελείετο Α. 5 ; Aor. Pass. Subj. δαμείω σ. 54, δαμήης, v. l. δαμείης, Γ. 436 ; 2 Aor. Subj. of Verbs in -μι, θείω II. 83, άνήη Β. 34, θέωμεν ω. 485, θείομεν Α. 143.

d. After the analogy of the contract Pres., the Ion. often extends the 2 Aor. Inf. in -ειν, as if formed by contraction, to -έειν : as, ιδέειν, φυγέειν, έλέειν, Ψ. 463, Β. 393 (φυγείν 401), λ. 205, Hdt. 1. 32, 1, 36.

e. In the Ion., εε followed by a distinct vowel, sometimes becomes ει, or loses one ε : as, μυθ(έ-εαι)είαι θ. 180, μυθέαι β. 202, νείαι λ. 114, αιδ(έεο)είο Ω. 503, πωλ(έ-εο)έο δ. 811, φοβέο Hdt. 7. 52 (φοβεύ 1. 9).

f. For the Doric contraction of εο and εου into ευ, and, in the stricter Dor., of εε into η, see 131 b, 130 c : έλέγευ Theoc. 1. 86, μάχευ 113, έρρευν 2. 89, εύσα 76 ; ποίη Ar. Lys. 1318. So, in Hom., άπειλήτην λ. 313.

324. III. THE FIRST VOWEL o. a. Here the IONIC and DORIC usually employ contraction, following the common rules, except that the Ion. sometimes uses ευ for ου, and the Dor. ω and ῳ for ου and οι (131 b, 130 c) : as, δικαιεύσι Hdt. 1. 133, μαστίγών Epich. 19 [1]. ·

b. The Dor. ω is likewise used by other dialects in ῥῑγόω *to be cold*, and in the Ion. ιδρόω *sweat :* as, ῥιγών Ar. Vesp. 446, ῥιγῷ Pl. Gorg.

c. The EPIC sometimes protracts the o to ω, and sometimes employs the combination ωω after the analogy of verbs in -άω (322 c) : as, ιδρώοντα Σ. 372, αρόωσιν ι. 108 ; 2 Aor. Subj. γνώω ξ. 118, δώῃ μ. 216, δώησιν Α. 324.

B. TENSE-SIGNS, AND UNION OF STEM AND AFFIX.

325. a. In verbs in -ζω, the Dor. commonly employs ξ for σ, in the Fut. and Aor.: as, καθίξας Theoc. 1. 12, for καθίσας from καθίζω, χαρίξη 5. 71, εκόμιξαν Pind. N. 2. 31. This change appears also in a few other verbs in which short α precedes : as, γελάξας (fr. γελάω, 310 e) Theoc. 7.

b. In the Fut. act. and mid., the Dor. commonly adds to the tensesign ε, which is then contracted with the connecting vowel : as, (ᾀ-σέ-ω) ᾀσώ Theoc. 1. 145, (ᾀ-σέ-ομαι) ᾀσεύμαι 3. 38, ποησείς 3. 9. See § 305 d.

c. For the doubling of σ by the poets, especially the Ep., see 171.

d. The omission of the tense-sign -κ- is extended, particularly in the Epic ; where we specially notice the Perf. Participles in -ώς pure. In these, the vowel preceding -ώς is more frequently lengthened ; and the Part. is then declined in -ότος or -ώτος, according to the metre. If the preceding vowel remains short, the form in -ώτος is commonly required. Thus, κεκμηότας Λ. 801, κεκμηώτα κ. 31, πεπτεώτα Φ. 503. See 320.

e. In the fem. of the Perf. Part., the Ep. sometimes shortens the antepenult on account of the verse : as, λελάκυια μ. 85 (λεληκώς X. 141).

C. CONNECTING VOWELS.

326. a. For the 2 Sing. and Inf. affixes -εις and -ειν, the Dor. has sometimes the old short forms -ες and -εν (291 a, 294 b) ; and sometimes prolongs these to -ης and -ην : as, συρίσδες, συρίσδεν, Theoc. 1. 3, 14, γαρύεν Pind. O. 1. 5 ; ευρήν, χαιρήν, ειπήν, Theoc. 11. 4, 14. 1, 19.

b. The Dor. and Æol. sometimes give to the Perf. the connecting vowel of the Pres. (276 a), especially in the Inf.: as, δεδοίκω Theoc. 15. 58, for δέδοικα, πεποίθει 5. 28 ; Inf. δεδύκειν Id. 1. 102, τεθνάκην Sap. 2. 15 ;

Part. κεχλάδοντας Pind. Instances likewise occur, in the Ep., of the Perf. passing over into the form of the Pres., and of the Plup. into that of the Impf.: as, κεκλήγοντας M. 125; ἐμέμηκον ι. 439, ἐπέφυκον Hes. Th. 152.

c. In this way new verbs arose, not confined to the Ep.: as, fr. ἄνωγα, ἀνώγω order, O. 43, Hdt. 7. 104, Impf. ἠνώγον Ι. 578 (ἠνώγεον H. 394), F. ἀνώξω π. 404, A. ἤνωξα, Hes. Sc. 479; fr. ὤλεκα, ὀλέκω destroy, Σ. 172.

d. Where the Ind. has a short connective, the Ep. often retains this in the Subj. (292. 2), for the sake of the metre: as, ἀγείρομεν Α. 142, ἴομεν Β. 440, φθίεται Υ. 173, μίσγεαι Β. 232, εἴδετε Θ. 18, λάβετον Κ. 545.

e. The poets, especially the Epic, much extended the use of nude affixes in the Pres., Impf., and 2 Aor.; introducing them into euphonic systems, and even using them after a diphthong or a consonant, chiefly in the Pass. and Mid.: as, ἀνύω, ἐρύω, τανύω (305 f), Pres. τάνυται P. 393, ἔρυσθαι ε. 484; Impf. ἤνῦτο ε. 243, ἄνυτο, ἄνυμες, Theoc. 2. 92, 7. 10; σεύω shake, στευ- stand, purpose, σεῦται Soph. Tr. 645, στεῦται Γ. 83, στεῦνται Æsch. Pers. 49, στεῦτο λ. 583; φέρω bear, φυλάσσω watch, Imv. φέρτε I. 171, (s. φυλακ-) φύλαχθε (cf. 320 f) Hom. Ap. 538; ἅλλομαι leap, γίγνομαι become, δέχομαι receive, μίγνῦμι mix, ὄρνῦμι rouse; 2 Aor. Ind. ἆλτο Α. 532, ἔγεντο Theoc. 1. 88, ἐδέγμην ι. 513, δέκτο O. 88, ἔμικτο a. 433, ὦρτο Æsch. Ag. 987; Imv. δέξο T. 10, δέχθε Ap. Rh. 4. 1554, ὄρσο Δ. 204; Inf. δέχθαι Α. 23, ὄρθαι Θ. 474; Pt. δέγμενος B. 794.

327. The 1 and 2 Aor. forms are *united,*

a.) In poetic, chiefly Ep., Aorists which have the tense-sign -σ- with the connectives -ο- and -ε- : as, βαίνω go, δύω sink, ἵκω come, οἱ-(φέρω) bear, ὄρνῦμι rouse; Aor. Ind. ἐβήσετο ν. 75, δύσετο H. 465, ἷξον E. 473; Imv. βήσεο E. 109, οἶσε χ. 106, ὄρσεο Γ. 250, contr. ὄρσευ Δ. 264.

b.) In forms, chiefly Alexandrine and Hellenistic, which attach the connectives and flexives of the 1 Aor. to 2 Aor. bases: as, ἐλθ- (ἔρχομαι) come, ἐλ- (αἱρέω) take, εὑρ- (εὑρίσκω) find, ὀσφρ- (ὀσφραίνω) smell; Aor. ἤλθατε Mt. 25. 36, ἦλθαν Acts 12. 10, ἀνειλάτο Ib. 7. 21, εὕρατο Ap. Rh. 4. 1133, ὀσφραντο Hdt. 1. 80. See 306.

c. These tenses of mixed formation are usually classed as 1 or 2 Aor., according to the connective: 1 A. ἦλθαν, 2 A. ἷξον.

D. FLEXIBLE ENDINGS.

328. a. 1 AND 3 PERSONS. The old flexives -τ and -ντ, *prolonged to* -τι *and* -ντι, remained in the Dor., which had also -μες for -μεν (Lat. *t, nt, mus;* 169 b, c): as, φατί Theoc. 1. 51, τίθητι 3. 48, τρέψοντι 6. 36; εἴδομες Theoc. 2. 25, δεδοίκαμες 1. 16 (Pind. uses the form -μεν).

b. Epic forms of the Subjunctive, with -μ *and* -τ *prolonged to* -μι *and* -σι, are not unfrequent: as, ἐθέλωμι Α. 549, ἴδωμι Σ. 63, ἐθέλῃσιν Α. 408.

329. The *change of ν into α* (142) is extended, especially in the Ion.

a. Here, the 3 Plur. endings -αται and -ατο, for -νται, -ντο (300 c), are usual in the Opt., and the Perf. and Plup. ind., and are also employed in the Impf., 2 Aor., and nude Pres. ind. Before these endings, a short vowel in the stem is not lengthened (310), except in the poets for the sake of the metre, the connective -ε- is used instead of -ο- (290 a), α and sometimes α become ε, and consonants are changed according to 300 c. Thus, οἰκέαται Hdt. 1. 142, for ᾤκηνται· ἔαται Γ. 134, εἴαται (134 a)B. 137, ἔατο H. 414, for ἧνται, ἧντο· πεφοβήατο Φ. 206; ἐβουλ(ο-ντο)έατο Hdt. 1. 4;

δυν(α-νται)έαται Id. 2. 142; κ(ει-ν)έαται Λ. 659, ἐκέατο Hdt. 1. 167 (so, with an intervening consonant, ἐρηρέδαται Ψ. 284, ἐρηρέδατο η. 95, from ἐρείδω); τετρίφαται (τριβ-, 39) Hdt. 2. 93, ἐσκευάδατο 7. 67 (so, as if from verbs in -ζω, ἐληλάδατο η. 86, ἐρράδαται v. 354, -το Μ. 431; βουλοίατο Hdt. 1. 3, πειρῶατο 68, γευσαίατο 2. 47. (b) The Opt. forms in -ατο are likewise used by the Att. poets: as, δεξαίατο Soph. (Ed. C. 44.

c. In a few cases, the poets seem to have simply dropped ν between two consonants, in the 3 Plur.: as, κεχείμ(αν-νται)αννται φρένες Pind. P. 9. 57, δέδο(κ-νται)κται . . φυγαί Id. Bac. 1350. Cf. 158.

d. For the Impf. ἐτίθην and ἦν, the Ion. has ἐτίθεα Hdt. 3. 155, and ἦα β. 313, unaugmented ἔα Δ. 321, Hdt. 2. 19. So ἔας Hdt. 1. 187, ἦεν A. 381, ἔατε Hdt. 4. 119, ἔασαν 9. 31. Cf. 306 c.

330. The flexives of the 3 Plur. are interchanged, especially in the Alex. and Hellen. Greek, and the Ep. and Dor. poets: thus,

a.) Alex. and Hellen., -ᾶν for -ᾶσι of the Perf., and -σαν for -ν or -εν: as, πέφρικαν Lyc. 252, ἔγνωκαν Jn. 17. 7 (so ἔοργαν Hom. Batr. 179); ἐσχάζοσαν Lyc. 21, ἦλθοσαν Ps. 79. 1, ποιήσαισαν Deut. 1. 44.

b.) In the Ep. and Dor. poets (sometimes imitated by the Att.), the older -ν for -σαν. (275 c): as, Aor. Pass. ἤγερθεν for ἠγέρθησαν, A. 57, τράφεν 251, φάανθεν 200, ἔκρυφθεν Eur. Hipp. 1247; -μι Form, ἔσταν A. 535 (ἔστησαν N. 488), ἴεν M. 33, τίθεν Pind. P. 3. 114, ἔφυν ε. 481.

331. 2 Pers. a. In the Subj. 2 sing., the uncontracted -ηαι (or shorter -εαι, 326 d) commonly remains in the Ep., and sometimes in Ion. prose: as, ἵκηαι Z. 143, ἴδηαι Hdt. 4. 9. Cf. 323.

b. The Ep. sometimes drops σ in the Perf. and Plup. pass.: as, μέμνηαι Φ. 442, contr. μέμνῃ O. 18, Theoc. 21. 41, βέβληαι E. 284, ἔσσυο Π. 585.

c. On the other hand, in the S. S., we find the σ retained in some contract forms, and in the Presents having the sense of the Fut. πίομαι, φάγομαι (305 f): as, καυχ(άεσαι)ᾶσαι Rom. 2. 17, πίεσαι, φάγεσαι Lk. 17. 8.

332. Iterative Form. a. The Ep., to express with more emphasis the idea of *repeated* or *continued action*, or sometimes perhaps for metrical effect, often formed the Impf. and Aor. in -σκον, -σκόμην.

b. This form, called the *iterative* (itĕro, *to repeat*), and akin to the Lat. formation in -sco, also appears in Ion. prose, and rarely in Dor. and Att. poets. (c) Of the connectives of the Impf. and Aor., it used -ε- and -α- (290 a), (d) sometimes dropping the -ε- after α or ε, and (e) rarely using -α- for -ε-. (f) It was almost strictly confined to the Ind. sing. and 3 plur., where it was inflected as an Impf. (-σκον, -σκες, -σκε, &c.), but commonly without the augment, which was now less needed. (g) Before the -σκ-, a short vowel was not lengthened. Thus,

(c, f) Impf. ἔχεσκον *I was in the habit of carrying*, N. 257, ἔχεσκες E. 472, ἔχεσκε 126, Hdt. 6. 12, 3 pl. ἔχεσκον δ. 627, for εἶχον, -ες, -ε, -ον; ὑφαίνεσκεν *she kept weaving*, β. 104, φέρεσκε Theoc. 25, 138, ἐμισγέσκοντο v. 7; 2 Aor. ἴδεσκε Γ. 217, γενέσκετο λ. 208; 1 Aor. (only poet.), στρέψασκον Σ. 546, μνησάσκετο Λ. 566; (d) ἔασκες for εἴας, T. 295, καλέεσκε ζ. 402, καλέσκετο Ο. 338; (e) ῥίπτασκον Ο. 23; (g) (ἔδων) δόσκον I. 331, (ἦν) ἔσκον H. 153, ἔσκεν Æsch. Per. 656, (ἐφάνη) φάνεσκεν Λ. 64.

333. Infinitive. a. In the Inf., instead of -ναι, the Dor. and Æol. commonly retain the old ending -ν (272 a), or, with the Ep., reduplicate this ending to -μεν, which may be still farther prolonged to -μεναι.

b. Thus the Æol. forms the Aor. pass. inf. in -ην, the Dor. in -ἦμεν, and the Ep. (which also employs the common form) in -ἦμεναι: as, μεθύσθην Alc. 28 [29], λασθῆμεν Theoc. 2. 18, ὁμοιωθήμεναι Α. 187.

c. In other tenses, the *nude* Inf. has commonly in the Dor. the form -μεν, in the Æol. -ν and -μεναι, and in the Ep. -ναι, -μεν, and -μεναι: as, θέμεν Theoc. 5. 21, λ. 315, θέμεναι Insc. Cum., B. 285, θεῖναι Δ. 26 (cf. Δ. 57), γνώμεναι α. 411; νίκᾶν (335 b) Alc. 86 [15]; τεθνάμεναι Ω. 225, ἴδμεν Λ. 719, ἴδμεναι Ν. 273. So ἐστάμεναι Hdt. 1. 17. Before -μεν and -μεναι, a short vowel in the 2 Aor. does not pass into a diphthong (314 d).

d. In like manner the non-Attic poets employ, for -ειν (originally -εν, 294 b), the prolonged -έμεν and -έμεναι: as, ἀκου(εν)έμεν Α. 547, Pind. O. 3. 44, Theoc. 8. 83, ἀκουέμεναι λ. 380, ἀξέμεν Ψ. 111, ἀξέμεναι 50.

e. Verbs in -άω and -έω have a contract form in -ἦμεναι: as, γο(ά-εν)ήμεναι Ξ. 502, πεινήμεναι υ. 137, καλ(έ-εν)ήμεναι Κ. 125, πενθήμεναι σ. 174.

334. PARTICIPLE. For the Fem. -ουσα, the Laconic uses -ωα: as, ἐκλιπ(οῦσα)ῶα, κλεῶα, θυρσα(ζουσῶν, 170 a)δδωᾶν, Ar. Lys. 1297, &c.

E. VERBS IN -μι.

335. a. The Ion. and Dor. employ more freely than the Att. the forms with a connecting vowel (315), especially in the Pres. sing. of verbs whose characteristic is ε or ο: as, τιθεῖς Pind. P. 8. 14, τιθεῖ α. 192, Hdt. 1. 133, διδοῖς Ι. 164, διδοῖ 519, Hdt. 1. 107, διδοῦσιν Β. 255; ἰστᾷ Hdt. 4.

b. On the other hand, the Æol., Dor., and Ep. retain the form in -μι in some verbs, which in the Att. and in Ion. prose have only the form in -ω: as, κάλημι Sap. 1. 16, ὄρημι 2. 11, νίκημι Theoc. 7. 40, for καλέω, &c.

c. The Ion. changes a *characteristic* before another α to ε (cf. 322 a), and sometimes inserts ε before α (135 a): as, ἱστ(ααοι, 156)έᾶσι Hdt. 5. 71, δυνέαται (329 a), ἱστέαιτο 4. 166. So, in the nude Perf., ἐστέατε 5. 49.

CHAPTER X.

STEM OF THE VERB.

336. The stem of the Greek verb, although not properly varied by inflection, yet *received many changes* in the progress of the language. These changes affected the different tenses unequally, so that there are but few *primitive* verbs in which the stem appears in only a single form.

a. The earliest form in which the stem of a verb appears is briefly called the *prime* or *old stem;* and other forms, *later* or *modified stems*. If a later form appears in the Present System, this is called the *new stem;* and any intermediate forms, *middle stems*.

b. The 2 Aor. and 2 Compound Systems are widely distinguished from the others by their *attachment to the original form* of the stem; and the

§ 339. DEFECTIVE AND REDUNDANT VERBS. 211

Pres. System no less by its *inclination to depart* from this form. The other systems differ comparatively little from each other in the form of the stem. If the verb has *three* stems, they are commonly formed from the *middle*. If it has only *two* stems, they are sometimes formed from the *earlier*, sometimes from the *later*, and are sometimes *divided :* as, in τάσ-σω (39), old stem ταγ- ἐτάγην τέταγμαι ἐτάχθην τέταχα ἔταξα τάξω, new stem τασσ- τάσσω ; in σήπω *to rot*, o. s. σαπ- ἐσάπην, n. s. σηπ- σέσημ-μαι ἐσήφθην σέσηπα ἔσηψα σήψω σήπω ; in φεύγω *flee*, o. s. φυγ- ἔφυγον πέφυγμαι, n. s. φευγ- ἐφεύχθην πέφευγα ἔφευξα φεύξομαι φεύξω.

c. The tenses may be arranged, with respect to the degree in which they exhibit the departure of the stem from its original form, as in 47 ; which shows a general table (with a few exceptions) for verbs having three forms of the stem.

337. Many verbs are DEFECTIVE, either from the *want of a complete formation,* or from the *disuse of some of their forms.*

a. In both cases, the defect is often supplied by other verbs having the same signification. In the poets, especially the older, we find many fragments of verbs belonging to the earlier language. These occur often in but a single tense, and sometimes in only a single form of that tense : as, 3 Sing. ἔβραχε *rang*, Δ. 420, δέατο (s. δεα-) *appeared*, ζ. 242.

338. On the other hand, many verbs are REDUNDANT, either through a *double formation* from the same stem, or the use of forms from *different stems.* It should be observed, however, that two or more forms of the same tense, with few exceptions, either,

(a) Belong to *different periods, dialects,* or *styles of composition :* thus, κτείνω, and later κτίννῦμι (50), *to kill ;* καίω (44), A. P. ἐκαύθην, and Ion. ἐκάην· πυνθάνομαι, and poet. πεύθομαι (50), *inquire.*

(b) *Differ* in their *use :* thus, 1 Pf. πέπεικα, transitive, *I have persuaded,* 2 Pf. πέποιθα, intransitive, *I trust* (39) ; πέφαγκα *I have shown*, πέφηνα *I have appeared* (40) ; 1 A. ἔστησα, trans., *I placed,* 2 A. ἔστην intrans., *I stood* (45). The *second tenses* are more inclined than the *first* to an intransitive use.

Or, (c) Are *supplementary* to each other. See 306 b, 320.

d. From the various changes which take place in the stem, many verbs, together with their common themes, have others, either older, derived, or collateral. In regard to some forms, it seems doubtful whether they should be rather viewed as redundant forms of the same verb, or as the forms of distinct but kindred verbs. Themes derived from the same root are termed *cognate.*

339. The changes in the stem of the Greek verb are of three kinds, EUPHONIC, EMPHATIC, and ADOPTIVE.

a. The same or similar terms are applied to the *modified stems* which result ; while special names have also been given to some of their more common forms.

b. The dialects increase greatly the number of these changes, especially of the euphonic : as, τάσσω, new Att. τάττω (169 a) ; ὁράω, Ion. ὁρέω.

c. In the following sections of this chapter, and in some of the tables, small Roman letters, and figures annexed, are used to mark classes of stems and their subdivisions : as, a, a¹, b².

212   THE VERB. — PRIME AND MODIFIED STEMS.   § 340.

I. PRIME STEMS (a).

340. 1. Prime Stems may be *roots*, either (a^1) giving rise to modified stems, or (a^2) remaining alone; or they may be *derived stems*, either (a^3) giving rise to other stems, or (a^4) remaining alone.

Thus, (a^1) the root τι-, *to pay* (itself found in the poet. Pres. τίω), gives rise to the stems τιν- and τινυ-, used in the later Presents τίνω and poet. τίνῡμαι; while (a^2) the root ἐλπ-, *to cause to hope*, remains alone in the Ep. verb ἔλπω. But these verbs have derivatives in the nouns ἐλπίς *hope*, and τιμή *honor*; and from these are taken derived stems for new verbs: viz., (a^3) ἐλπιδ-, giving rise to ἐλπιζ- in the Pres. ἐλπίζω *to hope*; and (a^4) τιμα-, the only stem of the verb τιμάω *to honor*.

2. Most verbs which have only the prime stem are *derivative pure verbs*: as, τιμάω, φιλέω, δηλόω (42).

3. Most roots are *monosyllabic*, and have a *short vowel*. Hence these became rules for the stem of the 2 Aor.; and some changes appear even in this stem, either for conformity to these rules, or to enable the tense to take the old nude inflection (313 b). See 342. 2, 3, 353 a. A very few forms from stems otherwise modified are used as 2 Aorists: as, 2 A. ἔτᾰμον, commonly ἔτεμον (341), *cut*. See 327.

4. The 2 Aor. System (except in a few defective forms, 337 a) belongs only to verbs which have more than one stem; and so, with very few exceptions, the 2 Compound System. Few verbs have both systems, and comparatively few have either; though among these are some of the most common verbs in the language.

II. EUPHONIC STEMS.

341. Euphonic changes in the stem are chiefly the following:

b. PRECESSION (*Attenuated Stems*). In some stems, a vowel is changed by precession, (b^1) ᾰ becoming ε, (b^2) ε or ο, ι (chiefly when consonants are annexed to the stem). (b^3) ᾱ, ω, &c.: as,

(b^1) 2 Aor. P. ἐδάρην, Pr. A. δέρω *flay*; ἐπλάκην, πλέκω *plait*; ἐτραπην, τρέπω *turn*; (b^2) 2 A. ἔτεκον, Pr. τίκτω *bring forth, beget*; ἀμβλόω and ἀμβλίσκω *miscarry*; (b^3) 2 A. ἔτρᾰγον, Pr. (τρᾱγ-) τρώγω *eat*.

342. c. CONTRACTION, SYNCOPE, METATHESIS, ANTITHESIS (103 s).

1. Some stems (c^1) are *contracted*: as, ἀείδω ᾄδω *sing*, ἀίσσω ᾄσσω *rush*, κληΐω κλῄω old Att. (later κλείω, cf. 222 a) *shut*.

2. Some stems are (c^2) *syncopated* in the *theme*, chiefly in cases of *reduplication*; (c^3) others, in the 2 *Aor.* (340. 3); and (c^4) others, in *other tenses*: as, (c^2) 2 A. ἐγενόμην, Pr. (γιγεν-) γίγνομαι *become* (cf. Lat. gig[e]no); ἔπετον (Dor.), πίπτω *fall*; μένω and poet. μίμνω *remain*; (c^3) (ἐγερ-, ἐγρ-) ἠγρόμην *awoke*; (c^4) καλέω CALI, Pf. (κλε-) κέκληκα, κέκλημαι.

3. In some stems there is *transposition*, chiefly by changing the place of a *liquid*. This occurs (c^5) in the *theme*; (c^6) in the 2 *Aor.*; (c^7) in *other tenses*: as, (c^6) 2 A. ἔθορον, Pr. (θρο-) θρώσκω *leap*; ἔθανον, (θνα-) θνῄσκω *die*; (c^6) (ταλ-, τλα-) ἔτλην *endured*, (σκαλ-, σκλα-) ἔσκλην *became dry*, (δαρκ-) ἔδρακον *saw* (340. 3); (c^7) βέβληκα, κέκμηκα (308).

4. (c^8) The substitution of one letter for another is chiefly presented under other heads (341, 343, &c.).

343. d. OMITTING OR ADDING ASPIRATION. 1. Some stems (d¹) are changed to avoid a *double aspiration*: as, (θρεφ-) τρέφω, (θρεχ-) τρέχω, (ἐχ-) ἔχω, (θε-) ἐτέθην, (θυ-) ἐτύθην (159 b, d, e).

2. A few stems (d²) have both aspirated and unaspirated forms: as, βρύχω and βρύκω; ψύχω *cool*, 2 A. P. ἐψύχην and ἐψύγην.

344. e. In some stems, a *consonant* is (e¹) *dropped* or (e²) *added* for the sake of euphony or the metre: as,

γίγνομαι, *become*, (γνο-, γιγνο-) γιγνώσκω [g]nosco, KNOW, later softened forms γίνομαι, γῑνώσκω; λείβω, poet. εἴβω, *pour*. In other verbs, the insertion of a consonant, especially ν, renders a syllable long, and thus relieves the succession of short syllables, particularly in objective forms. See 351.

345. f. (*Digamma Verbs*, &c.) In some verbs, the (f¹) dropping or (f²) change of F, or (f³) of σ, has led to different forms of the stem (140 s): as,

(πλεϝ-, πλε- f¹, πλευ- f²) πλέω, πλεύσομαι (42 g); (θεϝ-) θέω *run*, θεύσομαι· νέω *swim*, νεύσομαι· (χεϝ-, χε-, χευ-, χυ-) χέω *pour*, Aor. ἔχεα, Ep. ἔχευα, A. P. ἐχύθην; καίω (44): (σεχ-, σχ- c³, σχε- c⁶, ἐχ- 141, ἐχ- d¹) ἔχω *have*, F. (ἐχ-σω) ἕξω, 2 A. ἔσχον, Imv. σχές· (σεπ-, σπ- c³, ἐπ-, σεσπ- 284 e, ἐσπ-) ἕπω *be busy with*, 2 A. ἔσπον, ἐσπόμην, poet. ἑσπόμην.

III. EMPHATIC, OR PROTRACTED STEMS.

346. Most *impure* stems and many *pure* stems are PROTRACTED in the *Present System*, to express with more emphasis the idea of *continued*, or perhaps, in some cases, of *transitive* action. This protraction takes place, (A.) by lengthening short vowels; (B.) by adding syllables or letters.

347. A. By LENGTHENING SHORT VOWELS; either (g) to cognate LONG VOWELS (*Long Vowel Stems*); or (h) to DIPHTHONGS (*Diphthong Stems*):

(1.) In *mute* verbs, ἄ becomes η; in *liquid* verbs, and in some *mute* verbs, ῐ and ῠ are *simply lengthened*; in other cases, the short vowel is usually changed to a *diphthong*. (2.) In *mute* verbs, the change commonly extends to all the *regular tenses* (303 a). Thus,

◀(g) 2 A. P. ἐσάπην, ἐτάκην, Pr. σήπω *rot*, τήκω *melt*; ἐκλίνην, κλίνω *bend*; ἐτρίβην, τρίβω (39); ἐσύρην, σύρω *drag*; ἐτύφην, τύφω *fumigate*.

(h) Fut. φᾰνῶ, καθᾰρῶ, Pr. φαίνω (40), καθαίρω *purify*; σπερῶ, σπείρω *sow*; τενῶ, τείνω *stretch*; 2 A. ἔλιπον, ἔπιθον, Pr. λείπω, πείθω (38 s).

348. B. By ADDING SYLLABLES OR LETTERS. These may be *annexed*, *inserted*, or *prefixed* (32).

I. The CONSONANTS ANNEXED OR INSERTED are the consonant ι (with the resulting changes, 143), σκ, ν, τ, θ, &c.

349. Iota Form. i. The consonant ι unites (i¹) with a *palatal mute*, or less frequently (i²) with a *lingual* or (i³) *labial* mute, to form σσ (in later Att. ττ, 169 a): as,

(i¹) 2 A. P. ἐτάγην, ἐμάγην, Pr. τάσσω or τάττω (39), μάσσω *knead;* φυλάκ-, φυλάσσω *guard;* (i²) βλῖτ-, βλίττω *take honey;* κορῦθ-, poet. κορύσσω *arm;* (i³) F. (πεπ-σω) πέψω, Pr. πέσσω or πέττω *cook.*

j. The ι unites (j¹) with a *lingual mute*, or less frequently (j²) with a *palatal mute*, (j³) a *double palatal*, or (j⁴) a *labial mute*, to form ζ: as,

(j¹) φράδ-, φράζω *tell;* ὀνομᾱτ-, ὀνομάζω *name;* (j²) 2 A. ἔκραγον, ἐσφάγην, Pr. κράζω *cry,* σφάζω or σφάττω *slay;* στενάχ-, στενάζω *groan;* (j³) κλαγγ-, κλάζω *clang;* (j⁴) νίφ-, νίζω, later νίπτω, *wash.*

l (*for* k, *see* 350). The ι unites with λ, to form λλ: as,

F. βᾰλῶ, σφᾰλῶ, στελῶ, Pr. βάλλω *throw,* σφάλλω *deceive,* στέλλω *send.*

α. Palatals in -ζω are mostly *onomatopes* (words formed to imitate sounds). Some verbs in -ζω or -σσω have both palatal and lingual forms.

β. Linguals in -ζω are very numerous, particularly those in -ίζω. They are mostly derivatives, wanting the second tenses and, by reason of euphonic changes, nowhere showing the stem in its prime form. This may often, however, be ascertained from a cognate word. It ends most frequently in δ, and may be assumed to do so, if the contrary does not appear: as, ὀριδ-, ὀριζ- (39 d).

γ. Most linguals in -ζω may be *practically* regarded as having but a single form of the stem, with ζ as the stem-mark. And in some, (z) the stem may be regarded as having for an added consonant simply ζ, either (z¹) alone or (z²) with a vowel (the modified stem marked with z, to avoid double notation): as, (z¹) πρίω, and later πρίζω, *to saw;* οὐτάω and οὐτάζω *wound,* poet.; (z²) 2 A. ἔπορον, Pr. πορίζω *furnish.*

350. k (*for* l, *see* 349). Inceptive Form. In this form, -σκ- is annexed, (k¹) either alone, or (k²) with a vowel, commonly ι. When -σκ- alone is added, (k³) a consonant preceding is *dropped* or (k⁴) *transposed*, or (k⁵) rarely *unites with the* σ, excluding the κ; while a vowel preceding, particularly ο, (k⁶) may be *lengthened* or (k⁷) *changed to* ι. Thus,

(k¹) F. ἀρέσω, μεθύσω, Pr. ἀρέσκω *please,* μεθύσκω *intoxicate;* (k²) 2 A. εὗρον, Pr. εὑρίσκω *find;* (k³) ἔχανον, χάσκω (151) *gape;* ἔλακον, λάσκω *sound, utter,* poet.; ἔπαθον, (παθσκ-, 151, 159 g) πάσχω *suffer;* (k⁴,⁶) ἔθορον, (θορσκ-) θρώσκω *leap,* ἔθανον, (θανσκ-) θνήσκω *die* (342. 3); (k⁵) ἀλεκ-, (ἀλεκσκ-) ἀλέξω *ward off;* (k⁷) ἀμβλόω and ἀμβλίσκω (341); 2 A. (ἀλο-) ἐάλων, ἁλίσκομαι *to be taken.* So from r. μιγ-, with transposition, may be formed (μιγσκ-) μίσγω *mix;* cf. Lat. *misceo*, (*mics*)*mixtum*.

α. These verbs correspond in form and sometimes in force to the Lat. *inceptives* in -sco: as, γηράσκω *senesco, grow old,* ἡβάσκω *pubesco* (379 b).

351. n. Nasal Form. In this, ν is added, either alone, or with a vowel (chiefly as -ᾰν-, -νῠ-, or -νε-).

1. When -ν- alone is added, (n¹) it commonly *follows* the former stem-mark, which, (n²) if a short vowel, often becomes a long vowel or diphthong; but (n³) sometimes *precedes* it (chiefly α in a few poetic forms): as,

§ 354.   I, N, T, &C., ANNEXED.   215

(n¹) 2 A. ἔδακον, Pr. δάκνω *bite* (47); ἔκαμον, κάμνω *labor*; ἔτεμον, τέμνω *cut*; (n²) ἔπιον, πίνω, *drink*, (δῦ-) ἔδῦν, δύνω *enter*; (βᾰ-) ἔβην, βαίνω *go*; ἐλάω, commonly ἐλαύνω, *drive*; (n³) F. δαμάσω, poet. Pr. δαμνάω or δάμνημι *subduc*; (περᾰ-, περνᾰ-) πέρνημι poet., *sell*.

2. There are three ways of adding -ᾰν- : (n⁴) without further change, chiefly to *double-consonant* stems (already long); (n⁵) with ν *inserted* before a characteristic mute, to lengthen a short syllable (344); (n⁶) with -αν- *prolonged* to -αιν- or -ᾱν-: as,

(n⁴) αὔξω and αὐξάνω (41); 2 A. ἔβλαστον, βλαστάνω *bud*; ἔδαρθον, δαρθάνω *sleep*; ἥμαρτον, ἁμαρτάνω *err*; (n⁵) ἔλᾰθον, λανθάνω *lie hid*; ἔμαθον, μανθάνω *learn*; ἔλαβον, λαμβάνω (150) *take*; ἔτυχον, τυγχάνω *happen*; (n⁶) (ὀσφρ-) ὠσφρόμην, ὀσφραίνομαι *smell*; κερδ-, κερδαίνω *gain*; ἔκιχον, Ep. κιχάνω, Att. κιγχάνω n⁸, v. l. κιχᾱνω, *find*.

3. When -νν- is added, the preceding syllable is by rule long. Hence, while -νν- can be (n⁷) annexed without further change to *consonants* (chiefly palatals and liquids), (n⁸) *the ν is doubled* after a *short vowel* (o also becoming ω): as,

(n⁷) 2 A. ἐμίγην, μίγνῡμι *mingle*; ἔπταρον, πτάρνῠμαι *sneeze*; οἴγω and οἴγνῡμι *open*; F. ὄρσω, ὄρνῡμι *rouse*; (ἀγ-) ἄξω, ἄγνῡμι *break*; (n⁸) κερᾰσω, κεράννῡμι *mix*; σβέσω, σβέννῡμι *extinguish*; κορέσω, κορέννῡμι *satiate*; (ζο-) ζώσω, ζώννῡμι *gird*; χόω, and later χώννῡμι, *heap up*.

4. (n⁹) After a diphthong (securing in itself a long syllable), a lingual or liquid is dropped before -νυ-: as, δαιτ-, δαίνῡμι *feast*; κτείνω, later κτείνῡμι *kill*. In ὄλλῡμι (ὀλ-, ὀλνυ-) *destroy*, ν is assimilated.

5. (n¹⁰) A few stems receive -νε-: as, 2 A. ἱκόμην, ἱκνέομαι, and poet. ἱκάνω n⁶, *come*; 1 A. ἔκυσα, κυνέω *kiss*; βύω and βυνέω *stop up*.

352. t (*for* o, *see* 354). TAU FORM. In this, τ is added, either (t¹) alone, chiefly to *labial stems*, or (t²) with a vowel:

(t¹) 2 A. ἐκόπην, κόπτω *cut*; ἐτύπην, τύπτω *beat*; ἐβλάβην, βλάπτω (147) *hurt*; ἐκρύβην, κρύπτω *hide*; ἐβάφην, βάπτω *dip*; ἐρράφην, ῥάπτω *stitch*; ἔτεκον, τίκτω (341); ἀνύω and ἀνύτω *accomplish*; (t²) ἐρρίφην, ῥίπτω and ῥιπτέω *throw*; 1 A. (πεκ-) ἔπεξα, πεκτέω *comb*.

353. q (*for* p, *see* 356). THETA FORM. In this form, which is chiefly poetic, θ is annexed, (q¹) either alone, or (q²) with a vowel, commonly α or ε. (q³) A short vowel in the stem is oftener lengthened before θ. Thus,

(q¹) πελάω and πελάθω *approach*, poet.; (q²) φλέγω, poet. φλεγέθω, *burn*; (θαλ-) θάλλω 1, poet. θαλέθω *flourish*; φθίνω, poet. φθινύθω, *consume*; ἔδω, poet. (ἐδθω 147) ἔσθω, comm. ἐσθίω, *eat*; (q³) νέω and νήθω, *spin*.

a. A few verbs obtain, in this form, a 2 Aor. with a short penult (340. 3): as, διώκω *pursue*, ἐδιώκαθον · εἴκω *yield*, εἴκαθον. These extended Aorists, which are chiefly poet., are regarded by some as Present Systems.

354. o. A few stems receive *other consonants*, either (o¹) alone, or (o²) with vowels: as,

(o¹) ἀμερ-, ἀμέρδω and ἀμείρω h, *deprive*, poet.; δίω and δείδω h, *fear*, Ep.; τρύω and τρύχω *wear out*; ψάω and ψήχω *rub*; νέω and poet. νήχω *swim*; (o²) ἄω *to be sated*, Ep. A. (ἀδε-) ἄδησα · ἔχθω and ἐχθαίρω *hate*, mostly poet.; κυλίω, κυλίνδω n⁸, and κυλινδέω, *roll*.

355. u, v, w (*for* r *and* t, *see* 357, 352). II. Vowel Form. Vowels annexed to protract the stem are chiefly (u) *a* and (v) ε, but (w) sometimes others: as,

(u) 2 A. ἔγοον, γοάω *bewail;* ἔμῦκον, μῡκάομαι *low;* ἔμακον, μηκάομαι *bleat;* 2 Pf. βέβρῡχα, βρῡχάομαι *roar* (onomatopes, as also βληχάομαι, bālo, Germ. *blöken, bleat*) ; (v) γέγηθα, γηθέω poet., *rejoice;* 2 A. ἔκτυπον, κτυπέω *crash;* F. (δοκ-) δόξω, δρκέω *seem, think;* (ὠθ-) ὤσω, ὠθέω *push;* (w) ἕλκω, late ἑλκύω *draw;* (ὁμ-, ὀμνυ- n⁷, ὁμο-) ὄμνῡμι *swear*, F. ὀμόσω.

a. (u², v²) When **a** is affixed, **ε** in the preceding syllable usually becomes **ω**; but when **ε** is affixed, **o**: as, τρέπω, poet. τρωπάω and τροπέω, *turn;* στρέφω, chiefly poet. στρωφάω and στροφέω, *twist*.

356. p, r (*for* q, *see* 353). III. Preformatives lengthening the stem consist chiefly of (r) *three kinds of reduplication;* and (p) the few others may be rather *euphonic* than *emphatic:* as,

(p) σπαίρω and ἀσπαίρω *gasp;* δύρομαι and ὀδύρομαι *lament*.

357. r. Reduplicated Stems. Reduplication in the stem is most frequent in *verbs in* -μι *and* -σκω. It is of three kinds:

1. (r¹) Proper, prefixing the *first letter with* -ĭ- (rarely with -ε-) to stems beginning with a *single consonant*, with a *mute and liquid*, or with μν-: as,

(δο-, διδο-) δίδωμι, (θε-, θιθε-, 159 a) τίθημι (45) ; (χρα-, χιχρα-) κίχρημι *lend;* (πλα-, πι-μ-πλα-, 344) πίμπλημι *fill*, (πρα-) πίμπρημι *burn;* 2 A. ἔδαον poet., διδάσκω *teach;* ἔδραν (45 h), διδράσκω *run;* (γνο-) ἔγνων, γιγνώσκω k⁸, *know;* F. (τρα-) τρήσω, τετραίνω *bore*. Cf. Lat. *gigno,sisto*.

2. (r²) Attic, prefixing the *two first letters* to stems beginning with a *short vowel followed by a single consonant:* as,

(ἀρ-) ἀραρίσκω *fit*, poet. ; (ἀχ-, ἀχαχ-, 159 a) ἀκαχίζω *afflict*, Ep. So, with the familiar vowel of reduplication ι, in place of the initial vowel repeated, (ὀνα-) ὀνίνημι *benefit;* ἀτάλλω and ἀτιτάλλω *rear*, poet.

3. (r³) Improper, simply prefixing ι *with the rough breathing* to stems not included above: as, (στα-, σιστα-, 141) ἵστημι, (ἑ-, ἱ-ἑ) ἵημι (45) ; 2 A. ἐπτάμην, ἵπταμαι *fly*.

IV. Adopted Stems.
(*For* t, *see* 352 ; u, v, w, 355 ; z, 349 γ.)

358. x. Some themes, to complete their inflection, *adopt* tenses from stems that appear to be *radically distinct:* as,

αἱρέω *take*, 2 A. (ἑλ-) εἷλον; ἔρχομαι *come*, F. (ἐλυθ-, ἐλευθ- h) ἐλεύσομαι, 2 Pf. ἐλήλυθα; ἐσθίω *eat*, 2 A. ἔφαγον; ὁράω *see*, F. (ὀπ-) ὄψομαι, 2 A. (ἰδ-, 279 c) εἶδον; τρέχω *run*, 2 A. ἔδραμον; φέρω *bear*, F. οἴσω, Pf. (ἐνεκ-) ἐνήνοχα; ὠνέομαι *buy*, 2 A. ἐπριάμην (45 i).

CHAPTER XI.

FORMATION OF WORDS.

359. a. The Greek, like all other original languages, is the development, according to certain natural laws, of a *small number of germs*, or *primary elements*. These elements (termed by botanic figure *roots* or *radicals*) have a significance which is not arbitrary, but founded upon instinctive principles of the human constitution.

b. If a word contains only *one* radical, either with or without formative elements (172 b), it is termed *simple;* but, if *more than one, compound.* Of simple words containing the same radical, that which appears to have been the earliest is called the *primitive;* and the others, *derivatives.*

c. Of those words which are commonly distinguished as *primitive* and *derivative*, some are directly related to each other as parent and child; while others are merely formations from the same radical, which, however, may have a simpler form in the one than in the other. The parent of a word is sometimes called *its primitive*, even when it is itself the child of an older word. So the term *stem* is sometimes extended to the essence of a word which is not inflected (172 a).

360. The stem of a primitive sometimes remains *unchanged* in a derivative; but it is commonly *modified*, chiefly by annexing significant syllables or letters. These are termed *afformatives;* while the afformative, with the affix of the theme if this is added, may be distinguished as the *suffix.*

Thus, in ἄροτρον *plough* and λύτρον *ransom*, the stems ἀρο- and λυ- of the verbs ἀρόω *to plough*, λύω *to loose*, are modified by the addition of the afformative -τρ-, which denotes *instrument* or *means;* and thus give rise to the new stems ἀροτρ- and λυτρ-, to which again the affix of inflection -ον is added, making the themes ἀρο-τρ-ον and λύ-τρ-ον. These words are more briefly said to be formed by adding to the primitive stems the *suffix* -τρον.

361. Derivation shows also many euphonic changes, especially such as take place before the affixes of verbs: thus,

a.) Changes of consonants: as, τρῖ(β-τ)πτης *rubber*. Cf. 304.
b.) Precession or the use of a kindred vowel: as, (βασιλε-) βασιλεύς *king*, βασιλικός *kingly;* λέγω *to speak*, λόγος *speech.* Cf. 312.
c.) The lengthening of a short vowel, or the insertion of σ or η: as, ποιέω *to compose*, ποιητής *poet;* σείω *to shake*, σει-σ-μός *a shaking, shock;* αὔξω *to increase*, αὐξ-η-τικός *augmentative.* Cf. 307, 310, 311. Even an initial vowel is sometimes lengthened: as, ἦθος (ἔθω) *usage*, ὠφελέω (ὀφελος) *to help.*
d.) Contraction, Syncope, Metathesis, &c.: as, ἄεισμα ᾆσμα *song;* καλέω *to call*, (κλε-) κλητήρ *summoner;* τέμνω *to cut*, τμῆσις *cutting.* Cf. 342.
e. A union-vowel is often inserted.

I. FORMATION OF SIMPLE WORDS.

362. Simple words are divided in respect to their formation into three classes: (a) those which consist of the mere radical, without change, except for euphony or emphasis; (b) those which have, in addition, merely the affixes of inflection; (c) those which receive further modifications.

d. The Rules and Remarks which follow have respect chiefly to the last class.

e. Words derived from *verbs* are called VERBALS; from *nouns* (whether *substantive* or *adjective*, according to the old classification), DENOMINATIVES; from *pronouns*, PRONOMINALS.

f. Many derivative nouns are properly adjectives used substantively.

A. Nouns.

363. I. FROM VERBS. Nouns formed from verbs (or from common radicals, 359 c) denote,

1.) The ACTION or ABSTRACT IDEA of the verb. These are formed by adding to the stem of the verb,

a.) -σις (Gen. -σεως, fem.), or -σιᾰ (Gen. -σίᾱς, f.): as, μιμέ-ομαι *to imitate*, μίμη-σις *imitation*; πράσσω (r. πρᾱγ-) *to act*, πρᾱ(γ-σις)ξις *action*; θύω *to sacrifice*, θυσία *sacrifice*; δοκιμάζω *to try*, δοκιμασία *trial*.

b.) -η, -ᾰ (G. -ης, -ᾱς, f.): as, φεύγω (r. φυγ-) *to flee*, φυγ-ή *flight*; τρέφω *to nourish*, τροφή *nourishment*; χαίρω (r. χαρ-) *to rejoice*, χαρ-ά *joy*.

c.) -ος (G. -ου, m.): as, πλέω *to sail*, πλόος *sailing, voyage*.

d. -τος (G. -του, m.), -τη (G. -της, f.) and Ion. -τύς (G. -τύος, f.): as, κωκύ-ω *to wail*, κωκῡ-τός *wailing*; βιόω *to live*, βιοτή and βίοτος *life*.

e.) -μός (G. -μοῦ, m.), or -μη (G. -μης, f.): as, ὀδύρ-ομαι *to lament*, ὀδυρ-μός *lamentation*; μέ-μνη-μαι *to remember*, μνή-μη *remembrance*.

f.) -ος (G. -εος, n.): as, κήδ-ομαι *to care*, κῆδ-ος *care*.

g. Other suffixes appear in ὁ γέλως, -ωτος, *laughter*, ὄλεθρος *destruction*; ἡ ἀλγηδών *pain* (cf. Lat. *cupīdo*), δύναμις, -εως, *power*, &c.

h. From the tendency of *abstracts* to pass into *concretes*, verbals of Class 1 often express not so much the *action* itself, as an *effect, object, circumstance*, &c., of the action, and thus blend with other classes: as, γραμμή *line*, δόσις *gift*, λάχος *share*.

364. 2.) The EFFECT, or OBJECT of the action. These are formed by adding to the stem of the verb,

a.) -μα (G. -ματος, n.): as, πράσσω *to do*, πρᾶγ-μα (τὸ πεπραγμένον *factum, thing done*) *deed*; σπείρω *to sow*, σπέρμα *thing sown, seed*.

b. Other suffixes appear in τὸ δῶρον *gift*, πέταλον *leaf*, βέλεμνον *missile*.

365. 3.) The DOER. These are formed by adding to the stem of the verb,

a.) -της (G. -του, m.): as, ποιέω *to compose*, ποιητής *poēta, poet*.

b.) -τήρ (G. -τῆρος, m.) or -τωρ (G. -τορος, m.): as, σώζω *to save*, σωτήρ *servātor, savior*; r. ῥε-, *to speak*, ῥή-τωρ *orātor, speaker*. (c) The feminines corresponding to Classes a. and b. end in -τριᾰ or -τειρᾰ (proparoxytone, G. -ᾱς), or in -τρίς or -τις (G. -ιδος): as, ποιήτρια *poëtria, poetess*, σώτειρα *servātrix, female deliverer*, προφῆτις *prophetess*.

§ 368. NOUNS. 219

d.) -εύς (G. -έως, m.): as, γράφ-ω *to paint,* γραφ-εύς *painter.*
e.) -ός (G. -οῦ, m. f.): as, τρέφω *to nourish,* τροφός *nurse.*
f.) -μων (G. -μονος, m.): as, ἡγέ-ομαι *to lead,* ἡγε-μών *leader.*
g. Other suffixes appear in ὁ τέκτων, -ονος, *workman,* τρόχις, *runner,* &c.

366. 4.) The PLACE, INSTRUMENT, or other means or circumstances of the action. These are formed by adding to the stem of the verb,

a.) -τήριον (G. -ου, n.), more frequently expressing *place*: as, ἀκροάομαι *to hear,* ἀκροα-τήριον auditorium, *place of hearing, auditory.*
b.) -τρον (G. -ου, n.), or -τρᾰ (G. -ᾱς, f.), more frequently expressing *means*: as, ξύω *to curry,* ξύστρον and ξύστρα *currycomb,* ἄροτρον *plough.*
c. Other suffixes appear in τὸ κλεῖθρον *bar;* ὁ στέφανος *crown;* &c.
d. NOTE. Suffixes of verbals are annexed, in general, with the same euphonic changes as the similar affixes of inflection (361): i. e. those beginning with σ follow the analogy of -σω of the Fut. or -σαι of the Perf. pass.; those beginning with μ and τ, of -μαι and -ται of the Perf. pass.; and those beginning with a *vowel,* of the 2d Perf. It is convenient to remember, that verbal nouns following the 1st Pers. sing. of the Perf. pass. more frequently denote the *thing done;* the 2d, the *doing;* and the 3d, the *doer.* Thus,

πε-ποίη-μαι,   πε-ποίη-σαι,   πε-ποίη-ται,
  ποίη-μα, *poem,*   ποίη-σις, *poesy,*   ποιη-τής, *poet.*

367. II. FROM ADJECTIVES. Nouns formed from adjectives (or from common radicals, 359 c) usually express the ABSTRACT of the adjective, and are formed in,

a.) -ίᾱ (G. -ίᾱς, f.), or oftener, if the stem ends in ε or ο, -ιᾰ forming, with the stem-mark, -ειᾰ or -οιᾰ: as, σοφ-ός *wise,* σοφ-ίᾱ sapient-ia, *wisdom;* ἀληθής, -έ-ος, *true,* ἀλήθεια *truth;* εὔνο-ος, *kind,* εὔνοιᾰ *kindness.*
b.) -της (G. -τητος, f.), from adjectives in -ος and -υς: as, ἴσος *equal,* ἰσότης æqualitas, *equality;* ταχύς *swift,* ταχυτής celeritas, *swiftness.*
c.) -σύνη (G. -ης, f.), from adjectives in -ος and -ων: as, δίκαιος *just,* δικαιοσύνη *justice;* σώφρων *discreet,* σωφροσύνη *discretion.*
d.) -ος (G. -εος, n.), chiefly from adjectives in -υς: as, βαθύς *deep,* βάθος *depth;* εὐρύς *broad,* εὖρος *breadth;* ταχύς (b), τάχος *speed.*
e.) -άς (G. -άδος, f.), from numerals: as, δύο *two,* δυάς *duad;* τριάς.

368. III. FROM OTHER NOUNS. Nouns derived from other nouns are chiefly,

1.) PATRIALS, and similar words denoting *persons related to some object.* These end in,

a.) -της (G. -του, m.) and -τις (G. -τιδος, f.; 235 a), with the preceding vowel long in patrials (-ίτης, -ήτης, -άτης, -ιάτης, -ιώτης) and also in other nouns in ιτης, -ιτις: as, Σύβαρις *Sybaris,* Συβαρίτης, *a man of S.,* a *Sybarite,* Συβαρῖτις, *a woman of S.;* Αἰγινήτης, Πισάτης, Σπαρτιάτης, Σικελιώτης, *a man of Ægina,* &c.; τόξον *bow,* τοξότης *archer,* τοξότις *archeress.*
b.) -εύς (G. -έως, m.) and -ίς (G. -ίδος, f.; 217 f): as, Μέγαρα *Megara,* Μεγαρεύς *Megarian man,* Μεγαρίς M. *woman;* φάρμακον *drug,* φαρμακεύς *dealer in drugs, sorcerer,* φαρμακίς *sorceress;* ἵππος equus, ἱππεύς eques.
c. A PATRIAL NOUN (patria, *native land*) denotes a *person* belonging to a particular *country;* a GENTILE NOUN (gens, *nation*), one belonging to a particular *nation.* Adjectives have like distinctions.

369. 2.) PATRONYMICS (so called from containing the father's or an ancestor's name, πατρὸς ὄνομα). These end in,

a.) -δης (G. -δου, m.) and -ς (G. -δος, f.), preceded by -ᾰ- if from names in -ιος or of Dec. 1, but otherwise by -ι- (-ιδης uniting with a preceding ε or ο) : as, Βορέας Boreas, Βορεάδης son of B., Βορεάς daughter of B.; Θέστιος, Θεστιάδης, Θεστιάς · Πρίαμος, Πριαμίδης, Πριαμίς · Κέκροψ, Κεκροπίδης, Κεκροπίς · Πηλεύς, -έως, Πηλείδης Pelides ; Ἡρακλείδης (19 b); Λητώ, -όος, Λητοίδης. The Ep. often uses the form in -ιάδης after a long syllable, for the sake of the metre : Φηρητιάδης, B. 763 ; Πηληϊάδης, A. 1.

b.) -ίων (G. -ίωνος, rarely -ίονος, m.) and -ιώνη or -ίνη (G. -ης, f.), only poetic : as, Κρόνος Saturn, Κρονίων, -ίωνος or ίονος, son of S., A. 397; Πηλεύς, Πηλείων, v. l. -είων, A. 188 ; Ἀκρίσιος, Ἀκρισιώνη, daughter of A., Ξ. 319 ; Ἄδρηστος, Ἀδρηστίνη E. 412. The poets even blend the forms a. and b.; and use other freedoms : as, fr. Λάμπος, Λαμπετίδης, O. 526.

370. 3.) FEMALE APPELLATIVES. These end in,

a.) -ις (G. -ιδος), chiefly from masculines of Dec. 1, and from those in -εύς : as, δεσπότης master, δεσπότις mistress (also δέσποινα, cf. b).

b.) -αινᾰ (G. -ης), chiefly from masculines in -ων : as, λέων, -οντος, leo, lion, λέαινα leæna, lioness ; τέκτων, -ονος, artisan, τέκταινα.

c.) -ειᾰ (G. -είᾶς) : as, βασιλεύς rex, king, βασίλεια regīna, queen.

d.) -σσᾰ (-ττᾰ, 169 a ; G. -ης), from several endings of Dec. 3 : as, Κίλιξ, -ικος, Cilician, Κίλ(ικ)α, 143 c)ισσα · ἄναξ, -κτος, sovereign, ἄνασσα.

e.) -α, -η, &c.: as, θεά goddess (cf. b) ; ἀδελφός brother, ἀδελφή sister. See also 235, 365 c, 368, 369.

371. 4.) DIMINUTIVES (sometimes expressing *affection*, often *contempt*). These end in,

a.) -ιον (G. -ίου, n.), with a syllable often prefixed (-ίδιον, -άριον, -ύλλιον, -ύδριον, -ύφιον, &c.) ; (b) -ίσκος (G. -ου, m.), -ίσκη (G. -ης, f.) : as, παῖς puer, *child*, Diminutives, παιδίον *little child*, παιδίσκος, παιδαρίσκος, puerŭlus, puellus, puercŭlus, *young boy*, *little boy*, παιδίσκη puella, puellŭla, *young* or *little girl*, παιδάριον, παιδαρίδιον, παιδαρύλλιον, παιδισκάριον · Ὦ Σώκρατες, ὦ Σωκρατίδιον, *O Socrates! dear Socky!* Ar. Nub. 222.

c.) -ίς (G. -ίδος and -ῖδος, f.) : as, πίναξ tabula, *table*, πινακίς, -ίδος, tabella, *tablet ;* νῆσος isle, νησίς, -ῖδος, islet ; κρήνη fons, *fountain*, κρηνίς.

d.) -ιδεύς (G. -έως, m.; of the young of animals) : as, ἀετός *eagle*, ἀετιδεύς *eaglet ;* λαγώς *hare*, λαγιδεύς ; also υἱός, υἱϊδεύς *grandson*.

e.) -ίχνη, -άκνη, -ᾰλος, -ελος, -έλη, -ῖλος, -υλλίς, -ῡλος, -ύλη, &c.: as, πόλις *city*, πολίχνη · πίθος *wine-jar*, πιθάκνη · κόκκος *kernel*, κόκκαλος · σκοπός *peak*, σκόπελος scopŭlus ; νέφος nubes, *cloud*, νεφέλη nebŭla ; ναύτης *sailor*, ναυτίλος nautĭlus (*little sailor*); ἄκανθις *finch*, ἀκανθυλλίς.

f. Some diminutives (especially in -ιον) have lost their peculiar force : thus, θήρ, commonly in prose θηρίον *wild beast*.

372. 5.) AUGMENTATIVES, words implying *increase* or *largeness*, either of *number*, *size*, or *degree*. These end in,

a.) -ων (G. -ωνος, m.). This ending may express either a *place*, an *animal*, or a *person*, in which any thing exists *in numbers*, or *in large size* or *degree* : as, ἄμπελος *vine*, ἀμπελών vinētum, *vineyard*, ἱππών (ἵππος) *horse-stable*, γνάθος *jaw*, γνάθων *glutton*. Cf. Lat. Nāso, -ōnis, *Big-nose*.

b.) -αξ (G. -ᾱκος, m.), applied, like the preceding, to persons and animals, but harsher in its expression : as, πλοῦτος *wealth*, πλούταξ *a rich churl*. So λάβρος *greedy*, λάβραξ *sea-wolf*. Cf. Lat. adj. *loquax, rapax*.

B. ADJECTIVES.

373. Adjectives derived from *verbs* express, in general, *relations* (*active* or *passive* in their character) to the *actions* or *states* denoted by the verbs; and those derived from *nouns* express *relations* to the *persons* or *things* denoted by the nouns. But, from their very nature, *relations* are distinguished with less precision than *things* or *actions;* and, to some extent, the offices stated below blend with each other.

374. I. FROM VERBS. These end in,

a.) -ῐκός, -ή, -όν, *active:* as, ἄρχω *to rule,* ἀρχ-ικός *able to rule;* γράφω *to describe,* γραφικός *descriptive, graphic.* This ending is more frequently preceded by τ (cf. 365 a, b): as, ποιητικός (ποιέω) *poetic.* See 375 b.

b.) -τήριος, -ᾱ, -ον, *active* (τήρ + ιος, 365 b, 375 a): as, σώζω *to save,* σωτήρ, σωτήριος *saving, preservative.* Cf. Lat. *ora-tōr-ius.*

c.) -ῐμος, -ον (or -η, -ον), implying *fitness,* both *active* and *passive,* and annexed after the analogy of different verbal nouns: as, τρέφω, τροφή (363 b), τρόφ-ιμος *fitted to impart* or *to receive nourishment, nutritious, vigorous;* χρήσιμος (χράομαι, χρῆσις) *fit for use.*

d.) -μων, -μον (G. -μονος), *active:* as, ἐλεέω *to pity,* ἐλεή-μων *compassionate;* μνήμων (μέμνημαι) *mindful;* νοήμων (νοέω) *thoughtful.*

e.) -τός, -ή, -όν, *passive,* signifying *that which is done,* either as a matter of *fact* (like the Lat. Part. in *-tus* or *-sus*), or more commonly as a matter of *habit* or *possibility:* as, ὁράω *to see,* ὁρᾱ-τός visus, *seen,* visĭbĭlis, *visible;* φιλητός amātus, amābilis. See 269 d, 272 c.

f.) -τέος, -ᾱ, -ον, *passive* (269 d), expressing *necessity* or *obligation* (like the Lat. Part. in *-ndus*): as, ποιέω *to make,* ποιη-τέος faciendus, *that is to be made.* Often in neut. as impers.: γραπτέον scribendum.

g.) -νός, -ή, -όν, *passive* (compare the Part. in -μενος): as, σέβω *to revere,* (σεβ-νός, 148 c) σεμνός *revered,* ποθεινός (ποθέω) *longed for.*

h.) -ρός (-ᾱ, -όν), -άς (G. -άδος), -ός, &c.: as, χαλάω *to slacken,* χαλα-ρός *slack;* φέρω *to bear,* φοράς *fruitful;* λέγω *to choose,* λογάς *chosen.*

375. II. FROM NOUNS. These have the following endings, with, in general, the significations that are annexed:

a.) -ιος, *pertaining to;* if a vowel precedes, commonly uniting with it in a diphthong (-αιος, -ειος, -οιος, -ῳος, -υιος), and often, without respect to this, assuming the form -ειος (Ion. -ήιος, 132), especially from names of persons and animals (iv. 5. 31). Many *patrials* (properly adjectives, but often used substantively) belong to this class. Thus, οὐρανός *heaven,* οὐράν-ιος cœlestis, *pertaining to heaven, heavenly;* Ἀθηναῖος (Ἀθῆναι) *Athenian;* θεῖος (θε-ός) *divine,* Ἀργεῖος Argīvus; Ὁμήρειος (Ὅμηρος) *Homeric.*

b.) -ῐκός, -ή, -όν (commonly -κός or -ᾰκός after ι or υ, while -αιος often makes -ᾰϊκός), *relating to.* These adjectives in -κός are often formed from words that are themselves derivative. They apply to *things* rather than to *persons.* When used of the latter, they commonly signify *related to in quality,* or *fit for,* and are mostly derived from personal appellations. Thus, τέχνη *art,* τεχν-ικός *relating to art, artistic,* πολεμικός (πόλεμος) bellicus, *military;* νεᾱνι-κός (νεᾱνίας) *youthful,* Λίβυς *Libyan,* Λιβυκός *pertaining to the Libyans;* Ἀχαιός *Achæan,* Ἀχᾱϊκός. See 374 a.

c.) -εος, -ᾱ, -ον, and -ινος, -η, -ον (proparoxytone), denoting *material, -en:* as, χρυσός *gold,* χρύσ-εος aur-ĕus, *golden;* ξύλ-ινος (ξύλον) *wooden.*

d.) -ῐνός, seldom -ῐνός, expressing *time* or *prevalence:* as, ἠρ-ινός (ἦρ) vernus, *vernal,* πεδινός (πέδον) *level,* ὀρεινός (ὄρος, -ε-ος) *mountainous.*

e.) -ῑνος, -ηνός, -ᾱνός, *patrials,* from names of cities and countries out of Greece: as, Ταραντ-ῖνος (Τάρας, -αντος) *Tarentine*, Κυζικηνός (Κύζικος) *Cyzicene*, Σαρδιᾱνός (Σάρδεις) *Sardian*. Cf. Lat. *Latīnus, Romānus*, &c.

f.) -ρός, -ερός, -ηρός, -αλέος, -ηλός, -ωλός, -εις (-εσσᾰ, -εν, G. -εντος), -ώδης (-ες, G. -εος, contr., as most think, fr. -ο-ειδής, fr. εἶδος *form*), &c., expressing *fulness, quality*, &c.: as, αἰσχρός (αἶσχος) *shameful*, φοβερός (φόβος) *fearful*, πονηρός (πόνος) *painful*, θαρσαλέος (θάρσος) *courageous*.

376. III. FROM ADJECTIVES AND ADVERBS. a. From some adjectives and adverbs, derivatives are formed in the same manner as from nouns: thus, καθαρός *clean*, καθάριος *cleanly* ; ἐλευθέριος (ἐλεύθερος liber) liberālis, *liberal;* θηλυκός (θῆλυς), *feminine*.

b. The adjective has in Greek, as in other languages, two strengthened forms, of which one may be termed *dual*, applying to an object as *one of two*, and the other *plural*, applying to an object as *one of a number* (commonly more than two). The most obvious examples of these strengthened forms are the *comparative* and *superlative degrees*, commonly so called.

c. Other examples of the *comparative* or *dual strengthened form* are, (1) the correlatives πότερος; *whether of the two?* ποτερός, ἕτερος (formed from the 3d Pers. pron. as the positive, or, as some think, from the numeral εἷς) *one of the two*, οὐδέτερος, ὁπότερος, ἑκάτερος, ἀμφότερος (see 58, and compare the Lat. *uter, neuter, alter*, and the Eng. *whether, either, neither, other*) ; (2) the following, implying a consideration of *two objects* or *relations* : δεξιτερός (poet.) dexter, *right* (rather than left), ἀριστερός sinister, *left*, δεύτερος *second*, ἡμέτερος noster, *our* (rather than yours), ὑμέτερος vester, *your* (and, extending the analogy, σφέτερος *their*).

d. Other examples of the *superlative* or *plural strengthened form* are, (1) the *correlatives* πόστος; *which in order?* or, *one of how many?* ὁπόστος, ἕκαστος (58) ; (2) all *ordinals* except δεύτερος; see 240. 2, 264.

C. PRONOUNS.

377. For the formation of the most common pronouns, see 244 s. The Greek abounds in correlative pronouns and adverbs (53).

a. In respect to many of these, it will be observed that, when they begin with π-, they are *indefinite*, or *interrogative* (with a change of accent) ; with τ-, *definite* or *demonstrative;* with the *rough breathing, relative definite;* and with ὁπ-, *relative indefinite:* as, πόσος; *how much?* ποσός *of a certain quantity*, τόσος, τοσοῦτος, and τοσόσδε (252 a), *so much*, ὅσος *as much*, ὁπόσος *how much soever;* πότε; *when?* ποτέ *at some time*, τότε *then*, ὅτε *when*, ὁπότε *whensoever*.

D. VERBS.

378. I. FROM NOUNS AND ADJECTIVES. Of these the chief endings and prevailing significations are as follows :

a.) -έω, -εύω, and (mostly from nouns of Dec. 1) -άω, *to be* or *do* that which is pointed out by the primitive: as, φίλος *friend*, φιλ-έω *to be a friend, love*, βασιλεύω (βασιλεύς) regno, *reign*, τιμάω (τιμή) *honor*.

b.) **-όω** (mostly from words of Dec. 2), **-αίνω** and **-ύνω** (mostly from adjectives), *to make that which is pointed out by the primitive* : as, δῆλος *evident*, δηλ-όω *to make evident*, σημαίνω (σῆμα) *signify*, ἡδύνω (ἡδύς) *sweeten*.

c.) **-ίζω**, and (chiefly when formed from words which have α or η in the last syllable, or when preceded by ι, cf. 369 a, 375 b) **-άζω** ; from names of persons or animals, *imitative* (denoting the adoption of the *manners, language, opinions, party*, &c.) ; from other words, used in various senses, but mostly active : as, Μηδ-ίζω (Μῆδος) *to imitate or favor the Medes*, Ἑλληνίζω *speak Greek*, πλουτίζω (πλοῦτος) *make rich*, δικάζω (δίκη) *judge*.

d.) **-ιάω**, rarely **-άω**, expressing *desire* (Desideratives), or *morbid state* : as, μαθητής *disciple*, μαθητ-ιάω *to wish to become a disciple*, Ar. Nub. 183.

e. **-ω** with simply a strengthening of the penult, more frequently active : as, καθἁρός *pure*, καθαίρω *to purify*, μαλάσσω (μαλἄκός) *soften*.

f. Other endings appear in κονίω (κόνις) *to bedust*, δακρύω (δάκρυ) *weep*, φεύζω (φεῦ) and οἰμώζω (οἴμοι) *wail*, οἰκτείρω (οἶκτος) *pity*, &c.

379. II. From Other Verbs. These are,

a.) *Desideratives*, formed in **-σείω**, from the Fut.: as, γελάω *to laugh*, γελασείω *wish to laugh*, πολεμησείω (πολεμέω) *wish for war*, Th. i. 33.

b.) Various prolonged forms in **-ζω, -σκω, -λλω**, &c., sometimes *frequentative* or *intensive*, as, ῥίπτω jacio, *to throw*, ῥιπτάζω jacto, *throw to and fro*, στένω *sigh*, στενάζω *sigh deeply*, αἰτέω *ask*, αἰτίζω *beg ;* sometimes *inceptive* (350 a), as, ἡβάω *to be of age*, ἡβάσκω *become of age ;* sometimes *causative*, as, μεθύω *to be intoxicated*, μεθύσκω *intoxicate ;* sometimes *diminutive*, as, ἐξαπατάω *cheat*, ἐξαπατύλλω (cf. 371) *cheat a little, humbug*, Ar. Eq. 1144 ; but often scarce differing in force from the primitive form (336 s).

E. Adverbs.

380. Most adverbs belong to the following classes :

I. Oblique Cases of Nouns and Adjectives, employed as circumstantial adjuncts (see Syntax). With an adjective thus employed, a noun is strictly to be supplied. Many of these *oblique cases* have antique forms, and many belong to themes that are not in use. Thus,

a.) Accusatives : as, δωρεάν *as a gift*, gratis, ἀκμήν *at the moment*, χάριν in gratiam, *for the sake of*, δίκην instar, *like ;* and the Neut. sing. and pl. of adjectives, especially Comparatives and Superlatives (263).

b.) Genitives, (1) in **-θεν** (192), denoting the *place whence ;* (2) in **-ου**, denoting the *place where* : as, οὗ [sc. τόπου or χωρίου] *in which place, where*, αὐτοῦ *there*, ὁμοῦ *in the same place*, οὐδαμοῦ *nowhere ;* (3) in **-ης** : as, αἰφνης (and ἐξαίφνης, 382 a ; so Lat. *repente* and *derepente*) *of a sudden*.

c.) Datives, (1) in **-οι, -οθι** of Dec. 2 sing., and in **-ησι**(ν, **-ᾱσι**(ν, of Dec. 1 pl., denoting the *place where* (in adverbs in **-οι** derived from pronouns, this commonly passes into the idea of *whither ;* cf. the familiar use of *where, there*, &c., in Eng.) : as, Ἀθήνησι *at Athens*, Πλαταιᾶσι *at Plataeae*, θύρᾱσι *at the door ;* (2) in **-ῃ** (-η), **-ᾳ** (-α), **-αι** of Dec. 1, and in **-ι** of Dec. 3, denoting *way, place where*, or *time when* : as, ταύτῃ [sc. ὁδῷ] *in this way, thus*, [sc. χώρᾳ] *in this place, here*, πανταχῇ *every way, everywhere*, πεζῇ *on foot*, ἰδίᾳ *privately*, χαμαί humi, *on the ground*, πάλαι *in olden time*, ἕκητι *by the will of*, ἶφι (ἶς, 190) *with might*, A. 38, ἄγχι *near*.

d. For the old Dat. forms **-οι, -οθι, -αι**, and **-ησι** (for which **-ᾱσι** was common after ε, ι, or ρ, 115 a), see 187, 191, 198. The adverbial Dat. is usually written with ι subsc., when it has the same form in common Greek with a noun or adj. so written, and some carry the use of this ι still farther (109 a).

c. Some pronominal or kindred adverbs are strengthened by the insertion of -άχ-: as, ἀλλαχοῦ and ἀλλαχῇ *elsewhere*, πανταχῇ (c). See 58.

381. II. Derivatives signifying, (1.) Manner, in,

a.) **-ως**, from adjectives. The adverb may be formed by changing ν of the Gen. pl. into **ς**: as, σοφός, G. pl. σοφῶν, *wise*, σοφῶς sapienter, *wisely*; ταχύς, ταχέων, *swift*, ταχέως *swiftly*.

b.) **-ηδόν** or **-δον** (perhaps kindred with εἶδος, *form*), chiefly from nouns; **-δην** or **-άδην**, chiefly from verbs (those in -άδην conforming to 366 d; and **-δα**: as, πλινθηδόν (πλίνθος) *like bricks*, Hdt. 2. 96, βοτρυδόν (βότρυς) *in clusters*, B. 89, κρύβδην or -δα (κρύπτω) *secretly*. These appear to be Acc. forms (cf. 380 a): Sing. fem. **-δην**, neut. **-δον** and pl. **-δα**.

c. **-ί** or **-εί**, especially from imitative verbs (378 c; -ζω becoming -στί), and in compounds of ἀ- *privative*, αὐτός, and πᾶς· as, Μηδιστί *like the Medes*, Ἑλληνιστί *in the Greek language*; ἀμισθί (μισθός) *without pay*, αὐτοχειρί (χείρ) *with one's own hand*, πανδημεί (δῆμος) *with the whole people*. These appear to be Dat. forms (cf. 380 c).

d.) **-ξ**, mostly from palatal stems: as, ἀνα-μίγνυμι (r. μιγ-, 351. 3) *to mix up*, ἀναμίξ *confusedly, pellmell*, παραλλάξ (παρ-αλλάσσω) *alternately*.

(2.) Time when, in -τε (Dor. -κα, 168), or, for more specific expression, in -ίκα: as, ἀλλότε (ἄλλος) *at another time*, αὐτίκα (αὐτός) *at the very moment*. See 58.

(3.) Place whither, in -σε (which appears to be a softened form of -δε, 382 a, or at least kindred with it): as, πεδόσε *to the ground*, Eur. Bac. 137, = πεδόνδε Soph. Tr. 786; ἐκεῖσε *thither*.

382. III. Prepositional Forms and Phrases: as,

a.) Prepositions with their Cases, (πρὸ ἔργου) προὔργου *before the work, to the purpose*, παραχρῆμα *upon the affair, immediately*, (δι' ὅ) διό *on account of which, wherefore*, (ἐν ποδῶν ὁδῷ) ἐμποδών *in the way* of the feet, Θήβαζε (from Θῆβας and -δε, an inseparable preposition denoting *direction towards*, 137 d), poet. Θήβασδε Ψ. 679, *to Thebes*, Ἀθήναζε *to Athens*.

b. Prepositions used without Cases, πρός [sc. τούτῳ] *in addition to this, besides*, Æsch. Pr. 73; ἐν [sc. τούτοις] *meanwhile*, Soph. O. T. 27.

c. Derivatives from Prepositions, ἄνω (ἀνά) *up*, κάτω *down*, εἴσω, ἔξω, πρόσω, later πόρρω porro; ἔνδον (381 b), ἐντός intus, ἐκτός extra.

d. These adverbs in -ω, with Comparatives and Superlatives in -τέρω and -τάτω, as well as πώ *yet*, ὀπίσω *behind*, &c., have the Dat. form.

II. FORMATION OF COMPOUND WORDS.

383. In the union of two words to form a compound,

A.) The first word has commonly its stem-form with simply euphonic or imitative changes. These changes, besides those which the general rules of orthoëpy require, consist chiefly,

a.) In the addition of a *union-vowel* (termed the *composition-vowel*), which, after a *substantive* or *adjective*, is commonly -ο-, but sometimes -η-, -α-, -ι-, -οι-, or -αι-; and, after a *verb*, -ο-, -ε-, or -ι-: as, μυθ-ο-

§ 386.   FIRST AND LAST WORDS.   225

γράφος (μῦθ-ος, γράφω) *fable-writer*, θανατ-η-φόρος *death-bringing*, ποδ-ά-νιπτήρ *foot-bath*, πυρ-ί-γενής *fire-born*, ὁδ-οι-πόρος *wayfarer*, μεσ-αι-πόλιος *half-gray*; λειπ-ο-ταξία (λείπ-ω, τάξις) *leaving one's post*, ἀρχ-έ-χορος (ἀρχ-ω) *chorus-leading*, τερπ-ι-κέραυνος (τέρπ-ω) *delighting in thunder*.

b.) In the *contraction* of this vowel with an adjoining vowel: as, (ὀρε-ι-βάτης, fr. ὄρος, -ε-ος, and βαίνω) ὀρειβάτης *mountain-ranging*, (νᾱ-ο-κόρος, fr. να-ός and κορέω, 120 i) νεωκόρος *temple-sweeper*, (γα-ο-μετρία) γεωμετρία.

c.) In the *addition of* σ, commonly connected by a union-vowel either to the succeeding or preceding word, and sometimes even to both: as, παυ-σ-άνεμος (παύ-ω, ἄνεμος) *wind-allaying*, ναυ-σί-πορος *navigable*, θε-οσ-εχθρία *impiety*, ταμ-εσί-χρως (τέμνω, 340. 3) *flesh-cutting*, Δ. 511.

d.) In using a *shorter form*, sometimes, perhaps, suggested by the theme, or another stem: as, αἱμ-ο-βαφής (αἷμα, -ατος, βάπτω) *blood-bathed*, αἰ-πόλος (αἴξ, αἰγός) *goat-herd*. So, for ἥμισυς *half*, the old short stem ἡμι- is commonly used: ἡμι-θνής *half-dead*, ἡμί-ονος *mule*.

e.) In conforming to the theme with respect to *vowel-change*, &c.: as, βου-κόλος (βοῦς, βο-ός) *ox-herd*, ναυ-πηγός *ship-wright*, πολί-αρχος.

f.) It results from these changes or from direct adoption, that the first word has sometimes the form of one of the cases: as, Nom. νικη-φόρος *bringing victory*, ἀγορά-νόμος *clerk of the market*; Gen. νεώς-οικος *ship-house*; Dat. νυκτι-πόλος *roaming by night*, Eur. Ion 718. See 388 b.

384. If the first word is a *particle*, it is commonly unchanged except by the general laws of euphony.

a. For crasis in πρό, see 126 γ; for elision in prepositions, 127 s. Ἀμφί, like περί, often retains its vowel. In the other prepositions, the elision is rarely omitted, except in the Ion., particularly in the Ep. before some words which begin with the digamma: as, ἀποϜειπεῖν I. 309.

385. Some particles occur only in composition, and are hence called *inseparable*. Of these the most important are,

a.) ἀ-, commonly denoting *privation* or *negation*, and then called *a-privative*, as, ἄ-παις *without children*, ἄ-σοφος *unwise*; but sometimes denoting *union*, *likeness*, or *intensity* (the result of concentration), and then termed *a- copulative*, as, ἀ-κόλουθος (κέλευθος *way*) *going the same way, following*, ἀ-βρομος (βρέμω) *loud-shouting*, ἀ-τενής (τείνω) *strained*; while this prefix appears to be sometimes *euphonic* (356). A- *privative* has commonly its full form ἀν- before a vowel, except where Ϝ or σ has been lost; and is akin to ἄνευ *without*, to the Lat. *in-*, and to the Eng. and Germ. *un-*: ἀν-οπλος (ἄνευ ὅπλων) in-ermis, *un-armed*, ἀ-Ϝέκων Λ. 557 (Bek.), Att. ἄκων, *unwilling*. 'A- *copulative* (also ἁ-, as in ἅ-πας *all together*) appears to be akin to ἅμα *together*.

b.) νη-, akin to ἀν- *privative* (Lat. and Old Eng. *ne*): as, νή-ποινος (ποινή) *un-avenged*, (νη-ανεμος) νήνεμος *wind-less, calm*.

c.) δυσ-, *ill, mis-, un-*: as, δύσ-φημος *ill-omened*, δυσ-τυχία *misfortune*, δυσ-δαίμων *un-happy*, Δύσπαρις *accursed Paris*, Γ. 39.

d.) The *intensive* ἀρι- (kindred with ἀρε-, 261 a), by precession ἐρι-, ζα- and δα-, all mostly poetic: as, ἀρί-δακρυς *very tearful*, Æsch. Per. 947, ἐρί-δουπος *loud-sounding*, Υ. 50, ζά-πλουτος *per-dives, very rich*, Hdt.

386. B.) The form of the LAST WORD depends upon the part of speech to which the compound belongs.

I. If the compound is a NOUN or ADJECTIVE, it commonly takes the most obvious form which is appropriate to the class of words to which it belongs.

COMP. GR. 10*   O

a. Often the last word, if itself a *noun* or *adjective*, undergoes no change : as, ὁμό-δουλος con-servus, *fellow-slave*, μακρό-χειρ longi-manus.

b. If the last element is a *verb*, the compound adjective or masculine substantive ends commonly in,

1.) -ος. This ending (which is far the most common) has both an *active* and a *passive* sense, distinguished, for the most part, by the accent, which, if the penult is short, the *active* compound commonly takes upon the *penult*, but the *passive* upon the *antepenult* : as, λιθο-βόλος (λίθος, βάλλω) *throwing stones*, Th. 6. 69, λιθό-βολος *stoned*, Eur. Ph. 1063.

2.) -ης (-ες, G. -εος) : as, εὐ-πρεπής *becoming*, αὐτ-άρκης *self-sufficing*.

3.) -ης or -ας (G. -ου), and -ηρ or -ωρ, denoting the *agent* (365) : as, νομο-θέτης *legislator*, ὀρνιθο-θήρας *bird-catcher*, μηλοβοτήρ *shepherd*.

4.) -ς : as, ἀ-γνώς, -ῶτος (γνο-, 357. 1) *unknown*, ἀ-δμής, -ῆτος *untamed*.

c. In compounds of this class, if the last word begins with ἀ, ε, or ο, followed by a single consonant, this vowel is commonly lengthened to η or ω : as, στρατηγός (στράτος, ἄγω) *general*, δυσήλατος (δυσ-, ἐλαύνω) *hard for driving*, ἀνώνυμος (ἀ-, ὄνομα, 114d) *nameless*. The Att. uses the Dor. ᾱ in some compounds of ἄγω : as, λοχᾱγός *captain*, i. 7. 2.

387 II. If the compound is a VERB, it is important to observe that, with few exceptions, *verbs are compounded directly and without change with prepositions only ;* and that, in other cases, compound verbs have the form of derivatives from compound nouns or adjectives existing or assumed.

a. Thus, λαμβάνω, *to take*, unites directly with the prep. ἀνά *up*, to form ἀναλαμβάνω *to take up ;* but it cannot so unite with the noun ἔργον *work*, and hence the idea *to take work, contract*, is expressed by ἐργο-λαβέω, derived from the compound verbal ἐργο-λάβος *contractor*. So the verb compounded of ἵππος *horse*, and τρέφω *to feed*, is ἱπποτροφέω from ἱπποτρόφος *horse-keeper*. Sometimes the form of the verb happens not to be changed in passing through the compound verbal : thus, from σῖτος and ποιέω, is formed σιτο-ποιός *bread-maker*, and from this again σιτοποιέω *to make bread*.

388. *a.* Words formed by the direct union of others (as ἐργολάβος, ἱπποτρόφος, 387 a) are called *direct compounds ;* and derivatives from these (as ἐργολαβέω, ἱπποτροφέω) are called *indirect compounds* (the term *compound* extended beyond its strictest sense).

b. When the component words are joined without change except from the general laws of orthoëpy, the composition is termed *loose* (Gr. παράθεσις *putting side by side*), as liable to separation ; but when they are joined with further change, it is termed *close* (Gr. σύνθεσις *putting together*), as forming an inseparable word : thus, *loose*, or *parathetic compounds*, ἀναλαμβάνω, Διόσ-κοροι *sons of Jupiter*, Ἑλλήσ-ποντος *sea of Helle*, Ἀρηΐ-φιλος *dear to Mars ; close*, or *synthetic compounds*, ἐργο-λάβος, σιτο-ποιός.

c. Loose compounds are sometimes separated by other words, especially particles. This figure is called *Tmesis* (τμῆσις *cutting*). Thus, ἀπὸ λοιγὸν ἀμῦναι (= λοιγὸν ἀπαμῦναι), *to ward off death*, A. 67 ; ἐκ δὲ πηδήσας, *and leaping forth*, Eur. Hec. 1172.

d. The loose connection of the preposition with its verb (as if a modifying adverb) also explains 387 a, the intervention of prefixes (282), and the position, permitted by the Epic, of the preposition after its verb : as, ὀλέσας ἄπο, for ἀπολέσας, *having lost*, ι. 534.

e. A compound is distinguished as *double, triple, quadruple*, &c., ac-

§ 390. VARIOUS DISTINCTIONS. — LOOSE COMPOUNDS. 227

cording to the number of words of which it is composed : as, double, ὑπορρέω *to flow under;* triple, ὑπεκρέω *flow from under;* quadruple, ὑπεκπορέω *flow forth from under,* ʃ. 87. The extent to which the Greek permitted composition was sportively illustrated by Aristophanes in a *seventy-eight-syllable* compound, which follows, with Dr. Donaldson's translation : λεπαδο-τεμαχο-σελαχο-γαλεο-κρανιο-λειψανο-δριμ-υποτριμματο-σιλφιο-παραο[v. l. πρασο]-μελιτο-κατακεχυμενο-κιχλ-επι-κοσσυφο-φαττο-περιστερ-αλεκτρυον-οπτ-εγκεφαλο-κιγκλο-πελειο-λαγωο-σιραιο-βαφη-τραγανο-πτερύγ-ων, " a fricassee consisting of shellfish-saltfish-skate-shark-remainders-of-heads-besprinkled-with-sharp-sauce-of-laserpitium-leek-and-honey-thrushes-besides-blackbirds-pigeons-doves-roasted-cocks-brains-wagtails-cushats-haresflesh-steeped-in-a-sauce-of-boiled-new-wine-with-the-cartilages-and-wings," Eccl. 1169 s.

389. There is a loose form of composition, in which a PRONOUN or PARTICLE is attached to a word with which it is sometimes really and sometimes only apparently combined in sense.

1. The orthography here varies, the words being sometimes written together, especially if the last is an enclitic, and sometimes separately.
2. Among the chief words that are thus affixed to others are,

a. The INDEFINITE PRONOUN τὶς : as, ὅστις (or ὅς τις) *whoever,* οὔτις *no one,* εἴτις *if any one.* Cf. Lat. *quisquis, nequis, siquis.*

The following PARTICLES : b. ἄν (Ep. κέ or κέν, Dor. κά), contingent or indefinite : as, ὅς ἄν *whoever,* ὅταν or ὅτ' ἄν, ὁπόταν, ἐπειδάν (ἐπεὶ δὴ ἄν), *whenever, whensoever,* &c.

c. γέ (Dor. γά) *at least,* emphatic : as, ἔγωγε (accent drawn back) *I at least,* σύγε *you surely,* τοῦτό γε *this certainly,* ἐπεί γε *since at least.* See 247 h, and cf. Lat. *egomet, tumet, equidem.*

d. δή *now* (shorter form of ἤδη) : as, ὅστις δή *whoever now,* νῦν δή *just now.*

e. δήποτε (δή ποτε) *ever now:* as, ὁστισδήποτε *whosoever now ?* τί δήποτε ; *what in the world ?*

f. ἦ *surely, indeed:* as, τίη (Att. τιή) or τί ἦ; *why surely ?* ὁτιή *because indeed,* ἐπειή or ἐπεί ἦ *since indeed.*

g. οὖν (contr. fr. ἐόν, *it being so;* see εἰμί, 50) *then, therefore, yet,* often added to an indefinite pronoun or adverb to strengthen the expression of indefiniteness : ὁστισοῦν *whoever then,* ὁπωσδηποτοῦν *howsoever now then.*

h. πέρ (shorter form of περί) *very, particularly, just:* as, ὅσπερ *who in particular,* ὥσπερ *just as,* οἷόσπερ, ὅτιπερ, ὅθενπερ. Cf. Lat. *parumper.*

i. ποτέ *at any time, ever,* often added to interrogatives to strengthen the expression : as, τί ποτέ ἐστι τοῦτο ; [what at any time is this ?] *what in the world is this ?* or, *what can this be ?* Ep. τίπτε (sync. fr. τί ποτε).

j. τέ, the simplest sign of connection, and hence often joined to other connective words, before their use was established, to mark them as such. In the Ep. and Ion. this is found to a great extent : and even with an intervening particle, as ὅς ῥά τε O. 411, τάπερ τε Hdt. 1. 74. In the Att., it has remained in ἅτε and ὥστε, *as,* οἷός τε *able, possible,* and ἐφ' ᾧτε *on condition that.*

3. With some of the forms above, compare the Lat. *quicumque, quandocumque, quisque, uterque, ubique, quisnam ? quisquam, utpote,* &c.

390. For the mutual and external relations of the elements of compound words, see 722 s.

BOOK III.
SYNTAX.

Μύθους ὑφαίνειν.
Homer.

391. SYNTAX, as the DOCTRINE OF SENTENCES, treats either of the offices and relations of words as arranged in sentences, or of the offices and relations of these sentences themsélves.

392. The Greek is one of those languages whose syntax exhibits the greatest freedom and variety.

CHAPTER I.
SYNTAX OF THE SUBSTANTIVE.
I. AGREEMENT OF THE SUBSTANTIVE.

393. RULE I. An APPOSITIVE agrees in *case* with its *subject*. — Apposition may be

(a) Direct: Παρύσατις . . ἡ μήτηρ, *Parysatis, the mother,* i. 1. 4. (b) Predicate: Τὰ δὲ ἆθλα ἦσαν στλεγγίδες, *and the prizes were flesh-combs,* i. 2. 10. Ἧς αὐτὸν σατράπην ἐποίησε, *of which he had made him satrap,* i. 1. 2. Ὄνομα αὐτῷ εἶναι Ἀγάθωνα Pl. Prot. 315 e. (c) Modal: Λαβὼν Τισσαφέρνην ὡς φίλον, *taking T. as a friend,* i. 1. 2. (d) Partitive: Οὗτοι . . ἄλλος ἄλλα λέγει, *these say, one one thing, and another another,* ii. 1. 15. (e) Of generic and specific terms, especially of common and proper nouns: Ὁ Μαίανδρος ποταμός, *the river Mæander,* i. 2. 7. Ἄνδρες στρατιῶται, *gentlemen soldiers,* i. 3. 3. (f) Of a noun and a pronoun : Ἀλκιβιάδης . . κἀκεῖνος ἠμέλησεν, *A., he also neglected,* Mem. 1. 2. 24. (g) Of a sentence and word (396), &c.

h. Appositives, more frequently, agree with their subjects in *gender* and *number*, as well as in case: Ἐπύαξα, ἡ Συεννέσιος γυνή, τοῦ Κιλίκων βασιλέως, *E., the wife of S., the king of the Cilicians,* i. 2. 12.

394. a. ELLIPSIS. The appositive or the subject may be omitted, when it can be supplied from the connection : Λύκιος ὁ Πολυστράτου [sc. υἱός], L., the son of P., iii. 3. 20. Θεμιστοκλῆς ἥκω παρὰ σέ [sc. ἐγώ], I, T., have come to thee, Th. 1. 137.

b. The sign of *modal apposition* (commonly ὡς, *as*) is often omitted : Διφθέρας, ἃς εἶχον σκεπάσματα, *the skins which they had as coverings*, i. 5. 10.

c. SYNESIS. An appositive sometimes agrees with a subject which is implied in another word : Ἀθηναῖος ὢν πόλεως τῆς μεγίστης, *being an Athenian, a city the greatest*, Pl. Apol. 29 d (here πόλεως agrees with Ἀθηνῶν, *of Athens*, implied in Ἀθηναῖος). Ἀφίκοντο εἰς Κοτύωρα, πόλιν Ἑλληνίδα, Σινωπέων ἀποίκους [referring to πολίτας, implied in πόλιν] v. 5. 3.

395. a. In PARTITIVE APPOSITION, the statement of the parts is not always complete ; and sometimes the appositive denotes that which is *closely related* to the subject, rather than properly the *same person or thing*, even in part. With a participle, it may take the place of the *Gen. absolute*, in expressing some *circumstance*, as *cause, manner*, &c. Thus, Οἱ ξύμμαχοι τὰ δύο μέρη . . ἐσέβαλον, *the allies, two thirds of them, invaded*, Th. 2. 47. Εὔφλεκτα δὲ τὰ πρόθυρα αὐτῶν, φοινῖκος μὲν αἱ θύραι πεποιημέναι, *their portals are easily set on fire, the doors being made of the palm-tree*, Cyr. 7. 5. 22. Ὀδυρμὸς πολύς, Ῥαχὴλ κλαίουσα, Mat. 2. 18.

b. Hence by a poetic, especially Epic, construction, an appositive is used to specify the *part affected :* Βούλει πόνον μοι τῇδε προσθεῖναι χερί ; *do you wish to impose labor on me*, viz. *on this hand ?* Eur. Heracl. 63. Σθένος ἔμβαλ' ἑκάστῳ καρδίῃ, *imparted strength* [to each one, to the heart] *to the heart of each one*, Λ. 11. Ἀγαμέμνονι ἥνδανε θυμῷ Α. 24.

c. Some relations may be expressed either by an *appositive* or an *adjunct ;* and one of these constructions is sometimes used where the other would seem more appropriate : Τούτου τὸ εὖρος δύο πλέθρα, *of this the breadth is two plethra*, i. 2. 5 ; but, Τοῦ δὲ Μαρσύου τὸ εὖρός ἐστιν εἴκοσι καὶ πέντε ποδῶν, *and the breadth of the M. is twenty-five feet*, Ib. 8. Ποταμὸς . . εὖρος δύο πλέθρων Ib. 23. Δέκα μναῖ εἰσφορά· but, Δυοῖν μναῖν πρόσοδον, Vect. 3. Πόλιν Τροίην Α. 129 ; but, Τροίης ἱερὸν πτολίεθρον a. 2.

396. a. A word, in apposition with a *sentence not used substantively*, is commonly in the *Accusative*, as expressing the effect of the action ; but is sometimes in the *Nominative*, as if an inscription marking the character of the sentence : Ῥίψει . . ἀπὸ πύργου, λυγρὸν ὄλεθρον, *will hurl thee from a tower, a sad fate*, Ω. 735. Στέφη μιαίνεται, πόλει τ' ὄνειδος καὶ θεῶν ἀτιμία, *our garlands are profaned, a dishonor to the city, and an insult to the gods*, Eur. Heracl. 72. Ἑλένην κτάνωμεν, Μενέλεῳ λύπην πικράν Id. Or.

b. This use of the Nom. and Acc. may be often explained by *attraction* to the subject or object of the verb. Cf. 395 a.

c. ANACOLUTHON. Apposition is sometimes prevented by a change of construction : as, Μητρί τ', Ἐριβοιαν λέγω, *to my mother, Eribœa I mean* (for Μητρί τ' Ἐριβοίᾳ, *to my mother E.*), Soph. Aj. 569. See also 402.

II. USE OF THE CASES.

397. Cases serve to distinguish the relations of substantives. These relations are regarded, in Greek, (I.) as either DIRECT or INDIRECT, and (II.) as either *subjective, objective,* or *residual.*

I. Of these distinctions, the first is chiefly founded upon the *directness* with which the substantive is related to the *verb* of the sentence. The principal DIRECT RELATIONS are those of the *subject* and *direct object* of the verb, and that of *direct address*. Other relations are, for the most part, regarded as INDIRECT.

II. The second distinction is founded upon the *kind* or *character* of the relation. The relation is,

1. SUBJECTIVE, when the substantive denotes the SOURCE, or SUBJECT, of *motion, action,* or *influence;* or, in other words, THAT FROM WHICH ANY THING COMES.

2. OBJECTIVE, when the substantive denotes the END, or OBJECT, of *motion, action,* or *influence;* or, in other words, THAT TO WHICH ANY THING GOES.

3. RESIDUAL (residuus, *remaining*), when it is not referred to either of the two preceding classes.

398. a. The latter of the two distinctions appears to have had its origin in the *relations of place*, which relations are both the earliest understood, and, through life, the most familiar to the mind. These relations are of two kinds; those of MOTION, and those of REST.

b. Motion may be considered with respect either to its SOURCE or its END; and both of these may be regarded either as *direct* or *indirect*. We may regard as the DIRECT SOURCE of motion, that which *produces* the motion, or, in other words, that which *moves;* as the INDIRECT SOURCE, that *from* which the motion *proceeds;* as the DIRECT END, that which *receives* the motion, or that *to* or *into* which the motion *immediately goes;* and as the INDIRECT END, that *towards* which the motion *tends.*

c. By a natural analogy, the relations of *action and influence in general*, whether subjective or objective, may be referred to the relations of motion; while the relations which remain without being thus referred may be classed together as *relations of rest.* These *residual* relations, or relations of rest, may likewise be divided, according to their office in the sentence (397), into the *direct* and the *indirect.*

d. We have, thus, six kinds of relation, each of which, with a single exception, is represented in Greek by an appropriate case, denoting in general as follows:

I. DIRECT RELATIONS.

1. Subjective. THE NOMINATIVE. *That which acts.*
2. Objective. THE ACCUSATIVE. *That which is acted upon.*
3. Residual. THE VOCATIVE. *That which is addressed.*

II. INDIRECT RELATIONS.

1. Subjective. THE GENITIVE. *That from which any thing proceeds.*
2. Objective. THE DATIVE. *That towards which any thing tends.*
3. Residual. THE DATIVE. *That with which any thing is associated.*

399. a. For the historical development of the Greek cases, see 186 s. From the *primitive indirect case* (which remained as the Dat.), a special form was separated to express the *subjective* relations, but none to express the *objective*. The primitive form, therefore, continued to express the *objective* relations, as well as all those relations which, from any cause, were *not referred* to either of these two classes; and hence the Dat. is both an *objective* and a *residual* case.

b. In the Latin case-system, which so closely resembles the Greek, there is a partial separation of the *indirect objective* and *residual*, or, as they are termed in Lat., DATIVE and ABLATIVE cases.

c. A more important difference between the two languages appears in the extensive use of the Lat. ABLATIVE. The Romans were more controlled than the Greeks by the power of habit, while they were less observant of the minuter shades of thought, and niceties of relation. Hence, even after the full development of the Lat. case-system, the *primitive indirect case* continued to retain, as it were by the mere force of possession, many of the subjective relations.

d. As most verbs express *action*, and the Active is the leading voice, the use of the NOMINATIVE as the subject of a finite verb became so established, that it extended to verbs of *state* as well as of *action*, and to the Passive no less than the Active voice.

e. The NOMINATIVE, from its high office as denoting the subject of discourse, became the *leading case*, and was regarded as the representative of the word in all its forms (its *theme*, 172 c). Hence it was employed when the word was spoken of *as a word*, or was used *without grammatical construction* (401).

f. There are no dividing lines either between DIRECT and INDIRECT, or between *subjective, objective,* and *residual* relations. Some relations seem to fall with equal propriety under two, or even three heads, according to the view which the mind takes of them. Hence the use of the cases not only varies in different languages, and in different dialects of the same language, but even in the same dialect, and in the compositions of the same author.

g. A case may sustain the same relation to more than one word in the sentence: as, Κρέα ἔψοντες ἤσθιον, *they boiled and ate flesh*, ii. 1. 6.

A. THE NOMINATIVE.

400. RULE II. The SUBJECT OF A FINITE VERB is put in the Nominative: as,

Ἐπειδὴ δὲ ἐτελεύτησε Δαρεῖος, καὶ κατέστη εἰς τὴν βασιλείαν Ἀρταξέρξης, Τισσαφέρνης διαβάλλει τὸν Κῦρον, *and when now Darius was dead, and Artaxerxes was established in the royal authority*, Tissaphernes *accuses Cyrus*, i. 1. 3.

401. RULE III. SUBSTANTIVES INDEPENDENT OF GRAMMATICAL CONSTRUCTION are put in the Nominative.

NOTE. The Nom. thus employed is termed the *Nominative independent* or *absolute* (absolūtus, *released, free,* sc. from grammatical fetters).

To this rule may be referred the use of the Nominative,

a.) In the *inscription of names, titles,* and *divisions:* as, Κύρου Ἀνάβασις Cyri Expeditio, *The Expedition of Cyrus;* Βιβλίον Πρῶτον Liber Primus, *Book First.*

b. In *exclamations:* as, Θάλαττα, Θάλαττα, *the Sea! the Sea!* iv. 7. 24. Ὦ δυστάλαιν' ἐγώ, *O wretched me!* Eur.

c.) In *address.* — The appropriate case of address is the Voc. (186 g). But there is often no distinct form for this case, and even when there is, the Nom. is sometimes employed in its stead (182).

1. The Nom. is particularly used, when the address is *exclamatory* or *descriptive,* or when the *compellative* is the same with the *subject* of the sentence: Ἱππίας ὁ καλός τε καὶ σοφός, *O Hippias, the noble and the wise!* Pl. Hipp. Maj. 281 a. Χαῖρε, ὁ βασιλεύς Mat. 27. 29.

2. To the head of *descriptive address* belong those *authoritative, contemptuous,* and *familiar* forms, in which the person who is addressed is described or designated as if he were a *third person* (and in which οὗτος is often used): Οἱ δὲ οἰκέται, .. ἐπίθεσθε, *but the servants, do you put,* Pl. Conv. 218 b. Ὁ Φαληρεύς .. οὗτος Ἀπολλόδωρος, οὐ περιμενεῖς; *The Phalerian there, Apollodorus, stop! won't you?* Ib. 172 a.

3. In forms of address which are both direct, and likewise descriptive or exclamatory, the Voc. and Nom. may be associated: Πρόξενε καὶ οἱ ἄλλοι οἱ παρόντες Ἕλληνες, *O Proxenus and the other Greeks present,* i. 5. 16. Κύριε, υἱὸς Δαβίδ Mat. 20. 30. Ὦ φίλος, ὦ φίλε Βάκχιε Eur. Cycl.

402. ANACOLUTHON, &c. From the office of the Nom. in denoting the subject of discourse, and from its independent use, it is sometimes employed where the construction would demand a different case: as,

a.) In the *introduction* of a sentence: Ὑμεῖς δέ, .. νῦν δὴ καιρὸς ὑμῖν δοκεῖ εἶναι; *You then, .. does it now seem to you to be just the time?* vii. 6. 37. Ἐπιθυμῶν ὁ Κῦρος .., ἔδοξεν αὐτῷ, *Cyrus desiring, .. it seemed best to him,* Cyr. Μωυσῆς οὗτος, .. οὐκ οἴδαμεν τί γέγονεν αὐτῷ Acts 7. 40.

b.) In *specification, repetition,* or *description:* Ἄλλους δ' ὁ μέγας .. Νεῖλος ἔπεμψεν· Σουσισκάνης, Πηγασταγών, κ. τ. λ., *and others the vast Nile hath sent; Susiskānes, P., &c.,* Æsch. Per. 33. Θυγάτηρ μεγαλήτορος Ἠετίωνος, Ἠετίων, ὃς ἔναιεν Z. 395. Τὰ περὶ Πύλον ὑπ' ἀμφοτέρων κατὰ κράτος ἐπολεμεῖτο· Ἀθηναῖοι μέν .. περιπλέοντες Th. 4. 23.

c.) In speaking of *names* or *words* as such: Προσείληφε τὴν τῶν πονηρῶν κοινὴν ἐπωνυμίαν συκοφάντης, *he has obtained the common appellation of the vile,* "sycophant," Æschin. 41. 15.

B. THE GENITIVE.

403. THAT FROM WHICH ANY THING PROCEEDS (398 d) may be resolved into (I.) *That from which any thing proceeds, as its* POINT OF DEPARTURE; and (II.) *That from which any thing proceeds, as its* CAUSE.

Hence the Greek Genitive is either (I.) the GENITIVE OF DEPARTURE, or (II.) the GENITIVE OF CAUSE; and we have the following general rule for subjective adjuncts (397):

RULE A. THE POINT OF DEPARTURE AND THE CAUSE ARE PUT IN THE GENITIVE.

a. The *Genitive of departure* is commonly expressed in English by the preposition *from*; and the *Genitive of cause*, by the preposition *of*.
b. Hence the rule may take this general form:

The GENITIVE is used to express that OF or FROM which something is or is done.

c. The relations here denoted are, however, sometimes translated by other prepositions, and sometimes without a preposition.

I. GENITIVE OF DEPARTURE.

404. Departure may be either in *place*, in *time*, or in *character*. Hence,

RULE IV. Words of SEPARATION and DISTINCTION govern the Genitive.

(1.) *Genitive of Separation.*

405. a. Words of SEPARATION include those of *removal* and *distance*, of *exclusion* and *restraint*, of *cessation* and *failure*, of *abstinence* and *release*, of *deliverance* and *escape*, of *protection* and *freedom*, &c.: as,

Χωρίζεσθαι ἀλλήλων, *to be separated from each other*, Pl. Conv. 192 c. Χωρὶς τῶν ἄλλων, *apart from the rest*, i. 4. 13. Σώματος δίχα Cyr. 8. 7. 20. Διέσχον ἀλλήλων, *were distant from each other*, i. 10. 4. Πόρρω .. αὐτοῦ, *far from him*, i. 3. 12. Εἰ θαλάττης εἴργοιντο, *if they should be excluded from the sea*, Hel. 7. 1. 8. Κωλύσειε τοῦ καίειν, *he would prevent them from burning*, i. 6. 2. Τοῦ πρὸς ἐμὲ πολέμου παύσασθαι, *to cease from the war against me*, i. 6. 6. Οὗτος μὲν αὐτοῦ ἥμαρτεν, *this man missed him*, i. 5. 12. Σῶσαι κακοῦ, *to save from evil*, Soph. Ph. 919.

b. Words of SPARING imply *refraining from*, and those of CONCEDING, RESIGNING, REMITTING, and SURRENDERING, imply *parting with*, or *retiring from*. Hence, τῶν μὲν ὑμετέρων ἡδύ μοι φείδεσθαι, *it is my pleasure to spare your property*, Cyr. 3. 2. 28. Κἀκεῖνος ὑπεχώρησεν αὐτῷ τοῦ θρόνου, *and he* [Sophocles] *conceded to him* [Æschylus] *the throne*, Ar.

c. The Gen. denoting *that from which motion proceeds* is, in prose, commonly joined to *words not in themselves expressing separation* by a preposition; but in poetry, often without a preposition (cf. 450 b): Δόμων .. φέρουσαν, *bringing from the house*, Soph. El. 324. Τούσδε παῖδας γῆς ἐλᾷν, *to drive these children from the land*, Eur. Med. 70. Βάθρων ἵστασθε, *rise from your seats*, Soph. O. T. 142. (d) So *that from which action begins:* Ὕμνησαν Διὸς ἀρχόμεναι, *they sang beginning from Jove*, Pind. N. 5. 48.

e. In a few rare phrases, the Gen. without a preposition denotes that *from which time is computed* (forward or back) : Μετ' ὀλίγον δὲ τούτων, *and* [after a little from these things] *a little after these things*, Hel. 1. 1. 2.

(2.) Genitive of Distinction.

406. a. Words of DISTINCTION include those of *difference* and *exception*, of *superiority* and *inferiority*, &c. : as,

Διώρισται τέχνης, *is distinct from the art*, Pl. Polit. 260 c. Ἠλέκτρου οὐδὲν διέφερεν, *differed in nothing from amber*, ii. 3. 15. Πᾶσαι πλὴν Μιλήτου, *all except Milētus*, i. 1. 6. Διάφορον τῶν ἄλλων πόλεων, *superior to the other states*, Mem. 4. 4. 15. Πλούτου ἀρετὴ διέστηκεν Pl.

b. Λείπομαι, *to be left behind* [*from* or *by*, 405, 434 b], *to come short of*, governs the Gen. in these, and various derived or kindred senses : Πλήθει . . ἡμῶν λειφθέντες, [left behind us] *inferior to us in number*, vii. 7. 31.

407. Words of SUPERIORITY include,

1.) Words of *authority, power, precedence*, and *pre-eminence :*

Ἀνθρώπων ἄρχειν, *to rule men*, Cyr. 1. 1. 3. Ἐγκρατεῖς . . πάντων, *sovereign over all*, v. 4. 15. Ἡγεῖτο τοῦ στρατεύματος, *led the army*, iv. 1. 6. Πρεσβεύειν τῶν πολλῶν πόλεων, *to take rank of most cities*, Pl. Leg.

408. 2.) *Adjectives* and *adverbs* in the *comparative degree* (as denoting the possession of a property in a *higher degree*), and words *derived from them*.

RULE V. The COMPARATIVE DEGREE governs the Genitive : as,

Κρείττων ἑαυτοῦ, *more powerful than himself*, i. 2. 26. Τῶν ἵππων ἔτρεχον θᾶττον, *they ran faster than the horses*, i. 5. 2. Ἐμοῦ ὕστερον, [later than] *after me*, i. 5. 16. Ὑστέρησε τῆς μάχης, *came after the battle*.

a. So the other degrees, if used in the sense of the Comparative : Σεῖο . . μακάρτατος, *more completely happy than you*, λ. 482.

409. 3.) *Multiple* and *proportional* words (240) : as,

Πολλαπλασίους ὑμῶν αὐτῶν, *many times your own number*, iii. 2. 14.

II. GENITIVE OF CAUSE.

410. To the head of CAUSE may be referred, (*A*) That from which any thing is DERIVED, MADE, SUPPLIED, or TAKEN ; (*B*) That which exerts an influence, as an EXCITEMENT, OCCASION, or CONDITION ; (*C*) That which produces any thing, as its ACTIVE or EFFICIENT CAUSE ; and (*D*) That which CONSTITUTES any thing WHAT IT IS.

411. *A. That from which any thing is* DERIVED, MADE, SUPPLIED, *or* TAKEN. To this division belong, (1) the *Genitive of Origin*, (2) the *Genitive of Material*, (3) the *Genitive of Supply*, and (4) the *Genitive of the Whole*, or the *Genitive Partitive*.

1 and 2. *Genitive of Origin and of Material.*

412. RULE VI. The ORIGIN, SOURCE, and MATERIAL are put in the Genitive: as,

Δαρείου καὶ Παρυσάτιδος γίγνονται παῖδες δύο, *of D. and P. are born two children*, i. 1. 1. Τοῦ δ' ἔφυν, *from him I sprang*, Eur. Iph. T. 4. Τί ἀπολαύσαις ἂν τῆς ἀρχῆς; *what advantage should you derive from your authority?* Cyr. 7. 5. 56. Φοίνικος μὲν αἱ θύραι πεποιημέναι, *the doors being made of the palm-tree*, Ib. 22. Οἶνος φοινίκων ii. 3. 14 (cf. i. 5. 10).

a. The *Gen. of source* or *material* occurs, especially in the Epic poets, for other forms of construction, particularly the *instrumental Dat.*: as, Πρῆσαι δὲ πυρὸς δηίοιο θύρετρα, *burn the gates with raging fire* [from fire, as the source], B. 415. Χεῖρας νιψάμενος πολιῆς ἁλός, *having washed his hands* [with water from] *in the foaming sea*, β. 261.

413. That of which one discourses or thinks may be regarded as the *material* of his discourse or thoughts; thus we speak of the *matter of discourse*, a *matter of complaint*, the *subject-matter of a composition*, &c. Hence, not unfrequently, both in immediate dependence upon another word, and even in the introduction of a sentence,

RULE VII. The THEME OF DISCOURSE OR OF THOUGHT is put in the Genitive: as,

Τοῦ τοξότου οὐ καλῶς ἔχει λέγειν, ὅτι, κ. τ. λ., *it is not well to say of the bowman, that, &c.*, Pl. Rep. 439 b. Διαθεώμενος αὐτῶν, ὅσην μὲν χώραν.. ἔχοιεν, *observing in respect to them, how great a country they have*, iii. 1. 19. Τῆς δὲ γυναικός, εἰ.. κακοποιεῖ, *but in respect to the wife, if she manages ill*, Œc. 3. 11. Κλύων σου, *hearing of thee*, Soph. O. C. 307.

414. 3. *Genitive of Supply.*

Supply may be either *abundant* or *defective*. Hence,

RULE VIII. Words of PLENTY and WANT govern the Genitive: as,

a. OF PLENTY. Θηρίων πλήρης, *full of beasts*, i. 2. 7. Μεστὰ σίτου, *full of corn*, i. 4. 19. Διφθέρας.. ἐπίμπλασαν χόρτου, *they filled the skins with hay*, i. 5. 10. Τούτων ἅλις, *enough of these things*, v. 7. 12.
b. OF WANT. Ἀνθρώπων ἀπορῶν, *wanting in men*, i. 7. 3. Σφενδονητῶν.. δεῖ, *there is need of slingers*, iii. 3. 16. Οἵων ἂν ἐλπίδων ἐμαυτὸν στερήσαιμι, *of what hopes I should deprive myself*, ii. 5. 10. Μιᾶς δέουσαι τεσσαράκοντα, *40 less 1* (§ 242 c). Φίλων ἔρημος, *devoid of friends*.
c. The Gen. which belongs to δέομαι and χρῄζω as *verbs of want* may be retained by them in the derived senses, *to desire, to request, to entreat*: Οὗτινος ἂν δέησθε, *whatever you may desire*, i. 4. 15. Δικαίων δεῖσθαι, *to request what is reasonable*, Cyr. 8. 3. 20. Μακροῦ χρῄζειν βίου, *to desire long life*, Soph. Aj. 473.

4. Genitive Partitive.

415. RULE IX. The WHOLE OF WHICH A PART IS TAKEN is put in the Genitive : as,

Ἥμισυ τοῦ ὅλου στρατεύματος, *half of the whole army*, vi. 2. 10.

416. The partitive construction may be employed,

a.) To express *quantity, degree, condition, place, time*, &c., considered as a limitation of a general idea, or as a part of an extended whole (especially with a neuter adjective or an adverb) :

Μικρὸν δ' ὕπνου λαχών, *obtaining a little* [of] *sleep*, iii. 1. 11. Ἐν τοιούτῳ.. τοῦ κινδύνου προσιόντος, *in such imminent danger* [in such a degree of], i. 7. 5. Ὁ δ' εἰς τοῦθ' ὕβρεως ἐλήλυθεν, 'to such a pitch of insolence,' Dem. 51. 1. Ἦν μέσον ἡμέρας, *it was midday*, i. 8. 8. See 420 a, b.

b.) In presenting the whole as the sum of all the parts ; in denoting the whole and a part ; and in denying of all the parts :

Ἐν τοῖς ἀγαθοῖσι δὲ **πάντ'** ἔνεστιν σοφίας, *in the good dwell all the qualities of wisdom*, Eur. Alc. 601. Ἡμιόλιον.. οὗ πρότερον ἔφερον, *half* [and the whole of what] *as much again as they before received*, i. 3. 21. Τούτων.. οὐδένα οἶδα, *I know none of these*, Cyr. 7. 5. 45.

417. *a.* The whole is sometimes put in the case which belongs to the part, the part agreeing with the whole instead of governing it ; chiefly when different parts are successively mentioned (cf. 393 d, 395 a) : Ἀκούομεν ὑμᾶς.. ἐνίους σκηνοῦν ἐν ταῖς οἰκίαις, *we hear that you, some of you, quarter in the houses* [for ὑμῶν ἐνίους], v. 5. 11. Δίδυμα τέκεα πότερος ἄρα πότερον αἱμάξει; 'which of the two ?' Eur. Ph. 1289.

b. It is often at the option of the writer whether he will employ the Gen. partitive or a simpler form of construction ; and one form is sometimes found, where the other would rather have been expected. The two forms are sometimes combined : Εἴτ' οὖν θεὸς, εἴτε βροτῶν ἦν, *whether he was a god, or one of mortals*, Soph. El. 199.

418. According to Rule IX., a word referring to a part, whether *substantive, adjective, adverb*, or *verb*, may take with it a Gen. denoting the whole. Thus,

I. SUBSTANTIVES : Τὸ τρίτον **μέρος** τοῦ.. ἱππικοῦ, *the third part of the cavalry*, Cyr. Τῶν πελταστῶν τις ἀνήρ, *a certain man of the targeteers*..

a. When place is designated by mentioning both the *country* and the *town*, the former, as the whole, may be put in the Gen., and may precede the latter : Οἱ Ἀθηναῖοι ἐστράτευσαν τῆς Θεσσαλίας ἐπὶ Φάρσαλον, *the A. marched to Pharsalus* [of] *in Thessaly*, Th. 1. 111. Ἀφίκετο τῆς Ἀττικῆς ἐς Οἰνόην πρῶτον, *came upon Attica first at Œnoë*, Th. 2. 18.

b. The Gen., in all cases in which it is strictly *partitive*, may be regarded as properly depending upon a substantive denoting the part ; and therefore the use of this Gen. in connection with adjectives, verbs, and adverbs, may be referred to ellipsis or synesis : Πολέμου, καὶ μάχης οὐ μετῆν [sc. μέρος] αὐτῇ (421 a ; cf. ἀγαθοῦ τινὸς μετέσται.. μέρος Cyr. 2. 3. 6). Γῆς γε οὐδαμοῦ, i. e. ἐν οὐδενὶ μέρει τῆς γῆς (420 a).

c. If the substantive denoting the part is expressed, and that denoting the whole is a form of the same word, the latter is commonly omitted : Τρεῖς ἄνδρες τῶν γεραιτέρων [sc. ἀνδρῶν], *three men of the more aged*, v. 7.

419. II. ADJECTIVES. a. *The Article, and Adjective Pronouns:* Τοὐς μὲν αὑτῶν ἀπέκτεινε, τοὺς δ' ἐξέβαλεν, *slew some of them, and banished others*, i. 1. 7. Τῶν ἄλλων Ἑλλήνων τινές, *some of the other Greeks*, i. 7.

b. *Adjectives of Number:* Εἷς τῶν στρατηγῶν, *one of the generals*, vii. 2. 29. Ἡμῶν δ' οὐδείς, *none of us* (416 b), iii. 1. 16.

c *Superlatives, and words derived from them* (by virtue of the included adjective, cf. 408); and the *other degrees* when kindred in force: Ἐν τοῖς ἀρίστοις Περσῶν, *among the best of the Persians*, i. 6. 1. Τῶν . . ἀνθρώπων ἀριστεύσαντες [= ἄριστοι γενόμενοι], *being the best of the men*, Mem. 3. 5. 10. Ὦ φίλα γυναικῶν, *O* [beloved of] *dearest of women*, Eur. Alc. 460.

d. *Participles:* Σὺν τοῖς παροῦσι τῶν πιστῶν, *with those present of his faithful attendants*, i. 5. 15. Καὶ τῶν ἄλλων τὸν βουλόμενον i. 3. 9.

e. *Other Adjectives:* Ἔχων τῶν ὀπισθοφυλάκων τοὺς ἡμίσεις, *having half of the rear-guard*. Τοὺς ἀγαθοὺς τῶν ἀνθρώπων, *the good among men*, Ar.

f. Those adjectives which are most frequently employed to denote a part are termed *partitives*. A *neuter* adjective used substantively is often so employed. See 416 a.

420. III. ADVERBS. a. *Of Place and Time*, used literally or figuratively (416 a): Οὐδ' ὅπου γῆς ἐσμὲν οἶδα, *I know not where on earth* [upon what part of the earth] *we are*, Ar. Av. 9. Τηλοῦ γὰρ οἰκῶ τῶν ἀγρῶν, *I dwell* [in a remote part of the country] *far from town*, Ar. Nub. 138. Ἐνταῦθα ἤδη εἶ τῆς ἡλικίας, *you are now at that point of life*, Pl. Rep. 328 c. Ὁπηνίκα . . τῆς ὥρας, *at whatever point of time*, iii. 5. 18. Πρόσω δὲ τοῦ ποταμοῦ προβαίνειν, *to advance far into the river*, iv. 3. 28.

b. *Of State or Condition*, especially with the verbs ἔχω and ἥκω (416 a): Τῆς τύχης γὰρ ὧδ' ἔχω, *I am thus in* [have myself in this state of] *fortune*, Eur. Hel. 857. Πῶς οὖν ἔχεις δόξης; [in what state of opinion] *of what opinion are you?* Pl. Rep. 456 d. Πῶς ἀγῶνος ἥκομεν; *how do we come on in the strife* [with what progress of the strife]? Eur. El. 751.

c. *Of the Superlative Degree:* Ἀφειδέστατα πάντων ἐτιμωρεῖτο, *he punished most unsparingly of all* [he of all, 418 b] i. 9. 13.

421. IV. VERBS. The Genitive partitive, in connection with a verb, may perform the office either of a *subject*, an *appositive*, or a *complement;* taking the place of any case which the verb would require, if referring to the whole. See 418 b.

1.) *The Gen. Partitive as a Subject*. (a) *Of a Finite Verb:* Εἰσὶ δ' αὑτῶν, οὓς οὐδ' ἂν . . διαβαίητε, *there are some of them, which you could not pass*, ii. 5. 18. Πολέμου, καὶ μάχης οὐ μετῆν αὐτῇ, *of war and battle, there fell to her no share*, Cyr. 7. 2. 28. (b) *Of an Infinitive:* Ἐπιμιγνύναι σφῶν, *that some of them mingled*, iii. 5. 16. Ὤιετο προσήκειν οὐδενὶ ἀρχῆς, *he thought that* [a share of] *authority belonged to no one*, Cyr. 8. 1. 37.

422. 2.) *The Gen. Partitive in the place of an Appositive* is most common with *substantive verbs*, but is likewise found with other verbs, particularly those of *reckoning, esteeming*, and *making:* Οὐκ ἐγὼ τούτων εἰμί, *I am not one of these*, Cyr. 8. 3. 45. Ὕλας μακάρων ἀριθμεῖται, *Hylas is numbered as one of the blest*, Theoc. 13. Μουσικῆς . . τίθης λόγους; Pl.

423. 3.) *The Genitive Partitive is used as a Complement*,

a. *Generally*, with any verb, when its action affects not the whole object, but a *part* only: as,

Λαβόντας τοῦ βαρβαρικοῦ στρατοῦ, *taking a part of the barbarian army*, i. 5. 7. Τῶν κηρίων . . ἔφαγον, *ate of the honeycombs*, iv. 8. 20.

424. *β.*) *Particularly*, with verbs which, in their ordinary use, imply *divided* or *partial action*.

NOTE. The Gen. partitive may be connected with other parts of speech upon the same principle. Hence the rule is expressed in a general form.

RULE X. Words of SHARING, BEGINNING, and TOUCH govern the Genitive.

1. Words of SHARING include those of *partaking* (part-taking), *imparting*, *obtaining by distribution*, &c. Thus,

Τῶν κινδύνων μετέχειν, *to share in* [have a share of] *the dangers*, Hel. 2. 4. 9. Τῆσδε κοινωνῶ τύχης, *I partake of this fortune*, Eur. Med. 303. Τῶν εὐφροσυνῶν μεταδιδόντες, *imparting our joys*, Œc. 9. 12.

425. 2. The BEGINNING is, of course, only *part* of the work:

Τοῦ δὲ λόγου ἤρχετο, *he commenced his address*, iii. 2. 7. Φυγῆς ἄρχειν, *to begin flight*, Ib. 17. So ἐξάρχω, κατάρχω, καθηγέομαι, *to begin;* &c.

a. The partitive idea appears also in such expressions as Μεσοῦσι .. τῆς πορείας, *being in the middle of the way*, Pl. Pol. 265 b.

426. 3. TOUCH may be regarded as a species of partial action, affecting only the point of contact. To this head belong, either by direct connection or by obvious analogy, verbs of *laying hold of, hitting, meeting with*, &c. Thus,

Ἅπτεσθαι τῆς κάρφης, *to touch the hay*, i. 5. 10. Ἐπιλαμβάνεται αὐτοῦ τῆς ἴτυος, *lays hold of his shield-rim*, iv. 7. 12. Φεραύλα τυγχάνει, *hits P.*, Cyr. 8. 3. 28. Ἀνδρῶν ἀγαθῶν παιδὸς ὑπαντήσας, *having met with the son of brave heroes*, Soph. Ph. 719. Μέσσου δουρὸς ἑλών Γ. 78.

a. Hence, the *part taken hold of* is put in the Gen., in connection with other forms of construction: Ἔλαβον τῆς ζώνης τὸν Ὀρόντην, *they took Orontes by the girdle*, i. 6. 10. Νιν .. ψαύειν χερός Eur. Herc. 968.

b. To the analogy of verbs of touch may be referred expressions like the following: Τῆς κεφαλῆς κατέαγε, *he broke* [was fractured in] *his head*.

427. 4. Several words of *obtaining, attaining*, and *receiving*, govern the Genitive, from their referring primarily either to distribution or to touch. Thus,

Ἵνα τῆς προσηκούσης μοίρας λαγχάνῃ, *that it may receive its proper portion*, Pl. Leg. 903 e. Κληρονομεῖν οὐδενός, *to inherit nothing*, Dem. 1065. 25. Τῶν δικαίων τυγχάνειν, *to obtain your rights*, vii. 1. 30.

428. *B.* That which exerts an influence as an EXCITEMENT, OCCASION, or CONDITION. To this division belong the following rules, respecting, 1. *the motive, reason*, and *end in view;* 2. *price, value, merit*, and *crime;* 3. the *sensible* and *mental object;* and 4. *time* and *place*.

a. The Gen. so employed is often translated by other prepositions than *of* and *from*, especially by *for;* and sometimes without a preposition.

1. Genitive of Motive, &c.

429. RULE XI. The MOTIVE, REASON, and END IN VIEW are put in the Genitive.

To this rule may be referred the use of the Gen., both in *regular construction* and in *exclamation*, to express the person or thing, *on account of* which, *in consequence of* which, *for the sake of* which, *in honor of* which, or *to affect* which, any thing is done, said, felt, or existing. Thus,

a. WITH VERBS: Μισθοῦ ὑπηρετοῦντες, *serving* [from, *or* on account of] *for hire*, Cyr. 6. 2. 37. Τούτου σε .. ζηλῶ, *on this account I envy you*, Ib. 8. 4. 23. Μηδὲν αὐτῶν καταθείς, *paying nothing for them*, Ib. 3. 1. 37. Φίλου δείσας .. ἢ χαὐτοῦ, *fearing* [on account of] *for a friend or even himself*, Soph. O. T. 234. Ταύτης ἱκνοῦμαί σε, *I beseech you for her sake*, Eur. Or. 671. Ἱκετεύω σε τῶνδε γουνάτων, 'by these knees,' Id.

b. WITH ADJECTIVES: Εὐδαίμων .. τοῦ τρόπου, *happy* [by reason of] *from his character*, Pl. Phaedo 58 e. Ὦ μακάριε τῆς τέχνης, Ar. Av. 1423.

c. WITH ADVERBS: Πενθικῶς δὲ ἔχουσαν τοῦ ἀδελφοῦ, *in mourning for her brother*, Cyr. 5. 2. 7. Χαλεπῶς φέρειν αὐτῶν Th. 2. 62.

d. WITH NOUNS: Ὠδῖνας αὐτοῦ προσβαλών, *causing pangs on his account*, Soph. Tr. 41. Γενείου τοῦδ' .. λιτάς, *entreaties by this beard*, Eur.

e. WITH INTERJECTIONS: Φεῦ τοῦ ἀνδρός, *Alas for the noble man!*

f. IN SIMPLE EXCLAMATION: Τῆς τύχης, *My ill-luck!* Cyr. 2. 2. 3.

430. a. The Genitive of the END IN VIEW is put with some words of *direction*, *claim*, and *dispute*. Words of *direction* include those of *aiming at*, *throwing at*, *going towards*, and *reaching after*. Thus,

Ἀνθρώπων στοχάζεσθαι, *to take aim at men*, Cyr. 1. 6. 29. Αὐτοῦ χερμάδας .. ἔρριπτον, *they threw stones at him*, Eur. Bac. 1096. Εὐθὺ Πελλήνης πέτεσθαι, *to fly straight for Pellene*, Ar. Av. 1421. Τίς γὰρ αὐτῷ ἐστιν ὅστις τῆς ἀρχῆς ἀντιποιεῖται; *for who is there that disputes with him the sovereignty* [makes for the sovereignty in opposition to him]? ii. 1. 11.

b. The student cannot fail to remark the ease with which verbs of *motion* pass into those of simple *effort* and *desire* (432 e). Thus, ἵεμαι, and, more commonly, ἐφίεμαι, *to send one's self to, rush to, strive for, seek, desire;* ὀρέγομαι, *to reach after, strive for, seek, court, desire*: Δόξης ἐφιεμένοις, *eager for glory*. Ὀρέξασθαι τῆς ὁμιλίας αὐτοῦ, *to seek his company*.

2. Genitive of Price, Merit, &c.

431. RULE XII. PRICE, VALUE, MERIT, and CRIME are put in the Genitive.

a. PRICE: Ἵππον, ὃν .. ἀπέδοτο πεντήκοντα δαρεικῶν, *the horse, which he had sold for fifty darics*, vii. 8. 6. Δόξα δὲ χρημάτων οὐκ ὠνητή, *glory is not to be bought for money*, Isoc. 21 b.

b. VALUE AND MERIT: Ἄξιοι τῆς ἐλευθερίας, *worthy of freedom*, i. 7. 3. Πολλοῦ ἄξιος τῇ στρατιᾷ, *worth much to the army*, iv. 1. 28. Τῆς ἀξίας τιμᾶσθαι, *to estimate at the true desert*, Pl. Apol. 36 e.

c. CRIME: Ἀσεβείας φεύγοντα, *accused of impiety*, Pl. Apol. 35 d. Διώξομαί σε δειλίας, *I will prosecute you for cowardice*, Ar. Eq. 368.

d. The Gen. (chiefly θανάτου) is sometimes used to express the *punishment* (regarded either as the *desert* of the crime, or as the *end in view* in judicial proceedings): Θανάτου δὲ οὗτοι κρίνουσι, *these pronounce sentence of death* [adjudge worthy of]. Ὑπῆγον θανάτου, 'on a capital charge.'

3. *Genitive of Sensible or Mental Object.*

432. The object of sensation, thought, or emotion may be regarded as its *exciting cause*, and, in this view, may be put in the Genitive. Hence,

RULE XIII. Words of SENSATION, and of MENTAL STATE or ACTION govern the Genitive: as,

a. OF SENSATION: Σίτου ἐγεύσαντο, *tasted of food*, iii. 1. 3. Οἴνου.. ὀσφραίνεσθαι, *to smell wine*, v. 8. 3. Θορύβου ἤκουσε διὰ τῶν τάξεων ἰόντος, 'heard a murmur,' i. 8. 16.

b. OF PERCEPTION, KNOWLEDGE, REFLECTION, EXPERIENCE, and HABIT: Ἐπιβουλῆς οὐκ ᾔσθάνετο, *he did not perceive the plot*, i. 1. 8. Ἀλλήλων ξυνίεσαν, *understood each other*, Th. 1. 3. Ἐνθυμοῦ δὲ καὶ τῶν εἰδότων, *consider those who know*, Mem. 3. 6. 17. Πειρώμενοι ταύτης τῆς τάξεως, *making trial of this order*, iii. 2. 38.

c. OF MEMORY: Τούτων οὐδεὶς μέμνηται, *these things no one remembers*, v. 8. 25. Τούτων ἐμέμνητο, *made mention of these*, vii. 5. 8. Μή μ' ἀναμνήσῃς κακῶν, *do not remind me of my woes*, Eur. Alc. 1045. Τῶν πάροιθε μὲν λόγων λαθώμεθα, *let us forget the former words*, Eur. Hipp. 288.

d. OF CARE AND CONCERN: Κήδεσθαι Σεύθου, *to care for Seuthes*, vii. 5. 5. Τούτου σοι δεῖ μέλειν, *of this* [there must be to you a care] *you must take care*, Cyr. 1. 6. 16. Ἀμελεῖν ἡμῶν αὐτῶν, *to be careless of ourselves*, i. 3. 11. Μὴ μεταμέλειν σοι τῆς ἐμῆς δωρεᾶς, *that it may not repent thee* (old Eng.) *of thy gift to me*, Cyr. 8. 3. 32 (repentance or regret being *after-concern*). Φυλασσομένους τῶν νεῶν, *careful of the ships*, Th. 4. 11.

e. OF DESIRE: Ἐρῶντες τούτου, *desiring this*, iii. 1. 29. Χρημάτων ἐπιθυμεῖ, [sets his mind upon, cf. 430 b] *desires booty*, iii. 2. 39.

f. OF VARIOUS EMOTION: Ἄγαμαι λήματος, *I admire the spirit*, Eur. Rhes. 244. Ὑμῶν.. θαυμάζω, *I wonder at you*, Hel. 2. 3. 53. Οὓς οὐκ ἂν ἀνασχέσθαι αὐτοῦ βασιλεύοντος, *who would not endure him as their king*, ii. 2. 1. Ὧν ἐγώ σοι οὐ φθονήσω, *which I shall not grudge to you.*

g. The idea of *hearing* passes, by an easy transition, into that of *obedience* (obēdio, *to give ear to, listen to, obey,* fr. ob and audio). Hence, *words of obedience* often govern the Gen. (cf. 455 g): Τούτους.. βασιλέως οὐκ ἀκούειν, *that these did not obey* [or *were not subject to*] *the king*, iii. 5. 16. Ὑπήκοοι τῶν Μοσσυνοίκων, *subject to the M.*, v. 5. 1.

h. Verbs of *sight* commonly govern the Acc.; and many verbs which are followed by the Gen. according to this rule, sometimes or often take the Acc. (especially of a neuter adjective): Εἴδομεν τοὺς πολεμίους, *we have seen the enemy*, vi. 5. 10. Κλύω βοήν, *I hear a cry*. See 472 b, d.

4. *Genitive of Time and Place.*

433. The *time* and *place* in which any thing is done may be regarded as *essential conditions* of the action, or as *co-operating* to produce it. Hence,

RULE XIV. The TIME and PLACE *IN WHICH* are put in the Genitive (cf. 469, 482): as,

a. TIME: Ὤιχετο τῆς νυκτός, *he went in the night*, vii. 2. 17. Ποιεῖ δὲ τοῦτο πολλάκις τοῦ μηνός, 'many times [in the] a month,' Cyr. 1. 2. 9. Εἴτε νυκτὸς δέοι τι, εἴτε καὶ ἡμέρας, 'whether [*in the*] by night or by day,' iii. 1. 40. Βασιλεὺς οὐ μαχεῖται δέκα ἡμερῶν (cf. ἐν .. ταύταις ταῖς ἡμέραις), *the king will not fight* [within] *for ten days*, i. 7. 18. Πολλοῦ χρόνου, Μακροῦ χρόνου, Χρόνου συχνοῦ, *for a long time*, i. 9. 25 ; &c.

b. PLACE: Αὐτοῦ [sc. τόπου] μείναντες, *remaining in that place*, i. 10. 17. Ἦ οὔκ Ἄργεος ἦεν; *was he not in A.?* γ. 251. Ποτέρας τῆς χερός; Ἐν δεξιᾷ σου. *On which hand? On thy right.* Eur. Cycl. 681.

c. This use of the Gen., to denote the *place where*, rarely occurs in prose, except in those adverbs of place which are properly genitives (380 b): οὗ, αὐτοῦ, ὁμοῦ, οὐδαμοῦ, &c. Cf. 469 b.

d. This Gen. is sometimes employed, chiefly in the Epic, to denote the *place upon, over*, or *through which* any thing moves : Ἔρχονται πεδίοιο, *they advance* [in] *upon the plain*, B. 801. Πεδίων ἐπινίσσεται, Soph.

e. The ideas of *place* and *time* are combined in some expressions which relate to *journeying* (Fr. journée, *a day's-march*, fr. Lat. diurnus, fr. dies, *day*): Ἑπτακαίδεκα γὰρ σταθμῶν τῶν ἐγγυτάτω οὐδὲν εἴχομεν, '[in] during the last seventeen day's-marches,' ii. 2. 11.

f. The idea of *cause* appears especially in such expressions as Δώσειν .. τρία ἡμιδαρεικὰ τοῦ μηνός, *to pay three half-darics a month*, i. 3. 21.

434. *C.* That which produces any thing, as its ACTIVE or EFFICIENT CAUSE ; or, in other words, that *by* which, as its *author, agent*, or *giver*, any thing is *made, written, said, done, bestowed*, &c., or *from* which any thing is *obtained, heard, learned, inquired, requested, demanded*, &c.

To this division, which refers chiefly to *persons*, belongs the following rule, which will of course be understood as applying only to *adjuncts*.

Genitive Active.

RULE XV. The AUTHOR, AGENT, and GIVER are put in the Genitive: as,

a. With Verbs of Obtaining, Receiving, Hearing, Learning, Inquiring, Requesting, &c.: Ταῦτα δέ σου τυχόντες, *obtaining this of you*, vi. 6. 32. Ἐμοῦ ἀκούσεσθε πᾶσαν τὴν ἀλήθειαν, *you shall hear from me the whole truth*, Pl. Apol. Μάθε δέ μου καὶ τάδε, *learn from me this also*, Cyr.

b. With Passive Verbs and Verbals : Πληγεὶς θυγατρὸς τῆς ἐμῆς, *smitten by my daughter*, Eur. Or. 497. Φίλων ἄκλαυτος, *unwept of friends*, Soph. Ant. 847. Ἀγαπητοῖς Θεοῦ, *beloved of God*, Rom. 1. 7. — This use of the Gen. is rare in prose, and is most frequent with the Participle or Verbal.

c. With Substantives : Ξενοφῶντος Κύρου Ἀνάβασις, *Xenophon's Expedition of Cyrus.* Ἥρας ἀλατείαις, *wanderings caused by Juno*, Æsch. Pr. 900. Πολέμων φθορά, *destruction by wars*, Pl. Leg. 741 a.

435. *D.* That which CONSTITUTES any thing WHAT IT IS. To this head may be referred whatever serves to *complete the idea of a thing or property,* by adding some *distinction* or *characteristic.*

Genitive Constituent.

RULE XVI. An ADJUNCT DEFINING A THING OR PROPERTY is put in the Genitive: as,

Τὸ Μένωνος στράτευμα, *the army of Meno,* i. 2. 21.

a. Substantives simply denote *things* (including *persons*); and adjectives and adverbs, *properties.* Hence, if an adjunct is *simply viewed as modifying a substantive, adjective, or adverb,* it is put in the Gen.; and Rule XVI. might be thus expressed:

A SUBSTANTIVE, ADJECTIVE, or ADVERB, *as such,* governs the Genitive.

b. If, on the other hand, *the particular nature of the modification is to be expressed,* another case may be required; so that the same substantive, adjective, or adverb may either be followed by the Gen. as the *generic* case, or by the Dat. or Acc. as a *more specific* case. See 442 a, 463, &c.

436. a. The THING OR PROPERTY DEFINED may be either *distinctly expressed by its appropriate word,* or may be *involved in another word:* as βασιλεύς in βασιλεύω (442), πλησίον in πλησιάζω (445 c). Hence,

RULE B. A word may govern the Genitive, by virtue of an *included* substantive, adjective, or adverb.

b. Adjectives in which a substantive is compounded with **ἀ-** *privative* (385), have often a Gen. defining the substantive: as, Γήρως ἄλυπα, *free from the pains of age,* Soph. See 446 b. Hence the special rule,

RULE C. *Compounds of ἀ-Privative* govern the Genitive.

c. The verbs ὄζω *to smell,* πνέω *to breathe,* and προσβάλλω *to emit,* may take a Gen. defining a noun implied in these verbs or understood with them: Ὄζουσι πίττης, *they smell of pitch* [emit the smell of pitch], Ar. Ach. 190. Μύρου πνέον, *breathing of myrrh,* Soph. Fr. 147.

d. Some adverbs govern the Gen., as originally substantives (380), or by virtue of an included substantive: Τοῦδε τοῦ φόβου χάριν (or ἕνεκα), *on account of this fear,* Soph. El. 427, &c. So δίκην, δέμας poet., *after the manner* or *form of, like,* ἕκητι poet., *by the will of,* κύκλῳ *around,* &c.

437. A Genitive defining a substantive (a) is often connected with it through an *appositional verb.* Less frequently, (b) its connection is modified or strengthened by an *adjective* or *adverb.* These constructions may be often explained by ellipsis.

(a.) Πρόξενος .. ἦν [sc. ἄνθρωπος] ἐτῶν ὡς τριάκοντα, *P. was [a man] of about 30 years,* ii. 6. 20. See 440, 443, and cf. 422. (b.) Ἱερὸς ὁ χῶρος τῆς Ἀρτέμιδος, *the spot is sacred to Diana* [consecrated to be Diana's], v. 3. 13. Ἰδίων ἑαυτοῦ κτημάτων, *of his own acquisitions,* Pl. So with οἰκεῖος *proprius, own,* ἐπιχώριος *customary,* κοινός *communis, common,* &c.

c. The Gen. is often used in *emphatic periphrasis*, particularly with **χρῆμα** *thing* (446 a) and, by the poets, with **ὄνομα** *name*, **δέμας** *body*, **κάρα** *head*, **σχῆμα** *form*, and similar words : Ὦ φίλτατον .. ὄνομα Πολυνείκους, *O dearest* [name of P.] *P.*, Eur. Δέμας Ἀγαμέμνονος, for Ἀγαμέμνονα, Id.

d. A substantive governing the Gen., or (c) the Gen. itself, is sometimes used instead of an *adjective*, especially by the poets and Hellenistic writers: (d) **Χρυσὸν** .. ἐπῶν, *the gold of words*, for Ἔπη χρυσᾶ, *golden words*, Ar. (e) Πάθη ἀτιμίας, [passions of baseness] *base passions*, Rom. 1. 26.

438. ELLIPSIS. a. A substantive governing the Gen. is often *understood*, particularly words denoting *domestic relation* or *abode* (υἱός *son*, οἶκος *house*, &c.), and such as the context supplies: as,

Γλοῦς ὁ Ταμώ, *Glus, the son of Tamos*, ii. 1. 3. Βυρσίνης τῆς Ἱππίου [sc. γυναικός,] B., *the wife of H.*, Ar. Φοιτῶν εἰς διδασκάλου [sc. οἶκον], *resorting to the house of a teacher*, Pl. Alc. Ἐν Ἀσκληπιοῦ [sc. ἱερῷ *temple*] Mem. 3. 13. 3. Ἐν Ἅιδου Soph. Ant. 654 (cf. Εἰν Ἅιδου δόμοις 1241).

b. Instead of simple ellipsis, the *possessor* is sometimes put in the case belonging to the *thing possessed*, chiefly in *comparison:* as, Ἅρματα .. ὅμοια ἐκείνῳ [= τοῖς ἐκείνου ἅρμασι], *chariots like* [him] *his (chariots)*, Cyr.

439. An adjunct defining a THING either expresses a *property* of that thing, or points out *another thing related* to it. An adjunct defining a PROPERTY points out a *thing related* to that property. Hence the CONSTITUENT GENITIVE is either, (1) the *Genitive of Property*, or (2) the *Genitive of Relation*.

1. *Genitive of Property*

440. a. The GENITIVE OF PROPERTY expresses *dimension, age, quality*, &c. (often expressed by an adjective, 435 d) :

Ποταμὸν ὄντα τὸ εὖρος **πλέθρου** i. 4. 9, *a river being* [of] *a plethron in width* (cf. Ποταμὸν τὸ εὖρος **πλεθριαῖον** i. 5. 4, and see 395 c). Πρὶν εἴκοσιν **ἐτῶν** εἶναι, *before he was* [of 20 years] *20 years old*, Mem. See 437 a.

b. Except in the predicate, the Gen. of strict *quality* is chiefly poetic or Hellen. (437 c): Ὅσοι τῆς αὐτῆς **γνώμης** ἦσαν, *as many as were of the same mind*, Th. Στολίδα .. **τρυφᾶς**, *a* [dress of daintiness] *dainty dress*, Eur.

2. *Genitive of Relation.*

441. The GENITIVE OF RELATION, in its full extent, includes much that has been already adduced under other and more specific heads. The relations which remain to be considered are chiefly, (α) those of *domestic, social,* and *civil life ;* (β) those of *possession* and *ownership ;* (γ) that of the *object of an action* to the *action* or *agent ;* (δ) those of *time* and *place ;* (ε) those of *specification, explanation,* and *emphasis ;* while yet others are left for observation.

The Genitives expressing these relations may be termed, (α) the *Gen. of social relation,* (β) the *Gen. possessive,* (γ) the *Gen. objective,* (δ) the *Gen. of local* or *temporal relation,* (ε) the *Gen. of specification,* &c.

442. a. GENITIVE OF SOCIAL RELATION. Ὁ τῆς βασιλέως γυναικὸς ἀδελφός, *the brother of the king's wife*, ii. 3. 17. Βασιλεύων [= βασιλεὺς ὤν, 436 a] αὐτῶν, *being their king*, v. 6. 37 (cf. 407). Γείτων . . τῆς Ἑλλάδος, *a neighbor of Greece*; Τοὺς ἐκείνου ἐχθίστους, . . τοὺς Κύρου φίλους, *his worst foes, the friends of C.*; iii. 2. 4, 5. Cf. 450 a, 456.

a. To this analogy may be referred the use of the Gen. for the Dat., with some *adjectives* denoting *near connection* or *correspondence* (even compounds of σύν, ὁμοῦ, &c.): Συγγενὴς τοῦ Κύρου, *related to Cyrus*, or *a relative of Cyrus*, Cyr. Ζεὺς ὁμέστιος βροτῶν, *Jupiter dwelling with mortals*, Soph. Τούτων ἀντίρροπον, *counterpoising these*, Dem. Cf. 450 s.

b. In some of the examples falling under this head, an adjective may be regarded as used substantively.

443. β. GENITIVE POSSESSIVE. a. The Genitive possessive denotes that to which any thing *belongs* as a *possession, power, right, duty, office, quality, characteristic*, &c. Thus,

Τὰ Συεννέσιος βασίλεια, *the palace of S.*, i. 2. 23. Ἦσαν αἱ Ἰωνικαὶ πόλεις Τισσαφέρνους, *the Ionian cities belonged to T.*, i. 1. 6. Τῶν μὲν γὰρ νικώντων τὸ κατακαίνειν, τῶν δὲ ἡττωμένων τὸ ἀποθνῄσκειν ἐστί, *for it is the part of victors to kill, but of the vanquished to die*, iii. 2. 39.

b. A *neuter adjective used substantively* takes the Gen. possessive, in connection with some verbs of *praise, blame, wonder*, and the like: Τοῦτο ἐπαινῶ Ἀγησιλάου, *I commend this in Agesilaus* [this characteristic of Agesilaus], Ages. Ἕν σου δέδοικα, *one thing* [of you] *in you I fear*, Eur.

c. An adjective sometimes supplies the place of the *Gen. possessive* (435 d): Τὸ βασίλειον [= βασιλέως] σημεῖον, *the king's ensign*, i. 10. 12.

444. γ. GENITIVE OBJECTIVE. If an action, instead of being predicated by a verb, is simply presented in a substantive, adjective, or adverb, then its object is usually expressed by the Genitive (instead of an Acc., Dat., or preposition with its case, as with a verb, 435 a, b). Thus,

a. *Genitive of the Direct Object:* Ὁ φρούραρχος τὰς φυλακὰς ἐξετάζει, *the commander reviews the guards*, Œc. 9. 15; but, Κῦρος ἐξέτασιν ποιεῖται τῶν Ἑλλήνων, *C. makes a review of the Greeks*, i. 7. 1; Τῶν τοιούτων ἔργων ἐξεταστικόν, *fitted to review such matters*, Mem. 1. 1. 7. Λάθρα (or κρύφα) δὲ τῶν στρατιωτῶν, *without the knowledge of the soldiers*, i. 3. 8 (cf. Λαθεῖν αὐτὸν ἀπελθών 17), &c. Ἀρετῆς διδάσκαλος Pl. Meno 93 c.

b. *Genitive of the Indirect Object:* Εὔχεσθαι τοῖς . . θεοῖς, *to pray to the gods*, iv. 3. 13; but, Θεῶν εὐχάς, *prayers to the gods*, Pl. Phædr. 244 e. Τὴν τῶν κρεισσόνων δουλείαν, *subjection to the stronger*, Th. 1. 8.

c. *Genitive for a preposition with its case:* Ἀπέβη ἐς τὴν γῆν, *descended upon the land*; but, Ἐν ἀποβάσει τῆς γῆς, *in a descent upon the land*, Th.

d. In like manner, the *Gen.* is employed with *nouns*, to denote relations, which, with the corresponding *adjectives*, are denoted by the *Dat.:* Τῆς τῶν Ἑλλήνων εὐνοίας, *from good-will to the Greeks*, iv. 7. 20 (cf. Εὔνους δέ σοι ὤν vii. 3. 20). Ἀνδρὸς εὐμένειαν Soph. O. C. 631.

e. A *participle* may so perform the office of a substantive or common adjective, as to take the *Gen. objective:* Ὅ τ᾿ ἐκείνου τεκών, *his father*, Eur.

f. To the *Gen. of the direct object* may be referred the Gen. with αἴτιος and its derivatives: Ὁ ἐμὸς ἔρως τούτου αἴτιος, *my desire is* [causative of] *the cause of this*, ii. Τούτων οὐ σὺ αἰτία, *you are not responsible for this*, Œc.

g. The Gen. in its more active uses (when employed to denote *agent*,

§ 448.   POSSESSIVE, OBJECTIVE, LOCAL, &C.   245

possessor, &c.) has received the special designation of the *Gen. subjective*, in distinction from the *Gen. objective*. They may both modify the same word: Τὴν Πέλοπος μὲν ἁπάσης Πελοποννήσου κατάληψιν, *Pelops's seizure of all Peloponnesus*, Isoc. 249 a. Adjectives taking the place of the Gen. are, in like manner, used both *subjectively* and *objectively*.

445. 8. GENITIVE OF LOCAL OR TEMPORAL RELATION. a. *With Substantives:* Τόπον ἐλέους, *place for pity*, Polyb. 1. 88. Τριῶν ἡμερῶν ὁδόν, *a three days' march*, ii. 2. 12. Τελευτὴν τοῦ βίου, *end of life*, i. 1. 1.
b. *With Adjectives.* Ἐναντίος ἵστασ' ἐμεῖο, *stand opposed to me*, N. 448. Γάμου ἤδη ὡραία, *now of proper age for marriage*, Cyr. 4. 6. 9.
c. *With Adverbs.* The Gen. is used with many adverbs *of place* and *time:* Ἐγγὺς παραδείσου, *near a park*, ii. 4. 14. Ἐγγὺς μυρίων, *nearly 10,000*, v. 7. 9. Μέχρι ἑσπέρας, *until evening*, Cyr. 1. 4. 23.

446. ε. GENITIVE OF SPECIFICATION, EXPLANATION, or EMPHASIS. This makes the statement more precise or emphatic, by adding a more specific name, or by showing in what sense or with what special application (*in respect to what*) the statement is made, or by repetition, &c.

NOTE. In some of these uses, the Gen. rather denotes a relation between *two expressions for the same thing*, than between *two different things*. In some cases, an *appositive* might be substituted for it; and in others, we might regard the Gen. as in apposition with a substantive implied.

a. *With Substantives.* Τροίης πτολίεθρον, *city* OF *Troy* (395 c; cf. urbs Romæ). Θανάτου τελευτάν, *the end* [of life] *in death*, or simply, *death*, Eur. Med. 152 (cf. § 445 a). Τυράννου χρῆμα, *a* [thing of a tyrant] *vile tyrant*, Pl. Rep. 567 c. Ὑὸς χρῆμα μέγιστον, *a monster of a boar*, Hdt.
b. *With Adjectives.* Νεώτατος .. γόνοιο, *youngest of birth*, T. 409. Πληγῶν ἀθῷον, *free from the punishment of blows* (436 b), Ar. Nub. 1413. Ἄπαις δέ εἰμι ἀρρένων παίδων, *I am childless* [of] *as to male children*, Cyr.
c. *With Adverbs.* Ἀσφαλῶς τῆς δεῦρ' ὁδοῦ, *safely as to his journey hither*, Soph. O. C. 1165. Cf. 420 b, 429 c.
d. *With Verbs* (436 a). Τῆς ἐπωβελίας .. κινδυνεύοντα [= ἐν κινδύνῳ ὄντα], *being in danger of the prescribed fine*, Dem. 835. 14. Τάφου .. ἀτιμάσας, *having denied the honor of burial*, Soph. Ant. 21.
e. With words of number or quantity, the Gen. is often used to specify the *class* or *kind:* Καπίθην ἀλεύρων, *two quarts of flour*, i. 5. 6.

447. GENERAL REMARK. Great care is requisite in distinguishing the various uses of the Genitive.

C. THE DATIVE OBJECTIVE.

448. THAT TOWARDS WHICH ANY THING TENDS may be resolved into (I.) *That towards which any thing tends, as an* OBJECT OF APPROACH; and (II.) *That towards which any thing tends, as an* OBJECT OF INFLUENCE. Hence the Dative Objective is either

(I.) the DATIVE OF APPROACH, or (II.) the DATIVE OF INFLUENCE; and we have the following general rule :

RULE D. THE OBJECT OF APPROACH OR OF INFLUENCE IS PUT IN THE DATIVE ;

or, in other words, since neither approach nor influence are regarded as *direct action*,

AN INDIRECT OBJECT IS PUT IN THE DATIVE.

a. The *Dat. of approach* is commonly expressed in English by the preposition *to*, and the *Dat. of influence*, by the prepositions *to* and *for*; both, in Latin, by the Dative. An imitation of 403 b would give to the rule this form :

The DATIVE is used to express that TO or FOR which something is or is done.

b. The relations here denoted are, however, sometimes translated by other prepositions, especially by *with*; and sometimes without a preposition.

c. The *Dat. of approach* may denote either *person* or *thing*; the *Dat. of influence* oftener denotes *person*.

d. The DATIVE OBJECTIVE is the converse of the GENITIVE ; the *Dat. of approach* contrasting with the *Gen. of departure*, and the *Dat. of influence* with the *Gen. of cause*. See 397, 398, 403.

I. DATIVE OF APPROACH.

449. Approach, like its opposite, *departure* (404), may be either in *place*, in *time*, or in *character*. Hence,

RULE XVII. Words of NEARNESS and LIKENESS govern the Dative.

(1.) *Dative of Nearness.*

450. a. Words of nearness may imply either *being near*, *coming near*, or *bringing near*; and to this class may be referred words of *union* and *mixture*, of *companionship* and *intercourse*, of *meeting* and *following*, of *sending to* and *bringing to*, &c. : as,

Πελάσαι . . τῇ εἰσόδῳ, *to approach the entrance*, iv. 2. 3. Οἴνῳ κεράσας αὐτήν, *having mixed it with wine*, i. 2. 13. "Εψονται ὑμῖν, *they will follow you*, iii. 1. 36. Διάδοχος Κλεάνδρῳ, *successor to C.*, vii. 2. 5. Γείτων οἰκῶ τῇ Ἑλλάδι, *I dwell a neighbor to Greece*, ii. 3. 18 (cf. 442). Ἐπορεύετο . . ἅμα Τισσαφέρνει, *marched in company with T.*, ii. 4. 9.

b. So words which become *words of nearness* through their application : Κύρῳ ἰέναι, *to go to C.*, i. 2. 26. Πίπτοντος πέδῳ, *falling to the ground*, Soph. El. 747. Πέμπων αὐτῷ ἄγγελον, *sending a messenger to him*, i. 3. 8.

(2.) Dative of Likeness.

451. a. Words of likeness include those of *resemblance, assimilation, comparison, identity, equality,* &c. : as,

"Όμοιοι τοῖς ἄλλοις, *like the rest,* vi. 6. 16. Φιλοσόφῳ μὲν ἔοικας, *you resemble a philosopher,* ii. 1. 13. 'Εμὲ δὲ θεῷ μὲν οὐκ εἴκασεν, *but me he did not liken to a god,* Apol. 15. Τὸ ἀληθὲς ἐνόμιζε τὸ αὐτὸ τῷ ἠλιθίῳ εἶναι, *he thought sincerity to be the same with folly,* ii. 6. 22.

b. Many derivatives or compounds of σύν, ὁμοῦ, ὁμοῖος, and ἴσος, govern the Dat. by this rule.

II. DATIVE OF INFLUENCE.

452. The *Dative of Influence* expresses a person or thing which is *affected* by an action, property, &c., without being *directly acted upon*.

NOTE. Influence has every variety and degree. On the one hand, it may be so *immediate,* that it can scarcely be distinguished from direct action, and the Dat. expressing it is used interchangeably with the Acc.; and, on the other hand, it may be so *remote,* that it can scarcely be appreciated, and the Dat. expressing it might have been omitted without impairing the sense.

RULE XVIII. The OBJECT OF INFLUENCE is put in the Dative.

The Dative is governed, according to this rule, by,

a.) Words of ADDRESS, including those of *call* and *command,* of *conversation* and *reply,* of *declaration* and *confession,* of *exhortation* and *message,* of *oath* and *promise,* of *reproach* and *threatening,* &c. :

Οὗτος Κύρῳ εἶπεν, *this man said to C.,* i. 6. 2. Κλεάρχῳ ἐβόα, *called out to C.,* i. 8. 12. Διαλεχθέντες ἀλλήλοις, *having conversed with each other,* ii. 5. 42. Αὐτῷ μαντευτὸς, *pointed out to him by oracle,* vi. 1. 22.

453. b.) Words of ADVANTAGE and DISADVANTAGE, including those of *benefit* and *injury,* of *assistance* and *service,* of *favor* and *fidelity,* of *necessity* and *sufficiency,* of *fitness* and *unfitness,* of *convenience* and *trouble,* of *ease* and *difficulty,* of *safety* and *danger,* &c. :

Χρήσιμα . . τοῖς Κρησί, *useful to the Cretans,* iii. 4. 17. Ἀνθρώποισιν ὠφελήματα, *benefits to men,* Æsch. Pr. 501. Φίλοις ἀρήγειν, *to succor friends,* Cyr. 1. 5. 13. Παρύσατις . . ὑπῆρχε τῷ Κύρῳ, *P. favored C.,* i. 1. 4. Ἐγώ τινι ἐμποδών εἰμι ; *am I in the way* [to] *of any one ?* v. 7. 10. Τῇ ἡλικίᾳ ἔπρεπε, *it suited his age,* i. 9. 6. Οἴ μοι, *Woe to me ! Alas !*

454. c.) Words of APPEARANCE, including those of *seeming, showing, clearness, obscurity,* &c. :

Πᾶσι δῆλον ἐγένετο, *it became evident to all,* Hel. 6. 4. 20. Ἄδηλον μὲν παντί, *obscure to every one,* vi. 1. 21. Ἦν καὶ τοῖς ἄλλοις φανῇς οἷόσπερ ἐμοὶ δοκεῖς εἶναι, *if you appear to others such as you seem to me to be,* Cyr.

d.) Words of CAUSE, DESTINY, OBLIGATION, and VALUE :

Ἀγαθῶν αἴτιοι ἀλλήλοις, *authors of good to each other* (444 f), Cyr. 8. 5. 24. Πέπρωται σοι, *it is fated to you*, Æsch. Pr. 815. Τοῖς στρατιώταις ὠφείλετο μισθός, *pay was due to the soldiers*, i. 2. 11. Βασιλεῖ ἂν πολλοῦ ἄξιοι γένοιντο (431 b), *would be worth much to the king*, ii. 1. 14.

e.) Words of GIVING, including those of *granting, offering, paying, distributing, supplying*, &c. :

Δίδωμί σοι ἐμαυτόν, *I give myself to you*, Cyr. 4. 6. 2. Διανείμαι τοῖς στρατηγοῖς, *to distribute to the generals*, vii. 5. 2. Εἴπερ ἐμοὶ ἐτέλει τι Σεύθης, *if S. paid me anything*. Θεοῖς δωρήματα, *gifts to the gods*, Ar. Nub.

455. f.) Words of OPPOSITION, including those of *contention, dispute, enmity, resistance, rivalry, warfare*, &c. :

Λιμὸν ὑμῖν ἀντιτάξαι, *to oppose to you famine*, ii. 5. 19. Ἐρίζοντά οἱ περὶ σοφίας, *contending with him in skill*, i. 2. 8. Παλλάδι τ' ἔριν, *a dispute with P.*, Eur. Ἀντίοι ἰέναι τοῖς πολεμίοις, *to go against the enemy*, i. 8. 17. Οὐδεὶς αὐτῷ ἐμάχετο, *no one fought with him*, Ib. 23.

g.) Words of YIELDING, SUBJECTION, and WORSHIP, including those of *homage, obedience* (cf. 432 g), *prayer, sacrifice*, &c. :

Πάντα τοῖς θεοῖς ὑποχα, *all things are subject to the gods*, ii. 5. 7. Ἐμοὶ οὐ θέλετε πείθεσθαι, *you are not willing to obey me*, i. 3. 6. Ἐάν μοι πεισθῆτε, *if you will listen to me*, i. 4. 14. Εὔχεσθαι τοῖς .. θεοῖς, *to pray to the gods*, iv. 3. 13. Ἔθυε τῷ Διί, *sacrificed to Jupiter*, vii. 6. 44.

456. h. Words expressing a MENTAL ACT OF FEELING, which is regarded as *going out towards an object;* as those of *friendship* and *hatred, pleasure* and *displeasure, joy* and *sorrow, contentment* and *envy, belief* and *unbelief, trust* and *distrust*, &c.:

Κύρῳ φιλαίτερον, *more friendly to C.*, i. 9. 29. Τούτοις ἥσθη Κῦρος, *C. was pleased with these*, i. 9. 26. Ὧν ἐμοὶ χαλεπαίνετε, *for which you are angry with me* (429 a), vii. 6. 32. Χαίρεις .. φίλοις ἀγαθοῖς, *you delight in good friends*, Mem. Ἐπίστευον γὰρ αὐτῷ, *they trusted him*, i.

457. i.) Words expressing the ACT OF POWER OF EXCITING EMOTION : as *pleasure, displeasure, care, fear*, &c. :

Ἀρέσκειν ὑμῖν, *to please you*, Cyr. 3. 3. 39. Ἐμοὶ μελήσει, *it shall be [a care to me] my care*, i. 4. 16. Μεταμέλει μοι, *I repent*, Cyr. See 432 d.

458. j.) VERBAL ADJECTIVES in -τός and -τέος. With these the Dat. is used to express *relation to an agent* (for which, in Eng., *to* or *for* can be used, though other forms of expression are frequent) :

Θαυμαστὸν πᾶσι, *wonderful to all*, iv. 2. 15. Ἵνα μοι εὐπρακτότερον ᾖ, *that it may be easier for me to effect*, ii. 3. 20. Ποταμὸς .. ἡμῖν ἐστι διαβατέος, *there is a river for us to cross* [to be crossed by us], ii. 4. 6. Ἡμῖν .. πάντα ποιητέα, *everything* [is for us to do] *should be done by us*, iii. 1. 35.

NOTE. So rarely other verbals : Τοῖσι δυστυχοῦσιν εὐκταία θεός, Eur.

459. k.) SUBSTANTIVE VERBS implying *possession* (in forms of expression which may be variously translated).

§ 462   OF POSSESSOR, AGENT, &C.   249

Rule E.   *Substantive Verbs* take a *Dative of the Possessor :*

'Ενταῦθα Κύρῳ βασίλεια ἦν, *here* [there was a palace to C.] *C. had a palace*, i. 2. 7.   Τοῖς δὲ ὑποψία μὲν ἦν, *they had a suspicion*, or *they suspected*, i. 3. 21.   Ὑπάρχει γὰρ νῦν ἡμῖν οὐδέν, *we have now nothing*, ii. 2. 11. Ἀνάγκη δή μοι [sc. ἐστί], *I am now compelled*, i. 3. 5.   Πόλις . . ᾗ ὄνομα Σιττάκη, *a city* [to which there was the name] *named S.*, ii. 4. 13.   Δρόμος ἐγένετο τοῖς στρατιώταις, [to the soldiers there came to be a running] *the soldiers began to run*, i. 2. 17.   Ἔστιν ἀνθρώπῳ . . βλέπειν, [it is to a man to look] *a man can look*, Symp. 4. 58.   Νῦν σοι ἔξεστιν vii. 1. 21.

Note.   The relation is sometimes defined by a participle or adjective of *mental state*, joined with the Dat.: Ἐκείνῳ **βουλομένῳ** ταῦτ' ἐστί, *these things are* [to him willing] *according to his will*, or *agreeable to him*, Hel. 4. 1. 11.   Νικίᾳ **προσδεχομένῳ** ἦν, *were as N. had expected*, Th. 6. 46.

460.   l.) And, in general, words expressing *any action, property,* &c., which is represented as being *to* or *for* some person or thing :

Προπίνω σοι, *I drink to you*, vii. 3. 26.   Κενοτάφιον αὐτοῖς ἐποίησαν, *they made for them a cenotaph*, vi. 4. 9.   Μέγιστον κόσμον ἀνδρί, *the greatest ornament to a man*, i. 9. 23.   Ὥρα ἦν ἀπιέναι τοῖς πολεμίοις, *it was time for the enemy to withdraw*, iii. 4. 34.   Ἐγὼ σιωπῶ τῷδε ; *I be silent for this fellow ?* Ar. Ran. 1134.   Λοιπόν μοι εἰπεῖν, *left for me to say*, iii. 2. 29.

461. m.   A Dative of the Agent is sometimes joined with *passive verbs*, chiefly with the Perfect and Pluperfect :

Πάνθ' ἡμῖν πεποίηται, *all things have been done by us*, i. 8. 12.   Εἰ δέ τι καλὸν . . ἐπέπρακτο ὑμῖν, *if any honor had been gained by you*, vii. 6. 32. Τοῖς Ἕλλησι μισοῦντο, *would be hated by the Greeks* [hateful to them], Th.

Note.   This use seems to have come chiefly from the *possessive use* of the Dat. (459).   Thus, τοῦτό μοι γέγραπται, hoc *mihi est* scriptum, [this *is to me* written, *I have this written*] *I have written this*, or *this has been written by me*.   So the *possessive* has passed into the *active* idea, in the use of the auxiliary in our own and in other languages : *I have it written, I have written it* (Germ. *Ich habe geschrieben,* Fr. *J'ai écrit,* &c.).

462.   Remarks.   1.   The remoter relations expressed by the Dat. (452 N.) are various, having respect to *place, time, sensation, thought, feeling, expression, action,* &c.   They may be expressed (a) directly by a substantive in the Dat., with which (b) a participle is often joined ; (c) by the participle with its subject omitted ; or (d) by an elliptical form of construction, in which the Dat. is preceded by ὡς, *as :*

Πόλις ἐν δεξιᾷ ἐσπλέοντι [sc. τινὶ or σοί], *a city on the right to one sailing in*, or *as you sail in*, Th. 1. 24 (cf. vi. 4. 1).   Τὸ μὲν ἔξωθεν ἀπτομένῳ σῶμα οὐκ ἄγαν θερμὸν ἦν, ' to the external touch,' Th. 2. 49.   Εἰ γενναῖος, ὡς ἰδόντι [sc. φαίνει], 'as you appear to one beholding,' 'in appearance,' Soph. O. C. 75.   Καίτοι σ' ἐγὼ τίμησα τοῖς **φρονοῦσιν** εὖ, '[for] in the judgment of the wise,' Soph. Ant. 904.   Κρέων γὰρ ἦν ζηλωτὸς, ὡς ἐμοὶ [sc. ἐδόκει], 'as it seemed to me,' 'in my opinion,' Ib. 1161.

e. The Dat. is termed ETHICAL, when it is introduced, not as an essential part of the sentence, but to render it more emphatic or subjective, by referring to some one as interested (ἠθικός, *relating to the state of mind*). The pronouns of the 1st and 2d Pers. are especially so used : Μέμνησό μοι,

COMP. GR.   11*

μηδέποτε ἀναμένειν, remember [for me], *I pray you, never to defer*, Cyr. 1. 6. 10. Νοσεῖ δέ μοι πρόπας στόλος, *the whole nation is sick* [for me], *alas!* Soph. O. T. Τί σοι μαθήσομαι; *what shall I learn for you?* Ar. Nub. 1. The use of the *Dat. with a participle* in defining time, especially prevails in Hdt.: Θυομένῳ οἱ .. ὁ ἥλιος ἀμαυρώθη, *while he was sacrificing*, &c.

463. 2. Words governing the Gen. sometimes take a Dat. in its stead, to express the exertion of an influence:

Ἡγεῖτο δ᾽ αὐτοῖς ὁ κωμάρχης, *and the bailiff led the way for them*, i. e. *guided them*, iv. 6. 2. Ταφίοισι .. ἀνάσσω, *I am lord* [to] *of the T.*, a. 181. Δαρὸν γὰρ οὐκ ἄρξει θεοῖς, *he will not long rule the gods*, Æsch. Τοῖσιν ἀφείλετο νόστιμον ἦμαρ, *he took away* [for] *from them the day of return*, a. 9. Θέμιστι .. δέκτο δέπας, O. 87. Πέφευγεν ἐλπὶς τῶνδέ μοι, 'has fled [for] from me,' Eur. Τὰ ἄκρα ἡμῖν .. προκαταλαμβάνειν i. 3. 16.

464. 3. A *Dat. depending upon a verb* is often used instead of a *Gen. depending upon a substantive*:

Οἱ .. ἵπποι αὐτοῖς δέδενται, *the horses are tied for them*, = οἱ ἵπποι αὐτῶν δέδενται, *their horses are tied*, iii. 4. 35. Τοῖς βαρβάροις τῶν τε πεζῶν ἀπέθανον πολλοί, [for] *of the barbarians, many of the foot were slain*, iii. 4. 5. Ἡ .. τοῦ παντὸς ἀρχὴ Χειρισόφῳ ἐνταῦθα κατελύθη vi. 2. 12 (cf. 3. 1).

a. The Dat. for the Gen. is sometimes joined directly with a substantive, chiefly the Dat. of a personal pronoun : Οἱ δέ σφι βόες .. οὐ παρεγίνοντο, [the oxen for them] *their oxen did not come*, Hdt. 1. 31.

b. A Dat. is sometimes joined with a substantive, where the sense is more fully expressed by supplying a participle or adjective : Ἀπόβλεπε .. πρὸς τὴν νέαν ἡμῖν πόλιν, *look upon the new state* [planned] *for us*, Pl.

c. Except as above, substantives governing the Dat. are commonly derived from verbs or adjectives so construed. .

D. The Dative Residual.

465. The *Dative Residual* is used in expressing adjuncts, which are not viewed as either *subjective* or *objective* (397 s). It simply denotes *indirect relation*, without specifying the character of that relation; or, in other words, it denotes mere *association* or *connection*. Hence we have the general rule:

Rule F. An Attendant Thing or Circumstance, simply viewed as such, is put in the Dative.

a. In accordance with this rule, the Dat. is sometimes used in expressing an adjunct, which, upon a more exact discrimination of its character, would be expressed either by the *Gen.* or *Acc.* (399 a, f).

b. The Dative Residual is commonly expressed in Lat. by the *Ablative*; in Eng. most frequently by the preposition *with*, but likewise by the prepositions *at, in, by, through*, &c. Cf. 403 a, 448 a.

c. The Dative Residual may be resolved into (I.) the Instrumental and Modal .Dative, and (II.) the Temporal and Local Dative.

I. Instrumental and Modal Dative.

466. Rule XIX. The MEANS and MODE are put in the Dative.

Instrumentality and mode may be either *external* or *internal*, and mode may apply either to *action* or *condition*. Hence, to these heads may be referred,

1.) The *instrument, force*, or *other means*, with which any thing is done, or through which it comes to pass :

'Ακοντίζει τις παλτῷ, *one shoots with a dart*, i. 8. 27. Σχεδίαις διαβαίνοντες, *crossing with rafts*, i. 5. 10. Ἐφείποντο .. ἱππικῷ, *pursued with cavalry*, vii. 6. 29. Θανάτῳ ζημιοῦν, *to punish with death*, Cyr. 6. 3. 27. Ἀποθνῄσκει νόσῳ, *dies through disease*, vii. 2. 32. Εὐνοίᾳ ἑπομένους, ii. 6.

a. Means and Cause, to some extent, cover the same ground. Hence some of the examples above, and others like them, might be referred to a Dative of Cause (for which the Gen. could be used, 465 a).

b. **Χράομαι**, *to use* [to supply one's need with, 50], takes the Dat. (originally of *means*) : Τῷ ὄψῳ σίτῳ χρήσεται, *he will use meat as bread* (394 b), Mem. 3. 14. 4. (c) So the compounds ἀπο-χράομαι, &c.; and sometimes **νομίζω**, after the analogy of χράομαι· Φωνῇ .. νομίζουσι, Hdt.

467. 2.) a. The *way* or *manner*, in which any thing is done or affected, together with *attendant circumstances;* and also (b) the *respect* in which any thing is taken or applied :

(a) Οὐ γὰρ κραυγῇ, ἀλλὰ σιγῇ .. προσῇεσαν, *they advanced not with clamor, but in silence*, i. 8. 11. Ὥσπερ ὀργῇ ἐκέλευσε, *he commanded, as in anger*, i. 5. 8. Ἐλαύνων .. ἱδροῦντι τῷ ἵππῳ, *riding with his horse in a sweat*, i. 8. 1. Τούτῳ τῷ τρόπῳ ἐπορεύθησαν, *in this manner they marched*.

(b) Πλήθει γε ἡμῶν λειφθέντες, *inferior to us in* [respect to] *number* (406 b). Τῇ φωνῇ τραχύς, *rough in voice*, ii. 6. 9. Πόλις .. Θάψακος ὀνόματι, 'by name,' i. 4. 11. Τῇ ἐπιμελείᾳ περιεῖναι i. 9. 24.

c. The pronoun **αὐτός** is sometimes joined to the dative of an *associated object* to give emphasis ; and the preposition **σύν**, which is otherwise common with such adjuncts, is then usually omitted : Μὴ ἡμᾶς αὐταῖς ταῖς τριήρεσι καταδύσῃ, *lest he should sink us, triremes and all* [with the triremes themselves], i. 3. 17. Cf. Ξ. 498 and Τ. 482.

468. 3.) The *measure of difference*, especially with the Comparative :

Ἐνιαυτῷ πρεσβύτερος, *older by a year*, Ar. Ran. 18. Πόλι λογίμῳ ἡ Ἑλλὰς γέγονε ἀσθενεστέρη, *Greece has become weaker by an illustrious city*, Hdt. 6. 106. Χρόνῳ μετέπειτα πολλῷ Hdt. 2. 110. So often a neut. adjective (μακρῷ *by far*, ὀλίγῳ *by little*, &c.) : Οὐ πολλῷ δὲ ὕστερον, *not* [later by much] *long after*, ii. 5. 32. Ὅσῳ δὲ μᾶλλον πιστεύω, τοσούτῳ μᾶλλον ἀπορῶ, [by how much] *the more I believe*, [by so much] *the more I am at a loss*, Pl. Rep. 368 b. See i. 5. 9. Minor anno, Hor.

II. TEMPORAL AND LOCAL DATIVE.

469. RULE XX. The TIME and PLACE *AT WHICH* are put in the Dative (cf. 433, 482) : as,

a. TIME (in prose, chiefly in stating some *day, night, month, season, year,* or *festival,* as the *time at which* an event occurred): Τῇ πρώτῃ δὲ ἡμέρᾳ ἀφίκοντο, *the first day, they came,* iv. 8. 1. Τῷ δ' ἐπιόντι ἔτει, ᾧ ἦν Ὀλυμπιὰς, ᾗ τὸ στάδιον ἐνίκα Κροκίνας, *the following year, in which was the Olympic at which C. won the foot-race,* Hel. 2. 3. 1. Ὥρᾳ ἔτους Th.

b. PLACE (in prose, chiefly in *adverbs of place* which are properly datives, 380 c; and in stating some *town* or *Attic deme,* as the *place at which* an event occurred) : ταύτῃ and τῇδε [sc. χώρᾳ] *in this region, here,* iv. 5. 36, vii. 2. 13 ; ᾗπερ *where,* ii. 2. 21 ; κύκλῳ *in a circuit, around,* i. 5. 4 ; οἴκοι *at home,* i. 1. 10. Τὰ τρόπαια τά τε Μαραθῶνι καὶ Σαλαμῖνι καὶ Πλαταιαῖς, *the victories at M. and S. and P.,* Pl. Menex. 245 a. Κείμενον πέδῳ Αἰγισθον Eur. El. 763. Μίμνει ἀγρῷ λ. 188. Αἰθέρι ναίων B. 412.

c. This Dat., while *at* expresses its general idea, is often translated by *in, on,* &c.; or without a preposition.

d. To the LOCAL DATIVE may be referred the use of the Dat., chiefly poetic, to denote *persons among whom,* or *in whom any thing occurs* : Δύναμιν ἀνθρώποις ἔχειν, *to have power among men,* Eur. Bac. 310.

E. THE ACCUSATIVE.

470. The local idea upon which the uses of the Accusative are based (398), appears to be the idea of *that into which an action goes*.

a. Locally viewed, as the Gen. is the *Whence-Case,* the Dat. Residual the *Where-Case,* and the Dat. Objective the *Whither-Case,* so the Acc. is the *Whereinto-Case* (10).

b. Under the local form of conception, an action is conceived of as going *towards* or *to* an *indirect object,* but *into* a *direct object;* or, in familiar grammatical language, this is regarded as the *receiver* of the action. (c) In another view, the action passes into its *effect.* (d) It goes, in a special sense, into the *part affected.* And (e), in going *through* an object, it necessarily goes *into* successive parts. Hence,

471. Upon this general idea, are based (I.) the *Accusative of Direct Object,* (II.) the *Acc. of Effect,* (III.) the *Acc. of Specification* (specifying the particular *part, property, &c. affected*), and (IV.) the *Acc. of Extent* (denoting the *space, time, &c. through which* anything extends). (V.) In some uses, which may be referred to these heads or to its generic office (472 a), the Acc. has been termed *Adverbial.*

I., II. ACCUSATIVE OF DIRECT OBJECT AND EFFECT.

472. RULE XXI. The DIRECT OBJECT and the EFFECT of an action are put in the Accusative: as,

§ 474.   ACCUSATIVE OF DIRECT OBJECT, &C.   253

Λαβών Τισσαφέρνην, *taking T.*, i. 1. 2. Εἰρήνην ποιῆσαι, *to make peace*, Ages. 1. 7. Τρώπευε τελευτήν, i. 1. 1.

a. The term action is here used to denote *that which is signified by a verb;* since the verb, from its prevalent use, is grammatically regarded and treated as the word of action (cf. 435 a). And as *the direct* is more generic than *the indirect*, it results that

(RULE G.) An adjunct *simply considered as modifying a verb* is put in the Accusative. Hence,

b. Many verbs may take the Acc. as the *generic case*, which, according to preceding rules, govern the Gen. or Dat. as *more specific cases:* Προέχουσιν οἱ ἱππεῖς ἡμᾶς, *the cavalry surpass us* (406), iii. 2. 19. Σὲ αἰσθέσθαι, *to perceive you* (432), ii. 5. 4. Φίλους ὠφελεῖν, *to benefit friends* (453), Cyr. 1. 4. 25. Ἕκτορα εἶπε, *spake to H.* (452 a), M. 60. See e.

c. The same principle applies to circumstantial adjuncts (485 e). (d) This generic use of the Acc. is far more frequent in respect to *things* than *persons*, since the relations of the former are less varied and require less careful discrimination. For like reason, and also to distinguish the gender (181. 1), it is most frequent of all in the *neuter adjective* used substantively (478 a, 483 a). (e) It is sometimes chosen for distinction from a Gen. or Dat. modifying the same verb: as σοῦ θαυμάζω (432 f), but τούτου σε θαυμάζω (429 a), or τοῦτό σου θαυμάζω (443 b).

f. As many Greek verbs govern the Gen. or Dat. while the corresponding verbs in Eng. govern the Objective case; so many verbs governing the Acc. in Greek are translated into Eng. with a *preposition:* Ὄμνυμι θεοὺς καὶ θεάς, *I swear by gods and goddesses*, vi. 6. 17. Ἡμᾶς .. εὖ ποιῶν, *doing well* by *us*. Φυλαττόμενον .. ἡμᾶς, *guarding* against *us*, ii. 5. 3.

g. With verbs of motion, the *place where it ends* is commonly expressed with a preposition; but sometimes, chiefly in the poets, as a direct object: Ἀφίξεται τόπον ὑλώδη, *will come to a woody spot*, Ven. 10. 6. Σὲ πέμψαι φάος, *to send you into the light*, Eur. Alc. 456. Κνίση δ' οὐρανὸν ἷκε, *the savor ascended to heaven*, A. 317. (h) This construction applies less frequently to persons: Μνηστῆρας ἀφίκετο, *came to the suitors*, a. 332.

i. The poets sometimes even join an Acc. of the place with verbs of *standing, sitting*, or *lying* (as implying *occupation*): Ἕστηκε πέτραν, *stands on a rock*, Eur. Sup. 987. Τρίποδα καθίζων Φοῖβος Ib. 956.

j. This rule primarily applies only to the adjuncts of *verbs* (a). *Verbal adjectives* and *nouns*, however, sometimes take the Acc. by virtue of the included verb: Σὲ .. φύξιμος, *able to escape you*, Soph. Ant. 788; cf. Ἡ μὴ φύγω σε; Id. El. 1503. Τά τε μετέωρα φροντιστής, *a student of the heavens*, Pl. Apol. 18 b; cf. Τῶν μετεώρων φροντιστής Symp. 6. Cf. 477 a.

473. a. CAUSATIVES govern the Acc., together with the case of the included verb: as,

Μή μ' ἀναμνήσῃς κακῶν, *do not remind me of* [cause me to remember] *my woes* (432 c), Eur. Γάλα ὑμᾶς ἐπότισα, 'made you drink', 1 Cor. 3. 2.

b. The verbs δεῖ and χρή are sometimes construed by the poets as *causatives:* Σὲ δεῖ Προμηθέως, *you have need of* [it needs you of] *a Prometheus*, Æsch. Pr. 86 (414 b). Σὲ χρή .. αἰδοῦς, *you have need of modesty*, γ. 14. So χρεὼ ἔσται (as if a Fut. of χρή, 475 b) Φ. 322.

474. ATTRACTION. a. A word which is properly construed otherwise, sometimes becomes the direct object of a verb by *attraction*, especially in the poets. This sometimes results in *hypallage* (an interchange of construction) : Εἰ δέ μ' ὧδ' ἀεὶ λόγοις ἐξῆρχες [= μοι λόγους or λόγων], *if you had always begun your addresses to me thus*, Soph. El. 556.

b. A verb, of which the proper object or effect is a distinct sentence, often takes the subject (or some other prominent word) of that sentence in the Acc., by attraction : Ἤιδει αὐτὸν, ὅτι μέσον ἔχοι, *he knew* [him] *that he occupied the centre*, i. 8. 21. (c) Nor is this anticipation confined to the Acc.: Βαρβάρων ἐπεμελεῖτο, ὡς πολεμεῖν τε ἱκανοὶ εἴησαν, *he took care that the barbarians should be prepared for war*, i. 1. 5. See 402 a.

475. PERIPHRASIS. a. The place of a verb is often supplied by an *Acc. of the kindred noun* joined with such verbs as ποιέω (or more frequently ποιέομαι), ἄγω, ἔχω, τίθημι, &c.: Κῦρος ἐξέτασιν καὶ ἀριθμὸν τῶν Ἑλλήνων ἐποίησεν [= ἐξήτασε καὶ ἠρίθμησε τοὺς Ἕλληνας], *C. made a review and numbering of* [= reviewed and numbered] *the Greeks*, i. 2. 9.

b. These and like periphrases sometimes take an Acc. by virtue of the implied verb: Ἀνδράποδα ἁρπαγὴν ποιησάμενος [= ἁρπάσας], *having made seizure of slaves*, Th. 8. 62. Σῆμα τιθεὶς (= σημαίνων) . . νίκην, Θ. 171.

476. ELLIPSIS. 1. The *verb* which governs the Acc. is sometimes *omitted*; particularly,

a.) In EMPHATIC ADDRESS or EXCLAMATION: Οὗτος, ὦ σέ τοι [sc. λέγω or καλῶ], *You there, ho!* YOU *I mean*, Ar. Ἰώ, ἰώ, λιγείας μόρον ἀηδόνος [sc. ποθῶ], *oh, oh* [I long] *for the fate of the melodious nightingale!* Æsch.

b.) In ENTREATY: Μή, πρός σε θεῶν [sc. ἱκετεύω], τλῆς με προδοῦναι, *I beseech you by the gods, do not forsake me*, Eur. Alc. 275. Observe the hyperbaton, which is frequent in earnest entreaty.

c.) In PROHIBITION: Μὴ τριβὰς ἔτι [sc. ποιεῖτε], *No more delays!*

d.) In SWEARING: Οὐ, τόνδ' Ὄλυμπον [sc. ὀμνῦμι, 472 f], *No! by this Olympus!* Soph. Ant. 758. Οὐ, τὰν Διὸς ἀστραπάν Id. El. 1063. — By this ellipsis may be explained the use of the Acc. with the particles νή, ναί, and μά (of which the two first are *affirmative*, and the last, unless preceded by ναί, commonly *negative*), according to the following rule:

RULE H. ADVERBS OF SWEARING are followed by the Acc.:

Νὴ Δία, *Yes, by Jupiter!* i. 7. 9. Ναὶ τὼ Σιώ vi. 6. 34. Ἀλλὰ, μὰ τοὺς θεοὺς, οὐκ ἔγωγε αὐτοὺς διώξω, *but, by the gods, I will not pursue them*, i. 4. 8. Ναὶ μὰ Δία, *Yes, indeed!* v. 8. 6.

e.) Some familiar verbs: Ὁ τὸν κάνδυν [sc. ἔχων; in later writers], *he with the cloak*, Luc. D. C. 9.

2. The *Acc.* required by a transitive verb is sometimes *omitted*: cf. Διατελέσαι τὴν ὁδόν, *to finish the way*, iv. 5. 11, and πρὸς ὕδωρ βούλοιτο διατελέσαι i. 5. 7; Ἐλαύνοντος τὸν ἵππον, *riding his horse*, and Παρελαύνοντος, Cyr. 8. 3. 28, 29. Λύκιος ἦλασε i. 10. 15.

3. An elliptical or unusual construction of a verb and Acc. is sometimes employed, especially by the poets, for energy or brevity of expression: Φιλότητα . . τάμωμεν, *let us strike friendship* [a victim in pledge of friendship], Γ. 94 (cf. fœdus ferire). Cf. 474 s, 479.

Accusative of the Effect.

477. The EFFECT of a verb includes whatever the agent does or makes. Hence any verb may take an Acc. expressing or defining its action. The Acc. thus employed may be either (1) a *noun kindred, in its origin or signification, to the verb*;

§ 480.   DOUBLE ACCUSATIVE.   255

or (2) a *neuter adjective used substantively;* or (3) a *noun simply defining or characterizing the action.*

1. KINDRED NOUN (with this, the verb is often translated by a more general word): Εὐτύχησαν τοῦτο τὸ εὐτύχημα, *they had* [succeeded] *gained this success,* vi. 3. 6. Φυλακὰς φυλάξειν, *to keep guard,* ii. 6. 10. Ὡς ἀκίνδυνον βίον ζῶμεν, *how secure a life we live,* Eur. Med. 248.

   a. In like manner, an *adjective* sometimes takes an Acc. of the kindred noun : Σοφὸς ὢν τὴν ἐκείνων σοφίαν, *being wise with their wisdom,* Pl.

   b. It will be observed, that usually an adjective is joined with the Acc. of the kindred noun, and the whole phrase is an emphatic substitution for an adverb : Ὡς ἀκίνδυνον βίον ζῶμεν = Ὡς ἀκινδύνως ζῶμεν. This adjective not unfrequently occurs with an ellipsis of the noun : Τὸ Περσικὸν ὠρχεῖτο [sc. ὄρχημα], *he danced the Persian* [dance], vi. 1. 10. See 478.

478. 2. NEUTER ADJECTIVE (commonly translated by supplying a noun, or by an adverb) : Τοιαῦτα μὲν πεποίηκε, *such acts has he committed,* or *thus has he acted,* i. 6. 9. Λέγεις οὐκ ἀχάριστα, *you speak pleasantly enough,* ii. 1. 13. Κλέπτον βλέπει [sc. βλέμμα], *he looks* [a thievish look] *thievish,* Ar. Vesp. 900. Ἀνέκραγέ τε πολεμικόν vii. 3. 33.

   a. This construction of the *neuter adjective* is very extensive in its use, and often occurs where a *substantive* would be constructed differently (472 d) : Ὀσφραίνει τι; Τοῦ ψύχους, '*Do you smell any thing ?*' '*The cold.*' It is closely allied to the *adverbial use* of the neuter adjective (483).

479. 3. DEFINITIVE NOUN. Ἡ βουλὴ . . ἔβλεψε νᾶπυ, *the senate looked mustard,* Ar. Eq. 629. Μένεα πνείοντες, *breathing courage,* Γ. 8 ("breathing united force," *Milt.*). Ῥεῖτω γάλα, *let it flow milk,* Theoc.

Double Accusative.

480. 1. A word may take as many adjuncts, in the same or different cases, as the sense requires. Thus,

2. Many verbs govern TWO ACCUSATIVES, which may be,

   a.) The DIRECT OBJECT and the EFFECT, *in apposition* with each other (393) ; as with verbs of *making, appointing, choosing, esteeming, naming, dividing,* &c.: Βασιλέα σε ἐποίησαν, *they made you king,* vii. 7. 22. Στρατηγὸν δὲ αὐτὸν ἀπέδειξε, *he had appointed him general,* i. 1. 2. Πατέρα ἐμὲ ἐκαλεῖτε, *you called me father,* vii. 6. 38. Κῦρος τὸ στράτευμα κατένειμε δώδεκα μέρη, *C. divided the army into twelve parts* (393 d), Cyr. 7. 5. 13.

   b.) The DIRECT OBJECT and the EFFECT, *not in apposition ;* as with verbs of *doing, saying,* &c. (a neuter adj. often expressing the *effect,* 478 a) : Εἴ τίς τι ἀγαθὸν ἢ κακὸν ποιήσειεν αὐτόν, *if any one had done him any good or evil,* i. 9. 11. Ἀποτίσασθαι δίκην ἐχθρούς, *to wreak vengeance on his foes,* Eur. Heracl. 852. Ὅταν . . ἀλλήλους τὰ ἔσχατα λέγωσιν, *when they say the worst things of each other,* Mem. 2. 2. 9.

   c.) Two OBJECTS differently related, but which are both regarded as DIRECT ; as with verbs of *asking* and *requiring,* of *clothing* and *unclothing,* of *concealing* and *depriving,* of *persuading* and *teaching,* &c.: Κῦρον αἰτεῖν πλοῖα, *to ask vessels of Cyrus,* or *to ask Cyrus for vessels,* i. 3. 14. Τὸν δῆμον ὑμῶν χλαῖναν ἠμπισχον, *they clad your people in a mantle,* Ar. Lys. 1156. Μήτοι με κρύψῃς τοῦτο, *do not hide this from me,* Æsch. Pr. 625. Ἡμᾶς δὲ ἀποστερεῖ τὸν μισθόν, *but us he robs of our pay,* vii. 6. 9. Σὲ διδάσκειν τὴν στρατηγίαν, *to teach you the military art,* Mem. 3. 1. 5.

III. ACCUSATIVE OF SPECIFICATION.

481. RULE XXII. The Accusative is used in *specifying* to what PART, PROPERTY, &c., a word or expression applies :

The force of this Acc. is expressed in Eng. by *as to* (κατά, secundum), though other forms of translation are more frequent : Τὼ χεῖρε δεδεμένον, [bound as to the hands] *with his hands bound*, vi. 1. 8. Ποταμὸς, Κύδνος ὄνομα, εὖρος δύο πλέθρων, *a river, Cydnus by name, two plethra in breadth*, i. 2. 23. Πάντα κράτιστος, *best in every thing*, i. 9. 2 (cf. 416 b).

a. When a verb is in this way followed by two accusatives, the construction (which is most frequent in Epic poetry) may be often referred to partitive apposition : Τόνγε . . λίπ' ὀστέα θυμός Τ. 406. See 395 b.

b. An Acc. of specification sometimes introduces a sentence : Τὰ μὲν γὰρ παρελθόντα, ὑμεῖς μὲν Κῦρον ηὐξήσατε, *as to the past, you have exalted C.*, Cyr. 8. 6. 23. Τοὺς ἀγρονόμους τούτους, . . ὀνείδη φερέσθωσαν Pl. Leg.

IV. ACCUSATIVE OF EXTENT.

482. RULE XXIII. EXTENT OF TIME OR SPACE is put in the Accusative : as,

a. TIME : Ἔμεινεν ἡμέρας ἑπτά, mansit dies septem, *he remained* [through] *seven days*, i. 2. 6. Ἐδάκρυε πολὺν χρόνον, *he wept a long time*, i. 3. 2. Ἔπλεον ἡμέραν καὶ νύκτα vi. 1. 14. Εἴκοσιν ἔτη γεγονώς, viginti annos natus, *twenty years old*, Mem. 3. 6. 1. Ὅς τέθνηκε ταῦτα τρία ἔτη, ' these three years,' Lys. 109. 12. (b) So sometimes *repeated time*, as implying extent : Τὴν ὥρην ἐπαγινέειν σφι αἶγας, *to bring them goats at the proper hour* (each day), Hdt. 2. 2. (c) In stating a period ending with the present, an ordinal number is often used : Ἐνάτην ἡμέραν γεγαμημένην, *having been married* [the ninth day] *nine days*, iv. 5. 24.

d. SPACE : Ἐξελαύνει διὰ Φρυγίας σταθμὸν ἕνα, παρασάγγας ὀκτώ, *he advances through P. one day's-march, eight parasangs*, i. 2. 6. Μυρίας ἔμεγε κατὰ γῆς ὀργυιὰς γενέσθαι, *that I may be 10,000 fathoms under ground*, vii. 1. 30. Τὸ βέλος αὐτῶν καὶ διπλάσιον [sc. διάστημα] φέρεσθαι, *that their missile is sent double the distance*, iii. 3. 16.

e. In the simple designation of *time* and *place*, the GENITIVE commonly expresses the time and place *in which* (433), the DATIVE, *at which* (469), and the ACCUSATIVE, *through which;* the Gen. and Acc. differing like *in* and *through*, but both containing the idea of extension ; the Dat., like *at*, not containing this idea, but simply presenting the *when* or *where* as if a *point* in time or space. To some extent, however, the offices of the cases blend with each other ; and the more on account of their generic uses. See 485 c.

V. ADVERBIAL ACCUSATIVE.

483. RULE XXIV. The Accusative is often used ADVERBIALLY, to express *degree, manner, order,* &c.: as,

§ 485.   OF SPECIFICATION, EXTENT, &C.   VOCATIVE.   257

Τόνδε τὸν τρόπον, *in this way*, or *thus*, i. 1. 9. Κίρκην .. μιμήσομαι πάντας τρόπους, '*every way*,' Ar. Pl. 302. Τέλος δὲ εἶπε, [*at the end*] *finally he said*, ii. 3. 26. Ἀρχὴν μὴ πλουτῆσαι, '*in the first place*,' '*at all* (with negatives),' vii. 7. 28. Ἐμὴν χάριν, *for my sake*, Eur. Hec. 874.
 a. This rule applies especially to the *Acc. neut.* of *adjectives*, both sing. and plur.: Τὸ ἀρχαῖον, *formerly*, i. 1. 6. Τὰ μὲν .., τὰ δὲ, *partly* .., *partly*, iv. 1. 14. Μικρὸν ἐξέφυγε τὸ μὴ καταπετρωθῆναι i. 3. 2.
 b. An *Acc. neut. pronoun* is sometimes used to denote *that on account of which* something is done (especially an end in view) : Ταῦτ' ἐγὼ ἔσπευδον, [*on account of these things*] *therefore I made haste*, iv. 1. 21. Ἃ δ' ἦλθον, *what I came for*, Soph. O. C. 1291. Τί τὰ πυρὰ κατασβέσειαν, '*why*,' vi. 3. 25. (c) So with χρῆμα, *thing*, expressed : Τί χρῆμα κεῖσαι ; *why do you lie there ?* Eur. Heracl. 633.
 d. An adjective may be used adverbially in the *Acc. fem.*, with an ellipsis of ὁδόν *way*, or ὥραν *season* : Συντάττεσθαι τὴν ταχίστην, *to form* [in the quickest way] *immediately*, i. 3. 14. Τὴν πρώτην τρέχειν χρή, *we must first run*, Ar. Th. 662. So μακράν *a long way*, &c. .

F. THE VOCATIVE.

484. RULE XXV. The COMPELLATIVE of a sentence is put in the Vocative.

 a. The usual *sign of address*, in Greek, as in so many languages, is ὦ. It is commonly employed in prose, except (b) in abrupt or familiar address; and (c) is frequent in poetry. (d) It is commonly followed by the emphatic word in the address, unless (e) this has already preceded; and is (f) sometimes doubled for special emphasis.

 (a) Ὦ Φαλῖνε, θαυμάζω, *O Phalinus, I wonder*, ii. 1. 10. (b) Κλέαρχε καὶ Πρόξενε, .. οὐκ ἴστε ὅ τι ποιεῖτε, *Clearchus and Proxenus, you know not what you do*, i. 5. 16. (c) Ὦ Ἀχιλεῦ A. 74. (d) Ὦ θαυμασιώτατε ἄνθρωπε, *O most wonderful man*, iii. 1. 27. Ὦ κάκιστε ἀνθρώπων Ἀριαῖε ii. 5. 39. (e) Θαυμάσι' ὦ Κρίτων Pl. (f) Ὦ τέκνον ὦ γενναῖον Soph. Ph. 799.
 g. The term of respectful address to a company of men is ἄνδρες, with which may be likewise connected a more specific appellation : Ὁρᾶτε μὲν, ὦ ἄνδρες, *you see, gentlemen*, iii. 2. 4. Ἄνδρες στρατιῶται, i. 3. 3.

REMARKS ON THE CASES.

 485. It is important to distinguish not only the *specific offices* of the cases, but also their *generic* uses. Thus,
 a. The Nom. is the generic case for substantives independent of grammatical construction (401); while the Voc. is the specific case for *address*, and the other cases are also used in *exclamations* (429 e, f, 453, 476 a). — Hence the union of the Nom. and Voc. is not deemed a violation of the laws of agreement. An appositive with a Voc. is usually in the Nom.
 b. The Gen. is the generic case for the adjuncts of substantives, adjectives, and adverbs; and thus may even express *direct* or *indirect objects*, more specifically expressed by the Acc. or Dat. (435, 444).
 c. The Dat. is the generic case for a thing or circumstance simply viewed as an accompaniment (465).

d. The Acc. is the generic case for the adjuncts of verbs, and thus expresses much which is also expressed by the Dat. or Gen. (472 a, b). It often expresses as *simple object*, what is expressed by the Dat. as the *object of approach or influence*, or by the Gen. as the *point of departure* or the *cause :* 'Αφαιρεῖσθαι τοὺς ἐνοικοῦντας "Ελληνας τὴν γῆν, *to deprive the Greek inhabitants of their land* (480 c), i. 3. 4 ; Ὁ τοῖσιν ἀφείλετο νόστιμον ἦμαρ (463) ; Τῶν ἄλλων ἀφαιρούμενοι χρήματα, *taking money from others* (405), Mem. 1. 5. 3. Also, with a Gen. of the thing, or with a preposition (487), 'Αφαιροῦνται .. αὐτοὺς δὲ τῆς ὠφελείας, *deprive themselves of the benefit*, Ven. 6. 4 ; 'Απὸ τῆς ὀργῆς τὴν ἀκαλήφην ἀφελέσθαι, *to take away the nettle from his temper*, Ar. Vesp. 883 (with ἐκ, Ven. 12. 9). So the *Acc. of effect* may be supplied by another case : 'Ακίνδυνον βίον ζῶμεν (477. 1). Ζῶσαν ἀβλαβεῖ βίῳ, *living with unharmed life* (modal Dat., 467), Soph. El. 650.

e. If a *circumstance* is merely viewed as modifying a verb, it is put in the Acc.; if simply viewed as an accompaniment, in the Dat.; but if viewed as having some causal relation, in the Gen. These differences of view, and the prevalence of different analogies, have led to much variety of construction. Thus, (a) MANNER : Τὸν αὐτὸν τρόπον vi. 5. 6, Τῷ αὐτῷ τρόπῳ iv. 2. 13, *in the same manner* (483, 467). (β) MEASURE OF DIFFERENCE : Θυμοειδέστεροι δὲ πολύ, *much more spirited* (483), iv. 5. 36 ; Πολλῷ δὲ ὕστερον (468) ; Τοσοῦτον i. 8. 13 ; Τοσούτῳ i. 5. 9. (γ) RESPECT : Πλῆθος ὡς δισχίλιοι, *about 2,000 in number*, iv. 2. 2 ; Κῦδος ὄνομα (481) ; Πλήθει .. λειφθέντες, Θάψακος ὀνόματι (467 b) ; Νεώτατος .. γόνοιο (446 b ; cf. 413). (δ) PART AFFECTED : Τὼ χεῖρε δεδεμένον (481) ; Ψαύειν χειρός, *to take by the hand* (426 a). (ε) TIME : Τὸ λοιπόν ii. 2. 5, Τοῦ λοιποῦ (433 a), *afterwards ;* Τέλος, *at last* (483) ; Χρόνῳ ποτὲ εἶπεν, [with time] *at length he said*, Hel. 4. 1. 34. (ζ) CAUSE : Τοῦτ' ἐφικόμην, *on this account I came* (483 b), Soph. O. T. 1005 ; Τούτου σε .. ζηλῶ (429 a) ; Τῷ, *wherefore* (466).

486. The construction belonging to a word in its primary sense and form (a) is extensively retained in figurative or secondary senses, and in composition (414 c, 427, 432 g, &c.) ; but (b) is often changed to another more appropriate. Thus, (c) many verbs become transitive through a secondary sense, or through composition with a preposition, even though the preposition may not itself govern the Acc.: Κίνδυνον ἐξέστησαν, *they shrunk from danger*, Dem. 460. 2. In the same way, (d) other verbs from transitive become intransitive : Οἴκτῳ ἐνδῶτε, *you may* [give in] *yield to pity*, Th. 3. 37.

487. a. Most of the relations expressed by the cases may be more definitely expressed by the aid of *prepositions*. This definiteness was naturally more sought in prose than in poetry, and more in the later than in the earlier Greek.

b. The use of a preposition, or of one case rather than another, often avoids ambiguity, or distinguishes from other adjuncts, or gives emphasis, or favors the metre, or promotes euphony, &c.

III. USE OF THE NUMBERS, GENDERS, AND PERSONS.

488. NUMBERS. 1. The SINGULAR is sometimes used for the Plural in the Greek, as in other languages, to give to the expression greater *individuality* or *unity :* Τὸν Ἕλληνα, *the Greek* (= *the Greeks*), Hdt. 1. 69. Τὸν πολέμιον, *the enemy*, Th. 5. 9. Ἕρπει δάκρυον ὀμμάτων ἄπο, *the tear trickles from my eyes*, Soph.

§ 491.   NUMBERS AND GENDERS.   259

a. A *chorus*, from its unity and the action of the *coryphaeus* as its representative, is more frequently denoted by the singular (sometimes interchanged with the plural) : Ἡμῖν μὲν ἤδη πᾶν τετόξευται βέλος, μένω δέ, *every shaft has now been shot by us, and I wait*, Æsch. Eum. 676.

c. Some imperatives, used like interjections, are singular, though *more than one* are addressed : Ἄγε δή, ἀκούσατε, *Come now, hear*, Apol. 14.

d. In Greek, as in Eng., some nouns related individually to *more than one*, may be either singular or plural : Κράτιστοι . . τὴν ψυχήν, *strongest in heart*, Th. 2. 40 (or τὰς ψυχάς, *in their hearts;* cf. Mem. 4. 1. 2).

489. 2. The use of the PLURAL for the Singular is particularly frequent in Greek, especially in *abstract nouns*, in *neuter adjectives used substantively*, in the names of *things composed of distinct parts*, and in *vague expressions for persons or things*.

Ψύχη καὶ θάλπη καὶ πόνους φέρειν, *to endure cold, and heat, and labor* [in repeated instances], iii. 1. 23. Τὰ δεξιὰ τοῦ κέρατος, *the right* [portions] *of the wing*, i. 8. 4. Τὰ Συεννέσιος βασίλεια, *the palace* [royal buildings] *of Syennesis*, i. 2. 23. Ξὺν τοῖσδε τόξοις, *with this bow*.

b. An *individual* sometimes speaks of himself in the *plural* (with which the *sing.* may be combined), as if others were associated with him, especially in poetry ; and (c) a *woman* speaking of herself in this indefinite way, uses the *masculine* of the plur., as the generic gender (490 b) : (b) Αἰδούμεθα γὰρ τὰ λελεγμένα μοι, *I am ashamed of what I have said*, Eur. Hipp. 244. Ταῦτα πειρασόμεθα διηγήσασθαι, *these things we will endeavor to relate* (the author's plural), Cyr. 1. 1. 6. (c) Ἡμεῖς κτενοῦμεν, οἵπερ ἐξεφύσαμεν, *I will slay, who bore them*, Id. Med. 1241.

d. The *plural* for the *sing.* in neuter adjectives used substantively is especially frequent in their *appositive* use, in *adjective pronouns*, and in *verbals in* -τέος *and* -τός · Ὅταν μέν τι ἀγαθὸν ἔχωσι, παρακαλοῦσί με ἐπὶ ταῦτα, *whenever they have anything good, they invite me to* [these things] *this*, Symp. 4. 50. Πάτροκλος, ὅς σοι πατρὸς ἦν τὰ φίλτατα, P., *who was thy father's best-beloved*, Soph. Οὓς οὐ παραδοτέα τοῖς Ἀθηναίοις ἐστὶν Th.

490. GENDERS. 1. The MASCULINE is the generic gender for *persons* as such ; and hence is not only used when males are included, but even for *females only* in some indefinite or general forms of expression (489 c). See Mem. 2. 7. 2 s.

a. Where there are different forms for the two sexes, the masc. is also the form *common* to both : Οἱ καλοί, *the beautiful* (whether men or women).

b. When the masc. is applied to a woman, the expression becomes still more indefinite if the plural is used : Ξὺν οἷς τ' οὐ χρῆν μ' ὁμιλῶν, *consorting with those* [= her] *with whom I ought not*, Soph. O. T. 1184.

491. 2. The NEUTER is the generic gender for *objects of thought* considered without respect to personality (simply as *things*) ; and hence may even apply to persons so considered.

a. *Infinitives, clauses used substantively,* and *words or phrases spoken of as such,* are naturally regarded as neuter : Οὐ τὸ ζῆν περὶ πλείστου ποιητέον, ἀλλὰ τὸ εὖ ζῆν, *not* TO LIVE *is to be valued most highly, but* TO LIVE WELL, Pl. Crito 48 b. Δῆλον ἦν ὅτι ἐγγύς που βασιλεὺς ἦν, *it was evident that the king was somewhere near*, ii. 3. 6. Τὸ ΜΗ καὶ τὸ ΟΥ προτιθέμενα, *the* NOT *and the* NO *prefixed*, Pl. Soph. 257 b.

b. So clauses, phrases, or words, *not used substantively*, are accounted as *neuter* in any reference that may be made to them : Ἐνηδρεύσαμεν, ὅπερ ἡμᾶς καὶ ἀναπνεῦσαι ἐποίησε, *we ambushed, which enabled us to take breath,* iv. 1. 22. Φρόνιμός τε καὶ ἀγαθὸς ὁ ἄδικος, ὁ δὲ δίκαιος οὐδέτερα, *the unjust man is both wise and good, and the just man neither of these,* Pl.

c. As infinitives and clauses so often want strict singleness of conception and even of form, attributes and pronouns referring to them are often plural (489 a) : Ἀδύνατα ἦν ἐπιχειρεῖν, *it was impossible to undertake,* Th. 1. 125. Ἐβοήθησαν τῇ Λακεδαίμονι, καὶ ταῦτα [sc. ἐποίησαν] εἰδότες, *they aided L., and that* [they did] *knowing,* Ages. 1. 38.

AGREEMENT IN NUMBER, GENDER, &c.

492. The following table presents, for comparison, the general rules of agreement :

An APPOSITIVE ⎫ agrees ⎧   CASE.
An ADJECTIVE ⎬ with ⎨ GENDER, NUMBER, and CASE.
A PRONOUN   ⎪ its sub- ⎪ GENDER, NUMBER,   and PERSON.
A VERB   ⎭ ject in ⎩   NUMBER,   and PERSON.

a. These rules have the same general foundation, and to a great extent the same modifications and exceptions.

b. The agreement of an *attribute* with its subject is far less strict than that of an *epithet*; and the agreement of the *pronoun* is still less strict.

c. The use of the masculine form as feminine in adjectives and pronouns of three terminations (234 d, e) is not to be regarded as an exception to the laws of agreement.

493. RULE J. Agreement is commonly *according to form*, but often rather *according to sense.* See 70 p.

494. 1. The DUAL and PLURAL, as different modes of denoting *two* (178), very often agree with each other, or are interchanged :

Παῖδες δύο *two children,* τὼ παῖδε *the two children,* i. 1. 1. Τῶν ἀνδρῶν vi. 6. 29, τὼ ἀνδρε·30, τοὺς ἄνδρας, . . τούτων, . . τὼ ἄνδρε 31, &c. Προσέτρεχον δύο νεανίσκω, *two young men came running up,* iv. 3. 10. Ἐγελασάτην οὖν ἄμφω βλέψαντες εἰς ἀλλήλω, *both laughed, looking, &c.,* Pl.

a. In the old poetic language, a few passages occur in which the Dual appears to retain its application to more than two (186 g, 271 c) : Ξάνθε τε καὶ σύ, Πόδαργε, καὶ Αἴθων Λάμπε τε δῖε, νῦν μοι . . ἀποτίνετον Θ. 185.

495. 2. In COMPOUND CONSTRUCTION, both *syllepsis* and *zeugma* are common. See 68 f.

496. In SYLLEPSIS, (a) the combined number *may* be the *dual,* if only two are spoken of; but is otherwise the *plural* (with an exception in the verb, 569 b). — (b) For *persons of both sexes,* the combined gender is the *masculine* (490) ; (c) for *things,* or *persons and things,** it is the *neuter* (though it may

---

* Classed together as objects of thought (491). Zeugma, however, is here more common.

§ 499. COMPOUND CONSTRUCTION. SYNESIS. 261

be another gender, if all the subjects agree in that). — (d) The combined person, as in Lat. and Eng., is the *first*, if that is included in the subjects ; the *second*, if that is included and not the first ; but otherwise the *third*. Thus,

(a) Σωκράτει ὁμιλητὰ γενομένω Κριτίας τε καὶ Ἀλκιβιάδης πλεῖστα κακὰ τὴν πόλιν ἐποιησάτην, *C. and A., who had been associates of S., brought very many evils upon the city,* Mem. 1. 2. 12. Ἀπολελοίπασιν ἡμᾶς Ξενίας καὶ Πασίων, *X. and P. have left us,* i. 4. 8. (b) Εἶδε πατέρα τε καὶ μητέρα καὶ ἀδελφοὺς καὶ τὴν ἑαυτοῦ γυναῖκα αἰχμαλώτους γεγενημένους, *he saw father, and mother, and brothers, and his own wife taken captive,* Cyr. 3. 1. 6. (c) Πλίνθοι καὶ ξύλα καὶ κέραμος ἀτάκτως μὲν ἐρριμμένα οὐδὲν χρήσιμά ἐστιν, *bricks, wood, and tiles, thrown together in confusion, are of no use,* Mem. 3. 1. 7. (d) Ἐγὼ καὶ σφὼ.. πεπλήγμεθα, *I and you both are smitten,* Eur. Alc. 404. Οὐ σὺ μόνος οὐδὲ οἱ σοὶ φίλοι.. ἔσχετε Pl. Leg. 888 b.

e. Syllepsis is sometimes found, where the relation of the subjects to each other is disjunctive : Εἰ δέ κ' Ἄρης ἄρχωσι μάχης ἢ Φοῖβος Υ. 138.

497. In ZEUGMA, the agreement is sometimes with the *most prominent* substantive, sometimes with the *nearest :* as,

Βασιλεὺς δὲ καὶ οἱ σὺν αὐτῷ διώκων εἰσπίπτει, *the king and those with him, pursuing, attack,* i. 10. 1 (cf. διαρπάζουσι 2). Ἀπαλλαγέντες πολέμων καὶ κινδύνων καὶ ταραχῆς, εἰς ἣν.. καθέσταμεν, *delivered from the wars, perils, and trouble, in which we are now involved,* Isoc. 163 b.

a. Zeugma is the common construction of the adjective used as an epithet. It is least frequent in the pronoun.

b. In the construction of the verb, zeugma is especially frequent when the verb precedes or directly follows the first subject : Κύρου ἀποτέμνεται ἡ κεφαλὴ καὶ χεὶρ ἡ δεξιά, *the head of C. is cut off, and the right hand,* i. 10. 1. Σύ τε γὰρ Ἕλλην εἶ καὶ ἡμεῖς, *for you are a Greek, and we also.*

498. 3. SYNESIS. The agreement is sometimes with a *subject implied* in another word, especially a *Genitive* implied in an adjective (commonly a *possessive*) :

Τὸ σὸν [= σοῦ] μόνης δώρημα, tuum solius donum, [*your gift alone*] *the gift of you alone,* Soph. Tr. 775. Τἀμὰ [= ἐμοῦ] δυστήνου κακά, *the ills of wretched me,* Id. O. C. 344. Τῆς ἐμῆς ἐπεισόδου, ὃν μήτ' ὀκνεῖτε, *of my approach, whom do not fear,* Ib. 730. Τοῖς ἡμετέροις [= ἡμῶν] αὐτῶν φίλοις, *our own friends,* vii. 1. 29.

499. 4. Words may also agree *according to sense,*

a.) With *Collective Nouns,* and other words used collectively : Τὸ πλῆθος ἐψηφίσαντο, *the majority voted,* Th. 1. 125. See f.

b.) With the *plural used as singular* (especially ἡμεῖς for ἐγώ) ; and with the *singular used as plural,* or so modified as to render the idea plural : Πεπόνθαμεν, ἢ.. κενὴν κατέσχον ἐλπίδα, *we have suffered,* [yes I] *who cherished a vain hope,* Eur. Iph. A. 985 (see 489 b). Δημοσθένης μετὰ τῶν ξυστρατηγῶν.. σπένδονται, *D. with his colleagues makes a truce,* Th. 3. 109.

c.) Nouns *figuratively used to denote persons,* and others in which the *gender* does not follow the *sex :* Τόδ' ἔρνος.. κατθανόντα, *this scion* [son] *slain,* Eur. Bac. 1307. Μελέα ψυχά, ὃς.. ἤσθη Soph. Ὦ φίλτατ', ὦ περισσὰ τιμηθεὶς τέκνον, *O dearest, O most fondly cherished son,* Eur. Tro. 735.

d.) With a noun *forming a periphrasis* with a genitive or adjective : Φίλτατ' Αἰγίσθου βία, *dearest majesty of Æ.,* Æsch. Ch. 893. Ἐλθὼν.. βίη Ἡρακληείη, *the mighty Hercules coming,* Λ. 690.

e.) In general, with words for which others might have been used, or with which others are *implied* (as inhabitants with *places*, crews with *vessels*, troops with *commanders*, &c.) : Πᾶσα δὲ γέννα [= λαός] Φρυγῶν .. δώσων, *the whole race of the Phrygians, about to offer*, Eur. Tro. 531. Φεύγει .. ἐς Κέρκυραν, ὧν αὐτῶν εὐεργέτης, *he flees to Corcyra, being a benefactor of theirs*, Th. 1. 136. Πεντήκοντα τριήρεις .. οὐκ εἰδότες Ib. 110.

f. A double construction sometimes occurs, chiefly with intervening words. Thus, a collective noun may take a singular with reference to the united whole, and then a plural with reference to the individuals composing that whole ; &c.: Ἡ δὲ βουλὴ ἡσυχίαν εἶχεν, ὁρῶσα .., καὶ οὐκ ἀγνοοῦντες, *the senate remained quiet, seeing .., and not ignorant*, Hel. 2. 3. 55.

500. 5. ATTRACTION. An APPOSITIVE often attracts from the regular form of agreement:

Τὸ μέσον τῶν τειχῶν ἦσαν στάδιοι τρεῖς, *the distance between the walls was three stadia*, i. 4. 4. Ἐπὶ πύλαι· .. ἦσαν δὲ ταῦτα (for αὗται) δύο τείχη, *to the gates; now these were two walls*, i. 4. 4.

a. This construction occurs chiefly where the true subject is more remote or in a different clause ; and might be often referred to ellipsis or inversion : Ἑστίας, οὗ [sc. χωρίου] οὔτε ὁσιώτερον χωρίον, *the hearth, than which* [spot] *there is no holier spot*, Cyr. 7. 5. 56.

b. The attraction is sometimes *from an appositive* to its subject : Ἥλιος .. πάντων λαμπρότατος, *the sun, the brightest* [sc. *thing*] *of all things*, Mem. 4. 7. 8 (where the more regular λαμπρότατον, in the gender of the Gen. partitive, might also have been used). Indus fluminum maximus.

c. A word is sometimes attracted from its true subject by a noun governing the latter, chiefly in the poets : Τόδε νεῖκος ἀνδρῶν ξύναιμον [for ξυναίμων], *this* [kindred strife] *strife of kindred men*, Soph. Ant. 793.

501. 6. CHANGE OF NUMBER. The number is often changed for the sake of *individualizing* or *generalizing* the expression, especially when a *distributive* or *indefinite pronoun* is used :

Ἄλλους δ' ἐκέλευε λέγειν, διὰ τί ἕκαστος ἐπλήγη, *he bade the rest say, on what account each one had been struck*, v. 8. 12. Ἦν δέ τις τούτων τι παραβαίνει, ζημίαν αὐτοῖς ἐπέθεσαν, *if any one transgresses any of these laws, they have set a penalty for* [them] *him*, Cyr. 1. 2. 2.

a. When the subject is *divided* or *distributed*, the verb sometimes agrees with the *whole*, and sometimes with *one of the parts:* Ὅπῃ ἐδύναντο ἕκαστος, *where they each could*, iv. 2. 12. Ἀνεπαύοντο δὲ, ὅπου ἐτύγχανεν ἕκαστος, *they rested where each one happened to be*, iii. 1. 3.

502. 7. NEUTER ADJECTIVES are used in connection with words of different gender and number (commonly as appositives ; cf. 489 d, 491) :

Φοβερώτατον δ' ἐρημία, *solitude is the most terrible thing*, ii. 5. 9 (cf. Ξυμβουλὴ ἱερὸν χρῆμα Pl. Theag. 122 b). Ἔμοιγε φίλτατον πόλις, *to me the state is the dearest object*, Eur. Med. 329. Τί οὖν ταῦτά ἐστίν; *what then* [are these things] *is this?* ii. 1. 22.

503. 8. A CHANGE OF PERSON sometimes takes place,

a.) From the union of *direct* and *indirect* modes of speaking, especially in *quotation* : Ἄγοιτ' ἂν μάταιον ἀνδρ' ἐκποδών, ὃς .. κάκτανον, *take out of the way a senseless man, me, who have slain*, Soph. Ant. 1339.

b.) From a speaker's addressing a company, now as *one with them*, and now as *distinct from them:* Λανθάνειν ὑμᾶς εἰς ὅσην ταραχὴν ἡ πόλις ἡμῶν καθέστηκεν· ἐοίκατε γὰρ .., οἵτινες τεθύκαμεν Isoc. 141 d.

CHAPTER II.

SYNTAX OF THE ADJECTIVE AND PRONOUN.

I. AGREEMENT.

(See 492 s : for the union of the Dual and Plural, 494 ; for Compound Construction, 495 s ; for Synesis, 498 s ; for Attraction, 500 ; for change of Number and Person, 501 s.)

504. RULE XXVI. An ADJECTIVE agrees with its *subject* in *gender, number,* and *case.*

a. The word *adjective* is here used in its largest sense (173): Παράδεισος μέγας ἀγρίων θηρίων πλήρης, *a large park full of wild beasts,* i. 2. 7. Πόλιν οἰκουμένην, μεγάλην καὶ εὐδαίμονα, *an inhabited city, large and flourishing,* Ib. Τὼ παῖδε ἀμφοτέρω, *both the children,* i. 1. 1. Τοξότας Κρῆτας διακοσίους, 200 *Cretan archers,* i. 2. 9. Ταύτην τὴν πόλιν Ib. 24.

b. ANACOLUTHON. An adjective sometimes differs in case from its subject, through a *change of construction.* This occurs chiefly in the *participle,* as less closely joined to the subject, and especially with intervening words : Ἔδοξεν αὐτοῖς [= ἐψηφίσαντο] . ., ἐπικαλοῦντες, *it seemed best to them* [they voted], *alleging,* Th. 3. 36. Αἰδώς μ' ἔχει [= αἰδοῦμαι] ἐν τῷδε πότμῳ τυγχάνουσα, *I am ashamed, being in this state,* Eur. Hec. 970.

505. RULE XXVII. A PRONOUN agrees with its *subject* in *gender, number,* and *person.*

a. By the *subject of a pronoun* is meant the *substantive which it represents.* The rule, therefore, has respect either to *substantive pronouns,* or to *adjective pronouns used substantively:* Βασιλεὺς τῆς μὲν πρὸς ἑαυτὸν [i. e. βασιλέα] ἐπιβουλῆς οὐκ ᾐσθάνετο, *the king did not perceive the plot against himself,* i. 1. 8. Ἀπὸ τῆς ἀρχῆς, ἧς [sc. ἀρχῆς] αὐτὸν σατράπην ἐποίησε, *from the government, of which* [government] *he had made him satrap,* Ib. 2. Πρὸς τὸν ἀδελφὸν, ὡς ἐπιβουλεύοι αὐτῷ. Ὁ δὲ πείθεται, Ib. 3.

b. A pronoun, for the sake of perspicuity or emphasis, is often used in *anticipation or repetition of its subject,* or is *itself repeated:* Κεῖνο κάλλιον, τέκνον, ἰσότητα τιμᾶν, *that is nobler, my son, to honor equality,* Eur. Ph. 535. Βασιλέα . . δεῖ αὐτὸν ὀμόσαι ii. 4. 7. Οἶμαι δέ σοι . . ἔχειν ἂν ἐπιδεῖξαί σοι (Ec. 3. 16. (c) Intervening clauses often lead to this repetition.

d. Homer often uses the personal pron. οὗ, with its noun following : Ἥ μιν ἔγειρεν Ναυσικάαν εὔπεπλον, *who aroused* [her] *the well-clad N.*

II. OBSERVATIONS ON THE ADJECTIVE.

506. 1. ELLIPSIS. The subject of the adjective is often *omitted,* especially if it is a familiar word, or supplied by the context. The words most frequently omitted are,

a.) MASCULINE, ἀνήρ or ἄνθρωπος, *man,* χρόνος *time:* Συντάξαι δὲ ἕκαστον τοὺς ἑαυτοῦ [sc. ἄνδρας], *that each one should arrange his own* [men], i. 2. 15. Cf. ἐν τούτῳ i. 10. 6, and ἐν τούτῳ τῷ χρόνῳ iv. 2. 17.

b.) FEMININE, γυνή *woman,* γῆ or χώρα, *land,* ὁδός *way,* ἡμέρα *day,* χείρ *hand,* γνώμη *opinion,* μοῖρα *portion,* τέχνη *art,* ὥρα *season :* Ἡ Κιλίσσα [sc. γυνή] i. 2. 12. Τὴν λοιπήν [sc. ὁδόν] πορευσόμεθα, *we shall march the rest of the way*, iii. 4. 46. Ἐν δεξιᾷ [sc. χειρί], *on the right*, i. 5. 1.

c.) NEUTER, πρᾶγμα or χρῆμα, *affair, thing*, μέρος *part*, πλῆθος *collection, body*, στράτευμα *military force*, κέρας *wing of an army*, χωρίον *place, ground*, γένος or εἶδος, *class, sort, nature*: Τὰ ἡμέτερα, *our affairs*, i. 3. 9 (cf. τὰ Ὀδρυσῶν πράγματα vii. 2. 32). Τὸ κοινὸν [sc. πλῆθος], *the* [public body] *council*, v. 6. 27. Τὸ δὲ εὐώνυμον, *the left wing*, i. 2. 15.

d. In cases of familiar ellipsis, the adjective is commonly said to be used *substantively*.

e. The substantive omitted is sometimes contained or implied in another word: Ἀμυγδάλινον ἐκ τῶν πικρῶν [sc. ἀμυγδάλων], *of almonds (the bitter kind)*, iv. 4. 13. Γεωργεῖν τὸν μὲν πολλήν [sc. γῆν] Ar. Eccl. 592.

f. Many words which are commonly employed as substantives are properly adjectives, or may be used as such: Ὀρόντης δὲ Πέρσης ἀνήρ, *Orontes, a Persian man*, i. 6. 1. Ἕλλην ἐς οἶκον, *to a Greek home*, Eur. Ἑλλάδος γῆς Soph. These words, as substantives, are commonly appellations of persons or countries, ἀνήρ, γυνή, γῆ, &c., being understood.

507. 2. USE OF THE NEUTER. The substantive use of the neuter adjective exhibits itself in a variety of forms:

a. In the sing., a neuter adjective with the article has often the force of an *abstract*, or (b) *collective noun*; while (c) the plur. rather denotes *particulars* of the kind specified: (a) Τὸ δ' ἁπλοῦν καὶ τὸ ἀληθὲς ἐνόμιζε τὸ αὐτὸ τῷ ἡλιθίῳ εἶναι, *but* [the sincere and true thing] *sincerity and truth he thought to be the same with* [the foolish] *folly*, ii. 6. 22. (b) Τὸ Ἑλληνικὸν πᾶν, *the whole Greek race*, Hdt. 7. 139. Neuters in -ικόν are especially so used. (c) Τὰ.. Ἑλληνικά, *the Affairs of Greece*, Th. 1. 97.

d. Neuter adjectives (both with and without the article) are used with prepositions to form many *adverbial phrases*: Ἐν γε τῷ φανερῷ, *openly*, i. 3. 21. Διὰ ταχέων, *rapidly*, i. 5. 9. Διὰ παντός, *throughout*, vii. 8. 11.

e. The neuters πλεῖον or πλέον, μεῖον or ἔλαττον, ὅσον, μηδέν, and τί are sometimes used as indeclinable adjectives or substantives; and (f) from this, sometimes pass into an adverbial use: Μυριάδας πλεῖον ἢ δώδεκα, *myriads more than twelve in number*, v. 6. 9 (cf. Κρῆτες πλείους ἢ ἑξήκοντα iv. 8. 27). Ἄλυν, οὐ μεῖον δυοῖν σταδίοιν, *the H., not less than two stadia in breadth*, v. 6. 9. Ἀποκτείνουσι τῶν ἀνδρῶν οὐ μεῖον πεντακοσίους, non minus quingentos, vi. 4. 24. Πελτασταὶ ὅσον [= τοσοῦτοι ὅσοι] διακόσιοι, *targeteers as many as* (or *about*) 200, vii. 2. 20. Ἀπέχοι ὅσον παρασάγγην, 'about a parasang,' iv. 5. 10. Κρεῖσσω τῶν τὸ μηδέν, *better than those that are nothing*, Eur. Δοκούντων εἶναί τι, *appearing to be something*, Pl.

508. 3. An adjective (a) sometimes *agrees* with a substantive, instead of *governing* it in the *Genitive partitive;* and (b) often so *governs* it, instead of *agreeing* with it. In the latter construction, the adjective is either in the *same gender* with the substantive, or else in the *neuter* (commonly the *neut. sing.*).

(a) Περὶ μέσας νύκτας, *about midnight* [the middle of the night], i. 7. 1 (cf. ἐν μέσῳ νυκτῶν Cyr. 5. 3. 52). -Διὰ μέσης δὲ τῆς πόλεως, per urbem mediam, i. 2. 23. Τὸ ἄλλο στράτευμα, *the rest of the army*, Ib. 25.

(b) Μηδὲ τὰ σπουδαῖα τῶν πραγμάτων [for πράγματα], μηδὲ τοὺς εὖ φρονοῦντας τῶν ἀνθρώπων [for ἀνθρώπους], *neither virtuous actions* [the virtuous of actions], *nor wise men* [the wise of men], Isoc. 24 d. Λαμπρότητός τι, [something of distinction] *some distinction*, Th. 7. 69.

§ 511.   USE OF DEGREES.   265

509. 4. Adjectives are often used for *adverbs* and *adjuncts*, and, by the poets, even for *appositives*, and *dependent clauses*; to express,

a.) TIME: Προτέρα Κύρου . . ἀφίκετο, *she arrived before C.*, i. 2. 25.
b.) PLACE: Σκηνοῦμεν ὑπαίθριοι [= ὑπὸ τῆς αἰθρίας iv. 4. 14], *we encamp in the open air*, v. 5. 21. So demonstrative pronouns (especially ὅδε in poetry): Πολλὰ δ' ὁρῶ ταῦτα [= ταύτῃ, 469 b], πρόβατα, *I see here many sheep*, iii. 5. 9. Ὡς ἀνὴρ ὅδε, *as the man is here*, Soph. O. C. 32.
c.) MANNER: Συνεβάλλοντο . . πόλεις ἑκοῦσαι, *cities contributed willingly*, i. 1. 9. Εἵποντο ἄσμενοι, *sequebantur laeti*, vii. 2. 9.
d.) EFFECT: Εὔφημον [= ὥστε εὔφημον εἶναι] . . κοίμησον στόμα, *hush your mouth to silence* [so that it should be silent], Aesch. Ag. 1247.
e.) VARIOUS RELATIONS AND CIRCUMSTANCES: "Ἄλλοι δὲ ἦσαν ἑξακισχίλιοι ἱππεῖς, 'besides,' i. 7. 11. Ξύλιναι πεποιημέναι, *made of wood*, v. 2. 5. Πολύδακρυν ἀδονάν, *the joy of many tears*, Eur. El. 126.
f. This use of the adjective sometimes modifies the sense. Compare πρῶτον τοὺς θεοὺς ἐπαινῶ, *primum deos laudo*, *first* (before doing anything else), *I praise the gods*, with πρῶτος τοὺς θεοὺς ἐπαινῶ, *primus deos laudo*, *I first* (before any one else) *praise the gods*, and πρώτους τοὺς θεοὺς ἐπαινῶ, *primos deos laudo*, *I praise the* GODS *first* (before praising others).

III. USE OF THE DEGREES (256 s).

(The following observations apply both to ADJECTIVES and ADVERBS.)

510. 1. Words are compared not only by *inflection*, but also by the use of *adverbs* denoting *more* and *most*: as,

Μᾶλλον φίλον, *magis gratum*, *more agreeable*, Soph. Ph. 886. Τοὺς μάλιστα φίλους, *the most friendly*, vii. 8. 11. Ὦ πλεῖστα μῶροι Soph. El. 1326.
a. The two methods are sometimes united for emphasis or perspicuity (cf. 262 c, 512): Θανὼν δ' ἂν εἴη μᾶλλον εὐτυχέστερος ἢ ζῶν, *dying he would be happier, far happier than living*, Eur. Hec. 377.

511. 2. The COMPARATIVE is commonly construed with the particle ἤ, *than*, or with the *Genitive of distinction*; and the SUPERLATIVE, with the *Genitive partitive*: as,

Φιλοῦσα αὐτὸν μᾶλλον ἤ . . 'Ἀρταξέρξην, *loving him more than A.* (magis quam), i. 1. 4. Ἵππων θᾶττον (408). Ἀρίστοις Περσῶν (419 c).
a. The Comp. is sometimes construed with other particles, which commonly strengthen the expression through the union of two forms of construction (cf. 510 a): Κάλλιον . . πρὸ τοῦ φεύγειν, *more honorable than to flee* [honorable in preference to fleeing], Pl. Phaedo 99 a. Πέρα τοῦ δέοντος σοφώτεροι, *wiser than is proper* [wise beyond what is proper], Pl. Gorg.
b. The construction of the Gen. with the Comp. is often *elliptical*: Ἀθλιώτερόν ἐστι μὴ ὑγιοῦς σώματος μὴ ὑγιεῖ ψυχῇ συνοικεῖν, *it is more wretched to live with a diseased soul than* [to live with] *a diseased body*.
By a mixture of the two methods of construction which belong to the Comp., — (c) When a numeral, or other word of quantity, follows πλεῖον, μεῖον, or ἔλαττον, ἤ is sometimes omitted, though the Gen. is not employed (the Comp. being now construed as an *adverb*): Ἀποκτείνουσι τῶν ἀνδρῶν οὐ μεῖον πεντακοσίους, 'not less than 500' (507 e). (d) To the Gen. governed by the Comp., a specification is sometimes annexed with ἤ: Τί τοῦδ' ἂν εὕρημ' εὗρον εὐτυχέστερον, ἢ παῖδα γῆμαι βασιλέως; *what happier fortune could I have found than this*, [than] *to wed the daughter of a king?*

COMP. GR.   12

512. 3. The *positive* is sometimes added to the *superlative* for the sake of *emphasis*: as,

Ὦ κακῶν κάκιστε, *O vilest of the vile*, Soph. O. T. 334.

a. By *doubling* the *Pos.* or the *Sup.*, we obtain similar forms of expression, the one less and the other even more emphatic than the above: Δειλαία δειλαίων (419 c). Ἔσχατ' ἐσχάτων κακά, Soph. Ph. 65 (cf. 262 c).

b. From the doubling of the Sup., as in the last example, appears to have arisen the phrase ἐν τοῖς, which is used to modify the Sup.; and, as an adverbial expression, without change of gender: Ἐν τοῖς [sc. πρώτοις] πρῶτοι, [among the first also first] *among the very first*, Th. 1. 6.

c. The *numeral* εἷς is sometimes used with the Sup., to render the idea of *individuality* prominent: as, Δῶρα δὲ πλεῖστα . ., εἷς γε ὢν ἀνήρ, ἐλάμβανε, *he received the most presents*, [at least being one man] *for a single individual*, i. 9. 22. Urbem unam mihi amicissimam, *Cic.*

513. 4. Certain *special forms of comparison* deserve notice:

a.) The Comp., with a Gen. expressing *hope, duty, power of description*, &c.: Μεῖζον ἐλπίδος, majus spe, [greater than our hope] *above hope*, Æsch.

b.) The Comp. followed by ἢ κατά, or sometimes ἢ πρός: as, Μείζω, ἢ κατὰ δάκρυα [sc. ἐστιν], [greater than is in accordance with tears] *too great for tears*, Th. 7. 75. (c) Sometimes with an Inf. added : Μείζω . . ἢ κατ' ἐμὲ καὶ σὲ ἐξευρεῖν, *too great for me and you to discover*, Pl. Crat. 392 b.

d.) The Comp. followed by ἢ ὥστε (or ὡς) and the Inf. (sometimes another mode): Βραχύτερα ἠκόντιζον ἢ ὡς ἐξικνεῖσθαι, *they shot* [a shorter distance, than they must that they may reach] *too short a distance to reach*, iii. 3. 7. Μεῖζον ἢ ὥστε φέρειν Mem. 3. 5. 17. (e) We likewise find the Inf. without ὥστε or ὡς, and also the Pos. for the Comp.; Τὸ γὰρ νόσημα μεῖζον ἢ φέρειν, *for the malady is too great to bear*, Soph. Ταπεινὴ ὑμῶν ἡ διάνοια ἐγκαρτερεῖν, *your mind is too weak to persevere*, Th. 2. 61.

f.) The Comp. and Sup. (for the most part joined with αὐτός) followed by a *reflexive pronoun*, to denote the comparison of an object with itself; the Comp. representing it as above what it has been or would be in other circumstances, and the Sup. representing it as at its highest point : Ἀνδρειότερος γίγνεται αὐτὸς αὑτοῦ, *he becomes more manly* [himself than himself] *than he was before*, Pl. Rep. 411 c. Ἵν' αὐτὸς αὑτοῦ τυγχάνῃ βέλτιστος ὤν, *where he* [happens to be the best specimen of himself] *can do his best*, Eur. Ant. 20. (g) To the Comp. thus construed, a specification is sometimes annexed with ἤ (511 d): Αὐτοὶ ἑαυτῶν [θαρραλεώτεροί εἰσιν], ἐπειδὰν μάθωσιν, ἢ πρὶν μαθεῖν, *they have themselves more confidence when they have learned, than they had before learning*, Pl. Prot. 350 a.

h.) *Two comparatives connected by* ἤ, to denote that the one property exists in a higher degree than the other : Στρατηγοὶ πλείονες ἢ βελτίονες, *generals more numerous than good*, Ar. Ach. 1078.

i.) The omission of μᾶλλον before ἤ: Βούλομ' ἐγὼ λαὸν σόον ἔμμεναι [sc. μᾶλλον] ἢ ἀπολέσθαι, *I wish the people to be safe, rather than perish*, A. 117.

514. 5. The comparative and superlative are often used *without an express object of comparison*. In this case, the SUPERLATIVE *increases* the force of the positive, while the COMPARATIVE may either *increase* or *diminish* it, according to the object of comparison which is implied. Thus,

Ὦ θαυμασιώτατε ἄνθρωπε, *O most wonderful man*, iii. 1. 27. Τὴν ταχίστην, *immediately*, iii. 3. 16. Πλείω [sc. τοῦ δέοντος] λέλεκται, [more

§ 517.   USE OF THE ARTICLE.   267

than is proper] *too much has been said*, Eur. Alc. **Μακρότερον . . διηγήσασθαι**, *it is* [longer than it might be] *rather long to relate*, Pl. Conv. 203 a.

a. The Comp. and Sup., when used without direct comparison, are said to be used *absolutely;* otherwise, *relatively*. In the former use, the Comp. is often translated into Eng. by the simple Pos., or by the Pos. with *too* or *rather;* and the Sup. ("Sup. of Eminence"), by the Pos. with *very*.

515. 6. The degrees are more freely *interchanged* and *mixed*, than in English. It may be however remarked in general, that the use of a higher degree for a lower renders the discourse more emphatic, and the converse, less so. Thus,

Ταύτην **μάλιστα** [for πολὺ μᾶλλον] τῆς κόρης ἀσπάζεται, *this she chooses far rather than the virgin*, Eur. Iph. A. 1594. **Ἀξιολογώτατον** τῶν προγεγενημένων, [the most remarkable of those which had preceded it] *more remarkable than any which had preceded it*, Th. 1. 1. **Ὠκυμορώτατος** ἄλλων A. 505. Ἀνέκραγον πάντες ὡς ὀλίγας [sc. πληγὰς] παίσειεν, *they all cried out that he had given him too few blows*, v. 8. 12. Οἱ **πολλοί**, *the* [many] *most*, Mem. Πολλὰ ὦν οὐ **βέλτιον** αὐτοῖς στέρεσθαι, 'not well for them,' Cyr. (so, especially in negation or interrogation, ἄμεινον, χεῖρον, &c.).

IV. USE OF THE ARTICLE.

A. BROAD USE.

516. 1. EPIC. The article (**ὁ, ἡ, τό**) appears, in the Epic language, as a GENERAL DEFINITIVE, performing the office not only of an *article as usually understood*, but still more frequently of a *demonstrative, personal*, or *relative pronoun* (249 s): as,

Ὁ **γέρων**, *the old man*, A. 33 ; **Τά** τ' ἄποινα, *this ransom*, 20 ; **Τὸ** σὸν μένος, *that wrath of thine*, 207 ; Ὁ γὰρ ἦλθε, *for he came*, 12 ; **Τόν**, *whom*, 36.

NOTE. These uses are intimately allied, inasmuch as, — (a) The art., as usually understood, is simply a *less emphatic form* of the *demonstr. pron.;* and so, for the most part, the personal pron. of the 3 Pers. (but used as a substantive). Cf. "*That* man whom you see," and "*The* man whom you see"; "*Those* that love me," and "*Them* that love me," Prov. 8. 17, 21. (β) The demonstr. pron. used *connectively* becomes a *relative:* "Blessed are they *that* mourn."

In Epic poetry, — (a) The article, in its proper use as such, is commonly not expressed. The same omission prevails to a great extent in other kinds of elevated poetry. (b) When used as a personal pronoun, it is most frequently connected with the same particles as in Attic Greek (518) ; and is not unfrequently followed in the same sentence by the substantive to which it refers : Ἡ δ' ἕσπετο **Παλλάς**, *and she, Pallas, followed*, a. 125. Αἱ δ' ἐπέμυξαν **Ἀθηναίη** τε καὶ Ἥρη Δ. 20. Cf. 505 d. (c) As a demonstrative, it sometimes follows its substantive before a relative : Συνθεσιάων **τάων**, ἃς ἐπέτελλε, *those instructions which he gave*, E. 319. (d) The article when used as a personal or demonst. pron. has sometimes, from its position (518 f), or for the sake of the metre, the same form in the Nom. with the common relative : "Ὅς γὰρ δεύτατος ἦλθεν, *for he returned last*, a. 286.

517. 2. IONIC AND DORIC.* In the later Ion. and in the Dor. writers, this extended use of the article was, in great measure, retained. E. g. in Hdt., the relative has in the Nom. sing. and pl. the forms ὅς, ἥ, τό, οἵ, αἵ, τά · and has elsewhere the τ- forms of the article, except after prepositions which suffer elision, in the phrases of time, ἐν ᾧ, ἐξ οὗ, ἐς ὅ (or οὗ), μέχρι (or ἄχρι) οὗ, and in some doubtful readings.

518. 3. ATTIC. The use of the article as a *demonstrative and personal pronoun* remained in Attic Greek, (a) in connection with μέν and δέ; (b) in poetry with γάρ; and (c) as the subject of a verb, after καί, and :

(a) Ὁ δέ [sc. ἀδελφός] πείθεται, *and he* [the brother] *is persuaded*, i. 1. 3. Ἐκ δὲ τῶν (the common order after a prep.) μάλιστ' ἐγώ, *and of them I most*, Soph. O. C. 741. (b) Ὁ γὰρ μέγιστος αὐτοῖς τυγχάνει δορυξένων, *for he* [Phanoteus] *is the greatest of their allies*, Soph. El. 45.´ (c) Καὶ τὸν ἀποκρίνασθαι λέγεται, *and it is said that he answered*, Cyr. 4. 2. 13.

d. The article with μέν and δέ is commonly used for *contradistinction*, and we may translate ὁ μέν .., ὁ δέ, *this .., that, the one .., the other, one .., another*, &c. : Ὁ μὲν μαίνεται, ὁ δὲ σωφρονεῖ, *the one is mad, the other is rational*, Pl. Phædr. 244 a. Οἱ μὲν διώκοντες .., οἱ δ' ἁρπάζοντες, *these pursuing .., and those plundering*, i. 10. 4. Ἐν μὲν ἄρα τοῖς συμφωνοῦμεν, ἐν δὲ τοῖς οὔ, *in some things we agree, and in others not*, Pl. Phædr. 263 b.

e. Ὁ δέ, when used as a pronoun in the Nom. (even without ὁ μέν preceding), commonly denotes a different subject from that of the preceding sentence. The exceptions belong especially to the Epic and Ionic.

f. The *proclitics in the nominative* (ὁ, ἡ, οἱ, αἱ) require, from the very laws of accent, that the particle, in connection with which they are used, should follow them. If, therefore, it precedes, they become *orthotone*, or, in other words, take the forms which commonly belong to the *relative pronoun* (250). This change takes place with καί uniformly, and with δέ when it follows ἤ for ἔφη (45 u) : Καὶ ὅς ἐθαύμασε, *and he wondered*, i. 8. 16. Καὶ οἳ εἶπον vii. 6. 4. Ἣ δ' ὅς, ὁ Γλαύκων, *said he*, i. e. *Glauco*, Pl.

519. In its τ- *forms*, this use of the article also occurs, (a) before the *relatives* ὅς, ὅσος, and οἷος; (b) in some *special forms of expression*; and (c) sometimes, through *poetic imitation* of the earlier Greek; while (d) the *tragedians* even give these forms to the *relative pronoun* :

(a) Τοῦ δ' ἔστιν, *of that which is*, Pl. Phædo 92 d. Καὶ τὸν ὅς ἔφη, *he who said*, Lys. 167. 15. Προσήκει καὶ μισεῖν τοὺς οἱόσπερ οὗτος, *it is proper to hate* [those such as] *such men as this*, Dem. 613. 9.

(b) Πρὸ τοῦ (also written προτοῦ) *before this* ; τῷ *therefore* (cf. 466. 1) ; τό γε, followed by ὅτι · the article doubled with καί or ἤ : Πρὸ τοῦ παῖς ἦσθα, *you were once a child*, Pl. Alc. 109 e. Οἱ πρὸ τοῦ φίλοι, *former friends*, Eur. Med. 696. Τῷ . . σκεπτέον, *therefore we must consider*, Pl. Theæt. 179 d. Τό γε εὖ οἶδα, ὅτι . ., *this I well know, that . .*, Pl. Euthyd. 291 a. Εἰ τὸ καὶ τὸ ἐποίησεν ἄνθρωπος οὑτοσί, οὐκ ἂν ἀπέθανεν, *if this man had done this and that, he would not have died*, Dem. 308. 3.

(c) Τὸν . . φθίσον, *him destroy*, Soph. O. T. 200. Ταῖν μοι μέλεσθαι, *take care of these for me*, Ib. 1466.

(d) Τὸν θεόν, τὸν νῦν ψέγεις, *the god, whom you now blame*, Eur. Bac. 712. (e) This substitution of the τ- for the *aspirated* forms (250) in tragedy, scarce occurs, except to *avoid hiatus*, or *lengthen a short syllable*.

f. On the other hand, the *aspirated forms* are sometimes found with μέν and δέ for the τ- *forms* (518 a, d) : Πόλεις Ἑλληνίδας, ἃς μὲν ἀναιρῶν, εἰς ἃς δὲ τοὺς φυγάδας κατάγων, 'some destroying, and to others,' Dem. 248. 18. So, 'Ὁτὲ μέν . ., ὁτὲ δέ, *sometimes* . ., *at other times*, Th. 7. 27.

B. The Article Proper.

520. Rule XXVIII. The Article is prefixed to SUBSTANTIVES, to *mark* them as *definite*.

a. The Greek article, in its specific and later developed use *as an article proper*, corresponds in general to the definite article in our own and other modern languages. It is often, however, when used substantively, and sometimes when used adjectively, translated into Eng. by a *demonstrative pronoun* (527). With a *participle* following, it is most frequently translated by a *relative and verb*, preceded, if no antecedent is expressed, by a personal or demonstrative pronoun.

b. The article may be separated from its substantive by words modifying the latter (523 a), by particles which cannot stand first in the clause (as μέν, δέ, γάρ, γέ, τέ, δή), by the pronoun τὶς in Ionic, and sometimes by other words : Τῶν τις Περσέων, *one of the Persians*, Hdt. 1. 85.

521. A substantive used DEFINITELY is either *employed in its full extent, to denote that which is known*, or, if not employed in its full extent, *denotes a definite part*.

a. Compare, "Man is mortal," where *man* is used in its full extent of application, to denote every individual of a known race, and is therefore definite ; "The man whom we saw," where *man* is not used in its full extent of application, but is yet definite as denoting a particular and known individual ; and "If a man love me " (Jn. 14. 23), where *man* is indefinite, simply denoting any one of the race.

b. The article, according as it is joined with the substantive in the first or the second of these uses, is distinguished as the *generic* or the *limiting* article.

1. *Generic Article.*

522. A substantive *employed in its full extent, to denote that which is known*, may be,

a.) A substantive used *generically*, i. e. denoting *a whole class* or *kind ;* as ἡ γυνή, *woman* (for the whole sex), οἱ ἄνθρωποι, *men* (all men), οἱ Ἀθηναῖοι, *the Athenians* (the whole nation) : Ὁ ἄνθρωπος " ἄνθρωπος " ὠνομάσθη, *man was named* ἄνθρωπος Pl. See 533 c. (b) To this head may be referred substantives used *distributively*, which consequently take the article : Κῦρος ὑπισχνεῖται . . τρία ἡμιδαρεικὰ τοῦ μηνὸς τῷ στρατιώτῃ, *C. promises three half-darics* [the month to the soldier] *a month to each soldier*, i. 3. 21. If ἕκαστος, *each*, is expressed, the article may be used or omitted.

c.) A substantive expressing an *abstract* idea ; as ἡ ἀρετή, *virtue*.

d.) An *infinitive or clause used substantively*, or *a word spoken of as such* ; as Διὰ τὸ φοβεῖσθαι, *through fear*, v. 1. 13. Τὸ ὄνομα ὁ ἄνθρωπος Pl.

e.) The name of a *monadic object* (one which exists *singly* in nature, or is so regarded ; μοναδικός *single*) ; as ὁ ἥλιος, *the sun*, ἡ σελήνη, *the moon*.

f.) The name of an *art* or *science:* 'Η ἰατρικὴ καὶ ἡ χαλκευτικὴ καὶ ἡ τεκτονικὴ, *medicine and brasiery and carpentry*, Œc. 1. 1. See 533 c.

g.) A *proper name*, which has been before *mentioned* or *implied*, or which is *well known:* Διὰ Φρυγίας·.. τῆς Φρυγίας πόλιν, *through Phrygia;*
.. *a city of said* P., i. 2. 6, 7. Ὑπὲρ τῆς Ἑλλάδος, *in behalf of Greece*
(their native land), i. 3. 4. See 523 h, 533 a.

h. Proper names appear the rather to take the article, from their being so extensively, in their origin, either *adjectives used substantively* (506 f), or *common nouns used distinctively* (530). Thus, Ἡ Ἑλλάς [sc. γῆ], [the Greek land] *Greece*. (i) The adjective construction is frequent in the names of *rivers;* and is sometimes found in other names of places, where the gender and number permit : Ὁ Μαίανδρος ποταμός i. 2. 7.

2. Limiting Article.

523. I. A substantive *not employed in its full extent* may be rendered *definite* by a *limiting word, phrase*, or *clause*.

a. (ORDER OF DESCRIPTION.) A limiting word or phrase is usually placed, either (1) *between the article and its substantive*, or (2) *after the substantive with the article repeated*, or (3) as in the *second* order, but with *the article omitted before the substantive;* while these different positions may be repeated or combined : Ὁ ἀγαθὸς ἀνήρ, or ὁ ἀνὴρ ὁ ἀγαθός, or ἀνὴρ ὁ ἀγαθός, *the good man*. Τὸ βασίλειον σημεῖον (443 c). Τοὺς μὲν γὰρ κύνας τοὺς χαλεπούς, *savage dogs*, v. 8. 24. Σταθμῶν τῶν ἐγγυτάτω ii. 2. 11. Τὸ τῆς τοῦ ξαίνοντος τέχνης ἔργον, *the work of the carder's art*, Pl. Pol. 281 a. Τὰς μεγάλας ἡδονὰς καὶ τὰ ἀγαθὰ τὰ μεγάλα Cyr. 3. 3. 8.

b. (ORDER OF STATEMENT.) On the other hand, words and phrases not belonging to the definition or description of the substantive, but to *that which is said about it in the sentence*, regularly either (4) *precede the article*, or (5) *follow the substantive without a repetition of the article :* Ἀγαθὸς ὁ ἀνήρ or ὁ ἀνὴρ ἀγαθός [sc. ἐστιν], *the man is good*. Ὅτι κενὸς ὁ φόβος εἴη, καὶ οἱ ἄρχοντες σῶοι, *that the fear was groundless, and the generals safe*, ii. 2. 21. Ψιλὴν ἔχων τὴν κεφαλήν, *having the head bare*, i. 8. 6. Ἐν τῇ ἀγορᾷ μέσῃ, *in the midst of the forum*, Dem. 848. 13 (508 a ; but Τὸ μέσον στῖφος, *the centre division*, i. 8. 13). Τὸ κέρας ἑκάτερον vii. 1. 23.

c. A *modifying Genitive* has, however, much freedom of position, and other adjuncts are less strictly bound by these rules than adjectives or appositives. A *limiting* Genitive not only takes the first three orders according to the rule, but often the *5th order*, and sometimes (chiefly for emphasis) the *4th;* while the *Gen. partitive*, which regularly takes the *order of statement*, sometimes takes an *order of description :* Τοῦ δὲ κύκλου ἡ περίοδος, *the length of the circuit*, iii. 4. 11. Τῇ τελευτῇ τοῦ βίου i. 9. 30. Τοῖς Ἑλλήνων πλουσιωτάτοις Th. 1. 25. (d) A prepositional adjunct takes the *5th order* more freely after a verbal, or when another modifier has taken the place between the article and substantive : Ἡ ξυγκομιδὴ ἐκ τῶν ἀγρῶν ἐς τὸ ἄστυ, *the crowding from the country into the city*, Th. 2. 52.

e. Some modifiers may be placed in either of the two classes (b), according to the view which is taken of them : Πᾶσαν τὴν ὁδόν, *all the way*, i. 5. 9 (or τὴν πᾶσαν ὁδόν, *the whole way ;* without the art., πᾶσα μὲν ὁδός, *every way*, ii. 5. 9). Οἱ πάντες ἄνθρωποι, Πάντες οἱ ἄνθρωποι, *all men*, v. 6. 7 ; Œc. 17. 3 (πάντας ἀνθρώπους Cyr. 7. 5. 52). So ἅπας, σύμπας, ὅλος *whole*.

§ 526. LIMITING ARTICLE. 271

f. The use of the article with some adjectives, in representing a *part* as definite, should be observed : 'Αμφικράτης καὶ ἄλλοι, *A. and others*, iv. 2. 17. Ἐπορεύθησαν, ᾖ οἱ ἄλλοι, 'the others,' 'the rest,' Ib. 10. Ἄλλο δὲ στράτευμα, *and another army*, i. 1. 9. Τὸ ἄλλο στράτευμα, *the rest of the army*, i. 2. 25. Πολὺ τοῦ στρατεύματος, 'much of,' iv. 1. 11. Τὸ μὲν δὴ πολὺ τοῦ Ἑλληνικοῦ, 'the greater part,' i. 4. 13. Πολλοί, *many*, iv. 6. 26. Οἱ πολλοί (515). So often with *superlatives* and *ordinals*. See 419.

g. A *clause limiting a substantive* commonly begins with the relative pronoun ; and is usually placed according to *order 5th*, by which the immediate junction of the article proper and the relative (originally one, 249 s) is avoided. If it precedes the substantive, it commonly excludes the article. Thus, Ἀπὸ τῆς ἀρχῆς, ἧς αὐτὸν σατράπην ἐποίησε (505 a). Οὗτοι, οὓς ὁρᾶτε, βάρβαροι, *these barbarians whom you see* (524 b), i. 5. 16.

h. A proper name followed by an article in agreement with it, is rarely preceded by another, except with special demonstrative force.

i. In the *third order*, the substantive is sometimes *first introduced as indefinite*, and *then defined ;* and this subsequent definition sometimes respects simply the *kind* or *class*. Πολλοὶ δὲ στρουθοὶ οἱ μεγάλοι, *and many struthi, the large ones*, i. e. *ostriches*, i. 5. 2.

j. When the substantive is preceded or followed by *successive modifications*, the article is sometimes *repeated* with each : Τά τε τείχη τὰ ἑαυτῶν τὰ μακρὰ ἀπετέλεσαν, *they completed their own long walls*, Th. 1. 108.

k. A modification is sometimes divided between two positions (oftenest the 1*st* and 5*th*) : Τοῖς φήνασι θεοῖς τά τε ὀνείρατα, *to the gods who had sent the dream*, iv. 3. 13. Περσῶν τοὺς ἀρίστους τῶν περὶ αὐτὸν ἑπτά i. 6. 4.

524. REMARKS. 1. It is common to employ the article even when the substantive is rendered definite (a) by a *possessive* or (b) *demonstrative pronoun :*

(a) Ὁ ἐμὸς πατήρ, *my father*, i. 6. 6. Τῷ νόμῳ τῷ ὑμετέρῳ vii. 3. 39.

(b) The pronouns **οὗτος** and **ὅδε**, as themselves beginning with the article (252), do not take it immediately before them, and **ἐκεῖνος** follows their analogy. These pronouns are therefore placed according to 523 b, except when separated from the article by another modifier : Ταύτας τὰς πόλεις, *these cities*, Τόνδε τὸν τρόπον, Ἐκείνης τῆς ἡμέρας, Τὸν ἄνδρα τοῦτον, i. 1. 8, 9 ; 7. 18 ; 6. 9. Ἡ στενὴ αὕτη ὁδός, *this narrow way*, iv. 2. 6.

c. In prose, when the article is *omitted* with a demonstrative pronoun and a common noun (except as in 533, and in some special *deictic* uses, 543 s), the *pronoun* is regularly employed as a *subject*, and the *noun* as an *attribute :* Ἔστι μὲν γὰρ πενία αὕτη σαφής, *this is manifest poverty*, Œc. 8.

525. 2. Upon the same principle, the article is prefixed to words and phrases, which are joined with a *proper name* or a *personal pronoun* to give *definiteness* or *emphatic distinction :*

Τὸν βασιλεύοντα Ἀρταξέρξην, [the reigning Artaxerxes] *Artaxerxes the king*, i. 1. 4. Μένων ὁ Θετταλός i. 2. 6. Σὺ . . ὁ πρεσβύτατος Cyr. 4. 5.

a. If, on the other hand, *no distinction is designed*, the article is *omitted :* Ξενοφῶν Ἀθηναῖος, X., *an Athenian*, i. 8. 15. Παταγύας ἀνὴρ Πέρσης Ib. 1.

526. 3. An *adverb preceded by an article* has often the force of an *adjective*. This construction may be explained by supposing the ellipsis of a participle, commonly ὤν or γενόμενος :

Τὸν νῦν χρόνον, *the* [now time] *present time*, vi. 6. 13 (Τὸν ὄντα νῦν χρόνον Eur. Ion 1349). Τοῦ τότε βασιλέως, *the then king*, Cyr. 4. 6. 3.

a. So a *prep. with its case:* Τοῦ ἐν Δελφοῖς χρηστηρίου, *the Delphic oracle,* Cyr. 7. 3. 15. Ἀρμενία.. ἡ πρὸς ἑσπέραν, *Western Armenia,* iv. 4. 4.

b. This adjective may again, like any other adjective, be used either *substantively* or *adverbially* (527 s, 529).

527. 4. The substantive which is modified is often omitted, as a familiar word or supplied by the context; and in the former case, the article is commonly regarded as *used substantively with the word or phrase following* (506 d, 520 a):

Τῶν παρὰ βασιλέως [sc. ἀνδρῶν], *of those from the king,* i. 1. 5. Τὸ πέραν τοῦ ποταμοῦ, *the opposite side of the river,* iii. 5. 2. Ὁ μηδὲν ὤν (507 c).

a. The phrases οἱ ἀμφί and οἱ περί, followed by the name of a person, commonly include the *person himself,* with his attendants or associates; and sometimes, by a species of vague periphrasis, denote little more than the *person merely:* Οἱ δὲ ἀμφὶ Τισσαφέρνην, [those about T.] *T. and those with him,* iii. 5. 1 (cf. Τισσαφέρνης καὶ οἱ σὺν αὐτῷ Ib. 3). Οἱ περὶ Κέκροπα [i. e. Κέκροψ] Mem. 3. 5. 10. So Οἱ μετὰ Ἀριαίου i. 10. 1.

528. 5. When the *neuter article* is used *substantively* with a word or phrase following, (a) the precise idea (as, in English, of *'thing'* or *'things'*) must be determined from the connection, and (b) not unfrequently the whole expression may be regarded as a *periphrasis for an included substantive:*

(a) Τὰ τοῦ γήρως, *the evils of old age,* Apol. 6. Τὰ περὶ Προξένου, *the fate of Proxenus,* ii. 5. 37. Τὰ παρ' ἐμοὶ ἑλέσθαι ἀντὶ τῶν οἴκοι, *to prefer remaining with me to returning home,* i. 7. 4. Cf. 507.

(b) Τὸ τῆς τύχης, *the course of fortune,* = ἡ τύχη, *fortune,* Eur. Alc. 785. Ἐπῄνει τὰ βασιλέως, *extolled the king,* Hel. 7. 1. 38.

529. 6. The NEUTER ACCUSATIVE of the article is often used in forming *adverbial phrases,* in connection with,

a.) Adjectives (483 a): Τὸ πρῶτον, *at first,* i. Τὸ πρότερον, *before,* iv.

b.) Adverbs (526 b): Τὸ πάλαι [sc. ὄν], [as to that which was of old] *anciently,* Pl. Τὸ πρόσθεν, *before,* i. 10. 10. Τοὔμπαλιν, *back,* vi. 6. 38.

c.) Prepositions followed by their cases: Τὸ ἀπὸ τοῦδε, [as to that after this] *henceforth,* Cyr. 5. 1. 6. Τὸ πρὸς ἑσπέραν, *to the west,* vi. 4. 4.

530. II. A substantive *not employed in its full extent* may also be definite (a) from *previous mention, mutual understanding, general notoriety,* or *emphatic distinction;* (b) from *contrast;* and (c), in general, from the *connection* in which it is employed: as,

(a) Θορύβου ἤκουσε.., καὶ ἤρετο τίς ὁ θόρυβος εἴη, *he heard a noise, and inquired what* THE NOISE *was,* i. 8. 16. Τὸν ἄνδρα ὁρῶ, *I see* THE MAN, i. 8. 26. Ἀνακαλοῦντες τὸν προδότην, *exclaiming,* 'the traitor!' vi. 6. 7.

(b) Contrast may give a degree of definiteness to expressions which are otherwise quite indefinite; and may even lead to the employment of the article with the *indefinite pronoun* τις: Ἵππους.., τοὺς μέν τινας παρ' ἐμοί, τοὺς δὲ τῷ Κλεάρχῳ καταλελειμμένους, *horses, some with me, and others left by C.,* iii. 3. 19. So with numerals denoting part of a whole: Τὰ δύο μέρη, [the two parts from three, 242 d] *two thirds,* Th. Cf. 518 a.

(c) Ἐπειδὴ δὲ ἐτελεύτησε Δαρεῖος, καὶ κατέστη εἰς τὴν βασιλείαν Ἀρταξέρξης, 'had succeeded to the throne [sc. of Persia],' i. 1. 3.

d. A substantive is often definite as denoting that which is *natural, usual, necessary, proper*, &c., in the circumstances : Ἐν μὲν τῇ ἀριστερᾷ χειρὶ τὸ δόρυ ἔχων, ἐν δὲ τῇ δεξιᾷ βακτηρίαν, (Clearchus) *having in the left hand his spear, and in the right a staff* (the *spear* a part of his regular equipment, but not the *staff*), ii. 3. 11. See e.

e. With substantives which are rendered definite by the connection, a *possessive* or *genitive pronoun* is often implied in the article : Τισσαφέρνης διαβάλλει τὸν Κῦρον πρὸς τὸν ἀδελφόν, *T. accuses C. to* [the] *his brother*, i.

531. From a reference to something which precedes or is mutually understood, or for emphasis, the article may be even joined, (a) with an *interrogative pronoun*, (b) a *personal pronoun*, (c) a *pronoun of quality or quantity* :

(a) Ἄλλα . . θέλω σοι . . διηγήσασθαι . . . Τὰ ποῖα; "*I will relate to you other things.*" "[The what ?] *What are they?*" Œc. 10. 1. (b) Τὸν ἐμέ, *the me*, i. e. *me, of whom you speak*, Pl. Τὸν ἑαυτόν, [the himself] *his great self*, Id. (c) Τὸ τοιοῦτον ὄναρ, *such a dream as this*, iii. 1. 13.

d. The article is often joined with a *round number* used for comparison or general statement (especially with ἀμφί) : Εἰ μὲν τῶν μυρίων ἐλπίδων μία τις ὑμῖν ἐστι, *if you have one chance in* [the] *ten thousand*, ii. 1. 19. Πελτασταὶ δὲ ἀμφὶ τοὺς δισχιλίους, *targeteers about* [the] *two thousand*, i.

532. OBSERVATIONS. 1. The article is sometimes found without a substantive, through *anacolūthon* or *aposiopēsis* :

Ἡ τῶν ἄλλων Ἑλλήνων ——, εἴτε χρὴ κακίαν εἴτ᾿ ἄγνοιαν . . εἰπεῖν, *the* ——, *whether I should say cowardice or folly of the other Greeks*, Dem.

533. 2. OMISSION OF THE ARTICLE. With substantives which will be readily recognised as definite *without the article*, it is often *omitted* ; particularly with

a.) *Proper names*, and *other names resembling these* from their being *familiar titles of persons* or otherwise *specially appropriated* (522) : Πρὸς Κῦρον, Πρὸς τὸν Κῦρον, Ὁ δὲ Κῦρος, Κῦρος δέ, i. 1. 6, 7, 10 ; 2. 5. Ἅμα ἡλίῳ δύνοντι, Ἅμα τῷ ἡλίῳ δυομένῳ, ii. 2. 13, 16. (b) Hence βασιλεύς, in its familiar application to the *King of Persia*, commonly wants the article.

c.) *Abstract nouns, names of arts and sciences*, and *nouns used generically* (522) : Εὖρος . ., ὕψος δέ, Τὸ εὖρος . ., καὶ τὸ ὕψος, *in breadth . ., and in height*, ii. 4. 12 ; iii. 4. 10. Γεωργίαν τε καὶ τὴν πολεμικὴν τέχνην Œc. 4. 4. Θεοσεβέστατον . . ζώων ἄνθρωπος Pl. Leg. 902 b. Distributively, Ἕνα ἀπὸ φυλῆς, *one from* [a tribe] *each tribe*, Hel. 2. 4. 24.

d.) Familiar designations of *place, time*, and *related persons or objects* ; Εἰς τὸ ἄστυ, Εἰς ἄστυ, *into the city* ["into town"], Hel. 2. 4. 1, 7. Ἕως (ἑσπέρα) ἐγένετο, *it was morning* (evening), ii. 4. 24 ; iv. 7. 27. So with πόλις *city*, ἀγρός *country*, γῆ *land*, οἶκος *house*, νύξ *night*, πατήρ *father*, γυνή *wife*, παῖς *child*, σῶμα *body*, πούς *foot*, δόρυ *spear*, ἀσπίς *shield*, &c.

e.) *Ordinals* and *Superlatives* (523 f) : Καὶ τρίτον ἔτος τῷ πολέμῳ ἐτελεύτα, 'the third year,' Th. Εἰς Ἰσσοὺς, τῆς Κιλικίας ἐσχάτην πόλιν i. 4. 1.

f. The article is more freely omitted, as in Eng., when two or more nouns are coupled together ; and also after a preposition or governing adverb : Ἡλίου τε καὶ σελήνης καὶ ἄστρων καὶ γῆς καὶ αἰθέρος, *of sun, moon, stars, &c.*, Pl. Crat. 408 d. Θαυμάσιαι τὸ κάλλος καὶ τὸ μέγεθος, *wonderful for beauty and size*, ii. 3. 15. Ὑπὸ κάλλους καὶ μεγέθους ἀδιήγητον Cyr.

534. 3. The *subject of the sentence*, from its distinctive prominence, has the article more frequently than an adjunct; while a *predicate appositive* commonly wants it, as simply denoting that the subject is one (or more) of a class. Hence the article is often useful in distinguishing the *subject*, and sometimes appears to be used especially for this purpose : Μὴ φυγὴ εἴη ἡ **ἄφοδος**, *lest the departure should be a flight*, vii. 8. 16. Ἐμπόριον δ' ἦν τὸ χωρίον i. 4. 6. Τὰ **δὶς** πέντε δέκα ἐστίν, *twice five is ten*.

4. When words or phrases are coupled by conjunctions, they are more closely united in conception, if only a single article is used ; less closely, if the article is repeated : Τοὺς πιστοὺς καὶ εὔνους καὶ βεβαίους, *the faithful, friendly, and steadfast*, i. 9. 30. Τῶν Ἑλλήνων καὶ τῶν βαρβάρων, *of the Greeks and of the barbarians*, i. 2. 14.

V. OBSERVATIONS ON THE PRONOUNS.

535. a. Of the observations which follow, many apply equally to PRONOUNS and ADVERBS of the *same classes*.

b. In the use of pronouns, especially those first presented below, it is important to distinguish between the *stronger* and *weaker* forms of expression ; that is, between those forms which are *more distinctive, emphatic*, or *prominent*, and those which are *less* so.

A. Personal, Reflexive, and Possessive (27 s).

536. 1. The PERSONAL PRONOUNS (a) are commonly omitted in the Nom. (as implied in the affixes of the verb, 271), except for emphasis or distinctness of reference. (b) If needed in the Nom. of the 3d Pers., they are supplied by the *article*, or, as a stronger form, by the *demonstrative pronoun*. (c) They are also omitted in the other cases, when understood from the connection, more freely than in English. (d) In the *weaker form* for these cases, they are *enclitic* in the 1st and 2d Persons sing., and are commonly supplied in the 3d Person by αὐτός; while (e), in the *stronger form*, they are *orthotone* throughout, and are supplied in the 3d Pers. by the *article* or still stronger *demonstrative*. Thus,

Ἅπαντα σῶα ἀπέδωκά σοι, ἐπεὶ καὶ σὺ ἐμοὶ ἀπέδειξας τὸν ἄνδρα, *I gave you back everything safe, when you also had shown to me the man*, v. 8. 7. Ὁ δὲ ἐμπιπλὰς ἁπάντων τὴν γνώμην ἀπέπεμπε [sc. αὐτούς], *and he dismissed them, satisfying the wish of all*, i. 7. 8. Οὔτε σὺ ἐκείνας φιλεῖς, οὔτε ἐκεῖναι σέ, *neither do you love them, nor they you*, Mem. 2. 7. 9. "Ἡς" οὖν θανεῖται, *she then will die*, Soph. Ant. 751. Ἐγὼ μὲν, ὦ ἄνδρες, ἤδη ὑμᾶς ἐπαινῶ· ὅπως δὲ καὶ ὑμεῖς ἐμὲ ἐπαινέσετε, ἐμοὶ μελήσει, ἢ μηκέτι με Κῦρον νομίζετε i. 4. 16. Τούτῳ συγγενόμενος ὁ Κῦρος, ἠγάσθη τε **αὐτόν** i. 1. 9.

537. 2. In REFLEX REFERENCE, the *distinctive* and *emphatic* forms are those of the so-called *reflexives* (244); while the forms of the common personal pronouns and of αὐτός are also used as *weaker* forms, chiefly when the reference is both *indirect* and *unemphatic*.

'Εμαυτῷ γε δοκῶ συνειδέναι, *to* myself *at least I seem to be conscious*, vii. 6. 11. Αἰσχύνεσθαί μοι δοκῶ, [I seem to myself to be] *I feel ashamed*, i. 7. 4. 'Ορόντας, . . ὃν ᾤετο πιστόν οἱ εἶναι, ταχὺ αὐτὸν εὗρε Κύρῳ φιλαίτερον, ἢ ἑαυτῷ, *O. soon found the man whom he believed to be faithful to him, more a friend to C. than to himself* (O.), i. 9. 29.

a. If a *pronoun* used *reflexively* and its *subject* are both related the most closely to the *same verb* or *participle*, the former is termed a *direct reflexive*; (b) but otherwise, *indirect*: (a) Οὓς ἐγώ . . κατεθέμην ἐμοί, *which I laid up for myself*, i. 3. 3. (b) Πράττετε ὁποῖον ἄν τι ὑμῖν οἴησθε μάλιστα συμφέρειν, *do whatever you think will most benefit yourselves*, ii. 2. 2.

c. A *common reflexive* or *personal* pronoun is sometimes used for the *reciprocal* pronoun : 'Ἡμῖν αὐτοῖς διαλεξόμεθα, *we will confer with each other*, Dem. 1169. 5. Ἐπράξαμεν . . πρὸς ἡμᾶς εἰρήνην, *we made peace with each other*, Dem. 30. 16. Φθονοῦντες ἑαυτοῖς μισοῦσιν ἀλλήλους Mem.

538. 3. In the *stronger* form, (a) the *Gen. possessive* of the *personal* pronoun is commonly supplied in the 1st and 2d Persons, and sometimes in the 3d, by the *possessive adjective* (252. 5); and (b) so, of the *reflexive* plural, with the addition of αὐτῶν, while (c) a like substitution in the sing. is poetic :

(a) 'Εμὸς δὲ ἀδελφός, frater meus, *a brother of mine* (cf. τὸν ἀδελφόν, fratrem, 530 e), i. 7. 9. Τοὺς ἡμετέρους φίλους, *our friends*, Ib. 7. Τῶν ὧν τέκνων, *his children*, Soph. Tr. 266. (b) Τοῖς ἡμετέροις αὐτῶν φίλοις (498). (c) 'Εμὸν (ἐὸν) αὐτοῦ χρεῖος, *my (his) own interest*, β. 45; a. 409.

d. This substitution is sometimes made for the Gen. in its other uses with substantives, even the *Gen. objective* (444 g) : Τὸ σὸν λέχος, *the marriage you talk of*, Soph. Ant. 573. Φιλίᾳ τῇ σῇ, *love to you*, vii. 7. 29.

e. In Attic prose, the only possessive pronoun for the 3 Pers. is **σφέτερος**, which is used reflexively, and with no great frequency; while the poetic or dialectic ὅς, ἑός, and σφός (28 e, n) are very rarely used except as reflexive.

f. The *weaker* form of the Gen., from its want of distinctive emphasis, is rarely preceded by the article, and therefore follows the rule of position in 524 b; while the *stronger* form of the Gen., and the *possessive adjective* follow the rule in 523 a : Τῷ σώματι αὐτοῦ, Τὸ μὲν ἑαυτοῦ σῶμα, *his (own) body*, i. 9. 23. (g) The Gen. of αὐτός, however, in its stronger, and especially its reflexive uses, may take the position of ἑαυτοῦ.

539. 4. The *third person* being expressed *demonstratively* in other ways, the pronoun οὗ became simply a *retrospective* pronoun, i. e. a pronoun referring to a person or thing previously mentioned.

As such, it performed the office both (a) of an *unemphatic reflexive*, and (b) of a *simple personal pronoun*; rarely (c), in Epic, of a *general reflexive*, without respect to person. (d) This last use appears oftener in its derivatives (even in the Attic, in ἑαυτοῦ and σφέτερος). — (a) See 537. 2, a. (b) Συνέφασάν οἱ, *they agreed with him*, Cyr. 3. 2. 26. (c) Εἰο μὲν οὐδ' ἡβαιὸν ἀτύζομαι, *I tremble not in the least for* [one's self] *myself*, Ap. Rh. 2. 635. (d) Δώμασιν οἷσιν ἀνάσσοις, *may you rule* [one's own] *your own house*, a. 402. Δεῖ ἡμᾶς ἀνερέσθαι ἑαυτούς, *we ought to ask ourselves*, Pl. Phædo 78 b. Τῶν σφετέρων φρουρίων, *our fortresses*, Cyr. 6. 1. 10.

e. Some of the forms of οὗ are used with great latitude of number and gender. Thus, (a) μίν and νίν commonly sing., but also plur. (β) σφέ properly plur., but also (especially in the tragic poets) sing. (γ) σφίν rarely sing. (δ) ἕ commonly sing. masc. and fem., but sing. neut. A. 236, plur. Hom. Ven. 268. (ε) So the derived *possessives:* ἑός, *their*, Hes.; &c.

f. The place of οὗ as a reflexive is commonly supplied in Attic prose by ἑαυτοῦ, and as a simple personal pronoun, by αὑτός.

B. ΑΥΤΟΣ (251, 28 c).

540. The pronoun αὐτός marks a return of the mind to the same person or thing. This *return* takes place,

a.) In speaking of REFLEX ACTION or RELATION. Hence αὐτός is used with the personal pronouns in forming the REFLEXIVES. See 244.

b.) In designating a person or thing as THE SAME which has been previously mentioned or observed. When thus employed, αὐτός (like the corresponding *same* in English), being used for *distinction*, is preceded by the article (523 a):

Ὁ αὐτὸς ἀνήρ, rarely ὁ ἀνὴρ ὁ αὐτός or ἀνὴρ ὁ αὐτός, idem vir, *the same man*. Τῇ δὲ αὐτῇ ἡμέρᾳ, *and upon the same day*, i. 5. 12. See 451.

c.) For the sake of EMPHASIS, one of the most familiar modes of expressing which is *repetition*. When αὐτός is thus employed in connection with the article, it is placed in the *order of statement* (523 b):

Αὐτὸς ὁ ἀνήρ, less frequently ὁ ἀνὴρ αὐτός, vir ipse, *the man himself*. Αὐτὰ τὰ ἀπὸ τῶν οἰκιῶν ξύλα, *the very wood from the houses*, ii. 2. 16.

d. The emphatic αὐτός is joined with pronouns in both their *stronger* and their *weaker forms* (commonly preceding them); and (e) is often used in the *Nom.* with a pronoun *understood*. (d) Αὐτῷ μοι ἔοικεν, Αὐτῷ ἐμοὶ .. δόξει, *it seems (shall seem) to myself*, Pl. Phædo 60 c, 91 a. Αὐτοῦ τούτου ἕνεκεν, *on this very account*, iv. 1. 22. So in adverbs: Αὐτοῦ ταύτῃ, *in this very place, on the spot*, Hdt. 1. 214. (e) Αὐτὸς σὺ ἐπαίδευσας, Αὐτὸς ἐπαίδευσας, *you yourself educated*, Œc. 7. 4, 7. Αὐτοὶ καλοῦσιν iii. 5. 5.

f. In like manner, αὐτός is used without another pronoun expressed, in the *oblique cases of the third person:* Δῶρα ἄγοντες αὐτῷ τε καὶ τῇ γυναικί, *bringing presents both for himself and for his wife*, vii. 3. 16. (g) From the gradual extension of this use to cases in which there was no special emphasis, appears to have arisen the familiar employment of αὐτός in the *oblique cases*, as the *common pronoun of the third person* (536 d). In this unemphatic use, αὐτός must not begin a clause.

h. Sometimes (chiefly in the Epic), αὐτός occurs in the oblique cases, with the ellipsis of a pron. of the 1st or 2d Pers.: Αὐτῶν γὰρ ἀπωλόμεθ᾽ ἀφραδίῃσιν, *we were undone by our own folly*, κ. 27. Αὐτήν [sc. σέ] ζ. 27.

i. In the later Greek (e. g. the S. S.), αὐτός sometimes appears in the Nom., simply as a strong pronoun of the 3d Pers.: Ὅτι αὐτοὶ παρακληθήσονται, *for they shall be comforted*, Mat. 5. 4.

j. The emphasis of αὐτός sometimes lies in mere *contradistinction*.

541. The *emphatic force* of αὐτός has led to some special uses (see also 467 c):

a.) Χώρει αὐτός, *he goes* [himself only] *alone* (solus), iv. 7. 11.   (b) Αὐτοὶ "Ελληνες, οὐ μιξοβάρβαροι, '*pure Greeks,*' Pl. Menex. 245 d.   (c) Ἀλλά τις αὐτὸς ἴτω, '*of his own accord,*' sponte, P. 254.   (d) Οὐκ αὐτὸ δικαιοσύνην ἐπαινοῦντες, *not praising justice in and of itself*, Pl. Rep. 363 a.   (e) Πρὸς αὐτῷ τῷ στρατεύματι, [by the army itself] *close to the army*, i. 8. 14.   (f) Αὐτὸς ἔφα (Pythagorean), ipse dixit, [himself] *the Master said it*.   (g) After an *ordinal:* Περικλέους δεκάτου αὐτοῦ στρατηγοῦντος, *P. commanding* [himself the tenth] *with nine colleagues* (*Fr.* lui dixième), Th. 1. 116.

h.) A *reflexive* is frequently preceded by **αὐτός**, agreeing with the same subject ; and the two pronouns are often brought into close connection, in disregard of the natural order : Αἰσχύνεις πόλιν τὴν **αὐτὸς αὑτοῦ**, *you disgrace your own city* (539 d), Soph. O. C. 929.   See 513 f.

C. Demonstrative (28, 252).

542.   I. Of the primary demonstratives, the more *distant* and *emphatic* is ἐκεῖνος, ille, *that;* the nearer and more familiar is οὗτος or ὅδε, hic, *this:*

Ἐὰν ἐκείνοις δοκῇ, καὶ **τούτους** κακῶς ποιήσουσι, *if* those *should wish it, they will even injure* these, Pl. Phædr. 231 c.

a. The two may be combined to mark the connection of the MORE REMOTE with the NEARER; as of the *past* with the *present*, of a *saying* with its *illustration*, of that which *has been mentioned* with that which *is present before us*, &c.: Τοῦτ' [sc. ἐστὶ] ἐκεῖν' οὑγὼ 'λεγον, *this is that which I said,* Ar. Ach. 41. Τοῦτ' ἐκεῖνο, κτᾶσθ' ἑταίρους, *this* [is] *verifies that precept*, "Gain friends," Eur. Or. 804.   Hæc illa Charybdis, *Virg.*

b. Οὗτος sometimes marks the *ordinary* or *familiar*, and **ἐκεῖνος** the *extraordinary:* Ἔχοντες **τούτους** τε τοὺς πολυτελεῖς χιτῶνας, *having on the rich tunics which they are in the habit of wearing*, i. 5. 8.   Τὸν Ἀριστείδην ἐκεῖνον, *that remarkable A.*, Dem. 34. 20.   Ille Demosthenes, *Cic.*

543.   II. The pronouns οὗτος and ὅδε have in general the same force, and the choice between them often depends upon euphony or rhythm : Τούτω φιλεῖν χρή, τώδε χρὴ πάντας σέβειν, *these we must love, these all must revere,* Soph. El. 981.   Yet they are not without distinction.

a. Οὗτος, as formed by composition with **αὐτός**, is properly a pronoun of *identification* or *emphatic designation* (it may be regarded as a *weaker* form of ὁ αὐτός, *the same*, 540 b) ; while **ὅδε**, arising from composition with δέ, is strictly a *deictic* pronoun (δεικτικός, from δείκνυμι *to point out*), pointing to an object as before us (see 252).   Hence,

544.   1.) For reference to that which *precedes* or is *contained in a subordinate clause*, οὗτος is commonly used ; but for reference to that which *follows* and is *not* contained in a subordinate clause, ὅδε :

Τεκμήριον δὲ **τούτου** καὶ **τόδε**, *and of this* (which has been stated), *this* (which follows) *is also a proof*, i. 9. 29.   Οὗτοι, οὓς ὁρᾶτε, βάρβαροι (523 g).

To the *retrospective character* of **οὗτος** may be referred,

a.) Its use preceded by καί, in *making an addition to a sentence*, the pronoun either serving as a *repetition* of a *substantive* in the sentence, or, in the *neuter Acc.* or *Nom.* (commonly *plur.*, 491 c), of the *sentence* itself :

Ξένους προσήκει σοι πολλοὺς δέχεσθαι, καὶ τούτους [sc. δέχεσθαι] μεγαλοπρεπῶς, *it becomes you to entertain many guests, and these magnificently*, Œc. Ἐβοήθησαν τῇ Λακεδαίμονι, καὶ ταῦτα [sc. ἐποίησαν] εἰδότες (491 c).

b.) The use of τοῦτο and ταῦτα in *assent :* Δεῖ ὑπάρχειν καὶ δυνατούς. . ."Ἔστι ταῦτα. "They ought also to be competent." "This is so." Pl.

545. 2.) *Ὅδε* surpasses in *demonstrative vivacity;* but *οὗτος* in *emphatic force* and in the *extent of its substantive use :*

Ἦ τόνδε φράζεις; Τοῦτον, ὄνπερ εἰσορᾷς. "Is THIS the man you speak of?" "The VERY MAN, whom you behold." Soph. O. T. 1120.

a. To the *deictic* power of *ὅδε* may be referred the very frequent use of this pronoun by the Epic and Dramatic poets for an *adverb of place* (509 b), especially by the latter, in bringing a new person upon the stage.

546. 3.) In the emphatic designation of the *first* and *second persons* by a *demonstrative*, (a) the *first* person, as the nearer object, is regularly denoted by *ὅδε* (the speaker pointing, as it were, to himself, 543 a) ; and (b) the *second*, by *οὗτος*, which expresses *impatience, authority, contempt, familiarity,* &c., and (c) is used in *address*, both with and without *σύ* (401. 3) :

(a) Μὴ θνῇσχ' ὑπὲρ τοῦδ' ἀνδρός, οὐδ' ἐγὼ πρὸ σοῦ, *do not you die for this man* [for me], *nor yet I for you*, Eur. Alc. 690. (b) Οὑτοσὶ ἀνὴρ οὐ παύσεται φλυαρῶν, *this man* [you] *will not cease trifling*, Pl. Gorg. 489 b. (c) Οὗτος σύ, ὦ πρέσβυ, Heus tu, senex, [This you, *or* You there, 509 b], *Ho there! old man!* Soph. O. T. Οὗτος, τί σεμνὸν .. βλέπεις; Eur. Alc.

547. III. Other compounds of *αὐτός* and *δε* (252) are distinguished in like manner with *οὗτος* and *ὅδε* :

Ὁ Κῦρος ἀκούσας τοῦ Γωβρύου τοιαῦτα, τοιάδε πρὸς αὐτὸν ἔλεξε Cyr.

D. INDEFINITE (28, 253 s).

548. Of the indefinite pronouns, the most extensive in its use is *τὶς*, which is the *simplest expression of indefiniteness or general reference*.

a. Τὶς is variously translated : *any, some, certain, a, one,* &c.; Lat. *aliquis*, &c.; while it may be sometimes omitted in translation.

b. Τὶς more frequently *follows* the word with which it is most closely joined ; but may also *precede* it, yet not so as to commence a sentence. Sometimes, however, it begins a *clause ;* and sometimes separates closely connected words : Τί οὖν, τις ἂν εἴποι, ταῦτα λέγεις; *Why then, one might say, do you mention these things?* Dem. 13. 6. See 520 b.

c. The singular τὶς commonly refers to an individual (*some one, a certain one*) ; but sometimes to more than one (*some*, 488), or even to *any one concerned* (*every one*). The extent of the reference is sometimes marked by εἷς (οὐδείς, μηδείς), ἕκαστος, πᾶς, ἡ οὐδείς, &c. Ἄνθρωπός τις ἠρώτησε, *a certain man asked*, ii. 4. 15. Θεῶν τις, *some one of the gods*, v. 2. 24. Μισεῖ τις ἐκεῖνον, *there are those who hate him*, Dem. 42. 17. Εὖ μέν τις δόρυ θηξάσθω, *let each one sharpen well his spear*, B. 382. Ἔκαστος τις φοβούμενος, *each one fearing*, Cyr. 6. 1. 42. Adverbially, οὐδέν τι (Mem. 1. 2. 42), μηδέν τι, *not* [as to any one thing] *at all*, οὐ πάνυ τι vi. 1. 26, &c.

d. Τὶς often marks indefiniteness of *nature, character, quality, quantity,*

§ 550.   INDEFINITE AND RELATIVE.   279

number, degree, &c.   Ὁ σοφιστὴς τυγχάνει ὢν ἔμπορός τις ἢ κάπηλος, *the sophist is* [a certain] *a kind of trader or huckster*, Pl. Prot. 313 c.   Ἐγώ τις, ὡς ἔοικε, δυσμαθής, *I am, methinks, somewhat stupid*, Pl. Rep. 358 a. Ἡμέρας μὲν ἑβδομήκοντά τινας, *some* (i. e. *about*) *seventy days*, Th. 7. 87.

e.   Τὶς may be used to give a certain vagueness to a proper name, or a noun having the article : Παρὰ Χάρωνί τινι, *with a certain Charon*, Hel.

f.   Τὶς is sometimes *emphatic*, and may be then written as *orthotone* (yet editors here differ) : Ἤχεις τὶς εἶναι, *you boasted that you were somebody*.

g.   An *indefinite form of expression* is sometimes employed for a *definite :* Ποῖ τις τρέψεται; *whither can one* [= I] *turn*, Ar. Th. 603.   (h) So a *definite* for an *indefinite*, as ἴδοις ἄν, *you* [= one] *might see*, Pl. Conv. 177 c.

E. RELATIVE.

549.   I.   Relatives refer to an antecedent either as *definite* or as *indefinite;* and are, hence, divided into the DEFINITE and the INDEFINITE RELATIVES :

Ἡλίου ὃς πάντ᾽ ἐφορᾷ, *of the Sun, who seeth all things*, λ. 109.   Ἡγεμόνα αἰτεῖν Κῦρον, ὅστις . . ἀπάξει, *to ask C. for some guide who would conduct them*, i. 3. 14.

a.   INDEFINITE RELATIVES are formed, either from the *definite relatives* by adding τὶς or a particle (commonly ἄν), or from the *simple indefinites* by prefixing ὅς (in the shortened form ὁ-) : ὅστις or ὃς ἄν *whoever, ὁποῖος of what kind soever, ὁπόσος how much soever, ὁπότε whensoever*.   See 254, 377, 389.   (b) The use of an *indefinite relative* is sometimes explained by resolving it into an indefinite pronoun and a relative, the indefinite part seeming to belong more strictly to the antecedent clause : Ἔστιν ὅ τι σε ἠδίκησα; *is there aught in which I have wronged you?* i. 6. 7.

550.   II.   For one relative, another is sometimes used as a *simpler, more familiar*, or *more expressive* form.   This use may be sometimes explained by *ellipsis*.   Thus,

a.) A DEFINITE for an *indefinite* relative : Οὓς ἑώρα ἐθέλοντας κινδυνεύειν, τούτους καὶ ἄρχοντας ἐποίει, *whomsoever he saw willing to incur danger, these he made rulers*, i. 9. 14.

b.) An INDEFINITE for a *definite* relative : Ὁρᾶτε δὲ τὴν Τισσαφέρνους ἀπιστίαν, ὅστις λέγων .., *see the perfidy of T.,* [one] *a man who saying* .., iii. 2. 4.   See 549 b. — The use of *an indefinite relative referring to a definite antecedent* belongs particularly to those cases in which the relative clause is added, not to *distinguish*, but to *characterize*, thus representing the antecedent as *one of a class*.

c.) A SIMPLER RELATIVE for one of *quantity, quality, &c.*: Ἐπιθυμεῖν τοιαύτης δόξης ἧς [= οἴας] πολλοὶ τυγχάνουσιν, *to desire such glory* [which] *as many obtain*, Isoc. 408 d.   Ἕωσπερ ἂν ᾖς ὃς [= τοιοῦτος οἷος] εἶ, *as long as you are what* [= such, as] *you are*, Pl. Phædr. 243 e.

d.) A RELATIVE OF QUANTITY, QUALITY, &c., for a *simpler relative:* Ταῦτα . . χρὴ ποιεῖν, ὅσα [for ἅ, or sc. τοσαῦτα] ὁ θεὸς ἐκέλευσεν, *you must do these things,* [as many as] *which the god has commanded*, iii. 1. 7.

e.) A RELATIVE ADVERB for a *relative pronoun*, chiefly in designations of *place, time*, and *manner :* Εἰς χωρίον, ὅθεν ὄψονται θάλατταν, *to a place* [whence] *from which they would behold the sea*, iv. 7. 20.

f.   After the plural of πᾶς *all;* ὅστις and ὃς ἄν are regularly used in the *singular*, and ὅσοι, ὁπόσοι, and οἵ in the *plural :* Ἀσπάζεται πάντας, ᾧ ἂν περιτυγχάνῃ, *he salutes all* [whomsoever] *whom he may meet*, Pl. Rep. 566 d.   Πᾶσιν, οἷς ἐτύγχανεν, ἐβόα, *he shouted to all whom he met*, i. 8. 1.

551. III. ELLIPSIS. A word which belongs both to the antecedent and to the relative clause, is commonly expressed in but one; more frequently in the *earlier* clause, yet often in the *later;* while it may be omitted in *both*, if it is a word which will be readily supplied: as,

a.) A VERB or PARTICIPLE : Ὅ τι ἂν δέῃ [sc. πάσχειν], πείσομαι, *I will suffer whatever I must* [suffer], i. 3. 6.

b.) A PREPOSITION : Ἐν τρισὶ . . ἔτεσιν, [sc. ἐν] οἷς ἐπιπολάζει, *in three years, in which he has the upper hand*, Dem. 117. 16.

c.) The SUBJECT OF THE RELATIVE. Relative pronouns belong to the class of *adjectives* (173), and, as such, agree with a substantive expressed or understood; while a form of this substantive, or of one corresponding to it, is also the *antecedent* of the relative : Οὗτός ἐστιν ὁ ἀνὴρ, ὃν εἶδες ἄνδρα, *this is the man* [which man] *whom you saw*. But elliptic forms are far more common : Οὗτός ἐστιν ὁ ἀνὴρ, ὃν εἶδες, Οὗτός ἐστιν, ὃν εἶδες ἄνδρα, Οὗτός ἐστιν, ὃν εἶδες · or, with the antecedent clause preceding (an order more frequent in Greek than in Eng.), Ὃν εἶδες, οὗτός ἐστιν, &c.

Ἀπὸ τῆς ἀρχῆς, ἧς [sc. ἀρχῆς] αὐτὸν σατράπην ἐποίησε (505 a). Ἀποπέμψαι πρὸς ἑαυτὸν [sc. τὸ στράτευμα,] ὃ εἶχε στράτευμα, *to send back to him the force which he had* [what force he had], i. 2. 1. Κῦρος δὲ ἔχων οὓς εἴρηκα, *C. having the men whom I have mentioned*, Ib. 5.

d. If the relative and its subject are in the same clause, the latter is commonly put at the *end*, as though the rest of the clause were regarded as modifying it like an *adjective*. See 523 g. (e) The adjective character of a relative clause is sometimes made more prominent by placing it between a substantive and its article : Τοὺς ὁποιουσδήποθ' ὑμεῖς ἐξεπέμπετε στρατηγούς, [the WHAT SORT YOU SENT OUT generals] *the generals such as you sent out*, Dem. 276. 10.

f. A *demonstrative* or *indefinite pronoun* or *adverb* is very often omitted in the antecedent clause, as implied by the relative; but the simple ellipsis of the *relative pronoun* itself, which is so common in Eng., is not allowed in the Greek. Compare the ellipses in, Σὺν [sc. τούτοις] οἷς μάλιστα φιλεῖς, *with those* [sc. whom] *you love best* (cum iis quos), i. 9. 25.

g. Indefinite relatives are often used elliptically in expressing a *condition* or *circumstance* : Δόθ', ἥτις ἐστί, *give it* [to her, being whoever she is, *i. e.* let her be whoever she may], *whoever she may be*, Soph. El. 1123. (h) This has led to their use as *mere indefinites* (commonly with οὖν or δή) : Μηδ' ὁντιναοῦν μισθὸν [= μισθόν τινα, ὅστις οὖν εἴη] προσαιτήσας, *not demanding any pay whatever* [it might be], vii. 6. 27. Ὅτου δὴ παρεγγυήσαντος, *some one* [whoever it might have been] *having suggested it*, iv. 7. 4.

i. Observe the ellipses in such expressions as (α) ὅσαι ἡμέραι (united, ὁσημέραι), quot diebus *or* quotidie, [on as many days as there are] *daily*, ὅσοι μῆνες, quot mensibus, *monthly*. (β) Ὠκύμορος . . ἔσσεαι, οἷ' ἀγορεύεις, *you will be short-lived*, [according to such things as] *from what you say*, Σ. 95. (γ) Οἷος ἐκείνου θυμὸς ὑπέρβιος, οὐκ ἐθελήσει, *with* [such a spirit as is] *that violent spirit of his, he will not be willing*, Σ. 262.

552. IV. ATTRACTION. The intimate relation of clauses connected by a *relative pronoun* or a *kindred particle*, often produces an ATTRACTION, sometimes simply *affecting the position or form of particular words*, and sometimes even *uniting the two clauses into one*. Thus,

§ 554.   ELLIPSIS, ATTRACTION.   281

553. 1.) *Transfer.* A word or phrase is often made a part of the *relative*, instead of the *antecedent, clause;* and sometimes the two clauses are *blended in their arrangement* :

Ἔστιν ὅτῳ ἄλλῳ [for ἄλλος ὅτῳ] .. πλείω ἐπιτρέπεις; *is there* [to whom else] *any other to whom you entrust more?* Œc. 3. 12. Λόγους ἄκουσον, οὕς σοι δυστυχεῖς ἥκω φέρων, *hear the sad tidings which I bring you,* Eur. Or. 853. Οὗτοι, ἐπεὶ εὐθέως ᾔσθοντο τὸ πρᾶγμα, ἀπεχώρησαν, *these, when they understood the matter, immediately withdrew,* Hel. 3. 2. 4. Ὃν ἐγὼ ἀπεκεφάλισα Ἰωάννην, οὗτός ἐστιν Mk. 6. 16. See 554 s.

a. The SUPERLATIVE is often so placed, particularly in expressions of (b) *time* and (c) *possibility;* and with a frequent ellipsis of the word denoting *possibility :*

(a) Δοῦλον, ὃν εἶχε πιστότατον, ἔπεμψεν (De servis, quem habuit fidelissimum, misit, *Nep.*), *he sent the most faithful servant that he had.* Ἄρχεσθαι ἐπίσταμαι, ὥς τις καὶ ἄλλος μάλιστα ἀνθρώπων, *I know how to obey* [as even any other man knows at the best] *as well as any other man,* i. 3. 15.

(b) Πειρασόμεθα παρεῖναι, ὅταν τάχιστα διαπραξώμεθα [for π. τάχιστα, ὅταν δ.], *we shall endeavor to be present* [most quickly when] *as soon as we have accomplished,* Cyr. 4. 5. 33. Ἐπεὶ ἦλθε τάχιστα, ἀπέδοτο, *as soon as he had come, he sold,* vii. 2. 6. Ὡς τάχιστα ἕως ὑπέφαινεν, ἐθύοντο iv. 3. 9.

(c) Ἤγαγον .. ὁπόσους ἐγὼ πλείστους ἐδυνάμην, *I have brought* [the most that] *as many as I could,* Cyr. 4. 5. 29. Ἔχων ἱππέας ὡς ἂν δύνηται πλείστους, *bringing* [horsemen so as he could the most] *as many horse as he could,* i. 6. 3. Λαμβάνειν .. ὅτι πλείστους, *to take as many as possible,* i. 1. 6 (ὅτι the *neut.* of ὅστις, *according to whatever may be,* or *is possible;* though words denoting possibility are not expressed with it). Ὡς μάλιστα ἐδύνατο ἐπικρυπτόμενος, [concealing it as he best could] *as secretly as he could,* i. 1. 6. Ἐλαύνων ὡς δυνατὸν ἦν τάχιστα, *riding as fast as was possible,* Cyr. 5. 4. 3. Ὡς μάλιστα Cyr. 1. 6. 19, quam maxime, *as much as possible.* Ὅτι τάχιστα vii. 2. 8, *as quickly as possible.*

d. In the more elliptic of these constructions, ὡς, ὅτι, ὅπως, &c., are treated simply as *adverbs* strengthening the superlative.

554. 2.) *Assimilation.* a, b. The RELATIVE often takes the *case of its antecedent;* (c) far less frequently, the ANTECEDENT, the *case of a relative* following.

REMARK. The former, from its special frequency in Attic Greek, has been distinguished as *Attic,* and the latter as *Inverse* Attraction.

(a) *Attic Attraction.* This is the common construction, when the relative clause *limits* or *defines* an *antecedent in the Gen. or Dat.*, and the relative would properly be an *Acc. depending upon a verb :* Ἀπὸ τῶν πόλεων, ὧν [for ἅς] ἔπεισε, *from the cities which he persuaded,* Th. 7. 1. Σὺν τοῖς θησαυροῖς, οἷς ὁ πατὴρ κατέλιπεν, *with the treasures which my father left,* Cyr. 3. 1. 33. Ἄρχοντας ἐποίει ἧς κατεστρέφετο χώρας i. 9. 14. Χειμῶνός γε ὄντος οἵου λέγεις v. 8. 3. Μήδων μέντοι, ὅσων ἑώρακα Cyr. 1. 3. 2.

NOTE. If this ANTECEDENT is a *demonstrative pronoun,* it is commonly omitted (551 f) : Σὺν [sc. τούτοις] οἷς ἔχω, *with those whom I have,* vii. 3. 48.

(b) The *Dat.* and even *Nom.* are rarely attracted in like manner : Ὧν [= ἐκείνων, οἷς] ἠπίστει, πολλούς, *many of those whom he distrusted,* Cyr. 5. 4. 39. Βλάπτεσθαι ἀφ᾽ ὧν [= τούτων, ἃ] ἡμῖν παρεσκεύασται, *to be injured by those things which have been prepared by us* [in respect to which preparation has been made by us], Th. 7. 67. — When the *subject of a verb* is attracted, the verb, if retained, becomes impersonal.

(c) *Inverse Attraction.* The antecedent is here treated, except in position, as if a part of the relative clause; and sometimes omits an article, as if supplied by the relative (cf. 523 g) : 'Ανεῖλεν αὐτῷ ὁ 'Απόλλων θεοῖς οἶς [= τοὺς θεοὺς, οἶς] ἔδει θύειν, *Apollo made known to him* [to what gods] *the gods to whom he must sacrifice*, iii. 1. 6. Τάσδε [= Αἴδε] δ' ἅσπερ εἰσορᾷς, .. χωροῦσι πρὸς σέ, *these whom you behold, come to you,* Soph. Tr.

d. Assimilation appears also in *adverbs:* Ἐκ δὲ γῆς, ὅθεν [= οὖ] προύκειτο, *from the ground* [whence] *where it lay,* Soph. Tr. Inverse, Βῆναι κεῖθεν [= κεῖσε], ὅθεν περ ἥκει, *to return thither, whence he came,* Id. O. C.

555. 3.) *Condensation.* The two clauses may be *condensed into one* by the *omission of a substantive verb* either (a) from the antecedent clause or (β) from the relative clause.

(a) FROM THE ANTECEDENT CLAUSE. a. After a *demonstrative pronoun* or *article,* the RELATIVE is also *omitted,* and the ANTECEDENT takes its place in the construction. This form of condensation is particularly frequent in *questions, exclamations,* and *denials,* especially with the poets : Τί τόδ' αὐδᾷς [= Τί ἐστι τόδε, ὃ αὐδᾷς]; *what is this, which you say?* Eur. Alc. 106. Τί τοῦτ' ἀρχαῖον ἐννέπεις κακόν; *what is this old evil of which you speak?* Soph. O. T. 1033. Τοῦτο μὲν οὐδὲν θαυμαστὸν λέγεις Pl. Prot.

b. An *exclamation without a verb* and a relative clause may be united in like manner : Τοὺς ἐμὸς ἴδε πατὴρ θανάτους αἰκεῖς [= Ὢ θάνατοι αἰκεῖς, οὓς ἴδε πατὴρ ἐμός]! *the cruel death my father saw!* Soph. El. 205.

c. Expressions like the following are still more elliptical : Ἔνθα ἡ Τριπυργία [= ἐστί χωρίον, ὃ Τ.] καλεῖται, *where there is a place, which is called Tripyrgia,* Hel. 5. 1. 10. Ἐν ᾧ καλοῦμεν τὸ ζῆν Pl. Phædo 107 c.

556. (β) FROM THE RELATIVE CLAUSE. a. This occurs chiefly with a *relative of comparison* (οἶος, ὅσος, or ἡλίκος), which then, with any substantive or adjective in agreement, is assimilated to the corresponding demonstrative (expressed or understood) ; and the whole is construed as an adjective, sometimes even taking the article before it : Χαριζόμενον οἵῳ σοὶ ἀνδρί [= ἀνδρὶ τοιούτῳ, οἷος σὺ εἶ], *obliging a man such as you are* [a SUCH AS YOU man], Mem. 2. 9. 3. Οἱ δὲ οἷοί περ ὑμεῖς ἄνδρες, *but* [the SUCH AS YOU men] *men like you,* Cyr. 6. 2. 2 (cf. Τοὺς οἷος οὗτος ἀνθρώπους Dem. 421. 16). Ὄντος τοῦ πάγου οἵου δεινοτάτου [= τοιούτου, οἷός ἐστι δεινότατος], *the cold being* [such as is most dreadful] *of the most intense kind,* Pl. Conv. 220 b. — But if a substantive following οἷος as above is in a different number, it remains in the *Nominative:* Νεανίας δ' οἵους [= τοιούτους, οἷος] σύ, *young men such as you,* Ar. Ach. 601.

b. Some constructions may be explained either by the ellipsis of a substantive verb, or by the change of a finite verb to an infinitive depending upon this adjective : Ὅπως .. μὴ τοιοῦτοι ἔσονται οἱ πολῖται, οἷοι πονηροῦ τινος ἢ αἰσχροῦ ἔργου ἐφίεσθαι, *that the citizens should not be such as* [they would be] *to desire any wrong or base act* [or, such as would desire], Cyr. Ὅσον μόνον γεύσασθαι ἑαυτῷ καταλιπών, *leaving for himself only* [so much as] *sufficient to taste,* vii. 3. 22. Ὅσα μέντοι ἤδη δοκεῖν αὐτῷ, *but* [according to so much as now seemed to him,] *so far as he could now judge,* Th.

c. Through their frequent use as above, with the ellipsis of the corresponding demonstratives, οἶος and ὅσος (particularly the former with τέ, 389 j) came to be treated as mere adjectives of quality or quantity : Οἶοί τε ἔσεσθε ἡμῖν συμπρᾶξαι; . . Ἰκανοί ἐσμεν. "Shall you be [*such as to*] able to co-operate with us?" "We are able." v. 4. 9. Οὐκ οἷον τε ἦν . . διώκειν, [the state of things was not such as it should be to pursue] *it was*

§ 559.   CONDENSATION, COMBINATIONS.   283

not possible to pursue, iii. 3. 9. Λόγους οἴους εἰς τὰ δικαστήρια, *speeches* [such as for] *adapted to courts of justice*, Pl. Euthyd. 272 a.

d. In this construction, ὅσος is especially used in the *neuter form* ὅσον, as *indeclinable;* and often *substantively* or *adverbially* (507 e): Ὅσον ὅσον στίλην, *a mere, mere bit*, Ar. Vesp. 213. Ἐλείπετο τῆς νυκτὸς ὅσον σκοταίους διελθεῖν, *enough of the night remained for them to cross in the dark*, iv. 1. 5. Ὅσον ἀποζῆν, *sufficiently for subsistence*, Th. 1. 2.

557. 4.) A RELATIVE PRONOUN may take the place of a *definitive* (personal or demonstrative pronoun, or article), *and a connective particle.*

α.) When the DEFINITIVE belongs to the *first clause.* In this kind of attraction, the pronoun is commonly either *governed by a preposition or adverb*, or is itself *used adverbially:* Ἐφ᾽ ᾧ [= ἐπὶ τούτῳ, ὥστε] μὴ καίειν τὰς κώμας, *upon this condition, that they should not burn the villages*, iv. 2. 19 (cf. Ἐπὶ τοῖσδε, ὥστε Th. 3. 114). Ἐφ᾽ ᾧ τε [= ἐπὶ τούτῳ, ὥστε] πλοῖα συλλέγειν, *in order that we might collect transports*, vi. 6. 22. Μέχρι οὗ [= τοῦ χρόνου, ὅτε] εἶδον, *until* [the time when] *they saw*, v. 4. 16 (cf. Μέχρι τοσούτου, ἕως Th. 1. 90). Μέχρι (ἄχρι) οὗ [= τοῦ χωρίου, ἔνθα], *to the region where, as far as*, i. 7. 6. Ἐξ ὅτου (οὗ, οὗ τε), ex quo, *since*, vii. 8. 4.

a. The Attic poets sometimes use οὕνεκα, and Hdt. μέχρι οὗ (ὅτου), as compound adverbs governing the Gen.: Γυναικὸς οὕνεκα, *for the sake of a woman*, Æsch. Ag. 823. Μέχρι ὅτευ πληθώρης ἀγορῆς, Hdt. 2. 173.

558. β.) When the DEFINITIVE belongs to the *second clause:* Τίς οὕτω μαίνεται, ὅστις [= ὥστε ἐκεῖνος] οὐ βούλεταί σοι φίλος εἶναι; *who is so mad that he does not wish to be your friend?* ii. 5. 12. Ἀπόρων ἐστί .., οἵτινες ἐθέλουσι, *it is the part of those without resource* [that they should wish] *to wish*, ii. 5. 21. Οὐκ ἔστιν οὕτω μῶρος, ὃς θανεῖν ἐρᾷ, Soph. Ant.

a. Akin to this construction is the extensive use of the relative in *explanation*, or the *assignment of reason or purpose:* Θαυμαστὸν ποιεῖς, ὃς .. διδῶς, *you act strangely*, [who give] *that you give*, or *in giving* (qui des), Mem. 2. 7. 13. Ὅπλα κτῶνται, οἷς ἀμυνοῦνται τοὺς ἀδικοῦντας, *they prepare arms*, [with which they will repel] *that with these they may repel assailants*, Ib. 1. 14. Καὶ πόλει πέμψον τιν᾽, ὅστις σημανεῖ, *send some one to the city, to give notice*, Eur. Iph. T. 1208. Ἄγγελον ἧκαν, ὃς ἀγγείλειε γυναικί, *they sent a messenger to tell the woman* (qui nunciaret), o. 458. Equitatum præmittit, qui videant, *Cæs.*

b. RELATIVE ADVERBS likewise exhibit this form of attraction: Εὐδαίμων .. ὡς [= ὅτι οὕτως] ἀδεῶς καὶ γενναίως ἐτελεύτα, *happy that he died so fearlessly and nobly*, Pl. Phædo 58 e.

559. 5.) This attraction so unites some words, that the combinations are treated as *complex pronouns* or *adverbs*:

a.) Ἔστι with a relative, *the verb remaining unchanged*, whatever might be its appropriate number, tense, or mode: ἔστιν οἵ (αἵ, ἅ, ὧν, οἷς, αἷς, οὕς, ἅς· in questions οἵτινες; &c.), sunt qui, [there are who] *some;* ἔστιν ὅτε or ἔσθ᾽ ὅτε, est quando, [there is when] *sometimes*, ii. 6. 9; ἔστιν ἔνθα, est ubi, *in some places*, Cyr. 7. 4. 15; ἔστιν ὅπου (ὡς, ὅπως, ᾗ, ὅθεν, &c.). Προὐβάλλοντο πρέσβεις πρῶτον μὲν Χειρίσοφον .., ἔστι δ᾽ οἳ καὶ Ξενοφῶντα, *they proposed as ambassadors, first C., and some also* [there were also some who proposed] *X.*, vi. 2. 6. Ἔστιν οὕστινας ἀνθρώπων τεθαύμακας; *are there any men whom you have admired?* Mem. I. 4. 2.

b.) The relative followed by βούλει, and agreeing with the antecedent in any case (cf. Lat. *qui-vis, qui-libet*) : Περὶ Πολυγνώτου, ἢ ἄλλου ὅτου [= ὅντινα] βούλει, *respecting P., or any other one whom you please*, Pl.

c.) Ὅστις οὐ (sometimes ὅς οὐ) after οὐδείς or τίς : Οὐδεὶς ὅστις οὐκ ἀφέξεται, *there is no one, who will not refrain* (nemo non), Ven. 12. 14 (cf. Οὐδεὶς ἦν, ὅστις οὐκ ᾤετο Hel. 7. 5. 26). Οὐδεὶς ὃς οὐχὶ τῶνδ' ὀνειδιεῖ, *every one of these will reproach*, Soph. O. T. 373. Οὐδένα κίνδυνον [= οὐδεὶς κίνδυνος ἦν,] ὅντιν' οὐχ ὑπέμειναν, *there was no danger which they did not meet*, Dem. 295. 7. Οὐδενὸς ὅτου οὐ, Οὐδενὶ ὅτῳ οὐ, Pl. See also 556.

560. REMARK. FORMS OF COMPARISON are especially liable to attraction and ellipsis (cf. 438 b, 511 b) : Μόνοι τε ὄντες ὅμοια ἔπραττον, ἅπερ [= ἐκείνοις, ἅπερ] ἂν μετ' ἄλλων ὄντες, '[like things, which] things like to those which' (cf. *idem qui*) v. 4. 34.

561. v. A RELATIVE sometimes introduces a clause which (a) has *another connective* or a *participle absolute*, or which (b) is properly *coördinate* (as *imperative, interrogative*, &c.) ; and, on the other hand, a COÖRDINATE CLAUSE sometimes (c) takes the *place of a relative clause*, or (d) is used in *continuation of it:*

(a) Πολλὰ ἂν εἰπεῖν ἔχοιεν Ὀλύνθιοι νῦν, ἃ τότ' εἰ προείδοντο, οὐκ ἂν ἀπώλοντο, *the Olynthians could now mention many things, which had they then foreseen, they would not have perished*, Dem. 128. 17.

(b) Ψῆφον ἀμφ' ἡμῶν... "Ἡ κρινεῖ τί χρῆμα ; "The vote concerning us." "[Which will decide what ?] And what will this decide ?" Eur. Or. Κάτισον . . φυλάκους, οἳ λεγόντων, *station guards, and let them say*, Hdt. 1. 89.

(c) Ἐξετάσαι . . Ὀδυσσέα, ἢ Σίσυφον, ἢ ἄλλους μυρίους ἂν τις εἴποι, *to examine Ulysses, or Sisyphus, or* [one might mention ten thousand others] *ten thousand others whom one might mention*, Pl. Apol. 41 b.

(d) Κῦρον δὲ μεταπέμπεται ἀπὸ τῆς ἀρχῆς, ἧς αὐτὸν σατράπην ἐποίησε, καὶ στρατηγὸν δὲ αὐτὸν ἀπέδειξε i. 1. 2. This construction is adopted chiefly to avoid the repetition of the relative, in accordance with Rule K.

562. RULE K. The *repetition of the relative is commonly avoided*, either by *ellipsis*, or by the substitution of a *personal pronoun* or of a *demonstrative :* as,

Ἀριαῖος δέ, ὃν ἡμεῖς ἠθέλομεν βασιλέα καθιστάναι, καὶ [sc. ᾧ] ἐδώκαμεν καὶ [sc. παρ' οὗ] ἐλάβομεν πιστά, A., *whom we wished to make king, and to whom we gave and from whom we received pledges*, iii. 2. 5. Ὁ ἀνὴρ ὃς συνεθήρα ἡμῖν, καὶ σύ μοι μάλα ἐδόκεις θαυμάζειν αὐτόν, *the man who hunted with us, and whom you seemed to me greatly to admire*, Cyr. 3. 1. 38.

a. The relative is sometimes strengthened by a *personal pronoun* or a *demonstrative* in the same clause ; especially, after a Hebrew idiom, in the Hellenistic : "Ἡν χρῆν σ' ἐλαύνειν τήνδε, *whom you ought to drive* [her], Eur. And. 650. Οἷς ἐδόθη αὐτοῖς ἀδικῆσαι, *to whom it was given* [to them] *to hurt*, Rev. 7. 2. "Ὅπου τρέφεται ἐκεῖ Rev. 12. 14.

F. COMPLEMENTARY AND INTERROGATIVE.

563. 1. From the *connective*, and, at the same time, *indefinite* character of the complementary pronouns and adverbs, their proper forms are such as belong to *indefinite relatives* (549 a). But, when there is no danger of mistake, there is often employed, for the greater brevity and vivacity, in place of the full compound form, one or the other element, either the *relative* or the *indefinite*. Of these, the latter is far the more frequently used, but with this distinction from the *indefinite in its proper sense*, that the *accentuation of the compound form* is retained, as far as possible. Thus,

ὅστις, τίς, ὅς, quis, *who, what;* ὁπόσος, πόσος, ὅσος, quantus, *how much;* ὁπότε, πότε, ὅτε, quando, *when;* ὅποι, ποῖ, οἷ, quo, *whither;* &c.

Πρὶν δῆλον εἶναι, ὅ τι οἱ ἄλλοι Ἕλληνες ἀποκρινοῦνται, Πρὶν δῆλον εἶναι, τί ποιήσουσιν οἱ ἄλλοι στρατιῶται, *before it is known what the other Greeks will answer (soldiers will do),* i. 4. 14, 13. Ὡς δηλοίη, οὓς τιμᾷ i. 9. 28.

564. 2. The indefinites thus employed and accented are termed in Etymology, from the most prominent of their offices, INTERROGATIVES (253. 2, 377). As complementary words, they were employed in indirect question; and hence appears to have arisen their use as *direct interrogatives*, through an ellipsis.

Thus, from the indirect question, Εἰπὲ, **τίνα γνώμην ἔχεις περὶ τῆς πορείας**, *say, what opinion you have concerning the march* (ii. 2. 10), by the omission of εἰπὲ, comes the direct question, **Τίνα γνώμην ἔχεις περὶ τῆς πορείας;** *what opinion have you concerning the march?*

a. In other languages, as the Lat., with those derived from it, and the Eng., the complementary use of the *simple relatives* has prevailed; and hence, in these languages, the general identity of the *relatives* and the *interrogatives* (qui, quando, ubi, unde, *who, which, when, where*, &c.).

b. In direct question, the Greek employs only one of the two shorter forms above mentioned, but in *exclamation* it employs both: Οἴμοι, πάτερ, τί εἶπας; οἷά μ' εἴργασαι; *O my father, what have you said! how you treat me!* Soph. Tr. 1203. Ὅσα πράγματα ἔχεις! Cyr. 1. 3. 4.

c. The *neuter* τί unites with several *particles* to form *elliptical questions*; which, with various specific offices, serve in general to promote the *vigor* and *vivacity* of the discourse, commonly introducing other questions: Τί γάρ [sc. ἐστιν, or λέγετε]; . . ἐμποδὼν εἰμι; *What, indeed? Am I in the way?* v. 7. 10. Τί οὖν; *What then?* v. 8. 11. Τί δέ; Τί δή; Τί δῆτα;

d. A COMPLEMENTARY PRONOUN or ADVERB, used as *an echo to an interrogative*, has, for distinction's sake, its full form: Τίς γὰρ εἶ; [sc. Ἐρωτᾷς] Ὅστις; Πολίτης χρηστός. "*Who* are you?" "[Do you ask] WHO? A good citizen." Ar. Ach. 594. Οὗτος, τί ποιεῖς; Ὅ τι ποιῶ; "*Ho!* what are you doing?" "What am I doing?" Id. Ran. 198.

565. 3. CONDENSATION. a. Expressions like θαυμαστόν ἐστιν ὅσος (ὅσου, ὡς, &c.), *it is wonderful how much, &c.*, may be condensed into *complex adjectives* or *adverbs*: θαυμαστὸς ὅσος, θαυμαστοῦ ὅσου, θαυμαστῶς ὡς, &c. (cf. 555, 559):

Θαυμαστὴν ὅσην περὶ σὲ προθυμίαν ἔχει, *it is wonderful how much regard he has for you* (mirum quantum studium), Pl. Alc. 151 a. Μετὰ ἰδρῶτος θαυμαστοῦ ὅσου Id. Rep. 350 d. Θαυμαστῶς ὡς ἐπείσθην, *I was wonderfully convinced,* Id. Phædo 92 a. Ἀμήχανον ὅσον χρόνον, *an inconceivably long time,* Ib. 80 c. Ὑπερφυῶς ὡς χαίρω Id. Conv. 173 c.

b. A complementary word may take the place of a *connective particle* and a *demonstrative* (cf. 558): Κατοικτείρων τήν τε γυναῖκα, οἷον ἀνδρὸς [= ὅτι τοιούτου ἀνδρὸς] στεροῖτο, *commiserating the wife* [what a husband she had lost] *that she had lost such a husband,* Cyr. 7. 3. 13.

566. The Greek idiom (a) admits a *greater freedom* than the English, in the *construction* and *position* of both INTERROGATIVE and COMPLEMENTARY WORDS, especially in connecting them with dependent words and clauses; and even (b) allows the use of *more than one* in the same clause:

(a) Τί . . ἰδὼν ποιοῦντα, ταῦτα κατέγνωκας αὐτοῦ; [having seen him doing what, do you] *what have you seen him do, that you thus judge of him?* Mem. 1. 3. 10. Ὅταν τί ποιήσωσι, νομιεῖς αὐτοὺς σοῦ φροντίζειν; [when they have done what, will you think] *what must they do, before you will think that they care for you*, Ib. 4. 14. Ἵνα τί [sc. γένηται] ταῦτα λέγεις; [that what may be] *with what intent*, or *why, do you say this?* Id. Apol.

(b) Τίς τίνος αἴτιός ἐστι, γενήσεται φανερόν, *it will become evident who is guilty (and) of what*, Dem. 249. 8. Τίς πόθεν εἶς; *who are you (and) whence?* a. 170. Λεύσσετε, . . οἷα πρὸς οἵων ἀνδρῶν πάσχω Soph. Ant. 940.

G. "ΑΛΛΟΣ AND ΕΤΕΡΟΣ.

567. These pronouns are not only used *retrospectively*, but also *prospectively* and *distributively*: that is, they may denote, not only a different person or thing from one which *has been* mentioned, but also, from one which *is to be* mentioned; or they may, in general, denote a difference among the several individuals or parties which compose the whole number spoken of; but ἕτερος commonly with reference to two objects or sets of objects only. Compare *alius* and *alter*.

For modes of translation, see the following examples of ἄλλος, ἕτερος, and their derivatives, as used, (a) RETROSPECTIVELY. Ἱκανὸν ἔργον ἑνὶ ἕψειν κρέα, ἄλλῳ ὀπτᾶν, ἄλλῳ δὲ ἰχθὺν ἕψειν, ἄλλῳ ὀπτᾶν, *it is work enough for one man to boil meat, for another to roast it, &c.*, Cyr. 8. 2. 6. Μείναντες δὲ ταύτην τὴν ἡμέραν, τῇ ἄλλῃ ἐπορεύοντο, 'on the next," iii. 4. 1. (b) PROSPECTIVELY. Οὐδὲν ἄλλο πράξαντες ἢ δῃώσαντες, *having done nothing else than ravage*, Hel. 7. 4. 17. (c) PROSPECTIVELY and RETROSPECTIVELY. Ἄλλος ἄλλον εἶλκε, *one drew up another* (alius alium), v. 2. 15. Ὁ ἕτερος τὸν ἕτερον παίει, *the one strikes the other* (alter alterum), vi. 1. 5. (d) DISTRIBUTIVELY. Ἄλλοι ἄλλοθεν, [different persons in different directions] *some in this direction, and others in that*, i. 10. 13. Οὗτοι . . ἄλλος ἄλλα λέγει, *these say, one one thing, and another another* (393 d, 489 d). Εἰκαζον δὲ ἄλλοι ἄλλως, alii aliter, i. 6. 11.

e. The Greek idiom oddly permits these pronouns (esp. ἄλλος) to be used with reference to a larger class than the grammatical subject expresses: Βόες . . καὶ πρόβατα ἄλλα, *oxen and* [other sheep! *i. e.* other animals, *viz.* sheep] *also sheep*, vii. 3. 48. Ἔκτοθεν ἄλλων μνηστήρων, (Minerva was placed) *apart from the rest, the suitors*, a. 132. See 509 e, 515.

f. The neuter ἄλλο is often used prospectively with τί, τι, οὐδέν, or μηδέν, with the ellipsis of a verb, commonly ποιῶ, πράσσω, πάσχω, εἰμί, or γίγνομαι· Τί ἄλλο οὗτοι [sc. ἐποίησαν] ἢ ἐπεβούλευσαν; *what else have they done but plot against us?* Th. 3. 39. Οὐδὲν ἄλλο ἢ . . ἐθεᾶτο, *he did nothing but gaze*, Cyr. 1. 4. 24. Εἰ . . μηδὲν ἄλλο ἢ μετενέγκοις Ib. 6. 39.

g. Hence the phrase of *confident interrogation*, ἄλλο τι [sc. ἔστιν] ἤ, or the ἤ omitted, ἄλλο τι (also written ἀλλοτι), nonne, [is it any thing else than] *is it not certain that*: Ἄλλο τι ἢ οὐδὲν κωλύει; *is it not certain that nothing forbids?* iv. 7. 5. Ἄλλο τι οὖν οἵ γε φιλοκερδεῖς φιλοῦσι τὸ κέρδος; *do not then, surely, the covetous love gain?* Pl. Hipparch. 226 e.

CHAPTER III.

SYNTAX OF THE VERB.

I. AGREEMENT OF THE VERB.

(See also 492 s; for the union of Dual and Pl., 494; for Compound Construction, 495 s; for Synesis, 498 s; for Attraction, 500; for change of Number and Person, 501, 503; for construction with the Gen. Partitive, 421.)

568. RULE XXIX. A VERB agrees with its *subject* in *number* and *person*: as,

Ἐγὼ λήψομαι, *I shall take*, i. 7. 9. Σὺ ὁρᾷς, *tu vides*, ii. 1. 12. Ἠσθένει Δαρεῖος, *D. was sick;* Ὑμεῖς δόξετε, *you will seem;* Διειχέτην τὼ φάλαγγε, *the two lines were apart;* i. 1. 1; 4. 15; 8. 17. But,

569. RULE L. The NEUTER PLURAL has regularly its VERB in the *singular*: as,

Τὰ ἐπιτήδεια ἐπέλιπε, *provisions failed*, iv. 7. 1. Πλοῖα δ᾽ ὑμῖν πάρεστιν, *you have vessels*, v. 6. 20.

a. Exceptions to Rule L not unfrequently occur; chiefly, when things that have life are denoted, or when the idea of plurality is prominent, or in the non-Attic poets for the sake of the metre. Ἐνταῦθα ἦσαν τὰ Συεννέσιος βασίλεια, *here was the palace of S.* (489), i. 2. 23 (Βασίλεια ἦν 7). Ὑποζύγια νέμοιντο ii. 2. 15 (Ὑ. ἐλαύνετο iv. 7. 24). Τὰ τέλη . . ἐξέπεμψαν, *the magistrates sent forth*, Th. Φανερὰ ἦσαν καὶ ἵππων καὶ ἀνθρώπων ἴχνη πολλὰ i. 7. 17. Ἦσαν δὲ ταῦτα δύο τείχη i. 4. 4. Ἔργα γένοντο Λ. 310.

b. A compound subject with which a neut. pl. adjective agrees, is here commonly treated as if itself a single neuter plural (see 496 c).

c. A few passages occur, in which this rule applies to the *dual* as a form of the plural (494): Ὄσσε δαίεται, *the eyes burn*, ζ. 131.

570. When the *verb precedes*, it is sometimes singular, as if its subject were as yet *undetermined*, though a masc. or fem. plural follows. In Attic, this use is almost confined to ἔστι and ἦν (cf. the use of *il est* and *il y a* in Fr., and of *it is* in Eng.).

Ἔστι δὲ ἑπτὰ στάδιοι ἐξ Ἀβύδου ἐς τὴν ἀπαντίον, *it is seven stadia from Abydos to the opposite shore*, Hdt. 7. 34. Ἔστι . . ἄρχοντές τε καὶ δῆμος; *are there both rulers and people?* Pl. Rep. 462 e.

a. A few other examples of the Nom. pl. masc. or fem. with a verb in the sing. occur in the poets: Ὕμνοι . . τέλλεται, *hymns become*, Pind. Ol.

571. ELLIPSIS, &c. 1. The SUBJECT of the verb is commonly omitted, (a) if it is sufficiently indicated by the *affix of the verb* with the *context*, and is without emphasis; or (b), if it is a *pronoun* of the *third person*, referring to an agent *implied* in the verb itself, or (c) to *persons in general*, or (d) *vaguely* to some power, thing, or condition of things. In the last case, the verb is commonly termed *impersonal*. Thus,

288   SYNTAX.   R. XXIX. — VERB. — ELLIPSIS.   § 571.

(a) Ἐπεὶ δὲ ἠσθένει Δαρεῖος.., ἐβούλετο, *when D. was sick, he wished*, i. 1. 1.

(b) Ἐπεὶ ἐσάλπιγξε [sc. ὁ σαλπιγκτής], [when the trumpeter blew] *at the sound of the trumpet*, i. 2. 17 (cf. iv. 3. 32).   Ἐκήρυξε τοῖς Ἕλλησι [sc. ὁ κῆρυξ], *proclamation was made to the Greeks*, iii. 4. 36.

(c) Λέγουσιν, φασίν, dicunt, aiunt, *they* (men, people) *say*. Τοῦτον παθεῖν ἔφασαν (cf. Τοξευθῆναί τις ἐλέγετο) i. 8. 20. Ὅπερ πάσχουσιν ἐν τοῖς μεγάλοις ἀγῶσι, *as men are affected in great crises*, Th. 7. 69.

(d) Ὕει, νίφει, pluit, ningit, *it rains, it snows*. Ἐπεὶ συνεσκότασε, *when it grew dark*, Cyr. 4. 5. 5.   Μάχης δεῖ, *there is need of a battle*, ii. 3. 5 (see 473 b).   Μέλει μοι τούτων, [there is to me a care] *I take care of these*, Œc. 11. 9 (432 d, 457).   Μεταμέλει μοι, me pœnitet, *I repent*, Cyr.

e. An impersonal verb, from its very nature, is in the 3d *pers. sing.*; and an *adjective* joined with it is in the *neut. sing.*, or in the *neut. plur. for the sing.* (489 d, 491 c.) As it expresses an action or state without predicating it of any particular person or thing, its force may be commonly expressed by a *kindred noun* with a *substantive* (or *other appropriate*) *verb:* Δεῖ [= χρεία ἐστὶν] λόγων, opus est verbis, *there is need of words*, Cyr. 6. 1. 7. Παρεσκεύαστο, *preparation had been made*, Th. 4. 67.

f. A verb is often *introduced as impersonal*, of which the subject is afterwards expressed in an *Inf.* or *distinct clause:* Ἐδόκει αὐτῷ ἤδη πορεύεσθαι, *it now seemed best to him to march*, i. 2. 1.   Οὐκ ἦν λαβεῖν, [it was not for any one to take them] *it was not possible to take them*, i. 5. 2.

572.   2. The SUBSTANTIVE VERB is very often *omitted*, especially if it is merely a *copula;* most freely in the forms ἐστί and εἰσί.   Its omission is particularly frequent with *verbals in* -τέος, in *general remarks* and *relative clauses*, and with such words as ἀνάγκη, εἰκός, θέμις, καιρός, ὥρα, δῆλος, δυνατός, οἷός τε, ῥᾴδιος, χαλεπός :

Τοῦτο οὐ ποιητέον [sc. ἐστίν], hoc non faciendum, *this must not be done*, i. 3. 15. Ὁ μέγας ὄλβος οὐ μόνιμος, *great prosperity is not permanent*, Eur. Or. 340. Ποταμὸν, οὗ τὸ εὖρος στάδιον (cf. οὗ ἦν τὸ εὖρος), *a river, of which the width was a stade*, i. 4. 1.   Ὥρα λέγειν, *it is time to say*, i. 3. 12.

a. Other verbs may be omitted, if supplied by the context, or readily understood from the connection ; especially in familiar expressions, and familiar verbs, as of *coming, going, doing, saying, giving*, &c.: Οὔτε σὺ ἐκείνας φιλεῖς, οὔτε ἐκεῖναί σέ [sc. φιλοῦσι, 536]. Ἡ ἅμαξα τὸν βοῦν [sc. ἕλκει], "The cart before the horse," Luc. Ὦ φίλε Φαῖδρε, ποῖ δὴ καὶ πόθεν; *Dear P., whither now* (are you going) *and whence* (do you come)? Pl.

b. A verb expressed sometimes suggests a different, and even an opposite verb: Ἀμελήσας ὧνπερ οἱ πολλοί [sc. ἐπιμέλονται], *neglecting what the most seek*, Pl. Apol. 36 b.

573.   3. *Personal for Impersonal Construction.*   a. A verb, of which the proper subject is an *Infinitive* or *distinct clause*, often takes for a Nom. the *subject* of that Inf. or clause.   In this case, (b) the Inf. sometimes becomes a Part.; and (c) an adjective may be sometimes translated by an adverb.   Thus,

(a) Λέγεται Ἀπόλλων ἐκδεῖραι Μαρσύαν, *A. is said to have flayed M.*, = λέγεται, Ἀπόλλωνα ἐκδεῖραι Μαρσύαν, *it is said, that A. flayed M.*, i. 2. 8 (cf. i. 8. 7). Δῆλοι ἦσαν, ὅτι ἐπικείσονται, *it was evident that they would attack*, v. 2. 26. Δίκαιός εἰμι ἐγὼ κολάζειν, *it is just that I punish*, Ar. Nub. 1434. Πολλοὶ δὲ ἐπίδοξοι .. πείσεσθαι, *many are likely to suffer*, Hdt. 6. 12.

§ 576. PERSONAL CONSTRUCTION. VOICES. 289

(b) Ὁ μὲν οὖν πρεσβύτερος παρὼν ἐτύγχανε [= ἐτύγχανε τὸν πρεσβύτερον παρεῖναι], *the elder happened* [being] *to be present*, i. e. *it happened that the elder was present.* Ἀρκέσω θνῄσκουσ' ἐγώ, *it will be enough that I die.*

(c) Δῆλος ἦν ἀνιώμενος, *it was manifest that he was grieved*, or, *he was manifestly grieved.* Στέργων δὲ φανερὸς ἦν οὐδένα, *he evidently loved no one.*

d. This construction may occur in a dependent clause, and (c) is not confined to the finite verb; while (f) sometimes the two modes of construction are combined: (d) Ἦσαν δ' αὗται τετρακόσιαι, ὡς ἐλέγοντο, ἄμαξαι, *these wagons were* 400, *as* [they were said to be] *was said*, i. 10. 18. (e) Αὐτοῦ ὀλίγου δεήσαντος καταλευσθῆναι, *when he had wanted little of being stoned to death*, i. 5. 14. (f) Ἔδοξεν αὐτῷ, βροντῆς γενομένης, σκηπτὸς πεσεῖν εἰς τὴν πατρῴαν οἰκίαν, καὶ ἐκ τούτου λάμπεσθαι πᾶσαν, 'a thunderbolt seemed to fall, and [it seemed] that the whole house blazed.'

574. 4. The verb ἔφη is often separated from its subject by some of the words quoted; and is often thrown in *pleonastically:* "Εὖ λέγεις," ἔφη, "ὦ Σιμμία," ὁ Κέβης, "*You speak well, S.*," *said C.*, Pl. Phædo 77 c. Ἀποκρίνεται ὁ Χειρίσοφος· "Βλέψον," ἔφη, "πρὸς τὰ ὄρη," iv. 1. 20.

II. USE OF THE VOICES.

(For a general view, see 30, 266.)

575. RULE M. The uses of the VOICES are sometimes *interchanged.*

1. A *transition of meaning* sometimes gives to one voice the force of another voice of a different verb. Thus we find,

a.) The ACTIVE for the *passive:* Εὖ ἀκούω *to hear agreeably*, and hence, from the bewitching sweetness of praise, *to be spoken well of:* εὖ ἀκούειν ὑπό ... ἀνθρώπων, *to be praised by men* (bene audire), vii. 7. 23. Ἀπέθανεν ὑπὸ Νικάνδρου, *he* [died] *was killed by N.*, v. 1. 15. Οὕτως ἑάλω, *it was thus taken*, iii. 4. 12. See κτείνω, αἱρέω, 50. . Ἀσεβείας φεύγοντα (431 c).

b.) The MIDDLE for the *active:* Κόπτω *smite*, κόπτομαι *smite one's self through grief*, hence *bewail.* Τίνω *pay*, τίνομαι *take payment, punish.*

c.) The MIDDLE for the *passive:* Ἀπώλοντο ὑπό τε τῶν πολεμίων, [perished] *were destroyed by the enemy.* Ἀκούσομαι κακός, *I shall be called vile.*

d.) The PASSIVE for the *middle:* Ἐκπλαγεῖσά σε, [*struck out of* my wits by fear]*fearing you*, Soph. Ὄψιν ἀτυχθείς, *alarmed at the sight*, Z. 468.

576. 2. As the *middle* and *passive* had at first the same form throughout, and were afterwards separated in the Aor. and Fut. only (scarcely in the latter till after the age of Homer), it was but natural that the earlier freedom of use should sometimes prevail, especially in poetry, over the later distinction. This occurs chiefly in the use of a *shorter* for a *longer* form:

a.) In the use of the FUTURE MIDDLE for the *Future passive* (oftener in pures than in mutes, rarely in the contract Fut., 305): Οἱ δὲ ἀγαθοὶ τιμήσονται, *the good will be honored*, Th. 2. 87 (τιμηθήσονται 6. 80). Φιλήσεαι, *you will be kindly received*, a. 123. Εἰρξόμεθα, *we shall be excluded*, vi. 6. 16. Ὀνοδιεῖσθε, *you will be taunted*, Soph. O. T. 1500.

b.) In the use of the AORIST PASSIVE for the *Aorist middle.* This occurs chiefly in *deponents* (266 c), and in other verbs in which the proper passive is wanting or rare : as (M. marking verbs which have also an Aor. mid., less common or differing in sense), (a) *Deponents Passive*, ἄγαμαι M: (ἠγάσθη τε αὐτόν, *he admired him*, i. 1. 9, τὸν δ' ὁ γέρων ἠγάσσατο, *him the old man admired*, Γ. 181), βούλομαι *will*, δύναμαι M. *be able*, ἐπίσταμαι *understand*, οἴομαι M. *think ;* (β) *Other Verbs*, δέω (δεηθῆναι . . Κύρον, *to have requested C.*, i. 2. 14), μαίνω M. *madden*, στρέφω M. *turn*.

c. A few verbs belonging under b, extend the middle force to a *Fut. pass.*: διαλέγομαι (διαλέξομαι Isoc. 233 c, διαλεχθήσομαι Id. 195 c, *I will discourse*), ἄχθομαι M., ἥδω M. (Οὐκ ἀχθεσθήσῃ μοι; . . Ἡσθήσομαι. "*Will you not be displeased with me?*" "*I shall be pleased.*" Cyr.).

d. The use of the *Aor. mid.* as *passive* (except through simple transition of meaning, 575 c) is rare. It scarcely occurs, except in the 2 Aor. (originally the Impf. mid. and pass., 273 d) : Δουρὶ τυπεὶς ἢ βλήμενος ἰῷ, *struck by a spear or shot by an arrow*, Λ. 191. Κατέσχετο ἔρωτι Eur.

A. ACTIVE.

577. In many verbs, the active voice is both *transitive*, and *intransitive* or *reflexive*, in its use ; or both *causative* and *immediate*. (a) In some, the double use belongs to the same tenses ; but (b) in others, to different tenses, the intransitive sense falling especially to the complete tenses and 2 Aor. (c) In some verbs, the intransitive or reflexive use may be explained through the ellipsis of a noun or pronoun (476. 2);

(a) Στρέψαντες τὸ ἄγημα, *turning the corps*, Lac. 11. 9. Στρέψαντες ἔφευγον, *turning they fled*, iv. 3. 32 (cf. στραφέντες ἔφευγον iii. 5. 1).

(b) Τοὺς λόχους καθίστατε, *station your companies*, Cyr. 6. 3. 26. Προφύλακας καταστήσαντες, *having stationed sentinels*, iii. 2. 1. Κατέστη εἰς τὴν βασιλείαν, Εἰς τὴν βασιλείαν καθέστηκεν, *was* (is) *established on the throne*, i. 1. 3, Cyr. 5. 2. 27. Ἀπολώλεκεν, *has destroyed*, iii. 1. 38. Ἀπόλωλεν, *has perished*, Symp. 1. 15. See also, for intrans. 2 Aor. and 1 Pf., βαίνω, δύω, σβέννυμι, σκέλλω, φύω, 50 ; and for intrans. 2 Pf., chiefly preteritive, ἄγνυμι, ἐγείρω, μαίνω, ὄρνυμι, πείθω, πράσσω, σήπω, τήκω, 50.

(c) Ταύτῃ μὲν οὐκ ἦγεν, *he did not* [lead his army] *advance in this direction*, i. 10. 6 (cf. ἄγοιμι τὸ στράτευμα vii. 2. 25). Ἡδονῇ δούς [sc. ἑαυτόν], *giving* [himself] *up to pleasure*, Eur. Οὕτω δὲ ἔχει, *thus* [it has itself] *the matter stands*, v. 6. 12. Ἐδήλωσε, *showed itself*, ii. 2. 18.

d. Ἔχω used reflexively with an *adverb* is commonly equivalent to εἰμί with an *adjective* : Ἀθύμως ἔχοντες = Ἄθυμοι ὄντες, *being disheartened*. The poets even join ἔχω with an adj. : Ἔχ' ἥσυχος, [hold still] *be quiet*, Eur.

B. MIDDLE.

578. The middle voice, like the active, may be either *transitive* or *intransitive*. Its reflexive sense is far from being uniform either in kind or force. It not only varies in different verbs, but often in the same verb when used in different connections ; and is extensively not expressed in translation, but left to be understood. It is,

a.) DIRECT ; so that the middle is equivalent to the active with the *Acc.* of a *reflexive pronoun :* Λοῦται [= λούει ἑαυτόν], lavatur, *he is wash-*

§ 583.   ACTIVE AND MIDDLE.   291

ing himself, or *bathing*, Cyr. 1. 3. 11. Πάντες μὲν ἠλείφοντο, *they all anointed themselves*, Hel. 4. 5. 4. Λυόμην, ὑπέλυσα δ' ἐταίρους, ι. 463.

579. b.) INDIRECT ; so that the middle is equivalent to the active with the *Dat.* or *Gen.* of a *reflexive pronoun :* Στρατηγοὺς μὲν ἑλέσθαι [= ἑλεῖν ἑαυτοῖς] ἄλλους, τὰ δ' ἐπιτήδεια ἀγοράζεσθαι, *to* [take for themselves] *choose other generals, and buy* (for themselves) *provisions,* i. 3. 14. Παῖδα . . σὲ ποιοῦμαι, *I make you my son,* Cyr. 4. 6. 2. Ὅτι περὶ πλείστου ποιοῖτο, *that he* [made it to himself] *esteemed it of the utmost consequence* (582 γ), i. 9. 7.   Τρίτην ἐσηγάγετο γυναῖκα . . τὴν δευτέρην ἀποπεμψάμενος, *he took to himself a third wife, having* [sent from himself] *divorced the second,* Hdt. 6. 63.   Κῦρον δὲ μεταπέμπεται, *he sends for Cyrus* (to come to himself), i. 1. 2.   Τοῦτον φυλάττεσθαι, *to watch him for your own safety, to be on your guard against him,* i. 6. 9. Ἀποδίδομαι [give up for one's own profit], *sell ;* τίθεμαι or γράφομαι νόμον *make a law for one's self ;* βουλεύομαι *give counsel to one's self, deliberate ;* τιμωρέομαι *take vengeance for one's self, punish.* See χράω 50.

580. c.) RECIPROCAL ; so that the middle is equivalent to the active with a *reciprocal pronoun :* Μαχόμενοι καὶ βασιλεὺς καὶ Κῦρος, 'fighting with each other,' i. 8. 27.   Ἀμφὶ ὧν εἶχον διαφερόμενοι, 'quarrelling,' iv. 5. 17.   Διηλλάξαντο [τοὺς ἵππους], *exchanged,* Cyr. 8. 3. 32. — Hence the middle is extensively used in expressing actions which imply MUTUAL RELATION ; as those of *agreement* and *contention,* of *greeting* and *companionship,* of *intercourse* and *traffic,* of *question* and *answer,* &c.

581. d.) CAUSATIVE ; so that the middle denotes what a person *procures to be done* for himself : Ἐγὼ γάρ σε ταῦτα . . ἐδιδαξάμην, *I had you taught these things,* Cyr. 1. 6. 2.   Θώρακα ἐποιήσατο, *she had a corselet made,* Ib. 6. 1. 51.   Μισθόω *let for hire,* μισθόομαι [have let to one's self] *hire :* πλοῖον μισθωσάμενος vi. 4. 13.   Ἀποδώσουσιν οἱ δανεισάμενοι τοῖς δανείσασι, *the borrowers shall pay the lenders,* Dem. 926. 13. — The active is often so used, as in other languages, without the reflex reference.

582. e.) SUBJECTIVE ; so that the middle represents the action as *more nearly concerning the subject,* than the active (cf. 579).   Thus, (a) it may mark the close connection of the agent with that which is acted on ; (β) if the active is a *causative* verb, the middle may form the corresponding *immediate ;* (γ) if the active expresses an *external* or *physical* action, the middle may express the analogous *internal* or *mental* action ; (δ) if the active represents a person as *having* a particular office, condition, or character, the middle may represent him as making it more his own by *acting in accordance* with it.

(a). Ἔχω *have* (in general), ἔχομαι *have hold of, cling to* : ἑξόμεθα αὐτοῦ, *we shall keep hold of him,* vii. 6. 41.   Λαμβάνω *take,* λαμβάνομαι *take hold of.*   See 426.   (β) Γεύω *make another taste,* γεύομαι *taste for one's self* (432 a).   Παύω *cause to cease,* παύομαι *cease :* ἔπαυσε μὲν τούτων πολλούς Mem. 1. 2. 2 ; ταῦτα εἰπὼν ἐπαύσατο i. 3. 12.   Φοβέω *frighten,* φοβέομαι *fear ;* φαίνω *show,* φαίνομαι *appear.*   (γ) Σκοπέω *view,* σκοπέομαι *consider* (see v. 2. 20) ; ἀγάλλω *adorn,* ἀγάλλομαι *pride one's self ;* φράζω *tell,* φράζομαι *tell one's self, reflect.*   (δ) Πολιτεύω, ταμιεύω, *be a citizen (steward),* πολιτεύομαι, ταμιεύομαι, *act the citizen (steward), manage state* (or other) *affairs :* ταμιεύεσθαι, *to parcel out* (as a steward), ii. 5. 18.

583.   REMARKS.   1. If the reflex action is *direct,* it is oftener expressed by a *reflexive pronoun* with the *active,* or sometimes *middle ;* and in other cases, the pronoun is often added to make the expression more plain or emphatic : Ἐκεῖνος ἀπέσφαξεν ἑαυτόν, *he slew himself*, Dem. 127. 3. Ἑαυτὸν ἐπισφάξασθαι, *that he slew himself*, i. 8. 29. Ἐπισφαλεστέραν αὑτήν .. κατεσκεύακεν ἑαυτῷ, *he has rendered it less secure for himself*, Dem.

584. 2. As the Future so extensively denotes purpose (what a person will please himself by doing), it is the most *subjective* of the tenses ; and hence, in so many verbs (266 c), the middle here takes the place of the active. (a) In some of these, the Fut. act. is not used at all ; and (b) in others, only as a second, usually later or less common, form. (c) In some, the action of the body is thus connected with the state of the mind. E. g. (a) γιγνώσκω and οἶδα *know*, μανθάνω *learn*, εἰμί *be*, πάσχω *suffer*, θνήσκω *die*, λαγχάνω and τυγχάνω *obtain ;* (b) βιόω *live*, πνέω *breathe*, ἁμαρτάνω *err*, δείδω *fear*, τλάω *endure*, θαυμάζω *wonder*, ῥέω *flow*, τίκτω *bear ;* (c) ἀκούω *hear*, ὁράω *see*, ᾄδω *sing·* βοάω *shout*, γελάω *laugh*, γοάω *wail*, κλαίω *weep*, ὄμνυμι *swear*, ἐσθίω and τρώγω *eat*. See 50.

585. 3. In many cases, the reflex reference is so *obvious*, or so *indistinct*, that it may be either expressed or omitted without affecting the sense ; that is, the *active* or the *middle* may be employed at pleasure : Πολὺ φέροντες, Μικρὸν φερομένων, *bringing much (little)*, Mem. 3. 14. 1. Ἐσάγαγε γυναῖκα, Ἐσηγάγετο γυναῖκα, *take (took) a wife*, Hdt. 5. 40, 6. 63. — In some verbs, the use of the mid. form is poetic, especially Epic.

C. Passive.

586. The passive voice has for its SUBJECT a *complement of the active*, commonly (a) a *direct*, but sometimes (b) an *indirect* complement. (c) Any *other word* governed by the active, and not in apposition with this, may *remain unchanged* with the passive. (d) The SUBJECT OF THE ACTIVE is expressed, with the passive, by the *Gen. with a preposition* (commonly ὑπό, but sometimes ἀπό, ἐξ, παρά, or πρός), or (e), less frequently, by the *simple Gen. or Dat.*, or (f) yet more rarely (chiefly in poetry, especially Ep.), by the *Dat. with ὑπό*. Thus,

(a) ACT. governing ACC. Περιερρεῖτο δ' αὐτὴ ὑπὸ τοῦ Μάσκα, *it was surrounded by the Mascas* [= περιέρρει δ' αὐτὴν ὁ Μάσκας, *the M. surrounded it*], i. 5. 4. (b) ACT. governing GEN. Κατεφρονήθην ὑπ' αὐτοῖν, *I was despised by them* [= κατεφρονησάτην μου, *they despised me*,] Pl. ACT. governing DAT. Οὐκέτι δὲ ἀπειλοῦμαι, ἀλλ' ἤδη ἀπειλῶ ἄλλοις, *I am no longer threatened, but I now threaten others* (452 a), Symp. 4. 31.

(c) Ἱππέων ὁ λόφος ἐνεπλήσθη, *the height was filled with horsemen* (414), i. 10. 12. Εἰ θαλάττης εἴργοιντο (405). Δοθῆναί οἱ ταύτας, *that these should be given to him* (454 e), i. 1. 8. Μουσικὴν .. παιδευθείς, musicam doctus, *having been taught music* (480 c), Pl. But Στρατηγὸν δὲ αὐτὸν ἀπέδειξε πάντων (480 a), becomes Στρατηγὸς δὲ πάντων ἀπεδείχθη, i. 9. 7.

(d) Ὑπὸ δούλου ἄρχεσθαι, *to be ruled* [under] *by a slave*, Pl. Lys. 208 c. Γνῶμαι ἀφ' ἑκάστων ἐλέγοντο, *opinions were expressed* [from] *by each*, Th. 3. 36. Ἐκ βασιλέως δεδομέναι, *given* [from] *by the king*, i. 1. 6. Παρὰ πάντων ὁμολογεῖται, Ὁμολογεῖται πρὸς πάντων, *it is conceded by all*, i. 9. 1, 20. (e) See 434 b, 461. (f) Ὑπὸ τῷ πατρὶ τεθραμμένος, *brought up* [under] *by his father*, Pl. Rep. 558 d. Ἐφόβηθεν ὑφ' Ἕκτορι O. 637.

587. REMARKS. 1. When the active has more than one complement, it is commonly determined which shall be the subject of the passive by one or the other of the following preferences: (a) *The passive prefers, as its subject, a direct to an indirect complement of the active.* (b) *The passive prefers, as its subject, the name of a person to that of a thing.* If these preferences conflict, sometimes the one prevails, and sometimes the other. (a) Θώρᾱκες αὐτοῖς ἐπορίσθησαν, *they were furnished with breastplates* (454 c). (b) Οἱ τῶν Ἀθηναίων ἐπιτετραμμένοι τὴν φυλακήν, *those of the Athenians who had been intrusted with the guard*, Th. (cf. τοῖσι ἐπετέτραπτο ἡ φυλακή, *to whom the guard had been intrusted*, Hdt.).
2. The latter preference often leads to the construction in § 481.

588. 3. The passive is sometimes the converse of the *middle* rather than of the active; and hence *deponents* may have a passive: Μισθωθῆναι δὲ οὐκ ἐπὶ τούτῳ ἔφασαν, 'that they had not been hired,' i. 3. 1 (581). Θώρᾱκας εὖ εἰργασμένας, *corselets well made*, Mem. 3. 10. 9.

589. 4. If an active or middle which has *no complement* is changed to a passive, it becomes, *of course*, IMPERSONAL (571 d); and it *may* become so, with an *indirect complement:* Ὑπῆρκτο δ' αὐτοῦ, *a beginning of it had been made* [= ὑπῆρξαν αὐτοῦ, *they had begun it*], Th. 1. 93. Μάτην ἐμοὶ κεκλαύσεται, *I shall have wept in vain*, Ar. Nub. 1436.

III. USE OF THE TENSES.

(For a general view, see 30 b, 267.)

590. RULE XXX. The DEFINITE TENSES express the action as *doing at* the time; the INDEFINITE, simply as *performed in* the time; and the COMPLETE, as *complete at* the time. In the *Indicative*, this time is marked as PRESENT or FUTURE by the *primary tenses*, and as PAST by the *secondary;* in the *other modes*, it is not marked.

a. Hence the tense forms of the Indicative are distinguished, in general, as *chronic* (χρονικός *relating to time*); and those of the other modes, as *achronic* (ἀ- *not*). The Ind. Pres. and Impf. (more fully named *Present Imperfect* and *Past Imperfect*, since that which is *doing* is still unfinished) unite, for the other modes, in a tense which is simply *imperfect;* and in like manner, the Ind. Perf. and Plup. (which might properly be termed *Present Perfect* and *Past Perfect*) unite in a tense which is simply *perfect.* Another tense is commonly a *Past Aorist* (*Indefinite*, 267 d) in the Ind., but simply an *Aorist* tense in the other modes; and there are two Futures, a *Future Aorist* or *Indefinite*, and a *Future Perfect*, which, in respect to absolute time (607), are achronic out of the Indicative.

A. DEFINITE AND INDEFINITE.

591. The indefinite tenses present a *simple* (as it were, a *momentary*) view of the action as an *undivided whole;* the definite tenses present a *more extended* view of it as *in progress* (begun, going on, possibly never completed).

a. The former are distinguished in general as *narrative*, and the latter as *descriptive* tenses. If action is conceived of as *motion in a straight line*, the definite tenses may be said to present a *side view* of this line, so that it is seen *in its full length;* but the indefinite tenses to present only an *end view* of it, so that it appears as a *mere point.* Thus,

Definite View : ἔγραφε,   Indefinite View : ἔγραψε,

(————————)   (·)

scribebat, *he was writing,*   scripsit, *he wrote.*

592. Hence the ACTION is represented,

1.) By the definite tenses, as *continued* or *prolonged;* but by the Aorist, as *momentary* or *transient:* or by the former, as a *habit* or *continued course of conduct;* but by the latter, as a *single act:* ·

Τοὺς μὲν οὖν πελταστὰς ἐδέξαντο οἱ βάρβαροι καὶ ἐμάχοντο · ἐπειδὴ δὲ ἐγγὺς ἦσαν οἱ ὁπλῖται, ἐτράποντο · καὶ οἱ μὲν πελτασταὶ εὐθὺς εἵποντο διώκοντες · *the barbarians received the targeteers* (momentary) *and fought with them* (continued) *; but when now the hoplites were near, they turned to flight* (momentary) *; and the targeteers immediately followed pursuing them* (continued) *;* v. 4. 24. Λαβών . ., ἔχων, *having taken* (momentary), *having* (continued), i. 1. 2. Ἐπεὶ δὲ εἶδον αὐτὸν, οἵπερ πρόσθεν προσεκύνουν, καὶ τότε προσεκύνησαν, *when those saw him who previously used to bow before him* (habit), *they bowed even then* (single act), i. 6. 10.

a. Any dwelling of the mind upon the *agent, mode,* or *circumstances* of an action, or any attempt at *graphic description,* inclines to the use of the *definite tenses:* Ἀπεκρίναντο (Κλέαρχος δ' ἔλεγεν), *they answered (and Clearchus was the speaker),* ii. 3. 21.

b. In the IMPERATIVE, the momentary character of the Aor. is peculiarly favorable to *vivacity, energy,* and *earnestness* of expression : Ἀκούσατε οὖν'μου πρὸς θεῶν, *hear me, then, by the gods!* v. 7. 5.

c. The Aor. sometimes gives more vivacity or force to the *sequel* of another tense : Ὅς τε καὶ ἄλκιμον ἄνδρα φοβεῖ καὶ ἀφείλετο νίκην, *who puts to flight the valiant man, and* SNATCHES *victory from his grasp,* P. 177.

d. In verbs denoting *state,* the Aor. usually expresses *entrance* into the state (*becoming*), and the definite tenses *continuance* in it (*being*) : Βασιλεῦσαι ἄνδρα τυφλόν, .. ἐπὶ τούτου βασιλεύοντος, *that a blind man became king, and while he was reigning,* Hdt. 2. 137. So βουλεύω, πλουτέω, *I am senator, rich,* ἐβούλευσα, ἐπλούτησα, *I became senator, rich.*

593. 2.) By the definite tenses, as *doing at the time of,* or *until another action;* but by the Aorist, simply as *done in its own time:*

Ἐπορεύθησαν σταθμοὺς τέτταρας, ἡνίκα δὲ τὸν πέμπτον ἐπορεύοντο, εἶδον βασίλειόν τι, *they made four day's-marches, and while they were making the fifth, they saw a palace,* iii. 4. 23.

594. 3.) By the definite tenses, as *begun, attempted, designed,* or *imminent* (doing, not done) ; but by the Aorist, as *accomplished* (done):

§ 598. DEFINITE AND INDEFINITE. 295

Κλέαρχος τοὺς αὐτοῦ στρατιώτας ἐβιάζετο ἰέναι· οἱ δὲ αὐτόν τε ἔβαλλον.
.. Μικρὸν ἐξέφυγε τὸ μὴ καταπετρωθῆναι, ὕστερον δ' ἐπεὶ ἔγνω, ὅτι οὐ δυνήσεται βιάσασθαι. *C. attempted to force his soldiers to proceed; but they began to stone him.* He narrowly escaped being stoned to death (the completion of their act); *and afterwards, when he saw that he should not be able to prevail by force* (to accomplish his attempt). i. 3. 1 s. Ἔπειθον αὐτοὺς, καὶ οὓς ἔπεισα, *I tried to persuade them, and those whom I succeeded in persuading,* Cyr. Δῶρα δίδωσι, *he* (is for giving) *offers gifts,* I. 261.

a. Hence the definite tenses are often used with a negative to *deny the attempt* as well as the *accomplishment* of an action: Κλέαρχος οὐκ ἀνεβίβαζεν ἐπὶ τὸν λόφον, *C. did not undertake to march upon the hill,* i. 10. 14.

b. A person is often spoken of as *having done* what he *has attempted to do*: Δίκαια γὰρ τόνδ' εὐτυχεῖν κτείναντά με; 'having slain me,' Soph.

595. 4.) By the definite tenses, as *introductory;* but by the Aorist, as *conclusive:*

Ἠρώτων Κῦρον, .. ὁ δ' ἀπεκρίνατο, *they asked Cyrus, and he answered,* i. 3. 20. Ἀκούσαντες ταῦτα ἐπείθοντο καὶ διέβησαν i. 4. 16.

a. Verbs of *asking, inquiring, commanding, forbidding, deliberating, attempting, endeavoring, besieging,* and some others, are introductory in their very nature, and hence incline to the use of the definite tenses.

596. FUTURE. The dim, shadowy future has little occasion for precise forms to mark the *state* of the action. It is commonly enough to mark the action *simply as future.*

a. Hence the inflection of most verbs has but a single Fut., the *indefinite;* leaving the *definite* and *complete Futures,* if they require to be distinguished from this, to be expressed by a *Participle and substantive verb* (267 e): Σκῦρος ἐξαρκοῦσά μοι ἔσται τὸ λοιπόν, *Scyros shall hereafter content me* (continued, 592), Soph. Ἄνδρα κατακανόντες ἔσεσθε, vii. 6. 36.

597. In Greek, as in other languages, the Fut. furnishes indirect and variously expressive forms for the IMPERATIVE: (a) *Affirmation,* Ὡς οὖν ποιήσετε, καὶ πείθεσθέ μοι, *thus* [you will do] *do, and listen to me,* Pl. Prot. (b) *Negation,* Οὐ κλέψεις, *thou shalt not steal,* Rom. 13. 9. Μηδὲν τῶνδ' ἐρεῖς, *not a word of this!* Æsch. Th. 250. (c) *Question,* Ἆξά τις.. τὸν βοτῆρα; [will] *let some one bring the herdman,* Soph. O. T. 1069. (d) *Negative Question,* Οὐκ ἄξεθ' ὡς τάχιστα; καὶ.. ἄφετε μόνην, [will you not] *carry her away instantly, and leave her alone,* Soph. Ant. 885. (e) *Doubly Negative Question,* Οὐ μὴ λαλήσεις, ἀλλ' ἀκολουθήσεις ἐμοί; [Won't you not talk] *Don't talk, but follow me,* Ar. Nub. 505.

598. a. A future action may be represented more expressly as *close at hand,* or as *connected with destiny, necessity, will, purpose, expectation,* &c., by the verbs μέλλω, ἐθέλω or θέλω, βούλομαι, δεῖ, χρή, &c., with the Inf. This Inf. may be *Pres., Aor.* or *Fut.,* according to the view taken of the action in respect to definiteness and nearness: Μέλλω γὰρ ὑμᾶς διδάξειν, *I am about to teach you,* Pl. Ὁ σταθμὸς ἔνθα ἔμελλε καταλύειν, *the station where he was to halt,* i. 8. 1. Οὐκ ἐθέλω ἐλθεῖν, *I am not willing to go,* or *I will not go,* i. 3. 10. Βουλεύεσθαι, ὅ τι χρὴ ποιεῖν Ib. 11.

b. The ideas of *destiny, necessity, purpose,* &c. are often expressed by the simple Fut. Especially is the *Fut. Part.,* both with and without ὡς, used continually to express *purpose,* particularly with verbs of motion: Τί διαφέρουσι .., εἴ γε πεινήσουσι καὶ διψήσουσι; *what advantage have they, if they must hunger and thirst?* Mem. Οἶσθ' οὖν ὃ δράσεις; *do you know what you must do ?* Eur. Συλλαμβάνει Κῦρον ὡς ἀποκτενῶν, *he apprehends C.* [as about to put him to death] *with the design of putting him to death,* i. 1. 3. Ἔπεμψέ τινα ἐροῦντα, *he sent one to say,* ii. 5. 2.

c. Instead of the *Fut.* Part., the *Pres.* is sometimes employed to denote purpose, according to 594, especially with verbs of motion : Ταῦτ᾽ ἐκδικάζων ἦλθον, *I went to avenge this wrong,* Eur. Sup. 154.

B. COMPLETE.

599. a. While the indefinite tenses represent the action simply as *performed in* the time contemplated, the complete tenses represent it as *already finished (as having been already performed) at* the time contemplated. In the former, the view is directed to the *action* simply; in the latter, it is specially directed to the *completion* of the action, and to the *state consequent* upon its performance. Hence arise two special uses of the complete tenses : (b) the one to mark emphatically the *entire* (often *immediate*) *completion or termination* of an action ; (c) the other, to express the *continuance of the effects* of an action.

(a) Τοιαῦτα μὲν πεποίηκε, *such things has he done,* i. 6. 9. (b) Ἡ φεύγειν . . ἢ ταχὺ κατακεκαῦσθαι, *either to flee, or to be quickly and utterly consumed,* Cyr. (c) Εἶπον τὴν θύραν κεκλεῖσθαι, *they commanded the door* [to be closed and to remain so] *to be kept closed,* Hel. Ὅμηρον ἔγωγε μάλιστα τεθαύμακα, *Homer I have most admired* (as I still do), Mem. 1. 4. 3.

d. The Perf. Imv. *commands the completeness* of the action ; and hence may *forbid its continuance,* or may command emphatically its *full* (often *instant* and *final*) *performance :* Ταῦτα . . πεπαίσθω, *let* [so much have been played] *the sport end here,* Pl. Πεπεράσθω, *let a full trial be made,* Ar.

600. a. As the object of the complete tenses is to *ascribe the consequences* of the action, rather than *narrate* it, the transition in § 268 is natural and easy ; and we find verbs in different stages of the transition. Compare the Pres., Aor., and Preteritive, in examples like the following: Θνήσκω, *I am dying,* Eur. Alc. 284 ; Τεθνᾶσιν οἱ θανόντες, *those who have died* (the past event) *are dead* (the state consequent upon the event), Ib. 541. (b) The preteritive use has a far wider extent than is commonly recognized. In some verbs, however, it is dialectic or doubtful : βεβήκει, *she ascended,* or *had ascended,* A. 221 ; βεβλήκει, *he hit,* or *had hit,* E. 66.

601. FUTURE PERFECT. a. The Fut. Perf. expresses the sense of the Perf. with a change of the time ; that is, it represents the state consequent upon the completion of an action as *future.* (b) As it carries the mind at once over the act itself to its completion and results, it is sometimes used to express a future action as *immediate, rapid,* or *decisive.* (c) In some verbs these uses pass, more or less decidedly, into a preteritive use (268).

(a) Οὐ μὴν τοι μέλεος εἰρήσεται αἶνος, *your praise* (already spoken) *shall not have been spoken in vain,* Ψ. 795. Οὐδεὶς . . μετεγγραφήσεται, ἀλλ᾽, ὥσπερ ἦν τὸ πρῶτον, ἐγγεγράψεται, *no one shall be enrolled* (the simple act)

§ 604.   INTERCHANGE. — GENERIC USE.   297

elsewhere, but shall remain enrolled (the state consequent upon the act of enrolment) *as he was at first*, Id. Eq. 1370. (b) Νομίζετε .. ἐμέ τε κατακεκόψεσθαι, καὶ ὑμᾶς οὐ πολὺ ἐμοῦ ὕστερον, *be assured that I shall be immediately cut down, and you not long after*, i. 5. 16. (c) Πᾶν εἰρήσεται, *the whole* [shall have been] *shall be stated*, Hdt. 4. 16 (cf. a above). Πεπράσεται, *he shall be sold*, vii. 1. 36 (the classic Fut. pass. of πιπράσκω, 50).

C. INTERCHANGE.

602. RULE N. The uses of the TENSES are often *interchanged*.

a. This may be referred (I.) to *generic use*, especially where the formation is defective; (II.) to *gnomic use;* (III.) to varied use in respect to *relative* and *absolute time;* (IV.) to a *conception of the mind* varying from the reality of things, or to the choice of a *less direct form* of expression.

b. From the order in which the Greek tenses were historically developed (271 s), the Pres., in its *widest generic sense*, includes all the tenses; the Impf., all the past tenses; the Fut., all the future tenses; the Aor., all the indefinite and complete tenses, except those that are future; and the Perf., all the complete tenses.

c. The distinction of *generic* and *specific* belongs not merely to the tense-forms, but also to the ideas which these forms represent. Thus the idea of PRESENT TIME, which applies specifically only to the passing moment, extends in its generic application to any period including this moment; and we speak of the *present month*, the *present century*, &c. In its widest extent, therefore, it includes all time. (d) Hence *general truths* or *statements, existing states* or *habits*, and *oft-recurring facts*, belong appropriately to *present time:* Τίκτει τοι κόρος ὕβριν, *satiety begets insolence,* Theog. 153. A tense so employed to convey a general truth or statement is termed *gnomic* (γνωμικός *sententious*).

603. I. GENERIC USE. 1. Existing tenses are used generically to supply the places of those that are wanting.

a. The place of a *Present Indefinite* is commonly supplied by the Pres. Definite, as the generic *present* tense; but (b) sometimes, with stronger expression, by the Aor., as the generic *indefinite* tense. The latter, as the tense for the momentary, belongs especially to the vehement utterance of *lively feeling* or *quick thought* (chiefly in 1 sing.). Thus, (a) Τὸν ἄνδρα ὁρῶ, *I see the man*, i. 8. 26. (b) Ἥσθην ἀπειλαῖς, ἐγέλασα ψολοκομπίαις / *I smile at your threats, I laugh at your fury!* Ar. Eq. See 608 a.

c. In some verbs, (a) the Pres. supplies the place of a Fut.; or (β) the Impf., of an Aor.: (α) see 305 f, 326 c, 609 c; and εἶμι, νέομαι, χέω, βιόω, διδάσκω, κεῖμαι, in 50. (β) Ἦν *was*, ᾔειν *went*, ἔφην *said* (ἔφησα differing in sense, 50), &c.: Πέρσης μὲν ἔφη εἶναι, *he said that he was a Persian*, iv. 4. 17 (ὁ δὲ εἶπεν Ib. 18). Ἀπῄα and ἀπῆλθον, *deserted*, i. 9. 29.

604. 2. The definite tenses may express continuance (a) through a period *coming down* to their proper time (where we use the Perf. or Plup.); or (b) through a period *extending on* from this time (where the Fut. might be used): (a) Σφῷν ξυνοικῶ πόλλ' ἔτη, *I* [am] *have been living with you many years*, Ar. Pl. 437. Ταῦτ' ἄρ' ἐφυλάττου πάλαι, *this then you had been guarding against so long*, Ar. Eq. 125. (b) **Μένομεν** ἕως ἂν .. ληφθῶμεν; [do we wait] *shall we wait until we have been taken?* Th.

COMP. GR. 13*

605. 3. Unless the attention is specially directed to the *effect* of an action, the *generic Aor.* more frequently supplies the place of the *specific Perf. and Plup.* (602 b), as a more familiar, more vivacious, and often a shorter or more euphonic form:

Νυνὶ δὲ Θετταλοῖς .. ἐβοήθησε, *and now it has aided the Thessalians*, Dem. 22. 7. Ταύτην τὴν πόλιν ἐξέλιπον οἱ ἐνοικοῦντες, *this city its inhabitants had left*, i. 2. 24. Νῦν δ' ἦλθον, *I have now come*, a. 194.

a. This use prevails most in the *active*, as the voice which gives most prominence to the *action itself* (599 s); and is there especially frequent in the *participle:* Συλλέξας στράτευμα, ἐπολιόρκει Μίλητον, *having collected an army, he besieged M.*, i. 1. 7.   Τοῦτον διαβὰς ἐξελαύνει i. 2. 6.

b. The Aor. is so used in immediate connection with the Perf. or Plup., especially as a *sequel* (cf. 592 c): Ἀποδεδρακότες πατέρας καὶ μητέρας, οἱ δὲ καὶ τέκνα καταλιπόντες, *having run away from fathers and mothers, and others having even left children*, vi. 4. 8.

c. The use of the Aor. rather than the Plup., especially prevails after temporal and causal connectives, and in other dependent clauses: Ἐπεὶ δὲ συνῆλθον, ἔλεξε, *when they had assembled, he spake*, Cyr. 6. 2. 13.

606. II. GNOMIC USE. Past and future tenses may be used *gnomically*, as well as the Present (602 c).

a. If we can say "The wisest *err*" (the most general expression of the truth), we can also say "The wisest *have erred*" (the lesson of experience), or "The wisest *will err*"(a forethought for the future). Thus, Ὁ ἐπιεικὴς ἀνήρ .. τὸ τεθνάναι οὐ δεινὸν ἡγήσεται, *the good man will not account death an evil*, Pl. Rep. 387 d. Κάτθαν' ὁμῶς ὅ τ' ἀεργὸς ἀνὴρ ὅ τε πολλὰ ἐοργώς, *the indolent and energetic* [have died] *die alike*, I. 320.

b. GNOMIC AORIST. Especial *force, vividness*, or *actuality of expression* is often given to a general statement by the use of the Aor. (cf. 592, 603 b, 605): Ἀνὴρ δ' ὅταν τοῖς ἔνδον ἀχθηται ξυνών, ἔξω μολὼν ἔπαυσε καρδίαν ἄσης, *when a man becomes weary of the society of those at home, going abroad he* [has relieved] *relieves his heart at once of its disgust*, Eur. Med.

c. The general statements in *similes* are often expressed by the Aor., especially in Homer: Ἤριπε δ', ὡς ὅτε τις δρῦς ἤριπεν, *he fell, as when an oak falls*, Π. 482. See Γ. 33; and for Aor. with Pres. or Perf., Γ. 23. Λ. 62, H. 4. (d) A like use of the Fut. is doubtful or rare: Ὣς δ' ὅτε κινήσει Ζέφυρος, *as when the west-wind shall stir*, B. 147 v. l. (for κινήσῃ).

607. III. ABSOLUTE AND RELATIVE TIME. The time of an action is *absolute*, as simply viewed from the time of speaking or writing; but *relative*, as not so viewed, but from the time of another action.

a. The tense conforms to relative time far oftener in Greek than in English: in Ἔλεγεν ὅτι τὸ στράτευμα ἀποδίδωσι, *he said that he* [resigns] *resigned the army*, vii. 6. 3, ἀποδίδωσι conforms to the relative time, as the time of saying and resigning was the same, but *resigned* conforms to the absolute time, as the action was past when the author was writing.

608. IV. SYNESIS, &c. The relations of time have nothing sensible to fix the conceptions of the mind. It ranges therefore with freedom through all time, past, present, and future; and, at pleasure, transfers in thought the events of one period to another.

a. Even if the events are viewed in their proper time, a less direct mode of stating them sometimes spares the feelings, or is deemed more refined, courteous, or politic.

609. 1. VISION. That which is past or future is often seen in the imagination as *present*, and is so expressed. This figure of speech is called *vision ;* and the present tense so used is termed (a) the HISTORIC or (b) the PROPHETIC PRESENT, according as it expresses the past or the future :

(a) Τῷ τρόπῳ διόλλυνται; *how does* (did) *he perish?* Soph. (b) Μιᾷ μάχῃ τήνδε τε προσκτᾶσθε, *in one battle you* (will) *win this land,* Th. 4. 95.

c. That which *is to be* may be viewed as already *on the way :* Ἔρχεται ὥρα, *the hour is coming,* Jn. 4. 21. Εἶμι Φθίηνδε, *I* [am going] *shall go to Phthia,* A. 169. — This became the regular use of the Ind. εἶμι. See 603 c.

610. 2. *a.* A present or even future action, in view of the nearness or certainty of its completion, may be spoken of as *already accomplished ;* and (b) that which is present or even past is sometimes expressed by the Future, as though *not yet finished,* or for the sake of *less direct expression* (608 a) :

(a) Ἂν τοῦτο νικῶμεν, πάνθ' ἡμῖν πεποίηται, *if we conquer this, we have accomplished all,* i. 8. 12. (b) Τοὐμὸν . . σπέρμ' ἰδεῖν βουλήσομαι, *I* [shall] *choose to learn my origin,* Soph. Αἰτήσομαι, *I* [will] *beseech,* Eur. Alc.

611. 3. A past tense may be used, in *speaking of that which is present as related to some past opinion, feeling, remark, action, event,* or *obligation :* Κύπρις οὐκ ἄρ' ἦν θεός, *Venus* [was] *is not then a goddess* (as we supposed), Eur. Ἔφυν ἀμήχανος, *I* [was born] *am by nature incapable,* Soph. (§ 50 φύω). Ὤφελε μὲν Κῦρος ζῆν, [C. ought to be living] *Would that Cyrus were living !* ii. 1. 5. Οὐκ ἐχρῆν μέντοι σκοπεῖν; Apol. 3.

612. 4. The tense belonging to the *effect of an action* is sometimes used for the tense of the *action itself* (Pres. and Impf. for Perf. and Plup., or Aor.). So commonly in ἥκω and οἴχομαι (I *am* come, I *am* gone); often, as in Eng., in verbs of *hearing, learning,* and *saying ;* and sometimes in others : Εἰς καλὸν ἥκετε, *you* [are here, having come] *have come opportunely,* iv. 7. 3. Κῦρος δὲ οὔπω ἥκεν, *C. had not yet come,* i. 5. 12. Ὡς ἡμεῖς ἀκούομεν (audimus), *as we have heard* [are informed], v. 5. 8.

IV. USE OF THE MODES.

(For a general view, see 30 c, 269.)

A. INTELLECTIVE.

613. RULE XXXI. The INDICATIVE expresses *fact ;* the SUBJUNCTIVE, *present contingency ;* and the OPTATIVE, *past contingency.*

a. The Ind. presents the action as DECIDED IN POINT OF FACT (it *is* or *is not, has been* or *has not been, will be* or *will not be,* &c.), whether this decision is *declared* or *asked about,* is *known* or *unknown,* is according to the terms of the statement or *contrary* to them ; but the Subj. and Opt. present the action as UNDECIDED, and have respect to its CONTINGENCY or CHANCE (i. e. whether the action *may be* or *may not be*, *might be* or *might not be*, *might have been* or *might not have been*, &c.).

b. The Subj. and Opt. are *achronic* with respect to the *action itself* (590 a), but have a distinction of time with respect to its *contingency*. The Subj. expresses *present* contingency, i. e. some chance at the present time that the action will occur ; but the Opt., *past* contingency, i. e. some chance at some past time that the action would subsequently occur.

614. a. If there *will be* some chance that an event will occur, there *is* of course *now* some chance that it will occur ; and if there is now some chance, then, whether recognized or not, there always *has been*. *Future* contingency, therefore, is contained in *present* ; and all contingency, in *past*.

b. Hence, the past is the *generic time* for the contingent, as the present for the actual (602 c) ; and whatever is contingent is referred to past contingency, unless it is supposed with some degree of present expectation or looking forward to a decision, in which case it is referred to present contingency.

A. PRESENT CONTINGENCY : *I will go, if I can have leave* (and I intend to ask for it). *I think, that I may go, if I can have leave. I wish, that you may go. He reads, that he may learn.*

B. PAST CONTINGENCY. (1) Past supposition : *I thought, that I might go, if I could have leave. I wished, that you might go. He read, that he might learn.* (2) Present supposition not implying expectation or the looking forward to a decision : *I would go, if I should have leave* (but I have no thought of asking for it). *I could go with perfect ease. I should like to go.* (3) Present supposition contrary to fact : (α. In regard to the present.) *I would go, if I had leave* (but I have none, and therefore do not go). (β. In regard to the past.) *I would have gone, if I had had leave* (but I had none, and therefore did not go).

c. The range of past contingency is vast ; for there is nothing which it is proper for us to suppose at all, of which we may not conceive that there was some chance at some distant period in past eternity.

615. That which is *supposed contrary to fact* is regularly expressed in Greek by the Ind., as already decided (613 a) ; while the very act of supposition presents it as having been *at some time* contingent (614 c). It is therefore thrown back into the past as the time of its contingency ; and to a time *prior* to that of the opposing fact, as then only could there have been a chance in its favor. It is therefore expressed by what is termed a *prior tense*, i. e. a tense of the Ind. referring to this prior time.

a. *Supposition contrary to present fact* (what now *is*) *is regularly expressed by the Impf.*, i. e. the Pres. thrown back into the past ; and (b) *supposition contrary to past fact* (what *has been*), *by the Plup.* (the Perf. thrown back into the past), or (c) oftener by its equivalent *Aor.*: Εἰ μὴ ὑμεῖς ἤλθετε, ἐπορευόμεθα ἄν, *if you had not come, we should now be marching*, ii. 1. 4. Εἰ ἀπεκρίνω, ἴσως ἂν . . ἐμεμαθήκη, *if you had answered, I should perhaps have learned*, Pl. (d) So, "*If I had* time *to-day*, I would go"; "*If I had had* time *yesterday*, I should have gone."

e. Homer sometimes uses here the Opt. : Καί νό κεν ἔνθ' ἀπόλοιτο.., εἰ μὴ ἄρ' ὀξὺ νόησε, *he would have perished, had she not quick perceived,* E. 311.

f. If there will be no mistake respecting the time, the Impf. may take the place of the Aor. or Plup., to mark the act as continued or repeated (592): Οὐκ ἂν προέλεγεν, εἰ μὴ ἐπίστευεν ἀληθεύσειν, *he would not have predicted* (thus often), *had he not believed that his words would prove true.*

616. That which is *indefinite* is so far undecided ; and hence often employs the forms of contingent expression :

a.) The Subj. and Opt. are used in conditional, relative, and temporal clauses referring to the indefinite. See 634, 641.

b.) The secondary tenses of the Ind. are used with ἄν to denote indefinitely *any one* of a past series of acts. (c) This construction seems especially appropriate to the Aor. as the general expression for a single past act (592) : Πολλάκις.. ἠκούσαμεν ἄν τι κακῶς ὑμᾶς βουλευσαμένους, *we would often hear of your planning amiss* [used to hear], Ar. (d) The Impf. is so used (even in its iterative form, 332) ; though oftener and more appropriately without ἄν, as referring to the whole series (592, 632) : Διερώτων ἂν αὐτοὺς τί λέγοιεν, *I would ask them what they meant*, Pl. Apol. 22 b.

617. RULE O (*Law of Sequence*). The SUBJUNCTIVE regularly follows a tense referring to *present* or *future* time; and the OPTATIVE, a tense referring to *past* time.

a. In general, therefore, the primary tenses (269 c) and the Imv. are followed by the Subj.; the secondary tenses, by the Opt.; and the Inf. and Part., by either, according to the finite tenses whose places they occupy, or usually, according to those upon which they depend.

b. In the Att., the Subj. is scarce used, except in dependent clauses or those which can be so explained. In the Epic, it is sometimes independent, chiefly (with or without ἄν, 619 f) as a softer, or with a negative stronger, form for the Fut.: Καί ποτέ τις εἴπῃσι (ἐρέει), *some one may hereafter say* (*will say*), H. 87, 91. Οὐκ ἄν τοι χραίσμῃσι βιός *nought can* [*will*] *your bow avail,* Λ. 387.

c. The Greek Subj. is commonly translated by our Potential or Ind., rather than by our Subj., which, indeed, is now used far less than formerly. (d) In conditional and relative clauses, the Aor. subj. has often a force like that of the Lat. and Eng. Fut. Perf.: Ἐπειδὰν πάντα ἀκούσητε, κρίνατε, *when you shall have heard* (audiveritis), *all, judge*, Dem. 44. 2.

e. The Opt. is scarce used, except in dependent clauses and those which can be so explained, or as a conclusion dependent on some premise.

618. USE OF ἄν (Ep. κέ, 163 a, Dor. κά). This particle, which has no corresponding word in English, is a mark of contingence, and has two chief uses :

1.) Ἄν is joined with (a) the secondary tenses of the Indicative, (b) the Optative, (c) the Infinitive, and (d) the Participle, to mark them as depending on some condition expressed or implied.

(a, b) See 631 b, d. (c, d) The Inf. and Part. take ἄν, when it would belong to the finite modes of which they supply the place. See 621.

619. 2.) Ἄν is combined with various connectives before the subjunctive, thus forming *compound connectives,* of which the parts are sometimes distinct and sometimes united in form:

a.) With εἰ *if* (not as *whether*), uniting to form ἐάν, by contraction ἤν (so always in Hom., except as κέ is used for ἄν), and sometimes ἄν (distinguished by position, from simple ἄν, 621). See 631 c.

b.) With Relative Pronouns and Adverbs, and other Temporal Connectives: ὅς ἄν, ὅστις ἄν · ἕως ἄν, (ὅτε ἄν) ὅταν, (ὁπότε ἄν) ὁπόταν, (ἐπεί ἄν) ἐπήν or ἐπάν, (ἐπειδή ἄν) ἐπειδάν, εὖτ' ἄν · πρίν ἄν, μέχρι ἄν · &c. See 641.

c.) Sometimes with the final conjunctions ὅπως, ὡς, ὄφρα (thus expressing more distinctly the idea of contingency). See 624 a, e.

d.) That ἄν was thus combined before the Subj. (which grammatically it modifies), and not before the Opt., appears to have been due to the later and less strongly marked separation of the Subj. from the Ind. forms. (e) Dialectic, late, or rare exceptions, however, occur both ways (especially in the early poets): Εἰ μέγα νεῖκος ὄρηται, *if a mighty contest arise*, π. 98. Εἴ σου στερηθῶ, *if I lose you*, Soph. Ὣς κε .. δοίη δ' ᾧ κ' ἐθέλοι, *that he might give her to whom he pleased*, β. 53.

f. In the Epic, ἄν is sometimes joined more directly with the Subj.

620. a. In the Epic, ἄν is often used with the Fut. ind. as with the Subj. (chiefly in the form κέ): Εἴ κεν .. ἐθελήσει, *if he shall wish*, O. 213. (b) Rare and disputed cases also occur in the Attic, in which ἄν is used with the Fut.: Ποίᾳ δυνάμει συμμάχῳ χρησάμενοι μᾶλλον ἄν κολάσεσθε, *by using what auxiliary force you can better chastise them*, ii. 5. 13.

c. Critics deny that ἄν ever properly belongs to the Imv., or to the Pres. or Perf. ind. (d) Verbs with which ἄν is connected are commonly translated into Eng. by the potential mode.

621. The place of ἄν is after the verb which it modifies; or far oftener, after some prominent or characteristic word which is earlier in the sentence: as (a) a leading verb on which its own verb depends (especially such a verb as οἴομαι *think*, δοκῶ *seem*, οἶδα *know*, φημί *say*); (b) a participle or other word expressing the condition; (c) an interrogative, negative, or connective; (d) any emphatic word. (e) Hence it often shows an emphasis upon the word to which it is attached (and from which it is not regarded as parted by such particles as μέν, δέ, τέ, γάρ, &c., cf. 520 b). (f) Between ἄν and its verb, even another verb sometimes intervenes. Thus,

(a) Οἴομαι ἄν ὑμᾶς μέγα ὀνῆσαι, *I think that you would greatly benefit*, iii. 1. 38. (b) Λέγοντος ἄν τινος πιστεῦσαι οἴεσθε; *if one had said it, do you think they would have believed?* Dem. 71. 4. (c) Πῶς ἄν οὖν ἐγὼ ἢ βιασαίμην; *how could I compel?* v. 7. 8. (d) Εὐμενής ἄν δικαίως ἢ προδότης νομίζοιτο; *would he be justly considered* a friend *or* a traitor? Hel. 2. 3. 43. (e, f) Σύν ὑμῖν μέν ἄν οἶμαι εἶναι τίμιος, with you, *I think I should be honored*, i. 3. 6. (d, f) Χρήσιμοι ἄν ἐδόκουν εἶναι v. 6. 1.

622. a. For perspicuity, emphasis, or euphony, ἄν is often used more than once for a single verb; while (b) near verbs, *similarly used*, do not commonly require its repetition: (a) Στὰς ἄν ὥσπερ οὗτος .., λέγοιμ' ἄν, *standing as he does, I would say*, Cyr. 1. 3. 11. See i. 3. 6. (b) Κατακάνοι ἄν .., ἢ ζῶντας .. ἕλοι, καὶ κωλύσειε .., καὶ ποιήσειεν, *he would slay, or take alive*, &c., i. 6. 2. See ii. 5. 14; iv. 6. 13.

623. The general principles which govern the use of the intellective modes will now be applied to particular kinds of sentences, which may be termed, from their offices or connectives, *final, conditional, relative, temporal*, and *complementary*.

§ 627.   RULE P.   FINAL SENTENCES.   303

I. *Final (after* ἵνα, ὅπως, ὡς, μή · ὄφρα *poet.*).

624. RULE P. After a final conjunction, (a) an object of *present forethought* is expressed by the *Subjunctive*, or (b) in the *Future*, by the *Indicative;* but (c) an object of *past forethought*, by the *Optative*, or (d), to mark it as now contrary to fact, by a *prior tense* of the *Indicative:*

(a) Γράφω (γέγραφα, γράψω), ἵνα **μάθῃς** (**μανθάνῃς**), scribo (scripsi, scribam), ut discas, *I write (have written, shall write), that you may learn (be learning)*. Ἐμοὶ δὸς αὐτά, ὅπως.. διαδῶ, Cyr. Ὡς δ' ἂν μάθῃς.., ἀντάκουσον, *listen in turn, that you may learn (if you will)*, ii. 5. 16 (619 c).

(b) Instead of the Subj., the Fut. ind. is here commonly used after words of *attention, care,* or *effort*, and sometimes after others (regularly joined by ὅπως, sometimes by ὡς, ὄφρα, or μή): Ποιμένα δεῖ ἐπιμελεῖσθαι, ὅπως σῶαί τε ἔσονται αἱ οἶες, *a shepherd must take care,* [how his flock shall be safe] *that his flock be safe*, Mem. 3. 2. 1.

(c) Ἔγραψα (ἔγραφον, ἐγεγράφειν), ἵνα **μάθοις** (**μανθάνοις**), scripsi (scribebam, scripseram), ut disceres, *I wrote (was writing, had written), that you might learn (be learning)*. Φίλων ᾤετο δεῖσθαι, ὡς συνεργοὺς ἔχοι, *he thought he needed friends, that he might have coworkers*, i. 9. 21.

(d) Ἐχρῆν σε Πηγάσου ζεῦξαι πτερόν, ὅπως **ἐφαίνου**, *you ought* (rather) *to have saddled the wing of Pegasus, that you might appear*, Ar. Pax 135.

e. The final conjunctions ὡς, ὅπως, ἵνα, and ὄφρα are in their origin relatives; and μή seems to have become a connective through the ellipsis of one of these, the fuller form being still often retained: Οὕτω ποιεῖν, ὅπως.. φανείη, *to act* [in that way in which] *so that he might appear;* Cyr.

625. a. To the English reader, the use of the connectives after verbs of fearing often seems reversed, as in Latin, French, &c.; *apprehension for* being indicated rather than *apprehension against:* Ὅπως λάθω, δέδοικα, metuo ut lateam, [I am apprehensive for this, how I may elude] *I fear I cannot elude*, Eur. Δέδοιχ' ὅπως μὴ τεύξομαι, vereor ne inveniam, [I am concerned for this, how I may not find] *I fear that I shall find*, Ar.

b. Yet words of fear are sometimes followed by a complementary construction, as in Eng., especially if themselves modified by μή: Μὴ φοβοῦ, ὡς ἀπορήσεις, *do not fear that you will want*, Cyr. 5. 2. 12. Cf. 630.

626. ELLIPSIS. A word of *attention, care,* or *fear* is sometimes to be supplied before ὅπως or μή:

Ὅπως οὖν ἔσεσθε ἄνδρες [sc. ὁρᾶτε], *see then that you be men*, i. 7. 3. Ὅπως μὴ οὐχ οἷός τ' ἔσομαι [sc. δέδοικα], *I fear that I shall not be able*, Pl. Μή.. σοὺς διαφθείρῃ γάμους, *ah, lest she prevent thy marriage!* Eur.

627. This ellipsis appears to have introduced,

1.) The use of the *Subjunctive* or *Future Indicative* after οὐ μή, as a *future of strong denial:*

Οὐ γάρ [sc. φόβος ἐστὶ or δέδοικα] σε μὴ.. **γνῶσ'** οὐδ' **ὑποπτεύσουσιν**, [there is no danger that they may know or will suspect you] *they surely will not know or suspect you*, Soph. Οὔ σε μὴ **προδῶ**, Id. Οὐδεὶς μηκέτι **μείνῃ**, *no one will stay longer* (cf. βοηθήσει), iv. 8. 13.

628. 2.) The use of the *Subjunctive* as *Imperative*.

This occurs chiefly (a, b) in the 1 *Person* (where the Imv. is wanting, 270 a); and (c) in the *Aorist with* μή (including its compounds), according to this special rule for the 2 and 3 Persons: (RULE Q.) In prohibitions with μή, the *Pres.* is put in the *Imv.*, and the *Aor.* in the *Subj*. (d) Exceptions to this rule are doubtful in the Pres.; in the Aor., *t*hey are very rare in the 2 Person, but not in the 3d. Thus,

(a) Μή ἀναμείνωμεν . ., ἀλλὰ ἡμεῖς ἀρξωμεν [sc. ὁρᾶτε, or ὁρᾶτε ὅπως], [see that we do not wait] *let us not wait, but ourselves begin*, iii. 1. 24. (b) This Subj. is often preceded by ἄγε, φέρε, or some other Imv., after which a connective might be supplied: Φέρ', ἀκούσω, *come, let me hear*, Hdt. 1. 11. (c) Μή ποιήσῃς ταῦτα [sc. σκόπει], ne feceris hoc, [see that you do not do this] *beware of doing this*, vii. 1. 8. Μή θαυμάζετε, *do not be wondering* (as you now are), i. 3. 3. Μηδ' ἐπίκευθε, Μηδ' ἐπικεύσῃς, *do not conceal*, π. 168, o. 263. (d) Μηδείς . . νομισάτω, *let no one think*, Cyr.

629. a. Another form of ellipsis is found in such expressions as Ὡς δὲ συντέμω, *but to be concise* [I add this only], Eur. Tro. 441.
b. A final clause may refer elliptically to the *present* or even *past:* Φοβεῖσθε μή . . νῦν διάκειμαι, *you fear* [lest it prove] *that I am now affected*, Pl.

630. The use of final clauses blends with that of *infinitives* and *complementary clauses;* and one construction is sometimes found where another would rather have been expected; as, (a) ὅπως, &c. (Ep. and late, even ἵνα), after words of *entreating, exhorting, promising, commanding, forbidding, wishing*, and the like; (b) Inf. or Complementary Clause after words of *fear* or *care*; &c.: Θέλω ἵνα μοι δῷς Mk. 6. 25. See 625 b.

II. *Conditional (after* εἰ, αἰ D. E.; εἰ μή*).*

631. RULE R. In the HYPOTHETICAL PERIOD, (a, b) if the PREMISE is presented as *already decided in point of fact*, it takes the INDICATIVE; (c) if it is presented as *undecided, but with present expectation of decision*, it takes the SUBJUNCTIVE; (d) otherwise, it takes the OPTATIVE. In the first case, the CONCLUSION is commonly in the *Indicative* or *Imperative;* in the second, in the *Future Indicative* or an equivalent; and in the third, in the *Optative* with ἄν.

(a, b) If the *premise* is decided, the *conclusion* is also decided, so far as depends upon the premise; and is expressed accordingly, unless there is some reason, aside from the premise, for a different expression. There are here two constructions.

(FORM a.) If the premise is presented *as agreeing with fact*, or *without indication on this point*, any form of premise or conclusion consistent with such an agreement may be used: Εἰ γράφει, καλῶς ποιεῖ (καλῶς ἕξει, γραφέτω), *if he is writing, he is doing well* (*it will be well, let him write*). Εἰ ἔγραψε, καλῶς ἐποίησε (καλῶς ἔχει), *if he wrote, he did well* (*it is well*). Εἰ γράψει, καλῶς ποιήσει, *if he will write, he will do well*. Εἰ δοκεῖ σοι, στεῖχε (πλέωμεν), *if it seems best to you, go* (*let us sail*), Soph.

(FORM b.) If the premise is presented *as contrary to fact*, it takes a *prior tense* of the *Indicative;* and the conclusion, a *prior tense* with ἄν (615, 618 a): Εἰ ἔγραφε, καλῶς ἂν ἐποίει, si scriberet, bene faceret, *if he*

§ 634.   IN THE HYPOTHETICAL PERIOD.   305

were now writing, he would be doing well. Εἰ ἔγραψε, καλῶς ἂν ἐποίησεν (καλῶς ἂν εἶχεν), *if he had written* (yesterday), *he would have done well* (*it would* now *be well*). Οὐκ ἂν ἐποίησεν Ἀγασίας ταῦτα, εἰ μὴ ἐγὼ αὐτὸν ἐκέλευσα, *A. would not have done this, if I had not commanded him*, vi. 6. 15.

(FORM c.) Here the conclusion, as *depending upon a decision yet to be made*, is properly expressed by the *Fut. ind.*, or some other form referring to the future (as the Imv., Opt. of wish, &c.) : Ἐὰν γράφῃ (γράψῃ), καλῶς ποιήσει, si scribat (scribet), bene faciet, *if he write, he will do well*. Χρῶ αὑτοῖς, ἐὰν δέῃ τι, *use them, if you have any need*, Cyr. Ἦν . . ἀφέλωμαι . ., ἀπολοίμην, *may I perish, if I take*, Ar. — For ἐάν, &c., see 619 a.

(FORM d.) If the premise is *undecided and without present expectation of decision*, the conclusion must also be, so far as depends upon the premise ; and both are therefore appropriately expressed by the *Optative*, with ἄν in the conclusion (618). Εἰ γράφοι (γράψαι), καλῶς ἂν ποιοίη (ποιήσαι), si scribat, bene faciat, *if he should write, he would do well*. Οὐδὲ γὰρ ἂν Μῆδοκος . . ἐπαινοίη, εἰ ἐξελαύνοιμι τοὺς εὐεργέτας, *M. would not approve, if I should drive out our benefactors*, vii. 7. 11.

c. In forms b and d, ἄν is regularly used in the conclusion, but not in the premise, unless that is itself dependent upon some condition expressed or implied (618) : Εἴπερ ἄλλῳ τῳ ἀνθρώπων πειθοίμην ἄν, καὶ σοὶ πείθομαι, *if I would trust any other man* (should he so affirm), *I trust you*, Pl.

f. In the conclusion, the omission of ἄν with a past tense of the Ind. is chiefly for the sake of more decided expression ; (g) while its omission with the Opt. is almost wholly poetic, and chiefly Epic. See 632.

632. A *past tense of the Ind.* (commonly the Impf.) without ἄν may take the place of another form in the conclusion, to express *more decidedly* a *habit* or *series* of acts, a *continued, unfinished*, or *threatened* act or state, some *property* of an act (as possibility, propriety, necessity, &c.), or some *feeling* respecting an act, even though the particular acts themselves may be indefinite, contingent, or unreal (cf. 611) : Οὐδὲν ἤνυον, εἰ μὴ τούτους πείσαιμι, *I effected nothing, unless I should persuade these*, Cyr. Οὐδὲ γὰρ, εἰ πάνυ προθυμοῖτο, ῥᾴδιον ἦν, nor, *if he should greatly desire it, was it easy* (facile erat), iii. 4. 15. Ἠισχυνόμην μέντοι, εἰ . . ἐξηπατήθην, *I should be ashamed indeed, if I had been deceived*, vii. 6. 21. See 634.

633. a. If the conclusion is itself a dependent clause, its form is commonly determined by this dependence, and the condition usually conforms (617) : Ἐπορευόμην, ἵνα, εἴ τι δέοιτο, ὠφελοίην αὐτόν, *I went that I might aid him, if he should need*, i. 3. 4 (624).

b. The conclusion has sometimes a second condition, expressed or understood, to which its verb conforms : Ἐὰν δ' ἐμὲ ἕλησθε, οὐκ ἂν θαυμάσαιμι, εἴ τινα εὕροιτε, *if you elect me, I should not wonder if you should find*, vi. 1. 29. Εἰ διέλθοιεν . ., ἢν μὲν βούλωνται, διαβήσονται iv. 1. 3.

c. The true conclusion is sometimes implied, rather than expressed, in the grammatical apodosis ; or (d) is elliptically contained in it : (c) Οἱ δ' ᾤκτειρον, εἰ ἁλώσοιντο, *others pitied them* [for what they would suffer], *in case they should be taken*, i. 4. 7. (d) Εὕρημα ἐποιησάμην, εἴ πως δυναίμην, *I accounted it a godsend* [thought that it would be], *if I could in any way*.

634. INDEFINITE OR GENERAL PREMISE. If the premise refers indefinitely or generally to acts of a certain kind or series, (a) it sometimes takes the Indicative, from the *general decision of the kind or series as a whole ;* but oftener the Optative or Subjunctive, from the *want of definiteness in respect to*

COMP. GR.   T *particulars* (616), — (b) the Opt. if the kind or series is now past, (c) but otherwise the Subj. (d) The CONCLUSION has commonly the form appropriate to the kind or series as a whole, but (e) sometimes that appropriate to a single act. (f) Mixed constructions occur in both premise and conclusion.

(a, d) Εἴ τίς τι ἐπηρώτα, ἀπεκρίνοντο, *if any one put any question, they replied*, Th. 7. 10. (b, d) Εἴ τι μὴ φέροιμεν, ὤτρυνεν φέρειν, *if we should fail to bring anything, he bade us bring it*, Eur. Alc. (c, d) Ἢν δ' ἐγγὺς ἔλθῃ θάνατος, οὐδεὶς βούλεται θνῄσκειν, *if death come near, no one is willing to die*, Ib. (b, d, e) Εἴ τις αὐτῷ δοκοίη .. βλακεύειν, .. ἔπαισεν ἄν, καὶ ἅμα αὐτὸς προσελάμβανεν, *if any one seemed to him to shirk, he would give him a blow, and at the same time took hold himself*, ii. 3. 11.

635. INCORPORATION. The condition, instead of being expressed in a distinct clause, is often incorporated in the conclusion, especially in a *participial* form:

Λέγοις ἂν εὖ φρονῶν [= εἰ εὖ φρονοίης], *you would speak, if you were a friend*, Soph. O. T. Μαθοῦσ' ἐρῶ, Ib. Ὥσπερ ἂν δράμοι τις περὶ νίκης, *as one would run* [if he were running] *for victory*, i. 5. 8. Ἄλλως δὲ οὐκ ἂν τολμῷεν, *they would not venture otherwise* [if it were not so], v. 4. 34.

636. ELLIPSIS. In a hypothetical period, the premise or the conclusion is often omitted; the other part retaining its proper form (as also in 635):

I. PREMISE OMITTED. Among the conditions most naturally supplied, and therefore most frequently omitted, are those of *inclination* with-possibility and of *possibility* with inclination; since these are the two great conditions of human conduct.

a. Hence the frequent use of the Opt. and past tenses of the Ind. with ἄν (specially termed *potential Opt.* or *Ind.*), to denote one of these ideas, the other being implied as a condition. Other familiar ideas are also implied, as of *effort, necessity, propriety, occasion, existence, actuality*, &c.; and (b) the premise is often involved in an independent sentence, or otherwise supplied by the context. Thus, (a) Δύναιο ἄν . . εὑρεῖν ὅτῳ ἂν χαρίσαιο; [would you be able if you tried] *could you find one whom you might oblige* (if you should wish)? Cyr. Ἥδιστ' ἂν ἀκούσαιμι, *I should most gladly hear* (if I might), ii. 5. 15. (b) Οὔτε ἐσθίουσι πλείω ἢ δύνανται φέρειν, διαρράγειεν γὰρ ἄν, *they eat no more than they can bear, for they would burst* (if they did), Cyr. Ἔτι οὖν ἂν γένοιο .. φίλος; *would you yet become a friend* (if I should now forgive you)? i. 6. 8. See 637.

637. With the ellipsis of a premise, the Optative with ἄν may supply the place (a) of the Imperative, or (b) of the Indicative, especially (c) of the Fut. ind.; (d) or may express wish in the form of a question:

(a) As Imv., it expresses permission, or command in the softened language of permission, or prohibition in the strong form of denying permission: Κομίζοις ἂν σεαυτόν, *you may now betake yourself* [might if you should wish], Soph. Χωροῖς ἂν εἴσω, *go within*, Id. Οὐκ ἂν βασιλῆας ἀνὰ στόμ' ἔχων ἀγορεύοις, 'you must not harangue,' B. 250.

(b) Αὐτὸ ἂν τὸ δέον εἴη · θᾶττον γὰρ ἀναλώσουσι, *this* [would be, if we

§ 641.   RULE S.   RELATIVE AND TEMPORAL CLAUSES.   307

could have it] *is the very thing we want; for they will sooner expend*, iv. 7. 7.   Ποῦ δῆτ' ἄν εἶεν οἱ ξένοι; *where then* [might be] *are the strangers?* Soph.

(c) Οὐκέτ' ἄν κρύψαιμι, *no longer* [if I might, would I] *will I conceal it*, Ar.   Κλύοις ἄν ἤδη, *thou wilt now hear*, Soph. — So esp. in the 1 Pers.

(d) Πῶς ἄν ὀλοίμαν; [how might I die, if I should seek death?] *Would that I might die!* Eur.   Τίς ἄν .. δοίη; *O that one would give!* Soph.

638. II. CONCLUSION OMITTED.   To this ellipsis may be referred the common *expression of wish* (a) by the Optative, or (b) as contrary to fact, by a prior tense of the Indicative (615):

(a) Εἴ μοι γένοιτο φθόγγος [sc. ἡδοίμην ἄν], [if I might have a voice, I should be glad] *O that I might have a voice!* Eur. Hec. 836.   Εἰ γὰρ γένοιτο [sc. καλῶς ἄν ἔχοι], [for] *O if it might be* [it would be well]! Cyr. 6. 1. 38.

(b) Εἴθ' εἶχες .. βελτίους φρένας [sc. ἡδόμην ἄν], *if you but had a better mind!* Eur.   Εἰ γὰρ τοσαύτην δύναμιν εἶχον, *would I had such power!* Id.

c. From the great use of these elliptic forms, especially a, the connective εἰ (commonly in the forms εἴθε, εἰ γάρ, or αἴθε, αἰ γάρ D. E.) came to be regarded as a particle of wishing, and the Opt. as the appropriate mode for the expression of a wish (modus optātīvus, *the wishing mode*). (d) Hence it was so used without the connective; and (e) sometimes, as a less direct form, took the place of the Imv., especially in the 3 Pers. (the two modes being sometimes used together, and these again with the Subj.): (d). Οἱ θεοὶ ἀποτίσαιντο, *may the gods requite!* iii. 2. 6.   (e) Ἤ τις .. Ἀχιλῆϊ παρσταίη, *or* [may] *let one stand by A.*, Τ. 119.

f. Ἄν does not belong to this Opt. of direct wish, which is often thus distinguished from the Opt. in its other uses.

g. A wish in opposition to fact is also expressed by the 2 Aor., and rarely by the Impf., of ὀφείλω *ought* (50); the particles of wishing being often prefixed, to add strength : 'Ολέσθαι δ' ὤφελον, [I ought to have perished] *Would that I had perished!* Soph. O. T. 1157.   Ὤφελε μὲν Κῦρος ζῆν (611).   Εἴθ' ὄφελες ἄγονός τ' ἔμεναι, *Would you were unborn!* Γ. 40.   Ὡς πρὶν ὤφελλον ὀλέσθαι, *O that I had sooner died!* Ω. 764 (648 d).

639. a. The conditional form often takes the place of other forms, especially from Greek courtesy and moderation of speech (654 a); as, after verbs of *emotion;* in the frequent use of εἴ τις for ὅστις, and like substitutions, &c.: Τόδε ἐθαύμασα, εἰ [= ὅτι] .. τίθης, *this I wonder at*, [if] *that you place*, Pl. Rep. 348 e.   Ἔκαιον καὶ χῖλὸν καὶ εἴ τι ἄλλο χρήσιμον ἦν, *they burned both fodder and* [if anything] *whatever else was of use*, i.

III. *Relative or Temporal.*

640. RULE S. A RELATIVE CLAUSE commonly uses the modes like other sentences to which it is most nearly akin.

a. From such analogies, some relative clauses have been distinguished as *conditional relative, final relative,* &c.

641. 1. CONDITIONAL RELATIVE CLAUSES, &c. A relative or temporal clause referring to that which is *indefinite* or *general* or *not yet determined*, may be viewed as contingent (616); and then has regularly (a) the Subj., if it depends on a primary tense, but (b) the Opt., if it depends on a secondary.   For the form of the connective, see 619 d.

(c) Such a clause has commonly a form and force akin to those of an *indefinite premise* (634); while its leading clause resembles in form the corresponding conclusion. Thus,

308 MODES. R. T.—ORATIO OBLIQUA.—OPT., &C. OF WISH. § 641.

(a) "Ο τι ἄν [= ἐάν τι] δέῃ, πείσομαι, whatever [if any] evil must be met, I will suffer (551 a), i. 3. 5. Ὁπόταν καιρὸς ᾖ, ἥξω, when it is the proper time, I will come, vii. 3. 36. Ἐπειδὰν πάντα ἀκούσητε, κρίνατε Dem.

(b) Ἐθήρευεν ἀπὸ ἵππου, ὁπότε [= εἴ ποτε] γυμνάσαι βούλοιτο, he hunted on horseback, whenever [if at any time] he might wish to exercise, i. 2. 7. Φοβοίμην δ᾽ ἂν τῷ ἡγεμόνι, ᾧ δοίη, ἕπεσθαι, I should fear to follow the guide whom he might give us, Ib. 17. Ἐπεί τις διώκοι, προδραμόντες ἕστασαν, when any one gave chase, they would run before and stop, i. 5. 2.

d. Most temporal clauses are also relative (as above); and those which are not, usually follow the same analogy (introduced by πρίν, μέχρι, ἄχρι, &c.): Μὴ στενάξε, πρὶν μάθῃς (619 e), do not groan, before you [may] have learned, Soph. Ph. 917. . Ἰlpìν μάθοιμι Ib. 961. Ἀνέμενεν . ., ἔστε ἐμφάγοιεν, he waited until they [should have] had eaten, Cyr. 8. 1. 44.

e. Ὅστις, as requiring no additional mark of indefiniteness, is oftener joined with the Ind., than ὅς used indefinitely : Ὅστις δ᾽ ἀφικνεῖτο, i. 1. 5.

642. 2. FINAL RELATIVE CLAUSES. A relative clause having the force of a final clause (558 a) has commonly in Attic the Fut. (Ind., rarely Opt. except in Indirect Discourse, 643); but oftener in Epic the Subj. or Opt. (except Fut.) : Ὅπλα κτῶνται, οἷς ἀμυνοῦνται Mem., Πέμψον τῳ᾽, ὅστις σημανεῖ Eur., Ἄγγελον ἧκαν, ὃς ἀγγείλειε ο. 458, § 558 a.

a. In such relative clauses in Attic, the Subj. occurs chiefly after ἔχω (commonly without ἄν) ; and the Opt. chiefly after another Opt.

IV. *Complementary (Oratio Oblīqua, &c.).*

643. RULE T. The OPTATIVE is the finite mode appropriate to *Indirect Discourse in past time.* Thus,

a. Direct Discourse, Λέγει (εἶπεν), "ὁρῶ" ("εἶδον," "ὄψομαι"), he says (said), "I see" ("I saw," "I shall see"); Indirect Discourse in present time, Λέγει ὅτι ὁρᾷ (εἶδεν, ὄψεται), he says that he sees (saw, shall see); Ind. Discourse in past time, Εἶπεν ὅτι ὁρῷ (ἴδοι, ὄψοιτο), he said that he saw (had seen, should see). Ἀνηρώτα, τί βούλοιντο, he asked, what they wished (quid vellent), ii. 3. 4 (directly, τί βούλεσθε;). Ὅ τι δὲ ποιήσοι, οὐ διεσήμηνε, but what he would do, he did not indicate, ii. 1. 23. Ἠγνόει ὅ τι τὸ πάθος εἴη, he knew not what the matter was, iv. 5. 7.

b. In the change from Direct to Indirect Discourse, the *tense* is not commonly changed, even though the mode may be. It continues to express *relatively* (i. e. with reference to the time of the leading verb), the same time which it expressed *absolutely* in Direct Discourse; while the English idiom commonly requires us to translate it according to its absolute time as now used. See 607, and ὁρῷ, ἴδοι, ὄψοιτο, above ; and cf. 660.

c. The rule applies not only to leading verbs in the quotation, but to others connected with them : Ἔλεγον . ., ὅτι παντὸς ἄξια λέγοι Σεύθης, χειμὼν γὰρ εἴη, they said, that the proposal of S. was worth everything, for it was winter, vii. 3. 13 (directly, λέγει Σ., χ. γ. ἐστιν). Ἀπεκρίνατο γάρ, ὅτι . . βουλεύσοιτο περὶ αὐτῶν ὅ τι δύναιτο, he answered that he would provide for them what he could, vii. 1. 34 (directly, βουλεύσομαι ὅ τι ἂν δύνωμαι, § 641 a). Cf. 659 b. (d) But if a verb so connected expresses the writer's own thought, it must retain the form of Direct Discourse.

e. The rule may extend to various dependent clauses, which are thus referred to the speech or mind of another : Ἔφευγον ἔνθα μήποτ᾽ ὀψοίμην, I fled where (as I believed) I should never see, Soph. Ὤκτειρον, εἰ ἀλώσοιντο (633 c). (f) So rarely even to clauses elliptically expressed as independent: Ὑπέσχετο . . δηλώσειν ἀγῶν, οἴοιτο μὲν μάλισθ᾽ ἑκούσιον, Soph.

§ 647. SUBJUNCTIVE OF DOUBT. 309

g. That which is presented in Indirect Discourse, is not presented as fact, but as the statement, thought, or feeling of some person, and consequently as having some degree of contingency.

644. The Greek has here an especial love of VARIETY, either for its own sake, or for *euphony*, or to express in various degrees *contingency* or *positiveness* of conception ; so that

1.) Indirect and Direct Discourse are freely *blended;* commonly by a change to the latter, either (a) after the introductory particle ὅτι, or (b) in the body of the quotation, chiefly after a relative, a parenthetic clause, or one of the larger pauses : (a) Εἶπον, ὅτι "ἱκανοί ἐσμεν," *they said,* [that they were able] " *We are able,*" v. (b) Ἐπιδεικνὺς δὲ, ὡς εὔηθες εἴη, ἡγεμόνα αἰτεῖν παρὰ τούτου, " ᾧ λυμαινόμεθα τὴν πρᾶξιν," *showing, that it was folly to ask a guide from him, "whose plan* (said he) *we are frustrating,"* i.

645. 2.) Indirect Discourse (a) retains freely the modes and tenses of Direct Discourse ; and often blends them with its own proper forms, whether (b) in a leading and dependent verb, or (c) in verbs not so related : (a) Ἔλεγεν ὅτι ἀποδίδωσι (607), *he said that he* [resigns] *resigned* (a compromise between the regular ἀποδιδοίη and the direct "ἀποδίδωμι"). (b) Ἔλεγον, ὅτι περὶ σπονδῶν ἥκοιεν, ἄνδρες οἱ τινες ἱκανοὶ ἔσονται, 'that they had come respecting a truce, men who [will] would be competent,' ii. 3. 4. (c) Ἔλεγον, ὅτι Κῦρος μὲν τέθνηκεν, Ἀριαῖος δὲ .. λέγοι, *they stated that C.* [is] *was dead, and that A. said,* ii. 1. 3. See 652 a.

646. In the change from Direct to Indirect Discourse, (a) the Impf. and Plup. ind. are usually retained, lest, if changed to the Opt., they might be confounded with the Pres. and Perf. ind. so changed ; and (b) they are sometimes even used in Indirect Discourse, instead of these tenses. (c) Prior tenses, expressing supposition contrary to fact (615), require especially to be retained ; and (d) the Aor. Ind. is usually retained in dependent clauses of the quotation, for distinction from the Aor. Subj.

(a) Εἶχε γὰρ λέγειν, καὶ ὅτι .. συνεμάχοντο, *for he could say that they had assisted* (cf. στρατεύσαιντο), Hel. 7. 1. 34. (b) Ἐν πολλῇ δὴ ἀπορίᾳ ἦσαν οἱ Ἕλληνες, ἐννοούμενοι μὲν, ὅτι ἐπὶ ταῖς βασιλέως θύραις ἦσαν, .. προὐδεδώκεσαν δὲ αὐτοὺς καὶ οἱ .. βάρβαροι, 'reflecting that they were at the gates of the king, and had been betrayed by the barbarians,' iii. 1. 2. (c) Πυθοίμην .., τίν' ἂν ποτε γνώμην περὶ ἐμοῦ εἴχετε, εἰ .., 'what opinion you would have of me, if I had ..,' Dem. 1227. 2. (d) Ἔλεγον, ὡς ὁ Ξενοφῶν οἴχοιτο .. ἃ ὑπέσχετο αὐτῷ ἀποληψόμενος, 'had gone to receive what he had promised him,' vii. 7. 55.

647. SUBJUNCTIVE OF DOUBT (*Conjunctivus deliberativus*). a. In complementary clauses, where doubt respecting the future is expressed or implied, the Subjunctive is often used, chiefly in the 1 pers. (cf. 628 a). (b) The connective is sometimes omitted ; and (c) sometimes the leading verb itself.

(a) Οὐκ ἔχω τί λέγω, non habeo quid dicam, *I know not what* [I may call] *to call it,* Dem. 124. 24. Ἐρωτᾷ δὴ πῶς με θάπτῃ, *he asks how he shall bury me,* Pl. Phædo 115 d. (b) Βούλει [sc. ὡς] λάβωμαι; *wilt thou* [that] *I take ?* Soph. Ph. 761. (c) "Παραινῶ σοι σιωπᾶν." "[Sc. Παραινεῖς ὡς] Ἐγὼ σιωπῶ;" "*I advise you to be silent.*" "[Do you advise that] *I be silent ?*" Ar. Ran. 1132.

d. Hence the Subj. is used in asking *what one is to do, can do, &c.,* chiefly in the 1st pers. and the indefinite 3d : [Sc. Βούλει ὡς] Εἴπωμεν ἢ σιγῶμεν, ἢ τί δράσομεν; *shall we speak or be silent, or what shall we do?* Eur. Ion 758. Ποῖ βῶ; πᾶ στῶ; τί λέγω; *whither can I go? where stop? what say?* [sc. ἀπορῶ, I am at a loss whither, &c.] Eur. Alc. 864.

648. OPTATIVE OF DOUBT. a. Indirect Discourse in past time may change this Subj. to an Opt.: Ἐβουλεύετο .. εἰ πέμποιεν, *he consulted whether they should send,* i. 10. 5. Ἠπόρει ὅ τι χρήσαιτο Hel. 7. 4. 39.
(b) The connection must distinguish this use of the Opt. for the Subj. of present time, from its use in 643 a, for the Ind. of Direct Discourse.

c. Hence the Opt. is sometimes used without ἄν in questions, chiefly in poetry: Ποῖ τις φύγοι; *whither could one fly?* [sc. ἀποροίην ἄν]. Ar.

d. A different ellipsis explains the poetic use of the Opt. with ὡς to express wish: [Sc. Βουλοίμην ἄν] Ὡς ὄλοιτο παγκακῶς, *O* [*I should wish*] *that she might perish miserably!* Eur. Hipp. 407. Ὡς μὴ θάνοι o. 359.

v. *Interchange.*

649. RULE U. The uses of the FINITE MODES are often *interchanged.*

a. Especial freedom belongs here, as elsewhere, to the poets; particularly to Homer, and others who sung before the use of the modes became fixed.

b. The Greek has also great freedom here, as elsewhere, in combining different forms of construction (392); and (c) one part of a sentence often conforms to another, not as this *is* expressed, but as it *might have been* expressed: Εἰ μὲν ἐπαινῶ [= ἐπαινοῖμι] αὐτὸν, δικαίως ἄν με καὶ αἰτιῷσθε, *if I* [commend] *should commend him, you would justly blame me,* vii. 6. 15.

d. If the form of a leading verb does not agree with the time of its action, a dependent verb sometimes conforms to the one, and sometimes to the other: Hist. Pres., Γράφει .. ὅτι ἥξοι (v. l. ἥξει), *he writes that he* [would come] *will come,* i. 6. 3. Opt. of Wish, &c., Τεθναίην .., ἵνα μὴ ἐνθάδε μένω, *let me die, that I may not remain here,* Pl. Εἰρήνη .. ἔχοι πόλιν, ὄφρα μετ' ἄλλων κωμάζοιμι, *may peace possess the city, so that I may be merry with others,* Theog. Ποιήσαιτο (ἄν), ἵνα .. εἴη (v. l. ᾖ) ii. 4. 3.

650. I. Dependent sentences often conform to RELATIVE, instead of *absolute,* time (607):

Κατέκαυσεν, ἵνα μὴ Κῦρος διαβῇ, *he had burned* (the boats), *that C.* [may] *might not cross,* i. 4. 18. Ἔπρασσον ὅπως τις βοήθεια ἥξει, *they negotiated that some succor* [shall] *should come,* Th. 3. 4. Cf. 653.

651. II. GENERIC USE. This has a varied application to the modes:

1. The INDICATIVE is the generic mode; and hence may be used for the Subj. or Opt., if it is not deemed important to mark the contingency: Χρήσθων ὅ τι βούλονται, *let them use me as they* [may] *please,* Ar.

a. As the Impf. and Plup. have no separate forms out of the Ind., they often remain in this mode, for distinction from the Pres. and Perf., in cases where other tenses would take the Opt. or Subj.; especially the Impf. expressing a repeated or continued act or state in past time: Ἔλεγεν, ὅτι ὀρθῶς ᾐτιῶντο, καὶ αὐτὸ τὸ ἔργον αὐτοῖς μαρτυροίη, *he said that they had blamed him justly, and that the result sustained them,* iii. 3. 12 (directly, ᾐτιᾶσθε, ὑμῖν μαρτυρεῖ). See 632, 634, 646.

652. 2. The OPTATIVE is the generic *contingent mode,* as the earlier developed, and as expressing past contingency (614 b). It is, hence, often used for the Subj., especially to render the expression more general, indefinite, vague, or doubtful, or from a reference in the mind to something past, distant, or contingent : 'Αποτειχίζει, ὡς ἄπορος εἴη ἡ ὁδός, *he is building a wall, so that the way might be impassable* (for any one), ii. 4. 4.

a. We observe here, as elsewhere, the Greek love of variety, and the tendency to drop into a more general form, after the use of one that is more special or definite (cf. 592 c, 605 b) : Μετέρχομαι, ὡς ὕβριν δείξωμεν Αἰγίσθου θεοῖς, γόους τ' ἀφείην, *I go, that I may show to the gods the insolence of Æ., and* [might] *utter wailings*, Eur. El. 58.

653. III. The freedom of the mind in its conceptions of time affects the MODES, as well as the *tenses* (608 s).

a. Especially is the Subj. often used for the Opt., from a view of the past as present (or sometimes, as extending to the present). Cf. 650.

654. IV. The contingent is often conceived or spoken of as actual; and the actual, as contingent; especially from strong assurance or vivid fancy in the former case, and from courtesy or modesty in the latter. Cf. 608 a.

a. The taste, refinement, popular institutions, and civic life of the Greeks fostered a spirit of mutual concession and respect, which often led them, and especially the Athenians, to express even decided opinions and well-known facts, not as if asserted, but as if modestly and courteously suggested, and referred to others for a decision. Hence they often used the contingent modes, especially the Opt., instead of the Ind.; and the Opt., as being still less direct, instead of the Subj. See 637, 639, 652.

B. Volitive.

655. RULE XXXII. The IMPERATIVE is the most direct expression of an *act of the will*.

a. From the fondness of the Greeks for passing from indirect to direct forms of expression (cf. 644), the Imperative is sometimes found in *dependent* clauses : Θνητὸς δ' 'Ορέστης · ὥστε μὴ λίαν στένε, *O. was mortal; so that* [do not grieve] *you should not grieve to excess*, Soph. El. 1172.

656. a. In general but earnest address, the 2d Pers. of the Imv. is sometimes used with πᾶς, or τίς, or both, instead of the 3d : Χώρει δεῦρο πᾶς ὑπηρέτης · τόξευε, παῖε · σφενδόνην τίς μοι δότω. *Come hither every man of you! Shoot, smite. Let some one give me a sling.* Ar. Av. 1186.

b. Such familiar imperatives as ἄγε, φέρε, ἴθι, εἰπέ, and ἴσθι may be used in the singular, as interjections, though more than one are addressed ; and in the 2d Pers., though associated verbs are in the 3d : Ἄγε δή, ἀκούσατε, *come now, hear,* Apol. 14. Ἴθι . . τις . . δότω Ar.

C. Incorporated.

657. In dependent clauses, the Greek has great freedom in the employment of either distinct or incorporated forms, according as a more or less intimate union is desired ; and also in respect to the manner of incorporation. Thus (a) a dependent clause may be preserved *entirely distinct;* or (b) its *subject* or *most prominent substantive* may be *incorporated* in the leading clause, leaving it otherwise distinct; or (c) its *verb* may be also incorporated as an *Infinitive*, or (d) yet more closely as a *Participle*. The union often becomes still closer by an attraction, through which (e) the leading verb *adopts*, for a subject or object, the *subject* of the dependent clause; or the Inf. or Part. adopts, for its grammatical subject, either (f) the *subject* or (g) an *adjunct* of the leading verb. (h) Different forms are often combined or blended. E. g.,

(a, b) Ἤισθετο, ὅτι τὸ Μένωνος στράτευμα ἤδη ἐν Κιλικίᾳ ἦν (v. l. "Η. τό τε Μ. στράτευμα, ὅτι ἤδη ἐν Κ. ἦν), *he perceived, that the army of Meno was now in Cilicia (the army of M., that it was, &c.)*, i. 2. 21. Παρεσκευάζοντο, ὅπως . . ἐσβαλοῦσιν, *they prepared* [how they should invade, 624 b] *to invade*, Th. 2. 99. See 474 b, 573 a. (c, d) Παρεσκευάζοντο . . στρατεύειν (πολεμήσοντες, or ὡς πολεμήσοντες), *they prepared to make war*, Th. 1. 115; 2. 7. See 598 b. (e) See 573.

(f) Ἐνομίζομεν ἄξιοι εἶναι [= ἡμᾶς ἀξίους εἶναι], *we thought that we were worthy*, Cyr. 7. 5. 72 (cf. νομίζοιμι γὰρ ἐμαυτὸν ἐοικέναι Ib. 5. 1. 21). Νόμιζε . . ἄνδρα ἀγαθὸν ἀποκτείνων [= σεαυτὸν ἀποκτείνοντα], *consider yourself putting to death a good man*, vi. 6. 24. Οἶμαι εἶναι τίμιος (621; cf. οἶμαι μὲν ληρεῖν με Pl. Charm. 173 a). (g) Προσήκει ἄρχοντι φρονίμῳ εἶναι, *it becomes a ruler to be prudent*, Mag. Eq. 7. 1. See 667.

(h) Ἄλλῳ τε τρόπῳ πειράσαντες, καὶ μηχανὴν προσήγαγον, *both attempting in other ways, and* [they brought up] *bringing up an engine*, Th.

i. The Inf. and Part. may also be used *impersonally*. See 432 d.

j. An especial variety of construction appears with σύνοιδα, συγγιγνώσκω, ἔοικα, and some other words: Ἔοικας βασιλεὺς εἶναι (ἡδέμενος, δεδιότι), *you seem to be king* (pleased, like one fearing), Cyr., Hel., Pl. So Ὅμοιοι ἦσαν θαυμάζειν (v. l. θαυμάζοντες, = θαυμάζουσι), *they seemed to be wondering*, iii. 5. 13.

k. Some verbs may be followed either by the Inf. or the Part., with scarcely any difference of meaning, as in some of the examples above; and others, with an obvious difference. In the latter case, the Part. commonly denotes that which is less dependent on the action of the leading verb, or is a more immediate, positive, or personal object of perception : Τοῦτο μὲν οὐκ αἰσχύνομαι λέγων · τὸ δὲ αἰσχυνοίμην ἂν λέγειν · *I am not ashamed* [saying] *to say this* (which is said); *but I should be ashamed to say that* (which from the shame is not said); Cyr. 5. 1. 21. Ἂν ἅπαξ μάθωμεν ἀργοὶ ζῆν, *if we once learn to live in idleness*, iii. 2. 25; Ἵνα μάθῃ σοφιστὴς ὤν, *that he may learn that he is a schemer*, Æsch. Pr. 61.

658. The use of both the incorporated modes is even more extensive in Greek than in English.

1. Hence we often translate the Greek Inf. and Part. by finite verbs with connectives (*that, when, while, as, and, if, although, because, since, in order that*, &c.). Sometimes, also, from a difference of idiom, the Inf. and Part. are interchanged in translation : Παρὼν ἐτύγχανε, *happened to be present*, i. 1. 2. Ἐβούλετο ἑαυτὸν φιλεῖσθαι, *wished himself beloved*, Cyr.

a. With ἄν, the Inf. or Part. commonly supplies the place of the corresponding tense of the Opt., or past tense of the Ind. (618); and is usually translated by our potential mode: Καὶ δ᾽ ἂν τοῖς ἄλλοισιν ἔφη παραμυθήσασθαι, *he said he would advise the rest*, I. 684 (directly, ἂν . .

§ 661. INFINITIVE AND PARTICIPLE. 313

παραμυθησαίμην I. 417). 'Ως οὕτω περιγενόμενος ἄν, *as though he would thus prevail*, i. 1. 10 (directly, περιγενοίμην ἄν).

659. 2. The use of the incorporated modes, particularly the Inf., is very great in Indirect Discourse, sometimes (a) continuing through a series of sentences, or (b) even extending to relative, and rarely to other subsidiary clauses (cf. 661 a); and being interchanged and blended not only (c) with other forms of Indirect Discourse, but also (d) with those of Direct Discourse. For the use of the tenses here, see 660 b. E. g.,

(a) See Hdt. 1. 24; Cyr. 1. 3. 4 s. (b) Ἔφη δὲ, ἐπειδὴ οὗ ἐκβῆναι τὴν ψυχὴν, πορεύεσθαι .. εἰς τόπον .., ἐν ᾧ .. δύ' εἶναι χάσματε, *he said that, when his soul had left the body, it went to a place, in which were two openings*, Pl. (c) Ὡς μὲν στρατηγήσοντα ἐμὲ .. μηδεὶς ὑμῶν λεγέτω .., ὡς δὲ .. πείσομαι, *let none of you speak of me as to take command, but* (say rather) *that I will obey* (680), i. 3. 15. (d) Ἔφη ἐθέλειν πορεύεσθαι,.. "ἐγὼ γάρ," ἔφη, "οἶδα," *he said that he wished to go,* "for," *said he,* "I know," iv. 1. 27. See i. 3. 20, vii. 1. 39; and cf. § 644.

e. Ὅτι and ὡς are sometimes even followed, after intervening words, by an Inf. or Part., instead of a finite verb: Εἶπε δὲ, ὅτι, ἐπειδὰν τάχιστα ἡ στρατεία λήξῃ, εὐθὺς ἀποπέμψειν αὐτόν, *he said that, as soon as the campaign was ended, he would send him home*, iii. 1. 9. Cf. 644 a.

f. The use of the Inf. in Indirect Discourse after verbs of *saying, thinking, perceiving*, and the like (*verba sentiendi et declarandi*), is not broadly separated from its objective use after verbs of *commanding, advising, entreating, teaching, learning, wishing, intending*, and the like. (g) After verbs of *promising, hoping, expecting*, and the like, the Inf. is oftener in the Fut., according to the rule for Indirect Discourse.

660. a. The Inf. and Part. are *achronic* in respect to *absolute* time (590, 607). (b) But the Part., the Inf. Fut. and Fut. Perf., and the Inf. in Indirect Discourse (cf. 643 b), commonly express the same time *relatively* (i. e. with reference to the verb on which they depend), which the same tense of the Ind. would express *absolutely*. (c) For the use here of the Pres. and Perf. as also Impf. and Plup., see 269 c. (d) Otherwise the Inf., as in Eng., commonly expresses simply the relation of the action to the time (267 c), leaving the time itself to be inferred from the connection. This time is often a relative future; and then the less common Fut. Inf. might also be used, to give prominence to the time. E. g.,

(b) Ἤιει λέγων (λέξας, λέξων) *he went saying (having said, to say)*. Λέγει ὁρᾶν (ἰδεῖν, ὄψεσθαι), *he says that he sees (saw, shall see)*. Cf. 643 a. (c) Ἰᾶσθαι αὐτὸς τὸ τραῦμά φησι, *he says that he himself healed the wound*, i. 8. 26 (directly ἰώμην). (d) Βουλόμενοι .. ἔχειν (ἀποκλῇσασθαι, v. l. ἀποκλῄσεσθαι), *wishing* to have (to intercept), Th. 8. 9; 6. 101. See 598.

e. The Aor. Part. sometimes *agrees* in time with the leading verb, chiefly with another Aor. when both refer to a *single act*, and with such verbs as λανθάνω, τυγχάνω, φθάνω, and περιοράω: Τί ἂν εἰπών σέ τις ὀρθῶς προσείποι; *what could one call you and call you rightly?* Dem. 232. 20. Ἰδὼν εἶδον, [seeing] *surely I saw*, Luc. D. Mar. 4. Λήσομεν ἐπιπεσόντες, *we shall attack by surprise*, vii. 3. 43. See § 677.

661. a. Clauses depending upon the Inf. and Part. have usually the same form as if these were finite verbs: Ἕτοιμος ἦν ἀποτίνειν εἰ καταγνοῖεν, *he was ready to pay, if they should condemn him*, Isoc. 361 e.

b. From the familiar association of the Acc. with the Inf., and the Gen. with the Part., words commonly governing other cases are often followed by these in connection with an Inf. or Part.: Ὑμᾶς προσήκει

COMP. GR. 14

καὶ ἀμείνονας . . εἶναι, *it befits you to be* [that you should be] *braver*, iii. 2. 15 (cf. ὑμῖν προσήκει Ib. 11, § 450). "Ερποντος εἰσόρᾳς ἐμοῦ, *you see me going* (432 h), Soph. Tr. 394. (c) Sometimes the Acc. occurs for another case with the Part., if its use is analogous to that of the Inf.

d. In the use of the incorporated modes with adjuncts, there is often a union of two constructions : Ἀγγελλε δ' ὅρκῳ προστιθείς, *announce* [with an oath, adding it], *adding an oath*, Soph. El. 47.

662. From the intimate union subsisting between the Inf. or Part., and the leading finite verb, a word properly modifying the one is sometimes placed in immediate connection with the other. Thus we find (a) such adverbs as ἅμα, αὐτίκα, εὐθύς, ἐξαίφνης, μεταξύ, ὅμως, καίπερ, &c., joined with the Part. instead of the leading verb ; and sometimes (b) a particle joined with the leading verb instead of the Inf. or Part., particularly ἄν (621), and οὐκ with φημί : (a) Ἅμα ταῦτ' εἰπὼν ἀνέστη [having said this, he at the same time rose], *as soon as he had said this, he rose*, iii. 1. 47. Μεταξὺ παίζων εἰσέρχεται, [playing, meanwhile] *he enters in the midst of his play*, Pl. (b) Οὐκ ἔφασαν ἰέναι, *they said they would not go*, i. 3. 1.

I. *The Infinitive* (*Verb-Noun*, "Ὄνομα τοῦ Ῥήματος").

663. RULE XXXIII. The INFINITIVE is construed as a *neuter noun* (491 a). Hence,

(a) The Inf. may be the SUBJECT of any word which would agree with a noun, or (b) even of another Inf. ; (c) it may itself agree as an APPOSITIVE ; (d) it may DEPEND upon any word which would govern a noun ; or (e) it may be used, like a noun, to express a CIRCUMSTANCE ; particularly such as are denoted by the *Gen. of cause*, the *modal Dat.* (466 s), the *Acc. of specification* (481), and the *adverbial Acc.* (483). (f) The ARTICLE is often prefixed to the Inf. to give prominence to its substantive character, or to define the relation which it sustains as a substantive, by marking the case. If the Inf. is governed by a *preposition*, the insertion of the article is required.

(a) Φεύγειν αὐτοῖς ἀσφαλέστερόν ἐστιν, *to fly is safer for them*, iii. 2. 19. (b) Δοθῆναι αὐτῷ σώζειν τοὺς Ἕλληνας, *that it should be granted to him to save the Greeks*, ii. 3. 25. (c) Τὸ γὰρ γνῶναι ἐπιστήμην που λαβεῖν ἐστιν, *to learn is to acquire knowledge* (534. 3), Pl. Theæt. 209 e. (d) Θερμότερον πιεῖν, *warmer for drinking*, Mem. 3. 13. 3. Μανθάνειν γὰρ ἥκομεν, *we have come to learn*, Soph. O. C. 12. (e) Ἐξῆλθεν τοῦ σπεῖραι (429 a). Ὁρᾶν στυγνὸς ἦν, καὶ τῇ φωνῇ τραχύς, *he was stern in aspect, and rough in voice*, ii. 6. 9. (f) Διὰ τοῦ ἐπιορκεῖν, *through perjury*, ii. 6. 22.

g. In Greek, as in Eng., the Inf. *Act*. (or *Mid*.) is often used, where the Inf. *Pass*. might have been used with reference to a nearer, more explicit, or more natural subject : Ἄξιος θαυμάσαι, *worthy to* [admire] *be admired*, Th. 1. 138 (cf. θαυμάζεσθαι, Id. 2. 40). Θαῦμα ἰδέσθαι, E. 725.

h. The Inf. is often named from its special office : as, the *Inf. of Direct* or *Indirect Object*, of *Purpose*, of *Specification*, the *Adverbial Inf.*, &c.

664. ARTICLE WITH THE INF. a. The prevalent use of the Inf. as a *direct* or *indirect object* of a *verb* or *adjective*, is not commonly distinguished by the article; while its rarer *subjective* use as a *Gen.* is usually so distinguished. Hence it usually wants the article, where it would be naturally translated by the Eng. Inf., and also in Indirect Discourse; but commonly takes it when it modifies a noun, unless the noun is so joined with a verb, that the Inf. may seem related to them jointly (as together equivalent to some verb, &c.): See examples above. Πρόφασις τοῦ ἀθροίζειν (444 b). Ἔλαβον πρόφασιν στρατεύειν, *they seized a pretext for war*, Hel. Ἵνα . . φόβος εἴη . . στρατεύειν, *that they might fear*, &c., ii.

b. In some cases it seems indifferent whether the Inf. is regarded as the subject of a verb, or as depending upon the verb used impersonally. See 571 f. In such cases, or when the Inf. is the subject of ἐστί and an adjective, it commonly wants the article.

c. The article is often prefixed, especially in the tragedians, where it would not have been expected, and is often in the Acc. (of *direct object, effect*, or *specification*), where another case might have been expected. It is used the more freely, if some negation is expressed. Thus, Τὸ δρᾶν οὐκ ἠθέλησαν, [willed not the doing] *were not willing to do it*, Soph. Ὅς σε κωλύσει τὸ δρᾶν, *who will prevent thee* [as to] *from doing it* (405), Id.

665. a. The INF. OF SPECIFICATION and the ADVERBIAL INF. have a large range, and are variously translated. In some of these uses, the Inf. is often said, though not in the strict sense of the term (401 N.), to be *absolute*. E. g., Ἐκ δείματός του νυκτέρου, δοκεῖν ἐμοί, *from some night vision*, [according to the seeming] *as it seems to me*, or *methinks*, Soph. El. 410. Ἀλλ' εἰκάσαι μέν, ἡδύς, *but to guess, joyous*, Id. O. T. 82. Ὀλίγου δεῖν πλείους ἀπεκτόνασιν, *have slain* [to want little] *almost a greater number*, Hel. So μικροῦ δεῖν, ὀλίγου [sc. δεῖν], μικροῦ [sc. δεῖν], *almost*.

b. The use of εἶναι as the *Inf. of specification*, or the *adverbial Inf.*, will be particularly remarked with ἑκών, chiefly in negative sentences; and with some *adverbs*, or *prepositions followed by their cases*, chiefly preceded by τό: Οὔτε συνθήκας ἂν ψευδοίμην ἑκὼν εἶναι, *nor would I break my engagements willingly* [to be willing], or, *so far as depends on my will*, Cyr. Τὸ νῦν εἶναι, [as to the being, *or* state of affairs, *now*] *for the present*, iii. 2. 37. Τὸ κατὰ τοῦτον εἶναι, *so far as regards him*, i. 6. 9.

666. RULE XXXIV. The SUBJECT OF THE INFINITIVE is put in the *Accusative:* as,

Οἰόμενοι . . **Κῦρον** ζῆν, *supposing* [C. to be] *that Cyrus was alive*, ii. 1. 1 (cf. the finite Κῦρος ζῇ, *C. is alive*, 400). Ἤξίου . . δοθῆναί οἱ ταύτας τὰς πόλεις, *he requested that these cities should be given to him*, i. 1. 8.

a. The *subject of the Inf.* is very often, either properly or by attraction (474, 657 e), the *direct object* of a preceding verb, and consequently in the *Acc.* Hence has arisen an association between this case and the Inf., which has led to this rule. (b) The Inf., on the other hand, extensively constitutes an *indirect object* of the verb or other word on which it depends. From the prevalence of this use appears to have arisen the resemblance in form of the Greek and Lat. Inf. to the Dat., and the use of the prepositions *to* and *zu* before the Inf. in Eng. and German: Πέπεικε τὸν μάντιν λέγειν, *had persuaded the prophet* [to the saying] *to say*, vi. 4. 14.

667. a. This rule applies to the subject of the Inf. *simply as such.* (b) Very often, this subject has a *prior grammatical relation*, which determines its form; (c) even if its two uses are not in immediate connection. (d) Still, it is sometimes *repeated in the Acc.* for more distinct expression; and (e) is oftener *so understood.* (f) For clearness, emphasis,

or euphony, it is sometimes repeated in the same case, chiefly in the Nom.
(g) Attracted and mixed constructions also occur. Thus,
(b) Κύρου ἐδέοντο ὡς προθυμοτάτου.. γενέσθαι, they besought C. to be as strenuous as possible, Hel. 1. 5. 2. See 657 f, g. Ἰᾶσθαι αὐτὸς τὸ τραῦμά φησι (660 c). (c) Τοῦτο δ' ἐποίει ἐκ τοῦ χαλεπὸς εἶναι, he effected this by being severe, ii. 6. 9. (d) Οἶμαι δέ με ἀκηκοέναι, I think that I have heard, Pl. Rep. 400 b. Ἐνόμισε ἑωυτὸν εἶναι Hdt. 1. 34. (e) Δεομένων μου προστάτην [sc. με] γενέσθαι, entreating me [that I would become] to become leader, Cyr. 7. 2. 23. (f) Ἐπομνύω σοι .. ἐγὼ βούλεσθαι ἄν, I swear to you that I would choose, Cyr. 6. 4. 6. (g) Ἐλπίζων .. οὐδ' ὧν αὐτὸς, οὐδὲ οἱ [for τοὺς, attracted by αὐτὸς] ἐξ αὐτοῦ, παύσεσθαι, trusting that neither himself, nor his descendants, would lose, Hdt. 1. 56. Ἐννέπω σὲ .. ἐμμένειν, .. ὡς ὄντι (as if σοί had preceded), Soph. O. T. 350.

h. The subject of the Inf. is very often indefinite; and is then commonly omitted, though words may be expressed agreeing with it: "Οὐδαμῶς ἄρα δεῖ [sc. τινα] ἀδικεῖν." "Οὐ δῆτα." "Οὐδὲ ἀδικούμενον ἄρα ἀνταδικεῖν." "One ought then by no means to injure." "Surely not." "Not then, when injured, to injure in turn." Pl. Crito 49 b.

668. PLEONASM AND ELLIPSIS. I. The Infinitive (a) is sometimes *redundant*, and (b) is sometimes *omitted:*

(a) Χάριν ἀντιδιδῶσιν ἔχειν, *in return gives* [to have] *pleasure*, Soph. O. C. 232. Αἰτήσομαι δέ σ' οὐ μακρὸν γέρας λαχεῖν Id. Aj. 825. (b) Εἰς τὸ βαλανεῖον βούλομαι [sc. ἰέναι], *I wish to go to the bath*, Ar. Ἔφη ὁ Ὀρόντης [sc. οὕτω ποιῆσαι], *Orontes* [said that he had so done] *assented*, i. 6. 7.

669. II. The Infinitive often depends upon a word which is omitted or implied in another word.

1. This often occurs in Indirect Discourse:

Οἱ δὲ σφάττειν ἐκέλευον· οὐ γὰρ ἂν δύνασθαι πορευθῆναι [sc. ἔφασαν]· *but they bade him kill them; for* [they said that] *they were unable to proceed;* iv. 5. 16. Κατεφρόνουν .., μηδένα ἂν ἐπιχειρῆσαι, *they despised the foe,* (thinking that) *no one would attack*, Hel. 4. 5. 12.

670. 2. RULE V. The Inf. often forms an elliptical *command, request, counsel, salutation, exclamation,* or *question:*

Σύ μοι φράζειν [sc. ἔθελε], *do you* [please to] *tell me*, Pl. Soph. 262 e. Παῖδα δ' ἐμοὶ λῦσαι A. 20 (so esp. in Hom.). Ζεῦ πάτερ, ἢ Αἴαντα λαχεῖν, 'O [grant] that either Ajax may draw the lot,' H. 179 (cf. Ζεῦ ἄνα, δὸς τίσασθαι, 'grant that I may punish,' Γ. 351). Τὸν Ἴωνα χαίρειν [sc. κελεύω], *I bid Ion hail*, Pl. Ion 530 a. Ἐμὲ παθεῖν τάδε [sc. δεινόν ἐστι], φεῦ! *that I should suffer such things* [is horrible], *alas!* Æsch. Eum. 837. Ὦ βασιλεῦ, κότερον λέγεις .. ἢ σιγᾶν [sc. χρή, or κελεύεις]; Hdt. 1. 88.

a. So often in *proclamations, laws,* &c.: Τοὺς Θρᾷκας ἀπιέναι [sc. κελεύεται or δεῖ], *it is ordered that the Thracians depart, or the T. must d.*, Ar. Ach. 172. (b) In exclamation, the *article* is usually prefixed: Τῆς τύχης! τὸ ἐμὲ νῦν κληθέντα δεῦρο τυχεῖν! *My ill-luck! That I should happen now to have been summoned hither!* Cyr. 2. 2. 3 (429 f). (c) In a few poetic passages, the Inf. follows εἰ γάρ or εἴθε, to express wish: Εἰ γὰρ.. ἐχέμεν [sc. ὤφελες, 638 g], *would thou hadst*, η. 311. See ω. 376.

671. 3. RULE W. Some connectives are followed by the Infinitive; especially ὡς, ὥστε, οἷος, and ὅσος.

a. This construction, like similar constructions in our own and other languages, is plainly due to ellipsis, though it has extended to cases

§ 674.   INF. WITH 'ΩΣ, &C. PARTICIPLE.   317

where the ellipsis cannot be supplied without cumbering the discourse, and has some irregular forms. (b) It sometimes occurs where a connective seems needless; and (c) is often parenthetic (chiefly with ὡς). E. g.,
(a) Ἐπειδὰν δὲ σημήνῃ .., ὡς [sc. σημαίνοι ἂν] ἀναπαύεσθαι, *when the signal is given, as* [it would be given] *for resting*, ii. 2. 4. Ὑπελάσας ὡς συναντῆσαι, *riding up* [so as] *to meet him*, i. 8. 15. Βούλεται πονεῖν, ὥστε πολεμεῖν, *chooses toil, so as to be* [or *that he may be*] *at war*, ii. 6. 6. 'Ἐφ' ᾧ μὴ καίειν, 'Ἐφ' ᾧ τε πλοῖα συλλέγειν (557). Οἶον .. ἐφίεσθαι, "Οσον γεύσασθαι· see 556 b, c, d. (b) Ψυχρὸν ὥστε λούσασθαί ἐστιν, *it is cold* [so as to bathe in] *for bathing* (cf. λούσασθαι ψυχρότερον), Mem. 3. 13. 3. Ἐποίησα ὥστε δόξαι, *I had made* [things so result that it should seem] *it seem* (feceram ut), i. 6. 6. (c) Ὡς δὲ συντόμως (or συνελόντι, or ἐν βραχεῖ, sc. λόγῳ), εἰπεῖν, ut breviter dicam, [I say this so as to speak] *to speak briefly*, Œc. 12. 19, Ages. 5. 3, 7. 1. Ὡς ἔπος εἰπεῖν Pl., Ὡς λόγῳ εἰπαι Hdt., Ὡς εἰπεῖν Th., [that I may speak the word, &c.] *so to speak*. Ὡς μικρὸν μεγάλῳ εἰκάσαι, *to compare small with great*, Th. 4. 36.

d. Other modes are also used after these connectives, for the sake of greater precision, force, actuality, or independence of expression; while it is here the especial office of the Inf. to *describe, characterize*, or *modify* something that precedes: Κατέβαινον, ὡς ἐπὶ τὸν ἕτερον ἀναβαίνειν [v. l. ἀναβαῖεν], *they were descending, so as to ascend the second* [that they might ascend], iii. 4. 25. Κραυγὴν πολλὴν ἐποίουν .., ὥστε καὶ τοὺς πολεμίους ἀκούειν· ὥστε .. ἔφυγον· *they made so much noise that even the enemy heard* (characterizing the noise by showing its effect); [so that] *and therefore they fled* (narrating the result as a fact in the history); ii. 2. 17.

e. Ὡς and ὥστε, originally relative adverbs of manner, often express with the Inf. *purpose* or *consequence;* ὡς esp. the former, ὥστε the latter.

672. f. The Inf. is also used elliptically after ἤ, *than:* Μεῖζον ἢ φέρειν, [greater than it should be for one to bear] *too great to bear* (513 e).

II. *The Participle* (*Verb-Adjective*).

673. The Participle is either *circumstantial, complementary, definitive*, or *descriptive*, that is, it either expresses some *circumstance* or *complement* of the leading verb, or *defines* or *describes* some associated person or thing.

674. 1. The CIRCUMSTANTIAL PARTICIPLE is distinguished according to the circumstance denoted, as *time, cause, means, condition, purpose*, &c.; and also as (a) *preliminary*, (b) *contemporary*, or (c) *prospective*, according as its action precedes, is simultaneous with, or follows, that of the leading verb.

d. It is often translated into Eng. by a finite verb with a connective, an infinitive, a circumstantial adjunct, or an adverb (658). The Greek usually prefers a participle and verb, where the Eng. uses two verbs closely joined by '*and*.' (e) As a *preliminary part.*, the Aor. is especially used; for brevity, often translated by the Eng. Pres. The *prospective part.* is commonly in the Fut.; often translated by the Eng. Infinitive.
E. g., (a) Μάνθαν' ἐλθών, [having gone] *go and learn*, Ar. Nub. 89. Κῦρος ὑπολαβὼν τοὺς φεύγοντας, συλλέξας στράτευμα, ἐπολιόρκει Μίλητον, *C. received the exiles, and raising an army besieged M.*, i. 1. 7. (b) Οἱ ληϊζόμενοι ζῶσι, *who live by plundering*, Cyr. 3. 2. 25. Ἧκε .. ὁπλίτας ἔχων χιλίους, *he came with 1000 hoplites*, i. 2. 6 (so λαβών Ib. 3, ἄγων,

φέρων, = with). Τελευτῶν finally (509 a); ἀρχόμενος, at first, Th. 4. 64; ἐπικρυπτόμενος (553 c), or λαθών (677 f), secretly. Ὅ τι δέοι ποιοῦντας φίλους εἶναι, what they must [doing be] do to be friends, vi. 6. 4 (cf. iv. 2. 3). (c) Ἔπεμψέ τινα ἐροῦντα, he sent one to say (598). See 635.

f. For participles expressing *condition*, see 635. *Concession* is sometimes expressed by a finite verb (commonly preceded by καί εἰ or εἰ καί); but oftener by a participle with an appropriate particle, as καίπερ, καί, πέρ, καίτοι, οὐδέ, μηδέ, &c.: Προσεκύνησαν καίπερ εἰδότες, *they did him homage, even* [knowing] *though they knew*, i. 6. 10. See 662 a.

g. Ἔχων, both with and without an Acc., is joined with some verbs, chiefly of *trifling* or *delay*, to give the idea of *persistency* (cf. 679 b): Ληρεῖς ἔχων, *you trifle* [holding on] *continually*, Pl. Gorg. 497 a. (h) Μαθών or παθών, with τί or δ-τι, sometimes forms a sarcastic or wondering '*why*' or '*because*': Τί γὰρ μαθόντ' ἐς τοὺς θεοὺς ὑβριζέτην; [having learned what new notions, &c.] *what possessed you to insult the gods?* Ar. Nub. 1506. Τί παθοῦσαι . . εἰξᾶσι γυναιξίν; [having met with what, &c.] *what has happened to them that they resemble women?* Ib. 340.

675. The Circumstantial Participle is often so loosely connected with the leading verb, that it is said (though not in the strictest sense of the term, 401 N.) to be put *absolute*.

RULE XXXV. A PARTICIPLE AND SUBSTANTIVE are put absolute in the *Genitive*; an IMPERSONAL PARTICIPLE, in the *Accusative*: as,

Τούτων λεχθέντων, ἀνέβησαν, *these things having been said, they arose*, iii. 3. 1. Ἀνέβη ἐπὶ τὰ ὄρη, οὐδενὸς κωλύοντος, *he ascended the heights* [no one opposing] *without opposition*, i. 2. 22. Συνδόξαν τῷ πατρί . ., γαμεῖ, [it having seemed well to] *with the approval of his father, he marries*, Cyr. 8. 5. 28. Ἄδηλον ὄν, ὁπότε . . ἀφαιρήσεται, '*as it was uncertain*,' Th. 1. 2.

a. The *Gen. absolute* may be referred to the general head of the Gen. of Cause (often of *time*, 433 ; also of *motive*, *reason*, &c.). (b) The *impersonal participle absolute* commonly retained the generic Acc., the only form in which its proper gender, the neuter, could be distinguished (571 c); perhaps the rather, because this participle was so often akin to the *Acc. of time* or the *adverbial Acc.* (c) The Gen. is here more readily admitted when the subject is afterwards expressed by a finite clause, than when it is expressed by the Inf. (571 f): Δηλωθέντος, ὅτι . ., τὰ πράγματα ἐγένετο, *it having been shown that affairs depended*, Th. 1. 74. Προσταχθέν μοι . . ἀγειν, *it having been charged me to convey*, Dem.

d. The use of the neuter Acc. as absolute is sometimes extended, chiefly to participles not agreeing with *nouns*, or such as are often used impersonally: Κυρωθὲν δὲ οὐδέν, *nothing having been fixed*, Th. 4. 125. Προσῆκον αὐτῷ τοῦ κλήρου μέρος Isae. 51. 36. (c) Other genders sometimes appear as if in the Acc. absolute, after ὡς or ὥσπερ (680); a use which seems due to a verb of thinking or speaking expressed or understood, or to the influence of an associate construction: Ὡς μὲν στρατηγήσοντα ἐμέ . ., λεγέτω, *let him speak* [of me as to take], *as if I were to take command* (659 c; cf. 680 c). Εὔχετο δὲ πρὸς τοὺς θεούς . ., ὡς τοὺς θεοὺς (repeated) εἰδότας, *he prayed to the gods, as knowing*, Mem. 1. 3. 2.

676. a. In the absolute construction, the substantive is sometimes *omitted*, and sometimes, though less-frequently, the Part. of the substantive verb: Εἶπον, ἐρωτήσαντος [sc. αὐτοῦ], *when he asked, they replied*, iv.

§ 678. ABSOLUTE, COMPLEMENTARY, &C. 319

8. 5. Οὕτω δ' ἐχόντων [sc. πραγμάτων, 577 c], *affairs standing thus*, iii. 2. 10. Ἄκοντος βασιλέως [sc. ὄντος], *the king* [being] *unwilling*, ii. 1. 19.

b. Absolute and connected constructions of the Part. are, in various ways, interchanged and mixed ; the former giving more prominence to the Part., and sometimes arising from a change of subject ; the latter showing more clearly the relation of the Part. to the rest of the sentence: Δἰ ἡμᾶς, ἐν τάξει τε ἰόντων [sc. ἡμῶν], *by us, while marching in order*, v. 8. 13. Παρεσκευάζοντο, ὡς ταύτῃ προσιόντος καὶ δεξόμενοι, *they prepared for his coming that way and for receiving him* (680), i. 10. 6.

677. 2. The COMPLEMENTARY PARTICIPLE is used with verbs of *sensation*, of *mental state and action*, of *showing* and *informing*, of *appearance* and *discovery*, of *concealment* and *chance*, of *conduct* and *success*, of *permission* and *endurance*, of *commencement* and *continuance*, of *weariness* and *cessation*, of *anticipation* and *omission*, &c.

It may agree with (a) the *subject* or (b) an *adjunct* of the leading verb, or (c) may be used *impersonally;* and (d) is sometimes understood (chiefly ὤν). It is (e) variously translated, sometimes even by an independent verb (as expressing the chief idea), while its leading verb is translated by an adverb or circumstantial adjunct. E. g.,

(a) Ἐπαύσαντο πολεμοῦντες, *they ceased warring*, vi. 1. 28. Ἥδονται πράττοντες, *delight in doing*, Mem. 2. 1. 33. Ἐχθρὸς ὤν κυρεῖ, *happens to be a foe*, Eur. Δείξω .. σοφὸς γεγώς, *I will show that I have been wise*, Id. (b) Ἤκουσε Κῦρον ἐν Κιλικίᾳ ὄντα, *he heard* [of C. being] *that C. was in C.*, i. 4. 5. (c) Ἑώρα πλείονος ἐνδέον, *he saw* [there being need] *that there was need of more*, vi. 1. 31. (d) Σῶς ἴσθι [sc. ὤν], *know that you are safe*, Soph. (e) See f.

f. A few verbs, as λανθάνω *to escape notice, elude*, φθάνω *anticipate*, ἀνύω *despatch*, διαλείπω *leave an interval*, may either take complementary participles, or be themselves used as circumstantial participles ; and λανθάνω may express concealment either from others or from one's self, according to its object expressed or understood : Λαθεῖν αὐτὸν ἀπελθών, [to elude him departing] *to depart without his knowledge*, i. 3. 17. Τρεφόμενον ἐλάνθανεν, *was secretly maintained*, i. 1. 19. Ἐλάνθανε βόσκων, *he was fostering unawares*, Hdt. 1. 44. Ὅπως μὴ φθάσωσι .. οἱ Κίλικες καταλαβόντες, *that the Cilicians might not anticipate them in taking possession*, i. 3. 14. Οὐκ ἂν φθάνοις .. λέγων, *you cannot tell me too soon*, i. e. *tell me at once*, Mem. 2. 3. 11. Οὐκ ἔφθασαν πυθόμενοι .., καὶ .. ἧκον, *they no sooner heard than they came*, Isoc. 58 b. Κλέψαι .. λαθόντας καὶ ἁρπάσαι φθάσαντας, *to seize unobserved and take by surprise*, iv. 6. 11.

g. The Complementary Part. sometimes occurs with an impersonal expression, or with an adjective and verb supplying the place of a simple verb. When thus connected, the real subject of the sentence is sometimes implied in the Part.: Πολεμοῦσιν ἄμεινον ἔσται, *it will be better for them* [warring] *to go to war*, Th. 1. 118. Δῆλος ἦν ἀνιώμενος (573 c).

678. 3. The DEFINITIVE PARTICIPLE is equivalent to a *relative pronoun and finite verb*, and is most frequently translated by these. It is often used substantively, and may not unfrequently be translated by a noun. (a) It occurs chiefly with the article (the proper sign of this use, 520); but (b) sometimes without it, if the class only is defined. E. g.,

(a) Ὁ ἡγησόμενος οὐδείς ἔσται, *there will be no one who will guide us*, ii. 4. 5. Οἱ αὐτομολήσαντες, *the deserters*, i. 7.13. Τῶν ἄλλων τὸν βουλόμενον, *of the rest* [him that] *any one that wished*, i. 3. 9. (b) Ἅπαντα γὰρ τολμῶσι δεινὰ φαίνεται, '*appear fearful to the venturous*,' Eur.
c. Ὤν or γενόμενος *definitive* is often omitted. See 526. (d) The Part. used substantively sometimes takes the Gen. or a possessive adjective, instead of the proper case of the verb (chiefly in poetry) : Ὁ τ᾽ ἐκείνου [= ἐκεῖνον] τεκών, *his father*, Eur. Τῆς ἐμῆς κεκτημένης Ar.
e. A DESCRIPTIVE PARTICIPLE is sometimes joined with εἰμί: Ἦν . . φύσεως ἰσχὺν δηλώσας, *he was one who exhibited strength of genius*, Th.

679. The Participle with such verbs as εἰμί, γίγνομαι, ἔχω, ἔρχομαι, οἴχομαι, &c., often takes the place of a simple verb, either to supply some deficiency in inflection, or for the sake of more definite, emphatic, or metrical expression :

a.) With Substantive Verbs : Ἦν . . σπεύδων [= ἔσπευδεν], *he was seeking*, Eur. Ζῶντα ἐμὲ ἐᾶν εἶναι, *to permit me to live*, vii. 6. 30. Μὴ προδοὺς ἡμᾶς γένῃ, *do not abandon us*, Soph. (α) The substantive verb is sometimes omitted : Δεδογμέν᾽ [sc. ἐστίν], . . τῇδε κατθανεῖν, '*it is decided*,' Soph. (β) The *Perf. Part.* with εἰμί is especially common, either to supply the deficiencies in the inflection of the complete tenses (300 b, 317 s), or to direct the attention more expressly to the state consequent upon an action : Ἦσαν ἐκπεπτωκότες, *were fallen*, ii. 3. 10.

b.) Ἔχω commonly gives or strengthens the idea of *possession, continuance,* or *persistency* (holding on ; cf. 674 g) ; and is most frequent with the *Aor. act. part.*, and in the dramatists : Πολλὰ χρήματα ἔχομεν ἀνηρπακότες, *we have* [many things, having seized them] *seized many things*, i. 3. 14. Ἀτιμάσας ἔχει, *he has persistently dishonored*, Soph. Ant. 22.

c.) Ἔρχομαι with the *Fut. Part.* forms a more immediate Future. Ἔρχομαι ἀποθανούμενος νυνί, *I am going to die now*, Pl. Theag. 129 a.

d.) The Part. of a *verb of motion* with οἴχομαι is a stronger form of expression for the simple verb. Ὤιχετο ἀπιὼν νυκτός, *he* [departed going off] *went off in the night*, iii. 3. 5. So Βῆ φεύγων, *he fled*, B. 665.

680. RULE X. A PARTICIPLE is often preceded by ὡς or ὥσπερ, chiefly to mark it as *subjective;*

That is, as *expressing the view, opinion, feeling, intention, or statement of some one,* whether in accordance with or contrary to fact. The Part. thus construed may be either (a) *dependent* or (b) *absolute*. (c) It often supplies the place of a finite verb or Inf. ; and is sometimes *complementary* in *force*, though circumstantial in form (with words of *thinking, saying*, &c.). E. g.,

(a) Περικλέα ἐν αἰτίᾳ εἶχον ὡς πείσαντα, *they blamed P. as having persuaded* [because, as they complained, he had persuaded], Th. 2. 59. Συλλαμβάνει Κῦρον ὡς ἀποκτενῶν (598 b). (b) Παρήγγειλε . ., ὡς ἐπιβουλεύοντος Τισσαφέρνους, *he gave command*, [as he would, T. plotting] *as if T. were plotting*, i. e. on the ground alleged (whether truly or not), that T. was plotting, i. 1. 6. Κατακείμεθα, ὥσπερ ἐξόν, *we lie, as if it were permitted*, iii. 1. 14. (c) Ὡς μηδὲν εἰδότ᾽ ἴσθι με, [know me as knowing] *be assured that I know nothing*, Soph. Ph. 253. Ὡς πολέμου ὄντος, . . ἀπαγγελῶ, *I shall report* [as I should, war existing] *that there is war*, ii. 1. 21. Ὡς ἐμοῦ οὖν ἰόντος, . . οὕτω τὴν γνώμην ἔχετε [so have your opinion, as if I were going] *be assured that I shall go*, i. 3. 6.

681. So the particles ἅτε, οἷον, οἷα, ὥστε (Ion.), may precede the Part., especially in presenting a *cause* or other circumstance as *actual*: Κῦρος, ἅτε παῖς ὤν .., ἥδετο, *C.*, as [he naturally would be] *being a boy, was pleased*, Cyr. Οἷα δὴ παῖς φιλόστοργος ὢν φύσει, ἠσπάζετο Ib.

III. *Verbal in* -τέος (Lat. -*ndus*).

682. The passive verbal in -τέος, expressing *obligation* or *necessity*, is often used *impersonally*, in the neut. sing. or plur., with ἐστί· and from some verbs it can be only so used (571 e, 589; cf. Lat. -*dum est*). In this use, it is equivalent to the *Inf. act.* or *mid.* with δεῖ or χρή: Σκεπτέον ἐστίν [= σκέπτεσθαι δεῖ], considerandum est, *it is to be considered* [= *we ought to consider*]. See i. 3. 11. Hence it imitates this Inf. in two ways, as follows:

RULE Y. Impersonal verbals in -τέον, or -τέα, (a) govern the same cases as the verbs from which they are derived; and (b) have sometimes the agent in the *Acc.*, instead of the *Dat.* (458):

(a) Πάντα ποιητέον, *we must do all things* (572), iii. 1. 18 (cf. πάντα ποιητέα § 458). Οὓς οὐ παραδοτέα τοῖς Ἀθηναίοις ἐστίν, *whom we must not give up to the Athenians*, Th. 1. 86. (b) Καταβατέον οὖν ἐν μέρει ἕκαστον, *each one therefore must descend in turn*, Pl. Rep. 520 d.

683. Constructions are sometimes blended; as, (a) The *impersonal* with the *personal* construction of the verbal. (b) The *Dat.* of the agent with the *Acc.*: Ἡμῖν νευστέον .. ἐλπίζοντας, *we must swim, hoping*, Pl.

CHAPTER IV.

SYNTAX OF THE PARTICLE.

684. The PARTICLE, in its full extent, includes the *Adverb, Preposition, Conjunction,* and *Interjection.*

a. The name is specially given to short and familiar words of these classes, chiefly *characteristic adverbs* and *conjunctions* (66).

b. The INTERJECTION is *independent of grammatical construction*. But, as expressing *pleasure* or *pain* (and thus, indirectly, *good* or *evil*), *surprise*, &c., or as a sign of *address* or *exclamation* (65 c), it may itself be modified by a Gen. or Dat. (429 e, 453), or may introduce a Nom., Acc., or Voc. (401 b, 476 a, 484). Among the interjections, are ἆ, ἄ, ἔ, ἔ, ὖ, ὦ, ὤ, αἶ, οἶ, μῦ, ὀά, ἰώ, ἰαῦ, ἰού, εἶα eja, φεῦ, ὤπ, εὐοῖ evoe, οὐαί væ.

A. THE ADVERB.

685. RULE XXXVI. ADVERBS modify *sentences, phrases,* and *words;* chiefly *verbs, adjectives,* and *other adverbs:* as,

Πάλιν ἠρώτησεν, *again he asked*, i. 6. 8. Ὀρθία ἰσχυρῶς, *very steep*.

a. If an adverb proper modifies any other part of speech, it is through the *included idea* of a verb, adjective, or adverb: Τῆς.. πάλιν καταβάσεως, *the descent back*, Th. 7. 44 (καταβαίνω, *to descend*).

b. An adverb modifying a sentence or phrase is usually parsed as modifying the verb or leading word of the sentence or phrase; while it may also give a special emphasis or bear a special relation to some other word (57 d, 59 d): Ἡμεῖς γε νικῶμεν, WE *at least are victorious*, ii. 1. 4. Ἀριαῖος,.. καὶ οὗτος.. πειρᾶται, *Ariæus, even* HE *attempts*, iii. 2. 5.

c. Some classes of adverbs, specially termed *particles*, are chiefly CHARACTERISTIC in their use (684 a): as,

Negative οὐ, μή, *not* (regularly preceding the words which they modify); Interrogative, *Direct* ἆρα, ἦ, οὐ, μή, μῶν, *Indirect* εἰ, ἆρα, Ep. ἤ, *if, whether*, μή *whether not*, *Alternative* πότερον.. ἤ utrum.. an, εἰ.. ἤ, εἴτε.. εἴτε, Ep. ἤ.. ἦ, *whether.. or;* Contingent ἄν, κέ (618 s); Confirmative δή (389 d), δῆτα, δῆθεν, δαί, ἦ, μήν, τοί (27 f), Ep. θήν, *indeed, truly, surely, forsooth*, ναί, νή, μά (476 d); Emphatic or Intensive γέ, γοῦν (γέ οὖν), πέρ (389), καί *even*, οὐδέ, μηδέ, *not even*; Additive καὶ *also*, τέ et (389 j); Illative οὖν (389 g), ἄρα (Ep. ῥά, ἄρ) *accordingly, then*, νύν, Ep. νύ, *now*, γάρ (γέ ἄρ); Distinctive μέν *on the one hand*, δέ *on the other hand*.

686. NEGATIVE PARTICLES. The general rule for the use of οὐ and μή, whether simple or in composition, is this:—

Negation, as *desired, feared*, or *assumed*, uses μή; but otherwise, οὐ. Hence,

a. The Subjunctive and Imperative take μή; but (b) the Indicative and Optative, only in forms of wishing (638, 648 d), and in final and conditional clauses (including those in 641, 642). (c) The Infinitive usually takes μή, except in Indirect Discourse; and (d) the Participle, οὐ, except when it has the office of a conditional or indefinite relative clause (635, 641). (e) So where a participial or infinitive idea is involved. (a) Μὴ ποιήσῃς, Μηδ' ἐπίκευθε (628 c). (b) Οὔτ' ἂν δυναίμην, μήτ' ἐπισταίμην λέγειν, *I could not, and may I never be able to say*, Soph. Ant. 686. Εἰ μὴ ταῦτά [ἐστιν], οὐδὲ τάδε, *if that is not, neither is this*, Pl. See 624 s, 631 s. (c) Μὴ κλέπτειν, *not to steal*, Cyr. 1. 2. 2. Οὐ μεμνῆσθαί σέ φασιν, *they say that you will not remember* (609), i. 7. 5. (d) Μὴ γιγνομένων τῶν ἱερῶν, *if the sacrifices were adverse*, vi. 4. 19. Τὰ μὴ ὄντα ὡς οὐκ ὄντα, *to represent] whatever is not as not existing*, iv. 4. 15. (e) Οὗτοι φίλα τὰ μὴ φίλα [sc. ὄντα], *the displeasing cannot be pleasing*, Eur. Tro. 466.

f. The Epic Subj. for the Fut. ind. naturally takes οὐ (617 b).

g. After εἰ *whether*, and in dependent sentences of the form "*whether .. or not*," or "*what.. and what not*," both οὐ and μή are used.

h. After μή, a second negation in the same clause is usually expressed by οὐ; and after οὐ, by μή: Δέδοικα μὴ οὐκ ἔχω, *I fear lest I may not have*, i. 7. 7. Οὐ μὴ λαλήσεις; (597 e.) See 627.

i. Οὐ forms combinations with single words (akin to composition), in which it may remain where general rules require μή. These often belong to the figure *Litotes*, so prevalent in Greek (70 m, cf. 654). E. g., οὔ φημι *I* [do not say] *deny* (662 b), οὐκ ἐάω *I forbid*, οὐ πολλοί *few*.

687. INTERROGATIVE PARTICLES. a. The chief are ἆρα (Post-Homeric, a stronger form of ἄρα, *accordingly*) and ἦ (*indeed*). (b) These do not themselves indicate the answer expected; while ἆρα οὐ (or simply οὐ) implies that an answer is expected in the affirmative, but ἆρα μή (or ἢ μή, or simply μή, or μῶν contracted from μὴ οὖν), in the negative: Ἆρ' οὐκ ἂν ἐπὶ πᾶν ἔλθοι; *would he not resort to every means?* iii. 1. 18. Μή σοι δοκοῦμεν; [we do not seem to you, do we?] *do we seem to you?*

B. The Preposition.

688. Rule XXXVII. Prepositions govern *adjuncts*, and mark their relations (58 c): as,

Ὡρμᾶτο ἀπὸ Σάρδεων, καὶ ἐξελαύνει διὰ τῆς Λυδίας . . ἐπὶ τὸν Μαίανδρον, *he set out from Sardis, and marches through L. to the Mœander*, i. 2. 5.

a. More particularly, ἀντί, ἀπό, ἐξ, and πρό govern the Genitive; ἐν and σύν, the Dative; ἀνά and εἰς, the Accusative; ἀμφί, διά, κατά, μετά, and ὑπέρ, the Genitive and Accusative; ἐπί, παρά, περί, πρός, and ὑπό, the Genitive, Dative, and Accusative.

b. The Dat. sometimes follows ἀμφί, ἀνά, and μετά in the poets; and ἀμφί even in prose, chiefly Ion.: Ἀμφὶ τε μουσικῇ, *about music*, Hdt.

c. The eighteen words above mentioned are all which are commonly termed prepositions in Greek (from the use in 387), though other words may have a prepositional force (703 a). (d) Ἐν and πρό, by the addition of ς (expressing *motion* or *action*), become (ἐνς, cf. 156, 154) εἰς or ἐς, and πρός (689 a, i). Εἰς prevails in Att. prose, except Thuc.; but ἐς in Ion. and Dor.; while the poets may choose according to the metre.

e. To the prepositions governing the Acc., must be added the Ep. suffix -δε, *to* (cf. 252, 382): Οὐλυμπόνδε, *to Olympus*, A. 425 (cf. πρὸς Ὄλυμπον 420).

689. The prepositions have primary reference to the relations of *place*, and are used to express other relations by reason of some *analogy*, either real or fancied (many similar extensions of use appearing in our own and other languages). The use of the different cases with prepositions may be commonly referred with ease to familiar principles in the doctrine of cases.

1. Place. Some prepositions merely show *what place* is referred to, while the *relation* to this place is marked by the case employed; so that the same preposition may be used with different cases. *From* the place is expressed by the Gen.; *into* (or, with like sense, *to*) the place, by the Acc.; *in* or *at* the place by the Dat., or sometimes the Gen.; *through* the place, commonly by the Acc. Cf. 398, 433, 470 a, e. The following are the chief distinctions of PLACE denoted by the prepositions.

a. *Within.* Ἐν, Lat. *in* with Abl., [IN the space within] *in:* ἐν Μιλήτῳ, *in M.*, i. 1. 7. Εἰς, Lat. *in* with Acc., [INTO the space within] *into:* εἰς πεδίον, *into a plain*, i. 2. 22. Ἐξ, ex, [FROM within] *out of:* ἐκ τῆς χώρας, *out of the land*, i. 2. 1. Διά, akin to δύο and Lat. *dis-*, [THROUGH the space within, dividing it *in two*] *through:* with Acc. poet.; commonly with Gen.: διὰ Φρυγίας, [IN a line dividing] *through Phrygia*, i. 2. 6.

b. *With.* Σύν cum [IN the place with] *with:* σὺν ὑμῖν, *with you*, i. 3. 6. Ἀπό ab, [FROM the place with] *from:* ἀπ' ἀλλήλων, *from each other*, i. 8.

c. *Amid, among,* hence *with:* Μετά, akin to μέσος medius, and Germ. *mit:* νεκρῶν μετά, [IN the midst of] *among the dead*, Eur. Hec. 209; μετὰ Τρῶας, *into the midst of the Trojans*, Δ. 460. Μετὰ πρώτοισι Λ. 64.

d. *Beside.* Παρὰ μὲν Κύρου, [FROM beside] *from Cyrus*, i. 9. 29 ; παρὰ Κύρῳ, [AT the side of] *with C.*, i. 4. 3 ; παρὰ Κῦρον, [TO the side of] *to C.*
e. *About.* 'Αμφί, akin to ἄμφω and Lat. *ambo, amb-, on both sides of*, hence, *on different sides of, about :* ἀμφὶ τὰ ὅρια, [THROUGH the region on both sides of] *about the borders*, Cyr. 2. 4. 16 ; ἀμφὶ .. πόλιος, [IN the region] *about the city*, Hdt. 8. 104. See 527 a, 688 b.
f. *Around.* Περί, akin to Lat. *per :* περὶ τὸ στρατόπεδον, [THROUGH the circuit] *around the camp*, v. 1. 9 ; περὶ τοῖς στέρνοις, *around the breast.*
g. *On, upon,* or *against* (as in cases of *resting, leaning, pressing*, &c., *on* or *against*). 'Επὶ τοῦ ἵππου, [IN a position] *on his horse*, iii. 4. 49 ; ἐπὶ τῇ θαλάττῃ, *upon* [by] *the sea*, i. 4. 1.; ἀναβὰς ἐφ' ἵππον, *mounting* [TO a position] *on horseback*, iv. 7. 24 ; ἐπὶ θάλατταν, *to the seaside*, iv. 8. 22.
h. *Over against.* 'Αντί, akin to Lat. *ante*, very rare in its local sense.
i. *Before.* Πρό *præ*, pro : πρὸ ποδῶν, [IN the way] *before the feet*, iv. 6. 12. To mark more active relations, and the idea of *fronting*, s is added to πρό (688 d) : ἄγει πρὸς βασιλέα, *he is leading* [TO a position fronting] *against the king*, i. 3. 21 ; πρὸς Νεμέας, [IN the direction fronting] *towards Nemea*, Th. 5. 59 ; πρὸς Βαβυλῶνι, *in front of Babylon*, Cyr. 7. 5. 1.
j. *Over, above.* 'Υπέρ super : ὑπὲρ .. πέτρας, *from above the rock*, iv. 7. 4 ; ὑπὲρ κεφαλῆς, *over head*, Ages. 2. 20 ; ῥιπτέουσι ὑπὲρ τὸν ὦμον, *they throw it* [TO a place over and beyond] *over the shoulder*, Hdt. 4. 188.
k. *Under, beneath.* 'Υπό sub : ὑπὸ ζυγοῦ, ὑπὸ ἁμάξης, *from under the yoke*, δ. 39 ; vi. 4. 22 ; ὑπὸ τοῖς δίφροις, [IN the space] *under the seats*, i. 8. 10 ; εἶμ' ὑπὸ γαῖαν, *I shall go* [TO the region] *beneath the earth*, Σ. 333.
l. *Up.* 'Ανὰ .. μέλαθρον, *up to the roof*, χ. 239 ; ἀνὰ τὰ ὅρη, *up through the mountains*, iii. 5. 16 ; ἀνὰ σκήπτρῳ, *on a sceptre*, A. 15 (688 b).
m. *Down.* Κατὰ τῆς πέτρας, *down from the rock*, iv. 2. 17 ; κατὰ ῥόον, *down* [along] *stream ;* κατὰ τὴν ὁδόν, *along the way ;* κατὰ γῆν, *by land.*

690. 2. TIME. 'Εν τρισὶν ἡμέραις, *in three days*, iv. 8. 8. 'Εφ' ἡμῶν, *in our time*, i. 9. 12. Διὰ νυκτός, *through the night*, iv. 6. 22. 'Αμφὶ δείλην, *about evening*, ii. 2. 14. Πρὸ τῆς μάχης, *before the battle*, i. 7. 13. Μετὰ τὴν μάχην, *after the battle*, Ib. 'Απὸ γενεᾶς, *from birth*, ii. 6. 30.

691. 3. STATE. 'Εν πολέμῳ, εἰς πόλεμον, ἐκ πολέμου, *in (into, out of) a state of war*, vi. 1. 29 ; ἐξ ἴσου, [from equal ground] *on an equality*, iii. 4. 47. 'Επὶ τῷ ἀδελφῷ, *dependent upon his brother*, i. 1. 4 ; ἐφ' ἡμῖν, *in our power*, v. 5. 20. 'Υπό σοι, *under your power*, vii. 7. 32.

692. 4. COMPARISON. Πρό γε ἄλλων, *before* [more than] *others*, Pl. 'Υπὲρ ἐλπίδα, *above hope*, Soph. Ant. 366. Περὶ πάντων, *superior to all*, A. 287 (the greater *surrounding* the less). Παρὰ τὰ ἄλλα ζῷα, [by the side of] *in comparison with the other animals*, Mem. 1. 4. 14.

5. NUMBER, ADDITION, DISTRIBUTION. 'Αμφὶ τοὺς δισχιλίους (531 d). Εἰς χιλίους, *to the number of* 1,000, i. 8. 5. Πρὸς τούτοις, *in addition to these*, iii. 4. 13. 'Ανὰ ἑκατόν, [according to or by the hundred] *a hundred each*, iii. 4. 21. Κατ' ἐνιαυτόν, [by the year] *yearly*, iii. 2. 12.

693. 6. ORIGIN, SOURCE, MATERIAL, &c. Γεγονὼς ἀπὸ Δαμαράτου, *sprung from D.*, ii. 1. 3. Φῶς .. ἐκ Διός, *a light from Jove*, iii. 1. 12 ; ἐκ ξύλων, [out of] *of wood*, Hdt. 1. 194. Αἰτεῖν παρὰ τούτου, *to ask from him*, i. 3. 16. 'Ολίγοι ἀπὸ πολλῶν, *few* [from] *of many*, Th. 1. 110.

7. PROTECTION (defenders stand *before, over, around*). Μάχεσθαι .. πρὸ γυναικῶν, *to fight* [before] *for their wives*, Θ. 56 ; πρὸ ὑμῶν, *in your behalf*, vii. 6. 27. Μαχόμενοι ὑπὲρ Κύρου, *fighting* [over] *in defence of C.*, i. 9. 31. 'Αμύνονται περὶ τέκνων, *fight for their young*, M. 170.

§ 699. IN COMPOSITION. RULE Z. 325

694. 8. CAUSE, MOTIVE, END, AIM. Ἀπὸ τούτου, [from] *on account of this*, Hdt. 2. 42. Ἐξ ὑποψίας, [out of] *from suspicion*, ii. 5. 5. Διὰ πίστεως, *through confidence*, iii. 2. 8. Διὰ καύμα, [through] *by reason of the heat*, i. 7. 6. Περὶ νίκης, [about] *for victory*, i. 5. 8.

9. ACTION. This is commonly conceived of as proceeding *out of* the agent, or *from him*, or *from his sphere*, or *from under his influence* (ἐκ, ἀπό, παρά, πρός, ὑπό, 586, d, f).

695. 10. MEANS, INSTRUMENT, MANNER. Ἀπὸ ληστείας, [from] *by means of robbery*, vii. 7. 9. Σὺν αἰχμῇ, *with the spear*, Æsch.; σὺν τῷ δικαίῳ, *with justice, justly*, ii. 6. 18. Μετ' ἀδικίας, *unjustly*, Ib. Διὰ ταχέων, [through quick measures] *rapidly*, i. 5. 9. Ἀνὰ κράτος, [up to one's strength] *at full speed*, i. 10. 15. Πρὸς βίαν, [resorting to] *by force*, Æsch. Pr. 208. Ὑπὸ μαστίγων, *under the lash*, iii. 4. 25.

696. 11. CONNECTION, CONFORMITY, SEPARATION, OPPOSITION, SUBSTITUTION. Σὺν τοῖς θεοῖς, *with the help of the gods*, ii. 3. 23. Πρὸς τοῦ Κύρου τρόπου, [looking towards] *according to the character of C.*, i. 2. 11. Κατὰ σπουδήν, [according to haste] *hastily*, vii. 6. 28; see 513 b. Παρὰ φύσιν, [beside] *against nature*, Th. 6. 17. Λέγων καθ' ἡμῶν, *speaking against us*, Soph. Ph. 64. Ἀντὶ τούτων, [over against] *in return for this*, vi. 6. 32; ἀντ' ἐκείνου, *instead of him*, i. 1. 4.

697. 12. APPEAL, THEME, REFERENCE, SPECIFICATION, &c. Πρὸς θεῶν, [before] *by the gods*, vii. 6. 33. Ἀμφὶ σῆς λέγω παιδός, *I speak about your daughter*, Eur. Περὶ ἐμὲ ἄδικος, *unjust* [about] *towards me*, i. 6. 8. Κατὰ γνώμην, *as to intellect*, Soph. Πρὸς ταῦτα, *in view of this, upon this*, i. 6. 9. Ἐς φιλίαν, *in respect to friendship*, ii. 6. 30.

698. a. In many connections the preposition may be either employed or omitted, at pleasure: Κραυγῇ πολλῇ, Σὺν πολλῇ κραυγῇ, *with great clamor*, i. 7. 4; iv. 4. 14. (b) In Greek, as in other languages, prepositions with their cases form many adverbial phrases. See 382 a.

c. In *composition*, a preposition usually shows its original meaning, or one that is easily derived from it: ἀνα(κατα, εἰς, ἐκ) βαίνω, *to go up (down, in, out)*; κατανεύω *I* [nod down] *consent*, ἀνανεύω, *I* [nod up] *refuse*.

699. RULE Z. A PREPOSITION IN COMPOSITION often governs the same case as when it stands by itself.

a. A preposition in composition often retains its distinct force and government as such, according to this rule. (b) But oftener it seems to be regarded as a mere adverb (cf. 703 b), and the compound is construed just as a simple word would be of the same signification. See 486. (c) Hence the preposition may be repeated, or a similar preposition introduced. (d) This adverbial force is particularly obvious in *tmesis*, and (e) when the preposition is used with an ellipsis of its verb (chiefly ἐστί). E. g., (a) Συνέπεμψεν αὐτῇ στρατιώτας, *he sent with her soldiers*, i. 2. 20. Hence compounds of κατά, *against*, often take the Gen. (cf. 689 m, 696): Καταδικάζω ἐμαυτοῦ, *I give judgment against myself*, vi. 6. 15. (b) Ἐπιπλεύσας αὐτῷ, *sailing against him*, Hel. 1. 6. 23 (cf. πλεῖν ἐπ' αὐτούς Ib. 1. 11). (c) Ἐπειρῶντο εἰσβάλλειν εἰς τὴν Κιλικίαν, *they attempted to enter* [into] *C.*, i. 2. 21. (d) Ἐκ δὲ πηδήσας. See 388 c. (e) Ἀλλ' ἄνα [for ἀνάστηθι] ἐξ ἑδράνων, *but* [rise] *up from the seats*, Soph. Aj. 194. Εἰσελθεῖν πάρα [for πάρεστι], *it is permitted to enter*, Eur. Alc. 1114. Cf. 785.

f. The preposition, as such, and the general sense of the compound, often require the same case, as, particularly, in compounds of ἀντί, ἀπό, ἐξ, εἰς, πρό, and σύν : Ἀπέχοντες ἀλλήλων, *distant from each other* (405), ii. 4. 10. (g) Verbs compounded with ἐπί, παρά, or πρός, denoting *approach*, commonly take the Dat. (449), though the preposition by itself would govern the Acc.: Προσέρχεται τῷ Ξενοφῶντι, *comes to X.*, iv. 8. 4.

h. TMESIS, so called, occurs chiefly in the earlier (especially the Epic) Greek, when as yet the union of the preposition and verb had not become firmly cemented ; and is here often to be regarded as the adverbial use of the preposition (703 b), rather than the division of a word already compounded. (i) In Att. prose it is very rare, and even in Att. poetry (where it is most frequent in the lyric portions), it seldom inserts anything more than a mere particle or enclitic pronoun between the preposition and verb. (j) The preposition sometimes follows the verb ; and is sometimes repeated without the verb. E. g., (h) Ἀπὸ λοιγὸν ἀμῦναι (388 c) A. 67. (i) Διά μ' ἔφθειρας, κατὰ δ' ἔκτεινας, *you have ruined and slain me,* Eur. Hipp. 1357. (j) Πέμψαντος, ὦ γύναι, μέτα, 'having sent me for you,' Eur. Hec. 504. Ἀπολεῖ πόλιν, ἀπὸ δὲ πατέρα, *destroy the city and his father,* Id. Herc. 1055. So, Ὤρνυτο δ'.. Ἀγαμέμνων, ἂν [sc. ὤρνυτο] δ' Ὀδυσεύς, *then rose Agamemnon and* [up] *Ulysses,* Γ. 267.

C. THE CONJUNCTION.

700. RULE XXXVIII. CONJUNCTIONS connect *sentences* and *like parts* of a sentence : as,

Ἠσθένει Δαρεῖος καὶ ὑπώπτευε, *Darius was sick and apprehended,* i. 1. 1.

a. By *like* parts of a sentence are meant those of like construction, or performing like offices in the sentence, and which united by conjunctions form *compound* or *complex subjects, predicates, &c.* (62 g). They are commonly, but not necessarily, of the same part of speech and of similar form.

701. The chief conjunctions are the following, in two great classes according as they are used in coördination or subordination (62) :

1. COÖRDINATE. (a) *Copulative* (simply *coupling*) τέ (389 j), καί (the stronger and more emphatic), que, et, *and;* τέ .. τέ, καί .. καί, and closest τὲ καί, *both .. and;* compounds οὔτε .. οὔτε, μήτε .. μήτε, neque .. neque, *neither .. nor* (686). (b) *Adversative* (denoting *opposition*) ἀλλά, ἀτάρ, μέντοι, sed, at, *but, yet.* (c) *Distinctive* (weakly adversative, often approaching the copulative) δέ *but, and,* to which μέν corresponds ; compounds ἠδέ poet., ἰδέ and ἠμέν Ep.; οὐδέ, μηδέ, *and not, but not, neither, nor even.* (d) *Alternative* ἤ, ἠέ Ep., aut, vel, *or;* compounds ἤτε Ep. (389 j), strengthened ἤτοι ; ἤ .. ἤ, ἤτοι .. ἤ, *either .. or.*

2. SUBORDINATE. (e) *Final* (denoting *purpose,* or *end*) ἵνα, ὅπως, ὡς, ὄφρα poet., ut, quo, *in order that ;* μή ne, *lest.* See 624. (f) *Conditional* εἰ si (cf. 141), αἰ Dor. and Ep., ἐάν, ἤν, ἄν, εἰ κε Ep., *if;* εἴπερ siquidem, *if indeed;* εἰ μή, ἐὰν μή, nisi, *unless;* εἴτε .. εἴτε, rarer εἴτε .. ἤ, εἰ .. εἴτε poet., sive .. sive, *whether, or.* See 631, 619 a. For ἐφ' ᾧ, ἐφ' ᾧτε, *on condition that,* see 557 a. (g) *Concessive* (denoting *concession,* or *admission*) εἰ καί, καὶ εἰ, etsi, *even if, though ;* to which ὅμως tamen, *yet,* corresponds. See 674 f. (h) *Temporal* (marking a relation of *time*) πρίν *before,* akin to πρό and Lat. *prius ;* πρὶν ἤ priusquam ; μέχρι, ἄχρι, ἕως, ἔστε (ἐς, τέ, 389 j ; Post-Hom.), donec, *until.* Most temporal connectives are relative adverbs (641 d). (i) *Complementary* (66 d) ὅτι, ὅ Ep., quod, *that ;* ὡς, ὅπως chiefly poet., [how] *that ;* εἰ (f), ἤ Ep., num, *whether ;* πότερον

(πότερα).. ἤ, εἰ.. ἤ, εἴτε.. εἴτε, ἆρα.. ἤ, ἤ.. ἤ Ep., utrum.. an, whether.. or. See 643, 639 a. (j) *Causal* ὅτι quod, quia, *because;* ὡς, *as, since;* ὅτε, ἐπεί, quando, *since;* διότι (δι᾽ ὅ τι), οὕνεκα, ὁθούνεκα [on account of this that, 557 a] *because;* γάρ (γὲ ἄρα, *at least in accordance* with this, 685 c) nam, *for, since*. (k) *Consecutive* (denoting result, or consequence) ὥστε, ὡς, ut, *so that* (671 d, e). (l) *Comparative* ἤ quam, *than* (511, 513). (m) *Exceptive* πλήν, ἀλλ᾽ ἤ [*other than*, n], εἰ μή nisi, ὅτι μή (n ; after a negative), *except*, εἰ μὴ εἰ (714. 2) nisi si, *except* [if].

NOTE. In Greek, as in other languages, conjunctions have their origin, for the most part at least, in other parts of speech used connectively. E. g., (n) NEUTER PRONOUNS, ὅτι, ὅ, quod, *that*, as λέγει ὅτι ἄξει, *he says* [what follows] *that he will lead*, iv. 7. 20 ; ὅτι μή (m), as οὐδείς.. ὅτι μὴ γυνή, *no one* [that was not] *except a woman*, Hdt. 1. 181 ; διότι, οὕνεκα (j) ; ἀλλά (from neut. pl. of ἄλλος, 483 a) *otherwise, on the contrary, but;* ἀλλ᾽ ἤ (m), as ἀργύριον μὲν οὐκ ἔχω, ἀλλ᾽ ἢ μικρόν τι, *I have no money* [other than] *except a little*, vii. 7. 53. See h, 624 c.

702. a. Ὅτι (*that*, the *thing* which) is stronger, more *positive, direct*, or *actual* in expression than ὡς (*how*, the *manner* in which). Hence, in indirect discourse, ὅτι chiefly introduces what is simply *said* and not questioned ; ὡς, what is *described*, or what is *said* but *questioned*, or what is *not said*, or what is presented as *thought* or *not thought:* Λέγει ὡς ἀπεκόπησαν.., καὶ ὅτι τεθνᾶσι.. ἄλλοι, *he states* how *they had been beaten off, and that others are dead*, iv. 2. 17. Ἐνεκάλουν ἐμοί, ὡς μᾶλλον μέλοι μοι, *they brought against me the charge* (which I do not admit), *that I cared more*, vii. 7. 44. Οὐ τοῦτο λέγω, ὡς οὐ δεῖ, *I do not say this, that one ought not.*

b. A conjunction often connects the sentence which it introduces, not so much to the preceding sentence as a whole, as to some particular word or phrase in it: Προσβάλλουσι.. καταλιπόντες ἄφοδον τοῖς πολεμίοις, εἰ βούλοιντο φεύγειν, *they attack, leaving a way of escape for the enemy, if they should wish to flee*, iv. 2. 11.

c. In many connections, two forms of construction are equally admissible, the one with, and the other without, a connective. The two forms are sometimes blended. See 511, 644, 659 e, 671. A conjunction is sometimes used in Greek, where none would be usual in English.

A twofold construction is sometimes admissible, according as a word is regarded as belonging (d) to a compound part of a sentence, or (e) to a new sentence : (d) Πλουσιωτέρῳ μὲν ἂν.. ἢ ἐμοὶ ἐδίδους, *you would give to a richer man than I* [am], Cyr. (e) Τοῖς.. μᾶλλον ἀκμάζουσιν, ἢ ἐγὼ [sc. ἀκμάζω], παραινῶ, *I exhort those of greater vigor than myself*, Isoc.

OBSERVATIONS.

703. I. INTERCHANGE. In Greek, as in other languages, the uses of the PARTICLES are often *interchanged*. Thus,

1.) a. Adverbs sometimes take a case, as prepositions ; (b) prepositions are sometimes used without a case, as adverbs, especially in Hom. and Hdt. (πρός even in Att. prose) ; (c) the same particle is used both as an adverb and as a conjunction, or as a connective and a non-connective adverb.

(a) See 405 s, 436 d, 445 c, 450. Hom. uses εἴσω and ἔσω as protracted forms for εἰς : Ἀγάγῃσιν ἔσω κλισίην, 'into the tent'; Ἴλιον εἴσω, cf. εἰς

"Ίλιον · Ω. 155, 145, 143. (b) Τάδε λέγω, δράσω τε πρός [sc. τούτῳ], *this I say, and will do it* [in addition to this] *too*, Æsch. Πρὸς δ' ἔτι iii. 2. 2. Περί, [above others] *eminently*, θ. 44. (c) Κῦρον δὲ (*and*) μεταπέμπεται ... καὶ στρατηγὸν δὲ (*on the other hand, also*) αὐτὸν ἀπέδειξε i. 1. 2.

d. In the connection of sentences, **πρίν** is variously used: (a) as a *conjunction*, with a finite mode, or (β) as a *preposition*, with the Inf. ; (γ) as an *adverb* with ἤ and a finite mode or (δ) even the Inf., or (ε) in Hom. with ὅτε ; or (ζ) as a correlative (and so πάρος, πρόσθεν, πρότερον) preceding another πρίν : (a) Μὴ στενάζε πρὶν μάθῃς (641 d). (β) 'Εθύετο πρίν τινι εἰπεῖν, *he sacrificed before speaking to any one*, v. 6. 16. (γ) Πρὶν ἤ . . ἐγένοντο, [sooner than] *before they had come*, Ages. 2. 4. (δ) Πρὶν ἤ . . ἄσαι, *before he satiates*, E. 288. (ε) Πρίν γ' ὅτε . . δῶκεν, *until* [when] *he gave*, M. 437. (ζ) Οὐδέ τις ἔτλη πρὶν πιεῖν πρὶν λεῖψαι, *nor did any one dare to drink* [previously] *before offering*, H. 480.

e. When two prepositions are combined, which occurs most frequently in the Epic, either one or both of the prepositions are used adverbially, or one of the prepositions with its substantive forms the complement of the other : 'Αμφὶ περὶ κρήνην, *round about the fountain*, B. 305. 'Απόπρο, *far away*, Il. 669. Τπ' ἐκ βελέων, *from beneath the weapons*, Δ. 465.

704. 2.) One preposition or adverb is often used for another (or a preposition is used with one case for another), by reason of something associated or implied. This construction (especially frequent with ἐν, εἰς, and ἐκ, 689 a) is termed, from its elliptic expressiveness, *constructio prægnans*. Thus,

A sign of MOTION for one of REST. (a) PREPOSITION : Οἱ ἐκ τῆς ἀγορᾶς . . ἔφυγον [ἐκ for ἐν, by reason of ἔφυγον following], *those in the market fled* [from it], i. 2. 18. 'Εφάνη λὶς . . εἰς ὁδόν, *a lion appears* [having come into] *in the way*, O. 275. Παρῆσαν εἰς Σάρδεις i. 2. 2. (b) ADVERB : Τῶν ἔνδοθέν [for ἔνδον] τις εἰσενεγκάτω, *let one of those within* [coming from within] *carry in*, Ar. Pl. 228. (c) CASE : Πρὸς τὸ πῦρ καθήμενος, *going to the fire and sitting by it*, Ar. Vesp. 773.

A sign of REST for one of MOTION. (d) PREPOSITION : 'Εν γούνασι πίπτε, *fell* [and rested] *upon the knees*, E. 370. (e) ADVERB : "Οπου [for ὅποι] βέβηκεν, *where* [for *whither*] *he has gone*, Soph. Tr. 40. (f) CASE : Πρὸς πέτρῃσι βαλών, *dashing upon the rocks*, ι. 284.

705. 3.) The Greeks, especially the earlier writers, often employ the looser and more generic for the closer and more specific connectives (63 g), or for other forms of expression :

"Ἤδη τ' ἦν ἐν τῷ τρίτῳ σταθμῷ, καὶ Χειρίσοφος αὐτῷ ἐχαλεπάνθη, *it was now the third day, and C. was angry with him* [= when it was now, &c.], iv. 6. 2. 'Απειρήκεσαν μέν, ὅμως δ' ἐδόκει, [they were weary indeed, but yet] *although they were weary, yet it seemed*, vi. 5. 30.

The student will not fail to remark, — (a) The frequent use, in the Epic, of δέ for γάρ, and in general of *coördination* or *simple succession*, in the connection of sentences, for *subordination* (62) : Πίθεσθ', ἄμφω δὲ νεωτέρω ἐστόν, *be persuaded*, [and] *for ye are both younger*, A. 259. (b) The frequent use of γάρ in specification, where we should use *that, namely*, &c. : Τῷδε δῆλον ἦν · τῇ μὲν γὰρ πρόσθεν ἡμέρᾳ . . ἐκέλευε, *was plain from this, that on the preceding day he commanded*. (c) The use of καί after a word of *sameness, likeness*, or *anticipation* (677 f) : Τῇ αὐτῇ γλώσσῃ χρέονται καὶ Γελωνοί, *they use the same language* [and] *as the Geloni*, Hdt.

706. II. a. Adverbs and prepositional adjuncts are often used *substantively* or *adjectively*, in any case required: *Substantively*, Νομ. Ἦν .. ὑπὲρ ἡμισυ.. Ἀρκάδες, *above half were Arcadians*, vi. 2. 10. Acc. Εἰς μὲν ἅπαξ καὶ βραχὺν χρόνον, *for once and a short time*, Dem. 21. 1. *Adjectively*, Πελτασταὶ δὲ ἀμφὶ τοὺς δισχιλίους, *about 2,000 targeteers*, i. 2. 9. See 526 s. (b) An adverb and a preposition governing it are often written together as a compound word: ἐσαεί *forever*, ἔμπροσθεν.

707. III. In the doctrine of particles, especially connectives, the figures of syntax hold an important place: thus,

A. Ellipsis.

Ellipsis here consists either (α) in the omission of the particles themselves, or (β), far more frequently, in that of words, and even whole sentences, related to them.

a. A particle belonging alike to two parts of a sentence is either (a) expressed in both (the most distinct and emphatic form); or (b) in the first only; or (c) in the second only (more rarely and chiefly in poetry); or (d) is sometimes even omitted in both. (e) A like variety obtains in respect to other classes of words, and (f) when more than two parts of the sentence are affected. (a) Ἐν Αἰγύπτῳ καὶ ἐν Σικελίᾳ, *in E. and in S.*, Mem. 1. 4. 17. (b) Πρός τε ψύχη καὶ θάλπη, *to cold and heat*, Ib. 2. 1. 6. (c) Ἢ ἁλὸς ἢ ἐπὶ γῆς, *either on sea or land*, μ. 27. (d) Ἔγχος βριθύ, μέγα, στιβαρόν, *a spear, heavy, huge, stout*, Il. 801. (e) Οὐδὲν σὺ μᾶλλον ἤ τις ἄλλος ἔχει, *you have no more than any other one*. Pl. See g.

g. Copulative conjunctions are often omitted (especially if more than two particulars are joined); (h) less frequently, those of other classes. (i) When not joined by a connective, a clause is sometimes in *parenthetic* or *inverted* order, or placed in *apposition* with another clause. (g) Πόθου πατρίδων, γονέων, γυναικῶν, παίδων, *from longing for country, parents, wives, children*, iii. 1. 3. (h) Ὀμνύω .. [sc. ὅτι] ἐθυόμην, *I swear [that] I sacrificed*, vi. 1. 31. (i) Ταῦτα, .. ὄμνυμι .., ἔπαθον Cyr. v. 4. 31. Ἀφειλόμην, ὁμολογῶ, *I rescued him, I confess*, vi. 6. 17.

j. In annexing several particulars, the Eng. more frequently uses the copulative with the last only; but the Greek, with all or none: Πλίνθοι καὶ ξύλα καὶ κέραμος (496 c). Cf. d, g.

k. A secondary connective is sometimes used without its primary (66): Ὁμοίους μὲν φιλοσόφοις, *like philosophers indeed* [but not philosophers], Pl.

708. β. Connected sentences especially abound in ellipsis, from the ease with which the omission can be supplied from the connection. E. g., observe the frequent ellipses,

1.) In replies. These (a, b, c, d) have various forms. See 68 c.

e. In a dialogue or address, a speaker often commences with a connective (most frequently an adversative, distinctive, or causal conjunction), from reference to something which has been expressed or which is mutually understood: Ἀλλ᾽ ὁρᾶτε, *but you see*, iii. 2. 4. (f) In like manner, the Voc. is often followed by a connective: Ὦ γύναι, ὄνομα δέ σοι τί ἐστιν; *woman, but what is your name?* Mem. 2. 1. 26.

709. 2.) Between two connectives: Ἀλλὰ [sc. παύομαι] γὰρ καὶ περαίνειν ἤδη ὥρα, *but* [no more, for] *it is now quite time to stop* (sed enim),

iii. 2. 32. Παρὰ τὴν θάλατταν ᾔει · καὶ [sc. ταύτῃ ᾔει] γὰρ ἤδη ἠσθένει, *he went by the sea;* [and he so went,] *for he was now sick*, vi. 2. 18. — (a) And yet, perhaps, in such examples as these, ἀλλὰ γάρ or καὶ γάρ may be regarded as forming but a single compound connective, or one of the particles may be regarded as a mere adverb (703 c).

3.) With adversative and distinctive conjunctions, with which we must sometimes supply the opposite of that which has preceded : Μή μ' ἄτιμον τῆσδ' ἀποστείλητε γῆς, ἀλλ' ἀρχέπλουτον [sc. δέξασθε], '*dismiss me not, but receive me,*' Soph. Cf. 572 b. — For ellipsis with ἤ, see 513, 567 f.

710. 4.) With conditional conjunctions : Εἰ δ' [sc. βούλεαι] ἄγε, *if you will, come*, A. 302, and often in Hom. Εἰ δ' ἐθέλεις [sc. ἄγε] Φ. 487. Εἰ μὲν σύ τι ἔχεις πρὸς ἡμᾶς λέγειν [sc. λέγε δή] · εἰ δὲ μή [sc. ἔχεις], ἡμεῖς πρὸς σὲ ἔχομεν · *if you have anything to say to us, say it; if not, we have to you;* vii. 7. 15. Ἂν μὲν ὁ Κῦρος βούληται [καλῶς ἔχει] · εἰ δὲ μή Cyr.

711. 5.) With ὡς, especially in expressing *comparison, design, pretence, possibility*, &c. : Θᾶττον ἢ [sc. οὕτω ταχύ] ὥς τις ἂν ᾤετο, *quicker than* [so quick as] *one would have thought*, i. 5. 8. Ὡς εἰς μάχην παρεσκευασμένος, *arrayed as* [he would array] *for battle*, i. 8. 1. Ὡς ἐπὶ τὸ πολύ, *as things are for the most part, commonly*, iii. 1. 42. Ὡς ἀληθῶς, *truly*, Pl.

a. Ὡς, like our *as*, is remarkable for the variety of its use. It belongs to four classes of conjunctions (701), and also performs various offices as a connective adverb and as a modal sign (65 d). (b) It is often used to render expressions of quantity less positive : Ἔχων [sc. οὕτω πολλούς] ὡς πεντακοσίους, *having such a number as* 500, i. e. *about* 500, i. 2. 3. (c) From its frequent use with the accusative after verbs of motion to express the purposed end of the motion (472 g), it came at last to be even regarded as a *preposition*, supplying the place of πρός or εἰς, but chiefly before names of persons : Πορεύεται ὡς βασιλέα, *he goes* [as] *to the king*, i. 2. 4. Ὡς τὸν ὅμοιον, *to the like*, p. 217.

712. γ. Various ellipses occur with prepositions and adverbs : Ἱλαραὶ δὲ ἀντὶ σκυθρωπῶν [sc. γυναικῶν, or = ἀντὶ τοῦ εἶναι σκυθρωποί] ἦσαν, καὶ ἀντὶ ὑφορωμένων ἑαυτὰς ἡδέως ἀλλήλας ἑώρων, *they were cheerful instead of* [being] *downcast, &c.*, Mem. 2. 7. 12. Εἰς [sc. τὸν χρόνον] ὅτε, *for the time when*, β. 99. Σὺν οἷς ἔχω (554). See 557, 699 e, 703 b.

B. Pleonasm.

713. Under this head we remark,

1.) The redundant use of NEGATIVES. This appears chiefly,

a.) In connection with *indefinites*, which in a negative sentence are all regularly combined with a negative : Οὔποτε ἐρεῖ οὐδείς, *no one shall* [never] *ever say*, i. 3. 5. Οὐδενὶ οὐδαμῇ οὐδαμῶς οὐδεμίαν κοινωνίαν ἔχει Pl.

b.) In divided construction, and (c) in the emphatic use of οὐδέ and μηδέ : Μηδὲν τελείτω μήτε ἐμοὶ μήτε ἄλλῳ μηδενί, *let him pay nothing either to me or to any one else*, vii. 1. 6. Οὐ μὲν δὴ οὐδὲ τοῦτ' ἄν τις εἴποι, *nor surely could any one say this*, i. 9. 13. Μὴ τοίνυν μηδέ vii. 6. 19.

d.) In the common (but not necessary) use of μή with the Infinitive, after words implying some negation : Ναυκλήροις ἀπεῖπε μὴ διάγειν, *he forbade the shipmasters to transport* [saying that they should *not* transport], vii. 2. 12. Ἕξει τοῦ μὴ καταδῦναι, *will keep from sinking*. (e) Οὐ is sometimes used in like manner, with a finite verb after ὅτι or ὡς: Ἀρνεῖσθαι .., ὅτι οὐ παρῆν, *to deny that he was present*, Rep. A. 2. 17.

§ 716. PLEONASM. 331

f.) In the use of μή ού for μή, with the Infinitive (commonly) and Participle (sometimes), after *negative* and *interrogative* clauses (sometimes after expressions of *shame, fear*, and the like, from the negation implied). The ού (as simply continuing the general negation of the sentence, cf. a, b, c) may be here joined with μή, (g) even when this is redundant. E. g., (f) Ούδείς γέ μ' ἄν πείσειεν ἀνθρώπων τὸ μὴ ούκ ἐλθεῖν, *no one could persuade me not to go* [no], Ar. Ran. 65. Ού γὰρ ἄν μακρὰν ἰχνευον αὐτός, μὴ ούκ ἔχων τι σύμβολον, *I could not trace it far of myself*, [not having] *without some clew*, Soph. O. T. 220. Ώστε πᾶσιν αἰσχύνην εἶναι, μὴ ού συσπουδάζειν, *so that all were ashamed not to share his zeal*, ii. 3. 11. (g) Ούκ ἐναντιώσομαι τὸ μὴ ού γεγωνεῖν, *I will not refuse to speak*, Æsch. Pr. 787.

h.) In the occasional use of ού to strengthen the negative force of ή, than : Πόλιν ὅλην διαφθεῖραι μᾶλλον ή ού τοὺς αἰτίους, *to destroy a whole city, rather than* [and not rather] *the guilty ones*, Th. 3. 36.

Two negatives in the same sentence have their distinct force, when one applies to the whole sentence, and the other to a part only ; and so commonly (i) when the first is interrogative, or (j) the second is simple ού or μή, after a negative of its own class (686), or (k) the two negatives are of different classes : (i) Ού .. ούδέ .. δύνανται ; *are they not even unable ?* iii. 1. 29. (j) Ούδείς ούκ ἔπασχε, *no one was not affected*, Symp. See 559 c. (k) Ού .. δύναμαι μὴ γελᾶν, *I cannot help laughing*, Ar. Οὔτε σιγᾶν, οὔτε μὴ σιγᾶν Æsch. See 597 e. For apparent exceptions, see f, g, 627.

714. 2.) The repetition of various particles for greater clearness or strength of expression, particularly after intervening clauses, in divided construction, and with important or emphatic words ; but sometimes, especially in poetry, for mere euphony or rhythm :

Ἔλεγεν ὅτι, εἰ μή .. πείσονται, ὅτι κατακαύσει, *he said that, if they would not obey*, [that] *he would burn*, vii. 4. 5. Ούκ ἄν ἱκανὸς εἶναι οἶμαι, οὔτ' ἄν φίλον ὠφελῆσαι, οὔτ' ἄν ἐχθρὸν ἀλέξασθαι, *I do not think I should be able, either to aid a friend, or to repel a foe*, i. 3. 6. — And for like reasons,

3.) The addition of particles to words of similar meaning, and the use of needless connectives : Οἱόθεν οἷος, [solely] *all alone*, H. 226. Ἀπὸ βοῆς ἕνεκα, *from shouting* (*so far as this was concerned*), Th. 8. 92.

4.) Duplicate expressions with particles ; as (a) POSITIVE and NEGATIVE : Ούκ ἥκιστα, ἀλλὰ μάλιστα, *not the least, but the most*, Hdt. 2. 4. (b) WHOLE and PART (for special distinction) : Ὦ Ζεῦ καὶ θεοί Pl.

C. ATTRACTION AND ANACOLUTHON.

715. The influence of ATTRACTION sometimes passes even beyond a connective : as,

Ούδέν γε ἄλλο ἐστίν, ού ἐρῶσιν οἱ ἄνθρωποι, ἤ τοῦ ἀγαθοῦ [for τὸ ἀγαθόν, through the attraction of ού], *there is nothing else which men love, but the good*, Pl. Conv. 205 e. Πατρὸς, εἴπερ τινὸς [for τις], σθένοντος, *from a father powerful, if any one was*, Soph. Aj. 487. See 667 g, 702 d.

716. a. ANACOLUTHON is frequent in the connection of sentences, either from inadvertence or from preference (for the sake of ease, emphasis, &c.). The clause completing the construction is often changed in form, or even omitted ; or (b) the regular correspondence of particles may be neglected : as,

332   SYNTAX. — PARTICLES.   § 716.

(a) 'Ωs . . ἤκουσά τινος, ὅτι Κλέανδρος . . μέλλει ἥξειν [for ὡς ἤκουσα, Κ. μέλλει, or ἤκουσα, ὅτι Κ. μέλλει], as *I heard from some one*, [that] *C. is about to come*, vi. 4. 18. (b) Καὶ εἰ . . ἤ [for καὶ εἴ], *both if* . . [or] *and if*, Th. 6. 64. Τε . . ἔπειτα δέ, *both* . . [but then] *and*, v. 5. 8.

c. After a connective, a distinct sentence often takes the place of a part of a sentence, and (d) sometimes the reverse : (c) "Ἄλλῳ τε τρόπῳ πειράσαντες, καὶ μηχανὴν προσήγαγον, *both attempting in other ways, and* [they brought up] *bringing up an engine*, Th. 4. 100. See i. 10. 12 ; ii. 1. 7. (d) Παρημέλουν . ., οὔτε γάρ . . διδόντες [for ἐδίδοσαν, as if γάρ had been omitted], *they slighted them*, [not giving] *for they did not give*, Th. 1. 25.

717. IV. The Greek especially abounds in combinations of particles, and in elliptical phrases having the power of particles. The use of these sometimes extends farther than their origin and structure would strictly warrant. E. g.,

a. **ἄλλως τε καί**, *both otherwise and in particular, especially :* Οὐδὲν νομίζω ἀνδρί, ἄλλως τε καὶ ἄρχοντι, κάλλιον εἶναι κτῆμα vii. 7. 41.

b. **δῆλον ὅτι**, *it is evident that, evidently*, εὖ οἶδ' ὅτι, οἶδ' ὅτι, σάφ' ἴσθ' ὅτι, and similar phrases, which are often inserted in sentences (quite like adverbs), or annexed to them : Τὰ μὲν δὴ Κύρου δῆλον ὅτι οὕτως ἔχει i. 3. 9.

c. **εἰ δὲ μή**, *but if not, otherwise*, used even after- negative sentences : Μὴ ποιήσῃς ταῦτα · εἰ δὲ μή, αἰτίαν ἕξεις, *do not do this ; otherwise* [i. e. if you do] *you will have blame*, vii. 1. 8. So **εἰ δέ**, as adversative, sometimes implies negation : Εἰ μὲν βούλεται, ἐψέτω · εἰ δέ, . . ποιείτω, *if he wishes, let him boil ; if the contrary, let him do*, Pl. Euthyd. 285 c.

d. **μή τί γε**, *not to* [say aught surely] *mention*, i. e. *much less*, nedum : Οὐκ ἔνι . . τοῖς φίλοις ἐπιτάττειν . ., μή τί γε δὴ τοῖς θεοῖς Dem. 24. 21.

e. **οὐ γὰρ ἀλλά**, *for it is not otherwise, but*, i. e. *for indeed :* Οὐ γὰρ ἀλλ' ἡ γῆ βίᾳ ἕλκει, *for indeed the earth forcibly attracts*, Ar. Nub. 232.

f. **οὐ μέντοι ἀλλά**, *οὐ μὴν ἀλλά, yet no, but*, i. e. *nevertheless :* 'Ο ἵππος . . μικροῦ κἀκεῖνον ἐξετραχήλισεν · οὐ μὴν ἀλλ' ἐπέμεινεν ὁ Κῦρος Cyr. 1. 4. 8.

g. **οὐχ ὅτι, μὴ ὅτι**, οὐ μόνον ὅτι, οὐχ ὅσον, οὐχ ὅπως, μὴ ὅπως, οὐχ οἷον, *I do not say that, not to say that*, &c., i. e. *not only*, or *not only not :* Ἄχρηστοι γὰρ καὶ γυναιξὶν . ., μὴ ὅτι ἀνδράσι, *useless even to women, not to say men*, Pl. Οὐχ ὅπως δῶρα δούς, *not only bestowing no gifts*, vii. 7. 8.

CHAPTER V.

ARRANGEMENT.

718. In the *direct*, or *normal order* of arrangement, which, however, various influences are continually changing or modifying,

a.) A general *connective* or *interrogative* leads in its sentence : and (b) a *compellative-part* (60), as calling attention, is placed early, if not first ; though, as independent, it may have any place which will not interfere with the required connection of other words. (c) Of the remainder, the *subject-part* precedes the *predicate-part*. (d) *Exponents* precede the words whose offices or relations they mark (65). E. g., 'Αλλ' ἐγώ, ὦ Φαλῖνε, θαυμάζω . ., *but I, Phalinus, wonder*, ii. 1. 10.

§ 719. DIRECT ORDER OF ARRANGEMENT. 333

MODIFIERS (except as above, a) are thus placed in respect to their principals: (e) *Adverbs* and equivalent words or phrases precede them. (f) *Other modifiers* follow substantives without the article, (g) adjectives, and (h) adverbs; and (i) may either follow or precede verbs. (j) For the arrangement with the article, see 520, 523 s. (k) Of several modifiers of the same word, the more closely related are placed nearer to it (a *Dat. of person*, from more interest in the action, usually nearer than an *Acc. of thing*). E. g., (e) Ἐν ἴσῳ καὶ βραδέως προσῄεσαν, *they advanced evenly and slowly*, i. 8. 11. See 510. (f, g) Κῶμαι πολλαί, μεσταὶ σίτου, *many villages, full of corn*, i. 4. 19. (h) Χωρὶς τῶν ἄλλων (405 a). (i) Κύρῳ δοῦναι χρήματα, *to give C. money*, i. 2. 12. (k) Διαβάλλει τὸν Κῦρον πρὸς τὸν ἀδελφόν, *traduces C. to his brother*, i. 1. 3. Δίδωσιν αὐτῷ μυρίους δαρεικούς, *gives him* 10,000 *darics*, i. 1. 9.

l.) An *infinitive* follows the principal verb; (m) a *participle* follows or precedes it, according to the natural order of the thought. (n) *Coördinate sentences* follow each other according to the order in which they lie in the mind. (o) *Substantive* and *adjective clauses*, except the indefinite relative (641), follow the words upon which they depend. (p) *Adverbial clauses* may follow or precede the principal clauses, according to the natural order of the thought; and (q) are sometimes inserted in them, for the sake of a closer connection. E. g., (l, m) Συλλέξας στράτευμα.. ἐπειρᾶτο κατάγειν, *having raised an army, he* (then) *endeavored to restore*, i. 1. 7. See 571 f. (n) Ὁ δὲ πείθεταί τε καὶ συλλαμβάνει, *and he both believes and* (as a result) *apprehends*, i. 1. 3. (o, p, q) Ἐπειδὴ δὲ Κῦρος ἐκάλει, λαβὼν ὑμᾶς ἐπορευόμην, ἵνα, εἴ τι δέοιτο, ὠφελοίην αὐτὸν ἀνθ' ὧν εὖ ἔπαθον ὑπ' ἐκείνου i. 3. 4.

r. An order different from the preceding is termed, in general, *indirect, varied*, or *abnormal*; or, more particularly, *inverted, divided, parenthetic, mixed, confused*, &c., as the case may be. See 71.

t. If a complex or compound sentence is so arranged that there is no complete sense without the final clause, the structure is often termed *periodic*; but otherwise, *loose*: Εἰ δοκεῖ σοι, στεῖχε (631 a). Χρῶ αὐτοῖς, ἐὰν δέῃ τι (631 c). The Greek well illustrates the progress, in advancing civilization, from the looser to the closer connection of thought.

719. The order of the sentence is *varied*, chiefly,

a.) To render certain words more *emphatic* or *prominent*, or (b) through the *attraction* or *repulsion* of other words.

(a) α. The beginning and close of the sentence have a special prominence; and of other places, the earlier are in general more favorable to emphasis than the later. It is but natural, that a sentence should commence with that which is most prominent or foremost in the mind, and that it should then proceed with that which is closely related to this, or next in prominence; while the last word leaves the freshest impression. E. g., Μῆνιν ἄειδε.. οὐλομένην, *sing the fatal wrath*, A. 1. Περὶ Ὀρόντου τουτουΐ i. 6. 6. (β) Any unusual order attracts attention; and in prose, commonly expresses emphasis or emotion: Οὐκ ἀνθρώπων ἀπορῶν βαρβάρων, *not from want of* mere men, — barbarians, i. 7. 3. Οὗπερ αὐτὸς ἕνεκα i. 9. 21. (γ) See 476 b. (δ) See 708 f.

(b) ε. The desire of connecting kindred or contrasted words as closely as possible often varies the order; while a connection is avoided that would offend taste or might lead to mistake: Παρὰ φίλης φίλῳ φέρειν γυναικὸς ἀνδρί, *to bring from a* dear wife *to a* dear husband, Æsch. Ch. 89. Καὶ ἐποίουν οὕτως οὗτοι i. 1. 11. See 541 h, 567 d. (ζ) If a word modifying the verb comes early in the sentence, it often attracts the verb to a place before the subject : Ἐνταῦθα ἦσαν κῶμαι, *here were villages* (θ), i. 4. 19. Ἐπεὶ δὲ ἠσθένει Δαρεῖος, *and when D. was sick*, i. 1. 1. (η) A particle is sometimes attracted from its proper place : Οὐκ οἶδ' ἄν εἰ πείσαιμι, *I know not whether I could persuade* (πείσαιμι ἄν, 621 a), Eur. Med. 941. Καὶ νῦν ὅτι πολιορκοῦνται, *and that they are now besieged*, vi. 3. 11.

c.) In conformity to the *natural order and connection* of the thoughts ; or (d) to present *sooner* an *outline* of these, some details being deferred. Thus,

(c) Δαρείου καὶ Παρυσάτιδος γίγνονται παῖδες δύο (412 ; the well-known parents being naturally mentioned before their children). See ζ. (θ) A word referring or corresponding to what is contained in the preceding sentence, has commonly a leading place, as introducing the new thought and connecting the thoughts : Ὁ μὲν οὖν πρεσβύτερος παρὼν ἐτύγχανε · Κῦρον (corresponding to πρεσβύτερος) δὲ μεταπέμπεται ἀπὸ τῆς ἀρχῆς, ἧς (referring to ἀρχῆς) αὐτὸν σατράπην ἐποίησε · καὶ στρατηγὸν (corresponding to σατράπην) δὲ αὐτὸν ἀπέδειξε πάντων, ὅσοι (referring to πάντων) εἰς Καστωλοῦ πεδίον ἀθροίζονται. Ἀναβαίνει (the result of μεταπέμπεται) οὖν ὁ Κῦρος. i. 1. 2. (ι) When a question is made without an interrogative exponent, the predicate, as in Eng., often leads, as the part on which the force of the question most directly falls : Τέθνηκε Φίλιππος ; *is P. dead ?* Dem. 43. 10. (κ) A word pointing to a following sentence has naturally a late place : Διαβαίνοντες ὧδε, *crossing as follows*, i. 5. 10.

(d) Ἐνταῦθα ἀφικνεῖται Ἐπύαξα, ἡ Συεννέσιος γυνή, τοῦ Κιλίκων βασιλέως, παρὰ Κῦρον, *here comes E., the wife of S., king of the Cilicians, to C.*, i. 2. 12. An outline is here first presented in Ἐνταῦθα (θ) ἀφικνεῖται (ζ) Ἐ. ; then Ἐ. is defined by ἡ Σ. γυνή, Σ. by τοῦ Κ. βασιλέως, and ἀφικνεῖται by παρὰ Κ. The early presentation of the general idea is often aided, (λ) by placing first the shorter of two parts of the sentence ; (μ) by joining a word with the first of two or more words to which it is alike related ; (ν) by dividing or separating a modifying part, &c. : Ἐφαίνετο ἴχνια ἵππων καὶ κόπρος, *there appeared the tracks and dung of horses*. Περσῶν τοὺς ἀρίστους τῶν περὶ αὐτὸν ἑπτά, *the seven noblest of his Persian attendants*.

e.) For the *symmetry* of the sentence ; or (f) that it may *close* with a stronger or more important word. E. g.,

Οὔτε γὰρ ἡμεῖς ἐκείνου ἔτι στρατιῶται . . ., οὔτε ἐκεῖνος ἔτι ἡμῖν μισθοδότης, *for neither are we longer his soldiers, nor he longer our paymaster*, i. 3. 9 (see ε). Πολλάκις ἡδονὴ βραχεῖα μακρὰν λύπην τίκτει, PLEASURE *brief long* GRIEF *often brings* (71 a). Ὃς μόνος μὲν πρὸς θεῶν ἀσεβής, μόνος δὲ πρὸς ἀνθρώπων αἰσχρός, *which alone before the gods is impious, and before men base*, ii. 5. 20.

g.) For *euphony* or *rhythm*, especially in the poets ; (h) for *variety* itself ; or (i) for general *rhetorical effect*. E. g.,

Μάχην ἐς, *to battle* (the metre forbidding ἐς μάχην), O. 59. — The influence of these three causes was very great, and is often quite obvious, though its full extent and manner are now beyond our cognizance.

720. From their general want of emphasis, the following words cannot stand first in the sentence ; and are therefore called *post-positive:* the particles ἄν (not for ἐάν, 619 a ; Ep. κέ), ἄρα (not ἆρα, 685 c ; Ep. ῥά, ἄρ), αὖ (poet. αὖτε) and αὖθις (Ep. and Ion. αὖτις) *again*, γάρ, γέ, γοῦν, δαί, δέ, δή (exc. Ep. δὴ γάρ, δὴ τότε), δῆθεν, δῆτα, θήν, μέν, μέντοι, μήν,

§ 723.   PARTS OF COMPOUND WORDS.   335

νύν (not νῦν · Ep. νύ), οὖν, πέρ, τί, τοί, τοίνυν (see 685 c, 701); also τὶs, and the indefinites beginning with π (the rather for distinction from the interrogatives): Ὁ δὲ πείθεταί τε, καὶ συλλαμβάνει (718 n). See 518, 548.

a. When these words naturally lead a sentence or part of a sentence, they have commonly the second place or the earliest place allowable; and, from their frequent need of an early position and their lack of prominence, they are often permitted to separate closely related words; indeed they are often so inserted to give strength or emphasis to such words. Enclitic pronouns are sometimes placed in like manner. E. g., Ὁ μὲν οὖν πρεσβύτερος, *the elder, then,* i. 1. 1. Πρὸς δὲ ἄρκτον, *and to the north,* i. 7. 6. Ἐκ δὲ τῶν (518 a). Πρός σε θεῶν (476 b). See 520 b, 621 e.

721. a. Variation of place extends to *clauses,* as well as words and phrases: Ὅτι δὲ ἐπὶ βασιλέα ἄγοι, . . ἤκουσεν οὐδείς, *but, that he was leading against the king, no one heard,* i. 3. 21. Ὃν εἶδες, οὗτός ἐστιν (551 c).

b. A subject common to a dependent and principal clause often precedes the connective: Οἱ δ' ἄλλοι ἐπειδὴ ἧκον, . . διήρπασαν, *but when now the rest had come, they plundered,* i. 2. 26.

---

722. Postscript to Syntax. Syntactic relations belong not only to distinct words, but also to the PARTS OF COMPOUND WORDS (383 s). They are here either *internal,* between the parts themselves; or *external,* between these parts and other words.

1. INTERNAL RELATIONS. Of the *two* elements which commonly unite in the compound, one may modify the other as an (a) *adjective,* (b) *adverb,* (c – g) *adjunct,* or sometimes (h) *appositive;* or (i) one may belong to the other as an *exponent;* or (j) the two may be *coupled.* The same relations appear in compounds of more than two elements. E. g.,

(a) ἀκρό-πολις *upper city* (ἄκρης πόλιος Z. 257), *citadel;* κενο-τάφιον *empty tomb, cenotaph,* vi. 4. 9. (b) ὠκυ-πέτης *swiftly flying,* ἀ-γνώς *unknown.* (c) Direct Object: θανατη-φόρος *death-bringing* (θάνατον φέρων), νομο-θέτης *legis-lator.* (d) Indirect Object: ἰσό-θεος *god-like* (ἴσος θεῷ), ποδ-ηρής *reaching the feet,* i. 8. 9. (e) Agent: Διόσ-δοτος *given by Zeus* (ὑπὸ Διός), *heaven-sent.* (f) Instrument: χειρο-ποίητος manu-factus, *made by hand* (χειρί), iv. 3. 5. (g) Time, Place, Origin, &c.: νυκτι-πόλος nocti-vagus, *night-roaming,* οἰκο-γενής *born in the house* (ἐν οἴκῳ), ἀξιό-λογος *worthy of mention* (λόγου), πυρι-γενής *fire-born.* (h) ἰατρό-μαντις *physician-seer.* (i) ἔν-δοξος *in repute* (ἐν δόξῃ), ἀνθ-ύπατος pro-consul. (j) καλο-κ-ἀγαθία *honor and virtue,* Mem. 1. 6. 14; ᾠό-γαλα *eggs and milk,* Galen.

k. A modifier or exponent has commonly the first place in a compound, except that the object of a verb often follows it: φίλ-ιππος *horse-loving,* φέρ-ασπις *shield-bearing,* μισ-άνθρωπος *misanthropic.*

723. 2. EXTERNAL RELATIONS. An element of a compound has often the same relation to another word, expressed or implied, as if it stood by itself.

a.) It may so govern or be modified (see 436 a, b, 699 a). (b) It may so modify or be governed; often as a Gen. of property or relation: μήτηρ καλλί-παις, *a mother of beautiful children* (καλῶν παίδων), ὁμό-τροπος *of like character,* ὠκύ-πους celeri-pes, [of swift foot] *swift-footed.* In this use it often represents the object of an implied verb of possession: ὠκεῖς πόδας ἔχων, *having swift feet.* (c) Each part of a compound may have an external relation: ἀμφι-κίων having *pillars around* it.

BOOK IV.

PROSODY.

Γλώσσης μείλιγμα.
Æschylus, Eumen.

CHAPTER I.

QUANTITY AND VERSIFICATION.

725. In Greek all vowels and syllables are divided, in respect to QUANTITY (i. e. the *time of their utterance* according to the ancient pronunciation), into *long* and *short;* and the long are regarded as having *double* the time of the short.

a. Hence the unit in measuring metrical quantity is the short syllable, or the *breve* (brevis, *short*), and a long vowel or syllable is equal to *two breves*. For the marks of quantity (— ⏑), see 96 c.

b. Quantity is of two kinds, *natural* and *local*. Natural quantity has respect to the length of the vowel *in its own nature;* but local quantity, to the effect which is produced by the *position* of the vowel in connection with other letters or syllables. In ὄρτυξ, *quail*, both syllables are short by *nature*, i. e. in the natural quantity of the vowels; but both become long by the *position* of these short vowels before two consonants (137 d).

c. The quantity of a syllable is always the natural quantity of the vowel which it contains, unless some change is produced by position. Hence it is usual, in prosody, to regard the vowel as the *representative* of the syllable; and language is often applied to the *vowel* which in strict propriety belongs only to the *syllable*. Thus, in ὄρτυξ, it is common to say that the vowels are long by position; while, in strict accuracy, the quantity of the vowels themselves is not changed, but the *syllables* become long from the time occupied in the utterance of the successive consonants.

I. NATURAL QUANTITY.

726. RULE 1. ε and ο are short: as in φέρομεν.

RULE 2. η and ω, diphthongs, and all vowels that are circumflexed, or result from contraction or crasis, are long: as in ἡμῶν, πλείους, πᾶς, ἡμῖν, πῦρ· ῥῖς, δῦς (156); κἄν (126).

RULE 3. Other vowels are commonly short: as in χλἄμὔδῐ.

a. All vowels which result from the union of two vowels have, from their very nature, a double time. See 115 s. (b) To the *general rule for the doubtful vowels* (Rule 3) there are many exceptions; which renders it necessary to observe the ACCENT, the special laws of INFLECTION and DERIVATION, the DIALECT, and AUTHORITY, by which is here meant the *usage of the poets.*

727. A. ACCENT. From the general rules of accent (770 s), we learn, that in *natural quantity,*

a.) In *proparoxytones* and *properispomes,* the last vowel is short: as in ἄρουρα, δύναμις, τέλεκυς· βῶλαξ, πρᾶξις, διῶρυξ.

b.) In *paroxytones,* if the *last* vowel is *short,* the vowel of the *penult* is also short; and, on the other hand, if the vowel of the *penult* is *long,* the *last* vowel is also long: as in μαινάδος, καρκίνος, χλαμύδος· Λήδα, φοῖνιξ.

728. B. INFLECTION. In the common affixes of declension and conjugation, the doubtful vowels are short, except cases of contraction, -α in the Sing. of Dec. 1, and ᾱσί for νσί in the nude Present.

Thus, Dec. 1, Gen. sing. and Acc. pl. -ᾱς, Nom. du. -ᾱ (13, 122), Aor. Pt. -σᾱς, -σᾱσα (35 d), Pf. 3 pl. -κᾱσι (300 a). For special rules in regard to the Sing. of Dec. 1, see 194 s, 232 s; for -ἕᾱ, -ἕᾱς in Dec. 3, 220; for nude Pres. forms in -ᾱσι, 35 a, 156; for the dialectic affixes, 20, 48 a.

729. SPECIAL RULES OF DEC. III. 1. The doubtful vowels are *long* in the *last syllable* of the *stem,* — (a) If the stem-mark is ν: as, παιάν, -ᾶνος, δελφίς, -ῖνος, Φόρκυς, -ῡνος (208): except in the adjectives μέλᾱς, -ᾰνος, τάλᾱς, -ᾰνος (23 b, d), and the pronoun τίς, τίνος. (b) In most *palatals,* if a long syllable precede: θώραξ, -ᾱκος, μάστιξ, -ῑγος, πέρδιξ, -ῑκος, κῆρυξ, -ῡκος. (c) In words in -ις, -ιθος, and in some *oxytones* in -ις, ιδος: ὄρνις, -ῑθος, κνημίς, -ῖδος, σφραγίς, -ῖδος. (d) In a few other words: as, κέρας, -ᾱτος· ψάρ, ψᾱρός· γρύψ, γρῡπός.

2. Monosyllabic themes are long: κίς, κῑός· μῦς, μῡός· πῦρ, πῡρός. Except the pronoun τίς (208 d). — So the neuter πᾶν (23) is lengthened.

730. SPECIAL RULES OF CONJUGATION. 1. Before the OPEN AFFIXES (303), — (a) α is *short;* except in ἰάομαι *heal,* κάω, κλάω (309 b), and sometimes in the Epic and lyric poets for the sake of the metre. (b) ι is commonly *long*: κονίω *cover with dust,* πρίω *to saw;* but ἄῑω (ῐ), ἐσθίω, δέδια, ἔπιον from πίνω (50). (c) υ is *variable:* ἀνύω, λύω, θύω (ῡ).

2. Before the REGULAR CLOSE AFFIXES, — (d) In *lingual* and *liquid* verbs, the doubtful vowels are *short*: as, ὥρισα (39 d), κέκρῐκα, ἐκλίθην (304 a); except βρίθω *weigh down,* F. βρίσω. (e) In *pure verbs,* α is *short,* except when the theme ends in -άω pure, or -ράω; ι is commonly *long*: and υ *variable*: ἔσπᾱκα, ἐσκέδᾱσα (310 c, e), but εἴᾱσα, ἐθηράθην (310), ἔτῑσα (310), but φθίσω, ἐφθίμην (50); ἀνύσω, πέφῡκα, θύσω, τέθῡκα (310).

3. Before the AFFIXES OF VERBS IN -μι, the doubtful vowels are *short,* except in the *Ind. sing.* of the *Pres.* and *Impf. act.,* and in the 2d *Aor. act.*: δείκνῡμι, δείκνῠμεν, ἔδρᾱν. See 313 s.

4. Before a CONSONANT STEM-MARK, — (f) In the *theme,* α is commonly *short,* but ι and υ *long*: μανθάνω, κλίνω, ὀδύρομαι; but ἱκάνω, τίνω, φθίνω (50). (g) In the *liquid Fut.,* and in the 2d *Aor.* (340. 3), the doubtful vowels are *short,* but in the *liquid Aor.,* and in the 2d *Perf.,* they are *long:* κρινῶ, ἔκρῑνα (152); ἔλᾰβον, ἐτρίβην (347 g); κέκρᾱγα, κέκρῑγα, μέμῡκα (312 a): except 2 A. ἐάγην (50, ἄγνῡμι), ἐλήλῠθα, &c. (312 a).

- **731. C. DERIVATION.** RULE 4. DERIVATIVES follow the quantity of their *primitives*.

a. This rule applies to compounds, as well as to simple derivatives. In applying the rule, observe 366 d. E. g., θηράω, F. θηράσω, Pf. P. τεθήραμαι · θηράσιμος, θήραμα, θηρατής, θηρατός · ἔντιμος (ἐν, τιμή).

732. D. DIALECT. The Doric a for η is long; and a, where the Ionic uses η, is commonly long (130 a). See also 134.

733. E. AUTHORITY. For doubtful vowels which are long, and not determined by the rules already given, observe the usage of the poets, and the marks of quantity in the lexicons.

a. Familiar examples are ἄτη *destruction*, σφραγίς *seal*, τραχύς *rough*, μικρός *small*, νίκη *victory*, ὅμιλος *crowd*, σιγή *silence*, χαλινός *bridle*, πυρός *wheat*, συλάω *to plunder*, ὕλη *forest*, φυλή *tribe*, χρυσός *gold*, ψυχή *soul*.

II. LOCAL QUANTITY.

734. RULE 5. A vowel before two consonants or a double consonant is long (725 c, 137 d): as in ὄρτυξ, ἐλπίζοντες μάψ.

a. This *rule of position* holds, as in Latin, if the consonants are wholly or partly in the same word with the vowel; and commonly, also, if they are wholly in the next word.

735. EXCEPTION. When the two consonants are *a mute followed by a liquid in the same simple word*, the quantity of the vowel is often not affected, especially in Attic verse.

NOTE. This exception results from the easy flowing together of the mute and liquid, so as to produce the effect of a single consonant.

a. In the Attic, the quantity of the vowel is commonly not affected, if the mute is *smooth* or *rough*, or, if *middle*, is *followed by* ρ; but is regularly lengthened before a *middle* mute followed by μ, ν, or λ. Thus, the penult is regularly short in πέπλος, τέκνον, πότμος, ἴχνος, ἀγρός, ἔδρα · and long in δόγμα, ἔδνα, στρεβλός, as well as in the compound ἐκρεῖν.

736. A short vowel is sometimes *lengthened before a single consonant or another vowel*, especially in Epic poetry. This occurs chiefly in the following cases:

a.) When the consonant may be regarded as *doubled in pronunciation*. This applies mostly to the liquids, and in the case of these (chiefly initial ῥ, cf. 146) sometimes extends even to Attic verse: Αἰόλου [as if -ολλ-] κ. 36, δὲ νέφος Δ. 274, ἔδεισας X. 19, ἐμὲ ῥέπον Soph., μέγα ῥάκος Æsch.

b.) Where F has been dropped (138 s): γὰρ ἔθεν [Fέθεν, 27 f] I. 419, κέν ἑ κύνες X. 42, πρὸς οἶκον [Fοῖκον] I. 147. — Yet the Epic sometimes gives the digamma, if indeed used, only the force of a breathing (98 e).

c.) Before a *masculine cæsura*; and sometimes, without a cæsura, by the force of the *arsis* (745 c, 741): ὀνομᾶ · Οὗτιν ι. 366; ἀπόέρσῃ Φ. 283.

d. In Hexameter verse, one of three successive short syllables, a short between two long syllables, and a short syllable at the beginning of a line, must of necessity be made long. The second case sometimes occurs in the *thesis*. E. g., ἀπονέεσθαι Ξ. 46; Ἀσκληπιοῦ δύο B. 731 (cf. Ἀσκληπιοῦ υἱόν Δ. 194), Ἕως ὅ ταῦθ᾽ A. 193; Ἐπειδή (ε̄) X. 379, Ἄρες, Ἄρες E. 31.

737. Rule 6. A long vowel or diphthong at the end of a word may be shortened, if the next word begins with a vowel.

a. In the thesis of Hexameter and Pentameter verse, this shortening is the general rule: Ἡμετέρῳ ἐνὶ οἴκῳ ἐν Ἄργεϊ A. 30. Τίες, ὁ μὲν Κτεάτου, ὁ δ' ἄρ' Εὐρύτου, Ἀκτορίωνες B. 621. (b) This rule does not apply to the Iambic and Trochaic metres of the drama, as there the hiatus is scarce allowed. (c) Rarely, a long vowel or diphthong is shortened before a vowel in the same word: ἐμπαῖον v. 379, οἶος (οἴ) N. 275, τοιοῦτος Soph.

738. Rule 7. The last syllable of every verse is common.

a. That is, the *metrical pause* at the end of the verse renders the quantity of the last syllable indifferent; and it may be regarded as either long or short according to the metre. (b) In some kinds of verse, however, the scansion is continuous; i. e. the verses are formed into systems, at the end of which only this freedom is allowed, the preceding syllables being all subject to the rules of prosody, as if in a single verse.

739. *a.* In giving the rules of quantity, *position* should not be adduced, unless some change has been made from the natural length of the vowel. For convenient distinction in metrical analysis, a vowel whose quantity is to be referred to Rules 1 and 2 may be said to be long or short *by nature;* to Rule 3, *by the general rule* (i. e. for the doubtful vowels); to Rule 4, *by derivation;* to Rule 5, *by position* (i. e. before two consonants, or a double consonant); to Rule 6, *by position before a vowel;* to Rule 7, *at the end of the verse.*

III. VERSIFICATION.

740. Greek verse is founded upon RHYTHM; i. e. *the regular succession of long and short quantities.*

a. Elementary combinations of syllables, showing the rhythm, are termed FEET (as if *steps* in the rhythmic movement); regular combinations of feet, VERSES (versus, *a turn*); and regular combinations of verses, STANZAS, STROPHES, or SYSTEMS (744). For a table of feet, see 77.

b. A single foot, taken by itself, is called a *monopody* (πούς, *foot*); a combination of two feet, a *dipody;* of three, four, five, six, &c., a *tripody, tetrapody, pentapody, hexapody,* &c.; of a foot and a half, a *triemim* (τριημιμερής, *of three half-parts*); of two and a half, three and a half, four and a half, &c., *penthemim, hephthemim, enneëmim,* &c. See 745 c.

741. The long syllables are naturally pronounced with a greater stress of the voice than the short. This stress is termed ARSIS, (ἄρσις, *elevation*), while the alternate weaker tone is termed THESIS (θέσις, *depression*). These terms are also applied to the parts of the rhythm which are thus pronounced.

a. The arsis (also termed *metrical ictus* or *rhythmic accent*) is here marked thus (ˈ , ́ , or to indicate greater force, ⁋).

b. As one long syllable is equal to two short, the partial substitution of ⊥ ⌣ for ⊥ in the arsis (*resolution*), and of — for ⌣ ⌣ in the thesis (*contraction*), may be made without affecting the rhythm.

c. In the common kinds of verse, the metrical ictus is determined by the prevailing foot. Hence in Trochaic and Dactylic verse, every foot receives the ictus upon the *first* syllable ; while, in Iambic and Anapæstic verse, every foot receives it upon the *second*, except the anapæst and proceleusmatic, which receive it upon the *third*. (d) Iambic, Trochaic, and Anapæstic verse has commonly a stronger ictus upon every other foot ; and is hence measured, not by single feet, but by *dipodies* (740 b).

742. The simplest and most familiar rhythms are those in which a long syllable alternates with *one*, or with *two* short syllables ($\underline{} \smile \underline{} \smile \underline{} \smile$, or $\underline{} \smile \smile \underline{} \smile \smile \underline{} \smile \smile$). In the latter, the thesis is equal in time to the arsis, and the rhythm is termed *equal* or *quadruple* ($- \smile \smile = 4$ breves, 725 a); but in the former, the thesis is only half the arsis, and the rhythm is termed *triple* ($- \smile = 3$ breves).

a. Of these, the *equal* is the more stately in its movement, and the more appropriate to those kinds of verse which are farthest removed from common discourse ; while the *triple* has more nearly the movement of common conversation, and is hence better adapted to the more familiar kinds of verse, and to dialogue.
b. Other rhythms are formed by doubling the arsis, by prolonging the thesis, or by variously compounding simple rhythms. (c) Verses, in which the equal and triple rhythms are united, are termed *logœdic* (λόγος *discourse*, ἀοιδή *song*, see a).

743. VERSES are named,—(a) From the prevailing foot: *Iambic, Dactylic.* (b) From some poet who invented or used them, or the species of composition in which they were employed: *Alcaic*, from Alcæus; *Sapphic*, from Sappho; *Heroic*, as used in singing the deeds of heroes. (c) From the number of measures (i. e. feet, or dipodies, 741 d) which they contain: *monometer* (μονόμετρος, *of one measure*), *dimeter, trimeter, tetrameter, pentameter, hexameter.* (d) From their degree of completeness ; thus a verse is termed *catalectic* (καταλήγω, *to end* abruptly), when its last foot is incomplete; *brachycatalectic*, when it wants a whole foot at the end; *acatalectic*, when it has its just measure; *hypercatalectic*, when it has one or two syllables beyond; *hypermeter*, when it exceeds in any way its just measure; *acephalous* (ἀκέφαλος, *headless*), when it wants a syllable at the beginning; *anacrusic, basic*, or *syncopated*, when affected as below.
e. A long or short syllable or pyrrhic is sometimes prefixed to a lyric rhythm beginning with the arsis. This is called an *anacrūsis* (ἀνάκρουσις, *striking up*). A similar prefix of greater length is called a *basis* (a term sometimes applied to any monometer ; βάσις, *step*). (f) In the drama, exclamations often occur *extra metrum* (i. e. not included in the metre) : Φεῦ! Eur. Alc. 536. Τί φῶ; Soph. O. C. 315. Τάλαινα ! Ib. 318.
g. Metrical *syncope* is the omission of a thesis in the middle of a rhythm ; where we may suppose the time to have been supplied, as in modern music, by a *rest*, or by dwelling longer upon an adjoining arsis.

744. Metrical composition is either in MONOSTICHS, SYSTEMS, or STANZAS. (a) MONOSTICHS (μονόστιχος, *of a single line*) consist of the same verse repeated, as in Hexameter verse (748), Iambic Trimeter (756), &c. (b) SYSTEMS are formed by the repetition of similar rhythms, with continuous scansion (as if a single long line, 738 b)

§ 746.   KINDS OF VERSE. CÆSURA.   341

and an appropriate close. (c) STANZAS (also called *strophes*) are formed by the union of different kinds of verse. A stanza of two lines is called a *distich;* of three, a *tristich*, of four, a *tetrastich*.

d. The most common systems are easily arranged in dimeters, with here and there a monometer; and close with a dimeter catalectic.

e. The Greek choral odes were written in stanzas of very varied structure, but commonly arranged in *duads* or *triads* (sometimes in *tetrads* or *pentads*). A duad consists of two stanzas, corresponding in metre throughout. Of these, the first is termed the *strophe* (στροφή, *turning round, stanza*), and the second the *antistrophe* (ἀντιστροφή, *counter-turn* or *-stanza*). A triad consists of a strophe and antistrophe, preceded, divided, or followed by a third stanza of different metre, which according to its place is termed *proöde* (πρό *before*, ᾠδή *ode*), *mesode* (μέσος *middle*), or *epode* (ἐπί *after*). Of these, the epode is far the most common.

745. CÆSURA (*cædo, to cut*) is the *cutting* of the *metre* by a division in the *sense*. It may be (a) *of the foot*, or (b) *of the verse*. In the former, a foot is cut by the ending of a word; in the latter, a verse is cut by a pause permitted by the sense.

c. This pause, which is often slight, is called the *cæsural pause;* and the syllable preceding any cæsura, the *cæsural syllable*. When this syllable is pronounced with the *arsis*, the cæsura is termed *masculine;* with the *thesis, feminine*. A cæsura in the second foot is named *triemim*, from the portion of the verse which has preceded (740 b); in the third, *penthemim;* in the fourth, *hephthemim;* &c.

d. The cæsura of the verse (often called simply *the cæsura*) is more frequently, but not necessarily, a cæsura of the foot. A prominent exception is the cæsura often occurring in Hexameter verse after the fourth foot (which is then commonly a dactyl), named the *bucolic* or *pastoral cæsura* from its prevalence in pastoral poetry. See also 757, 761.

746. a. HIATUS between words was admitted the most freely in Epic poetry, where however it may be often removed by the insertion of the digamma (98 e, 99 b). It was the most studiously avoided in Attic poetry, especially in the Tragic Trimeter (756).

SYNIZESIS (117). b. In Epic poetry synizesis is very frequent, especially when the first vowel is ε; thus, ἐᾱ, ἐᾳ, ἐαί; ἐο, ἐοί, ἐου; ἐω, ἐῳ: Πηληϊάδεω, χρυσέῳ ἀ|νά, A. 1, 15; see 27 f, 197 c, 222 b, 323 c. We find more rarely ἀε; ἰα, ἰαι, ἰη, ἰῃ, ἰο; οο; ὐα, ὐοί; &c. Synizesis sometimes occurs between two words, when the first is ἤ, ᾗ, δή, μή, ἐπεί, or a word ending in the affix -η or -ῳ: ἤ οὐχ E. 349, δὴ ὀγδοον η. 261, ἐπεί οὐ.

c. In Attic poetry, synizesis occurs chiefly in the endings -εως, -εων, -εα of Dec. 3 (220 d); in a few single words and forms (as θεός Eur. Or. 399); in the combinations ἤ οὐ and μή οὐ, regularly pronounced as one syllable; in some other combinations in which the first word is ἤ, ᾗ, μή, ἐπεί, or ἐγώ: μὴ εἰδέναι Eur. Hipp. 1335, ἐπεὶ οὐδέν, ἐγὼ εἰμ᾽ Soph. Ph. 585.

d. In SCANNING, observe not only the division into dipodies and feet, but also the arsis or metrical ictus (741), and the verse-cæsura (745). Unless these are carefully marked, the metrical character and expression of the verse are, to a great extent, lost. (e) In the following exhibition of metres, the division of feet will be marked by a single bar (|); the division of dipodies by a double bar (‖); the verse-cæsura by an obelisk (†), sometimes doubled (‡); and sometimes the omission of a syllable by a caret (ʌ). An anacrusis will be denoted by A, and a basis by B; and of syllables metrically long or short (whether by nature or position), the former will be printed in full-face, and the latter in common Greek type.

A. Dactylic Verse.

747. The place of the fundamental dactyl is often supplied by a spondee ($-\smile\smile = - -$). See 741 b.

748. I. The common HEXAMETER or HEROIC VERSE consists of six feet, of which the first four are either dactyls or spondees, the fifth commonly a dactyl, and the sixth always a spondee.

a. When the fifth is a spondee, the verse is termed *spondaic*, and has commonly an expression of greater weight or dignity. This occurs most frequently when the verse ends with a word of four syllables. (b) The favorite caesura of the verse is the penthemim (the "*heroic caesura*"), which is almost equally masculine and feminine (745 c). After this, the most frequent caesuras are the masculine hephthemim (often preceded by a triemim), and the pastoral (745 d). (c) Even when the penthemim is not the principal verse-caesura, it is yet seldom wanting as a foot-caesura.

d. SCHEME AND EXAMPLES.

$$\begin{array}{cccccc} 1. & 2. & 3. & 4. & 5. & 6. \\ -\smile\smile & -\smile\smile & -\dagger\dagger & -\dagger\dagger & -\smile\smile\dagger & -\smile \\ - - & - - & -\dagger - & -\dagger - -\dagger & (- -) \end{array}$$

'Αλλὰ κα|κῶς ἀφί|η, † κρατε|ρὸν δ' ἐπὶ | μῦθον ἔ|τελλεν. A. 25.
Εἴ κέν | πως ἀρ|ινῶν κνί|σης † αἰ|γῶν τε τε|λείων. A. 66.
Στέμματ' ἔ|χων ἐν | χερσὶν † ἑ|κηβόλου | 'Απόλ|λωνος. A. 14.

749. II. The ELEGIAC PENTAMETER consists of two dactylic penthemims (740 b), the first containing two dactyls or spondees with a caesural syllable, and the second, two dactyls with a final syllable. It commonly alternates with the Hexameter, forming what is termed, from its early use in plaintive song, the Elegiac Metre.

$$-\smile\smile | -\smile\smile | -\dagger | -\smile\smile | -\smile\smile | -$$
$$- - | - -$$

Εὐχομέ|νῳ μοι | κλῦθι, † κα|κὰς δ' ἀπὸ | κῆρας ἄ|λαλκε·
Σοὶ μὲν | τοῦτο, θε|ά, † | σμικρὸν, ἐ|μοὶ δὲ μέ|γα. Theog. 13.

750. III. Other Dactylic Metres are, (a) *Pure*, consisting of dactyls only; (b) *Impure*, consisting of dactyls and spondees; (c) *Æolic*, containing, in place of the first foot, a basis or anacrusis (743 e); (d) *Logaœdic* (742 c), in which dactyls are united with trochees. Thus,

1. Dimeter.

(a) Μυστοδό|κος δόμος. Ar. Nub. 303.
(b) ADONIC ($-\smile\smile | - -$). Πότνια, | θῦμον. Sapph. 1. 4.

2. Trimeter.

(b) Πολλὰ γὰρ | ὥστ' ἀκά|μαντος. Soph. Tr. 112.
(c) PHERECRATIC (B. | $-\smile\smile | - -$). Ἔλδε|αι φίλον | ἦτορ. Pind. O. 1. 6.
   Vix dū|rārĕ că|rīnæ. Hor. Od. 1. 14.
GLYCONIC.   Τὸν σὸν | δαίμονα, | τὸν σὸν, ὦ
   (B. | $-\smile\smile | -\smile\smile$) Τλᾶμον | Οἰδιπό|δα, βροτῶν. Soph. O. T. 1193.

§ 755.   ANAPÆSTIC. IAMBIC.   343

3. Tetrameter.

(a) ALCMANIAN. Μῶσ', ἄγε, | Καλλιό|πα θύγα|τερ Διός. Alcm. 36 [4].
(d) GREATER ALCAIC (A. | $\perp \smile$ | $\perp \smile$ | $\perp \smile \smile$ | $\perp \smile \smile$).
    Κάβ|βαλλε | τὸν χεί|μων', ἐπὶ | μὲν τιθείς. Alc. 34 [27].
LESSER ALCAIC ($\perp \smile \smile$ | $\perp \smile \smile$ | $\perp \smile$ | $\perp \smile$).
    Χρυσοκό|μᾳ Ζεφύ|ρῳ μί|γεισα. Alc. 5 [24].

4. Pentameter.

(b) 'Ατρεί|δας μαχί|μους, † ἐδά|η λαγο|δαίτας. Æsch. Ag. 123.
(d) SAPPHIC ($\perp \smile$ | $\perp \smile$ | $\perp \smile \smile$ | $\perp \smile$ | $\perp \smile$).
    Αἱ δὲ | δῶρα | μὴ δέκετ', | ἀλλὰ | δώσει. Sapph. 1. 22.

B. ANAPÆSTIC VERSE.

751. The place of the fundamental anapæst is often supplied by a spondee or dactyl, and, very rarely, by a proceleusmatic ($\smile \smile \perp = -\perp = -\perp \smile = \smile \smile \perp \smile$).

752. I. The Anapæstic, from its strong, even movement, was a favorite metre for marching songs; and was greatly employed in SYSTEMS, by the dramatic poets, as intermediate between the Iambic of the common dialogue, and the lyric metres of the choral odes.

a. These systems are scanned continuously (738 b), but are usually arranged so far as convenient, in dimeters (whence the common name of this species of verse, the ANAPÆSTIC DIMETER). They uniformly close with the dimeter catalectic, called, from its use in proverbs (παροιμίαι) the *parœmiac* verse (744 d). (b) This verse requires a *cæsura* after each dipody, except in the parœmiac.

Πελάσει|ε δόμοις, † ‖ ὧν τ' ἐπί|νοιαν
Σπεύδεις | κατέχων † ‖ πράξει|ας, ἐπεὶ
Γενναῖ|ος ἀνὴρ,
Αἰγεῦ, | παρ' ἐμοὶ ‖ δεδόκη|σαι. Eur. Med. 759.

753. II. The combination of the regular dimeter with the parœmiac (cf. 757, 761) forms the ANAPÆSTIC TETRAMETER CATALECTIC of comedy, also called the *Aristophanic*.

$\smile \smile \perp$ | $\smile \smile \underline{\perp}$ † ‖ $\smile \smile \perp$ | $\smile \smile \underline{\perp}$ † ‖ $\smile \smile \perp$ | $\smile \smile \underline{\perp}$ ‖ $\smile \smile \perp$ | $-$: &c.

Τί γὰρ εὔ'δαιμον † ‖ καὶ μακα|ριστὸν ‡ ‖ μᾶλλον | νῦν ἐσ‖τι δικασ|τοῦ.

754. III. Examples are added, from lyric poetry, of other kinds of Anapæstic verse, both common and *logaœdic* (742 c):

Dim. Hyperc. Τότε μὲν | περισα‖μότατος | καὶ ἄρισ‖τος. Eur. Herc. 1018.
LOGAŒDIC. 1 An., 1 Iam. Νεμέᾳ | δὲ τρὶς. Pind. N. 6. 34.
1 An., 3 Iam. Cat. Μακαρί|ζομέν | σε, τέτ|τιξ. Anacreontic.
3 An., 2 Iam. Δολερὸν | μὲν ἀεὶ | κατὰ πάν|τα δὴ | τρόπον. Ar. Av. 451.

C. IAMBIC VERSE.

755. The place of the fundamental iambus may be supplied by a tribrach ($\smile \perp = \smile \perp \smile$), except at the end of a line. To add dignity and variety to the verse, the *first foot* of a dipody (where the arsis is less strong) is very often lengthened to a spondee, and not unfrequently to a dactyl or anapæst.

a. Comedy admits the anapæst in every place except the last of a verse or system; and also tragedy, when it is wholly contained in a proper name.

756. I. The IAMBIC TRIMETER ACATALECTIC (also called, from the number of its feet, the *Senarius*) is the principal metre of dramatic dialogue (752).

a. This verse has for its cæsura the penthemim or, much less frequently, the hephthemim. The latter is sometimes *anticipated* by the elision of the syllable after which it would properly fall, forming what has been termed by Porson the *quasi-cæsura*. Lines occur, though rarely, which have neither of these cæsuras.

b. The Tragic Trimeter admits the tribrach in every place but the last; the spondee in the 1st, 3d, and 5th places; the dactyl in the 1st and 3d; and the anapæst in the 1st. The feet which are admitted only in proper names or in comedy (755 a) are placed, below, in parentheses.

```
             1.        2.         3.        4.        5.        6.
c. Iambus.   ⏑ ⊥  |  ⏑ ⊥   ‖  ⏑† ⊥  | ⏑† ⊥  ‖  ⏑ ⊥   |  ⏑ ⊥
   Tribrach. ⏑⏑⏑  |  ⏑†⏑⏑  ‖  ⏑†⏑⏑  | ⏑†⏑⏑  ‖  ⏑⏑⏑   |
   Spondee.  ⎯ ⊥  |        ‖  ⏑† ⊥  |       ‖  ⎯ ⊥   |
   Dactyl.   ⎯⏑⏑  |        ‖  ⏑†⏑⏑  |       ‖  (⎯⏑⏑) |
   Anapæst.  ⏑⏑⊥  | (⏑⏑ ⊥) ‖  ⏑ ⎯⊥  | ⏑ ⏑ ⊥  ‖        | (⏑⏑⊥)
```

Ἐγὼ | δ᾽ ἀτολ‖μός εἰ|μι † συγ‖γενῆ | θεόν. Æsch. Pr. 14.
Θορύβῳ | τε πίσυ‖νος † κά|μαθεῖ ‖ παῤῥη|σίᾳ,
Πιθανὸς | ἔτ᾽ αὐ‖τοὺς † περι|βαλεῖν ‖ κακῷ | τινι. Eur. Or. 905.

757. II. The IAMBIC TETRAMETER CATALECTIC is peculiar to comedy. It consists of two dimeters, the second catalectic (cf. 753, 761); and has commonly a cæsura after the first.

Ὅτου | χάριν ‖ μ᾽ ὁ δεσ|πότης † ‖ ὁ σὸς | κέκλη‖κε δεῦ|ρο. Ar. Pl. 260.

758. III. The Iambic verse sometimes occurs in SYSTEMS of the common form (744 d).

759. IV. Examples are added, from lyric poetry, of other kinds of Iambic verse (for logaœdic examples, see 754):

Tripody. Ὕπεσ|τί μοι | θράσος. Soph. El. 479.
Dim. Cat. Θέλω | λέγειν ‖ Ἀτρεί|δας. Anacreontic.
Dim. Hyperc. Σύ τοι, | σύ τοι ‖ κατη|ξίω‖σας. Soph. Ph. 1095.

D. TROCHAIC VERSE.

760. The place of the fundamental trochee may be supplied in any part of the verse by a tribrach (⊥ ⏑ = ⏑ ⏑ ⏑). The *last foot* of a dipody (where the ictus is less strong) is often lengthened to a spondee or anapæst. In proper names, the dactyl is admitted in some places.

§ 766. TROCHAIC, &C. — ACCENT. 345

761. I. The TROCHAIC TETRAMETER CATALECTIC occurs in both tragedy and comedy. It consists of two dimeters, the second catalectic (753, 757); and has commonly a cæsura after the first.
Πολλα|χοῦ σκο||ποῦντες | ἡμᾶς † || εἰς ἅ|πανθ' εὑ||ρήσε|τε. Ar. Vesp. 1101.

762. II. The Trochaic verse sometimes occurs in SYSTEMS of the common form (744 d).

763. III. Examples are added, from lyric poetry, of other kinds of Trochaic verse (for logaœdic examples, see 750):
Tripody (ITHYPHALLIC). Πάντρο|φος πε|λειάς. Æsch. Th. 294.
Trim. Δωρί|ῳ φω||νὰν ἐν|ἁρμόξ||αι πε|δίλῳ. Pind. O. 3. 9.
Trim. Cat. Τὴν γὰρ | ἐν πόν||τῳ κυ|βερνῶν||ται θο|αί. Ib. 12. 4.
Tetram. Ἔστι | μοι θε||ῶν ἕ|κατι || μυρί|α παν||τᾶ κέ|λευθος. Pind. I. 4. 1.

a. Syncope sometimes explains a seeming interchange of Iambic and Trochaic rhythm (743 g): Βοᾶν· ἰώ, ⁀ κλάει· ὠβολοστάται. Ar. Nub. 1155.

E. OTHER METRES.

764. The metres which remain are LYRIC, and for the most part admit with great freedom isochronous feet, or the substitution of two short syllables for one long, or of one long for two short:
 a. Cretic (⊥ ⌣ ⊥). Φρόντισον | καὶ γενοῦ. Æsch. Sup. 418.
 b. Bacchic (⌣ ⊥ ⊥). Τίς ἀχώ, | τίς ὁδμὰ | προσέπτα | μ' ἀφεγγής. Æsch.
 c. Choriambic (⊥ ⌣ ⌣ ⊥). Γυμνασίου | λέγειν τι δεῖ. Ar. Vesp. 527.
 d. Rising Ionic (⌣ ⌣ ⊥ ⊥). Πεπέρακεν | μὲν ὁ περσέ|πτολις ἤδη. Æsch.
 e. Pæonic (⊥ ⌣ ⌣ ⌣). Ὦ μακάρι' | Αὐτόμενες, † | ὥς σε μακα|ρίζομεν. Ar.

765. f. An *Antispast*, combining an iambic with a trochaic rhythm, admits in the first part any foot which is admitted into Iambic verse, and in the second any foot which is admitted into Trochaic, each with the appropriate ictus. The addition of a long syllable (which may be resolved into two short) forms the *Dochmius;* which has consequently a triple ictus, with great variety of structure (thirty-two forms having been counted):
Dochmiac (⌣ ⊥ ⊥ ⌣ ⊥). Μεθεῖται στρατὸς | στρατόπεδον λιπών. Æsch.

CHAPTER II.

ACCENT.

766. In every Greek word, one of the *three last* syllables was distinguished by a *special tone* of the voice.

1. This tone is commonly spoken of simply as *the tone*, or *the accent*.
2. The versification of the ancient Greeks was founded upon quantity without regard to accent; that of the modern Greeks is founded upon accent without regard to quantity.
3. The accent, even if not regarded in pronunciation, is still useful, as serving, — (a) To distinguish *different words*, or *different senses* of the same word: εἰμί *to be*, εἶμι *to go;* ὁ *the*, ὅ *which* (249 c) ; πότε; *when?*

COMP. GR. 15*

ποτέ *once;* ἄλλα *other things,* ἀλλά *but;* λιθοβόλος *throwing stones,* λιθόβολος *stoned* (386. 1). (b) To distinguish *different forms* of the same word : Opt. ἐκ-λύσαι, Inf. ἐκ-λῦσαι, Imv. ἔκ-λυσαι, (37 f, h). (c) To aid in ascertaining *quantity* (727). (d) To show the *original form* of a word : thus the circumflex over τιμῶ, φιλῶ, δηλῶ, marks them as contract forms of τιμάω, φιλέω, δηλόω. (e) To show how a word is employed in the sentence ; as in cases of anastrophe, and where the accent is retained by a proclitic or enclitic (785 s).

767. a. In a final or initial, and often in an intermediate syllable, a long vowel is treated in accentuation as consisting of two vowels (108, 115), and thus forming two *tone-places* (i. e. places in respect to accent). (b) But *final* -αι and -οι *in affixes* are regarded in accentuation as short vowels, except in the Optative.

c. By *long vowels*, in accentuation, are meant those that are long *by nature*, including diphthongs ; and by *short vowels*, those that are short in *natural quantity*, without regard to their position (725).

d. It is not strange that this treatment of final -αι and -οι should have at length resulted from the natural hurrying of the voice over such familiar endings. For the exception in the Opt., see 272 d.

e. The Greek grammarians adopted an ascending line (΄) as the mark of an accented place, and a descending line (`) as the mark of an unaccented place. A syllable in which an unaccented followed an accented place was entitled, of course, to a double mark (῀).

f. In counting tone-places, the ultima is counted as the first place if its vowel is short, but as the first and second if its vowel is long. If the ultima forms two places, the penult makes the third, and completes the number allowed. If the ultima forms only a single place, then a short vowel in the penult forms the second ; and a long vowel, the second and third. One of these, however, a long penult often gives up to the antepenult, contenting itself with a single place. Thus the antepenult forms the third place, if the ultima and penult are both short by nature ; and often also, if the ultima is short and the penult long. No account is taken of any place beyond the third, or beyond the accent if this is sooner reached. In the following words, which are all accented on the highest place, the several places would be thus numbered and marked :

```
   1     21    2 1    3 21   2  1     3 21    32 1     32  1     3 21      32 1
  θές,  παῖς, δόλὸς,  δόλὺ,  δόλοὶ,   ταυρὺ,  ταύρὸς,  ταύροί,  ἐκούσαὶς,  ἐκούσᾶ',
  32  1       3 2 1   3 2 1  3 2 1             3 21    3    2 1     3    2 1
  ἐκούσαί,   πολέμὺς, πόλὲμὸς, πόλὲμοί,       ἀνθρώπὸὶς, ἄνθρὼπὸς,       ἄνθρὼποί.
```

g. It is evidently needless, except for grammatical illustration, to mark unaccented syllables, and when the two marks (῀) fall upon the same syllable, it is more convenient in writing to unite them into one (^, or, as rounded for greater ease, ῀ or ˜). Dropping, therefore, the marks over the unaccented syllables, and uniting the double marks, we write thus :

θές, παῖς, δόλος, δόλον, δόλοι, ταύρον, ταῦρος, ταῦροι, ἐκούσαις, ἐκοῦσα, ἐκοῦσαι, πολέμους, πόλεμος, πόλεμοι, ἀνθρώποις, ἄνθρωπος, ἄνθρωποι.

768. A syllable or vowel is termed *grave*, if it has no accent ; *circumflexed*, if it forms an accented followed by an unaccented place ; *acute*, if it forms an accented place not so fol-

§ 772.   GENERAL LAWS.   IN VOWEL CHANGES.   347

lowed: as the final syllables and vowels in λύρα, νῆσος, λύω· μνᾶ, τῆς, θεᾷ, ᾠοῦ, γυπῶν, τιμῶ· ᾠδή, τό, ᾠόν, αἴξ, αἰγός, ἐμοί.

A word is termed
{
  OXYTONE,
  PERISPOME,   } if its Ultima is   { Acute. / Circumflexed.
  BARYTONE,   { Grave.
  PAROXYTONE,
  PROPERISPOME, } if its Penult is   { Acute. / Circumflexed.
  PROPAROXYTONE, if its Antepenult is Acute.
}

a. The terms above, and those applied to the *marks* of accent (94), are formed from the Greek and Latin words τόνος accentus, *tone*, ὀξύς acūtus, *sharp*, περισπώμενος circumflexus, *bent round*, βαρύς gravis, *heavy*, παρά *beside*, and πρό *before*. (b) The *paroxytones*, *properispomes*, and *proparoxytones* are all included in the general class of *barytones*. See § 5.

769. The accent is termed *final*, when it falls upon the ultima. According as it goes back from this, or forward towards it, it is said to *recede* or *advance*. When it recedes as far as the general laws permit, it is termed *recessive*. When it retains the same place as in the theme, so far as these laws permit, it is termed *retentive*.

I. GENERAL LAWS OF ACCENT.

770. LAW I. The ACUTE ACCENT cannot recede beyond the *antepenult;* and can fall upon this, only when the *ultima* is *short*.

a. Hence the accent of ὄνομα *name*, τράπεζα, ἄγγελος (15 s), must advance in the Gen. to the second syllable: ὀνόματος, τραπέζης, ἀγγέλου.

b. In accentuation, ε before ω in the endings of the Gen. and of the Attic Dec. 2 is not regarded as forming a distinct syllable (120 i, 200, 220 c): hence, Ἀτρείδεω, πόλεως, πόλεων· εὔγεως. So, in some compound adjectives, even with an intervening liquid: as, φιλόγελως (237 b).

c. Final ξ and ψ, making position after a short vowel (734), forbid the acute on the antepenult, though not the circumflex on the penult: hence ἐριβῶλαξ, -ἀκος, though ἐρίβωλος, *fertile*.

771. LAW II. a. The CIRCUMFLEX can only fall upon a *long vowel*. (b) It cannot recede beyond the *penult*; and can fall upon this, only when the *last vowel* is *short*, — (c) being the only accent which a *penult long by nature* can then receive.

Hence, (a) βοῦς, μῦς, πᾶς (19, 23), become in the Nom. pl. βόες, μύες, πάντες: (b) μοῦσα, νῆσος (15 s), in the Gen. μούσης, νήσου: (c) αἴξ, θήρ (17 s), Ἀτρείδης (15), in the Nom. pl. αἶγες, θῆρες, Ἀτρεῖδαι (767 b).

II. ACCENT IN VOWEL CHANGES.

772. A. CONTRACTION. LAW III. In contraction, the acute *followed* by the grave produces the circumflex: νόος νοῦς, ὀστέον ὀστοῦν (16), τιμάω τιμῶ, φιλέειν φιλεῖν (42).

1. Otherwise the accent is not affected by contraction, except as the general laws may require : τίμαε τίμα, τιμαέτω τιμάτω, τιμαοίμην τιμῴμην· ἕσταϐτος ἑστῶτος (261, 771 c). See 120 s.

2. Some contract forms are accented as though made by inflection without contraction; or fall into the analogy of other words. Thus,

In contracts of Dec. 2, — (a) The accent remains throughout upon the same syllable as in the theme: εὔνοος, εὐνόου, cont. εὔνους, εὔνου (Nom. pl. εὖνοι or εὔνοι, 767 b), *kind*. (b) The Nom. dual, if accented upon the ultima, is always oxytone : νώ, ὀστώ (16). (c) Except in the Nom. dual, all simple contracts in -ους or -ουν are perispome : χρύσεος χρυσοῦς (23), κάνεον κανοῦν, *basket*. — (d) Oxytones of the Attic Dec. retain throughout the accent of the theme : νεώς, νεώ, νεῴ (16); ἀγήρω (22). Cf. 120 e.

In contracts of Dec. 3, — (e) The Acc. of nouns in -ώ is oxytone : ἠχόα ἠχώ (19 a). So Dat. χρωτί χρῷ perispome (207 a). These cases follow the analogy of 775. (f) The contract Gen. pl. of τριήρης (213 c) and some like compounds is made by some paroxytone : as, τριηρέων τριήρων.

g.) The Subj. and Opt. pass. of *verbs in* -μι and *preterites* are accented by some without regard to their contraction : thus, τιθώμαι, τίθῃ, τιθῆται, διδοῖτο (45 c); κέκτωμαι, μέμνῃτο (317 c). (h) This is usual in the deponents δύναμαι, ἐπίσταμαι, κρέμαμαι, and the 2 aorists δύνασθαι, πρίασθαι (50).

3. In the resolution or extension of a vowel, a circumflex is resolved into its acute and grave (767 g) : ταῖς πάϊς, φῶς φόως (105 a, 103 b).

773. B. CRASIS. In crasis, the accent of the *first* word is *lost;* while that of the *second remains* without change, except as required by 771 c : ταὐτό for τὸ αὐτό, κἄν for καὶ ἄν, τἆλλα for τὰ ἄλλα.

774. C. APOSTROPHE. The accent of an elided vowel is *thrown back* upon the penult, except in *prepositions* and *conjunctions*: δείν' ἔπη for δεινὰ ἔπη, κατ' ἐμέ (κατά), ἀλλ' ἐγώ (ἀλλά). See 128.

III. ACCENT IN INFLECTION.

775. LAW IV. A *long affix of declension* can only take the *acute* in the *direct*, and the *circumflex* in the *indirect* cases.

a. Hence, ᾠδή, -ῆς, -ῇ, -ήν (15); χοροῦ, -ῷ, -ῶν, -οῖς, -ούς (16); γυπῶν, -οῖν (17). (b) Except in the datives ἐμοί, μοί, σοί (27 a). See also 772 d.

776. LAW V. The accent is RETENTIVE in *declension;* but RECESSIVE in *comparison* and *conjugation*: ᾠδόν, ᾠδοῦ, ᾠδά (16); κακός, κακίων, κάκιστος (260 a); λύω, ἔλυον, λέλυκα (37).

777. A. DECLENSION. 1. In DEC. 1, the affix- ων of the Gen. pl. is circumflexed, as contracted from -άων (197 c) : τράπεζα, τραπεζῶν.

2. In adjectives in -ος, the feminine is accented throughout, so far as the general laws permit, upon the same syllable as the masc.: thus, φίλιος, φιλίᾱ, *friendly*, Pl. φίλιοι, φίλιαι, Gen. masc. and fem. φιλίων ; while, from the noun ἡ φιλία, *friendship*, φιλίαι, φιλιῶν. (a) In most other adjectives, the fem. retains the accent of the theme, but subject to the same changes as in nouns of Dec. 1 : μέλας, μέλαινα, μελαίνης, μελαινῶν (22).

778. 3. In DEC. 3, *dissyllabic Genitives and Datives* throw the accent upon the *affix*.

a. Hence, from γύψ, &c. (17 s), γυπός, αἰγί, πατρός, ἀνδρῶν, κυσί, ἀρνί.

b. Except those which have become dissyllabic by *contraction*, *participles*, and the *Gen. pl.* and *dual* of these ten nouns, ὀᾴς, ὀμώς, θώς, κάρα, οὖς, παῖς, σῆς, Τρώς, φῴς, φῶς (*light*), and of the adjective πᾶς (also Dat. πᾶσι, 23): πόλεϊ πόλει (19), ἔαρος ἦρος (209 a); ὀδόντος, θέντι, δῦσι (26); παίδων, φώτων, ὤτοιν (17). (c) The contraction is not regarded in accenting the Gen. and Dat. of οἶς (19 d), οὖς, στέαρ, φρέαρ (207 ; yet see b), and Θρᾷξ (G. -κός). (d) Observe the accentuation of οὐδείς (25), τίς, τὶς (28), γυνή (203 a), θυγάτηρ (210 b); and of datives in -ᾴσι, from liquids (145 a).

779. 4. The natural tone of frequent address gives RECESSIVE ACCENT to the Voc. in a few familiar words: as, Dec. 1, δεσπότης, *master*; Dec. 2, ἀδελφός, *brother*; Dec. 3, γυνή (203 a), 'Απόλλων, &c. (208 f); Voc. δέσποτἄ, ἄδελφε, γύναι, Ἄπολλον. So V. δύσμητερ ψ. 97.
a. In the Voc. sing., -ευ and -οι final are always circumflexed: ἱππεῦ.
5. From the tendency to recessive accent in comparatives and compounds (795), the Voc. and Neut. sing. forms are so accented — (b) In most compound paroxytones in -ων and -ης, except those in -φρων, -ώδης, -ώλης, -ήρης, -ώρης, and -έτης: εὐδαίμων *fortunate*, Neut. and Voc. εὔδαιμον· V. Σώκρατες, Ἡράκλεες (19). So a few other neuter adjectives, when used adverbially: ἀληθές, *really*? (c) In comparatives in -ων: ἡδίων, ἥδιον.
d. Recessive accent appears also in some Nom. forms in -α for -ης (197 b): εὐρύοπα. (e) Observe the accentuation of μήτηρ, θυγάτηρ, Δημήτηρ (210 b). (f) In the forms in -φι, -θι, -θεν (190 s), the accent usually falls upon a short vowel in the penult, but is otherwise retentive. (g) For peculiarities in the accentuation of the numerals and pronouns, see 25, 27 s.

780. B. CONJUGATION has exceptions to the law of *recessive accent*; chiefly in the *Infinitive* and *Participle*.
1. These forms are accented upon the PENULT: — (a) All Infinitives in -αι *not preceded by* -σθ- or -μεν-: λῦσαι, λελυκέναι, λυθῆναι, τιθέναι· but λύσασθαι, τίθεσθαι (37, 45), θέμεναι (333). (b) The 2 Aor. mid. Inf.: λιπέσθαι (38), ἀπο-δόσθαι (45 i); but πρίασθαι, ὄνασθαι (50; as if pres.). (c) The Perf. pass. Inf. and Part.: λελῦσθαι, λελυμένος; except a few preteritive participles, and Epic infinitives, as ἥμενος, ἀκάχησθαι Τ. 335.

781. 2. These forms are OXYTONE: — (a) Participles in -s, Gen. -τος, except in the 1st Aor. act.: λελυκώς, λυθείς, ἰστάς, δούς· but λύσας (37, 45). (b) The 2 Aor. act. Part.: λιπών (38). (c) The Pres. participles (as if 2 Aor.) ἰών (45 m), κιών (fr. κίω *go*, poet., II. 263), ἐών E. I. (50 εἰμί a). (d) The 2 Aor. Imv. forms εἰπέ *say*, ἐλθέ *come*, εὑρέ *find*; and in Attic, ἰδέ *see*, and λαβέ *take*; except in composition, as ἔξ-ελθε, εἰσ-ιδε.

782. 3. These forms are PERISPOME: — (a) The 2 Aor. Inf. in -ειν: λιπεῖν (38). (b) The 2 Pers. in -ου, of the 2 Aor. Imv.: λιποῦ (38), θοῦ, δοῦ (45 i); except in compounds of more than two syllables from verbs in -μι, as ἀπόδου, but προδοῦ.
NOTES. c. That the *final accent* in the preceding forms should be acute on the theme of the Part., and circumflex on the Inf. (considered as a Dat., 666 b), is in accordance with Law IV. (775). (d) The circumflex in λυθῶ, ἱστῶ, τιθῶμαι, δῶ, λυθείεν, τιθείο (37, 45), and like Subj. and Opt. forms, is due to contraction (772). (e) Monosyllabic forms *long by nature*, except Participles, are generally circumflexed: εἶ, ἦν, ἦ, ὦν (45 l).

783. a. The accent of a verb in COMPOSITION can never recede beyond a prefix (277); or beyond the nearest syllable of the preposition: thus, ἐπέχω (ἐπί, ἔχω, 50), ἐπεῖχον, ἐπέσχον, ἐπίσχες. (b) The preteritive οἶδα (46) is treated as without reduplication: σύν-οιδα. (c) The accent of εἰμί recedes in composition only in the Pres. Ind. and Imv.

d. For the accent in εἰμί and φημί, see 45, 787 c; for κεῖμαι, 50. Other examples of *irregular* or *various accentuation* are χρή, ἐχρῆν (50 χράω d); 1 Aor. Imv. εἶπον or εἰπόν (50 φημί c); εἶs or εἷs (50, εἰμί 1), ἰδού as exclam. (50 ὁράω); forms noticed in 316 c; &c.

IV. ACCENT IN CONSTRUCTION.

784. A. GRAVE ACCENT. LAW VI. Oxytones, followed by other words in closely connected discourse, *soften* their tone, and are then marked with the *grave accent* (`): Στρατηγὸν δὲ αὐτὸν ἀπέδειξε (480). Ἐπὶ τὰ καλὰ καὶ ἀγαθά.

a. Except the interrogative τίς (253 a), and words followed by enclitics.

b. The terms *acute* and *oxytone* are still applied to the syllable and word, although the tone is softened. Syllables *strictly grave* are never marked, except for grammatical illustration, as in 767.

785. B. ANASTROPHE. In *prepositions of two short syllables*, the accent commonly recedes to the penult, when they *follow* the words which they would regularly precede, or take the place of *compound verbs*: thus,

Σοφίας πέρι, *about wisdom*, Pl. (the like placing of other prepositions is poetic); ὀλέσας ἄπο for ἀπολέσας, *having lost*, ι. 534 (§ 699 j); ἄνα, πάρα, ἔνι (699 e). This recession is termed ἀναστροφή, *turning back*.

a. Some so write πέρι and ἄπο when used adverbially.

786. C. PROCLITICS. Ten monosyllables, beginning with a vowel, are called *proclitics* (προκλίνω, *to lean forward*), because they commonly so lean upon the *following* word as to lose their proper accent. They are the *aspirated* forms of the art., ὁ, ἡ, οἱ, αἱ, and the particles οὐ *not*, εἰs *into*, ἐν *in*, ἐξ *out of*, εἰ *if*, ὡs *as*.

a. These forms of the article are written with the accent, when used in Epic as *relative*, and by some, when used as *personal pronouns*: ὃ . . ἤλυθες, *who camest*, β. 262; ὁ γάρ, but ὃ γάρ Bek., *for he*, A. 9. (b) The proclitics retain their accent when they close a sentence, or in poetry follow a word whose relation they denote (718 d), or are followed by an enclitic: οὐ δῆτα, *no, indeed*, but πῶς γὰρ οὔ; *how not?* ὡs βόες, but βόες ὥs χ. 299, *as kine*; ἐκ κακῶν, but κακῶν ἔξ, *from the base*; εἴ ποτε, *if ever*.

787. D. ENCLITICS. LAW VII. The accent of an enclitic falls, as *acute*, upon the *ultima* of the preceding word, or upon its *penult* if it is a *paroxytone*, uniting with any accent already upon the syllable: as,

Ἄνθρωποί τε, hóminés-que, *and men*, δεῖξόν μοι, *show me*; εἴ ποτε (786 b): ἀνήρ τις (784 a); φίλος μου, *my friend*; ἤ ῥά νύ μοί τι πίθοιο (705 a; each enclitic throwing its accent back). — But see 788 d.

Enclitics are so named as *leaning* in pronunciation upon the preceding word (ἐγκλίνω, *to lean upon*). They are these familiar words of one or two syllables: (a) These *oblique cases of the personal pronouns*: 1 Pers. μοῦ, μοί, μέ · 2 P. σοῦ, σοί, σέ · 3 P. οὗ, οἷ, ἕ · νίν, σφίσι, σφέ. For other enclitic forms of the personal pronouns, see 27 f, g. (b) The *indefinite pronoun* τὶς, through all its cases (but not ἄττα); and the *indefinite adverbs* πή, ποί, πού, πώ, πώς, ποθί, ποθέν, ποτέ (53). (c) The Pres. ind. of εἰμί *to be*, and φημί *to say*, except the 2d Pers. sing.; and even here in the Ep. form εἶς: νήπιός εἰς, stultus es, ι. 273. (d) The *particles* γέ, νύν (νύ), πέρ, τέ, τοί, with the poetic θήν, κέ, ῥά, and -δέ (688 e).

e. Some familiar combinations of this kind are commonly, and others sometimes, joined in writing, and viewed as compounds: εἴτε, ἤτοι, μήτις, ὅστις (observe the accent, 28 h), οὐδέποτε, ὥσπερ, ὥστε. (f) The preposition -δέ, *to* (688 c), is always so attached: Ὀλυμπόνδε, δόμονδε. (g) In pronouns and adverbs compounded with -δέ (252, 53 ix.), the syllable preceding -δέ always takes the accent, which is acute or circumflex according to the law in 775. (h) In ἐγώ, ἐμοί, and ἐμέ, the accent is drawn back when γέ is affixed (389 c): ἔγωγε, ἔμοιγε, ἔμεγε. (i) Εἴθε and ναίχί are accented as ending in enclitics; and οἴκαδε (225 i) as a single word.

788. An enclitic *retains* its accent, (a) At the *beginning* of a clause or verse, or after a parenthetic insertion: φημὶ γάρ, *for I say*. (b) After the *apostrophe*: πολλοὶ δ' εἰσίν, *but they are many*. (c) If it is *emphatic* or *strongly reflexive*: οὐ Κῦρον, ἀλλὰ σέ, *not C., but* YOU. (d) If it is a *dissyllable*, preceded by a *paroxytone*, or by a *properispome* in -ξ or -ψ (770 c): ἄνδρες τινές, *some men*. (e) If it is a *personal pronoun*, preceded by an *orthotone preposition* which governs it and is not itself more emphatic: παρὰ σοί, περὶ σοῦ, πρὸς σέ· but ἐπί σε ἢ σύν σοι, against *you* rather than with *you*, vii. 7. 32. Yet πρός με (sometimes σε) iii. 2. 2; and some exceptions occur, chiefly in the poets, with other prepositions.

f. When ἐστί is prominent in the sentence, it becomes a paroxytone (as at the beginning, or when it expresses *existence* or *possibility*, and commonly after such words as οὐ, μή, ἀλλά, εἰ, καί, ὅτι, ὡς, τοῦτο): Ἔστιν οἵ (559 a); ἔστι λαμβάνειν, *one can take*, i. 5. 3; τοῦτ' ἔστιν, *it is so*.

g. A word which neither *leans* upon the following nor upon the preceding word, but stands, as it were, *erect*, is called, in distinction from the proclitics and enclitics, an *orthotone* (ὀρθότονος, *erect in tone*).

V. ACCENT IN FORMATION.

789. GENERAL PRINCIPLE. In each word, the accent belongs to that syllable *upon which the attention is most strongly fixed*. — If, from some law of language, this syllable cannot receive the accent, it draws it as near to itself as possible.

1. In the origin of language, the attention is absorbed by the greater distinctions of thought; but, as these become familiar to the mind, it passes to the less, and then to those that are still subordinate. In the Greek, as in other languages, the accent originally belonged to the syllables containing the essential ideas of words, i. e. to their *radical syllables*. But, in proportion as these became familiar, there was a tendency to throw the accent upon those syllables by which these ideas were modified, either through inflection, derivation, or composition. Compare γράφω *I* WRITE, with ἔγραφον *I* WAS *writing*, γέγραφα *I* HAVE *written*, γραφή the ACT *of writing*, γραφεύς the PERSON *who writes*, γραφικός SUITED *to writing*.

790. a. The Doric was characterized by its adherence to general rules and old usage; (b) the Lesbian Æolic, by its tendency to throw the accent as far back as possible; (c) the Attic (which the Ionic appears to have more nearly approached), by an expressive variety of accent.

791. The accent of the THEME IN DECLENSION, and of UNINFLECTED WORDS must be learned from special rules and from observation.

NOTE. For derivatives, the marks of accent in § 363 – 382 should be carefully noticed. The rules below are not intended for proper names.

A. *Special Rules for Simple Words.*

1.) OF DEC. I. All contracts are perispome : Ἑρμῆς, μνᾶ. Of other words, — (a) Those in -ας are paroxytone : ταμίας. (b) Most in -ης are paroxytone, except *verbals in* -της *from mute and pure stems of verbs in* -ω, which are commonly oxytone : Ἀτρείδης (so all patronymics in -δης), ναύτης, ψάλτης, προφήτης, προστάτης · δικαστής, ποιητής. (c) Nouns in -α short (194) have recessive accent : μυῖα, μοῦσα, τράπεζα, ἀλήθεια. (d) Most abstracts in -ιᾱ, those in -συνη, and those in -εια from verbs in -εύω (363, 367), are paroxytone : σοφία, σωφροσύνη, παιδεία. (e) Most other verbals in -α long or -η are oxytone : φυγή, φθορά, φυλακή.

792. 2.) OF DEC. II. (a) *Adjectives in* -ος *preceded by a mute* are commonly oxytone, especially those in -κος, verbals in -τος, and ordinals in -στος : κακός, ἀρχικός, ὁρατός, εἰκοστός, χαλεπός, σοφός, δολιχός, ἀγαθός. So *verbal nouns* in -ος denoting the *agent:* ἀρχός, τροφός. (b) On the contrary, in *primitive nouns with a mute stem,* the accent is more frequently recessive : κῆπος, κρόκος, πλοῦτος, ψάμαθος. (c) All ordinals not ending in -στος have recessive accent : δέκατος. (d) Adjectives in -λος, -ρος, and -νος (except those in -ινος denoting *material* or *country,* 375 c, e) are commonly oxytone : ψιλός, φοβερός, σεμνός, πεδινός · ξύλινος, Ταραντῖνος. (e) *Nouns* in -μος with a *long penult* are commonly oxytone ; while in *adjectives* in -μος the accent is commonly recessive : ὀδυρμός, βωμός · χρήσιμος. (f) Nouns in -ος *pure* are more frequently oxytone : ναός, θεός, υἱός, νυός. (g) Verbals in -τεος (374 f), numerals in -αιος and -πλοος (240), and most adjectives in -αιος from nouns of Dec. 1, in -οιος, and in -ῳος, are accented upon the penult : ποιητέος, διπλόος, ἀγοραῖος, ὁποῖος, ἑῷος. (h) Adjectives in -ειος, in -ιος *preceded by a consonant,* and in -εος joined immediately to the root, have commonly recessive accent : θήρειος, οὐράνιος, χρύσεος. (i) Very few neuters are oxytone ; and in most neuters the accent is recessive : μόριον, ποτήριον, ὄρνεον, ἔλαιον. But a diminutive in -ιον, forming a dactyl, is commonly paroxytone : παιδίον.

793. 3.) OF DEC. III. (a) Nouns in -αν, -ευς, -ω, -ως -οος, -ας -ᾱδος, -ῑς -ῑδος, masculines in -ηρ, and almost all nouns in which the stem-mark is ν preceded by ᾱ, ε, η, or ῑ, are oxytone : παιδν, ἱππεύς, ἠχώ, αἰδώς, λαμπάς, -άδος, πατήρ, λιμήν, -ένος. (b) Nouns in -εων, names of months in -ων, and most feminines and augmentatives in -ων, are oxytone ; other words in -ων are more frequently paroxytone : κυκεών, χελιδών, ἀμπελών · κλύδων. (c) Monosyllabic nouns which have the Acc. in -α are commonly oxytone ; those which are neuter (see d), and most which have the Acc. in -ν, perispome : αἴξ, πούς, θήρ, θώς · τὸ φῶς, τὸ πῦρ (so πᾶς, πᾶν, 23) ; βοῦς, ναῦς. (d) In neuter nouns, in words in -ξ and -ψ, in verbals in -τωρ, and in nouns in -ις or -υς with the Gen. in -εως, the accent is recessive : κέρας, βούλευμα · κόραξ ; δύναμις, πέλεκυς. (e) Female appellatives in -ις (365 c, 368 s) have the accent upon the same syllable as the masculine, except when this is a proparoxytone or dissyllabic barytone (in which case the feminine commonly becomes oxytone) : πολῖτις,

πολῖτις· Πριαμίδης, Πριαμίς· αἰχμάλωτος, αἰχμαλωτίς· Πέρσης, Περσίς.
(f) Simple adjectives are commonly oxytone, if the stem-mark is a vowel; paroxytone, if it is a consonant: σαφής, ἡδύς· μέλας, χαρίεις (22 s).

794. 4.) ADVERBS. (a) Adverbs in -ως derived from adjectives are, with very few exceptions, accented like the Gen. pl. of their primitives (381 a): σοφῶς, ταχέως. (b) Derivative adverbs in -δον, -δα, -ι, -ει, and -ξ are commonly oxytone; those in -δην, -ακις and -ω, paroxytone (381 s): πλινθηδόν, Μηδιστί, ἀμαχεί, παραλλάξ· σποράδην, πολλάκις, ἔξω.
5.) PREPOSITIONS. The eighteen prepositions proper (688 c) are all oxytone: ἀπό, κατά. For the removal or loss of the accent, see 785, 786.

B. *Rules for Compound Words.*

795. In composition, there is a general tendency to recessive accent. But, — (a) Compound adjectives in -ης are more frequently oxytone: as, εὐπρεπής. (b) Compounds in which -ος is affixed to the stem of a verb united with a noun are commonly oxytone, if the *penult is long;* but if the *penult is short*, they are commonly paroxytone when *active* in sense, and proparoxytone when *passive* (386 b): σιτοποιός (387 a); λιθοβόλος and λιθόβολος (386. 1). (c) Compound adjectives of Dec. 3, with a palatal or lingual stem-mark, in which the latter part is a monosyllable derived from a verb, are commonly oxytone: ἀπορρώξ, ἡμιθνής. (d) Words derived from compound words are commonly not accented as though themselves compounded; but their compounds again follow the general rule: thus, κατασκευάζω, κατασκευαστός (792 a), ἀ-κατασκεύαστος.

---

797. INDEX I.—GREEK.

The references are here made, as in other parts of the Grammar, to sections and their parts. The letter s (from the Lat. *sequens*) is often added, as elsewhere, to signify *and the following;* but is often omitted as needless, where it might have been added. The signs < and > represent the forms at the angle as arising by contraction or some other change, chiefly euphonic, from the forms at the opening, or as used in their stead. The sign × denotes opposition or distinction. Dialectic use is marked by an older style of figures in the references (as, 329). For abbreviations, see 798. To increase the practical value of the Index, the form or construction of a word is sometimes referred to the appropriate rule or remark, although the particular word may not have been cited as an example in the present edition, perhaps not even in the larger Grammar. In the latter case, the reference is marked with an accent ('). The index for the conjugation of verbs is contained in § 50.

A 4, 106; <ν 138, 142.
ἀ- cop. 385: priv. 385, compounds w. gen. 436.
ᾳ 109 s, 118 d, 7, 11 s.
ἀγαθός cp. 262 b, 260 a, 261 a, b; w. acc. 481'.
ἀγάλλω mid. 582 γ.
ἄγαμαι w. acc., gen., 429 a, 443 b, 432 f.

ἀγανακτέω w. dat. 456, w. pt. 677'. [pt. 677'.
ἀγαπάω w. dat. 456, w. ἄγγελος dec. 16.
ἄγε imv. 656 b.
ἀγήραος, -ως, dec. 22.
ἀγνώς 386, w. gen. 432 b.
ἄγχι, -οῦ, cp. 262 d, 263 d; w. gen. 445 c.

ἀδελφός w. gen. 442 a, w. dat. 451; ἀδελφε 779.
Ἅιδης dec. 225 b; Ἀϊδόσδε 688 e; 483 a.
ἀδικέω w. 2 acc. 480 b, w. pt. 677 a; pres. as ἄδικος dec. 22. [pf. 612.
-αθ- in 2 aor. 353 a.
Ἄθως, -ω acc. 199. 3.

αι 108 ; in accent. 767.
αἴ, D., E., for εἰ ἴ/, 701 f.
αἰδώς 219 b, 214, 215 c.
αἴξ dec. 17.
αἱρέω w. 2 acc. 480 a ;
 mid. 579, pass. 588'.
-αισι old dat. pl. 198. 3.
αἰσθάνομαι w.gen. 432 b,
 h, w. dep. verb 657, 677.
αἰσχρός, -ρῶς, cp. 260,
 261 c, 263.
αἰσχύνομαι w. acc. 472 f,
 w. inf. × pt. 657 k.
αἰτέω w. 2 acc. 480 c.
αἴτιος, -άομαι, w. gen.
 444 f, 431 c, dat. 454 d.
ἀκόλουθος w. gen. 442 a,
 w. dat. 450.
ἀκούω w. gen. and acc.
 432g, h, 434 a ; as pass.
 575 a ; pres. as pf. 612 ;
 w. inf. or pt. 657 k, 677.
ἄκρος, use 508 a.
ἀλγεινός cp. 260, 261 e.
ἅλις w. gen. 414 a.
ἀλίσκομαι w. gen. 431 c,
 w. pt. 677'.
ἀλλά 701 b, n, × ἄλλα
 766 a ; introd. 708 e ;
 ἀλλὰ γάρ 709, ἀλλ' ἤ
 700 m, n.
ἀλλάσσω w. gen. 429 a.
ἀλλήλων 27, 244. 3.
ἀλλοῖος w. gen. 406 a.
ἄλλος dec. 28 l ; use 567 ;
 w. gen. 406 a ; as adv.
 509 e, 567 e ; × ὁ ἄλλος
 523 f ; ἄλλο τι (ἤ) 567 g.
ἄλλως τε καὶ 717 a.
ἅλς dec. 208.
ἀλώπηξ dec. 203 b.
ἅλως dec. 225 j. [662.
ἅμα w. dat. 450 ; w. pt.
ἁμαρτάνω w. gen. 405.
ἀμείνων compt. 261 a, f,
 262 b.
ἀμπέχω w. 2 acc. 480 c.
ἀμφί 688, 689 e ; οἱ ἀμφί
 527 a. [480 c'.
ἀμφιέννυμι w. 2 acc.
ἄμφω dec. 25, 240 c.
ἄν conting. w. ind., opt.,
 inf., pt., 618, 658 a ; w.
 sub. 619 ; w. fut. ind.
 620 ; pos. 621, 662 b ;

repeated 622, omitted
 631 e – g ; w. pot. opt.
 or ind. 636 s ; w. ind.
 of habit 616 b ; not w.
 opt. of wish 638 f.
ἄν conj., < ἐάν, 619 a.
ἀνά 688, 6891 ; sc. στῆθι
 699 e, 785 ; w. num.
 239 f, 692. 5.
ἀναμιμνῄσκω const. 473.
ἀνέχομαι w. gen. 432 f.
ἀνήρ dec. 18, 210, 208 f ;
 ἴη address 484 g ; ἀνήρ,
 ὠνήρ, 125.
ἀντί 688, 689 h ; ἀνθ' ὧν,
 because, 557 ; derivat.
 w. gen. 445, w. dat. 455.
ἀντιποιέομαι w.gen. 430.
ἄντρον dec. 16.
ἀνύω const. 677 f.
ἄνω cp. 262 d, 263.
ἄξιος, &c., w. gen. 431 b ;
 w. dat. 454 d.
ἀπειθέω w. dat. 456.
ἁπλόος, -οῦς, dec. 23 ;
 cp. 257 c, d.
ἀπό 688, 689 b ; form
 136 b ; cp. 263' ; w.
 pass. 586 d. [gen. 431 a.
ἀποδίδομαι sell, 579, w.
ἀποδιδράσκω 472 f.
ἀπολαύω w. gen. 412.
Ἀπόλλων dec. 208 f,
 211 a. [w. dat. 456.
ἀπορέω w. gen. 414 b ;
ἀποστερέω w.gen.414 b';
 w. 2 acc. 480 c.
ἅπτω, mid. w. gen. 426.
ἄρα (ῥά, ἄρ) 685 c ; pos.
 720 ; ἦν as pres. 611.
ἆρα (οὐ, μή) ; 687. [262 b.
ἀρείων, ἄριστος, cp. 261 a,
ἀρέσκω w. dat. 457.
Ἄρης 21, 216 c, 220 a.
ἀρι- in compos. 385 d.
ἀριστεύω w. gen. 419 c.
ἀρκέω w. dat. 453 ; per-
 sonally 573.
ἄρκυς dec. 219 f.
ἀρνέομαι ὅτι οὐ 713 d.
ἀρνός dec. 18, 210.
ἅρπαξ 230 a ; cp. 259.
ἄρρην dec. 22, 208 a.
ἄρχω w. gen. 407, 425 ;
 pt. as adv. 674 b.

ἅσσα, ἄσσα (-ττα), 253 a,
 254 b, 28. [226 g.
ἀστήρ, -τράσι 145 a ;
ἄστυ dec. 19, 215 b.
-αται, -ατο < -νται, -ντο
 158, 300 b, 329.
ἀτάρ conj. 701 b.
ἅτε as, w. pt. 681.
ἅτερος = ἕτερος 125 b.
Ἀτρείδης 369', dec. 15.
ἀτυχέω w. gen. 405, 427.
αὐ 4, 108 ; < aF 142.
αὖ, αὖθις, pos. 720.
αὐτίκα w. pt. 662.
αὐτός dec. 28,251, 255 b ;
 cp. 262 d ; use 540 s ;
 w. dat. of assoc. obj.
 467 c ; w. compt. and
 sup. 513 f ; as pers.
 pron. 540 g ; ὁ αὐτός
 540 b, w. dat. 451.
αὑτοῦ < ἑαυτοῦ 244.
ἀφαιρέομαι const. 485 d.
ἀφειδέω w. gen. 405 b.
ἄχθομαι w. dat. 456 ;
 w. pt. 661 b, 677'.
ἄχρι(s) 164 ; w. gen.
 445 c ; ἄχρι οὗ 557 a.
B 4, 137 ; < π, φ, 147.
βασιλεύς (sc. ὁ) 533 b ;
 cp. 262 d.
βασιλεύω w. gen. 407 ;
 aor. × pres. 592 d.
βελτίων, &c., 260, 261 e.
βοηθέω, &c., w. dat. 453.
βορέας, -ῤῥᾶς dec. 15,
 196, 198. 1.
βουλεύω, mid. 579.
βούλομαι, βούλει 559 c,
 647 b ; βουλομένῳ 455 N.
βοῦς dec. 19, 214 s, 217.
Γ 4, 137 c ; < κ, χ, 147.
γάρ 701 j ; in specif.
 705 b ; anacol. 716 a ;
 pos. 720 ; ὁ γάρ 518 b.
γέ 389 c, 685 b, c ; pos.
 720 ; encl. 787 d, h.
γείτων const. 442, 450.
γέλως dec. 207 c ; com-
 pounds 237 b.
γένος, γέρας, dec. 19,
 216 s. [473.
γεύω w. gen., acc., 432 a,
γίγας dec. 17, 205.
γίγνομαι w. gen. 412,

§ 797.   γίγνομαι   GREEK.   Ἑρμέας   355

437 a'; w. dat. 449;
w. pt. 679. [657 k.
γιγνώσκω w. inf. × pt.
Γλοῦς dec. 21, 227 b.
γόνυ dec. 224 c.
γράφω, mid. 579, 581, w.
gen., acc., 431 c, 480 c.
γυνή dec. 203, 779.
γύψ dec. 17, 203.
Γωβρύας dec. 15, 198. 1.
Δ 4, 137; in dec. 217.
δαίμων dec. 18, 208.
δάκρυον,-ρυ dec.14,225f.
δάμαρ dec. 17, 153 a.
δανείζω, mid. 581.
δέ 685 c, 701 c; for γάρ
705 a; introd. 708 c;
pos. 720 : ὁ δέ 518.
-δε local 688 e, 382, 252;
enclit. 787 d, f, g.
δεῖνα dec. 27, 245.
δένδρον, -εον, dec. 225 f.
δέσποτα voc. 779.
δέω need, w. gen. 414 b;
w. num. 242 c : δεῖ w.
acc.473 b; w.inf.598 a;
μικροῦ [δεῖν], &c., 665 :
δέομαι w. gen. 414 c,
434 a.
δή, δήθεν, δῆτα, δαί,685 c,
389; pos. 673.
δηλός εἰμι 573, 677 g;
δῆλον ὅτι 717 b.
δηλόω w. pt. 677. [208 f.
Δημήτηρ dec. 210 b,
διά 688, 689 a.
διαλέγομαι 580, w. dat.
452 a. [677 f.
διαλείπω, pt. or w. pt.
διατρίβω w. pt. 677 a.
διαφέρω (-φορος) w.gen.
406; mid. w. dat. 455'.
διδάσκω w. 2 acc. 480 c;
mid. 581.
δίδωμι, pres. × aor. 594.
δίκαιός εἰμι w. inf. 573.
δίκην w. gen. 436 d.
διότι conj. 701 j.
διπλάσιος w. gen. 409.
δίπους dec. 22, 231 c.
δοκέω personally 573;
(ὡς) δοκεῖν ἐμοί 665,
671 c'; pt. abs. 675 c, d.
δόλος dec. 14, 11 s.
δόρυ dec. 21, 224 c.

δούς dec. 26, 205, 233.
δύναμαι w. acc. 472 f;
or -τος, w. rel. 553 c.
δύο, δύω, dec. 25, 240 c.
δύς dec. 26, 205, 233.
δυσ- 385 c; aug. 283.
δωρεάν adv. acc. 380 a.
δῶρον dec. 14, 11 s.
Ἐ ψιλόν 4, 98 b, 106;
< σ 138, 142, 152 s;
ins. in cont. 120 i.
-εα- in plup. 291 c : -εᾱ,
-εᾱς, in acc. 220.
ἐάν (εἰ ἄν) 701 f, 619 a.
ἑαυτοῦ > αὑτοῦ dec. 27,
244, 248; use 537 s;
as gen. refl. 539 d.
ἐάω w. οὐ, forbid, 686 i.
ἐγγύς cp. 263 d; w. gen.
445 c; w. dat. 450.
ἐγώ dec. 27, 243, 246;
use,536 s; ἔγωγε 787 h.
ἔθεν for οὗ 27 f, 247 f.
εἰ, εἴπερ, εἰ μή, εἴτε, εἰ
καί, εἰ μή εἰ, 701 f, g, i,
m, 631 s, 639 a, 643 s,
674 f; εἰ γάρ, εἴθε, εἰ,
in wish 638 ; εἴ τις 639;
ell. w. εἰ δέ, εἰ δὲ μή, &c.,
710, 717 c; εἰ procl.786.
-εια- in opt. 293 d, c.
εἰδώς dec. 26, 233 c.
εἴκοσι(ν) 52, 163 a.
εἴκω w. dat., gen., 455 g,
εἰκών dec. 224 a. [405 b.
εἰμί be × εἶμι go 766. 3 ;
enclit. 787 c : w. gen.
421 s, 437; w. dat.
459; w. pt. 679; ἔστιν
οἱ, &c.,559; ἔστι, ἦν, w.
pl. nom. 570; ἦν as aor.
603 b, as pr. 611.
εἰπέ, -όν, acc. 781, 783 c;
εἴργω w. gen. 405. [656.
-εις adj., 155; cp. 258.
εἰς dec. 24, 240 b; w.
dat. 451, sup. 512 c.
εἰς, ἐς, 688, 689 a; w.
num. 239 f, 692. 5;
proclit. 786 ; εἰς ὅτε
712. [480 c'.
εἰς(ἐκ)πράττω w. 2 acc.
ἕκαστος 376 d; const.
501, 548 c.
ἐκδύω w. 2 acc. 480 c.

ἐκεῖνος 28 l, 252; ἐκει-
νοσί 252 c; use 542;
w. art. 524.
ἑκών εἶναι 665 b.
ἐλάσσων,-ττων,cp.261 b,
262 b; ἔλαττον as indec.,
adv., 507 c, f, 511 c.
ἐλαύνω as intrans. 577 c.
Ἑλλάς, -ην, as adj. 506 f.
ἐλπίς dec. 17, 204.
ἐμαυτοῦ dec. 27, 244,
248; use 537 s.
ἐμός 252. 5; use 538.
ἐμοῦ, ἐμοί, ἐμέ × μοῦ, μοί,
μέ, 246 c, 536 s, 787 s.
-εν, inf. in, 309 c, 326.
ἐν (ἐνί) 688,689 a; proclit.
786; in compos. 166,
698 c; as adv. 703 b;
for εἰς 704 d : ἐν τοῖς
w. sup. 512 b; ἔνι for
ἔνεστι 699 c, 785.
ἐνδίδωμι intrans. 486 d.
ἔνδον, -οθεν, -οθι, w. gen.
445 c; interch. 704.
ἕνεκα,-κεν, w. gen. 436 d.
ἔνοχος w. gen. 431 c, d.
ἐξ, ἐκ, 688, 689 a, 165;
proclit. 786 ; cp. 262 d;
w. pass. 586; for ἐν
704 : ἐξ ὅτου, &c., 557 a.
ἐξαίφνης w. part. 662.
ἐξάρχω in hypall. 474.
ἔξαρνος w. acc. 472 j.
ἑξῆς w. gen. 445 c, w.
dat. 450 a. [426.
ἐξ(ἐφ)ικνέομαι w. gen.
ἐξόν absolute 675'.
ἔξω cp. 262 d, 263.
ἔοικα const. 657 j.
ἐπαινέω w. gen. 429 a,
443 b; w. 2 acc. 480 b'.
ἐπεί(δή) w. aor. 605 c,
617 d ; w. εὐθέως, τά-
χιστα, &c., 553. 1, b.
ἐπί 688, 689 g; w. num.,
240 f,692.5; in compos.
699 g: ἐφ᾽ ᾧ (τε) 557 a,
w. inf. 671 ; ἔτι 785.
ἐπιχώριος w. gen. 437 b.
ἔρημος,-όω, w.gen.414 b.
ἐρι- in compos. 385 d.
ἔρις, -ιζω, w. dat. 455 ;
dec. 17, 204.
Ἑρμέας,-ῆς, dec. 15,196.

ἐρρωμένος cp. 257 d.
ἔρχομαι w. pt. 598 b, c; pr. for fut. 609 c:
ἐλθέ oxyt. 781 d,
ἐρῶν dec. 26, 152, 121.
ἐρωτάω w. 2 acc. 480 c.
ἔστε (ἐς, τέ) conj. 701 h.
ἑστώς dec. 26, 233 a.
ἔσχατος cp. 262 d, c.
ἑταῖρος cp. 262 d.
ἕτερος 376 c; use 567; w. gen. 406.
ευ < εF 142, 217 b; < εο, &c., 131 b, 323 c, f.
εὔγεως dec. 200 b.
εὐθύ(ς) 164; w. gen. 430; w. part. 662.
εὔνοος accent. 772 a.
εὑρίσκω w. pt. 677; εὑρέ, oxyt. 781.
ἐΰς, ἠΰς, dec. 237 d.
εὔχαρις dec. 22, 204.
ἐφελκυστικόν (ν) 163 c.
ἐχθρός cp. 260, 261 e.
ἔχω reflex. 577 c, d, w. gen. 420 b; w. pt. 679; ληρεῖς ἔχων 674 g; mid. w. gen. 426.
-εως, -εων, Att. gen. 220.
ἕως dec. 225 j, 199.
F 4, 98 e, 100, 138 s; in dec. 217; in cj. 345; in pron. 27 f, g, 246 s; in pros. 736 b.
Z 4, 137 d; < mute & I 143 c, 261 b, 349.
ζα-, δα-, insep. 385 d.
ζάω w. acc., dat. 485 d: ζάων, ζῶν, dec. 26.
Ζεύς, Ζάν, dec. 21, 224 f.
-ζω, verbs in, 349, 378 s.
H 4, 106; ins. 311.
ᾖ 109 s, 118 d, 7, 11 s.
ἤ or, than, 701 d, i, l; w. compt. 511, 513, om. 511 c; ἢ κατά, ἢ ὡς, &c., 513; ἢ οὐ 713 h.
ἦ indeed, 685 c, 687.
ἦ δ' ὅς 518 f. [553 c.
ἦ as adv. 380 c'; w. sup.
ἠδέ (ἰδέ E.) conj. 701 c.
ἥδομαι w. dat. 456; in dat. 459 N.; w. pt. 677.
ἡδύς dec. 23, 213 s, 217, 233; cp. 260.

ἥκιστος sup. 262 b: ἥκιστα no, 708 b.
ἥκω w. adv. and gen. 420 b; as perf. 612.
ἡλίκος 53; in condens., 556, 565'.
ἡμέρα, gen. 433, dat. 469 a, acc. 482; wt. art. 533 d; om. 507 b.
ἡμῖν, ἡμᾶς, &c., 247 g, i.
ἥμισυς dec. 220 g; compounds 242 e.
ἤν < ἐάν 619 a, 631 s.
ἦπαρ dec. 17, 206.
ἦρ < ἔαρ, ἦρος, 209, 778 b.
Ἡρακλέης dec. 19, 219 c, 779 f, 222 d.
ἥρως dec. 19, 216.
-ῆς < -έες nom. 121 e.
-ης, -ησι, dat. pl. 198.
-ης in form. 386. 2; cp. 258. [262 b.
ἥσσων, -ττων, compt.
ἥσυχος cp. 257 d, 259 a.
ἦτε, ἦτοι, 701 d. [779 a.
ἠχώ dec. 19, 214 s, 772 e, ἠώς, dec. 225 j, 219 b.
Θ 4, 137; changes 147 s.
θανάτου, use 431 d.
θάσσων (ταχύς) 261 b.
θάτερον, -ου, 125 b.
θαυμάζω w. acc. & gen. 432 f, 472 e; w. εἰ 639.
θαυμαστὸν ὅσον, &c., 565.
θεά dec. 15, 194 s.
θείς dec. 26, 205, 233.
Θέμις dec., use, 224 g.
-θεν, gen. in, 192, 380 b.
θήν 685 c; pos. 720; encl. 787 d.
θήρ dec. 18, 208.
-θι, dat. in, 191. 2.
θνήσκω, tenses, 600 a.
θρίξ dec. 17, 203 b.
θυγάτηρ dec. 210 b, 208 f.
θύραζε, θύρασι, 382, 380 c.
Ι 4, 106; ι subs. 109.
I consonant 138 s, 143.
ἰδέ, ἴθι, imv. 656 b; 781 d.
ἴδιος w. gen. 437 b.
ἵεμαι w. gen. 430 b.
ἱερός w. gen. 437 b.
-ιη- in opt. 293. [566 a.
ἵνα 701 c, 624 e; ἵνα τι; ἱππεύς dec. 19, 21, 213 s.

ἰσόμοιρος w. gen. or dat. 442 a.
ἴσος & der. w. dat. 451.
ἰχθύς dec. 19, 217, 219 f.
-ίων, -ιστος, in cp. 260 s.
K 4, 137; tense-s. 288.
καί 701 a, 685 c; crasis 126; w. num. 242; w. οὗτος 544 a; w. pt. 674 f; for other connectives, 705: καὶ τόν (ὅς) 518 c, f; καὶ εἰ 701 g; πολὺς καί 702 c; καὶ γάρ 709; καίπερ 674 f, 662. [262 b.
κακός cp. 260 s, 261 e,
καλέω w. 2 acc. 480 a.
καλός cp. 260 [dec. 226.
κάρα in periphr. 437 c;
κατά 688, 689 m; in cp. 513 b; compounds w. gen. 699 a: κάτ 136.
κατανέμω w. 2 acc. 480 a.
κέ(ν), κά, 163 a; = ἄν 618; pos. 720; encl. 787 d.
κεῖνος 281, 255 c.
κέρας dec. 17, 207, 222 e; compounds 237 b.
κερδαλέος cp. 260.
κεφαλῆς const. 426 b.
κηρύσσει (ὁ κήρυξ) 571 b.
κινδυνεύω w. gen. 446 d.
κίς dec. 19, 216 b, 217 c.
κλείς dec. 17, 207, 222 a.
κλέπτης cp. 262 d.
κλύω w. gen. 432 a, 434 a', 413; as pass. 575 a; as perf. 612'.
κοινός & der., w. gen. & dat. 424, 437 b, 450.
κόπτομαι as act. 575 b.
κόραξ dec. 17, 203.
κόρυς dec. 17, 204.
κορέννυμι w. gen. 414 a.
κράτος & der. w. gen. 407.
κρείσσων, κράτιστος, cp. 261 b, 262 b.
κρύπτω w. 2 acc. 480 c.
κρύφα w. gen. 444 a.
κύρω, -έω, w. gen. or dat. 427, 450'; w. pt. 677 a.
κύων dec. 18, 210.
Λ 4, 137; λλ < ρλ, λΙ, 150, 143 a, 349 l; changes of λσ 152.

λαγχάνω w. gen. 427.
λάθρᾳ w. gen. 444 a.
λάλος cp. 257 d.
λαμβάνω w. gen. 423, 426; λαβέ oxyt. 781.
λανθάνω const. 677 f.
λαός, λεώς, dec. 200'.
λέγω w. 2 acc. 480 b; λέγουσιν 571 c.
λείπω w. gen. 405', 406 b.
λέων dec. 17, 205.
λίμην dec. 18, 208.
λιπών dec. 26, 781.
λούω, mid. 578.
λύγξ dec. 17, 203.
λύρα dec. 14, 194 s.
λύω w. gen. 405 : λύων, λύσας, dec. 26.
λώων, λῷστος, 261 a, 262 b.
M 4, 137; changes of & w. 148, 150, 152, 160.
μά × νή w. acc. 476 d, 685 c ; μὰ τόν — 532.
μάκαρ, -αιρα, 235 d.
μακρός cp. 261 b, e; μακρῷ, by far, 468.
μάλα cp. 263 a; μᾶλλον, μάλιστα, in cp. 510; μᾶλλον om. 513 i.
μάλης, ὑπό, 228 c.
μανθάνω w. gen. 434 a, 413; w. inf. × pt. 657 k; τί μαθών; 674 h.
Μασκᾶς dec. 227 b.
μέγας dec. 24, 236 ; cp., 261 b ; μείζων dec. 22, 211.
-μεθα, -μεσθα, 299: -μεθον 299 b, 9 c, page 7.
μείων cp. 261 a; μεῖον as indecl. 507 e. [cp. 259.
μέλας dec. 23, 208 c, 233;
μέλλω w. inf. 598 a.
μέλει & der. w. gen. 432 d; w. dat. 457 : 571 d.
μέν, μέντοι, 685 c, 701 b, c; pos. 720: ὁ μέν 518; ἆς μέν 519 f.
μέσος cp. 257 d, e; use 508 : -όω w. gen. 425 a.
μεστός, -όω, w. gen. 414 a.
μετά 688, 689 c; compounds w. gen. 424.
μεταπέμπω, mid. 579.
μεταξύ w. part. 662.

μέτεστι w. gen., dat., 421, 459.
μέχρι(s) 164; w. gen. 445 c ; w. οὗ, &c., 557; conj. 701 h, 703 c.
μή adv. × οὐ, 686 s; redund. 713 ; μηδέ emph., μὴ οὐ, 713 c, f ; μή τί γε, μὴ ὅτι (ὅπως), 717 d, g : conj. 701 e, 624 s : μηδέ, μήτε, conj. 701 c, a.
μηδείς dec. 25, 240 b; μηδέν as indecl. 507 e.
μηκέτι < μὴ ἔτι 165 c.
μῆλον dec. 16, 11 s, 771.
μήν 685 c ; pos. 720.
μήτηρ dec. 210 b.
-μι form 45, 313 s, 335.
μικρός cp. 261 a, e, 262 b; μικροῦ (δεῖν) 665.
μιμνήσκω w. gen., acc., 432 c, 473.
μίν acc. 27 i ; use 539 e.
μισθόω, mid. hire 581.
μνάα, μνᾶ, dec. 15, 196.
μόριον dec. 16, 770.
μόσσυν dec. 225 f.
μου, μοί, μέ, encl. 787 ; × ἐμοῦ, &c., 246 c, 536 s; μοί ethical 462 e.
μοῦσα, μυῖα, dec. 15.
μῶρος dec. 23, 232.
N 4, 137; corresp. to α 138, 142, 156, changes 8, 150 s, of νς 152 s, ιν < νΙ 142 a; ν final 160 ; movable 162 s.
ναί × μά w. acc. 476 d.
ναός, νεώς, dec. 16, 200.
ναῦς dec. 19, 21, 216 s, 222 f ; ναῦφι 190 a.
ναύτης dec. 14, 194 s.
νέατος sup. 257 e.
νεώς dec. 16, 200, 772 d.
νή × μά w. acc. 476, 685 c.
νη- privative 385 b.
νῆσος dec. 16, 771.
νίν acc. 27 g ; use 539 e.
νομίζω w. dat. 466 c.
νόος, νοῦς, dec. 16, 225 g.
νύ(ν) 163 a, 685 c; pos. 720 ; encl. 787 d.
νύξ 17 f ; gen., dat., acc., 433, 469, 482.

Ξ 4, 137 ; < κσ, γσ, χσ, 151.
ξύν = σύν 170, 688 s.
Ὁ μικρόν 4, 98 c, 106 ; kind. w. α, ε, 114, 312 b.
ὁ art. 28, 249 s; accent. 786; in crasis 125 ; τώ for τά 234 e ; in form ὅs 518 e : use as pron. 516 s ; as art. 520 s, generic 522, limiting 523 s ; w. inf. 663 f, 664; arrangement 523 ; ellipsis 527 s, 532 s : ὁ μέν (δέ, γάρ), καὶ τὸν (ὅs) 518 ; ἐν τοῖς 512 b.
ὅδε dec. 28, 252; use 542 s;
× οὗτος 543 s ; = adv. 545 a ; = ἐγώ 546 ; w. art. 524 : ὁδὶ 252 c.
ὁδούς dec. 17, 205 a.
Ὀδυσ[σ]εύς dec. 21, 222.
ὄζω w. gen. 412, 436 c.
-οθεν, -οθι, 191 s, 380.
ὁθούνεκα 126 δ; use 701 j.
οἱ 4 ; in accent. 767.
οἶδα w. pt. 677 ; οἶδ' ὅτι 717 b ; οἶσθ' ὃ δρᾶσον 655.
Οἰδίπους dec. 21, 214 s.
οἰκεῖος w. gen. 437 b ; w. dat. 450.
οἶκος om. w. gen. 438.
οἰκτρός cp. 260.
οἴμοι 453 ; w. gen. 429 e.
-οιο Thessal. gen. 201.
οἴομαι > οἶμαι parenth. 313 e ; w. gen. 413.
οἷος 53 ; use 549 s, 563 s ; in condens. 555 s, 565 ; in exclam. 564 b ; w. inf. 671 : οἷός τε 556 c; οἷον, οἷα, w. pt. 681.
ὄϊς, οἶς, dec. 19, 21.
-οισι dat. pl. 201 d. [679.
οἴχομαι as pf. 612 ; w. pt.
ὀλίγος cp. 261 b, 262 b ; w. art. 523 f : ὀλίγου (δεῖν) 665 ; ὀλίγῳ 486.
ὅλος w. & wt. art. 523 e.
ὄμνυμι w. acc. 472 f.
ὁμοῦ & der. w. dat. 450 s, w. gen. 442 a ; w. καί 705 c; ὁμοιός εἰμι const. 657 j ; ὅμως w. pt. 662.

ὄνομα in periphr. 437 c ; acc., dat., 485 γ.
ὀπ- in pron. & adv. 377.
ὅπου, ὅποι· ποῦ, ποῖ· οὗ, οἷ, 53 ; w. gen. 420 ; interchanged 704.
Ὀπούς dec. 17, 207 c.
ὅπως adv. 53, 559 a, 624 c ; conj. 701 e, 624 s ; in ell. 626.
ὁράω w. ὅπως, μή, 626 ; w. pt. 677.
ὀρέγομαι w. gen. 430 b.
ὄρνις dec. 224 e.
ὀρχέομαι w. acc. 477 b.
ὅς rel., dec. 28, 250 : use as rel. 549 s, as complem. 563 s ; attr. 552 s, Att. 554 a, inverse 554 c ; w. modes 640 s : ὃς βούλει 559 b : ὅς as demonst. 518 f, 519 f : ὅς possess. 252. 5 ; use 538 s.
ὅσος 53 ; use 549 s, 563 s ; in condens. 556, 565 ; in exclam. 564 b ; w. inf. 671 : ὅσον as indecl. or adv. 507 c, f, 556 d ; ὅσῳ 468 : ὁσημέραι 551 i.
ὀστέον, -οῦν, dec. 16, 772.
ὅστις, ὅτις, ὅτου, &c., dec. 28, 254, 255 c : use as rel. 549 s, as complem. 563 s ; x ὅς 549 s ; w. modes 640 s : ὅ τι μαθών (παθών) 674 h.
ὅτε (ὅταν 619 b) w. modes 640 s'; w. sup., aor., 553 b, 605.
ὅτι 701 i, j, n, 643 s ; x ὡς 702 ; not elided 129 a ; redund. 644, 659 e ; repeated 714 ; in anacol. 716 ; pos. 719 η : w. sup. 553 c ; ὅτι μή 701 m.
οὐ 4, 115 a ; < οF 217 b.
οὗ, οἷ, ἕ, dec. 27, 246 ; encl. 787 ; use 539.
οὐ > οὐκ, οὐχ, οὐχί, 165, 685 c ; x μή 686 ; interrog. 687 ; redund. 713 ; wt. μά 476 d : οὐ μή w. subj. or fut.

597, 627 ; οὔ φημι, &c., 686 i ; οὔτε, οὐδέ, 701 a, c, 713 b, c ; οὐ γὰρ ἀλλά, οὐ μέντοι (μὴν) ἀλλά, οὐχ ὅτι (ὅσον, ὅπως), 717.
οὐδείς (οὐδὲ εἷς 240 b) 24 : οὐδεὶς ὅστις οὐ 559.
οὐκοῦν therefore 687 c.
οὖν < ἐόν (ὤν D., I.) 389 g, 685 c ; pos. 720.
οὕνεκα 126, 557 a, 701 j.
οὖς dec. 17, 207, 778 c.
οὗτος dec. 28, 252 : use 542 s ; x ὅδε 543 s ; in repetition, assent, 544 ; in address 401. 3, 546 ; pl. for sing. 489 d ; w. art. 524 : οὑτοσί, 252 c.
οὕτω(ς) 164 ; x ὧδε 547.
ὀφείλω in wish 638 g.
ὄφρα 701 c, 624, 53 v.
ὀψέ cp. 263 a ; w. gen. 420 ; w. ἦν 571 d.
Π 4, 137 ; changes 147 s.
παιάν dec. 18, 208.
παῖς dec. 17, 204, 778 b.
παλαιός cp. 257 d.
πάλιν in compos. 166.
παρά (παραί 134, πάρ 136) 686, 689 d ; in cp. 511 a ; w. pass. 586 d ; in compos. 699 g: πάρα 699 c, 785.
Παράρτημα, App., 80.
πᾶς dec. 23, 729. 2, 778 b, 793 c ; w. gen. 416 b ; w. art. 523 c ; w. τίς 548 c ; w. rel. 550 f ; w. imv. 656 : πᾶν in compos. 166. [674 h.
πάσχω 575 a'; τί παθών ;
πατήρ dec. 18, 210, 208 f. [222 d.
Πάτροκλος dec. 21, παύω w. gen. 405 ; mid. 582 β ; w. pt. 677.
πείθω w. 2 acc. 480 c ; w. dat. 455 g, 456.
Πειραιεύς dec. 220 c.
πέλας & der. w. gen. 445 c ; w. dat. 450.
πέμπω w. dat. 450 b ; w. 2 acc. 472 g. [414 b.
πένης cp. 258 ; w. gen.
πενθικῶς w. gen. 429 c.

πέρ 389 h, 685 c ; w. pt. 674 f ; pos. 720 ; encl. 787 d.
περί (πέριξ) 688, 689 f ; not elided 129 ; as adv. 703 b : πέρι 785 ; οἱ περί πέρυσι(ν) 163 a. [527 a.
πηνίκα ; w. gen. 420 a.
πῆχυς dec. 19, 213 s.
πλείων, -έων, -εῖστος, -εῖν, 261 a, d ; πλεῖον as indecl. 507 e, 511 c ; πλεῖον, -είστα, in cp. 510.
πλεονέκτης cp. 258 a.
πλέως dec. 236 b ; & der. w. gen. 414 a.
πλῆθος acc., dat., 485 γ ; w. pl. 499 a.
πλήν w. gen. 406 ; conj. 701 m : πλὴν εἰ 710.
πλούσιος, -τέω, w. gen., 414 a. [acc. 479.
πνέω w. gen. 436 c, w.
Πνύξ dec. 224 h.
πόθεν, ποῖ, ποῦ, πῶς, 53 ; w. gen. 420.
ποιέω w. dat., 2 acc., 460, 480 b ; mid. 579, 581, 585 ; w. gen. 430, 431 b ; in periph. 475.
ποιητής 15, 366 d, 791 b.
πόλις dec. 19, 21, 217 g, h, 222 c.
πολιτεύω, mid. 582 δ.
πολύς dec. 24, 236 ; w. art. 523 f ; cp. 261 ; w. καί 702 c : πολλοῦ 431 a, πολλῷ 468.
πόρρω, πρόσω, w. gen. 405, 420 a.
πορφύρεος cp. 257 c.
Ποσειδῶν dec. 208 f, 211 a.
ποτέ, πού, πώς, &c., x πότε ; &c., 53, 563 s ; pos. 720 ; encl. 787 b : ποτέ w. interrog. 389 i. [n.
πότερος 376 s : -ον 701 i, πότνια, -να, fem. 238 b.
πούς dec. 17, 214 s, 231 c.
πρᾶος dec. 24, 236 c.
πρίν const. 703 d.
πρό 688, 689 i ; in crasis 126 : cp. 262 d ; w. comp. 511 a ; πρὸ τοῦ 519 b.

πρός (προτί, ποτί, πότ, 136) 688, 689 i ; in cp. 511 a ; w. pass. 586 d ; as adv. 703 b ; in compos. 699 g ; in accent. 788 e.
προσβάλλω w. gen. 436 c.
προσήκει w. gen., dat., 421, 450 ; -ον abs. 675 d.
πρόσθε(ν 164 a), πρότερον, w. πρίν 703 d.
πρότερος cp. 262 c, d.
προὔργου 382 ; cp. 262 d.
πρῶτος cp. 262 c, d.
πῦρ dcc. 14, 225 f.
πῶς ἄν in wish 637 d.
Ρ 4, 137 ; aspirated, doubl., 93 d, 146, 159 e ; changes of ρσ 152 s.
ῥᾴδιος cp. 261.
ῥήτωρ dec. 18, 153.
ῥίς dec. 18, 208.
Σ, σ or s, 4, 90. 1, 137 ; corresp. to ε 138, 142, 152 s ; final 160, 164 ; σ, σι, σσ < mute & Ι 143.
σαλπίζει (sc. ὁ σ.) 571 b.
σαφής dec. 22, 213 ; -ής, -ῶς, cp. 258.
σεαυτοῦ, σαυτοῦ, dec. 27, 244, 248 ; use 537.
-σθα in 2 pers. 297 b.
-σκον, -σκόμην, iter. 332.
σκοπέω, mid. 582 γ ; w. ὅπως, μή, 624, 626.
σός 252. 5 ; use 538.
σοφός dec. 23, 232 ; -ός, -ῶς, cp. 257, 263.
σπέος dec. 21, 222 d.
σταθμός dec. 226 b.
στοχάζομαι w. gen. 430.
σύ dec. 27, 246 s ; use 536 s ; σοῦ, σοί, σέ, encl. 787 s ; σοί ethical 462 e : σύγε 389 c. [442 a.
συγγενής w. gen., dat., συγγιγνώσκω const. 657 j.
σύν (ξύν 170) 688, 689 b ; in compos. 166 ; w. num. 240 f : compounds w. dat. 451, 699 f ; w. gen. 424.
συνελόντι 671 c.
σύνοιδα const. 657 j.
σῦς, ἧς, dec. 14, 141.
σφέ, ι φίσι, σφίν, 27,

246 d, 247 ; use 539 ; encl. 787 s.
σφέτερος 252. 5, 538 s.
σφοδρός cp. 257 a.
σφώ, σφωέ, &c., 27, 246 s.
Σχῆμα Ἀλκμανικόν 497 c;
Ἀττικόν, Πινδαρικόν (Βοιώτιον), 569 d.
σώζω w. gen. 405 a.
Σωκράτης dec. 19, 213 s.
σῶμα dcc. 17, 206.
σῶς, σῶος, dec. 236 d.
σωτήρ dec. 208 f.
σώφρων cp. 259.
Τ 4, 137 ; changes 147 s.
τάλας cp. 259.
τἀμά = ἐγώ 428 b.
ταμίας dec. 15, 195.
ταύτῃ adv. 380 c.
ταὐτόν, ταὐτό, 199 a.
ταχύς, -έως, cp. 261 b, e, 263 : τὴν ταχίστην 483 d; ὡς τάχιστα, &c., 553 b, c.
τέ 389 c, 685 c, 701 a ; pos. 720 ; encl. 787 d.
τελευτάω w. gen. 405 ; pt. as adv. 674 b.
τέλος adv. acc. 483.
-τέος, verb. in, 269 d, 374 f; w. dat. 458 ; const. 682, 572. [257 s.
-τερος, -τατος, cp. in,
τέσσαρες dec. 25, 240 e.
τηλίκος, -οῦτος, -όσδε, 53, 252, 547′.
τίθημι, mid. 579.
τιμάω w. gen. 431 b.
τιμωρέω, mid. 579.
τὶς indef. dec. 28, 253, 255 e ; pos. 548 b, 720, 520 b ; encl. 787 b ; affixed 389 a : use 548 ; w. pl. 489 d, 501 ; τί as indecl. 507 e, g.
τίς interrog. dec. 28, 253, 255 e ; use 563 s ; w. art. 531 a ; in condens. 555 : τί γάρ, τί δέ, &c., 564 c ; ἵνα τί 566 a.
Τισσαφέρνης dec. 225 d.
τό γε, τὸ καὶ τὸ, πρὸ τοῦ, 519 b ; τὸ νῦν εἶναι 665 b : τοί, ταί, = οἱ, αἱ, 28 j. [pos. 720.
τοί encl. 685 c, 787 d ;

τοῖος, -οῦτος, -όσδε, 53, 252, 199 a, 547.
τοξεύω w. gen. 430.
-τος, verbal in, 374 e, w. dat. 458.
τόσος, -οῦτος, -όσδε, 53, 252, 199 a, 547. [253.
τοῦ = τινος, &c., 28 f, g,
τράπεζα dec. 15, 791 c.
τρεῖς dcc. 25, 240 e.
τριήρης dec. 213 c, 219 a.
τρίτον ἡμιτάλαντον 242 c.
τρόπῳ, -ον, -ους, 485 a.
τυγχάνω w. gen. 426 s, 434 ; w. part. 677.
τύννος, -οῦτος, 53, 252 a.
τῷ th(wh)erefore 519 b.
Υ ψιλόν 4, 98 b, 106 ;
υ- 93 c, υ- 93 c ; υ < F,
εF, 138, 142, 217 b, c.
ὑβριστής cp. 259 a.
ὑγιής cont. 120 f.
ὕδωρ dec. 206.
υἱός dec. 21 ; om. 438.
-υμι, less Att. -ύω, 315 a.
ὑμῖν, ὑμᾶς, &c., 247 g, i.
ὑπάγω θανάτου 431 d.
ὑπακούω, -ήκοος, w. gen., dat., 432 g, 455 g.
ὑπάρχω w. gen. 425 ; w. dat. 459 ; w. pt. 677′.
ὑπέρ (ὑπείρ 134′) 688, 689 j ; cp. 262 d.
ὑπό (ὑπαί, ὑπ, 136) 688, 689 k ; cp. 262 d ; w. pass. 586.
-υς adj. 213 c ; cp. 258.
ὑστερέω, -ίζω, -αῖος, w. gen. 408.
ὕστερος, -τατος, cp. 262 d.
Φ 4, 137 ; 147 s, 159, 167.
φαίνω, mid. 582 β.
φανερός εἰμι 573 c.
φέρτερος, -ιστος, &c., cp. 262 b.
φέρω, mid. 578 a, 585 :
φέρε 656 b.
φεῦ 684 b ; w. gen. 429 e.
φεύγω as pass. 575 a.
φημί, φασίν 571 c ; ἔφη 574 ; οὔ φημι 686 i.
φθάνω, p. or w. pt. 677 f ; w. καί 705 c. [432 f.
φθονέω w. gen., dat.,
-φι(ν) old dat. 190, 163.

φίλος cp. 257 d, 261 e.
φλέψ dec. 17, 151, 778.
φοβέω, mid. 582 β; or
 φόβος, w. ὅπως, μή,
 624 s; om. 626 s.
φροντιστής const. 472 j.
φυλάσσω, mid. 579.
φύξιμος w. acc. 472 j.
φύω w. gen. 412.
φῶς dec. 17, 206, 224 f.
Χ 4, 137; 147 s, 159.
χαίρω w. dat. 456.
χαρίεις dec. 23; cp. 258.
χαλεπαίνω w. dat. 456.
χάρις dec. 203 a; χάριν
 380 a, w. gen. 436 d.
χείρ dec. 18, 224 f: χει-
 ρῶν, -ιστος, 261, 262 b.
χορός dec. 16, 775.
χράομαι w. dat., acc.,
 466 b, 478.

χρή w. gen., acc., 473 b;
 w. inf. 595 : ipf. 611.
χρῄζω w. gen. 414 c.
χρῆμα in periph. 446 a;
 τί χρῆμα why 483 c.
χρόνος, gen. 433, dat.
 469, 485 ε, acc. 482.
χρύσεος dec. 23, 772 c.
χρώς dec. 224 e, 207 a.
Ψ 4, 137; < πσ, βσ, φσ,
ψαύω w. gen. 426. [151.
Ὦ μέγα 4, 98 c, 106 :
-ω & -μι forms 270 c.
ᾦ 109 s, in cont. 7, 118 d,
 119 s; in dec. 11 s.
ὦ, ὤ, 684 b: ὦ in address
 484, 401. 3; crasis 126.
ὧδε × οὕτως 547, 53.
ᾠδή dec. 15, 195, 775.
ᾠόν dec. 16, 775.
ὡς proclit. 786; use 711 a,

53, 701 e, i, j, k; w.
 gen. 420 b; w. dat.
 462 d; w. sup. 553; in
 condens. 558 b, 565; w.
 pt. 598 b, 680, 675 c; final 624 s; complem. 643 s,
 × ὅτι 702 a, om. 647 b;
 in wish 648 d; w. inf.
 671, 513 d; w. adv.
 711; w. num. 711 b;
 as prep. 711 c; in ell.
 711: ἔστιν ὡς 559 a.
ὥσπερ 389 h; w. pt. 680,
 675 e; in ell. 711.
ὥστε 389 j, 787 e; consec.
 701 k, 671 d; w. imv.
 655; w. inf. 671, 513 d.
ὦν Ion. 131 e.
ὠφελέω w. dat. 453; w.
 acc. 472 b.   [638 g.
ὤφελον in wish, 611,

798. INDEX II. — LATIN AND ENGLISH.

This Index is designed, not only for prominent subjects and words, but also for the authors most cited, and for abbreviations. The writings of Xenophon are commonly cited without naming the author, and the Anabasis without even naming the work (by book, chapter, and section, according to the usual division: as, iv. 3. 12). The Iliad and Odyssey are cited by book-letter and verse as numbered by Wolf, Bekker, &c.; a capital referring to the Iliad, and a small letter to the Odyssey (Δ. 25, for Il. iv. 25; δ. 134, for Od. iv. 134). In Pindar, the references are made to the verses of Heyne; and in the Dramatists, to those of Dindorf. The Historians are commonly cited by book and chapter, according to the usual division; Demosthenes, by the pages and lines of Reiske; the other Orators and Plato (including Timæus Locrus), by the pages and lines or division-letters of Stephens; &c. Figures indicating the times at or about which the authors flourished are here subjoined to their names, from the latest edition of Liddell & Scott's excellent Lexicon. It will be understood that the year before Christ is denoted, unless the number is followed by "A. D." In most cases, the meaning of the abbreviations used in this work will be plain from their familiar use, or from the connection and the following list of words; in other cases, special aid will be given below. For some explanations applying to the Index itself, see § 797.

ABSOLUTE nom. 401; compt. & sup. 514; time 607; inf. 665; gen., acc.
Absorption of vowels 118. [(pt.) 675.
Acatalectic verse 743.
Accent 766 s; final, recessive, retentive, 769: rhythmic 741. See page 12.
Accusative 10, 186 d, 398, 485 d; local idea 470: in appos. w. sent. 396; of rel. attracted 554 n; subj. of inf. 666; abs. 675; w. verbal in τέον 682 s; w. prep. 688 s. See page 12.

Achronic forms 590 a, 613 b, 660.
Active *Voice* 30, 271 e; for pass. 575;
 trans. and intrans., = mid., 577, 585:
 Verbals w. gen. 444; w. acc. 472 j.
Actual sentence 61 f: mode 30 c, 613;
 interch. w. contingent 654.
Acute accent 94, 767 e; > grave 784;
Additive particle 685 c. [syll. 768.
Address 57; voc. 484, nom. 401. 3.
Adjective 55, 173; *dec.* 22 s, 229 s;
 num. 25, 239; *pron.* 28, 249: *compar.*

§ 798. ADJU LATIN & ENGLISH. ATTR 361

256: *der.* 373; compos. 385 s: SYNT.
492 s, 506 s: pos. 718 f, s: Adj. *Clause*
62 h; pos. 718 o.   [circumst., 58.
Adjunct, prepos. × nude, complem. ×
Adopted stems 358.
Adverb 55,685; num. 52,241, pronom.
53, 377, charact., neg., interrog., &c.,
685 s: cp. 263, 262 d; der. 380: *synt.*
685, 703 s; w. art. = adj. 526; attracted
554 d, 558 b; as prep., as conn. and
non-conn., 703; used subst. 706: pos.
18 e, s.
Adverbial clause 62 h, pos. 718 p;
acc. 483, 380, gen., dat., 380; phrases
529, 698; inf. 655; pt. 674 d.
Adversative conjunctions 701 b.
Æolic dialect (Æol., Æ.) 82, 84, 87 a;
opt. 293 e; verse 750.   [tor, § 85.
Æschines (Æschin.) fl. 345, Att. ora-
Æschylus (Æsch.) fl. 484, Att. tragedian, § 85: Agamemnon, Choëphori,
Eumenides, Persæ, Prometheus, Septem contra Thebas (Th.), Supplices.
Affixes, open × close, 172 c; nude ×
euph. 183, 303: of *dec.* 11, 180 s, 20,
analyzed and compared 12 s: of *pers.
pron.* 27 e: of *cj.*, subjective × obj., pri-
mary × sec., imv., inf., partic., 32,35 s,
285 s, 48, 321 s; nude 290 a, 313, 320;
regular 303; union w. s. 304 s.
Affirmatives 360, 32 f.
Agent, suff. of, 365; w. pass., gen.
586, 434, dat. 586, 461, 458, acc. 682 b.
Agesilāus, see Xenophon.
Agreement 63 a, 492 s; acc. to form ×
sense 493 s; of subst. 393, adj. 504,
pron. 505, verb 568.
Alcæus (Alc.) fl. 606, Æol. lyrist.
Alpha privative 385, 436.
Alphabet 1 s, 90 s; hist. 97.
Alternative adv. 685 c; conj. 701 d.
Anabasis, see Xenophon.
Anacolūthon 70 t; in synt. of appos.
396 c, nom. 402, adj. and pt. 504 b,
compt. 511, art. 532, fin. verb 644 s,
649 s, 655, inf. and pt. 659, 667 g, ver-
bal 683, particle 716.
Anacreon fl. 540, Ion. lyrist: poems
in imitation of, *Anacreontica* (Anact.).
Analysis of sentences 57 s, 72 s, words
75 e, cp. 29, verb 32, affixes 12 s, 27 e,
32, 35 s, metres 78.   [verse 751.
Anapæst 77: anapæstic rhythm 742.
Anastrophe 71 a; of accent 785.
Antecedent, def. or indef., 549; in
clause w. rel. or om. 551; attracted
553 s: *clause* un. w. rel. clause 555 s.
Antepenult 111, 767 f, 770.
Antistrophe 744 e.

Antithesis 6, 104; or *contrast,* 71 a.
Aorist 30 b, 267 c, 273 s; w. σ changed
or om. 152, 306: *second* 289, in pures
313 b; stem 47, 336, 340; accent 780 s;
redupl. 284 e; intrans. 338 b: SYNT.,
× def. and compl. tenses, 590 s; as sequel 592 c, 605 b; generic use 602 b,
603,605; gnomic 606; × ipf. as conting.
or indef. 615 s; × pres. w. μή 628; inf.
660, 598; pt. 674 e, 660 e; pass. and
mid. interch. 576; aor. sub. = fut. pf.
Aphæresis 6, 103 c, 124 b.   [617 c.
Apocope 6, 103 c; in particles 136.
Apodosis 62 j; see Conclusion.
Apollonius Rhodius fl. 200, Epic poet.
Apologia (Apol.), see Xenophon.
Aposiopēsis 68 e, 532.
Apostrophe 6, 103 d, 127, 135 b;
accent 774, 788 b: rhetor. 70 g.
Apposition, -tive, 58; dir., pred.,
modal, &c., 393; partitive 395, 417:
synt. 393 s; w. sentence 396, w. voc.
485 a, by synesis 394 c: appositional
verb 59 a, 437.
Apud (ap.) = *quoted in.*
Aristophanes (Ar.) fl. 427, Att. come-
dian, § 85: Acharnenses, Aves, Eccle-
siazūsæ, Equites, Lysistrata, Nubes,
Pax, Plutus, Ranæ, Thesmophoria-
zūsæ, Vespæ: Aristophanic verse 753.
Aristoteles (Aristl.) fl. 347, philosopher (§ 85 b): Rhetorica, &c.
Arrangement, log., rhet., rhythm.,
64; hyperb. 71; dir. or normal × indir.
or varied, periodic × loose, 718; why
varied 719 s.
Arsis 741; affecting quant. 736 c.
Article, prepos. × postpos., 28, 249 s;
in crasis 125; proclit. 786: SYNT., use
as *gen. defin.* 518 s: as *art. proper* 520 s;
generic, 522: *limiting* 523 s; order of
description × statement 523; w. αὐτός
540 b; w. ἀμφί, περί, 527 a; in contrast,
&c., = poss. pron., 530: repeated 523 b,
j, 534. 4; omitted 533 s.
Aspirate mute 4, 137: breathing 93:
aspiration om. 159, 343, 167; transferred 159 g, 167.   [554.
Assimilation 104; of rel. or antec.
Asyndeton 68 d, 707; Eng. × Gr. 707 j.
Attenuation of vowels 107, 114: attenuated stems 341.
Athenæus fl. 228 A. D., scholar.
Attic dialect 82, 85; old, mid., new,
> Common, 85 a, b: dec. 200; gen.
220 f; redupl. 281 d, 357. 2; opt. 293 c;
imv. 300 d; fut. 305; accent 790.
Attraction 70 q: in synt. of appos.
396 b, acc., &c., 474, agreement 500,

COMP. GR. 16

adj. 508 s, pron. 552 s, 565, verb 573, 649 d, inf. and pt. 657, 666 s, particle 715, 702 d; affecting pos. 719, 553, 662.
Attribute 60 b, 492 b.
Augment, syll. × temp., 277 ; rules 278 s; in dial. 284; in accent 783.
Authority in prosody 726 b, 733.
Auxiliary verbs 274, 285 a, 317, 679.
BASE in cp. 29, 256 a ; in cj. 289 c.
Bekker's Edition of Homer, 1858
Bœotic (Bœot., n.) dialect 82. [(Bek.).
Breathings 4, 93 ; < F, Σ, 141 ; in dial. 167 c: marks 98 b. ·
Breve (short syllable) 725 a.
CÆSŪRA, of foot, verse, masc., fem., &c., cæsural pause, syll., 745; affecting quantity 736 c.
Cases, dir. or indir., right or oblique, subjective, obj., or resid, 10, 179, 397 s; affixes 11 s, 180 s; hist. 186 s: *use* 397 s, generic 485, in denoting place or time 470, 482 e, absolute 675, w. prep. 689: Latin 399 b, c.
Catalectic verse 743.
Causal conjunctions 701 j.
Causative verbs 379, 473, 577, 581.
Cf. = confer, *compare, consult.*
Characteristic 172 d : exponents 66.
Chief = principal clauses 626 : chief = primary tenses 267 b : -ly (ch.).
Choral odes 744 e.
Chorus using sing. 488 a.
Chronic × achronic forms 590 a.
Circumflex accent 94, 767 e, g; 771 : -flexed syll. or vow. 768; long 771, 726.
Circumstantial adjunct, or circum-
Cj. = conjugation. [stance, 58 d, s.
Clauses 57 ; kinds 62, 58 h ; pos. 718 o, s, 721. [compos. 388 b.
Close vowels 107 a : affixes 172 c :
Cognate vowels 4, 110 b : consonants 4, 137 b, 167: themes 338 d.
Collectives 55 ; w. pl. 499.
Comedy, comic (com.), 85 s.
Common dialect 85 a : gend. 174 : commonly (comm.).
Comparison (cp.) 29 (anal.), 256 s ; by use of adv. 510; accent 776: see p. 11: Comparative (compt., comp.) w. gen., w. ἤ, &c., 408, 511 s; w. dat. of mensure 468; abs.,*too*, as pos., 514 s: Comp. conjunction ἤ 701 l.
Compellative 57, 484 s : -part 60.
Complementary adjunct, or complement, 58 d, e, 63 f: pron., adv., 66 d, 563 s: conjunction 701 l: clause 643 s.
Complete tenses 30 b, 267 c; redupl. 280; auxil.and nude forms 317 s, 679 a:

× def. and indef. 590, 599: special uses 599; preter. 268, 600; as pres. or fut. 610. [and parts 62 b, g.
Complex modification 59 : sentence
Composition 359, 383 s ; dir. × indir. loose × close, double, &c., 387 s; vowel 383 a; elision 128 a, 282 a; augm., &c., 282; synt. relations 722; accent 783.
Compound *word* 359 b ; verb 387, 699: *sentence* 62 c: *vowel* (diphthong) 108: *system* 267 f: *constr.* 68 f, 495.
Concession expr. by pt. or w. conj. 674 f, 701 g. [631 s; omitted 638.
Conclusion × premise 62 j ; forms of,
Condensation, 555, 565.
Condition 62 j ; see Premise : Conditional *conj.* 701 f; *sentences*, forms of, 631 s, rel. 641; for oth. forms, 689.
Conjugation (cj.), distinctions 30, 265 s; hist. 271 s; anal. 32, 35 s, 277 s; paradigms 37 s, 48 b; prefixes 277, 284; affixes 285, 48, 321 ; stem 47, 49, 336: quant. 728 s; accent 776, 780.
Conjunctions (conj.) 55, 65 s, 700, classes, origin, 701; om. 707; repeated 714; pos. 718 a, 720.
Connecting vowels, or connectives, of dec. 12 s, 183, cp. 29, 256 s, cj. 32 h, 35 s, 290 s, 326, compos. 383.
Connective exponents, conj. × conn. pron. or adv., primary × sec., 66: pos. 718 a, 720.
Consecutive conj. 701 k, 671 d, e.
Consonants 4, 137 s ; in Gr. alph. 98; old 138; changes 139 s; final 160; movable 162; dial. and poet. var. 167 s; added or om. in s. 217, 344 s, 348.
Construction, personal for impers. 573 : *Constructio prægnans* 704.
.Contingent *sentence* 61 f; modes 30 c ; 613 s; particle 618, 685 c: Contingency, pres. × past, fut., 613 s.
Contraction (cont., ct.) 7, 117 s, 131; quant. 726; accent. 772: note, in *versif.* 741 b: Contr. verbs 42, 309, in Lat. 43.
Coördinate vowels 110 b; consonants 137 b, 168; sentences 62 c; conjunctions 701: Coördination 62 c; for subord.
Copula 60 b ; omitted 572. [705.
Copulative conjunctions 701 a.
Correlatives, pronominal, 53, 377.
Corresponding vowels and consonants 138; connectives 66 f.
Cp., in § 50 = compounded ; in the Indexes = comparison. [accent 773.
Crasis 117, 124, 133 ; quant. 726 ;
Ct. = contracted.
Cyropædia, see Xenophon.
DACTYL 77 : -ic verse 742, 747.

Dative 10, 186 f, 190, 393, double office 399: w. prep. 688 s, w. comp. verbs 699 f, g. See page 12.
Declarative sentence 61.
Declension 10 s, 173 s; distinctions 173; three methods 180; gen. rules 181; affixes 11 s, 183; hist. 186; paradigms compared w. Lat. 14, &c.: Dec. I. 14 s, 189, 193; Dec. II. 14, 16, 187, 199; Dec. III. 14, 17, 186, 202; dial. 20 s; irreg. 21, 223; def. 227: adj. 22, 229; num. 25, 240 s; pt. 26, 234; pron. 27, 239: quant. 728, accent 775 s. [verbs 337.
Defective nouns 227; adj. 238;
Definite *tenses* 30 b, 267 c; × indef. 590 s; for oth. tenses 602 s: *article* 520: *relatives* 549. [479.
Definitive, old, 249, 516: noun (acc.)
Degrees of compar. 256; use 510; interch. 515: Degree-sign 256 a, 29.
Demonstrative pron. and adv. 28, 53, 252, 377; SYNT. 542; om. bef. rel. 551 f; in attr. 552 s; for rel. 562.
Demosthenes fl. 355, Att. orator, § 85.
Dependent sentences 62 b, 58. 3, h.
Deponent, mid. × pass., 266 c, 576 b.
Derivation, -tive, 54, 359 s; euph. changes 361; quant. 731; accent 789 s.
Diæresis 6, 105; accent 772. 3; mark 96 b, 110 a: in versif. 745 h.
Dialects 81 s: variations in orthog. and orthoëpy 130, 167, dec. 20 s, &c., cj. 48, 284, 321, accent 790: Dialectic Forms (*D. F.*).
Digamma = Vau; see F, before Z, in Greek Index: verbs 345.
Diminutives, gend. 175; der. 371.
Diphthongs 4, 106; prop. × improp. 108; corresp. 115 a; resolved 105, 132; quant. 526, 737; in accent. 767.
Direct *cases* 10, 179, 397, 186 c, in accent. 775: *complement*, *obj.*, 58 e: *discourse*, *quot.*, 62 k, 643, w. indir. 644, 659: *compounds* 388: *order* 718.
Distinct sentence, verb, mode, 62 a, 30 c; in depend. clauses, × incorp., 657.
Distinctive adv. 685 c: conj. 701 c.
Distributive pronouns 55, 501.
Division of syllables 111.
Doric dialect (Dor., D.) 82, 86 s: future 305 d, 325 b: accent. 790.
Double *accusative* 480: *consonants* 4, 137 u, d, 170; affecting quant. 725, 734: *d. cons. verbs* 41, 270 c, 311.
Doubtful vowels 4, 106, 726. 3.
Dual number 178; old plur. 186 g, 271 c; in cj. 299: used w. pl. 494.
ELEGIAC poets 83: verse 749.

Elements of the *sentence* 57: of the *word* 172; in dec. 183, cp. 256, cj. 32, der. 359 s, compos. 383 s.
Elision, see Apostrophe.
Ellipsis 68; in synt. of appos. 394 s, gen. 418 b, 438, dat. 450 d, 462, acc. 476, adj. 506, 511 b, art. 527, 533, pron. 536, 551, 555, 562, 565, verb 571, 626, 636, 647, inf. 668, pt. 676, 678 c, particle 707.
Emphatic *changes* in s. 346: *particles* 685 c: *repetition* 69 b: *position*
Enclitics 787; accent. 788. [719 a.
Ending, see Flexible.
Epenthesis 6, 103; see Insertion.
Epic, or Homeric, language (EP., E.)
Episēma 1, 91, 98 d. [83.
Epithet × predicate adj. 59 a, 492 b.
Equestri, De Re, see Xenophon.
Equal, or quadruple, rhythm 742.
Essential × inflective 172 a, c.
Ethical dative 462 e.
Etymology 172 s; tables 9 s.
Euphonic *changes* 99; of vowels 7, 113 s, of consonants 8, 139 s, 147 s: *affixes*, *dec.*, *cj.*, 183, 187, 303, 271 f.
Euripides fl. 441, Att. tragedian, § 85: Alcestis, Andromache, Bacchæ, Cyclops, Electra, Hecuba, Helena, Heraclīdæ, Hercules Furens, Hippolytus, Ion, Iphigenīa in Aulide, Iphigenīa in Tauris, Medēa, Orestes, Phœnissæ, Rhesus, Supplices, Troades.
Exclamation, nom. in, 401 b, gen. 429 f, dat. 453, acc. 476 a, pron. or adv. 564 b, inf. 670, interj. 684 b: exclamatory sentence 61 d.
Exempli gratia (e. g.), *for example*.
Exponents for words 65, sentences 66; pos. 718 d, 720: exponential adjunct 58 c. [324 c, 48 c.
Extension of vowels 103 b, 135, 322 c,
FEET 77, 740; interch. 741 b, 747, 751, 755; ictus 741 c; cæsura 745.
Feminine gender 174 s; in adj. 232; w. masc. form 234: *cæsura* 745 c.
Figures affecting letters and sounds 6, 99: of syntax, of rhetoric, 67 s.
Final *consonants* 160, movable 162: *conjunctions* 701 e: *clauses*, modes in, 624: *syll.* of verse 738: *accent* 769.
Finite modes, sentences 62 a; synt. of, 568 s; interch. w. incorporated 657, 659, 671.
Flexible endings, or flexives, of dec. 12, 183; of cj. 32 i, 295, 328.
Flourishing (of authors; fl.).
Fluents (λ, ρ) 4, 137.

Formation 172, 359; of simple words 362, compound 383; quant. 731; accent 789: formative × radical 172 b.
Fractional numbers 242 d, e.
Fragment (Fr.). — French (Fr.).
Future *indef.* 30 b, 266 s, 273 s; subjective tense 584; wants sub. and imv. 269 b; liquid 152; Att., Dor., 305, 325 b: second 289: SYNT. 596 s; for imv. 597; gnomic 606; for pres. or past 610; in final clause 624 b; inf. 598, 660; pt. 674 e, expr. purpose 598 b; mid. for act. 584, for pass., *v. v.*, 576 a, c: *def.* and *complete* 596 at *Contingency* 614.
Future Perfect 30 b, 267 e, 273 e, 319: use 601. [490 s.
GENDER 174; rules 175 s: in synt.
General or indef. premise, 634, 641.
Generic *use* 63 g, 392 a; of cases, 485, tenses 602 s, modes 651, connectives 705: *time* for fact 602 c, contingency 614 b: *article* 522.
Genitive 10, 186 e, 398, 485 b: w. art. 523 c; in pron. 538; abs. 675; w. prep. 688 s. See page 12.
Gentile × patrial noun or adj. 368 c.
Gnomic use of pres. 602 d, aor., &c.,
Government, or regimen, 63. [606.
Grammatical × logical parts 60. [768.
Grave accent 94, 767 e, 784: syllable
HDT. = Herodotus.
Hellenica (HeL), or Historia Græca, see Xenophon. [pated 756 a.
Hephthemim 740 b, 745 c; antici-
Herodotus (Hdt.) fl. 443, Ion. historian, § 83. [748.
Heroic (Epic) poetry 83: verse 743,
Hesiodus (Hes.) fl. 800 ?, poet (Ep.): Opera et Dies, Scutum Herculis, Theogonia.
Heteroclites 223, 225.
Heterogeneous nouns 223, 226.
Hexameter 743, 748: -pody 740 b.
Hiātus, how avoided, 99 s, 117 s, 162, 217; 190; in poetry, 746 a, 737 s.
Hiero, see Xenophon.
Hippocrates fl. 430, medical writer in Ion., § 83. [ondary tenses 267 b.
Historic present 609: historical = sec-
History of Greek lang. 81, 359, orthog. 97, dec. 187, pron. 246, 249 s, cp. 264, cj. 271, 336, accent 789.
Homērus fl. 900 ?, Ep. poet, § 83: Ilias, Odyssēa, Hymni (in Apollinem, Bacchum, Cererem, Martem, Mercurium, Venerem), Batrachomyomachia.
Hypallage 70 r, 474 a.
Hyperbaton 71, 719 s.

Hypercatalectic verse 743.
Hypothetical period 62 j, 631 s.
IAMBUS, Iamb, 77: Iambic rhythm 742, verse 755. [part of a work.
Ibidem (Ib.) = in the same work or
Ictus in pronunc. 79 c: metrical 741.
Id est (i. e.) = that is.
Idem (Id.) = the same author.
Illative, or inferential, adverbs 685 c.
Imitative verbs 378 c.
Immediate = nude adjunct 58 c: immediate, or included, × causative verbs 473, 582 β.
Imperative (imv.) 30 c, 269 s, 272 e, 655; in perf. 318, 599 d; × sub. w. μή 628: *sentence* 61 c.
Imperfect (impf., ipf.) 30 b, 267, 271 d; × aor. 591 s; × aor. and plup. as conting. or indef. 615 a, 616 b, in wish 638 b, g; for aor. or plup. 603 c, 604, 612, pres. 611.
Impersonal *verbs* 571, pass. 589; inf. and pt. 657 i; pt. abs. in acc. 675: *verbal* 682.
Improper diph. 4, 108: redupl. 357.3.
Impure vowel, affix, stem, word, 112.
Imv. = Imperative.
Inceptive verbs 350, 379 a.
Incorporation, -ated sentence, verb, mode, × distinct or finite, 62 a, 30 c, 657. See Infinitive, Participle.
Indeclinable (aptote) 227 a.
Indefinite (indef.) *pron.* and *adv.* 27 s, 53, 245, 253, 548: *rel.* 549: *subject of* verb 571, inf. 667 h: *tenses* 30 b, 267 c; × def. 590 s, complete 599; how supplied 603: *action* 616: *premise* 634.
Independent sentence 62 e: elements 57 f: nominative 401.
Indicative (ind.) 30 c, 269, 271 s: SYNT., × sub. and opt. 613; expr. suppos. contrary to fact 615, habit w. ἄν 616, purpose 624, wish 638; in hypoth. period 631 s, 634 s; in indir. disc. 643 s; generic use 651.
Indirect cases 10, 179, 186 c, 397 s: complement, obj. 58 e: compounds 388: disc. or quot 62 k: order 718 r.
Infinitive 30 c, 269, 272: SYNT. 657 s; × pt. 657 d, k; in indir. disc. 659; relation to time 660; as neut. noun, w. or wt. art., 663 s; of specif., adv., abs., 665; w. acc. 666, other cases 667; redund. or om. 668; as imv., &c., 670; w. connectives 671: pos. 718 l; accent 780 s.
Inferential, or illative, adverbs 685 c.
Inflection 172; three periods 276.
Inflective × essential 172 a, c.

Inseparable particles 385, 252, 688 e.
Insertion of cons. to prevent hiatus 99 s, 217, 190; of ε in contr. 120 i; of ρ, mid. mute, 146; for metre 171; of σ, η, &c., in cj. 307, 311; of ν in s. 351. 1; of vowel and σ in compos. 383.
Intellective sentence 61 : modes 30 c, 613 s.
Intensive verbs 379 b : adv. 685 c.
Interchange, -ed (interch.).
Interjection 55, 684 b.
Interrogative *pron.* or *adv.* 28 g, 53, 253, 564; w. art. 531; doubled 566 b; pos. 718, 720: *particles*, dir., indir., altern., 685 c, 687: *sentence* 61, expressing wish 597.
Intransitive use of act., esp. in second and complete tenses, 577 b, 338 b.
Inversion 71 a : inverse attr. 554.
Ionic dialect (Ion., I.), old, mid., new, 82 s: forms in 3 pl. 300 d, 329: feet and verse 77, 764: accent. 790.
Iota *subscript* 109 : *form* of verbs 349.
Ipf., impf., = Imperfect.
Irregular nouns 223 : adj. 236 : cp. 262: verbs 50, 336 s.
Isocrates fl. 380, Att. orator, § 85 b.
Iterative *pron.*, see αὐτός : *form* in cj.
KINDRED vowels 114 b. [332.
LABIALS 4, 137 ; changes 147 s : in Dec. III. 17, 203: l. verbs 38 s, 270 c.
Lacedæmoniōrum Respublica (Lac.), see Xenophon.
Laconic dialect 82, 141 a.
Language, significant elements 55, gen. synt. 56 s; Indo-European 81.
Last syllable of verse common 738.
Late (l.), *i. e.* during the long period of decline which followed the loss of freedom.
Lesbian dialect 82, 84, 87 a, 790 b.
Letters, Gr., Heb., Lat., 1 s, 90, 98.
Limiting article 523 s.
Linguals 4, 137 ; changes of and w., 147 s; in Dec. III. 17, 204, contr. 207: lingual verbs 39, 270 c.
Liquids 4, 137 ; changes of and w., 144 s, 168 s; Dec. III. 18, 208: liquid verbs 40, 152, 311 b, 342. 3, 347.
Local quantity 725, 734 s.
Logical parts 60 : order 64.
Long *vowel* 4, 106 ; = 2 short 115, 725; shortened bef. vowel 737; forming 2 tone-places 767: *syll.*, by nature or pos., 725 s. [718 t.
Loose compounds 388 b : structure
Luciānus fl. 160 ? A. D., essayist and wit: De Historia Scribenda, Deōrum

Concilium, Dialogi Deōrum (D. D.), Deōrum Marinōrum (D. Mar.), Mortuōrum (D. M.), Parasitus.
Lysias fl. 411, Att. orator, § 85.
MAGISTER Equitum, see Xenophon.
Masculine 174 ; form as fem., esp. in du. and pl., 234 d, e, 489 c, 490: cœ-
Megarian dialect 82. [*sura* 745 c.
Memorabilia Socratis, see Xenophon.
Metaplasm, -asts, 223 s.
Metathesis 6, 104, 145 ; in cj. 308, 342; in der. 361 d.
Metre 740 s : metrical ictus 741.
Middle *Mutes* 4, 137 ; ins. 146 b ; changes 146 s; see β, γ, δ: *Stem* 47, 386: *Voice* 30, 266; synt. 575s, 578.
Modal sign 65 : appos. 393 c, 394 b.
Modern Greek pronunc. 79. 2.
Modes 30 c, 265, 269 s ; hist. 272 ; affixes 286 s; conn. vowels 290, 326; flex. endings 295, 328: SYNT. 613 s. See page 12.
Modified stems 49, 339 a.
Modifiers 57 g, 58 ; pos. 718 s.
Monosyllables, roots 340. 3, 359 f ; quant. 729. 2; accent 782 e, 786, 793 c.
Movable consonants 162.
Mutes 4, 137 ; changes of and w., 147 s, 167 s; m. and liquid as affecting quant. 735: in Dec. III. 17, 203: in cj. 38 s, 270 c, 347.
NASALS 4, 137 ; changes of and w., 139 s: nasal form in cj. 351.
Nature, long or short by, 725 s.
Negative *pron.* and *adv.*, object. × subj., 53, 686; as interrog. or affirm. 687; redund. w. indef., inf., &c., 713 ; οὐ μή w. sub. or fut. 627 : *sentence* 61 e.
Neuter (neut., N.) 174 ; dec. 188 ; in adj. 231: as generic gend. 491, 496 c, 502; pl. w. sing. verb 569; impers. 571 e: as adv. or acc. of effect 380 a, New stem in cj. 47, 336. [483, 478.
Nominative (nom., N.) 10, 186 d, 398 s, 485; for voc. 182, 401 c; in appos. w. sent. 396: as subject 400, 568; om. 571; by attr. 573, 657: independ. 401.
Noun 55 ; dec. 14 s, 193 s ; deriv. 363; compos. 386; synt. 393 s; quant. 728 s; accent 775 s, 791.
Nude *affixes, dec.,* 183, 187, *cj.* 303, 313, 320, 326 e, 335: adjunct 58 c.
Number 178, 270 ; signs 12, 33 a ; use and interch. 488 s, 494 s.
Numerals 25, 52, 239 s ; how combined 242; letters as, 1, 91.
OBELISK (†) 96 c. [448, 470 s.
Object 58 c, 63 f ; dir. × indir. 397 s,

Objective *affixes* 36, 285 : *voice* 271 e, 274: *cases* 10, 397 s; gen., adj., 444g; dat. 448 s: *negative* 686, 53 III.
Oblique cases 179 b ; as adv. 380.
Odes, choral, 744 e.
Œconomicus, see Xenophon.
Old stem 47, 386. [rhet. 68. 2.
Omitted (om.) : omission as fig. of
Open *vowels* 107 a : *affixes* 172 c.
Optative 30 c, 269, 272 d, Att., Æol., 293 c, e; conn. vow. 293: SYNT., x ind., sub., 613; law of sequence 617; in final clauses 624, the hypoth. per. 631, rel. and temp. clauses 640, complem., indir. disc., 643; potential 636; for imv. or ind., esp. fut., 637, 654 a; of wish 638, 637 d, 648 d; of doubt 648; generic conting. mode, for sub., 652, 654 a. [blended 644.
Oratio recta x obliqua 62 k, 643 ; Order, direct or normal x indirect or varied 718; why varied 719.
Orthotone 5, 788 g.
Other Examples (O. E.).
Oxytone 768 ; w. grave mark 784.

PALATALS 4, 137 ; changes of and w., 147 s, 169 s: in Dec. III. 17, 203: in cj. 39, 270 c, 349 s. [162 s; ι 252 d.
Paragōge 6, 103 : paragogic cons.
Parenthesis, -thetic, 71 c.
Paroxytone 768.
Participle 30 c, 269 s, 272 b, c; dec. 26, 205, 234: SYNT., 657 s, 673 s; as *adj.*, w. anacol., 504; x inf. 657 d, k; relation to time 660; *circumst.*, as adv., 674 s, w. dat. 462, expr. purpose 598 b, 674 e, condition 635, concession 674 f, abs., impers., 675; *complem.* 677; *defin.*, *desc.*, 678; w. aux. verb 679; w. ὥς, &c., 680: pos. 718 m; accent 780 s.
Particles elided 128 ; in compos. 384 s, 389 : SYNT., classes, 684 s ; interch. 703; ellips. 707; pleon. 713; attr. 715; anacol. 716; combin. 717: pos. 718, 720; accent 785 s, 794.
Partitive appos. 393 d, 395 : gen. 415 s: adj. 419 f.
Parts of sentences 56 s.
Passive *Voice* 30 ; synt. 575 s, 586 s; w. gen., dat., 586, 434 b, 461; impers. 589: *Verbals* 364, 374; w. dat. 458.
Pastoral, or bucolic, cæsura 745 d.
Patrials x gentiles, der., 368, 375 e.
Patronymics, der. 369.
Pause cæsural 745 c : final 738.
Pentameter 743, 749.
Penthemim 740 b, 745 c.
Penult 111 a ; in accent. 768 s.

Perfect (perf., pf.) ; see Complete.
Period, hypothetical, 62 j, 631 s.
Periphrasis 69 d ; in synt. of gen. and adj. 437 c, 499 d, acc. 475, art. 527 s, verb 598, 637.
Perispome 768 : verbs 309.
Person 246, 270 ; signs 246, 249 ; in cj. 33 a, 271: agreement 492, 496; change 503, 539 c, 644.
Personal *Pronouns* 27, 243, 247 ; hist. 246; encl. 787: SYNT., 536 s; eth. dat. 462 e: *Construction* for impers.
Pf., perf., = Perfect. [573.
Phrases x clauses 56 a.
Pindarus fl. 490, lyric poet, § 84 : Isthmia, Nemea, Olympia, Pythia.
Plato fl. 399, Att. philosopher, § 85 : Apologia, de Republica, &c.
Pleonasm 69 ; in synt. of gen. 446, dat. 462 e, acc. 477, pron. 505 b, cp. 510 s, art. 523 j, verb 574, inf. 668, prep. 699, neg., &c., 713.
Pluperfect (plup., plp.), aug. 280 s ; ἐα >η, ει, 291 c; cont. 615: see Complete.
Plural (plur., pl., p.) 178, 186, 271 ; signs 12, 33 a: interch. or joined w. sing. or dual 488 s, 494 s, 499 s, 569.
Plutarchus fl. 80 A. D., biographer and philosopher: Pompeius, &c.
Poetic (poet., po., P.), poetry, 83 s.
Polysyndeton 69 f.
Position of words and clauses 718 s, 721 e: in prosody 725, 734 s.
Positive *degree* 256 ; joined or interch. w. sup. or compt. 512, 515: *sent.* 61 e.
Possessive *pronoun* 28, 252. 5, 538 ; w. or implied in art. 524, 530 e: *genitive* 443. [*cles*, &c., 720.
Postpositive *article* 249 b, 250 : *particles*
Potential *opt.*, *ind.*, 636 a.
Precession of vowels 107, 114 s, 130 ; in contr. 115 s; in affix 195; in s. of dec. 114 d, 217, of cj. 341; &c.
Predicate 57 ; -part, log. x gram., 60 ; pos. 718 c, s: adj., &c., 59 a.
Prefixes 172 c ; of verbs 32, 277 s, Preformatives 32 c, 356. [284.
Premise 62 j ; forms 631 ; indef. or gen. 634; om. 636.
Preposition 55 ; elided 128 ; apoc. 136; w. and wt. case as adv. 382, 703: SYNT. 688 s, 487; in compos., tmesis, 699, 486; constr. præg. 704; pos., accent, 718 d, 785 s, 794. 5.
Prepositional adjunct 58 c, 706.
Prepositive *vowel* 106 : *article* 249 b.
Present *definite* 30 b, 267 : generic tense, gnomic, 602 s; historic, pro-

§ 798.   PRET   LATIN & ENGLISH.   SUBJ   367

phetic, 609; for perf. 612; × aor. w.
μή 628: *contingency* 613 s. [600.
Preteritive use, verbs, &c., 46, 268,
Primary *tenses* 30 b, 267 b, 271 s;
followed by sub. 617: *affixes* 32 i, 35 s,
286: *elements* of sent. 57.
Primitive × derivative 359.
Principal *word* 57 h : *sentence* 62 b.
Prior tense (impf., aor., plup.) 615.
Proclitics, or atona, 786.
Prohibition w. μή 628.
Prolepsis 71 b, 474 b, 657. [377.
Pronominal correlatives 53, 362 e,
Pronoun 55, 27 s, 243 s, 509, 535 s.
See Article; Substantive, Personal,
Adjective, Indefinite, Relative, &c.
Pronunciation, four methods, 79.
Proparoxytone 768, 770.
Proper *diphthong* 4, 108 : *redupl.*
357: *name* w. or wt. art. 522 g, 533 a.
Properispome 768, 771.
Protracted Stems 346 s.
Protasis = premise 62 j.
Pt., part., = participle.
Pure vowel, affix, stem, word, 112 :
nouns in Dec. III. 19, 212 s; verbs
42 s, 270 c, 309, 313.
Q. v. = quod vide, *which see*.
Quadruple, or equal, rhythm 742.
Quantity, natural × local, 725 s ; in
dec. 728 s, cj. 728, 730, der. 731.
Quotation or disc., dir. × indir., 62 k.
RADICAL × formative 172 b, 359.
Rare (r.). [769.
Recessive × retentive or final accent
Reciprocal *pronoun* 27, 244. 3.
Redundant nouns 233 b : verbs 338.
Reduplication 280, 273 e, 284 ; Att.,
281 d; in compos. 282; in 2 aor. and
fut. 284 e, s: in s., proper, &c., 357.
Reflexive *pronoun* 27, 244, 248 ; use,
dir. × indir., 537 s, 513 f, 541 h.
Regular affixes of verb 303, 35 s.
Relative *Pronoun* and *Adverb* 28, 53,
250, 243 s, 377: SYNT. 549 s; *attr.*
522 s; condens. 555; rel. for defin. and
conn. particle 557: w. another conn.,
&c , 561: *Clauses* 640 s. [Xenophon.
Republica Atheniensium, De, see
Residual cases, 10, 397 s : dat. 465 s.
Retention, fig. of synt., 70 v. [769.
Retentive × recessive or final accent
Rhythm 740 s; affecting pos. 718 g.
Root 172 b, 340. 3, 359.
Rough *breathing* 93 ; w. init. υ and ρ
93 c, d; <F, Σ, 141, 345; *mutes* 4, 137;
changes of and w., 147 s, 159, 167.

SAPPHO fl. 611, Æol. lyrist : Sapphic
verse 750. 4. [738 b, 744 b.
Scanning 746 d : continuous scansion
Scholia, notes of Greek grammarians.
Scilicet (sc.) = namely.
Scripta Sacra (S. S.) : *Septuagint*
(Lxx.), Psalms, Proverbs, &c.; *New
Testament*, Matthew (Mat., Mt.), Mark
(Mk.), Luke (Lk.), John (Jn.), &c.
Second tenses and systems 289 ; rel. to
stem 47, 336 b, 340. 4; use 338 b.
Secondary *tenses* 30 b, 267 b, 271 d, s ;
conting. and indef. 615 s; w. opt. 617;
w. ἄν 618; in hypoth. per. 631 s; expr.
wish 638: *affixes* 32 i, 35 s, 286.
Semivowels 4, 137 ; four old, 138 ;
changes of and w., 139 s, 147 s, 168 s.
Sentence 56 ; parts 57 s ; kinds, connection, 61 s; condensed 555, 565; pos.
718 n, s, 721: words in appos. w., 396:
sentential *analysis* 57 s, 72 s; *exponents*
Sequence of modes, law of, 615. [66.
Sequens (s) = *following*.
Short vow. and syll. 4, 106, 725 s ;
elided 127; >long in dec. 194, 213 s,
cp. 257, cj. 275 d, 288 a, 310, 314, 347,
compos. 386 c. [139 s, 151 s, 169 s.
Sibilants 4, 137 s ; changes of or w.,
Signs of relation or case, number,
and gender, in dec., 12; of degree, in
cp., 29; of person, number, voice,
mode, and relation, in cj., 32 i, 33; of
tense 32 g, 35 s.
Simple *sentence* 62 e : *vowels* × diphthongs 4, 106: *words* 359; der. 362 s;
accent 791 s: *succession* 62 d, 705 a.
Singular (sing., s.) 178 ; interch. or
joined w. pl. 488 s, 499 s, 569.
Smooth, or soft, *breathing* 93; for
rough 93 c, 167 c; <F 141: *mutes* 4,
137; changes of and w., 147 s, 167 s.
Sophocles fl. 468, Att. tragedian,
§ 85: Ajax, Antigone, Electra, Œdipus Colonēus, Œdipus Tyrannus, Philoctētes, Trachiniæ; Fragmenta.
Specification, acc. of, 481 : nom. in,
Spirants 4, 137 s. See Σ, F, I. [402 b.
Stanza × system 740 a, 744.
Stem (s) × root 172 ; of *noun* 180 b:
of *verb* 270 b, 32, 47, 336 s.
Stem-mark, or characteristic, 172 d.
Subject of *sentence* 57 ; -part, log. ×
gram. 60; pos. 718 c, s: of *word* 63 a,
492, finite verb 400, pass. 586, inf. 666;
om., subj. of appos. 394, adj. 506, art.
527, rel. 551, verb 571, pt. 676.
Subjective *cases* 10, 397 s: *gen., adj.*,
444 g: *affixes* 285, 32 i, 35: *sense of
middle* 582: *neg.* 666, 53 iv.

Subjunctive (sub.) *vowel* 108 : *mode* 30 c, 269, 272 d; × ind., opt., 613, 269 c, 617 g; w. prim. tenses 617; w. ἄν combined 619; in final clauses 624, as fut. 627, as imv. 628; in hypoth. per. 631 s, as indef. prem. 634; in rel und temp. clauses 640 s; of doubt 647: for opt. 560, 653, fut. 617 b.
Subordination, -ate *clause*, 62 b, h ; see Dependent: *conjunctions* 701. 2.
Subscript, see I in Greek Index.
Substantive 55, 57 s ; dec. 173 ; cp. 262 d; der. 362 s; synt. 393 s: *pron.* 27, 243; synt. 536: *verb* w. gen. 437; w. dat. 459; om. 572, 676, 678 c, in conden. 555,565: *clause* 62 h, 66 d, 643.
Succession, Simple, 68 d ; early use
Suffixes in der. 360. [705 a.
Superlative 256 s, 510 s ; w. gen. 419 c; w. dat. 468; w. positive, ἐν τοῖς, εἷς, doubled, 512; w. reflex. 513 f; abs., "of eminence," interch., 514 s.
Syllables, division 111 ; union 117 ; quant. 725 c; accent 766 s: syllabic *augment* 277: syllabication 111.
Syllepsis × zeugma 68 f, g, 495 s.
Symposium, or Convivium, see Xen-
Synæresis 6, 105. [ophon.
Syncope 6, 103, 140, 144 ; in Dec. III. 207, 210, 217; in fut. 305 b; in s. 342; in der. 361 d: *metrical* 743 g, 763 a.
Synecdoche 70 j, 481, 587. 2.
Synesis 70 p; in appos. 394 c, adj., pron., verb, 498 s, 569, tense 608 s, mode 653 s.
Synizēsis, or Synecphonēsis, 117 b, 220 d, 222 b, 323 c, 746 b, c. [744.
System in cj. 267 f ; in versif. 740 a,
TAU form in cj. 352.
Temporal *numbers* 52, 243 : *augment* 277 s: *conjunctions* 701 h: *clauses* 641.
Tenses 30 b, 265, 267 ; systems 267 f, 289 b; formation 31; hist. 271 s; signs 32 g, 288, changed 152, 305 s, 325; base, or tense-stem, 289 e; first × second 289, 336, 338 b, 340: SYNT. 590 s.
Tense-sign, -stem, -system, see Tenses.
Tetrameter 743. [cj. 270 b.
Theme 172 e ; in Dec. III. 202 ; in
Theocritus fl. 280, Dor. poet, § 86.
Theognis fl. 544, Ion. elegiac poet.
Thesis 741 ; quant. in, 736 d, 737.
Theta form in cj. 353.
Third future, see Fut. Perf. [§ 85.
Thucydides fl. 423, Att. historian,
Time of *verb* 267 ; absolute × relative 607; generic 602 c, 614 b: of *vow.* and *syll.* 725: cases expr , 482 e· 485 e.
Tmesis 388 c, 699 d, h, s.

Tone, or accent, 766 s : places 767.
Transitive *verb* 55, 486 c ; or intrans. 577 : *sense* 70 c. [740 b, 745 c.
Trimeter 743 ; Iambic 756 : tricmim
Trochee 77 : -aic verse 742, 760.
ULTIMA 111 a ; in accent. 767 s.
Union of syllables 117 s ; accent. in, Usually (usu.). [722 s : vow. 383 a.
V. l. = varia lectio, *various reading*: *v. v.*, vice versa = *and the converse.*
Variable stems 49, 336 s : varied order 719.
Vectigalia, Venatio, see Xenophon.
Verb 55, 57 c ; *cj.*, distinctions 30, 265 s; classes, in -ω × -μι, 270 c, deponent 266, irregular, &c., 336 s, 378 s, appositional 59 a; hist. 271; forms analyzed 32, translated 34; prefixes 277; affixes 35 s, 285, 48, 325 s; general paradigm 37, 48 b; mute, liquid, &c., 38 s, 304 s; contract 42, 309. 48 c, 321 s; in -μι 45, 313, 335; preteritive 46, 268, 317 s; stem 49, 336; catalogue 50: *der.* 378 s; compos: 387: SYNT, agreement 568 s, 492 s, w. subj. om., impers., 571; om. 572; pers. for impers. 573: use of voices 575, tenses 590. modes 613: *quant.* 728, 730; accent 776, 780.
Verbal 362 e ; *noun* 363, adj. 269 d, 874, *adv.* 381: w. gen. 444, dat. 458, acc. 472 j; impers. 682.
Verse, versification, 740 s, 766. 2 ; kinds 742 s; cæsura 745; dact. 747, anap. 751, iamb. 755, troch. 760.
Vision, fig. of, 70 u, 609.
Vocal elements 4, 106 s.
Vocative 10, 179, 186 g ; same w. nom. 181 s, 203, 208 f; in Dec. I. 194. 2: *synt.* 484 s: *accent* 775, 779.
Voices 30, 265 s ; hist. 271 e, 274 : *synt.* 575 s. [655. See Imperative.
Volitive sentence 61 : mode 30 c,
Vowels 4, 106 s ; open × close 107 s ; pure × impure 112; precession, kindred, 114; union 117 s; dial. var. 130: connect. of dec. 12, 183 s, of cj. 32 h, 35 s, 290, 326, of compos. 383; v. form in cj. 355: quant. 725 s; accent 767 s.
WITH (w.). — Without (wt.).
XENOPHON fl. 401, historian, biographer, and essayist (Att., § 55): Agesilaus, Anabasis, Apologia Socratis, Cyropædia, De Re Equestri (Eq.), Hellenica (Hel.), or Historia Græca, Hiero, Lacedæmoniorum Respublica, Magister Equitum, Memorabilia Socratis, Œconomicus, De Republica Atheniensium, Symposium, Vectigalia, Venatio.
ZEUGMA × syllepsis 68 f, g, 495 s.

799. TABLE OF SECTIONS.

In each division below, the numbers in the first column indicate paragraphs or sections in former editions of the Grammar; while those in the second refer to corresponding sections in the Revised and Compendious Editions. A small s signifies *and the following*.

Old. ¶	New. §	Old. §	New. §	Old. §	New. §	Old. §	New. §	Old. §	New. §	Old. §	New. §	Old. §	New. §
1	1	14 s	94 s	83 s	186	153	254 s	217	304	306	364 s
2	3	16	96	86	187	154	249 c	γ	148 a	307	366
3	4	17 s	79	87	188	155 s	256 s	218 s	310	308	367
4	9	21	2	88	189	157	258	220	345	309	368
5	11		97	89	190	158	259	221	307	310	369
6	12	22 s	98	90	191	159	260 s	222	311	311	370
7	15	24	106 s	91	192	160 s	262	223	308	312	371
8	20 a	25	108 s	92	194	162 s	263	224	313 s	313	372
9	16	26	110	93	195	164	265	225 s	315 s	314	373 s
10	20 b	27	113	94	196	165 s	30 a	227	313 b	315	375
11	17	28	114	95 s	197 s		266	β	840	316	376
12	18	29	115	97	199	167 s	267	228 s	50	317	377
13	17	30	117	98	200	169	269	233	268	318	378
14	19	31	118	99	201	170	270	234	317	319	379
15	20 c	32	119	100	202	171 s	271	235	318	320	380
16	21	33 s	120 s	101	203	176 s	272	236	312	321	381
17	22	38	124	102	204	178 s	273	237 s	320	322	382
18 s	23	39	125	103	206	180	274	239	319	323	722 k
20	24	40	126	104	207	181	275	240	317	324	383
21	25	41	127 s	105	208	α,β	328	241	321	325	384 s
22	26	42	129	106	210	3	297 c	242	322	326	386
23	27	43 s	130	107	211	182	297	243	323	327	387 s
24	28	45	131	108	209	183	275 d	244	324	328	389
25	52	46	132 s	109	204 s	N.	326 a	245	325	329	391
26 s	30	47	134	110	212	184	298	246	326		56 s
28	31	48	135 s	111 s	213 s	185	276 a	247 s	328 s	330	392
29	35	49	137	113	215		313 s	249	332	331 s	393 s
30	36	50	138 s	114	216	δ	326 e	250	333 s	333 s	395 s
31	32	51	151	115	219	ε,ζ	327	251	335	335	488
32	48	N.	137 d	116	220	186	276 b	252	50	336	489
33	34	52	147	117 s	217	187	277	253.1	325 d	337	494
34 s	37	53	148	119	218	188	278	2		338	397
	44	54	150	120	221	189	279	254 s	47	339	398
36 s	38 s	55	151	121	222	190	280		336	340 s	399
41 s	40	56	152	122	223	191	281		340	342	400
43 s	41	57	153 s	123	224	192	282	257.2	337	343	401
45 s	42	58	156	124	225	193	283	3	338	344	402
48 s	45	59.7	145 a	125	226	194	284	258	339	345	403
53	45 u	8	157	126	227	195	285	259	341	346	404
54 s	45 k	60	158	127	228	196	286	260 s	342	347 s	405
	s	61	149	128	229	197	287	263	343 s	349	406
57	45 h	62	159	129	230	198	288	264	345	350	407
58 s	46	63	160	130	231	199	289	265	346		425
60	45 q	64	145 s	131	232	200	305	266 s	347	351	408
61	49	65	161	132	233	201	306	271	348	352	409
62	54	66	162 s	133	234	202	290	272	352	353	410
63	53	67	164	134	235		289 e	273 s	349	354	411
64	76	68	165 s	135	236	203	291	277 s	351	355	412
65	74	69	167	136	237 s	204	292		349 1	356	413
66	72	70	169 s	137 s	239 s	205	293	279 s	350	357	414
67	78	71	171	139	241	206 s	294	282	353 s	358	415
§ 1	81 s	72	172	140	242	208.1	290 a	283 s	357	359	416
2 s	83 s	73	173	141	243	2	313	287 s	355	360	417
3	84	74	174	142	247	3	320	289 s	351	361	418
4	85	75	175	143	246	209	295 s	296	350	362	419
5	86	76	176 s	144 s	244	210	297	297	349 γ	363	420
6	85 c	77	178		248	211	298	298	352 s	364	421
7	87	78	10	146	245	N.	163 b	299	353 a	365	422
8 s	88 s		179	147	249	212	299	300	345	366	423
10	90	79	180	148	250	213	300	301	358	367	424
11	91	80	181	149	251	214	301 s	302 s	359 s	368 s	426
12	92	81	182	150 s	252	215	303	304	362	370	427
13	93	82	183 s	152	253	216	309	305	363	371	428

SECTIONS COMPARED. § 800.

Old.	New.	Old.	New.	Old.	New.	Old.	New.	Old.	New.	Old.	New.
372	429	437 s	481	515	546	570 s	592	627	667	689	735
373	430	439	482	516	547	572	593	628 s	671 s	690	736
374	431	440 s	483	517 s	548	573	594	629.1	556 c	691	737
375 s	432	442 s	484	519	549	574	595	630	673	692	738
378 s	433	444	504	520 s	550	575	603	631 s	674	693	739
380 s	434		492	522 s	551		606	633 s	677	694	740
382	435	445	491	524	552	576	609	634 β	657 k	695	741
383 s	436 s	446	495 s	525	553		603	635	674	696	742
386	439	447 s	506	526 s	554	577 s	599 s	636	678	697	77
387	440	449	507	γ	559 b	580	605	637	679	β	741 d
388	441	450 γ	502	528	555	581	596	638 s	675 s	698	743
389	442	δ	507 e	2	559 c	582	601	640	680	699	745
390	443	451	489	529	556	583	598	641 α	504 b	700	744
391 a	437 b		491	530	557	584 s	610	β	657 h	701 s	746
β	443 b	452	508	531	558	586 s	613 s	642 s	652	703	747
γ	438 b	453	499*	532	560	588	618 s	644	683	704	748
δ	436 c	454	498	N.	556 d	589 s	614 s	645	684	705	749
392 s	444	455	500	533	561	591 s	269	646	685	706	750
394	445	456	508	534	562		617	647	686 s	707	751
395	446	457 s	509	535	563	593	615	648	688	708	752
396	447	459	504 b	536 s	564	γ	620	649 s	689 s	709	753
397	448	460	510	537 3	551 g	594	616		707	710	754
398	449	461	511	538	565	595 α	637 b		712	711	755
399	450	462	512	539	564	β	637 c	652 s	699	712	756
400	451	468 s	513	539.2	566	γ	647 d	654 s	700 s	713	757
401 s	452	465	514	540 s	567	δ	627	656	705	714 s	758 s
403	453	466	515	543	568	596	623 -	657	703	716	760
404	454	467 s	516 s	544	495 s	597 s	597	658	706	717	761
405	455	469	520	a	501 a	598	628	659	704	718 s	762 s
406	456	470 s	521 s	545 s	671	599 s	638	660	707	720	764
407	457 s	472	523	547	572		648 d	661	708 s	721	765
408	459	473	524	548	499	601	624	662	711	722	766
409	460	474	525	549	569 s	602.1	650 s	663	709 s	723 s	767
410	462	475	526	550	500	2	625	664 s	713	725	768
411	463	476	527	551	573	3	626	667	714	726	770 s
412	464	477	528	552	574	603	631	668	715	727 s	772 s
413	395 b	478	529	553 s	575 s	604	635 s	669 s	716	729	784
414	465	479	530	555	577	605	632 s	671	717	730	785
415 s	466	480	531	556	575 s	605.5	639	672	718 d	731	786
417	461	481 s	530	557	578	606	640 s	N.	719 e	732 s	787 s
418	467	484	532	558	579	607 s	643	673.2	718 a	734	789
419.4	468	485 s	533 s	559	580 s	609	644	α	720	735	790
5	466 b	490 s	518	560	582	610	645	β	719 η	786	791
420 s	469	492 s	519	561	583 s	611	643	γ	708 f	737	792
422	470 s	494	505	562	586		647	674.4	621 f	738	793
423 s	472	495 s	489 s	563	587	612	655	5	484	739	795
425	474 s	499	505 b	564	588 s	613	656	675 s	725	740	776 s
426 s	476	500	503	565	590	614 s	657 s	678 s	726	741	778
428	472 f	501 s	535 s	566	602	616 s	601 s	681	727	742 s	779
429	472 g	503 s	537 s	567	608 s	617.5	657 i	682	728	744	775
	i	506 s	539	β	606	618 s	658 s	683	729	745	776
430	473	507.7	537 c	γ	611	620 s	663	684	730	746	776
431	477	508 s	540 s	568	607	623	665	685	731		780
432	478	512	542		643 b	624	668 s	686	732	747	781
433	479	513	543 s		660	625	670	687	733	748 s	782 s
434 s	480	514	545	569	591	626	666	688	734		750	794

800. "Let me repeat, that so far from dissuading from the study of Greek as a branch of general education, I do but echo the universal opinion of all persons competent to pronounce on the subject, in expressing my own conviction that the language and literature of ancient Greece constitute *the most efficient instrument of mental training* ever enjoyed by man; and that a familiarity with that wonderful speech, its poetry, its philosophy, its eloquence, and the history it embalms, is incomparably THE MOST VALUABLE OF INTELLECTUAL POSSESSIONS."—MARSH's *Lectures on the English Language.*

THE END.

www.ingramcontent.com/pod-product-compliance
Lightning Source LLC
Chambersburg PA
CBHW020305240426
43673CB00039B/713